Paul Karoly

PSYCHOPATHOLOGY FROM INFANCY THROUGH ADOLESCENCE

PSYCHOPATHOLOGY FROM INFANCY THROUGH ADOLESCENCE

A DEVELOPMENTAL APPROACH

■

CHARLES WENAR

Ohio State University

Random House *New York*

To Solveig

First Edition
987654321

Library of Congress Cataloging in Publication Data

Wenar, Charles.
Psychopathology from Infancy through Adolescence

Bibliography:
Includes indexes.
1. Psychology, pathological. 2. Child psychopathology.
I. Title. [DNLM: 1. Human development. 2. Mental disorders—Etiology. 3. Child development disorders.
WS 350.6 W467d]
RC454.4.W37 1982 616.89 82-7698
ISBN 0-394-32396-3 AACR2

Text and Cover design: Lorraine Hohman

Manufactured in the United States of America

A Note to the Instructor

The primary goal of this book is to place child psychopathology in a truly *developmental context*. This involves more than merely locating various disturbances in infancy, the preschool period, middle childhood, and adolescence, as is usually done. Above all, it means viewing each psychopathology within the context of its history and future consequences. Thus, the description of a given disturbance is just the starting point of an exploration of its early roots and its impact upon future behavior. It is this interest in a broad span of time that defines a developmental approach. The developmental perspective of this book is its distinguishing characteristic.

However, the book goes further by defining psychopathology as *normal development gone awry*. Disturbed infants, children, and adolescents are not a breed apart; rather they are individuals whose growth has been diverted from the normal path. The time-honored explanation of psychopathology in terms of fixations or regressions is the best-known example of normal development gone awry, but it is too limited to cover all that is now known about disturbed behavior. Therefore, in exploring the various psychopathologies, this book also discusses other kinds of deviations. By the same token, the chapter on normal development is not an isolated unit as it is in many texts. Rather, the interplay between normality and abnormality is a theme that runs through the discussion from beginning to end.

In addition to examining the ways in which normal development can go awry, this book raises the question of *why* it does. Answers are sought in what are called contexts: the organic context (e.g., the central nervous system, genetic factors), the intrapersonal context (e.g., the child's affects and cognitions), and the interpersonal context (e.g., parent-child and peer relations), as well as the superordinate context (e.g., the family, groups, socioeconomic status). To help answer the question of how present disturbances may affect future development, considerable use is made of longitudinal studies, many of which challenge long-held beliefs, such as the close relation between childhood and adult neuroses.

The theoretical orientation of the book is *eclectic*. Freudian, behavioral, Piagetian, and other theories are introduced where they help to explain the psychopathology under consideration. Special attention is paid to research findings and methodology, and a variety of methodologies are discussed and illustrated along with their advantages and limitations.

Treatment is presented at both a specific and general level. A section on the treatment of choice follows the discussion of each psychopathology. Research and reviews, rather than clinical reports, are the primary sources for these sections. Then, three of the major schools of psychotherapy (Freudian, Rogerian, and behavioral) are examined in detail, with special attention to their developmental underpinnings. Family and group therapies are also discussed. *Prevention* is dealt with in the context of the community mental health movement along with such topical issues as child advocacy and children's rights. *Assessment* is reviewed from two vantage points. The first concerns the general problem of defining and classifying childhood disturbances. The descriptive psychiatric approach is contrasted with factor analysis, and controversies surrounding the medical model and DSM-III are discussed. One chapter is given to a detailed description of the techniques available for clinical assessment, including the interview, tests, and behavior assessment, not forgetting the clinician's own experience and sensitivity. Finally, clinical vignettes interspersed throughout the book are part of a general effort to convey to the student what it is actually like to *function as a professional* concerned with understanding and helping children.

The book is intended for advanced undergraduates and beginning graduate students. It is assumed that such students will have had an introductory course in child development. While not essential, such a course provides a desirable background for the references to normal development in this text.

A Note to the Student

Question: How can you tell developmental psychologists from other psychologists?

Answer: Instead of asking "*How* are you?" they ask, "*Where* are you in your life?"

This modest joke undoubtedly contains more truth than humor; it captures the spirit of a special viewpoint, which is called developmental. The present is important, yes, but the quest for understanding extends back into the known past and forward into the speculative future. How you were as an infant, a preschooler, a school-aged child, and a teenager has left its imprint on how you are today, just as how you are today has implications for your adult years and old age. It is this special time perspective, viewing the present within the context of the entire life span, that is at the heart of developmental psychology.

One of the primary goals of this book is to help you to think about *disturbed behavior* in developmental terms. You will be introduced to a number of psychopathologies, or behavioral abnormalities—preschoolers who are almost oblivious of their environment; school-aged boys who cannot resist the impulse of the moment to steal or fight or "go wild" with excitement; teenagers who literally starve themselves to death trying to achieve what they believe to be an ideally slim figure. Fascinating as the descriptions are, they serve only as a point of departure in the quest for answers to the questions, What events in these children's past might account for their current plight? and How will their present disturbance affect their future development?

The key to understanding disturbed infants, children, and adolescents is that something has gone wrong with their development. They are not a breed apart; quite to the contrary, they have much in common with their normal counterparts, except that something along the way diverted them from the path of normal growth. Thus childhood psychopathology can be viewed as *"normal development gone awry."* What is this something that prevents healthy growth? The possibilities are numerous and range from a damaged brain to a bleak or brutal home to a punitive or indifferent society. In the search for the (typically) multiple roots of a given psychopathology, you will become acquainted with both the theories and the research that best account for it.

If psychopathology is "normal development gone awry," then a general guide to the normal growth is necessary to understand it. Such a guide will be provided and it will figure prominently in all discussions. Another reason for knowing the details of normal development is that behavior is sometimes considered psychopathological because of *when* it occurs rather than *what* it is; thus the willful defiance of authority that is normal during the "terrible twos" would be regarded as disturbed behavior in a teenager, and rightfully so. Since psychopathology can be a failure to outgrow or a subsequent return to behavior that was once age appropriate, a knowledge of when behaviors appear and when they should disappear is essential.

However, this book is concerned not only with the nature, origins, and consequences of disturbed behavior but also with *prevention* and *remediation.* What can be done to decrease the likelihood that a particular psychopathology will occur? And once it has occurred, what can be done to set the child back on the path of healthy growth? You will learn what specific remedial measures are most effective with specific disturbances and you will be introduced to the major types of psychotherapies and preventive programs.

And there is more. You will learn something of the history of the study of disturbances from infancy to adulthood, the problems involved in defining and categorizing these disturbances, how professionals go about deciding whether a given child is disturbed and, if so, what kind of disturbance exists. Finally, it is hoped, you will begin to get something of the "feel" of what it is like to work as a professional—the special personal demands, the surprises, the disappointments and rewards, and the problems involved in dealing not only with parents but with other health care professionals, school principals, judges, and politicians as well.

To understand and to help children whose development has gone awry is surely a demanding and frustrating undertaking. Fortunately it is also a very exciting one.

Acknowledgments

Two colleagues have helped me immeasurably in my efforts to view all childhood psychopathology developmentally. As always, I am most indebted to Ann Garner for her encouragement, her critical eye, and constructive comments. I am also grateful to Ping Serafica for being a sounding board for my ideas and a source of enlightenment.

At Random House, Virginia Hoitsma was enthusiastic about the manuscript from the beginning, but continually implied, however gently, that a good thing could be made better. Sylvia Shepard was unerringly on target in her specific critiques. Judith Kromm was endlessly patient in her attention to the myriad of details involved in turning the manuscript into a book.

And I am grateful to my wife, Solveig, for providing me with my model of a model child clinician—merely by being herself.

Contents

PSYCHOPATHOLOGY FROM INFANCY THROUGH ADOLESCENCE

1 ▪ The Developmental Approach

You are a clinical child psychologist.[1] A mother telephones your office frantic over the sudden personality change in her boy. "He used to be so sweet and then, out of the clear blue sky, he started being sassy and sulky and throwing a fit if anybody asked him to do the least little thing. What really scared me was last night he got so mad at his brother, he ran at him and started hitting him with all his might. His brother was really hurt and started screaming, and my husband and I had to pull them apart. I don't know what would have happened if we hadn't been there. I just never saw anybody in a rage like that before."

What is the first question you ask?

You are at a cocktail party and, after learning that you are a clinical child psychologist, a former star-quarterback-turned-successful-business-executive takes you aside. After some rambling about "believing in sexual equality as much as the next fellow," he comes to the point. "Last week my son turned to my wife and announced that when he got old enough, he was going to become a girl. When my wife asked him where he got a crazy idea like that, he said that he thought boys were too rough, and he liked to be with girls more. I know he's always been a 'mama's boy,' but I'll be damned if I want any son of mine to have one of those sex changes done on him."

[1] This and subsequent sections will concern the experiences of a hypothetical clinical child psychologist. However, the experiences themselves might apply to any professional who is involved with the mental health of children. All names are fictitious.

What is the first question you ask?

YOU ARE A CLINICAL CHILD PSYCHOLOGIST CONDUCTING an initial interview with a mother who has brought her daughter to a child guidance clinic. "She has always been a sensitive child and a loner, but I thought she was getting along all right—except that recently she has started having some really strange ideas. The other day we were driving on the highway to town, and she said, 'I could make all these cars wreck if I just raised my hand.' I thought she was joking, but she had a serious expression on her face and wasn't even looking at me. Then, another time she wanted to go outside when the weather was bad, and she got furious at me because I didn't make it stop raining. And now she's started pleading and pleading with me every night to look in on her after she has gone to sleep to be sure her leg isn't hanging over the side of the bed. She says there are some kind of crab creatures in the dark waiting to grab her if her foot touches the floor. What worries me is that she believes all these things can really happen. I don't know if she's crazy or watching too much TV or what's going on."

What is the first question you ask?

The first question is the same in all three cases: *How old is your child?*

OVERVIEW

Our general concern is with time—or, more precisely, with change over time.

Our specific charge is to understand psychopathological disturbances of childhood.

Our procedure will involve placing various psychopathologies within a developmental context and examining them as instances of *normal development gone awry*.

The three vignettes illustrate this procedure. Whether the described behaviors are regarded as normal or pathological depends upon when they occur in the developmental sequence. All three are to be expected in toddlers and preschoolers but would be suspect at later ages. It is not unusual for a docile infant to become a willful, negativistic, temperamental tyrant during the "terrible twos." If the child were 10, however, his attack on his brother may well represent a serious lapse in self-control. In a like manner it is not unusual for preschool boys to believe that they can grow up to be women because they have not grasped the fact that sex remains constant throughout life. If an adolescent boy seriously contemplated a sex change, this would be cause for parental concern and professional attention. And finally, ideas of omnipotence and a failure to clearly separate fantasy from reality are part of normal cognitive development in toddlers and preschoolers; their presence from middle childhood on suggests the possibility of a serious thought disturbance and an ominous lack of reality contact.

The vignettes also provide us with our first clue to understanding child psychopathology as normal development gone awry: psychopathology is behavior which once was but no longer can be considered appropriate to the child's level of development. This was one of Freud's most brilliant and influential insights. The general thesis that adult disturbances have their roots in childhood continues to be a pervasive etiological hypothesis accepted even by those who reject all other aspects of Freudian theory. We shall make use of the same developmental hypothesis but apply it within childhood itself. As we examine various psychopathologies we shall discover that there are many variations on this theme of psychopathology as developmentally inappropriate behavior; therefore we shall constantly be seeking the specific developmental model which best fits the data at hand. We shall also come across some unexpected exceptions for which the model itself does not seem to hold.

At the applied level, the developmental approach underlies the child clinician's deceptively simple statement, "There's nothing to worry about—most children act that way at this age, and your child will probably outgrow it"; or its more ominous version, "The behavior is unusual and should be attended to, since it might not be outgrown." A considerable amount of information concerning normal development must be mastered in order to judge whether the behavior at hand is age appropriate, as well as whether a suspect behavior is likely to disappear in the course of a child's progress from infancy to adulthood. In addition, the child clinician must know which frankly psychopathological behaviors stand a good chance of being outgrown with or without therapeutic intervention and which are apt to persist.

Incidentally, to state that behavior is outgrown is not as much an explanation as a label for ignorance. While certain psychopathologies tend to disappear with time, exactly what happens developmentally to cause their disappearance is not known. In fact, the phenomenon has rarely been investigated. The best we can do is to recognize that "outgrown" is a nonexplanation.

Before we set out to understand child psychopathology as normal development gone awry, there are a number of preliminary matters to be attended to. First, we must present a *general developmental model* in order to examine various characteristics of development itself. Then we must select those *variables* which are particularly important to the understanding of childhood psychopathology and trace their normal developmental course. Our vignettes, for example, suggest that the variables of self-control, sex, and cognition should be included in the list. We shall also have to select the *theories* which will contribute most to the developmental approach. Next, we shall turn to a descriptive account of the *behaviors comprising childhood psychopathology,* since these are the behaviors we must understand in terms of our developmental perspective. And, finally, we must examine *longitudinal studies* which have followed groups of normal and disturbed children into adulthood, since these studies will provide a general guide as to which psychopathologies are apt to persist and which are likely to be outgrown.

The General Developmental Model

Our general developmental model includes the time dimension along with intrapersonal, interpersonal, superordinate, and organic variables. These five categories will be referred to as *contexts.* They can be represented schematically as shown in Table 1.1.

TIME. Since our general concern is with change over time, our task would be simpler if there were agreement as to how change should be conceptualized. There is not.

Some psychologists anchor change in chronological time. Gesell is a prime exemplar, since he links crucial behavioral changes to chronological age. In tracing the child's relation to the parents, for example, he describes age 6 as a time of high ambivalence toward the mother, cravings for affection being followed by tantrums and rebellion. Age 7 is calm and inward, the child being companionable, sympathetic, anxious to please. Age 8 is stormy again, with the child demanding the mother's attention while being exacting, rude, and "fresh," while 9 marks a return to self-sufficiency, eagerness to please, and affectionate behavior. And so it goes (Gesell and Ilg, 1946).

A different way of conceptualizing change

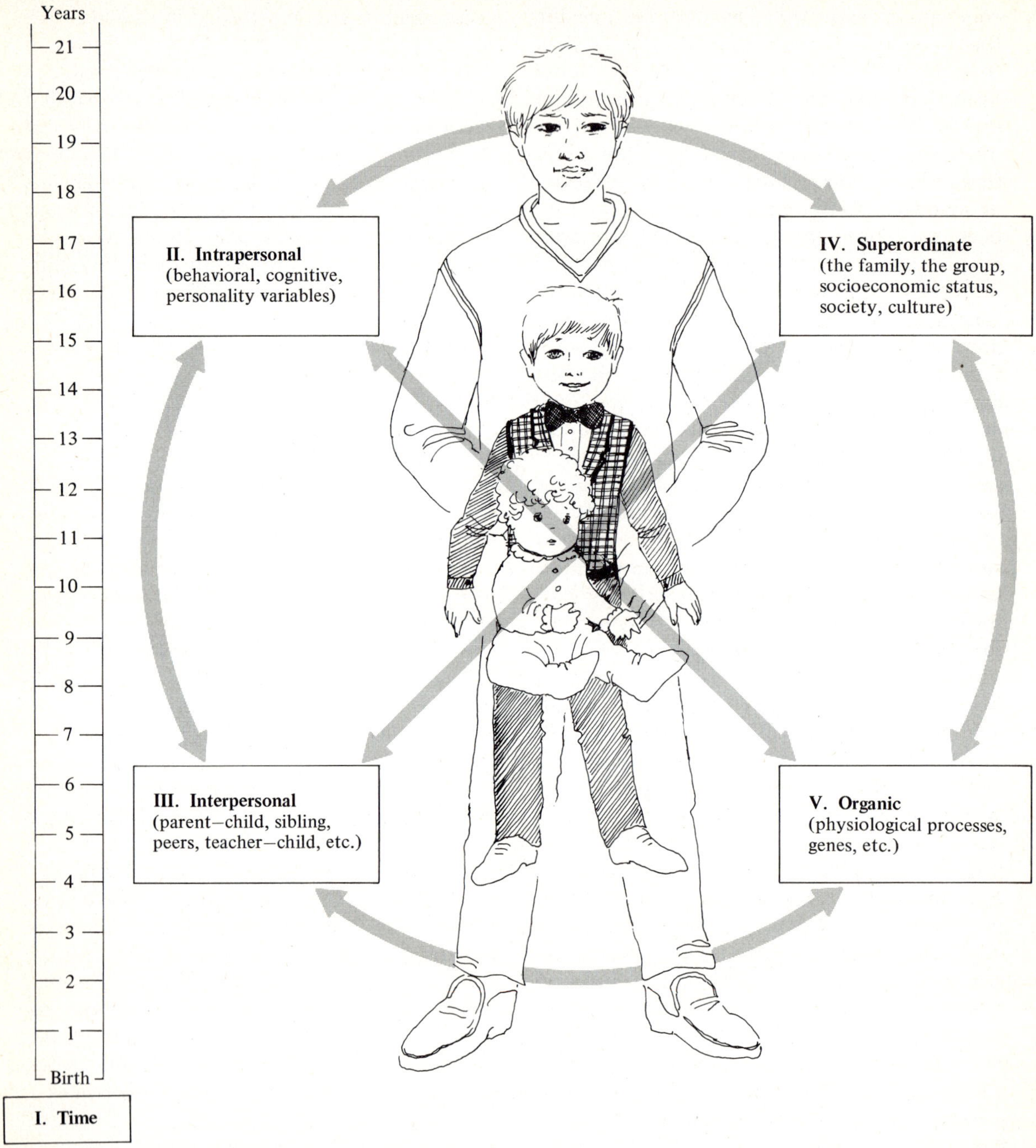

Contexts II–V interact at all points in time as well as over time.

is in terms of *stages* of development, Piaget's cognitive theory and Freud's psychosexual theory being two prominent examples. Stage theories are more concerned with change itself than with chronological age. Typically they make two assumptions: stages represent qualitative reorganizations of behavior rather than "more of the same"; and the sequence of stages is unalterable. Thus, something new emerges at each stage, and the order of emergence is fixed. For both Piaget and Freud, the question "How old is the child?" is not as important as "What stage is the child in?" Fortunately for the clinician, the developments they depict can be translated into chronological age guidelines.

The conceptualization of change over time is of more than academic interest. A characteristic of stage theories is that they often regard the transition between stages as a time of increased tension, unrest, and even reversion to less mature behaviors. The psychosexual stages have this characteristic, while Piaget describes the child's return to immature ways of thinking during cognitive transitions. Even Gesell, whose maturational theory does not include specific stages, describes development in terms of periods of unstable expansion alternating with ones of stable consolidation. All such conceptualizations stand in contrast to radical environmentalism, which claims that stability or instability is primarily the consequence of the experiences the child is having. The important point for us to note is that normal development may entail built-in times of stress and upset; the transitions from infancy to the preschool period and from middle childhood to adolescence, for example, are two potentially stressful periods. Knowledge as to when disturbed behavior is part of normal growth helps the clinician decide whether to tell a parent, "Most children act like that, and yours is likely to outgrow it."

There is another aspect of the time dimension. Our developmental approach implies that, in order to evaluate the meaning and import of an event in a child's life, it is essential to know not only *what* happened but also *when* it happened. To illustrate: a lengthy separation from the mother may have few adverse effects in early infancy before an attachment to her has developed but may trigger a dramatic reaction of protest and extreme withdrawal after an attachment has been formed. Being hospitalized becomes progressively less upsetting between 2 and 12 years of age and also may have different meanings, the younger children being distressed over separation, the 4- to 6-year-olds fearing mutilation or death or viewing hospitalization as punishment. Whether obese adults regard their body with disgust or not depends, among other things, on whether they were obese during adolescence, a period when body consciousness is at a height.

It is also widely believed that events happening in the first few years of life have a more lasting effect on development than events happening subsequently. However, this so-called critical-period or sensitive-period hypothesis has not gone unchallenged and is viewed with a certain amount of skepticism (see Clarke and Clarke, 1976). While the controversy over the critical or sensitive period will play only a minor role in our presentations, we will not accept either hypothesis as a universally valid principle of human development. Rather we prefer to test its validity in regard to the particular aspect of development under discussion.

THE INTRAPERSONAL CONTEXT. The intrapersonal context will figure most prominently in our discussions of psychopathology, since it contains the greatest amount of developmental data. However, here, as with the context of time, we are confronted by the problem of how best to conceptualize the individual child. Once past the obvious variables of age and sex, in what direction should we go? Traditional behaviorists would persuade us to deal exclusively with manifest behavior and avoid all mentalistic or inferential concepts; Freudians urge us to examine the child's ego strength and monitor the battles between id and superego; Piaget reminds us not to neglect egocentrism and the balancing act between assimilation and accommodation; Erikson points to the centrality of ego identity; and Werner insists on the importance of differentiation and hierarchical integration. (The technicalities of the various theories need not concern us here. However, it would be helpful to have the kind of general familiarity with the major developmental theories to be found in introductory texts in child development. See, for example, Yussen and Santrock, 1978.)

The choice among conceptualizations has important clinical implications. The behavioral viewpoint leans toward a statistical and social approach to psychopathology. Since there is nothing in behavior itself which designates it as abnormal, the judgment must be based on its infrequency or on the fact that a given society chooses to label certain behaviors as psychopathological. In another society the same behavior might go unnoticed or even be regarded as a special gift.

The psychoanalysts, on the contrary, maintain that behavior is important only as it furnishes clues to the child's inner life; psychopathology is not a matter of behavior per se, but of the meaning of such behavior. The frequency of masturbation in adolescence, for example, is not as important as the stage-appropriateness of the fantasies which accompany masturbation. (We shall elaborate on this difference between the behavioral and the psychoanalytic approach when we discuss the nature of neurosis in chapter 7. The more recent interest in cognitive behaviorism will also be discussed in chapters 7 and 14.)

Since our primary goal is to understand rather than to champion a particular conceptualization of the intrapersonal context, we shall utilize various theories only as they throw light on the psychopathology at hand. Such eclecticism assumes that no one theory offers a satisfactory account of all of childhood psychopathology, while various individual theories are apposite in accounting for specific disturbances.

THE INTERPERSONAL AND SUPERORDINATE CONTEXTS. Interpersonal variables are concerned with the interaction of individuals—of child with parents, of child with siblings, and so on. Superordinate variables deal with aggregates of individuals taken as a unit—the family, the adolescent clique, the middle class, the industrialized society, and so on. Superordinate variables are primarily the province of social psychologists, sociologists, and cultural anthropologists. We shall refer to such variables only on occasion, since we shall be concerned primarily with psychological ones. Our neglect should not be taken to imply that the superordinate context is unimportant; rather it represents a different approach to psychopathology from the one we are adopting.

THE ORGANIC CONTEXT. The psychological representation of the body should be distinguished from the purely organic body. The two clearly cannot be equated: many physiological processes do not and cannot have any representation in consciousness; most people have only a sketchy and inaccurate image of how their bodies look; in the case of phantom limbs, pain is still felt in a toe which has been amputated; and severe psychopathology may be marked by somatic delusions, such as believing that one's bowels are turning to stone.

The effects of psychological disturbances on the organic body will be central to our examination of obesity and anorexia nervosa in chapter 5, and reversing the direction of influence, the behavioral consequences of blindness and of certain brain psychopathologies will be explored in chapter 12. The organic context also includes genes, which, as transmitters of hereditary characteristics, will figure in our discussion of the etiology of schizophrenia (see chapter 10). Aberrations in an individual's genetic structure itself produce Down's syndrome, the specific kind of mental retardation which we shall study in detail in chapter 11.

Interaction

We have been discussing the contexts as static entities. In reality, they are constantly interacting. An emergency appendectomy may arouse anxiety not only in the child but in parents and siblings as well, just as a stellar performance in soccer may elevate self-esteem while raising status among parents, peers, and teachers.

More important, interactions among contexts change with time. While we are accustomed to thinking of the child as changing, all the other contexts are changing also. Parents who are 25 years old when their infant daughter is born are not at the same stage in their development as they will be at 40 when she is entering adolescence. Nor is the single-child family the same after other children are added, while the casual, improvised peer group of the preschool period differs from the adolescent clique, which is the arbiter of taste in clothes, music, language, and social deportment. Being a member of the lower class in the socially stable 1950s had a different meaning than it did in the 1960s when riots and protests made the plight of the urban poor a matter of national concern. The social ferment of the 1960s has had other effects as well. The family as a social institution is being markedly changed by the willingness of parents to place toddlers and preschoolers in day-care facilities, by the increasing number of working mothers, by the emphasis on negotiable rather than assigned parental roles, and by the increase in divorce and single-parent families. Our society has become increasingly tolerant of early sexual experiences and of couples living together without being married, while the emphasis on doing "your own thing" has broadened the spectrum of acceptable behavior. All these changes have an impact on our concern with differentiating normal from deviant development.

The changes described above are well known. Not so well known is the fact that the concept of childhood itself is changing. In the pioneer days, children were workers and miniature adults; since they were born into sin, their parents were advised—often by the clergy—to beat the devil out of them. Quite a different image from our present one, with its emphasis on the uniqueness of childhood and the importance of child-centeredness on the part of the parents! (For a more detailed account, see Abramowitz, 1976.) To cite another example: in 1874 a brutally abused, starving, and mutilated child named Mary Ellen received legal protection from her parents only after she had been legally defined as an animal so that the laws against animal cruelty could be applied to her. This is a far cry from the current concern for children's rights, where serious consideration is even being given to children suing their parents under certain conditions.

Just as the concept of childhood is changing, so is the concept of childhood psychopathology. Some changes have come from within the profession, such as Kanner's delineation of early infantile autism in 1943; others have resulted from social forces, such as the elimination of homosexuality as a psychiatric disturbance in 1974. The social ferment of the 1960s forced professionals to recognize that poverty vastly increases the risk of a variety of psychopathologies, thereby changing the course of the mental health movement from an individual to a community orientation. (See chapter 14. For a comprehensive historical account, see H. E. Rie, 1971.) Thus, there is nothing final about the list of psychopathologies that will be introduced in chapter 3. The list has changed and will continue to change in response both to theoretical and empirical progress within the profession and to social pressures and values outside the profession. In fact, a consistent application of our developmental model requires that this be so.

While we are in the context of historical time, it will be worthwhile to examine in some detail the history of childhood psychopathology. After tracing its past roots, we shall turn to current conceptualizations of psychopathology and the diverse methods by which understanding of abnormal behavior of children has been advanced.

CHILDHOOD PSYCHOPATHOLOGY: THE HISTORICAL CONTEXT

The history of childhood psychopathology is characterized by sameness in the relative degree of concern, fluctuation in humanitarian attitudes, and progress in scientific understanding.

Throughout history and up to the present moment, *concern* for children has consistently lagged behind similar concern for adults. Regardless of what aspect of psychopathology one examines, interest has initially focused on the disturbed adult and only subsequently spilled over to children. In its *attitude* toward disturbed individuals, society has fluctuated between viewing them as deserving of respect and special care at one extreme and as "crazy" or "inferior imbeciles" who should be chained up in dungeons or isolated in bleak, brutal institutions at the other. When Philippe Pinel, chief physician at Bicêtre Hospital in Paris, unchained the disturbed inmates in 1792, his act symbolized the beginning of humanitarian treatment in modern times, and during the first half of the nineteenth century the former hopelessness about finding a cure for mental disorders was replaced by an equally unrealistic optimism. The second half of that century saw the return of pessimism, isolation, neglect, and brutality, reinforced in part by a perverse reading of Darwin, which stated that the healthy, the industrious, and the affluent were selected by nature for survival, while the indigent, the feebleminded, and the insane were obviously unfit. In the twentieth century the humanitarian battle had once again to be fought, and while major advances can be claimed, total victory lies in the future. It is in the area of *scientific understanding* of childhood psychopathology that there has been the clearest progress since the turn of the century. The image of children as miniature adults, which deluded scientists and professionals alike into regarding their psychopathology as merely an extension of adult disturbances, is slowly—ever so slowly—being dispelled by the recognition of the many unique features of early development. It is not by chance that this reorientation forward from infancy, rather than backward from adulthood, has gone hand in hand with the impressive progress made in understanding normal development in the last half-century. In fact, it is the interdependence of normal and psychopathological development that will provide the substance for most of our discussions.

With this general orientation, we are now ready to examine the historical context in detail (our presentation follows Rie, 1971, pp. 3–50).

Precursors

Before the twentieth century "one could not confidently point to disordered behavior in children as a field of study, or . . . identify a body of knowledge. The virtual absence of proposed treatment of the described conditions is [also] significant" (Rie, 1971, p. 26). While this is true, there were precursors which set the stage for the developments to come.

Certain of the more florid childhood psychopathologies have been known and described for centuries, while the connection between childhood and adult disturbances has also been fleetingly glimpsed. In 1622, for example, Baddeley described a boy with "many strange fits and much distemper" who was thought to be possessed by the devil, demonology being the prevalent explanation of abnormal behavior since the fifth century (Hunter and Macalpine, 1963). In addition, Burton's classic *The Anatomy of Melancholy,* first published in 1621, lists harsh discipline and "evil bringing up" among the many causes of what we would now call depression (Burton, 1968). Yet, such attention to childhood psychopathology was fitful indeed, and it was not until the beginning of the nineteenth century that the Enlightenment generated a social movement sufficiently broad to nurture a sustained interest. In terms of the general trends we shall discuss, concern with treatment preceded a concern with diagnosis and etiology, while interest in the mentally retarded child preceded an interest in the psychopathologically disturbed one.

MORAL TREATMENT. After unchaining the inmates at Bicêtre, Pinel inaugurated a humanitarian and basically psychological approach to therapy called moral treatment. Consisting of considerate, respectful, individualized attention, occupational therapy, mild exercise, entertainment, good food, and comfortable quarters, the treatment has a modern ring, being compatible with what we would term milieu therapy today. However, because it was primarily implemented in institutions, called corporate asylums, and because psychopathologically disturbed children (unlike mentally retarded ones) were rarely institutionalized, moral treatment had little direct impact on childhood disorders.

THE ORGANIC EMPHASIS. The second half of the nineteenth century saw a disillusionment with moral treatment because of its failure to fulfill the promise of a quick cure for rich and poor alike. It was replaced by an essentially anti-individual, nonpsychological emphasis on organic factors to explain severely disordered behavior. The model of the organic approach was the medical research on paresis which first revealed inflammation of the brain and finally a syphilitic infection as the cause. If the delusions, loss of memory, failure of judgment, spatial disorientation, and deterioration of speech, locomotion, and handwriting characteristic of paresis were due to organic factors, could not all other severe psychopathology have a similar basis? The argument was persuasive and, in a modified form, is the basis of the current medical model of psychopathology, as we shall soon see.

MENTAL RETARDATION. However crude, a distinction has been made, at least since the seventeenth century, between those who have lost their reason, that is, "madmen" and "lunatics," and those who never developed reason, that is, "fools" and "idiots." While children in the former category received only sporadic attention, the mentally retarded child was the center of lively interest in the latter half of the nineteenth century. The movement began with Jean Itard's attempt to educate Victor, the Wild Boy of Aveyron, an 11- or 12-year-old discovered living like a wild animal in the forest. Itard's belief that the untutored savage could be civilized through sensory-motor techniques used with deaf-mutes met with moderate success, even though he ultimately concluded that the boy was fundamentally retarded. Itard's student, Edward Seguin, carried on his tradition of sensory stimulation to develop the retardate's "dormant faculties" as much as possible. Like Itard, Seguin was motivated not by scientific interest but by a moral concern with using education to elevate the lowly and the social outcast, as mandated by the gospel. During this period, institutions for the training of retardates were being established, utilizing educational approaches in the hope of making the retardates self-supporting.

As with the institutionalized disturbed adults, however, optimism turned to pessimism and even hostility, so that by the turn of the century retardates were being blamed for most crimes and social ills. Furthermore, the rediscovery of Mendel's laws of heredity in 1900 provided a "scientific" rationale for regarding retardates as genetically inferior and for returning to the period of social isolation, neglect, and brutal treatment.

THE SEVERELY DISTURBED CHILD. Interest in the nature and etiology of severe childhood disturbances was not totally absent during the nineteenth century. We shall briefly describe the tentative beginnings of a psychopathology of childhood.

There was recognition of the fact that severe disorders in children were not as stable, pervasive, or resistant to change as were those in adults. It was also noted that certain psychopathological characteristics such as delusions did not occur until a given developmental level had been reached. For example, in 1812 Benjamin Rush, America's first psychiatrist, claimed that "madness" was rare before puberty because of children's "unstable brains"; hence the "mental impressions" which frequently cause madness in adults were too transient to lead to a permanent disease (Rubinstein, 1948).

The origin of adult psychopathology in childhood and the influence of parental discipline were both recognized, although the latter was not emphasized because of the prevailing tendency to conceptualize etiology in organic terms. There were even scattered references to the ego or the self, to repression, and to the unconscious. Griesinger, for example, wrote of ill-treatment and intimidation producing the "cerebral irritability" leading to psychopathology and of strong affect rendering certain ideas unavailable to the self, a concept we would term repression (Alexander and Selesnick, 1966).

Detailed descriptions of specific psychopathologies were written, and attempts were made to evolve diagnostic categories. Thus, two of the basic steps in the development of a naturalistic science were taken—description and classification. Maudsley's 1867 *Physiology and Pathology of the Mind* is usually considered the first classification of childhood psychopathology (Harms, 1967). The classifications, however, were crude: for instance, Griesinger listed "maniacal insanity," which would include the present-day categories of acting-out aggressive disorders, schizophrenia, and hyperactivity, and "melancholic insanity," which would include hypochondria, suicidal states, generalized anxiety states, and ideas of demonic possession. In light of the general neglect of childhood disturbances, it is understandable that only the severe psychopathologies were described and discussed; milder disturbances were rarely mentioned.

The classifications were not only crude but sometimes inaccurate as well, as witnessed by the prevalent diagnosis of "masturbatory insanity," which was viewed as the only unique disorder of the young and was thought by some authorities to account for as many as 25 percent of all cases of mental disorders in children (Hare, 1962). First proposed as a cause of epilepsy in 1758, masturbation was seen 100 years later as the basis for many mental disturbances—imbecility, shyness, suspiciousness, aggression, lethargy, suicidal impulses, and dementia among them. Predictably, the specific mechanism was often an organic one, such as masturbation impairing nutrition of the brain and spinal column.

In spite of these precursors for the study of childhood psychopathology, one does not have the impression of a rich and fertile field waiting to be cultivated by twentieth-century investigators. The writings of the nineteenth century have an antiquated flavor, not solely because of the excessive concern with moral issues at one extreme and organic etiology at the other but rather because of the almost total absence of an empirical and theoretical context regarding child development. The isolated observations dangle in space, having few antecedents or consequences and lacking a corpus of empirical findings to support or refute them. In such a state, masturbation could readily be accepted as a cause of insanity, while the significance of intra- and interpersonal influences or the child's own developmental status could be overlooked almost entirely.

The Twentieth Century

The twentieth century has witnessed major advances in regard to all aspects of child psychopathology. Spearheaded by the psychoanalytic movement and later by behaviorism, along with Adolph Meyer's commonsense psychiatry, William Healy's study of juvenile delinquents, and Lightner Witmer's clinic for psychoeducational problems, the scientific investigation of childhood disorders came into its own. With the advent of the psychometric movement, behavior descriptions could be supplemented by measuring instruments, while professionals concerned with diagnosis strove for a comprehensive accounting of the entire range of childhood disorders. On the professional front, the mental hygiene movement was launched, child psychotherapies and residential treatment centers for children proliferated, child guidance clinics—typically staffed with an interdisciplinary team of psychiatrist, psychologist, and social worker—came into being, and targets for remediation were extended down the age span to infancy and outward from the child to include parents, entire families, and the community. As a sign of the vitality of the field, scientific and professional organizations and publications devoted to childhood psychopathology appeared at an accelerated rate.

We shall have time only to sample this rich fare, highlighting the developments most germane to our interests.

THE PSYCHOANALYTIC MOVEMENT. The landmark event in the scientific study of childhood psychopathology was the publication of Sigmund Freud's "Three Essays on the Theory of Sexuality" (1905). Freud's thesis that early development held the key to the understanding of adult neurosis moved the study of childhood from the periphery to the center of inquiry. Moreover, the psychosexual theory provided a detailed model whereby developments in the first six years of life could be related to subsequent adult disturbances. And finally, Freud was explicit in attributing a sexual drive to children, in regarding conflict over sexuality as the etiological factor in neurosis, and in postulating repression and the unconscious as two factors crucial to the production of a neurosis: "An alertness for the unconscious, the sexual and the infantile may be called the psychoanalytic point of view'' (Waelder, 1960). (We shall present the psychoanalytic theory of neurosis in detail in chapter 7.)

Freud and his followers continued to elaborate upon and revise psychoanalytic theory. Freud himself was most interested in exploring the motivational aspects of his theory, in particular the sexual and aggressive drives and the workings of the unconscious. His followers, notably Hartman and Kris, expanded his concept of the ego or the reality-oriented, adaptive functions of the psyche (Hartman, 1964), the superego, or conscience (Jacobson, 1964), and the defense mechanisms (Freud, 1946), while enlarging the interpersonal context from the nuclear family to society (Erikson, 1950). The initial emphasis on a single trauma as the origin of neurosis concomitantly shifted to a consideration of the complex interaction among intra- and interpersonal variables.

Freud himself never studied children. His famous psychoanalysis of a phobic boy, little Hans, was conducted through Hans's father and led Freud to conclude that he had learned little which he had not already known through his investigation of adults! It remained for Melanie Klein and Anna Freud to study children directly. Through such studies, the mother–infant relationship came into prominence, play came to be viewed not as a trivial pastime but as a disguised expression of unconscious wishes and conflicts, psychoanalytic concepts were applied to the entire array of childhood disorders from psychosis to situational disturbances, and the traditional psychosexual variables were expanded to include self-reliance, companionship, and work (A. Freud, 1965). (For a more detailed account of the psychoanalytic movement, see Rie, 1971.)

Of the many disciples who broke with Freud, often over the issue of the central role of sexuality, Adler was one who made major contributions to the understanding of childhood psychopathology. Adler regarded human nature as basically social rather than sexual and the striving for superiority as more important than the need for sexual gratification. Because of their social nature, children should be viewed within the context of the entire family rather than within the narrow triangle of the oedipal situation, and both siblings and peers play a central role in children's development. The striving for superiority, as Adler came to view it in his later writings, is a striving for mastery, for fulfillment, for growth. This striving can be undermined by excessive parental indulgence or excessive discipline, either of which paves the way to psychopathology. Far from using discipline to "break the child's will," for example, parents should strive to preserve the child's sense of autonomy, confidence, and expansiveness. (A detailed presentation of the Adlerian approach is to be found in Ansbacher and Ansbacher, 1956.)

THE BEHAVIORAL MOVEMENT. The behavioral movement was formally launched in 1913 by John B. Watson's paper, "Psychology as the Behaviorist Views It." In defiance of the current tradition, Watson proclaimed that the study of overt behavior, not consciousness, was the sole basis for a scientific psychology. Just as we need not trouble ourselves with the thoughts and introspections of animals in order to predict and control their behavior, neither should we trouble ourselves with those of human beings. While allowing for the importance of hereditary equipment, Watson championed a radical environmentalism in which it was possible to produce any kind of behavior one wished, given the proper learning conditions. The learning model itself, involving the building up of habits through stimulus–response connections, had a refreshing simplicity, especially in contrast to the complexities of the Freudian theory. And if one could mold human behavior as one wished, one could both prevent psychopathology from occurring and change it to normality after it had taken place. This mixture of simplicity and unbounded optimism was a heady brew.

Specifically in regard to children, Watson prescribed rigid schedules for child rearing which would mold children to be independent, require little affection, have no unnecessary fears, and fit comfortably into a socially prescribed niche. Laboratory experiments, especially with little Albert (the behavioral counterpart of little Hans) indicated that fears could be both acquired and eliminated utilizing learning principles. However, Watson's contribution to childhood psychopathology was rather like a promissory note that has only been redeemed in recent years.

Recently, the behavioral tradition has undergone both a narrowing and a broadening. B. F. Skinner goes Watson one better in rejecting not only mentalism but also physiological explanations of the link between stimulus and response. And just for good measure, he eschews theory construction and hypothetical constructs as aids to explaining behavior. His learning model relies heavily on the simple principles of reinforcement, extinction, generalization, and discrimination to account for a large spectrum of normal and disordered behavior. Like Watson, Skinner enthusiastically champions a cradle-to-grave environment in which scientifically proven learning principles would be utilized to produce an ideally adjusted society. (The best-known statement of Skinner's environmental engineering is *Walden Two,* 1948. For a general statement of his position, see *Science and Human Behavior,* 1953.)

The behavioral tradition has been broadened by social-learning theorists who insist that imitation or modeling must be added to the list of learning principles responsible for behavioral change. The thesis was defended by Miller and Dollard (1941) and subsequently by Bandura and Walters (1963). The learning theorists are "social" because they are primarily concerned with learning that takes place in a social context, such as between parent and child or among peers.

Among social-learning theorists, Bandura has been one of the most venturesome in making "private events" such as ideas, plans, wishes, and feelings, compatible with the scientific tenets of behaviorism. The study of private events, he argues, need not involve a return to the mentalism of the past, since these events can be operationally defined in terms of antecedents and consequences. The time-honored concept of a "mental" image, for example, can be anchored in behavioral antecedents, such as instructions to "Imagine you are lifting a weight," and measurable consequences, such as changes in muscle potential in the arms. Moreover, having the concept of an image accounts for the observed behavior better than if the concept were excluded. Thus, the requirements of objective inquiry are satisfied. In general, Bandura argues that a host of cognitive variables, such as symbolic representations of experiences, expectancies, and problem solving, can be encompassed within the social-learning framework with no loss of rigor and with significant gains in explanatory scope. Rejecting Skinner's exclusive emphasis on observable antecedents and consequences, Bandura maintains that external events affect behavior through intermediary cognitive processes which "partly determine which external events will be observed, how they will be perceived, whether they leave any lasting effects, what valence and efficacy they have, and how the information they convey will be organized for future use" (Bandura, 1977, p. 160).

Bandura also counters the charge that behaviorism makes the individual into a mere recipient of environmental events. He has his own version of initiative which he calls *self-efficacy*. In the initial stages, observing the differential effect of one's actions enables individuals to respond appropriately to various situations; for example, a preschool boy learns that playing in a day-care center will be rewarding and fighting will be punished, and behaves appropriately. Next, individuals come to anticipate not only that a given behavior will produce a given outcome, but more important, they also come to estimate whether they can successfully execute such a behavior. This conviction of success is called an efficacy expectation. Such an expectation of mastery affects both the initiation and persistence of coping behavior, people fearing and avoiding situations they believe exceed their coping skills, behaving assuredly in those which they believe themselves capable of handling. Therefore, self-efficacy influences both the choice of activities and persistence in the face of obstacles. It is important to note that Bandura's concept of self-efficacy is not merely speculative but also buttressed by empirical data (Bandura, 1977).

One final development in the behavioral movement may prove the most significant in regard to the study of childhood psychopathology. It is the appearance of a cluster of remedial techniques called *behavior therapies*. The behavior therapies have taken a number of behaviorists out of the rarefied atmosphere of the laboratory and challenged them to apply their scientific principles to the complexities of social interactions. In the process these therapies have firmly secured a place for the behavioral movement in the clinical arena while raising searching issues concerning the adequacy of a simple learning model to account for the changes which take place. (We shall take up this thread in chapter 14.) For many reasons, then, the behavior therapies have become the leading edge of the behavioral movement today.

OTHER CONTRIBUTORS. The commonsense psychiatry of Adolph Meyer occupies a kind of middle ground between the psychoanalytic and the behavioral movements. Like Freud, Meyer emphasized the importance of childhood precursors of adult disturbance and the dynamic balance of psychological forces within the individual. He was also critical of the overemphasis on organic determinants that was so prevalent at the turn of the century. He called his own approach *psychobiological*, in recognition of the importance of genetic and organic factors, on the one hand, and psychological and social factors, on the other. Yet he found Freud's emphasis on sexuality and the unconscious, along with his elaborate theorizing concerning the symbolism of symptoms, uncongenial. In his down-to-earth manner, Meyer viewed symptoms as well-learned reaction patterns that, though they originally seemed adjustive to the environment, proved to be maladjustive in the long run. Characteristically, he preferred the term "unsuccessful adjustment" to the then popular "insanity." In keeping with his eclecticism, he advocated medical, psychological, educational, and sociological treatment as well as preventive measures to help people before their faulty reactions became symptoms (see Leif, 1948). It was this emphasis on behavior and adaptation to the environment which linked Meyer with the behaviorist tradition; indeed, when Meyer, as head of the Phipps Clinic of Johns Hopkins University, started the first course in psychology for medical students, one of his instructors was John B. Watson.

Another pioneer, and one more concerned with children than Meyer, was William Healy, who devoted his professional career to understanding and helping juvenile delinquents. In 1899 a juvenile court was established in Chicago in order to give juvenile delinquents special legal consideration, and in 1909, Healy founded what is now known as the Institute for Juvenile Research as a court-affiliated clinic. Like other pioneers, Healy emphasized the importance of social and cultural factors rather than biological ones in the production of juvenile delinquency. Because we now take it for granted that children who are in conflict with society must be understood in terms of their social context, it is difficult to realize that the idea once was far from self-evident (see Healy and Bronner, 1948).

The *psychometric tradition* began auspiciously in 1905 when Alfred Binet, a French psychologist, together with Theophile Simon, developed the first test for differentiating feebleminded children from other students in the Paris school system. The test was designed to serve the practical purpose of providing a relatively objective procedure for determining whether a given child's intellectual functioning was sufficiently below average to justify special education. Binet clearly regarded his intelligence test as an estimate of current functioning rather than an evaluation of some hypothetical potential or some fixed intellectual level. He also realized that test results provided no information as to the reasons why a child was functioning at a given level, such as heredity or environment. (For a translation of the original article, see Binet and Simon, 1916.) Unfortunately, these crucial insights tended to be ignored as the testing movement gained in popularity and the IQ score began to be perceived as having an immutability which was never intended.

As school attendance became mandatory and as children with academic and emotional problems came increasingly to the attention of professionals charged with evaluating them, tests became diversified to include abilities, achievement, personality, social maturity, and psychopathology itself.

The rise of the *child study movement* is particularly relevant to our interest in understanding psychopathology as normal development gone awry. The very idea that children might be worthy of study in their own right is a relatively recent one. (See Ariès, 1962, and for an alternate interpretation, see de Mause, 1974.) The medieval world probably regarded children as nothing more than miniature adults; they dressed as adults, had no special play activities or games, were economic pawns for their elders, were educated only if they belonged to the privileged class, while, in the lower classes, livestock took precedence over wives and children alike. Misbehavior was viewed as evidence of inherent wickedness to be suppressed by frequent corporal punishment. After the fourteenth century, children began to be regarded as "charming toys," providing amusement and relaxation for adults. By the seventeenth century, children's behavior was viewed in moralistic terms, and there was concern over making the now inherently innocent children into "good Christians." Biased as it was, this moralistic view at least recognized the separateness of childhood and created an interest in child rearing and education.

One product of this interest was the philosopher John Locke's influential notion, published in 1690, that the mind of the newborn was a *tabula rasa,* a blank slate, and that experience determined how the mind would develop. In such radical empiricism one catches a glimpse of the radical environmentalism of the twentieth-century behaviorists. In the eighteenth century, Jean Jacques Rousseau, the father of modern educational philosophy, argued that children were innately good and would develop optimally if their natural activities were not interfered with—an idea very much in keeping with the present-day humanistic belief that each individual has the potential for maximal growth and self-realization. The latter half of the nineteenth century saw Darwin using his powers of observation to demonstrate that infant development contained adaptive mechanisms which paralleled those occurring in the evolution of the human species. Yet the scientific study of childhood, like that of childhood psychopathology, had to wait until the twentieth century before coming into its own.

The pivotal figure was G. Stanley Hall, the first promoter of the psychological study of children in the United States. He was concerned with understanding, within an evolutionary framework, how individuals develop and adapt to their environment. Because of this interest in origins or genesis, his is called a genetic psychology. In his research, for example, he distributed questionnaires to parents, teachers, and children to obtain developmental data on thinking, fears, motor abilities, dreams, and prayers. His most famous book was on adolescence (1904), whose thesis that this is a period of inherent turmoil is still being debated.

The subsequent history of the child study movement up until World War II is largely a history of child development institutes. (Our presentation follows Sears, 1975, chap. 1—a chapter which deserves to be read in its entirety.) In 1906, Mrs. Cora Bussey Hillis reasoned that, if agricultural colleges in Iowa could study ways to improve livestock and disseminate the information efficiently to farmers, why couldn't a similar model be set up to research, teach, and disseminate information about children? The idea was difficult to sell because, although the "agricultural public believed in science for hogs . . . children were another matter. . . . Could the human soul be subjected to Science?" (Sears, 1975, p. 19). In 1917 the Iowa legislature finally appropriated funds for the Iowa Child Welfare Research Station at the State University of Iowa. After World War I had sensitized the public to the deplorable state of literacy in the male population, the Rockefeller interests followed suit by dedicating approximately $12 million for research, teaching, and dissemination of knowledge in the field of child development. The era of the institutes had been launched. The research conducted in such settings in large measure defined the content of the study of child development:

The Iowa Child Welfare Research Station studied physical growth first and then mental growth, becoming an environmentalist stronghold particularly in regard to intellectual development.

The University of Minnesota Institute of Child Welfare's research program emphasized the development of school-aged children, personality, and objective measures of behavior.

The Yale Clinic of Child Development, under the direction of Arnold Gesell, meticulously observed and documented a variety of behaviors, particularly in infants but also in preschoolers. Gesell also championed a theory of maturational unfolding of behavior and published influential books for parents. In addition, Gesell came closer than any of his contemporaries to having a theoretically oriented, objectively documented developmental psychopathology.

Teachers College's Child Development Institute emphasized personality development.

The University of California's Institute of Child Welfare at Berkeley concentrated on longitudinal studies of personality and intellectual development as well as the physical, physiological, and social development of adolescents. The rich data from the Berkeley Growth Study continue to be mined and we shall refer to them on more than one occasion.

The Fels Research Institute at Yellow Springs, Ohio, studied physiological and personality development from birth to maturity.

Thus, during the interwar period there was a giant leap forward in terms of factual information and research methodology, while physical, mental, and personality development were explored from infancy to adulthood. World War II almost decimated the child development movement, which was rescued only by massive federal funding. While institutes continued to exist, child development moved into departments of psychology, both learning from and adding a developmental dimension to general psychology. The combination of financial support and intellectual challenges has produced the current state of widespread interest and high productivity. We will not cover the current substantive issues (see Sears, 1975) because we are more concerned with current models of psychopathology. However, before examining these, we need to summarize one more important historical trend—the mental hygiene movement.

The *mental hygiene movement* for children began in 1896 when Lightner Witmer established the first clinic for children in this country at the University of Pennsylvania. He also coined the terms "clinical psychology" and "psychological clinic." (Our presentation again follows Rie, 1971.) Witmer's initial presentation of clinical psychology to the American Psychological Association was received with cool indifference, but, undaunted, he went on to found both a journal, *Psychological Clinic,* and an orthogenic school for prolonged observation and training. During this period, Healy was pioneering a tridisciplinary clinic for juvenile delinquents in which psychiatrists, psychologists, and psychiatric social workers joined in a team approach to deal with problems of diagnosis and remediation. In 1921 the Commonwealth Fund, together with the National Committee of Mental Hygiene, sponsored a conference on the prevention of juvenile delinquency, which resulted in the launching of a five-year demonstration program of child guidance clinics. This "may well have been the single most important step toward the goal of the definition, prevention and remediation of behavior disorders in children" (Rie, 1971, p. 33). The clinics were basically atheoretical and eclectic, learning primarily from firsthand experience. The contributions to childhood psychopathology were numerous. The addition of mild and moderate disorders expanded the range of psychopathologies and countered the tendency to concentrate only on the severely disturbed child. Early influences, rather than heredity, came to be viewed as the major determinants of behavior disorders. However, there was also evidence that, instead of a one-to-one correspondence between childhood experiences and subsequent disturbance, similar situations could be followed by dissimilar behavior patterns in adults, while dissimilar early experiences might eventuate in similar adult behavior. There was little evidence to support the old belief that disturbances were due to the impact of a single traumatic event; rather, they resulted from the cumulative weight of untoward events. Undoubtedly buttressed by the team approach, interest shifted from symptom to the "whole-child" approach, requiring a comprehensive evaluation of the children's current functioning, their interactions at home and at school, and their histories—what we have called the intra- and interpersonal contexts and the context of time.

As for the clinics themselves, they expanded from a handful in 1922 to 285 exclusively serving children and 350 serving children and adults by 1946 (see Rie, 1971). This growth was accompanied by an expansion of organizations and journals devoted to clinical and professional issues.

The Interplay of Ideas

Before bringing the historical context up to the present, it is worth noting that the trends discussed were described separately only for convenience in presentation. In reality, interest in childhood psychopathology was vitalized by the continual interaction among the various trends. The desire to help went hand in hand with the desire to learn and to teach; the basic and the applied, the laboratory and the clinic, were in constant interaction. Psychoanalysis was at once a therapeutic technique and a device for exploring personality. To celebrate Clark University's twentieth anniversary, Hall invited Meyer and Freud to speak, and the latter received an honorary degree. Watson dedicated *Psychology from the Standpoint of the Behaviorist* (1919) to an academic psychologist, J. McKeen Cattell, and to Meyer and established the pattern of applying findings from laboratory experiments to the practical problems of preventing and remedying disturbed behavior. Finally, the child guidance clinics, while carrying out their service mission, uncovered valuable leads as to the nature and etiology of childhood psychopathologies. It is this same picture of diversity with component elements overlapping, complementing, and conflicting with one another which continues to lend a special excitement to the quest for understanding and, ultimately, eradicating childhood psychopathology.

CHILDHOOD PSYCHOPATHOLOGY: CURRENT MODELS

There are, at present, a variety of models of childhood psychopathology, most of which are rooted in the historical developments we have just examined. While having distinctive features, the models are not necessarily incompatible. Some share common features. Others are complementary or tangential. Still others represent irreconcilable differences. Each has merit; none is totally satisfactory. Moreover, few efforts have been made to integrate them all, as there is tacit agreement that such a unification lies far in the future. Therefore we must reconcile ourselves to living with diversity and partial truths. (For a more comprehensive coverage of models of psychopathology than we shall give, see Bootzin, 1980.)

The term "model" is best interpreted as a frame of reference, since it has little of the precision and explanatory potency of models in the physical sciences, such as a model for the structure of the atom or the DNA molecule. Each model has its own concepts, often couched in terms of a specialized vocabulary, its own assumptions concerning which are relevant variables, its own view of etiology and remediation, and its own stand on the nature of scientific inquiry. In addition to its expected functions of organizing existing facts and generating new ones, a model of psychopathology must also serve the pragmatic function of being useful to the professionals concerned with understanding and remedying childhood disturbances.

The Medical Model

The medical model is the present-day version of the organic emphasis, which, by replacing the demonology of the Middle Ages, was a step forward in the scientific study of psychopathology but which, in its exclusion of all other etiological factors in the nineteenth century, became a roadblock to progress. Currently, the organic emphasis is more temperate and buttressed by a more substantial body of empirical findings than it was 100 years ago. The present-day medical model consists of two different components. The first involves the general etiological hypothesis that certain psychopathologies result from organic dysfunctions. The second involves classifying and interpreting psychopathological behavior in the same way as physical diseases, namely, in terms of diagnostic entities.

ORGANIC ETIOLOGY. There is evidence that organic factors play a major role in certain kinds of adult schizophrenia and depression, and in certain kinds of mental retardation and schizophrenia in children. Organic factors have also been implicated in the etiology of autism and in certain kinds of antisocial acting-out behaviors, hyperactivity, and learning disabilities in children, although the evidence varies in definitiveness. Thus, the list of psychopathologies having a possible organic etiology continues to be impressive. Note the modifier "certain kinds of," however: a given psychopathology—adult depression, for example—may have an organic basis in some cases while being psychogenic in others.

There are three specific models of organic etiology. In the first, *genetic* factors are responsible for the appearance of a given psychopathology. Research has centered around three related areas of inquiry. The first of these concerns which psychopathologies have a significant genetic component; for example, there is compelling evidence for the inheritance of certain kinds of schizophrenia. The second area concerns the mode by which a genetic abnormality is transmitted. This involves tracing the path from gene to behavior and understanding all the mediators involved. The third area concerns the extent of hereditability in a given psychopathology. Extremists maintain that genes per se determine the abnormal behavior; moderates counter that only vulnerability to a psychopathology is inherited, while its actual appearance depends on environmental conditions. For example, one child may become schizophrenic because of a genetic vulnerability interacting with a series of traumatic life experiences, while another child with the same genetic vulnerability may make an adequate adjustment because of a sympathetic, benign environment.

The *biochemical model* seeks to discover the biochemical agents which may contribute to the etiology of psychopathological behavior. Again, schizophrenia has been the most frequently targeted disturbance, each new advance in medical science leading to new hope that the psychotoxic agent has been discovered. When bacteria were found to cause physical disease, it was also suggested that they were involved in mental illness; then attention shifted to viruses and, most recently, to alterations in the metabolism of certain brain chemicals, or neurochemicals, particularly a group of naturally occurring neurochemical substances called monoamines. In spite of promising leads, the gap between chemistry and behavior is far from being closed—as is the case with genes—and the assumption of a direct causal relation seems a highly oversimplified one.

The *neurophysiological model* assumes that abnormal behavior is due to inherited, congenital, or acquired brain pathology. Obviously, it overlaps the genetic and biochemical models but includes other etiological agents such as intrauterine disease, premature birth, or traumatic brain insult. What this model does is to make brain functioning the key to understanding psychopathological conditions. Because of the difficulties and uncertainties involved in doing research on the human brain, however, less is known about neurophysiological factors in relation to psychopathology than is known about genetic or biochemical models.

At the most general level, the medical model is part of the quest to build a bridge between human behavior and human physiology. The quest is an ancient one and is currently being facilitated by astonishing advances in modern technology. However, to claim at this point that psychopathology is "nothing but" organic dysfunctioning would be as erroneous as to claim that it is "nothing but" problems in adjustment. The organic contexts interact with the intra- and interpersonal contexts, and knowledge of this interaction is necessary if progress is to be made in understanding the etiology of psychopathology. (For further details concerning the organic basis of psychopathological behavior, see Knopf, 1979.)

THE MEDICAL MODEL OF DIAGNOSIS. At one level, diagnosis can be viewed as a variation on the age-old scientific exercise of classification. Psychopathologies, like insects and flowers, are so diverse that viewing each separately would be overwhelming. In order to simplify their task, therefore, investigators assume that there are classes in nature and that keen observation will reveal what these classes are.

Classifications based on the medical model require answering two basic questions: What is the rationale for regarding the behaviors as abnormal rather than normal? and, Are the specific classifications valid or true to nature? The first question establishes the general criteria for inclusion and exclusion and, among classifications utilizing the medical model, has been answered in a variety of ways. The least satisfactory is based on an analogy of mental health and illness to physical health and illness. An analogy is not an acceptable rationale and can be both incorrect and misleading. Yet it is the analogy which has crept into and dominates the very vocabulary we have used in dealing with psychopathology—mental illness, mental health, mental hygiene, syndrome, patient, treatment, cure, and, indeed, psychopathology itself all derive from medicine.

Whether a classification is really there in nature involves validation, with diverse professionals and investigators putting the classification to empirical and statistical tests which either affirm or cast doubt upon its soundness. As we shall see, some classifications, such as autism, have met the test of subsequent validation; others, such as minimal brain damage, have not.

But the medical model has always entailed more than a descriptive classification; the classifications themselves are called diagnoses, and these have both etiological and prognostic implications. It is the former which is most troublesome. Kraepelin, who published the landmark classification of adult psychopathologies in 1833, set the stage by assuming an organic etiology for each class of psychopathology. While it is an erroneous overgeneralization, the equation "classification = diagnosis = organic etiology" lingers on, particularly in the ceaseless professional skirmishes between psychiatrists and other mental health professionals. The former claim that their medical background makes them the ultimate arbiters of diagnosis and therapy in mental as well as physical illness. Psychologists are particularly incensed by this stand, and heated legal battles are being fought over what constitutes the legitimate province of each professional.

There is another problem with medical terminology, involving the use of the word "symptom." To designate a given psychopathology, say, a phobia, as a symptom means that there is an underlying cause, just as in medicine a virus may be the underlying cause of the symptoms of the flu. The underlying cause need not be organic, however; it might just as well be psychological. Thus, a phobia might be considered as a symbolic expression of an underlying fear of a powerful mother. The issue of underlying causes is a complex and controversial one which will occupy us later (see chapter 7). Suffice it to say at this point that the evidence is too inconclusive to resolve the controversies satisfactorily, but the word itself remains a bone of contention.

Since the term "medical model" has become so affect-laden among professionals, it is important to disentangle relevant from irrelevant issues. Purely as a classification system, one based on the medical model should stand or fall on the basis of proven validity and clinical utility—that is, on independent evidence that clusters of symptoms do, in fact, exist in nature, that etiology and prognosis are, in fact, what the system claims them to be, and on practitioners' reports of the fit between described classifications and observed behavior. Currently, there are two dangers. One is that classifications based on the medical model will be used as a vehicle for making unwarranted assumptions concerning organic etiology and for extending the province of psychiatrists into childhood disturbances which have little or nothing to do with medical training and expertise. The second danger is that nonmedical professionals and researchers will reject the classification out of hand because of the label "medical model," thus turning their backs on its empirical merits and clinical utility.

The Behavioral Model

Three characteristics distinguish behavioral psychology. First is the assertion that *observable behavior* comprises the basic data of a scientific psychology. The more radical theorists would limit psychology to the response organisms make to environmental stimuli, excluding all mentalistic and inferential variables such as thoughts, images, drives, and memory traces. More moderate theorists admit inferential concepts under two conditions: such terms can be defined behaviorally, and their introduction facilitates the fundamental goals of predicting and controlling behavior. Next, behaviorists favor *research conducted under highly controlled conditions,* the laboratory experiment being the technique par excellence for establishing the necessary and sufficient conditions for producing the behavior being investigated. Measurement and quantification are highly valued as part of the overall emphasis on precision. Third, behaviorists assume that a limited number of *learning principles* can account for a wide array of behavior in animals and humans. True, there are other forces at work—genetic, instinctual, maturational, temperamental—but the acquisition, maintenance, change, or elimination of much behavior can be adequately and concisely accounted for in terms of learning principles.

PRINCIPLES OF LEARNING. The three principles of learning which form the basis of the behavioral approach are *classical conditioning* (also called respondent or Pavlovian conditioning), *operant conditioning* (also called instrumental conditioning), and *imitation* (also called modeling or observational learning).

In classical conditioning a stimulus (the conditioned stimulus, or CS) which initially is incapable of eliciting a response (the unconditioned response, UR) is successively paired with a stimulus (the unconditioned stimulus, US) which is the UR's uniform or innate elicitor. After a given number of pairings, the previously neutral stimulus (the CS) comes to elicit the response (the UR) which is now known as the conditioned response, or CR. To vary the well-known example of a dog being conditioned to salivate to the sound of a bell, a tone (the CS) that is successively paired with a puff of air to the eyelid (the US)—a stimulus which naturally elicits a blinking response (the UR)—will, with time, itself come to elicit the blinking response (now called the CR), even when the air puff is omitted.

Two other principles derived from classical conditioning have proved useful in accounting for the development and elimination of psychopathological behavior. *Stimulus generalization* is the tendency for stimuli similar to the conditioned stimulus also to elicit the conditioned response, the greater the degree of similarity the more vigorous the response. In the above example, the blinking response can be elicited by tones similar to the CR. The increase in efficiency is obvious since the organism does not have to learn to respond anew to each variation in the stimulus. *Discrimination learning* is the opposite of generalization in that it involves learning to distinguish among stimuli and to respond only to the appropriate one. Typically, the discrimination is established through nonreinforcement or punishment. Thus, a preschooler who has learned that a dog is a wolf-wolf might label a number of animals wolf-wolf until the parent supplies another, more appropriate label.

In *operant conditioning* the organism operates upon or does something to the environment in order to achieve a given result. In essence, it is a process by which an organism learns to associate certain results with certain actions it has taken. These results may serve either to increase or decrease the likelihood of the behavior's being repeated. The term used to designate an increase in the likelihood of occurrence is reinforcement. Reinforcement can be positive or negative. In *positive reinforcement* behavior is followed by a reward; for example, the father of an 8-year-old treats his son's soccer team to ice cream after a victory. In *negative reinforcement* an aversive stimulus is removed; for example, a 10-year-old girl is excused from washing dishes for a week after improving her grade in history.

The two terms used to designate a decrease in the likelihood of a behavior's being repeated are extinction and punishment. In *extinction* the reinforcement maintaining a response is removed; for example, upon her therapist's advice, a mother no longer gives in to her 4-year-old's demands every time he has a temper tantrum, and the tantrums disappear. In *punishment* a response is followed by an aversive stimulus; for example, a 5-year-old is spanked after running into the streets.

A distinction is also made between *primary* and *secondary reinforcers*. The first are unlearned, having a biological base: primary positive reinforcers include food, water, warmth, and sex, while primary negative reinforcers include pain, extremes of heat and cold, and intensely loud sounds. Most reinforcers are learned in association with primary reinforcers and are called secondary or conditioned reinforcers; the cuddly blanket which provided the infant with warmth becomes a security blanket during the toddler and preschool years, just as mother's harsh voice preceding punishment becomes feared in its own right. Subsequently words, the mere symbols of reinforcement, acquire great potency, and much of the child's behavior is regulated by the value judgments of "Good" and "Bad."

One consequence of punishment is particularly relevant to our interest in psychopathology. Once exposed to an aversive stimulus, an organism will try in the future to avoid reexposure, a process which is called *avoidance learning*. Avoidance learning is a two-edged sword. It protects the organism from a repeated encounter with a possibly harmful situation; for example, once burned, a 2-year-old does not continually touch the burner of a stove. But avoidance learning can also lead to unrealistic avoidance of situations after they are no longer noxious; for example, an adult may be terrified of his reasonable, benevolent boss because, as a child, he was brutally beaten by his father. Thus, avoidance prevents the individual from adopting new behaviors which are appropriate to changed circumstances.

The final concept which will be useful in subsequent discussions is *shaping*. Operant conditioning depends on the natural occurrence of the operant response. Yet, some of these responses have a very low rate of occurrence or, indeed, do not occur at all. In such instances the response must be shaped by reinforcing successive approximations to the desired one; for example, young children are progressively taught to swim by first getting them accustomed to the water, teaching them to float, then to kick their legs or tread water while floating, and so on, until the basic skill of swimming has been mastered.

The third in the triad of learning principles is *imitation,* which involves learning a new behavior by observing and imitating another person's performance of that behavior. Thus, without any direct parental tutelage preschoolers will pretend to clean the house or hammer a nail as their parents do or will answer the phone with the exact words and intonation that they have heard adults use. While learning theorists have devoted a good deal of attention to studying the possible mechanisms involved in imitation, their research and theorizing will not be relevant to our discussions.

NORMAL AND ABNORMAL DEVELOPMENT. The behaviorists' credo is that all behavior is one and—once allowance has been made for genetic, maturational, and temperamental factors—all behavior conforms to the basic principles of learning just described. Of course, one may divide behavior into categories, such as infant or adolescent, normal or abnormal, but this is done only to stake out territory of special interest to the investigator. The basic task is to discover how the principles of learning can be utilized to account for the special behaviors one has chosen.

According to the behaviorists, some children grow up with the kinds of learning experiences which maximize their chances of making a successful adaptation to environmental demands, while others have experiences which minimize such an outcome. In the latter instance, behaviorists prefer to talk in terms of "maladaptive" rather than "abnormal" behavior to avoid any suspicion of a qualitatively different developmental outcome. Implicit in their stand is also a cultural relativism: What would be adaptive in one society may be maladaptive in another.

In addition to being cultural relativists, behaviorists have a penchant for quantification which leads them to define psychopathology as deviations in the frequency or intensity of behavior. Note A. O. Ross's definition of a psychological disorder as behavior which "deviates from an arbitrary and relative social norm in that it occurs with a frequency or intensity that authoritative adults . . . judge . . . to be either too high or too low" (Ross, 1980, p. 9).

Utilizing such a definition, psychopathologies can be grouped in terms of behavioral deficit or excess. In *behavior deficit,* behaviors occur at a lower frequency or intensity than is expected within society so that the child's social, intellectual, or practical skills are impaired. Autism, learning disabilities, mental retardation, and even juvenile delinquency are examples, the last resulting from deficient behavioral controls. In *behavior excess,* behavior occurs at a higher frequency or intensity than is adaptive to the standards of society. The hyperactive child who is in a continual state of excitement, the compulsive child who repeatedly washes his hands, and the anxious child who is constantly terrified by real and imagined dangers would all be examples.

However, other kinds of deviations are also recognized, one being the appropriateness of the stimulus–response relationships. In *inappropriate stimulus control,* either a response occurs in the absence of any appropriate stimulus, or a stimulus fails to elicit the appropriate response. A psychotic boy's delusion that his therapist will bite his head off if he enters the therapy room is an example, as is the anorectic girl's conviction that she is still too fat when she is on the verge of starving herself to death.

In addition to categorizing types of maladaptations, behaviorists have also conceptualized traditional psychopathologies in terms of learning principles. A phobia, for example, could readily be regarded as an example of maladaptive avoidance behavior, in which the child is too terrified to learn how harmless the feared object really is; depression may be interpreted as the result of extinction, in which significant positive reinforcements are withdrawn, and the person becomes passive and hopeless; while autism, with its imperviousness to the human environment, may result from a failure of parents to acquire secondary reinforcing value.

For the past decade or so, however, behaviorists have not been particularly vigorous in testing hypotheses concerning etiology. This is primarily because they have concentrated on changing maladaptive behavior by means of a host of behavioral techniques; therapy, not pursuit of etiology, has been the vitalizing force. And as practical clinicians, they implicitly raise the question, If we can enable people to change their maladaptive behavior, is it so important to understand how they came to be that way? Watson's pragmatic spirit is still very much alive.

The Psychodynamic Model

The psychodynamic school of thought was generated by Freud and his followers, some of whom ultimately rebelled against the Freudian tenets of psychoanalysis. What they all shared was an interest in discovering the dynamics—the basic motives, the prime movers—of human behavior. This concern with intrapersonal forces immediately sets them apart from the behaviorists, with their concern for the environmental factors which shape behavior. As with the other two approaches discussed so far, our coverage of the psychodynamic approach will not be comprehensive; instead, we shall concentrate on the two aspects of Freudian theory that are most relevant to understanding childhood psychopathology—the structural and genetic theories. (For more extensive coverage, see Bootzin, 1980.)

THE STRUCTURAL THEORY. Freud arrived at a tripartite conceptualization of the human psyche: the id, the ego, and the superego.

According to classical Freudian theory, the id is the source of all psychic energy, which in turn derives from biological drives. Among these, the sexual drive is prepotent in its import for personality development. (Freud subsequently added the death instinct, which included aggression as the other primary motivating force, but its conceptualization was unsatisfactory and its status remains controversial.) The drives of the id are alogical, demanding immediate and complete satisfaction, or what Freud called discharge. The id's ceaseless striving for immediate discharge, Freud termed the *pleasure principle*. Ideation in the id is also at the service of the pleasure principle, resembling the irrational images and sequencing of events in dreams. Freud called such ideation *primary process thinking* to distinguish it from rational thought. Developmentally speaking, the infant is an id-dominated creature, concerned only with reducing the tensions generated by physiological needs, having no capacity for delay and no awareness of the realistic parameters of the world he or she has entered.

In the classical formulation, the ego arises from the id's need for maximal gratification. Unlike the id, the ego is endowed with functions such as perception, memory, and reasoning which enable it to learn realistic means of satisfying the id. A 2-year-old's ego may advise, "You can do anything you want with your teddy bear when you're mad; but when you get mad at your baby brother, better wait until no one is around or else the pain of punishment will outweigh the pleasure of hitting him." Thus, the ego functions on what Freud called the *reality principle;* he called the rational thinking which is in tune with the parameters of reality *secondary process thinking.* Note that the ego requires the id to postpone immediate gratification, although this is inimical to its nature, and that secondary process thinking both delays and guides behavior. Subsequently, the ego psychologists made a major revision in the classical theory by postulating that the ego initially is endowed with its own energy and can function autonomously rather than being subservient to the id. Important as this change is, it will not directly bear on our discussions.

The ego begins to emerge at about 6 months of life, and the third structure, the superego, comes into its own at about 5 to 6 years of age. It contains the moral standards of right and wrong which the preschooler takes over from his or her parents and which become an internalized judge of the moral rectitude of the child's behavior. In case of transgression, the superego punishes the child with guilt feelings. The superego is comparable to the conscience, but it is an absolutistic, implacable conscience and demands continual obedience to its standard of proper behavior.

From middle childhood on, then, the ego must find ways of obtaining as much id gratification as reality will allow without arousing the superego, which in its way is as irrational in its demands as the id itself. The image of the beleaguered ego contending with inevitable conflict between irreconcilable intrapersonal forces has been regarded as stern and heroic by some, bleak and dour by others. It certainly has little of the behaviorist's belief in the malleability and therefore the potential perfectability of human behavior and none of the humanist's belief that humans inherently desire to grow and maximize themselves.

Finally, Freud's structural theory interrelates with his topographical approach, which is concerned with levels of consciousness. The *perceptual conscious* contains the mental events in immediate awareness, while the *preconscious* consists of whatever a person can remember upon making an effort to do so. The largest level is the *unconscious,* which contains all of the id and part of the ego and superego as well as the material which has been banished from consciousness by repression because of its anxiety-producing content. Such repressed material, however, continues to seek readmittance into consciousness, reappearing in fantasies and dreams, in "accidental" forgetting or slips of the tongue, or on other occasions when the vigilance of the ego is relaxed.

While Freud's structural theory is relevant to our concern with psychopathology, his genetic theory of psychosexual development will figure more prominently in subsequent discussions.

THE PSYCHOSEXUAL THEORY. Freud's psychosexual theory assumes that eroticized intimacy exists throughout the life span, adult sexuality being only the culmination of a process begun in earliest infancy. Our bodies themselves are so constituted that stimulation of certain areas arouse exquisitely pleasurable sensations. Once having experienced them, we are forever driven to obtain the maximum bodily pleasures which society will allow. Freud called this biologically determined drive to obtain erotic bodily sensations *libido.* Furthermore, the body is constituted so that the mouth, the anus, and the genitals are particularly rich in erotic sensations when stimulated. Freud assumed that there is an inevitable progression, whereby first the mouth, then the anus, and finally the genitals predominate as sources of pleasure. Equally important, each progression of libido is accompanied by a psychological change in the intimate relations with the parents or primary caretakers. The label *psychosexual* epitomizes the complementary relation between psychological and erotic development.

The three specific stages of psychosexual development are called the oral, the anal, and the phallic. These are true stages in that their sequencing is unalterable and each represents a qualitative change in personality. The Oedipal complex, which is the climax of the psychosexual stages, occurs toward the end of the preschool period. Finally, Freud stated that progression is never complete; even in normal development, residuals of prior stages can be found. Such residuals are called *fixations.* We will briefly describe both the stages themselves and their normal residuals.

In the *oral stage* the infant derives pleasure first from sucking and, after teeth appear, from biting. In the context of being fed, the first emotional attachment or, to use the Freudian term, the first *object relation* is formed. This initial intimacy is particularly potent in setting the tone for all future intimacies. Sensitive, loving caretaking engenders a positive image both of mother and of being mothered; caretaking marked by distress and frustration will engender an image in which love is mixed with anxiety and rage. And at a primitive level, being loved and being fed are forever equated.

Normal fixations include pleasure in sucking candy and chewing gum as well as smoking and kissing. In religion, the Madonna preserves the image of the all-loving, all-powerful mother figure, while in literature the witch epitomizes the angry, destructive mother, the poisoned apple or poison in general representing love contaminated by the destructiveness of hostility. "There's no apple pie like mother's apple pie" and "The way to a man's heart is through his stomach" derive from the basic equation: being well loved equals being well fed.

In the *anal stage* the toddler achieves erotic gratification from retaining and evacuating feces or from manual manipulation of the anus. For the first time, the toddler also has control of the source of pleasure: whereas the infant is totally dependent on the caretaker for feeding, the toddler alone can decide when, where, and how to have a bowel movement. Toilet training requires the relinquishing of this pleasurable autonomy. For such a sacrifice the toddler should be adequately compensated by love. If training is punitive, unloving, or coercive, the toddler becomes rebellious and stubbornly resistive or anxious and overly compliant.

One normal residual of the anal stage is the cult of regularity; laxatives always sell well, and there are adults whose daily mood is contingent upon a daily evacuation. Preschoolers call one another "You old BM" or "You old pooh-pooh," and adult cursing continues the tradition by substituting adult for childhood equivalents of feces. The preschooler's fascination with mud and clay derive from the earlier interest in feces. In addition, any number of behaviors can be categorized as being "clean" or "dirty"—being personally clean, neat, orderly, being clean minded and clean living as contrasted with being messy and slovenly, being a dirty dealer, having a dirty mind, and telling dirty jokes, dirt being only a thin disguise for feces.

In the *phallic stage* masturbation and curiosity about anatomical differences are at their height, so that the desire to peek and to show, to look and to exhibit, run high. The period is also marked by expansiveness, assertiveness, and an intoxicating sense of power as the child feels that he or she is now—or soon will be—"big" and "grown up." Normal residuals include an abiding interest in the human body, sexual techniques, and intercourse evidenced in scholarly descriptions, pinup magazines and pornography alike. The desire to show off also harks back to the phallic stage and is evident in the "sex symbol," the muscle man on the beach, the actress who tries to captivate the audience, the physicist who tries to dazzle the scientific community, or even the conspicuous sufferer who proclaims that no one else has ever known such misery.

The *Oedipus complex* and *castration anxiety* climax early psychosexual development for boys, the girls experiencing a variation called the *Electra complex.* The preschool boy is incapable of feeling generous about his attachment to his mother; he feels possessive and jealous. In the exuberance of the phallic stage he wants to be the only person in his mother's life. This passionate attachment makes him his father's rival, which in turn leads to a wish that the father would disappear. The desire to possess the mother and destroy the father is called the Oedipus complex.

The Oedipus complex precipitates a crisis because of the boy's terrifying fantasy that the rivalrous, retaliatory father will cut off his penis. Freud claimed that castration anxiety is inevitable, even with the most benevolent of fathers, since it is essentially of the child's own making. Remember that we are dealing with the 4- to 5-year-old who is still in the egocentric stage of assuming that others feel as he does. Thus, the boy reasons that if he wants to destroy the father, the father must have similar wishes toward him. It is the projection of his own hostility which makes castration anxiety inevitable. The typical resolution of the oedipal conflict is for the boy to renounce his sexual feelings and his claim on the mother and identify with the powerful father. In essence he says, "I am not your rival, I am like you."

The boy's relations with the mother during the Oedipus complex set the tone of his future heterosexual strivings. If the relationship is positive, he will unconsciously seek to replicate it at the adult level; if the relationship is mixed with anxiety and/or anger, other kinds of relationships will prove attractive. Fear of physical injury, operations, or vigorous contact sports as well as a negative attitude toward same-sex competition may be a residual of castration anxiety. "I'm afraid to stick my neck out because someone will cut it off" is a thinly disguised expression of the preschooler's castration terror that assertiveness will lead to destruction by a powerful rival.

Freud erroneously regarded middle childhood as a period of diminished sexual activity caused by the repression which resolved the Oedipus complex along with an inherent decrease in the libidinal drive. Physiological maturation at puberty revives all the difficulties of psychosexual development in the first six years, which once again must be dealt with and mastered. However, Freud's contributions to understanding both the middle years and adolescence have been minor. More relevant to our subsequent discussion of homosexuality is the Freudian concept of normal and deviant sexuality in adulthood.

Adult sexuality remains a psychosexual development. Sexually, all the erotic elements of the first six years of life are revived as components of foreplay, except that oral, anal, and genital stimulation along with exhibition of the body serve the function of heightening the pleasure of the ultimate goal of mature sexuality, which is genital union. It may be that the idiosyncratic reactions of pleasure, indifference, and disgust in regard to specific aspects of foreplay are rooted in comparable experiences during the first three stages of psychosexual development. Sexual *perversions* result when elements of foreplay become goals in themselves; for example, the psychopathology called exhibitionism involves an irresistible desire to display one's genitals in public, while voyeurism involves Peeping Tom activities or the irresistible urge to view nude bodies. Both pathologies result from a failure to develop beyond the phallic period.

Mature sexuality is a psychological achievement as well. It too involves components of the early stages of psychological development: from the oral period comes the need for and ability to provide tender care, along with trust that the partner will be there in times of distress; from the anal period comes a willingness to negotiate the many areas of adult responsibility and decision making, such as how money will be spent, work loads apportioned, or discipline enforced; from the phallic period comes pride in those achievements that make the partner proud, whether it be a bowling trophy or a PhD; from the oedipal period comes confidence that one is as good as the next person. However, maturity entails a mutuality, a givingness, and an appreciation of the partner's point of view which counteracts the basic egocentricism (using the term in the Freudian sense) of the early psychosexual stages.

And, just as is true of the sexual act, the psychological relationship is immature if any one of the initial psychosexual stages becomes a goal in itself—a woman who is primarily seeking someone to protect her from feeling helpless and to pamper and baby her, a man whose primary purpose is to impose his will and crush the autonomy of his partner, or an adult who only wants an audience to admire him or her for real or imagined achievements. Note that the psychosexual theory maintains that sexual maturity is only incidentally related to the performance of the sexual act. A man who has intercourse five times a week just to prove his prowess or three times a week because he read that this is the average for a person his age, is fixated or, quite literally, childlike in his behavior. Maturity is a matter of the psychological qualities one brings to the sexual experience itself and to the intimacy it entails.

PSYCHOPATHOLOGY. The title of one of Freud's books, *The Psychopathology of Everyday Life,* succinctly states his thesis that normality imperceptibly blends into psychopathology. The difference between the two is quantitative rather than qualitative.

In structural terms, psychopathology is a matter of a significant imbalance between id, ego, and superego. If the id is excessively strong, either because of innate endowment or a weak ego and superego, the result is impulsive aggressive or sexual behavior. If the superego is excessively strong, the result is overly inhibited behavior in which the child is tortured by guilt feelings for the slightest transgression, real or imagined.

However, psychosexual theory contains the richest source of clues as to both the nature and form of psychopathology. While fixations are normal, as we have seen, excessive fixations lay the groundwork for psychological disturbances, either because they hamper further development or because they increase the possibility that, having progressed, the child will return to the fixated, less mature stage. This latter process is called *regression.* The greater the fixation, the more vulnerable the child to regression. Excessive fixations can result either from inadequate libidinal gratification, such as inadequate love during the oral period, or excessive gratification, such as an oversolicitous, overprotective mother during the oedipal phase. The psychosexual stage of fixation determines both the severity and the kind of psychopathology. In general, the earlier the fixation, the more severe the psychopathology, so that a child who is either fixated at or regresses to the oral stage is more disturbed than one who is fixated at or regresses to the anal stage. In addition, each stage is apt to produce a particular kind of disturbance: the Oedipus complex is associated with hysterical and phobic disturbances, the anal stage with obsessive-compulsive disorders, and the oral stage with psychosis. (These classifications will be discussed in chapter 3.) Thus, for example, the bizarre ideation of the schizophrenic, which is determined more by idiosyncratic needs, longings, and fears than by a desire to communicate intelligibly, marks a return to the primary process thinking of the id-dominated oral stage.

As a developmental theory of psychopathology, the psychodynamic model has no peer. Yet it is also mentalistic, inferential, exceedingly complex, peppered with contingencies, and lacking just those clear behavioral referents and accessibility to tightly controlled research which behaviorists claim are essential to a scientific psychology. It is also true that neither the preferred method of investigation, namely psychoanalysis or psychoanalytically oriented psychotherapy, nor the data it produces are available to the general scientific community. But to conclude, as some have done, that psychodynamic concepts are unscientific because they cannot be tested by the usual controlled procedures is unjustified. Psychodynamic theory has generated more research than any other personality theory, and while older reviews claimed that the theory was totally lacking in scientific credibility, a more recent review found it to be faring surprisingly well (Fisher and Greenberg, 1977). It is also true that a number of psychodynamic concepts are either taken for granted by the general scientific community or regarded as tenable hypotheses: that adult psychopathologies have their roots in early childhood; that anxiety may be conceptualized as the anticipation of pain, and that defense mechanisms are utilized to reduce it; that early conscience is the internalization of parental values by means of identification; that the infantile conscience is particularly absolutistic and punitive; that frustration is one of the conditions leading to aggression; that behavior may be determined by ideas and impulses which are unconscious; that there is a cognitive progression from irrational to rational thinking in the first eight years of life; that adequate maternal care during infancy is essential to subsequent healthy personality development; and even the once shocking idea that sexuality is present throughout childhood. Like all other models, the psychodynamic one has its advantages and limitations, but the charge that it lies beyond the pale of science or that it has been discredited by controlled studies is patently false.

The Cognitive Models

Strictly speaking, there is no cognitive model of childhood psychopathology. This is a puzzling state of affairs in light of the fact that since midcentury interest has shifted from motivation to cognition and Piaget has been the towering figure in developmental psychology. While a number of researchers have utilized Piagetian concepts to account for specific psychopathological phenomena, there has been no attempt to integrate all the relevant aspects of Piagetian theory with the psychopathological thinking and behavior of children. Consequently the current situation resembles a patchwork more than a comprehensive frame of reference. However, we shall be referring to Piaget with sufficient frequency to justify a review of some of his major concepts.

GENERAL REMARKS. Newborns know practically nothing about the world they have entered. In particular, they do not know that they are individuals and that they are entering a world composed of animate and inanimate objects. All they know is the stream of sensations they are experiencing. There is nothing about the sensation of hunger which informs infants, "I am coming from your stomach"; there is nothing in two vaguely seen dots which says, "I am your mother's eyes"; nor does a sound announce itself as coming from a rattle. The infant must learn to distinguish experiences comprising "me" from those comprising "not-me," and among the latter he or she must learn to distinguish things from people. Depending upon what aspect of cognitive development one studies, evidence of this kind of learning can be found until middle childhood.

Cognitive development is not a simple matter of accumulating increasingly large pieces of correct information until a comprehensive understanding of the self and the environment is achieved. On the contrary, initial understandings are erroneous and must be revised in light of experience, and these revisions, in turn, must be further revised, until an accurate grasp of reality is achieved. Since erroneous understandings contain the seeds of psychopathology, it is essential that the child remains open to growth, so that, by constant testing, the validity of erroneous beliefs can be revised and corrected.

PIAGET'S STAGE THEORY. While most psychologists would agree with the above picture of cognitive development, Piaget makes the additional assumption that successive modifications in thinking occur in orderly, fixed stages. Each stage of cognitive development is qualitatively distinct, and no higher type of thinking can evolve until the child has gone through all the preceding stages. The timetable may differ from child to child, but the order can never vary. It is these stages and the significant cognitive advances within each which will concern us next. (One of the most succinct and clearest expositions of Piaget's theory is found in chapters 1 and 2 of Piaget, 1967.)

The *sensorimotor stage* lasts for approximately the first two years of life and is so called because the vehicle for intellectual growth is the sensory and motor apparatus. Incapable of symbolization, except toward the end of the period, infants and toddlers must explore and learn by acting directly upon the environment motorically and by watching and listening.

For our purposes, the significant development in this period is that of the *object concept*, or *object permanence*. For the first few months, infants give no evidence of missing an object they can no longer see or hold. Thus, the world exists only when they are acting upon it or perceiving it. Out of sight not only means out of mind but out of existence as well. Only gradually, through a succession of cognitive steps, do they come to realize that objects exist regardless of their own actions or perceptions—objects exist "out there" as part of the environment, while actions exist "in here" as part of the self. Instead of being the center or even the creator of the universe, toddlers grasp the fact that they are only one of the many furnishings of the world. A giant step has been taken toward separating me from not-me.

The *preoperational stage* lasts from approximately 2 to 7 years of age and marks the appearance of symbolic functions. The most obvious but by no means the exclusive manifestation of symbolization is language, which develops rapidly in this period. However, the preschooler tends literally to believe what he or she sees. Consequently, something which looks different is different. Piaget's well-known documentation of this thesis dazzled the psychological world. If, before their very eyes, water is poured from a wide squat glass into a tall narrow glass or a ball of clay is rolled out into an elongated snake, children will claim that there is now more water or more clay. It looks like more, so it must be more. Piaget calls such literal thinking *intuitive*, to contrast it with thinking based on reason.

The *concrete-operational stage* extends from approximately 7 to 11 years of age. The triumph of middle childhood is that the children are capable of understanding the world in terms of reason rather than in terms of naive perception. They grasp the notion that an object remains the same despite perceptual variations. Piaget's term for this achievement is *conservation,* denoting that objects conserve or maintain their identity in the face of manifold changes in appearance. Although realistic, the child's thinking is still tied to concrete reality, however, and bound to the here and now.

The *formal-operational stage* begins around the twelfth year and lasts into adulthood. It is in this period that general ideas and abstract constructions flourish. The ability to draw conclusions from hypotheses rather than relying totally on actual observation is called *hypothetic-deductive thinking*. Adolescents can go wherever their thoughts lead them. They discuss, they write, they ruminate. They create a philosophy of life and explain the universe. They are also capable of being truly self-critical for the first time because they can reflect on and scrutinize their own ideas.

We have emphasized Piaget's cognitive theory because it best suits our purposes. However, it is not the only theory we shall use. When we discuss learning disabilities we will have to adopt a frame of reference that deals with perceptual development, and when discussing mental retardation, we shall refer to an information-processing model (see chapters 9 and 11).

OTHER MODELS. There are sundry models of psychopathology that we will do little more than catalog, since they have not addressed themselves extensively to child psychopathology or have not generated sufficient empirical evidence to be considered anything more than speculative. (For a more detailed presentation see Bootzin, 1980.) At times the models overlap one another as well as the three we have already presented.

The *deviance model* takes many forms, but they all share the definition of abnormal as a deviation from the norm. In its most precise form, the norm is a *statistical* one epitomized by the bell-shaped curve that results from measuring a particular trait, such as intelligence. Deviance itself is defined in terms of scores that lie a certain number of standard deviations above and below the mean. However, the statistical model lacks criteria for differentiating between desirable and undesirable behavior and so considers the creative genius as abnormal as the severe retardate. The model also implies that as infrequent behaviors such as learning disabilities and violent crimes become more frequent, they become normal, and it makes conformity the primary goal of treatment. Both ideas are obviously unacceptable. Next, there are *cultural* norms, which are approved standards of behavior that a given society establishes for its members. Particular deviations from these norms are considered psychopathological. Certain of these deviations are culture-specific, while others, such as delusions, hallucinations, phobias, and sexual deviations, seem to be universal. The cultural model belongs in the superordinate context and, as we have stated, will not be our concern. However, the final category, deviations from *developmental* norms, will play a central role in our discussions.

The *humanistic model* is based on an image of humanity as innately good, capable of growth, and striving for self-actualization. It emphasizes the uniqueness of each individual, the potential for fulfilling capabilities, freedom of choice, and responsibility for one's own destiny. It follows that psychopathology is the inability to accept or express one's true nature, to take responsibility for one's actions, and to make self-generated choices. Since the model has been more influential in the area of child psychotherapy than child psychopathology, we shall postpone further discussion of it until we take up Carl Rogers's nondirective therapy (see chapter 14).

Finally, there are limited models which focus on specialized psychological functions: in the *interpersonal* model, the child is unable to cope successfully in his or her relations with others, particularly in the family; abnormality in the realm of *emotional control* consists of impulsivity, inhibition, blandness, or inappropriate emotional expression; the *cognitive* perspective includes both gross distortions of reality, such as delusions and hallucinations, and less severe but still crippling distortions, such as chronically viewing oneself as a failure.

The Developmental Model

Any theory of human behavior can contain a developmental component and can attempt to account for both normal and psychopathological development. In this sense there is no developmental model that is somehow different from other models of abnormal behavior. It is just a historical fact that few theories have accepted the developmental challenge and fewer still have generated a body of empirical findings which would take them out of the category of the merely speculative. The three models we have discussed in detail are the exceptions. The medical model is best exemplified by the number of eminent child psychiatrists who have distinguished themselves as diagnosticians, investigators, and textbook writers, Leo Kanner and his classic *Child Psychiatry* (1977) being among the most notable. Development lies at the heart of the psychodynamic model and is indispensable. Its adherents were the first to grasp the meaning of a developmental psychopathology and it has evolved into the most comprehensive theory extant. For behaviorists, concerned as they are with general laws applicable to all living organisms at any age, childhood psychopathology is one of many areas of interest rather than one occupying a special status; thus, behaviorists are relative latecomers, although vigorous ones. They bring with them a clear-eyed view of psychology as a science and a pragmatic orientation to clinical practice, which serve to correct the tendency toward obscurity and the infatuation with complexity that can become roadblocks to progress.

In sum, there is no satisfactory comprehensive theory of psychopathological development, but there are three models which have significantly advanced our understanding. In addition, there is a body of nontheoretically aligned research which furnishes valuable data concerning childhood disturbances. In light of the current situation we have adopted a loose conceptualization—psychopathology as normal development gone awry—whose very openness allows us to select from any model and from any body of data what we need in order to understand the psychopathology at hand. The question of how well our conceptualization has fared will be raised in each of our discussions and will be dealt with in detail in chapter 15.

SOME COMMENTS ABOUT METHODOLOGY

In discussing research, Meehl referred to the five "noble traditions" in clinical psychology that he speculates will be around long after current fads have faded: descriptive clinical psychiatry; psychometric assessment; behavior genetics; behavior modification (with its remarkable technical power); and psychoanalytic theory (with its unsurpassed level of interest.) Two relative newcomers that seem to merit addition to this list are the cognitive theories of Piaget and information processing, whose impact on developmental psychopathology is just beginning to be felt. We shall have many encounters with all of these noble traditions, for they make up the rich and varied foundation on which clinical psychology rests.

Meehl's point concerning traditions is equally applicable to methodologies. The three giants of psychology—Pavlov, Freud, and Piaget—utilized quite different research methodologies. Thus the progress of psychology as a science has taken place by means of diverse investigatory strategies. Note that we said "as a science." Science is defined as the search for knowledge. Different sciences have found different methodologies to be most fruitful in this quest: astronomy, the oldest science, advanced through observation of naturally occurring events, while physics and chemistry advanced through highly controlled laboratory experiments. Psychology, in contrast, has not settled on a method of choice. What is true of psychology in general is doubly true of developmental psychopathology, which owes as much to the Darwinian tradition of *natural observation* as it does to the *laboratory experiment*. The research of choice is the research which is clearly conceived and elegantly executed, regardless of the methodology.

Instead of looking at methodology in the abstract, we shall approach it through research which has actually advanced our understanding of childhood psychopathology. (For a more formal discussion, see Achenbach, 1978.) We shall use illustrations taken from studies that we shall discuss in detail in subsequent chapters. (These illustrations are set apart from the main text. The first words are in bold type and the format is a single, wide column.)

The Naturalistic Tradition

THE CLINICAL EYE. In developmental psychopathology, the naturalistic tradition in pure culture is carried on by individuals with a clinical eye, which is at the opposite extreme from the innocent eye. "The Emperor's New Clothes" notwithstanding, inexperienced individuals quite literally see very little of the behavior occurring around them. As Piaget has taught us, current stimuli, in order to register, must be assimilated into organized bodies of meaningful concepts, which in turn have grown out of meaningful observations in the past. Thus, the clinical eye requires, first of all, sensitive and disciplined observation with the intent of maximizing understanding. The challenge may well last a lifetime. But observation is not enough: the clinical eye must nourish a conceptualizing mind. A vast quantity of accumulated clinical wisdom goes no further than the application of past experience to present problems. To make the leap from the applied to the conceptual is rare among clinicians, but it marks the transition from personal experience to embryonic scientific knowledge.

Naturalistic observation aims at describing and understanding naturally occurring behavior. It maximizes the chances of obtaining ecologically valid ("true to life") data and of capturing the multiplicity of variables which may be responsible for producing such behavior. By selecting comparative and contrasting populations and settings, the researcher takes a step toward disentangling relevant from irrevelant and confounding variables. However, there are practical limits to the extent to which such disentangling can be done. Limitations in the degree of control over the data should not be equated with a lessening of investigatory rigor, however. There is no reason to claim, for example, that Darwin or Piaget were less rigorous than Pavlov just because they chose to examine naturally occurring behavior rather than to work in a laboratory. Or in the research we are about to cite it would be unthinkable to view the investigators as lacking in rigor (see Shakow, 1953).

Our three examples of the use of the clinical eye represent three successive levels of understanding. Kanner's delineation of autism (chapter 4) is a model of *descriptive classification,* in which the entity is clearly and accurately described in its own right while also being differentiated from other disturbances which resemble and therefore could be mistaken for it. Redl (chapter 8), through his keen observation of a small group of impulsive, acting-out boys, was able to analyze their behavior according to a number of separate psychological *functions,* such as memory, anticipation, and social perspective-taking, and to discover how each function deviated from normal. And finally, Fraiberg (chapter 12), aided by some of the most brilliant developmental psychologists of the day and by the technology of videotaping, which permits repeated viewing of behavior, was able to reconstruct some of the psychological *processes* in which blind infants and toddlers engage while traveling their deviant path to normal functioning.

OBJECTIVE PROCEDURES. The clinical eye has undoubtedly made major contributions to our science. But like all research procedures, it has its disadvantages. What if one observer fails to verify what another has reported? What if two observers disagree as to what has occurred? Behavior such as guilt or anxiety is not objectively "out there" like a fossil or a plant. In order to correct for the possible error involved in individual observation, objective procedures have been devised. Such procedures have two advantages: their reliability can be tested, and they can be used by all members of the scientific community. In certain instances, naturally occurring behavior still comprises the basic data; for example, observers can be trained reliably to record the number of friendly overtures made to normally achieving and learning disabled fourth-graders during recess. In addition, special instruments may be used to measure naturally occurring behavior: standardized interviews, behavioral checklists, and personality tests are examples. These instruments must be shown to be both reliable and valid, so that there is evidence that they do, indeed, measure the behavior they purport to evaluate.

We shall encounter studies which utilize objective procedures both for descriptive purposes and for hypothesis testing. Hetherington, a master of the art of multitechnique research, utilized observation, interviews, personality tests, and tests of sex-role typing to uncover the differential effects of paternal death and divorce on the personality development of adolescent girls (see chapter 5). Olweus, in his research on bullies, utilized procedures ranging from teachers' reports to projective techniques to eliminate hypotheses concerning the contribution of various superordinate, interpersonal, and intrapersonal variables before concluding that the aggression in these boys most likely resulted from an innate predisposition (see chapter 8).

The Laboratory Tradition

While it is possible to introduce objective procedures and control of variables into naturalistic research, it takes considerable ingenuity (and often good luck) to do so (see Wenar, 1976). Both objectivity and control are built into laboratory studies. The instruments are objective and available to the scientific community, while the actual conduct of the research is explicitly described so others may replicate it. The investigators' control of the situation allows them systematically to manipulate the variable or variables being studied, while holding all others constant. The result is a powerful tool for disentangling crucial from confounding and tangential variables as well as for revealing processes responsible for the psychopathological behavior being investigated.

Of the many admirable examples of controlled studies we shall encounter, we shall select only four. A series of interrelated investigations provided evidence that mental retardation is not synonymous with a slow rate of learning but may be, in part, due to a failure to generate appropriate hypotheses for learning and remembering or—and this is the most intriguing puzzle—a failure to utilize potentially efficient strategies even when they are available (see chapter 11). Controlled studies of autism are separating mental retardation as a confounding variable and isolating other variables that seem specific to the psychopathology: difficulty with processing patterned information and a deficiency in imitation being two of the most important (see chapter 4). Gibson's reconstruction of the processes underlying both reading and reading disabilities is likewise based on a host of laboratory findings (see chapter 9). Finally, Douglas's elegant programmatic research is exploring hyperactivity as the product of a defect in sustaining attention. Douglas has also isolated a variable of impulsivity, which undermines the hyperactive child's ability to stop, look, listen—and think (see chapter 12).

Along with its many assets, the laboratory study has a potential disadvantage which is the mirror image of that of the naturalistic study—the maximizing of control might result in artificial data. Instead of being a paradigm of reality, the findings may have little ecological validity, being applicable only to the highly rarefied setting of the laboratory (see Bronfenbrenner, 1977).

In general, naturalistic studies rate high on ecological validity and, in certain instances, on objectivity of procedures, but controlling variables is exceedingly difficult. Laboratory studies rate high on objectivity and control but are marred by the question of ecological validity. In actuality, the subjective, uncontrolled naturalistic study has taught us as much about childhood psychopathology as the highly controlled, objective laboratory study. While particular psychologists may stoutly defend one methodology as being scientific, science itself is capricious. So far at least, it has no favorites.

A RETURN TO OUR MODEL

It would be interesting to view the medical, behavioral, and psychodynamic models of psychopathological development in terms of the variables of our own developmental model. In doing so, we shall have to oversimplify them somewhat for the sake of emphasizing their distinctive features, since each is more broadly based than we shall allow.

The medical model is primarily concerned with the interaction between the organic and the intrapersonal contexts. The genetic, biochemical, and neurophysiological components all aim at relating organic variables to specific intrapersonal abnormalities, such as schizophrenia and hyperactivity. When interpersonal variables enter, for example, as stressors aggravating the basic physiological vulnerability, typically they are not explored in depth. The conservative behavorists hew closely to the interpersonal context, allowing only for observable responses to observable stimuli. The more venturesome behaviorists and social-learning theorists, however, are exploring the intrapersonal context, admitting both "private events" and variables connected with the self, such as self-efficacy, under the strict condition that they be objectively defined and enhance prediction and control. The psychodynamic advocates are most at home in the intrapersonal realm and the limited interpersonal context of the nuclear family. The drama of id–ego–superego is acted out on the intrapersonal stage, while psychosexual development is closely tied to the transactions between parents and child. Although some notable efforts have been made to broaden the interpersonal scope and to introduce the superordinate context of societal values, they have not become part of the mainstream of psychodynamic thought.

If each of these models is complex, our own model, which embraces all three, might seem to raise complexity to the point of unworkability. Indeed, the image of multiple variables in diverse interactions which change over time boggles the mind. But remember, this is only a model, an ideal that suggests what we should know in order to give a comprehensive accounting of psychopathological development. In reality, we know very little—a fragment here, a tag end there. Far from being overwhelmed by the complexity of the field of childhood psychopathology, we will more frequently protest: We must know more than we now do! The field has suffered from neglect in the past and is just now coming into its own. With the aid of our comprehensive model, we will be able to see which details of the total picture have been filled, thereby putting the present stage of knowledge into proper perspective. Knowing the important variables will also serve to organize our thinking in regard to a given psychopathology, the model serving as a topical guide to areas which might be explored as the clinician attempts to answer the two simplest but most baffling questions: Is this child disturbed? And, if so, how disturbed is he or she? (As an illustration, see the checklist of variables affecting enuresis in chapter 5.)

Having outlined our general developmental model, we are now ready to describe the normal development of the intra- and interpersonal variables that will have a bearing on our subsequent discussions of the various childhood psychopathologies. Then, in chapter 3, we shall be ready to build a bridge to the psychopathologies themselves and learn which ones tend to persist and which ones tend to disappear with time.

2 ▪ Normal Development

We are now in something of a quandary. If we are to understand childhood psychopathology as normal development gone awry, obviously we must first chart normal development. But having decided not to follow any one of the current models in favor of a looser, more inclusive framework, we still need a conceptual guide for selecting variables to discuss. Fortunately, it is still possible to draw up a list of variables crucial to a child's well-being so that, if anything went radically wrong with any one of them, we would be willing to regard the child as disturbed.

First there are a group of variables binding the child to the human environment. Prominent in this group is the bond of love that develops between infant and mother in the first year of life, which we shall call *attachment*. Throughout childhood and throughout life the ability to feel deeply about and become attached to another individual lies at the core of the human experience. Attachments may become erotic, resulting in *sexual* relationships, or at a more moderate and diffuse level, the human bond may be expressed in friendships and companionableness, which we shall call *social feelings*. If something goes radically awry with any of these bonds—if, for example, the loving overtures of a parent are met with rage or profound indifference, if sexual intimacy is a source of terror rather than pleasure, if the child is socially isolated and friendless—we would rightfully be concerned.

Another basic variable involves *initiative* or self-reliant expansiveness.

The bright-eyed infant scanning the environment for new and interesting sights epitomizes this urge to explore and to master. In many of their ventures children are free to follow their own interests; but increasingly with age they are required to stay with a task whether they want to or not. We shall call this combination of initiative and necessity *work*, the special setting for work during childhood being the classroom. If, instead of initiative and the capacity for work, the child is apathetic or distracted or fearful of any kind of venturing out, if there is a persistent, self-defeating rebelliousness at being told what to do no matter how benign and reasonable, again we have cause to be concerned about the child.

Perhaps the most obvious variable for us to examine is *self-control*, the control of *aggression* looming particularly large in the public mind. Socializing children often involves curbing their preferred behaviors; with time, children take over this monitoring, controlling function themselves, eventually adding another mechanism specifically concerned with judging the moral content of behavior, the *conscience*. Self-control also involves the generation of *anxiety*, which serves as one of the principle deterrents to performing socially disapproved actions. Having "everything under control" is a sign of healthy growth, while both excessive and deficient control are deviations; the child who is plagued by anxiety and guilt as well as the violently destructive child concern parent and clinician alike.

Finally, it is essential for the child to understand the physical and social environment as well as him- or herself, a variable we shall call *cognition*. As we have already seen in chapter 1, reality can be distorted by magical ideas in the first few years of life because of cognitive immaturity. Therefore it is essential that these distortions be replaced by realistic understanding; the persistence of bizarre, magical ideas, such as a 10-year-old believing that he can hear through his "bellybutton" and can control television pictures by merely thinking about them, is generally recognized as a sign of disturbed development.

In sum, the ten variables we have selected in our developmental approach to childhood psychopathology are: attachment, initiative, self-control, conscience, cognition, anxiety, sex, aggression, social relations, and work. (Much of the material which follows is condensed from Wenar, 1971.)

ATTACHMENT

The bond of love between parents and child is one of the pivotal variables determining the course of development throughout childhood. We shall be referring to it in many of our discussions of psychopathology—the failure of the bond to develop in infancy, the rupture of the bond by death or divorce, the contamination of the bond with excessive anger or anxiety, the atrophy of the bond through neglect. It is essential, therefore, to understand how this bond is established in infancy and how it develops throughout childhood. While labeled differently in various theories, we shall call the bond *attachment*. (For a discussion of various conceptualizations, see Ainsworth, 1969.)

The Formation of Attachment

Two reminders are in order before starting our descriptive account. First, neonates have practically no knowledge of the world of people or the world of things; they even lack knowledge of themselves as a separate entity. They do not know who their mother is or how she differs from a rattle or a stomachache.

Their experience consists of various sensations, out of which they must grasp the fundamental distinction between people, things, and self. How they go about doing this is discussed in the section on cognitive development.

The second point is that human beings have the longest period of helpless infancy of any species. In order to survive they must be cared for by more mature human beings for many months. Thus, attachment takes place in the caretaking situation; the kind of care infants receive determines, to a significant degree, the kind of attachment they form. While most of our information comes from the infant's attachment to the mother, psychologists have begun to recognize and investigate the importance of father–infant attachment as well. (See Parke, 1979. For a summary of research on mother–infant attachment, see Osofsky and Connors, 1979.)

The development of attachment to the mother or primary caretaker (for convenience, the two terms will be used synonymously) follows a reasonably predictable course. Neonates are no more or less interested in the caretaker than in any other object that comes their way. However, by two weeks of age they prefer the human voice over other sounds and, by four weeks, prefer the mother's voice over other human voices. In the second month, eye contact is established. Between the third and fourth months, these precursors of attachment reach a cognitive and emotional climax: the pattern of stimuli comprising the human face is perceived with sufficient cohesiveness and detail to be distinguished from other patterns of stimuli and, equally important, is a source of special delight. The percept "people" and the affect "pleasure" are fused into what is called the *social smile.* The social smile is indiscriminate and hedonistic: infants light up when anyone hits upon that combination of grimacing and vocalizing and bouncing and tickling which delights them. On their part, adults will go through all kinds of absurd antics in order to elicit such a smile. The simple fact that delighting the infant is highly rewarding to the adult is one of the strongest guarantees that an attachment will be formed.

Between the sixth and ninth month, indiscriminate responsiveness gives way to selectivity as infants show a strong preference for the mother and other special caretakers. This inner circle of caretakers elicits greater delight than anyone else and can most readily comfort the infant in times of distress. In addition, two negative affects come to the fore. The first is *separation anxiety* when the mother leaves. In spite of the label, the distress is not akin to fear, as are most anxieties, but is better described as anguish—that painful blend of protest and despair which wells up when a crucial source of pleasure disappears and one is helpless to bring it back. Thus, separation anguish is more closely related to depression than to terror. *Stranger anxiety,* or the fear of unfamiliar persons, is not as prevalent as it was once believed to be. However, the indiscriminate pleasure which marked the era of the social smile is replaced with a more cautious, wary response to unfamiliar adults.

Separation anxiety has implications for many aspects of normal and deviant development. First, we learn that intense anxiety is part of normal development. Indeed, there are those who claim that the absence of such anxiety is suggestive of deviant development: for example, some children reared in impersonal institutions will subsequently respond to anyone who shows them affection (like the infant during the stage of the indiscriminate social smile) while failing to form an enduring relationship and being unaffected by loss (see chapter 4). We also learn that, from the beginning, intense affection and intense anguish over loss go hand in hand. Dare I love deeply and risk abandonment? is one of those life-long questions which each individual must answer in his or her own way. Certain delinquents, for example, are difficult to help because they fear that if they let themselves become emotionally attached to their therapist, the therapist will desert them as other adults have done in the past.

Hostility is also a consequence of attachment, although it has received less attention than anxiety. In reunions after separations, such as hospitalization, it is not unusual for infants and toddlers first to ignore their parents and then become unusually angry and touchy for the next few days or even weeks. Infants and toddlers are cognitively incapable of grasping the reality of the situation, such as the fact that the separation was for good reason and unavoidable; all they can understand is that they needed the mother and she was not there. In their eyes she becomes a "bad" mother and the target for anger (see Bowlby, 1973).

Thus we see that attachment, even in its normal manifestations, is never purely positive; it is inevitably a mixture of love and anguish and fear and anger. It is when the negative components begin to dominate that the chances for deviant development are increased. (For a general discussion of affective development in infancy, see Sroufe, 1979.)

Caretaking

A few comments concerning *caretaking* are relevant to the discussions to come. The traditional image has been that of the mother caring for a totally helpless, passive infant, who is capable only of responding to environmental inputs. However, there is now convincing evidence that infants are never merely passive recipients. From the beginning they are actively taking in and trying to cope with their environment (see Appleton, Clifton, and Goldberg, 1975). They also have their special temperament—their individualized tempo and activity level, their characteristic mood and adaptability, their special set of vulnerabilities and resiliencies, their preferences and dislikes. Psychologists have verified what mothers have known for many years—namely, that certain infants are temperamentally easy to care for while others are difficult, regardless of the kind of care they receive. Thus, caretaking is now viewed as an interaction between mother and infant in which each has to accommodate the other. If all goes well, the result is a mutual enhancement of development in which not only the infant grows but the mother also in terms of her caretaking skills, feelings of competence, and sources of gratification. This interdependence of mother and infant has sometimes been called *symbiosis;* when we discuss symbiotic psychosis we shall see the devastating consequences to certain toddlers when it fails to exert its growth-promoting influence (chapter 5.)

Caretaking itself is conceptualized as a combination of *comforting* and *stimulation.* Comforting and relieving the infant's distress has been the traditional view of mothering. More recently, attention has turned to the mother as stimulator. The very fact that she is human means that she is a source of fascinating and delightful visual and auditory stimuli, since infants seem to be preprogrammed to respond most intensely to stimuli characteristic of the human. The mother is also a mediator of stimulation, bringing the infant in contact with a variety of interesting sights and sounds such as rattles and rings and mobiles. Hers is a dual role of comforter and stimulator, so her sensitivity to the infant's needs and the promptness and appropriateness with which she responds to them is more important than the sheer amount of time she spends with the infant. And through her comforting and stimulation, the mother provides both the emotional security and the varied environmental input that are necessary to normal development.

Attachment has two important consequences. If caretaking is consistently and sensitively administered, the infant develops a *loving, trusting* relationship. Those who accept the critical-period hypothesis would say that this relationship sets the infants to view future closeness in terms of love and trust; they can subsequently reveal intimate thoughts and feelings without fear of betrayal, and they know that their cry for help will be answered, however this cry may be expressed. Well-cared-for infants are also apt to develop a positive self-image and confidence in their ability to cope successfully with problems as they arise. There is evidence, for example, that the securely attached infant becomes the effective problem solver as a toddler and the flexible, resourceful and curious preschooler who is enthusiastically involved with school tasks and peers (Arend, Gove, and Sroufe, 1979).

Second, attachment is a prerequisite for successful *socialization.* Infants and toddlers have no natural desire to be neat and clean or to respect property; quite to the contrary, they want to explore and mess and possess at will. Why, then, should they ever give up the pleasure of immediate gratification? Because the love of the parents is at stake. The behavior which the parents regard as good is rewarded with love; the behavior which they regard as bad is punished by the withdrawal of love. In normal development, toddlers and preschoolers for the most part acquiesce, since the love they receive compensates for the autonomy they lose. But already we can sense the possibilities for abuse of parental love: suppose parental demands are excessive and entail total subjugation, as may happen in certain cases of anorexia nervosa (see chapter 5)? Or suppose demands are made with inadequate compensations of love, as in certain cases of juvenile delinquency (see chapter 8)? We would rightly suspect that chances of deviant development would be increased.

Attachment and the Older Child

With regard to attachment, the developmental picture grows dim in middle childhood. Gesell's previously summarized account of the relationship of the 6- to 9-year-old child to the parents is one of the most complete descriptions (see chapter 1). In adolescence, however, the issue of attachment comes again to the fore. Adolescence is a time of major revolutions: a biological revolution brought about by sexual maturation, an interpersonal revolution involving a shift away from the family and toward the peer group, an identity revolution involving a search for a fulfilling adult role. While we now know that the picture of adolescence as necessarily a time of "storm and stress" is exaggerated and that there are significant continuities between the generations alongside the more highly publicized alienation and rebelliousness of youth, the cultural expectation of independence still marks the period as a time of significant change in the relation between parent and child. Attachment is caught up in this change. Parental expressions of affection become an embarrassment, offers of comfort and help are apt to be met with the standard outcry, "I'm not a baby any more!" (To a clinician, the vigorousness of the protest suggests that the underlying longing for love and comfort and help might still be a strong but unacceptable one.) If the adolescent is having problems with growing up and becoming independent, however, parents are also having problems with growing older and no longer being needed. A change in status and function is occurring in all parties involved in the interaction, as the interpersonal context of our developmental model would indicate.

While adolescence can go relatively smoothly, it still stands as a time of increased vulnerability for those individuals whose relations with their parents make the challenge of independence an exceptionally threatening one. In examining schizophrenia, for example, we shall be dealing with an instance in which the stresses cannot be managed and contribute to the production of a severe psychological breakdown (chapter 10).

Independence from parents is not the ultimate or necessary fate of attachment. While adulthood is not our concern, we should note that it often brings with it a rapprochement between parent and child if a rift had taken place in adolescence. The ability to express love for parents without embarrassment or guilt over being close marks the return of an old theme in a mature variation. By the same token, the adult who must continue to protest vigorously against any show of parental affection or any sign of closeness gives the impression of being inappropriately adolescent.

INITIATIVE

If attachment is central in the first year of life, initiative is central in the second, toddlers literally and figuratively standing on their own two feet and turning their backs on their mothers. Intoxication with a newfound sense of power propels them into a stage of *willfulness* and *negativism*. The selfsame 2-year-old who, a few months ago, was terrified at the mother's departure, now counters her every request with an imperious "No!" For her part, the mother finds that she must increasingly restrict her child, who is into everything and all over the place. Thus begins the conflict between freedom to do what one wants and conformity to the requirements of society, a conflict which will last a lifetime. We will take a closer look at the toddler's self-reliant venturing forth, which we shall call *initiative,* tracing its roots in infancy and commenting further on some of its manifestations during the "terrible twos."

Origins in Infancy

Initiative in the toddler period has a number of roots in infancy, a primary one being *curiosity* and *exploration*. The old image of the infant's life as being totally dominated by physiological needs such as hunger, thirst, and sleep is erroneous. (The landmark article is White, 1959.) As soon as there are periods of alert wakefulness, neonates begin exploring their environment. Their searching eyes and receptive ears lead the way, followed increasingly by motoric exploration as they outgrow their body's initial clumsiness. In the first month of life exploratory behaviors are remarkably mature, characterized by orientation, concentration, perseverance, gratification with success, or annoyance at failure. Infants are as hungry for stimulation as they are for food, their endless fascination undergirding the giant steps taken in comprehending their environment in the first year (Appleton, Clifton, and Goldberg, 1975).

But infants not only want to take in the environment; they want actively to control it as well. Eight-week-old infants who were placed in a specially designed crib discovered they could make a mobile move by turning their head and repeatedly did so with great glee (Watson and Ramey, 1972). Around 20 weeks of age infants begin to take the initiative in establishing, sustaining, and renewing contact and interaction with the mother, lifting their arms in greeting her, clinging to her, following her when they are able to crawl. By the end of the first year they may be so adept and insistent in their demands for attention that some mothers become resentful (Sander, 1964). Other evidence of an early need to control is the many "battles" between mother and infant: 8-month-olds who have had the experience of holding the bottle, thereby taking feeding "into their own hands," may strongly resist attempts to make them drink from a cup (Spock, 1963); the "battle of the bottle" is subsequently replaced by the "battle of the spoon," as 1-year-olds insist on feeding themselves, although their ineptness results in bringing the oatmeal to their nose or ear or hair as often as to their mouth. The mother who cannot stand the ensuing mess and tries to take the spoon away by sheer force might be met with a tenacious determination to hold onto it and a rage reaction when the infant is overpowered. Just over the horizon—during the toddler period—lies the "battle of the potty."

There is an important cognitive component to this desire to control the environment. Neonates are too immature cognitively to grasp the relation between their actions and environmental events. By the middle of the first year the connection has been established, but—and this is the important point—it is an unrealistic, magical one. After discovering that their vigorous, jerky movements can make a mobile on their crib dance, they proceed to repeat these movements and look at the television set or the clock or other familiar objects, expecting them to dance also. Again, infants whose attentive mothers come when they cry initially believe that their cry actually produces the mother's presence. But how could it be otherwise? How could infants grasp the reality of the sequence—that the mother was in another room, that she heard the cry, that she could decide either to ignore it or come to the infant, and that she chose the latter? While unable to grasp reality, infants can make sense of their immediate experience, which is, "I make jerky movements, objects dance; I cry, mother appears; *ergo* my actions alone cause environmental events to happen." In short, infants have an *omnipotent* concept of causality. While such thinking would be a sign of severe psychopathology in adolescence, it is not only developmentally appropriate but represents a significant advance over the prior period when the notion of causality itself was not grasped (see Piaget, 1967).

The desire to venture out in infancy continues into the toddler period, locomotion literally opening up a whole new world for the toddler to explore and master. It is important to underscore the spontaneous, *intrinsically rewarding* nature of this exploration, in contrast to the socializing parents' directives and prohibitions, many of which go against the grain. Also, as toddlers explore they continue to develop the concept of the *self-as-agent*, and as their explorations are successful and pleasurable, they develop *self-confidence* and a healthy self-pride. This self-reliant venturing out, which we call initiative, has variously been labeled autonomy, mastery, competence, and independence by others. While differences exist, all the terms share an emphasis on the self-as-agent and on expansiveness.

We now have a better appreciation of why anything which impedes the toddler's self-reliant exploration is apt to be resented and resisted. Typically such resistance takes the form of negativism, which may be an active noncompliance (shouting "I won't" or throwing a tantrum) or a passive noncompliance (ignoring the parent or doing nothing). And typically, impediments take the form of the socializing adult's "No" and "Don't." The evidence indicates that the toddler will bridle regardless of how sweetly reasonable the parent is (Wenar, 1982). Just as the self-centered infant only knew, "Mother is not here when I need her," the self-centered toddler only knows, "My parents are preventing me from doing what I want to do." The terrible twos are, by and large, of the toddler's own making. By the same token, exasperated parents can take comfort in the fact that, while nothing they do will prevent or shorten its reign, negativism is usually "outgrown" in a couple of years.

We have emphasized the toddler's physical venturing forth because it sets the stage for the conflict between compliance and defiance which will figure so prominently in our discussion of psychopathology. However, not all initiative is physical. Producing varied sounds seems to have an intrinsic appeal and the toddler soon learns that certain of these sounds, made either fortuitously or in imitation of adult speech, have the magical property of eliciting responses of great delight from parents. "Baby's first word" typically becomes the occasion for rejoicing. The toddler also learns that words as well as gestures can be used to communicate, subsequently realizing that they are also more versatile and require less effort. In addition to their communicative value, *words and language* play an important role in self-control and cognition. Subsequently, when we turn to the psychopathologies, we shall learn that the absence or breakdown of communicative speech plays a crucial role in two of the most severe childhood disturbances—autism and schizophrenia (see chapters 4 and 10).

Developmental Course of Initiative

The toddler's fascination with objects continues throughout childhood. "What is it?" and "How does it work?"—questions first asked of ordinary household objects—expand to include objects in the wider physical environment and, eventually, in outer space. In the realm of tools, the toy hammer is replaced by the tool kit, the blunt scissors by the sewing machine; ahead lies the computer. The ten-word vocabulary of the 19-month-old increases to the 80,000-word vocabulary of the high school freshman. In the social realm, playing house with the preschoolers next door develops into the complex gangs and cliques of adolescence.

We could go on, but we are not so much interested in areas of self-reliant expansion as in certain consequences of initiative for the self. First, discovering what one can do plays a central role in *self-definition*. The 3-year-old who announces excitedly, "I can jump" and the high school sophomore who says, "I was elected class treasurer," have defined themselves through their various ventures. As they succeed they are accruing a sense of *self-worth* and pride. Such healthy self-love can be as important as a healthy love relation with another person. Finally, enterprising individuals are developing a sense of being in charge of their own destinies, which psychologists have studied under the heading of *locus of control*. Individuals who perceive events as contingent upon their own behavior or some characteristic of themselves have an *internal* locus of control; individuals who believe that events are the result of factors other than themselves, such as luck or chance or fate, have an *external* locus of control. Thus, initiative affects the individual's perception of personal responsibility for events. Such perceptions have been shown to be significantly correlated with academic achievement; for example, children who believe that education does not matter because they will never have a chance to make anything of themselves do poorly compared to children who believe that they can use education to make a difference to their future (Phares, 1976).

Adolescence may be a period which presents special problems in regard to initiative, as it did for attachment. The adolescent must negotiate the transition from dependent child to independent adult, a transition made difficult by conflicts at many levels. In our society an independent adult holds down a good job, gets married, and moves into his or her own home. However, the minimal age for working and voting and driving a car implies that the adolescent is incapable of assuming most of these responsibilities, while the emphasis on higher education often entails continued financial dependence on the family. Parents, for their part, want their adolescent to take on responsibilities, earn money, date, and be popular, but they also want to retain their parental role as guide to proper conduct and as decision maker. And adolescents themselves are ambivalent about independence. Physically, sexually, and intellectually they are young adults, not children; they have the capacity to work and devote themselves to an ideal; they are socially sensitive and can form meaningful friendships. For the first time the adult world is within their grasp. Yet, they also sense that they might lack the experience, judgment, and psychological maturity to utilize such assets appropriately. They cannot become adults overnight; finding a niche in a complex society and mastering the intricacies of vocational and sexual relations are often a matter of trial and error. Setbacks are apt to bruise their egos and remind them that, if they are no longer children, they are also not quite adults. When all the conflicts within and between family members boil over, the last of the normal battles of childhood is fought—the battle of the generations. The adolescent is viewed as wild, disrespectful, and amoral, the parents are seen as old-fashioned, self-centered, and lacking in understanding.

Like attachment, initiative is fundamental to normal development. A significant diminution of initiative is an ominous sign, while a lack of initiative, as evidenced in autism, indicates severe psychopathology (chapter 4). We shall see how certain bleak institutional settings can crush initiative so that normal infants and mentally retarded children are no longer motivated to utilize their abilities and skills (chapters 4 and 11). A special kind of loss of initiative called learned helplessness may underlie the defeatist attitude which characterizes depression (chapter 5). Both the normal negativism of the terrible twos and the normal transitional problems of adolescence can become exaggerated to the point where they block further growth (chapter 5) or in the case of adolescence eventuate in drug use and abuse (chapter 10).

SELF-CONTROL

In a number of psychopathologies, self-control figures more prominently than any other single variable. In early childhood, control of bodily functions is a basic aspect of self-control. Toddlers may fail to learn to control their bladders and continue to wet their beds at night or, less frequently, their pants during the day. Eating may get out of control, leading to obesity at one extreme or self-starvation even to the point of death at the other (chapter 5). When self-control is excessive in middle childhood, the groundwork for neurosis is laid; when self-control is weak, acting-out behavior such as aggression and juvenile delinquency may result (chapters 7 and 8). Therefore, it is essential that we understand the development of self-control from infancy to adulthood and the factors that enable the child to achieve normal self-control. In the following sections we shall examine that special kind of control exercised by the conscience, the role cognition and anxiety play in achieving self-control, and finally, the two most important behaviors the child must learn to control—sex and aggression.

Factors Involved in Self-Control

Descriptively, the situation could not be simpler. The exploring toddler reaches for a vase on the living room table. Her mother rushes in, says "No," and slaps her hand. She withdraws. She may reach again, and again be punished. The pattern is repeated many times. Eventually, however, as the toddler approaches the vase and begins reaching for it, she suddenly stops, shakes her head, and even slaps her own hand. Then she withdraws. She never again reaches for the forbidden vase. She has achieved self-control. However, teasing out the factors involved in this achievement and understanding how they work is far from simple (Wenar, 1971). Let us examine certain important ingredients.

As our example clearly suggests, there is *reward and punishment.* These may be physical: a toddler who puts his toy away at mother's request may get to lick the chocolate-pudding bowl, while another toddler who pokes a finger into the light socket may get slapped or spanked. Rewards and punishments may also be psychological. As we have just seen, attachment enables parents to bestow love for conformity to their directives; it also enables them to withdraw love when disobeyed, thus creating a situation akin to separation anguish in the child. Thus, the child's concern about being loveworthy is a major force in the motivation to seek parental approval and avoid parental disapproval by complying with socializing directives.

In rewarding and punishing the child, parents convey more meaning than they intend, since they are also serving as a model of either controlled or uncontrolled behavior. Children are adept imitators. A parent can be taken aback on hearing a toddler, during a pretend telephone conversation, turn around and shout, "Be quiet! Can't you see I'm on the phone?" in an exact duplication of the parent's own words and tone of voice. Children imitate spontaneously; no reward and punishment is necessary, and at times the imitated behavior appears full-blown. In certain instances, *modeling* or *imitation* may serve to undermine socialization; a father who punishes aggression by losing his temper and beating the child is simultaneously serving as a model of uncontrolled behavior.

A host of *cognitive* variables are involved in self-control. At the simplest level, toddlers must be able to grasp cause-and-effect relations and remember what behavior leads to reward or punishment; only then will they be able to apply past experiences to the situation at hand. They must then be able to integrate fragmentary experiences into guiding principles of behavior, so that "I should not take that toy" will eventually become "I should not take anything that belongs to somebody else." Words play a pivotal role in this process of achieving higher levels of self-control. The simple "No" becomes, "Mustn't touch," and then, "That's Jimmy's truck, not yours," and finally, "You shouldn't take other people's things without asking them first." As the directives become increasingly complex, they serve to guide behavior in an increasingly wide variety of situations. And as the cognitively developing child can both verbalize these directives and grasp their meaning, built-in controls become increasingly effective. Since "saying things to oneself" is one aspect of thinking, we can see why *thinking* is regarded as the ally of control: the very fact that the child must stop and think serves to check immediate action, while the content of the thought itself serves to guide behavior into socially acceptable channels. As thinking serves its *inhibiting* and *guiding* functions, control is enhanced.

However, thought is not the only aid to

counteracting impulsivity; interpersonal *trust* is equally important. Socialization consists not only of prohibitions but also of delayed gratification. The child's capacity to wait is enhanced if the promised rewards are consistently forthcoming. If parents are unreliable or if the environment is disorganized and unpredictable, children are less likely to tolerate the tensions of delay and more apt to seize upon the pleasures of the moment. Finally, the availability of *substitute gratifications* helps the child master the frustration of being forbidden to pursue a desired goal. The sensitive parent who has prohibited a toddler from touching a treasured vase may then present the child with a favorite set of pots and pans to play with. As children grow older they become increasingly capable of redirecting their own activities into acceptable substitutes. Note that some substitutes involve the relinquishing of the original goal, as with our toddler; others provide alternate, socially acceptable ways of achieving or partially achieving the goal; a boy who is forbidden to fight with a peer can defeat him in athletics, for example. One function of play and fantasy is to provide safe substitutes for achieving forbidden goals; the girl recently punished by her mother can spank her doll for being a "mean old mommy," while adults continue to fantasy victories and glories in situations too threatening to undertake in real life (Mischel, 1974). Our discussion of a group of impulse-ridden boys enables us to see what happens when many of these factors involved in self-control fail to develop adequately (chapter 8).

Parental Discipline

Unlike their pioneer ancestors, modern parents no longer feel it is their duty to break their child's will; child centeredness prevails, with its emphasis on affection, understanding, and respect for the child's individuality. However, the modern parent is concerned that child centeredness might be corrupted into a laissez-faire permissiveness that weakens the child's self-control by placing insufficient demands upon him or her. The perennial problem of the optimal mix of parental love and authority is yet to be solved, but we do have some important leads.

It is convenient to divide parental discipline into *love-oriented, power-assertive,* and *authoritative.* Let us concentrate on the first two for the time being. Love-oriented discipline uses praise and reasoning on the one hand and threats of withdrawal of love on the other. Power-assertive techniques rely on physical punishment and physical threats. Love-oriented parents also tend to be warm and to give reasons for their discipline; power-assertive parents tend to be hostile and adopt an authoritarian stance: "Do what I tell you because I tell you to do it." Finally, parents can differ in the degree of control they exercise, some imposing many demands, others few.

Extremes of rejection, brutality, neglect, and protectiveness should be avoided. An inconsistent alternation between neglect and harsh punishment is apt to result in antisocial behavior; the child receives no love to make self-control worthwhile, while parental punitiveness both foments rebellion and serves as a model of impulsive hostility. A boy with a remote, rejecting father is apt to be withdrawn, particularly if he has a close relationship with a dominating mother. Excessive maternal indulgence with few restrictions is apt to produce children who are impudent, demanding, disrespectful tyrants at home, in addition to being bossy and uncooperative with peers—and friendless.

Once we leave extremes of discipline, children fare considerably better. A love-oriented, reasoning parent tends to have children who are socially responsible, cooperative, and introspective concerning their role in incurring disapproval. They tend to be nonaggressive in social relations and to feel guilty. Power-assertive techniques are apt to produce aggressive, uncooperative children who tend to blame others for wrongdoing and to use power-assertive tactics with peers. Warm, restrictive discipline tends to be correlated with a compliant, dependent, docile child, while warm permissive discipline tends to be correlated with an independent, friendly, creative child, whose assertiveness may take the form of hostility and bossiness but who nevertheless enjoys high status among peers (Becker, 1964).

Recently, authoritative discipline has been differentiated from authoritarian discipline. The parents are warm, dynamic, demanding, and communicative. They are highly involved with their children, loving yet requiring age-appropriate behaviors. While explicitly communicating the reasons for their actions and listening to and respecting the child's point of view, they reserve the ultimate power of decision for themselves. Their preschoolers are self-reliant, self-controlled, curious, and content. They take pleasure in mastering new tasks, are involved in decision making, and have leadership qualities.

Our conclusion is that there is no one ideal parental discipline suited to all children, since healthy growth itself can take many forms. One parent may value assertiveness and creativity, another conformity and docility; a sensitive, introspective child may have advantages in certain settings, a tough-skinned scrapper in another. We are now dealing in stylistic differences in normal development and are no longer in the realm of healthy versus unhealthy adjustment. If there is no absolute answer to the question, What discipline is best? such absolutism does not seem necessary in light of the diversity of healthy personality development itself. (For a general review of the topic, see Martin, 1975.)

Developmental Trends

To tell infants to wait a minute when they cry or to punish them for having a bowel movement makes no sense. It is only in the toddler period that requirements for self-control begin to be developmentally appropriate. Such requirements are apt to precipitate the angry storms, the temper tempests, the shouts of defiance of the terrible twos and threes. However, gradually the storm subsides. Not only are controls being strengthened but affective investments are being diversified, the intense involvement with parents and siblings now being supplemented by extrafamiliar adults and peers. Diversification aids modulation so that the preschooler is increasingly capable of managing feelings which are becoming increasingly manageable.

The period between 6 and 9 years of age is the high point of self-control. The early anxieties and jealousies within the nuclear family, the accommodation to peer groups, and the transition from home to school have all been weathered, and no comparably dramatic new adjustments need to be made. Children are variously described as conforming, practical, industrious, self-motivated, and self-controlled. They have more insight into their own behavior and the behavior of others than they did formerly and are more orderly, organized, and persistent. They are less aggressive and possessive than before, while the tendencies to blame and ridicule, to be greedy and possessive, or to snatch and steal are all on the wane. There is also a general tendency to be more inward rather than acting on the feelings and impulses of the moment.

The calm of middle childhood is shattered by the physiological changes and explosive growth of puberty. The period between 12 and 14 years of age may be marked by turmoil: some preadolescents are confused, touchy, negativistic and solitary, aggressive, deliberately provocative, and resistant to authority. Little wonder that some developmentalists have seen a similarity between this period and the terrible twos, even while recognizing that the preadolescent is vastly more complex.

Adolescence itself is not so dramatically unstable, although, as we have seen, the many problems involved in the transition to adulthood still make it a time of vulnerability rather than stability in regard to self-control.

At this point we can anticipate a question which bedevils the clinician: If adolescence is a period of "normal upset" for some individuals, at what point does moody or impulsive behavior become psychopathological? This issue will have to be faced squarely in the discussion of drug abuse in chapter 10; as we shall see, there is no clear answer. Rather, there is a large gray area in which the normal shades into the deviant and even the experts disagree as to where a given adolescent stands.

CONSCIENCE

Self-control evolves from parental prohibitions epitomized by "No" and "Wait." Conscience develops from parental evaluations typified by "good boy" or "good girl," "bad boy" or "bad girl." It is this added element of evaluation which makes conscience a special kind of control mechanism. Since conscience is a complex psychological creation, we had best describe it before discussing its development.

Description

Conscience grows out of evaluations of the child's behavior. "Evaluation" suggests that conscience is intimately connected with *values.* Typically we think of moral values as residing in the conscience and rightfully so. But the human conscience contains values from many other sources: some, such as success, achievement, and self-reliance, are cultural values; some, such as cleanliness and an unwillingness to waste food, derive from the family's style of living and parental idiosyncrasies; some, such as fair play and cooperativeness, come from peers. To various degrees, such values exist in harmony, conflict, and isolation. Their psychological potency is not determined by their moral weight; a man who is unconcerned over beating his children may suffer a pang of conscience over having forgotten to send his mother a birthday card.

Next, conscience involves *thinking, feeling,* and *behaving*—understanding what is morally right or wrong, feeling appropriate satisfaction or guilt, and acting in a moral manner. But this is the description of the ideal, integrated conscience. In reality, one element can overshadow the other two: the Devil can quote Scripture, people can feel righteous or guilty over acts which have nothing to do with morality, and moral behavior can serve immoral or amoral ends.

A special word should be said about the feelings originating in the conscience. Interestingly, we have a ready label for the negative affect accompanying transgressions, which is *guilt:* but we have no such label for the positive affect accompanying obedience, so we will arbitrarily call it *self-satisfaction.* Both affects derive from the parental evaluations "good boy" or "good girl," "bad boy" or "bad girl"; the former implies that the child is worthy of love, the latter that he or she is not. Because of the bond of love, being loveworthy is a source of one of the greatest pleasures of early childhood, while not being loveworthy subjects the child to intense anguish. As toddlers and preschoolers develop, they begin to internalize these two judgments; they judge their own behavior as being good or bad. And as they say "good boy" or "good girl," "bad boy" or "bad girl" to themselves, they also experience the same pleasure and anguish that accompanied parental evaluations. The pleasure becomes self-satisfaction, the anguish becomes guilt.

Already we can sense the importance and potential dangers of guilt. Certainly guilt is essential to normal development, but the preschooler's negative self-judgment enters the scene long before it can be employed judiciously. And this raises the possibility of all kinds of problems. It is time for us to look at the developmental picture and find out why.

The Development of Conscience

Freud, in trying to understand the childhood origins of adult psychopathology, and Piaget, in trying to understand the cognitive development of children, arrived at a similar picture of the early conscience as an absolutistic, punitive, irrational tyrant. They hypothesized different but complementary reasons why the early conscience was such a monster; Freud emphasized the emotional turmoil created by the Oedipus complex, whereas Piaget emphasized the cognitive immaturity which characterizes the preschool period. But they both believed that the early conscience is the child's own creation. It is not necessarily a reflection of rigid, punitive socialization on the parents' part.

The punitiveness of the early conscience has been documented in preschoolers, who, for example, might believe that if they are naughty God will drown the world or they will be killed or starved or shut out of their homes or pursued and eaten by large animals. Piaget (1932) provided the richest documentation of the cognitive distortions which characterize moral judgment in the preschool period and the beginning of middle childhood. He demonstrated that the seriousness of a transgression is judged by its physical consequences; breaking five cups is worse than breaking one cup, for example, even if the former were accidental and the latter intentional. Wrongdoing must be punished unconditionally, and in certain cases, the more severe the punishment the better. Punishment is an end in itself and there is little concern that it fit the crime or serve to help the child avoid similar misdeeds in the future. In regard to justice, the child believes that what the adult in authority does is, by its very nature, justified; if a child is punished when there is no evidence of wrongdoing, for example, then the child must have done something wrong anyway. The next stage in the development of conscience is marked by an inflexible equalitarianism: the child believes in "an eye for an eye" in regard to retaliation and, in regard to altruism, believes that one does something nice for someone else so he or she will do something nice in return! Even in nonmoral areas such as playing marbles, the child believes that rules are absolute and immutable, that they always existed and never can be broken. In short, the absolutistic, unconditional, punitive nature of the child's thinking is clear. It is only during the latter part of middle childhood that children begin to take intentions into account and consider degrees of punishment which match the seriousness of the transgression. Punishment itself serves a constructive purpose. Children begin to realize that people in authority can be wrong, that rules exist for social regulation and can be altered by common consent, and that fairness requires that an issue be considered from the points of view of all parties involved.

Piaget (1932) calls the early stages of thinking *moral realism,* which might seem a strange term except that by realism Piaget means literalness rather than rationality. Just as infants literally believe their cries produce the mother's presence, preschoolers literally believe what they see and hear. They can see a broken cup, they cannot see an intention, so naughtiness is manifested by its physical consequences. His father can carry a tool box which the boy cannot budge, her mother can read books which do not even have pictures; therefore, how could such omnipotent and omniscient parents be wrong? And parents unwittingly cater to the child's literalism. When they tell their toddler or preschooler that he is a "bad boy" or that she is a "bad girl," they have two perspectives which the child lacks: they know that what their child is doing is no worse than what other children his or her age do and that the behavior is only temporary. But the child is incapable of thinking, "This is just a phase and I will outgrow it"; instead, "bad" takes on an absolute connotation. Piaget would add that, even if the parent tried to provide reasons and perspective, the child's immature mind could not grasp them.

Elaborating and expanding on Piaget, Kohlberg (1976) reconstructs the stages of moral development in the following manner. At the *preconventional* level the child is concerned only with the reward or punishment an act will lead to. During the *morality of conventional role conformity* stage, the child adopts the conventional standards of "good boy" or "good girl" behavior in order to maintain the approval of others or conform to some moral authority such as religion. In the *postconventional or principled stage,* children judge behavior in terms of the morality of contract, of individual rights, of democratically accepted law, and of individual conscience, holding themselves personally accountable for moral decisions. Between 6 and 16, the preconventional level gradually declines while the other two levels increase, although only about one-quarter of 16-year-olds have achieved the highest level.

Although we know that the tyrannical conscience changes, we do not know why. Piaget emphasized the importance of the cognitive give and take during peer interaction as counteracting the rigid authoritarianism of early moral reasoning, but the evidence has not been clearly supportive. The parent who confronts the child with such simply stated challenges as, "How would you feel if someone did that to you?" may help the child think of transgressions in terms of all the parties involved. Dramatic play requiring children to assume various roles, such as those involved in playing house or grocery store or space travel, may also help the child realize that the same situation can be seen from different perspectives depending on the individual's role, thus counteracting the rigidity of absolutist thinking. When the mystery concerning the agents of change has been solved, we will be in a better position than we now are to insure that normal children "outgrow" their primitive consciences and to help disturbed children who continue to suffer needlessly from its tyranny.

This would be a good place to pause in order to emphasize a point which has come up in previous sections: there is a significant gap between reality and the young child's understanding of reality. Separation anxiety is an unrealistic fear in most instances, as is the infant's anger with the mother for not being there when needed regardless of the reason for her absence; the toddler can throw a tantrum in response to the most reasonable request from the most loving mother; and now we see a conscience developing that has little resemblance to the values the parent is trying to teach, no matter how simply those values are presented and how patiently they are explained. One implication is that good parenting cannot protect the child from the inevitable distresses and distortions of early childhood; however, good parenting can prevent such distresses and distortions from being magnified and, equally important, can maximize the corrective forces inherent in continued growth. For the child clinician, the implication is that the child's view of family and friends and school is just that, rather than an accurate report of reality; age-appropriate distortions can result in an attentive mother being perceived as a "mean old witch," while a competent father may be seen as a destructive giant. Especially before middle childhood, the child is capable of creating a chamber of horrors out of personal needs and cognitive distortions.

To return to conscience: up to this point we have been dealing with the thinking aspect of conscience, not with feeling or acting. Fortunately for the child, there is no evidence that primitive ideas of wrongdoing are inevitably accompanied by guilt. Unfortunately for our interests, the developmental picture of guilt itself is incomplete. Clinical reports indicate that guilt can exist in the preschool period; however, studies which rely on older children's verbal responses present a different picture. Young school-age children are concerned primarily with punishment rather than with guilt over transgressions; they think an act is wrong because it entails the pain of physical punishment and their main worry is being caught. Thus, they have an *externally oriented* conscience. Subsequently the theme of confession increases and is a kind of halfway house between externally oriented fear of punishment and internally oriented guilt. Children are inwardly troubled and driven to confession even if they could get away with the transgression because of what others might think of them. However, confession can also be used manipulatively by children learning the trick of saying "I'm sorry" in order to forestall punishment. It is only in the preadolescent period that true guilt in the sense of an *internal judgment* and self-criticism appears. Punishment or even the love and opinion of others are not central; rather, preadolescents are concerned with the damage done to their own self-image and self-respect.

Before proceeding to cognition, let us take time out to compare self-control and conscience in terms of the complexities of the general developmental model discussed in chapter 1. The courses of the two variables differ. Self-control is at its height during middle childhood, is badly shaken during preadolescence, and remains rather tenuous throughout adolescence. Conscience has a more linear progression from primitive to mature, the cognitive stages, for instance, appearing in an orderly sequence. While we may wish that the development of all variables were linear since this would immeasurably simplify our task of understanding, no such uniformity exists. The course of each variable must be charted rather than assumed, and we must be prepared to find various patterns of change as each progresses along its normal course.

COGNITION

The aspect of cognitive development most pertinent to understanding the relation between normal and psychopathological development is the separation of the self from the social and physical environment—what has been called the separation of the "me" from the "not-me." Within this general domain, we shall explore the development of causal thinking and the concept of egocentrism, both of which will figure in future discussions.

Causality

An adolescent girl who will not speak for fear that feces would come out of her mouth, or a young man who always sleeps on his back in the belief that, if he did not, he would turn into a woman, would be regarded as psychopathologically disturbed, since they are convinced that they can cause events which, in reality, are beyond their control. This magical notion is called *omnipotence.* Yet omnipotence is not the creation of the mature mind—all concepts of causality are initially magical. Piaget tells us that, between 5 and 8 months of age, the infant is beginning to grasp the idea that events, rather than being discrete, are related to one another: if A happens, then B is likely to follow. Yet infants mistakenly believe causal relations are dependent on their own activity. We have already seen two examples of such omnipotent thinking: infants who believe their cries produce the mother's presence and those who believe their bodily movements can cause any object in the room to jiggle and dance. Their thinking is omnipotent because it has not become *spatialized:* while they can understand their motor activity affecting an object (such as the motion of their hand causing a rattle to make noise), they cannot grasp the idea of causal relations among objects (such as a ball knocking a tower of blocks down). Understanding that objects in space can affect one another, thereby causing change, does not occur until the middle of the second year of life (Piaget, 1954).

Why, then, does not magical thinking disappear from the scene? Because the arena of cognitive development shifts from action, where it was during the sensorimotor stage, to verbal symbols or words, where it remains from the preschool period on. Instead of being able to transfer the insights of the earlier period, preschoolers once again revert to magical notions of causality when they think and reason with verbal symbols.

As in infancy, preschoolers revive the error of viewing all causality in terms of human activity. They conceptualize the physical environment in terms of animism—objects have life and consciousness—and the world becomes conscious, purposeful, and industrious, just as preschoolers themselves are. Piaget calls this thinking *precausal.* When asked to explain natural phenomena, such as the movement of clouds, the child may respond in terms of a humanized God who, for example, pushes the clouds with his hands or pulls them by a string or presses a button to make them move. The child can also cause natural events to happen so that, for example, the clouds move because the child moves. This last example is particularly interesting because when the child walks clouds and the entire landscape do seem to move. Because children in the preoperational stage literally believe what they see, they distort the physical environment, just as did the medieval astronomers who believed the sun went around the earth.

In subsequent stages, children no longer believe human or humanlike agents cause events in nature; instead, they grasp the idea that causation is totally "out there." However, they still cling to their animistic orientation because now objects themselves are humanized: the sun makes clouds move by pushing them with its rays, or the air makes them move by chasing them. Only by 8 to 10 years of age does the child completely divest the physical world of human qualities by conceptualizing causality in purely physical and mechanical terms (Piaget, 1932).

Let us now consider the implications of magical thinking for early development. The first six years are unmatched in terms of intense affect and fateful beginnings: attachment brings with it anxieties over loss and jealousy over competition, socialization requires the control of initiative, anger, and sexual behavior, evaluations in terms of good and bad are internalized and become sources of self-satisfaction and guilt, and as we shall soon see, peers place their special demands on social participation. All of these momentous events occur at a time when the child is cognitively incapable of fully understanding the reality of what is happening. Distortions are highly likely to occur. If, for example, a 5-year-old girl's parents are going through a stormy period in their marriage marked by quarreling and accusations, the child might not understand the reality of the situation (indeed, how could she?) but instead distort it in terms of her own "badness," causing the disharmony. Or if a father is drafted when his preschool son happens to be angry with him, there is a chance that the boy will blame himself for the father's disappearance from the family group. Thus, omnipotence can create fears and guilts which have no basis in reality. As we shall see, it is just such highly charged distortions of reality which may block development and eventuate in a childhood neurosis (chapter 7).

Egocentrism

Piaget defines egocentrism as conceiving the physical and social world exclusively from one's own point of view. Consequently, characteristics of the self are used to define or interpret characteristics of the objective environment: the "me" is confused with the "not-me."

Egocentristic thinking appears at all stages of cognitive development. The infant believes that the very existence of objects depends on its actions, while from the toddler period to middle childhood physical causation is interpreted in terms of the child's activities or humanlike agents. Egocentrism has an important social consequence, since it prevents the preschooler from understanding that other people not only have an independent existence but also their own point of view. The ability to view the same situation from multiple vantage points—for example, to see an episode of classroom cheating from the viewpoint of the boy who cheated, the boy who was pressured into helping him cheat, and the teacher responsible for disciplining the classroom—represents a giant step forward in cooperative social interactions. In fact, a lively research interest has sprung up around what is called *social-perspective taking* and its consequences for social behavior. We will have an opportunity to explore some of this literature when we discuss impulsive and delinquent behavior in chapter 8. (For a review of the literature, see Shantz, 1975.)

Egocentrism also prevents true *communication,* since it deludes children into thinking that everything they say is immediately understood. Only as they can view themselves from the perspective of others can they adjust their speech to the inferred level of comprehension of the listener—just as a father unconsciously adjusts his language depending on whether he is talking to a toddler, a teenager, or his wife. While Piaget maintained that nonegocentric communication does not appear until the beginning of middle childhood, subsequent evidence suggests that it might be found in the preschool period (Shantz, 1975).

Egocentrism makes its last childhood stand in early adolescence. Piaget assumed that times of cognitive transition are times when primitive modes of thought are apt to reappear. One aspect of egocentrism may be expressed as self-consciousness; if someone laughs on the bus while the adolescent boy is fumbling to find the correct change for the fare, he is certain that he is being laughed at. Another aspect of the adolescent's egocentrism is the belief that ideas alone will win the day and that their ideas hold the key to solving the world's problems—if only the world would listen! "Make love, not war!" "Do your own thing!" "If it feels right, it is right!" Such egocentrism is overcome by the realities of adult life. Adolescents discover that they cannot impose their answers on the world, but that they must moderate their idealism if it is to have any effect. They realize that the purpose of reflection is not to reorder experience but to interpret it and to offer realistic guides for future conduct. (For a more extensive discussion of egocentrism, see Elkind, 1976.)

While we have been following Piaget's concept, it is important to note that egocentrism plays a central role in other theories. The psychoanalysts have a particularly relevant definition in terms of our concern with deviant development. They emphasize the *affective* aspects rather than the purely cognitive ones. In psychodynamic theory egocentrism is the tendency to evaluate events in terms of their hedonistic value to the self: the behavior of others is good if it brings the child pleasure; it is bad if it brings pain. A father is good to the extent that he fixes his son's toy car or puts money in a candy machine; he is bad to the extent that he does not let the child hold his pocket watch and orders him to go to bed. The Freudians would agree with Piaget that the child must realize that parents are independent individuals governed by their own motives and feelings, but they add that it is equally important for the child to develop to the point where the bond of love can be maintained over and above the individual pleasures and pain which comprise the relationship. When we study children raised in bleak institutional settings, we shall see how certain of them never develop to this point but continue to relate to adults in terms of the pleasures and distresses of the moment (chapter 4).

Reality Testing

No one knows for certain how cognitive growth takes place. However, many theories postulate a progressive change as the child tests faulty ideas against reality. The psychoanalysts in fact call this process *reality testing*. When faulty ideas fail to serve their function as guides to realistic behavior, they are modified to bring them in line with reality. Healthy growth requires that reality testing be kept vigorously alive. If not, stagnation with the possibility of deviant development may occur. In fact, one limitation of Piaget for our purposes is that he did not fully explore the conditions which block and divert cognitive growth. Indeed, he was never interested in such a project. Freud, by contrast, was endlessly fascinated by the failure of rational people to behave rationally and provided some of the keenest insights into the reasons for irrationality. One of the most important of these is anxiety, the topic which will concern us next.

ANXIETY

While anxiety has diverse definitions, its conceptualization as anticipation of pain is of greatest interest to us. The concept itself originated with Freud, who used the term *signal anxiety* to designate the moderately painful anticipation of a noxious situation which warns, "Danger ahead!" Forewarned, the child can take steps to avoid reexposure to the situation. As we have seen in our discussion of self-control, anxiety lies at the heart of socialization, the child foregoing various pleasures in order to avoid the pain of parental discipline.

The Developmental Picture

INFANCY. There may be innate differences in neonatal anxiety, some infants being rugged and resilient, others sensitive and vulnerable. However, every infant is relatively helpless in regard to coping with anxiety. Having learned, for example, that a mild hunger pang will be followed by intense hunger, there is little the infant can do except endure both the pain of anticipation and of the hunger itself. It is the caretaker who must protect the infant from this dual distress. If the caretaking is sensitively administered and a source of satisfaction and pleasure, the anticipation of hunger will now signal "Pleasure ahead!" rather than "Danger!" The result will be a happy, secure infant rather than an insecure one.

THE PRESCHOOL PERIOD. The descriptive literature notes that fear of noise, strangers, pain, falling, and unexpected movement declines between 2 and 6 years of age, while fear of the dark, imaginary creatures, being alone, physical harm, and wild animals increases. There are striking individual differences in the stimuli eliciting fear and in the ways normal children cope with it. Girls tend to have more fears than boys, bright children more than average or dull ones. Psychoanalytic theory claims that the prepotent fears center around loss of parental love, castration, or physical injury, while guilt is called "moral anxiety" (Hurlock, 1964).

MIDDLE CHILDHOOD. Middle childhood is a particularly interesting time. Studies conducted thirty years ago found that the most potent fears involved imaginary, supernatural, and improbable dangers such as being attacked by a lion or by witches or ghosts. More recent surveys, however, indicate that fear of war and being taken over by communists rank highest (Croake and Knox, 1973). While the manifest content has changed, the fears still have an air of improbability: Why should a 9-year-old be frightened of a communist takeover? Our suspicions concerning an underlying consistency are reinforced by the fact that the realistic fears of receiving low grades in school and of not doing a good job at home are less potent than these two political fears.

Why fears in middle childhood continue to have an air of unreality is not known. The phenomenon is puzzling in light of the fact that during this period children are capable of grasping the nature of reality uncontaminated by egocentric distortions. One would expect them to realize that political fears were farfetched, thereby exorcizing them. Regardless of the explanation, however, the finding contains an important general lesson: normal development does not consist of a grand march forward on all fronts. In the natural course of events some areas advance, others lag. Knowing that the stable self-control and the realistic thinking of middle childhood can also be accompanied by unrealistic fears is particularly important for the clinician confronting the question of how deviant an individual child's behavior might be.

ADOLESCENCE. During adolescence fears become developmentally appropriate. Some reflect self-consciousness, such as fear of making a mistake, looking ridiculous, or being teased. Adolescents fear loss of prestige with the group through failure to live up to group-prescribed behavior. Boys in particular are concerned with their ability to assume responsibilities and to find a suitable job. Sexual fears involve doubts concerning physical attractiveness and sexual adequacy as well as fear of being sexually deviant.

Defense Mechanisms

The major features of defense mechanisms are so well known that they need be only briefly reviewed. Freud stated that signal anxiety can itself become so painful that certain maneuvers are undertaken to defend the individual against it. The basic defense is *repression,* in which both the dangerous impulse and the ideas and fantasies associated with it are banished from consciousness. In essence, the child says, "What I am not aware of does not exist"; for example, a girl who is frightened of being angry with her mother no longer is aware of such ideas and feelings after repression. If repression is insufficient, *reaction formation* might be called into play so that the child thinks and feels in a manner diametrically opposed to the anxiety-provoking impulse; continuing our example, the girl now feels particularly loving toward her mother and would not dream of being angry. In *projection*, the forbidden impulse is both repressed and attributed to others, so that the little girl might be upset that "all of the other girls" she knows are so sassy and disrespectful of their mothers. In *displacement*, the impulse is allowed expression but is directed toward a different object; for example, our little girl becomes angry with her older sister or with a teacher.

We would like to call attention to certain *congnitive* and *developmental* implications of defense mechanisms. Defense mechanisms inevitably persuade the individual that a distorted image of reality is an accurate reflection. The child who claims to have no hostility toward her parents on the basis of repression is as convinced as if, in reality, the relationship were an unusually congenial one. The point illustrates the Freudian thesis that if affect is sufficiently intense, it can readily twist reason into endless distortions, which are then mistaken for the truth.

But also recall that, in discussing cognition, we stressed the importance of continual reality testing in order for development to proceed along acceptable lines. If defense mechanisms prevent this process from taking place by protecting the child from his or her fear of facing a given reality, are they not pathogenic by their very nature? In answering this question we must rely on the clinical wisdom of Anna Freud (1965), who has been studying children all her professional life within a psychoanalytic framework. While acknowledging their potential danger, Anna Freud sees no inherent incompatibility between defense mechanisms and the general goals of socialization. Neatness and orderliness, which might be a reaction formation against the messiness of the toddler period, can be an adaptive, serviceable defense through adulthood; a political activist who is displacing anger toward parents onto anger toward entrenched political corruption still has a useful and meaningful direction to his life. In addition, the healthy child can use defenses flexibly, relying on them to manage a particularly painful episode in development but discarding them when they are no longer needed. It is when defenses become rigid, pervasive, and extreme and when the child's repertoire of defenses becomes unduly narrow that they are in danger of jeopardizing future growth.

The Dual Nature of Anxiety

Anxiety, like other variables we have discussed, can either promote or block development. On the positive side, it prevents constant reexposure to painful and destructive situations, it raises the level of motivation enabling the child to make maximal use of abilities, and it engenders defenses which may be socially adaptive and growth promoting. However, anxiety can also perpetuate inappropriate, self-defeating defenses and can bizarrely distort both thought and action; an individual may cling to the most extreme form of deviant behavior out of sheer terror over what might happen if it were relinquished. Clearly, anxiety will figure prominently in our discussions of psychopathologies and of psychotherapies as well (chapter 14).

SEX

Sexuality has been approached from a learning-cognitive point of view and from an affective point of view; both will be relevant to the subsequent exploration of homosexuality (chapter 10). Infants, lacking innate knowledge, must learn to classify themselves as "boys" or "girls." This sex classification of humans is called *gender identity,* and the cognitive processes it involves will be examined here. In addition, society prescribes behaviors and feelings which are appropriate to boys and to girls and children must learn such appropriate *sex-role behavior.* Finally, sexuality involves intense *erotic pleasures* which, at the very least, must be controlled through socialization or which, if psychoanalytic theory is correct, form the leading edge of major personality developments and changes in interpersonal relations.

Gender Identity

While the typical 3-year-old male child has grasped the idea that "boy" applies to him and can correctly answer the question, "Are you a boy or a girl?" he does not comprehend the real meaning of the label nor has he grasped the principle of categorizing people by sex. Confronted with a family of dolls, for example, he might blithely say, "Johnny is a boy, Mommy is a boy, Daddy is a boy." The 4-year-old can label the sexes correctly by relying on external cues of size, clothing, and hairstyle. Remember that the preschooler is still cognitively in the preoperational stage, literally believing what he sees, so his categorizations by sex are on the basis of manifest differences. Since children this age are incapable of conservation, they also believe that as appearances change so do essences—things that look different are different. Consequently, it is perfectly possible that boys change into girls and vice versa just by altering their clothes, hairstyle, and behavior to that of the opposite sex. And, referring to our vignette in chapter 1, it is perfectly possible for a child to grow up to be a "mommy" or a "daddy" regardless of his or her present status. It is only around 6 or 7, when conservation is cognitively possible, that children grasp the idea that gender is permanent and immutable. They also come to realize that the genitals are the crucial factor determining gender (McConaghy, 1979).

Sex Role

Every society prescribes behaviors and feelings which are appropriate and inappropriate to each sex. Traditionally in our society, boys should be dominant, aggressive, unsentimental, stoic in the face of pain, pragmatic, and work-oriented; girls should be nurturing, sociable, nonaggressive, emotionally expressive, and concerned with domestic and child-care pursuits. The message is redundant: parents know it, advertisers know it, television directors know it, gym teachers and car sales people know it. And now that there is a strong movement afoot to change the traditional stereotypes so as to foster equality between the sexes, the same social forces are being mobilized to send the new message. Society is never subtle about an issue so important as sex role. Along with the image go rewards for conforming to and punishments for deviation from the prescribed role. In fact, it was society's punitiveness toward women who deviated from their traditionally prescribed role which eventually led to the rebellion against the narrowness of the prescriptions themselves.

It is too early to tell the effects of the movement toward sexual equality on child development. However, the literature on traditional sex roles shows how pervasive the influence of such roles can be. They influence preference in games and toys: boys prefer toy cars and trucks, sports equipment, and activities capitalizing on speed and power, while girls prefer dolls and home-centered activities and fantasy themselves as nurses or secretaries. Girls more frequently express a desire to be boys than boys express a desire to be girls. In regard to intellectual functioning, boys ask more "how" and "why" questions, girls are more concerned with social rules and correct labels for objects. The stage is set for boys to be more analytic in their thinking, girls more conventional. Mathematics, science, and mechanical reasoning are viewed as being in the masculine domain, and girls perform less well in such areas. On the other hand, grade school is typically taught by women who reward the traditionally feminine values of docility and compliance, and girls consistently outperform boys. It is only toward adolescence, when the boys become concerned with their future as workers, that the situation is reversed. In all probability, the new definition of sex roles will make an equally indelible imprint on personality characteristics and on recreation, intellectual functioning, school performance, and vocational choice. (See Hetherington and Parke, 1979, chapter 15, for a more detailed presentation.)

It is easy to see how readily the concept of sex role conforms to the principles of social-learning theory, with diverse socializing agents not only rewarding appropriate behavior and punishing inappropriate behavior but also serving as models for a particular kind of sex role. It is interesting to note, for example, how the media is now presenting women as successful business executives, athletes, police officers, sexual aggressors, and superheroes.

Erotic Pleasure

In addition to learning gender and sex role, children also have erotic experiences of intense pleasure when stimulating their genitals and are curious about anatomic differences and intercourse. Having already discussed psychosexual development (see chapter 1), we shall focus here on the literature describing the development of erotic pleasure.

An infant's erect penis unmistakably points to the presence of at least one precursor of adult sexuality in the first year of life. The toddler may derive sporadic pleasure from genital stimulation, and by the preschool period the child is frequently practicing masturbation as a source of pleasurable sensations, looking at the genitals of adults and peers, asking questions concerning anatomical sex differences and the origin of babies. Erotic feelings may be aroused by the tickling and teasing and generally pleasurable excitement of caretaking during the toddler preschool period, and a mother may become concerned when her preschooler wants to masturbate while lying in bed with her or a father may realize that his little girl is becoming too excited by "riding horsy" on his foot (Gesell and Ilg, 1949).

While informed parents no longer socialize sexual behavior with threats to cut the boy's penis off or with terrifying visions of the insanity and depravity which will be his certain fate, even the most enlightened ones must inevitably require a certain amount of self-control. Typically, the parent wants to curb socially disapproved expressions of sexual behavior without alienating the child from natural feelings and curiosities. Instead of judging the child as bad, the parent conveys the message that there is a proper time and place for sexual behavior. Without such socialization, there might well be an increase in heterosexual activity throughout middle childhood, as there is in cultures with different sexual taboos. As it is, boys during middle childhood talk and joke about sex in their gangs, sometimes experimenting with mutual masturbation, while girls talk more about love and have powerful sexual fantasies, although engaging less in actual experimentation. Sexual curiosity is evidenced by an interest in peeking, seeking pornographic or sex-education books, and exchanging sex information with same-sex friends. Middle childhood is also the time of sex cleavage between boys and girls in regard to peer relations (Gesell and Ilg, 1949).

Puberty ushers in physiological maturity, the period extending from around 11 to 15 years of age for girls and from around 12 to 16 years of age for boys. The complexities of sexuality now clearly occupy the center of the stage. At the simplest level, there is the matter of obtaining accurate information, and since society rarely provides ready access to factual material, the adolescent is apt to accumulate both correct and incorrect information, to have areas of uncertainty and ignorance. In the search for personally gratifying sexual techniques, however, instructions in lovemaking are of limited value. Sexual techniques are intrinsically interpersonal, each partner having idiosyncratic sources of erotic arousal and having to adapt to those of the other partner. Thus, adolescents are dealing not merely with the awkwardness of inexperience, but also with individual differences that make the same technique exquisitely pleasurable to one partner and deeply repugnant to another. And because intense pleasures are at stake, frustration readily becomes rage, insensitivity touches off anxiety or disgust. In addition, each sexual venture involves the question, What kind of sexual being am I? Adolescents know that society will judge them, and they in turn will judge themselves in terms of the success or failure of their ventures. Most important of all, sexuality is part of the questions, "Whom can I love?" and "With whom can I share my life?" Such questions transcend those of information, technique, and social criteria of adequacy. In sum, the adolescent is searching for a physically and psychologically fulfilling relationship with a person of the opposite sex under the pressure of irresistible demands for periodic sexual gratification.

AGGRESSION

While there has been a notable relaxation of controls on sexual behavior, as evidenced by earlier sexual experiences for both boys and girls and the increase of unmarried couples living together, concern over the control of aggression may well have increased. It is not clear whether there has been a quantitative increase in violence, but certainly the possibility for massive destruction has vastly accelerated. Among the psychopathologies, uncontrolled aggression is a much more serious problem from a prognostic point of view than is excessive inhibition and neurosis, although, ironically, it is receiving insufficient attention from the professional community and from society at large (chapters 3 and 8).

As with sex, there is no consensus concerning the definition of aggression. The one adopted here defines aggression as behavior which has injury or destruction as its goal, and anger or hatred as its accompanying affect.

The Developmental Picture

INFANCY. Anger can be differentiated from general distress in the 6-month-old baby and is marked by crying, random and overall body movements such as kicking, flailing of arms and legs, and arching of the back. (For details of this developmental picture, see Wenar, 1971.)

THE TODDLER/PRESCHOOL PERIOD. The period between 1 and 4 years of age is the high-water mark for unvarnished expressions of rage, the developmental trend being from explosive, undirected outbursts of temper to directed attacks, and from physical violence to symbolic expression of aggression. Thus, temper tantrums which include kicking, biting, striking, and screaming peak around $3\frac{1}{2}$ years of age and gradually decline. On the other hand, the more directed expressions of aggression, such as retaliation, are negligible in the first year but increase, until about one-third of the outbursts of 4- and 5-year-old children are of this nature. Concomitantly, verbal forms of aggression such as name calling, arguing, and refusals also increase. Self-aggression is not uncommon in this early period, children hitting themselves, pulling their hair, or even occasionally biting themselves during a tantrum.

The descriptive picture makes sense in light of what we have learned about development. The infant cannot be angry *at* anyone because the independent existence of others has not been grasped; only after the object concept is understood is directed anger possible. While the toddler can intend to aggress, the idea that an attack actually hurts does not register until around the third year of life. Thus only from 3 years of age on is the child capable of meeting all the criteria of our definition of aggression. Subsequently, attack becomes less physical and more verbal and "psychological." While it would be comforting to believe that the transition from physical to verbal aggression represents an intrinsic diminution in aggression rather than merely a change in form, this does not appear to be the case. A blow to self-esteem can be as painful as a blow to the face; a humiliation can be more destructive than a beating.

The situations likely to evoke aggression also follow a developmentally meaningful trend: frustrations in relation to feeding, sleeping, and receiving attention in the first year; toileting in the second year, particularly being forced to remain on the toilet when the toddler is ready to leave. Thwarting of initiative, either by an authoritarian caretaker's refusal to permit an activity or, to a much less extent, by the child's own ineptness in achieving a goal, also begins to trigger aggression in the toddler period and continues to do so through the preschool period. Anger over having to share or not being able to appropriate an object belonging to another child peaks in the 3- to 4-year-old. Typically, aggressive episodes are brief, preschool quarrels lasting less than half a minute.

The meaning of aggressive behavior itself changes according to the intra- and interpersonal context. In certain emotionally unstable children, extremes of aggression alternate with extremes of withdrawal and fearfulness. On the other hand, vigorous social participation and the formation of mutual friendships also increase the incidence of aggressive behavior. Thus, while aggression solely as a desire to harm and destroy may be undesirable and aggression accompanied by withdrawal and fearfulness may be part of a general emotional instability, aggression which results from a high level of sociability may be regarded as innocuous or even healthy. In this illustration, the importance of the individual and interpersonal contexts in understanding the meaning of behavior can be seen: in any discussion of psychopathology, placing a given behavior in the context of other behaviors can change our evaluation of it.

MIDDLE CHILDHOOD. After the preschool period, aggression in the form of a crude physical attack in reaction to the immediate situation declines, and children's behavior becomes progressively more intentional, retaliatory, and symbolic. Children are concerned with getting even and paying back in kind, while their aggressive repertoire proliferates: bickering, quarreling, teasing, and swearing abound, along with bullying, prejudice, and cruelty. In keeping with the development of conscience, children now can be troubled by their outbursts. To counterbalance this gain, their increased time perspective also enables them to hold a grudge and have both more delayed and sustained aggression than was possible in the preschool period.

The situations provoking anger continue to reflect the situations which are of great concern to the child. Anger over cheating and lying, unjust punishment, neglect by others, teasing, bossing, lecturing, ineptness, and poor grades in school reflect children's concern with strict justice, their growing desire for independence, their need to be valued in their own right, and resentment over being ignored. On the other hand, their pride dictates that they should not be pushed around or mocked or treated as less than they are. From the earlier period they retain irritation over their own shortcomings and jealousy of siblings, especially when siblings take their property and when parents hold them up as models.

In general, then, anger is developmentally appropriate in middle childhood, unlike anxiety, which is developmentally inappropriate. Thus, the developmentally oriented clinician knows that it is "normal" for an 8- or 9-year-old boy to have the unrealistic fear that World War III is about to break out, but it is not "normal" for him to have a tantrum when he is told to finish all the food on his plate or when his mother continues talking on the phone after he asks her a question.

ADOLESCENCE. The early phase of adolescence, often called preadolescence, is a generally unstable time. The more infantile modes of expressing anger, such as stamping feet, throwing objects, and crying, may reappear for a while and disappear subsequently. In adolescence verbal expressions of anger predominate, such as sarcasm, name calling, swearing, ridiculing, and humiliating. Sulking frequently follows an angry outburst. The situations evoking anger resemble those of middle childhood—unfair treatment, encroachment on rights, refusal of privileges, being treated as a child, and being incapable of achieving a goal.

Further Characteristics of Aggression

Societies and classes within societies differ in the amount and kinds of aggressive behavior they consider acceptable. In our society, boys are uniformly more aggressive and more physically aggressive than girls, who rely more on verbal aggression. A child is more likely to behave aggressively in a crowded playroom than in an uncrowded one and when ill and tired rather than when well and rested. Thus, variables ranging from situation specific to societal, all have an effect on aggression.

More important for our purposes are the multiform variations of aggressive behavior. First, let us consider the effect of certain defense mechanisms on the expression of aggression. In *displacement,* changing the object of anger reduces the fear of retaliation. The familiar example is the man who, after failing to get a raise at work, comes home and punishes his child. In the turbulent 1960s, adolescent anger toward "the establishment" might well have been displaced anger toward parents in certain instances. Next, aggression can be *sublimated;* that is, both the affect and the destructive intent are sufficiently modified so as to become socially acceptable. Competitive athletics are a prime example: anger is sublimated into a "fighting spirit" and the intent to destroy becomes a determination to defeat; the cheerleaders shout, "Yea team, fight, fight, fight!" and the following day, sportswriters describe the home team as having been "slaughtered" and "annihilated."

Aggression can assume *passive* disguises. Dawdling, or complying with parental demands in slow motion, is an exquisite form of revenge that both exasperates the parents and robs them of their right to punish the child for open defiance. As we shall see (in chapter 9), underachievement in school may represent a child's unconscious revenge on parents who have demanded too much intellectually and given too little emotionally. In general, the clinician must be aware of the possibility that an unrealistic ineptness in an area highly valued by parents (such as physical awkwardness in a healthy boy whose father wants him to be an outstanding athlete) may at least be partly motivated by unconscious hostility.

Finally, aggressive behavior itself can serve nonaggressive goals. The toddler who realizes that her genuine temper tantrum always monopolizes parental attention may soon learn to use anger as a highly effective manipulative behavior. The adolescent, experiencing the loneliness of becoming independent of the family, may adopt the face-saving tactic of maintaining contact through contrived confrontations. Certain acting-out children—toddlers and juvenile delinquents alike—are not so much angry as in desperate need of being loved and valued; despairing of that, they at least can settle for getting attention. "It is better to be wanted for murder than not to be wanted at all."

As we describe the many disguises and uses of aggression, we have our first taste of the complexity that lies ahead. Aggression may or may not appear as aggressive behavior, may or may not be appropriate to the target, may motivate constructive as well as destructive behavior, and may itself be serving needs in addition to the one to destroy. Yet complexities such as these are inherent in human behavior itself, and oversimplification would lead to distortion of the very psychopathologies we are trying to understand.

Is Aggression Instinctive?

A fundamental issue among behavioral scientists concerns whether aggression is instinctive or learned. Proponents of both points of view marshal impressive supportive evidence, but the issue itself remains unresolved. Nor is the issue academic; it has major implications for understanding normal and deviant behavior as well as for remediation. If aggression is an instinct, then it must be tamed so as to find expression in socially acceptable outlets. Some outlets may be direct so that, for example, a certain amount of fighting would be regarded as desirable, as long as it did not result in serious injury. It would also be healthy for a child to get anger "off his chest" by various verbal confrontations. There should also be varied sublimated outlets for aggression, such as sports for the athletically inclined and debates for the intellectual, as well as Jaycee and 4-H awards for the aggressive salespersons and farmers of the future. If direct and indirect outlets are denied the child, aggression will accumulate and, when it no longer can be contained, will likely produce either terrifying anxiety or irrational, explosive outbursts.

Learning theorists would claim that such an image of human behavior is totally untenable. Aggression is no different from other kinds of behavior and there is ample evidence that aggressive behavior obeys the same principles of learning—classical conditioning, reinforcement and imitation. If, for example, a boy is rewarded with attention when he is angry, he will not be getting anger "off his chest" but, on the contrary, will be increasingly likely to behave aggressively in the future. Comparison of different societies indicates that the amount of aggressive behavior varies widely and that the socialization of the children and the models they encounter play an important role in this variability. To assume that some direct expression of aggression is essential runs counter to what is known concerning the environmental control of behavior; to assume that the nonaggressive child is, of necessity, a seething caldron of pent-up rage is unwarranted. Violence and wars become imminent only when other forms of aggressive behaviors are condoned and even regarded as "healthy" or desirable.

It would be difficult to find a split among scholars which has more far-reaching implications.

THE MANAGEMENT OF AGGRESSION. In spite of their fundamental disagreements as to the basic nature of aggression, proponents of both the instinctual and learning theories have similar ideas concerning the constructive management of aggressive behavior as it actually exists in childhood. Parents should be affectionate and serve as models of self-control. Love-oriented discipline and consistently prescribed standards of behavior favor control of aggression, while punitiveness, rejection, neglect, and inconsistency undermine it. The heightened arousal characterizing aggression should be channeled into alternate, constructive behaviors; it can motivate the sprinter, the satirist, the social reformer, as well as the delinquent. Attention should be paid to the problems underlying aggressive behavior—the feeling of being unloved, the humiliating sense of insignificance, the self-loathing. The aggressive child, in turn, should be helped to find constructive ways of coping with anger and to focus on its source (Berkowitz, 1973).

We have now finished our discussion of self-control and the major behaviors which the child is required to control. However, we have not exhausted our list of important developmental variables. In concentrating on socialization and on the socializing parents we have neglected peer relations as well as school, work, and occupational choice. These are the topics which will concern us next.

SOCIAL RELATIONS

A number of factors have conspired to prevent peer relations from receiving the attention they deserve. The impact of Freudian theory riveted attention on parents as the prime determiners of personality development, with peers occupying a tertiary role at best. The Freudian orientation was congruent with American societal values, which emphasize the primacy of the parents in charting the course of the child's development at least until adolescence. This neglect of peer relations is being corrected from two sources: the increased interest in peer interaction in the early years and—of direct concern to us—the finding that peer relations are a potent predictor of subsequent psychopathology (chapter 10).

In our discussion we shall distinguish a general interest in peers, which we shall call *sociability,* from *friendship,* which represents a more intense involvement with particular peers—both of which differ from groups, which are organizations of individuals possessing norms or values regulating the behavior of the individual. In interpreting the significance of social relations we shall refer to Sullivan (1953), one of the few authorities on child development who fully appreciated their significance. (For a more empirically oriented evaluation, see Hartup, 1976.)

The Early Years

There is no lack of dramatic developments in the first six years, but we shall treat such developments summarily, since they have yet to be linked with psychopathology. (For details, see Wenar, 1971.) Two-month-old infants are interested in looking at one another, and by 10 months of age there is a more varied and sustained reaction expressed in mimicking, patting, hitting, and imitation of laughing. By 15 months of age affection appears and by 2 years there is participation in games, although the toddler's short attention span and limited ability both to communicate and to control the behavior of others give sociability a fleeting, improvisational quality. However, toddlers have been observed to select one member of the group to be an object of attention, concern, or affection, the relationship suggesting the intensity and focus of a friendship, except that it is often not reciprocated.

Clearly, all early social behaviors are less stable and intense than attachments, and for good reason. Peers have no interest in assuming the caretaking role of relieving distress and providing stimulation; nor do they have the caretaker's skill in responding quickly and appropriately to needs. However, they have one inherent advantage over adults in that, being at comparable developmental levels, they are naturally attracted to one another's activities. A parent may love a child for what he or she is; peer attraction is based on interest. Peer relations are important not because they represent diluted versions of attachment, but because they add a new dimension to development.

A number of dramatic changes take place in the preschool period. One is the well-known shift from *parallel play*, in which toddlers play beside one another but not with one another, to *cooperative play*, such as playing house or grocery store, in which each child must perform an assigned role in order to achieve a common goal. Cooperativeness, respect for property, constructiveness, and adaptability are the basis of general social attraction; the child who is highly aggressive, quarrelsome, or dictatorial, who refuses to play with others or is dependent on adults for attention and affection rates low on attractiveness and sociability.

Friendships now have that combination of sharing and quarreling which will characterize them throughout childhood. They are unrelated to general sociability, as will also be true into adulthood. Finally, under special circumstances, such as having no adult caretaker in a concentration camp, preschoolers can form remarkably cohesive groups, caring for one another with great warmth and sharing responsibilities with a total lack of the jealousy, possessiveness, and competition that so often mark peer and sibling relations.

Friendship

According to Sullivan (1953) friendships in middle childhood and adolescence are essential in order to make the transition from the egocentrism of the preschool period to the mutuality, sharing, and concern for the partner which marks mature heterosexual relations. We can see the beginnings of that shift in middle childhood. Anger does not lead to disruption of the relationship as it did in the preschool years, but friendship is now sufficiently important to be sustained in the face of difficulties. The child is also beginning to want his or her friend to be happy and is concerned about the friend's attitude toward himself or herself. Thus, the concept of a friend as an independent individual is beginning to register. What is more, being with a friend is rewarding in its own right, whereas formerly the pleasure of friendship was limited to sharing specific activities. However, the readiness with which friends are shifted and the dependence of friendship on propinquity, along with a tendency to make a public show of friendship, attest to the superficiality of the relationship.

In adolescence friendships become even

more sustained and personalized. Being together rather than doing together is now paramount and is apt to involve the sharing of forbidden and disturbing feelings, especially sexual feelings and problems with parents. In the process, the friend can gain support, relieve guilt, and check reality with a trusted confidante. However, adolescents are also more frank and critical of their friends than they were as children or than they will be as adults. Anyone who knows adolescents is aware of their ability to be pitiless critics, to epitomize faults with a nickname, while all the virtues and extenuations, all the overlooking and covering up vanish. Finally, friendship teaches the adolescent the responsibility and respect of intimacy—tolerance of others, a balance of giving and receiving, knowing the limits to expression and confession (Coleman, 1980).

Such a developmental progression through middle childhood and adolescence fits nicely with Sullivan's concept of friendship as a prelude to adult intimacy, in which sexuality is united with mutuality, sharing, intimate exchange, concern for the partner, and steadfastness. Finally, Sullivan states that friendship increases self-knowledge. The critical confrontations in adolescence are particularly valuable, since parents have difficulty with playing the role of critic or are either too involved with or isolated from their adolescent to play the role constructively. (For recent studies, see Asher and Gottman, 1981.)

Sociability

The qualities making for sociability in the preschool years continue to hold sway in middle childhood. The child who is accepted by others is resourceful, intelligent, emotionally stable, dependable, cooperative, and sensitive to the feelings of others. Popular boys are strong, agile, active, aggressive, daring; popular girls traditionally have been sociable, neat, and docile, although toward preadolescence they are more assertive, vigorous, and given to fair play. The child low on social acceptability is retiring, nonadaptive to others, negativistic, individualistic, insensitive, and overbearing. Boys who run counter to the masculine stereotype by being effeminate or "sissified" suffer greater ridicule than girls who run counter to the traditional stereotype by being tomboys.

These characteristics are not as important as the psychological significance of peer relations. Sullivan claims that the shift from "me" to "we" is highly unlikely in the parent-child relationship and highly likely among peers. The child literally and figuratively looks up to parents as the source of love and of socializing directives which must be obeyed because of parental authority. By contrast, the child can look peers in the eye, literally and figuratively, the word "peer" itself meaning "equal." Consequently, the possibility of mutuality is greatly enhanced. As we have seen, shared interests form one of the primary bonds among peers. In this context of sharing, children learn what Sullivan calls *accommodation:* instead of thinking of themselves as unique or special, as they might at home, they begin to learn how to get along with others.

There is another important dimension which sociability adds to the child's development. At home the child has to be *loveworthy* because affection and obedience lie at the heart of the parent-child relationship. With peers the child must be *respect-worthy,* which is a matter of proven competence. Children must expose themselves to comparisons with other children in regard to athletic ability, manual skills, resourcefulness in suggesting and implementing interesting activities, and so on. They are valued in terms of their actual contributions to the activities that peers themselves value.

In sum, sociability prepares the child to live in the adult world of peers, just as friendship is preparation for adult heterosexuality.

The Group

MIDDLE CHILDHOOD. The insubstantial, play-oriented groups of the preschool period become the middle childhood *gang,* which, by the time children are 8 to 10 years of age, is sufficiently potent to compete with the family in terms of interest, loyalty, and emotional involvement. The child begins to subordinate personal interests to the goals of the group, tries to live up to group standards, and criticizes those who do not. Thus, "we" become more important than "I." The gang no longer needs to rely on stereotyped games and activities such as hopscotch or jump rope but is sufficiently autonomous to respond to general suggestions such as, "Let's make a clubhouse," or "Let's give a party." Names, insignia, and secret passwords help give the gang a special identity. In addition to being identifiable social units, gangs traditionally have been segregated by sex, boys being action-oriented, girls being sociable and domestic in their interests. The striking antagonism between the sexes peaks around 9 to 11 years of age when boys and girls disparage one another with bickering, quarreling, and name calling. (There are no data sufficiently recent to determine whether this pattern changed significantly by the 1980s.)

Just as friendship advances mutuality, the gang advances the sense of belongingness. It offers training in interdependent behavior, ventures out further than the individual could go alone, and through its cohesiveness buttresses the individual member's self-control. Sullivan notes that by being able to test one's feelings against those of the group, the individual is less apt to exaggerate them, either positively or negatively.

ADOLESCENCE. Group involvement reaches a high point in adolescence . The adolescent group is an autonomous social organization with purposes, values, standards of behaviors, and means of enforcing them. In its stability and differentiation it resembles adult groups rather than those of middle childhood. Conformity peaks in 11- to 13-year-olds and gradually declines; it is greatest in those adolescents low in status and high in self-blame.

Adolescent groups vary in structure and nature. There is the small, close-knit *clique* whose members are bound together by a high degree of personal compatibility and mutual admiration. The *crowd* is a larger aggregate than the clique, is concerned with social activities such as parties and dances, and does not demand the same high personal involvement. Crowds vary in status; being a member of a high-status crowd is one of the surest ways of gaining popularity. An important function is that of providing a transition from unisexual to heterosexual relations. The *gang* still survives and requires more loyalty than the crowd. It is often hostile to adult society and has a specific goal—sexual, athletic, delinquent. It retains its emphasis on adventure and excitement as well as on the formal trappings of organization, such as name, dress, and initiation ritual.

The group serves as the adolescent's primary bridge to the future. It provides a sense of belonging, which is especially important during this period of transition between being a child and being an adult. It helps adolescents master uncertainty by prescribing behavior down to what clothes to wear, what music to listen to, and what language to use. It provides both provocation and protection in changing from a same-sex to a heterosexual orientation. Finally, it supports individuals in their opposition to their parents. This does not imply that the majority of adolescents are rebellious and alienated; the battle of the generations is fought only fitfully and the values of the group, such as cooperation, self-control, and dependability, are congruent with or even reflections of parental values (Coleman, 1980).

What mars adolescent groups is their rigidity and demands for conformity. Adolescence is a high-water mark for group prejudice, when caste and class lines are sharply drawn, and inclusions and exclusions are absolute. For all their rebelliousness against adult society, adolescents are more slavishly conforming to the group than they have been before or will be in the future. In short, in middle childhood and especially in adolescence there is a narrow group centeredness, which is the counterpart of the child's earlier egocentrism. Perspective and flexibility, evaluation of individuals in terms of personal worth, loyalty without chauvinism, social commitments which transcend immediate group interests—all these lie in the future.

As we shall see, peer relations play an important role in both juvenile delinquency and drug abuse. However, there is a question as to whether they play a leading etiological role. Does the juvenile gang force its members to defy the law whether they want to or not? Or do angry, defiant youths seek out juvenile gangs? While peer pressure is a potent force in drug abuse, does it also *cause* drug abuse? Or are the adolescents who become addicted those who are particularly disturbed to begin with? These questions will be discussed in chapters 8 and 10.

WORK

Why discuss work? Work is what adults do. It is important to the adult's self-esteem and self-definition: the question, Who is X? usually being answered in terms of what X does. Work both expresses and determines personal values while playing a central role in determining friends, social activities, and conduct. The decision to enter the labor market on a full-time basis marks the end of childhood as much as any single decision can. What children do is play. So why not discuss play? The principal reason is that, while there are no psychopathologies of play, there are psychopathologies of work as it is conceptualized here (Wenar, 1971).

Work and Requiredness in Middle Childhood

Work derives from initiative. Watch toddlers exploring the environment and you will see an embryonic worker. They are totally absorbed in what they are doing, distracted neither by extraneous inner needs nor by external events; they experiment, construct, and solve problems within the limits of their intelligence and skill; they persist in the face of frustration. Note that we have described an *embryonic* worker, not a miniature one. A host of developments lie ahead. The one which concerns us now is *requiredness.*

Initiative in pure culture is the toddlers' paradise. They can do what they want just because they want to do it. As we have seen, socialization, with its "No," "Wait," "good boy" and "bad girl," is an intrusion, although sensitive parents seek to preserve initiative while requiring self-control. The next major development in regard to initiative is school. As with socialization, children cannot choose *not* to go to school, nor can they choose not to learn what they are supposed to. With the introduction of requiredness, initiative takes on an important characteristic of adult work—work is something you do whether you want to or not. Ideally, work will be intrinsically rewarding and pleasurable, but these are not of the essence.

Interestingly, disagreements among educators concerning requiredness echo disagreements among parents concerning socialization. Some educators, like some parents, favor giving the child's spontaneous interests free rein, capitalizing on natural curiosity and the ability to learn through discovery. Other educators, like other kinds of parents, emphasize formal instruction, along with the adult's ability to guide wisely and to serve as models of disciplined thinking. Good teachers from both camps share a concern with keeping spontaneous curiosity alive while enabling children to master the content of their intellectual heritage. And good teachers are concerned when children fail to live up to their potential. A special group of such children, the learning disabled, will be discussed in chapter 9.

There are other aspects of school which make it a halfway house between the free exercise of initiative and the constraints of adult occupation. School is often the child's first encounter with an extrafamilial organization empowered to make significant decisions concerning the regulation of his or her daily life. The boy entering kindergarten, for example, is one among many children whom he has not chosen to be with; he is also with an adult on whom he has no special claim and who feels obliged to show him no favoritism. His physiological needs cannot be gratified at will since neither the refrigerator nor the toilet is available on demand. Rather there are both schedules and rules which apply to all. Thus, school is an *impersonal* environment compared to home.

What is more, the products of children's efforts are valued as never before. Children are with an adult whose principle function is to scrutinize what they do and help them do even better. Grades introduce an element of public evaluation so that not only the teacher but parents and peers as well have knowledge of the quality of the children's products. "Right" and "wrong" enter the picture and take a place alongside "good" and "bad" as preconditions for adult approval or disapproval. In sum, school is *product oriented.* School children add "student" to the list of self-characterizations, and their success or failure in this new role contributes significantly to their self-esteem.

While school has many other influences on personality development, we are interested primarily in the requiredness, impersonality, and product evaluation it brings to initiative, thereby placing initiative in a context which resembles the adult work situation to a greater extent than does the home.

School failure figures prominently in discussions of psychopathology. Both the future delinquent and the future schizophrenic might be variously described as disruptive and inattentive in class, defiant and truant, for example, while the devaluing of achievement in school is an important factor determining drug use in adolescence (see chapters 8 and 10). Thus, the ability to harness and direct initiative into the work-oriented demands of school takes its place alongside other facets of self-control as a determinant of normality or psychopathology.

Vocational Choice and Identity in Adolescence

In addition to being students, adolescents begin to think of themselves as potential workers. The complexities of vocational choice are such that exploring them will continue into young adulthood. The job market itself is complicated and constantly changing, and today's adolescents probably are as poorly prepared for a vocation as they are for mature sexual behavior. The world of work has its own structure of class- and sex-appropriate occupations, its hierarchy of prestige, its requirements for occupational preparation. But work is not only doing a job; it is relating to others as well. In fact, more jobs are lost for interpersonal reasons than for lack of skill and inadequate preparation. Fellow workers have different needs—to dominate and protect, to destroy and seduce, to expand and conserve, to placate and manipulate. Finding a congenial interpersonal setting introduces an unpredictable element into the adolescent quest since there is no sure way of knowing how their idiosyncratic needs will mesh with those of fellow workers.

Along with interpersonal factors, intrapersonal factors are important in choosing a vocation. Ideally, adolescents' interests, values and talents should all find full expression in the work they choose. Yet, development itself decreases the probability of such a harmonious outcome. Vocational self-knowledge lags behind other cognitive developments, and most high school seniors make important choices concerning education or work on the basis of little accurate information concerning their aptitudes. Fortunately, they have progressed in other areas, so that the unrealistic idealism of middle childhood, such as an airy dedication to "helping others," has been replaced by a realistic set of vocational values.

In sum, adolescents must engage in a long period of trying to define their vocational as well as sexual selves. In a special form of reality testing, they set out to discover the most rewarding fit between their peculiar set of ideals, values, and talents and the world of work. Since the work they do will be an important aspect of self-definition and self-esteem, more is at stake than just finding a "good job."

Interestingly, the adolescent's search for a vocation in the broad sense has much in common with Erikson's (1968) well-known concept of the adolescent *search for identity*. (See also Marcia, 1980.) For Erikson, the adolescent's question, Who am I? is closely related to the question, What can I do that will be fulfilling? Similar intra- and interpersonal variables are involved. Adolescents bring with them a unique constellation of aptitudes, interests, values, and personality traits, which are their heritage from the past. Their occupation must offer an opportunity to continue and fulfill this special heritage, so that what they value most will be valued by others, whether such "others" be the nation, an industry, the neighborhood, or a handful of close friends.

The instability of the adolescent period makes this search for identity a difficult period of trial and error with two inherent dangers: at one extreme there may be premature occupational choice, the adolescent latching on to a stereotyped image of the "successful executive" or "prestigious doctor" only to be trapped in meaningless activities. At the other extreme, uncertainty becomes pervasive and immobilizing, so that the adolescent bogs down in what Erikson calls role diffusion. However, such untoward outcomes need not be discussed now. In successful vocational choice, as in successful socialization, the individual wants to do what is required by maturity. If he or she can no longer live in the toddler's paradise, it does not matter; finding fulfillment in the adult world is far better.

KEY POINTS TO REMEMBER

This review of normal development has taught us a number of lessons which will stand us in good stead as we discuss childhood psychopathology.

First, we have seen the importance of *context* to the understanding of behavior. The context of time is essential; when a behavior or an event occurs is as vital to understanding it as what it is (see chapter 1). The intra- and interpersonal contexts are equally important. We saw, for example, that aggressive behavior may alienate a preschooler from the group or serve as part of sociability and friendship. Other examples anticipate the discussion of psychopathology: enuresis is different in a 6-year-old boy whose negligent parents have not troubled to toilet-train him than in a child whose parents have trained him "according to the books"; juvenile delinquency can represent an impulsive lashing out at society, a desperate bid to be noticed, or a need to be accepted by a delinquent gang; homosexuality can be the most fulfilling or the most terrifying of sexual impulses.

The emphasis on context will also return when psychological assessment is discussed in chapter 13. What kinds of information are needed to make the crucial decision concerning the deviance of a given behavior or the chances of it being outgrown? And what techniques are available that can provide data relevant to making such decisions?

Next, we have seen the *complexity of growth patterns* characterizing normal development. Some patterns conform to a simple incremental model: just as children become taller and heavier, they become more intelligent with age. Other variables follow different patterns. Self-control is low during the terrible twos, increases to a high point during middle childhood, declines dramatically during preadolescence, and recovers again during adolescence, although still remaining on the unstable side. Piagetian egocentrism is conquered during the first eighteen months of life but reappears in the preschool period to distort the verbalized concepts of causality, and returns again in the self-referrent thinking of the adolescent. Negativism peaks in the early preschool period, only to vanish from the developmental scene except for a brief return during preadolescence. Differences in rates of development result in unrealistic fears during middle childhood, when the provocations to and expressions of anger are developmentally appropriate.

As was noted in chapter 1, the professional must be mindful of the many complexities of development in making a judgment concerning the possibility of psychopathology. But even more is needed. Knowledge of norms does not in and of itself answer the question of whether a child's behavior is pathological or not. Knowing that most children behave in such and such a way does not mean that this particular child is developing normally, and the child clinician is typically concerned with a given child. To return to the opening clinical vignettes in chapter 1: knowing that the child is a toddler or preschooler rather than an adolescent significantly increases the possibility that his furious attack on his sibling or his desire to change sex or her magical thinking is normal. However, the possibility still remains that this particular toddler or preschooler is severely disturbed. The conscientious clinician still proceeds to examine the context variables of history, general personality, interpersonal relations, and physiological intactness before coming to a final decision.

While we have not quite finished with normal development, we are now at a point where we can begin to make a bridge to psychopathology. We shall need to know the kinds of behaviors that have been designated pathological so we can understand what we have to account for in our quest to view psychopathology as normal development gone awry. Finally, we need a general overview as to which psychopathologies are apt to be outgrown and which are apt to continue into adulthood. All these matters will occupy us next.

3 ▪ The Bridge to the Psychopathologies

We now have a general developmental model and a working knowledge of the variables we shall use in understanding psychopathology as normal development gone awry. It is time to focus on the psychopathologies themselves. First, there will be a discussion of the way that normality shades imperceptibly into psychopathology both conceptually and empirically; then the major psychopathologies of childhood will be described; and, finally, longitudinal studies of normal and disturbed children will be summarized in order to learn which psychopathologies tend to persist, and which tend to be outgrown. Then, in chapters 4 to 12 selected psychopathologies will be explored.

THE CONCEPTUAL BRIDGE

Again and again in our previous discussion we have seen that the same variables that facilitate development have the potential of impeding its course. Attachment goes hand in hand with separation anguish, which, if exaggerated, may undermine the preschooler's self-reliant expansiveness; initiative can become a self-defeating negativism in which the child strikes out at all authorities, even those who can be genuinely helpful; self-control can become a prison and conscience a punitive inquisitor; realistic anxiety can become unrealistic terror; peer groups can mercilessly torment the outsider; schoolwork can become drudgery. This affinity between growth and failure to grow is our first, tentative support for viewing psychopathology as normal development gone awry. Note the word "tentative," since we have yet to put the view to the test in regard to specific psychopathologies.

In fact, one of the major unresolved issues in the study of psychopathology concerns the continuity or discontinuity between normal and disturbed behavior, which at times is referred to as the *quantity versus quality* debate. Is all pathological behavior on a continuum with normal behavior so that, for example, a phobia is just an exaggeration of normal fearfulness, delinquency is just an exaggeration of minor antisocial acts (such as the mischievous stealing of hubcaps), or the sexual perversion of exhibitionism is just an exaggeration of "streaking"? Or do we find, particularly among the severe psychopathologies, either certain kinds of behaviors or certain patterns of development which have little or no counterpart in normal behavior and normal development? We are in no position to debate the issue now, but we should keep it in mind as we examine specific psychopathologies.

THE EMPIRICAL BRIDGE

If stress is built into normal development, we should expect problem behavior to increase during certain periods from infancy to adulthood. There is evidence that this is the case. The data presented come from the Berkeley Growth Study (Macfarlane, Allen, and Honzik, 1954). Since this study will be referred to on other occasions, a brief summary is in order.

A total of 252 children, constituting a representative sample of the population of Berkeley, California, and born between January 1928 and June 1929, were seen at 21 months of age for a comprehensive physical and psychological evaluation. The parents were largely middle and upper lower class, with more formal education but lower income than the population at large. The subjects were subsequently seen at yearly intervals into adulthood and were evaluated by means of observation and interview. The particular data we are concerned with here were derived from 126 mothers and children in a control group. (The parents of the so-called guidance group, unlike those in the control group, were involved in discussions of marital relations, parenting, child rearing, and so forth.) As inevitably happens, the population dwindled with time, so that when the children were 14 years of age, only 86 children and 41 mothers participated in the study.

The data on behavior problems contain some confirmations of our expectations concerning *normal periods of stress*, as well as some surprises. In every instance, the behaviors to be discussed appeared in at least one-third of the population. The outcropping of certain problems was specific to certain stages of normal development. Enuresis, food finickiness, and thumb sucking were prevalent in the age group ranging from 21 months to 3 years, a time when toddlers are being pressured to control their urination and appetite and take refuge in one of the earliest and most readily available of solaces—thumb sucking. Except for a brief reappearance of food finickiness, all three problems vanished from the developmental scene. As might be expected, negativism characterized the preschool period and also disappeared subsequently. Certain problems marked transition periods: the 5- to 6-year-olds tended to have disturbing dreams and loss of appetite, to be finicky eaters, and to become somber, while preadolescents tended also to be troubled by disturbing dreams, moodiness, and shyness.

Other problems, however, were fairly common throughout childhood: temper displays, oversensitivity, jealousy, and specific fears at least up to 12 years of age. To some extent this consistency may have been the result of individual children who were "temperamentally" touchy or shy and so on, but it also may not be unusual for many children at one time or another to go through periods of fearfulness or anger or jealousy or hypersensitivity.

Before leaving these data, some comments of a methodological and clinical nature are in order. First, in longitudinal studies there is an inevitable shrinkage in the number of participants, with no guarantee that the final population will be comparable to the initial one (although this problem did not significantly affect the data we have just presented). The second lesson concerning longitudinal studies is more subtle. The Berkeley Growth Study was begun in 1929. Now think back to what was said concerning the ever-changing nature of the contexts in the developmental model. There are undoubtedly significant differences between children growing up in the 1930s and those growing up fifty years later in the 1980s. And these differences may well affect the appearance of normal behavior problems. While the data from the Berkeley Growth Study are the best available for our purposes, we must also realize that their applicability to the current scene is uncertain.

At the clinical level we have learned that, paradoxical as it sounds, there is such a thing as normal problem behavior. It would be a mistake either to expect a normal child to be problem-free or to assume that the existence of problem behavior per se is a sign that development has gone awry. However, there is a cautionary note here: we have been dealing with behavior which, taken singly, may be considered normal. This does not mean that the appearance of a number of such behaviors in a given child is also to be expected. On the contrary, as the number increases, so does the chance that the child may indeed be psychopathologically disturbed.

THE DIAGNOSTIC BRIDGE

There is some question as to whether diagnostic classifications of childhood psychopathologies do, in fact, represent a bridge between normal and deviant development. We have seen the historical reasons for this ironic state of affairs: childhood diagnoses have long been modeled on adult disturbances, which in turn have been regarded as more or less static. While there has been some recognition of the fact that certain psychopathologies are unique to childhood while others depend upon the developmental level of the child, classificatory systems are only slowly outgrowing their static, adultomorphic biases. (It might be helpful, therefore, to refer to Table 3.1 in order to locate various psychopathologies in their developmental context.) However, the concept of abnormality requires the complementary concept of normality and every classification must take into account the relationship between the two. The particular classification we shall use explicitly traces the steps whereby the normal shades, almost imperceptibly, into the psychopathological.

Classification Systems

There is no agreed upon classification of childhood psychopathologies. Some derive from a single theory (such as the psychoanalytic or behavioral); others are in the psychiatric tradition of accurate descriptions of symptoms; others stress the statistical manipulation of readily observed behaviors, while still others are a grab bag from sundry traditions. (For a more detailed discussion, see Kessler, 1971.) However, there are characteristics which all classification systems should share. There should be a *rationale* for regarding behaviors as psychopathological rather than normal, and the rationale should be appropriate to the population being studied. There should be a reason for including bedwetting as a psychopathology, for example, while excluding unpopularity. The classifications should be more than variations of adult categories since, as we have seen, pathological adult behavior can be developmentally appropriate in children, while a number of childhood psychopathologies, such as autism, enuresis, learning disabilities, truancy, and certain types of hyperactivity, have little or no counterpart in adulthood.

Next, the range of psychopathologies should be *comprehensive;* each specific category should be *clearly delineated* in terms of its behavioral characteristics and *differentiated* from other categories it may resemble. Ironically, at present, there is an inverse relation between a detailed coverage of the various psychopathologies and the reliability of the categories themselves: specific disturbances such as school phobias or compulsions tend to have low reliability as measured by agreement among experts as to diagnosis, while broad-gauged classifications, such as neurotic versus psychotic behavior, fare better.

One purpose classification systems serve is that of parceling an unwieldly mass of information into meaningful and manageable units. However, they do more than help place a given child in a given category: they are points of departure for exploring *etiology* on the one hand, *prognosis* on the other. Thus, the diagnosis of adolescent schizophrenia should carry with it implications as to causative factors and prognosis, both in regard to the chances of outgrowing the disturbance and the effectiveness of therapeutic intervention. At present, we are far from realizing such an ideal goal.

While classification may be essential, children rarely fit neatly into a single diagnostic category. Consequently, *multiple diagnoses* are often preferable to a single diagnostic label. There should also be statements as to *acuteness* or *chronicity* based on the history of the disturbance, an evaluation of the *severity* of disturbance, a specification of the *developmental period* the child is in, and a description of the *specific behaviors* which comprise the psychopathology. Thus, a child's diagnosis might read: a severe, acute reactive disorder of middle childhood, with phobic and compulsive features, manifested by persistent restlessness, irritability, fitful sleep, along with occasional panic while waiting for the school bus and a frequent need to retrace his paper route to make sure each paper was properly delivered.

In many classifications the categories themselves carry connotations concerning severity of disturbance. Reactive disorders (which we shall soon discuss) are regarded as the least severe because of their close relation to realistic events. Severity increases as the disturbance becomes progressively more internalized in the sense of being self-perpetuating and independent of reality, more pervasive and more disruptive of normal functioning. Psychoneurotic disorders, for example, are regarded as more serious than reactive disorders because the problem is internalized to a greater degree; for example, an adolescent girl may realize that her bus phobia is irrational, since there is little chance of being killed in an accident, yet the terror persists. A personality disorder is more serious still, since the problem affects a wider range of behavior than is affected in the psychoneurosis. Psychotic disorders repre-

Chronological time	The Context of Time						
	Developmental periods	Piagetian stages	Freudian stages	Eriksonian stages	Attachment	Initiative and Work	Self-contro
Birth	Infancy: 0–12 months	Sensorimotor: 0–2 years	Oral	Trust *vs.* mistrust	Social smile, 3–4 months Attachment: separation anguish, hostility, 6–9 months	Exploration; self-as-agent; battle of bottle and spoon	Not required
1 year	Toddlerhood: 1–2½ years						
2 years	Preschool age: 2½–6 years	Preoperational: 2–6 years	Anal	Autonomy *vs.* shame, doubt		Willful, negativistic; battle of the potty	Low: “terrible two
3 years						Expansion of skills: verbal, social, intellectual, etc.	Increasing
4 years							
5 years			Phallic Oedipal	Industry *vs.* inferiority			
6 years	Middle childhood: 6–11 years	Concrete operations: 6–11 years	Latency	Initiative *vs.* guilt	Fluctuation	School: requiredness, impersonality, product orientation	High
7 years							
8 years							
9 years							
10 years							
11 years	Preadolescence: 11–13 years	Formal operations: 11 years on			Vigorous denial		Low
12 years							
13 years	Adolescence: 13–18 years		Genital	Identity *vs.* role diffusion	Emancipation	Vocational choice; identity	Increasing
14 years							
15 years							
16 years							
17 years							
18 years	Young adulthood: 18–20 years			Intimacy *vs.* isolation	Rapprochement		High
19 years							
20 years							

Personality Variables*								
Conscience		Cognition		Anxiety	Sex			
...gnitive	Affective	Causality	Social, Self		Gender	Erotic Feelings	Psychosexual Developments
		Omnipotence of action		Innate differences? differentiated from distress (6 months)			Mouth libidinized; object relation
			Egocentrism				Anus libidinized; autonomy
...l realism: ...lute, rigid, ...l; ...nventional	Guilt (Freudian theory)	Omnipotence of words; precausal thinking		Dark, imaginary creatures, etc.; defense mechanisms (timetable uncertain)	Determined by external clues; changeable	Masturbation; sexual curiousity	Genitals libidinized; exhibitionism; castration anxiety; Oedipus complex
...lity of ...eration; ...entional ...lity	Punishment is sole concern		Social perspective taking; cooperation; communication; reflection	Age inappropriate: imaginary and supernatural dangers	Determined by genitals; immutable		Diminution of sexuality
	Troubled; confesses; others' reactions are important						
...ccepted ... principles	Guilt: self-oriented regardless of others	Realistic grasp of physical causality		Age-appropriate: prestige, sex, responsibility, etc.		Central concerns: information, techniques, adequacy, love	Revival of earlier conflicts
							Integration of previous stages into mature love

*Each entry marks the *beginning* of a continuous developmental process.

Chronological time	Personality Variables (continued)*			
	Aggression	Social Relations		
		Sociability	Friendship	Groups
Birth	Rage differentiated from distress (6 months)	Interest in peers		
1 year	Peak for uncontrolled aggression; age-appropriate provocations		Unreciprocated "friendships"	
2 years		Parallel play		
3 years	Intentional attack, tantrums, retaliation			
4 years		Cooperative play	Insubstantial, activity oriented	Insubstantial play groups
5 years				
6 years	Increasingly verbal-symbolic, intentional, retaliatory; age-appropriate provocations	Accommodation to others; respectworthiness	More sustained, other oriented; superficial	Gangs: identifiable units
7 years				
8 years				
9 years				
10 years				
11 years	Immature modes reappear, e.g., tantrums			
12 years				
13 years	Verbal expressions predominate: name calling, sarcasm, etc.; age-appropriate provocations		Sustained; personalized; sharing, frank, critical	Stable groups with potent control: clique, crowd, gang
14 years				
15 years				
16 years				
17 years				
18 years				
19 years				
20 years				

*Each entry marks the *beginning* of a continuous developmental process.

Onset of Psychopathologies†

Autism: 0–30 months

Depression: any age
Brain syndrome: any age
Mental retardation: any age
Developmental deviations: any age

Pica: 1–2 years

Symbiotic psychosis: 2½–5 years

Separation-anxiety disorder: preschool period

Attention-deficit disorder with hyperactivity: 3 years — Oppositional disorder: 3 years; more common in middle childhood and adolescence

Encopresis: 4–8 years — Sleep terrors: 4–12 years

Enuresis: 5–8 years

School phobia: 7–12 years — Learning disabilities: beginning school years — Schizophreniform psychotic disorders: 6–12 years

Personality disorders: middle childhood and adolescence — Psychoneurotic disorders: middle childhood, but more usual in adolescence

Conversion symptoms: middle childhood, but more typically in adolescence

Impulse-ridden personality: preadolescence — Homosexuality: early adolescence

Psychoses of adolescence — Suicide: increases in adolescence — Substance abuse: adolescence

Sociosyntonic personality disorder: adolescence — Bulimia: adolescence

Identity disorder: late adolescence — Anorexia nervosa: adolescence

†Our entries follow DSM-III. Special qualifications are noted following specific psychopathologies.

sent the extreme of disturbance because the behavior is more bizarre and further removed from normal functioning than in the other classifications.

Most classifications differentiate disturbances which are psychological, or—to use the technical term—*functional*, in origin from those which are *organic* in origin. In "pure cases" of brain syndrome, for example, organic brain pathology is established and affects behavior in characteristic ways; in "pure cases" of psychophysiological disorders, an otherwise healthy body begins to malfunction because of some psychological distress. In actuality, pure cases are all too rare, since a number of disorders may have an organic and a functional component. Mental retardation is a case in point: organic and functional factors, either singly or in combination, may play a major etiological role, while subnormal intellectual functioning itself may place a child at risk for developing psychological problems.

Finally, a number of specific psychopathologies can be ordered along a dimension of *internalization–externalization* of children's problems. When children themselves suffer they are regarded as internalizers. Neurotic children, for example, generally are well behaved but are tormented by fears or guilt. Delinquents, on the other hand, engage in antisocial behavior; the form their disturbance takes differs from that of the internalizer in that they act out their problems in relation to society. Thus, they are called externalizers. Internalization–externalization is a dimension of behavior, not a typology; while a certain percent of children fall at either extreme, many of them are mixtures of both elements; that is, they can be both anxious and aggressive or have a "nervous stomach" and steal.

The current scene in regard to classifying childhood psychopathologies is a lively one. The appearance of a new revision of a widely used diagnostic manual has occasioned a rethinking of the traditional questions: What are the basic requirements of a diagnostic system that relies upon clinical observation? How well does the present revision meet such requirements? At the same time, a classification based on the statistical manipulation of discrete behavioral items is coming into prominence and promises to be an alternative to traditional clinical diagnosis. It will be worthwhile to examine both of these developments in detail.

A TRADITIONAL APPROACH: DSM-III

The Diagnostic and Statistical Manual of Mental Disorders, Third Edition, or DSM-III (American Psychiatric Association, 1980) is the latest in the tradition of classification based on naturalistic observations. The tradition has primarily been carried on by psychiatrists and relies heavily upon the observational skills of clinicians. After describing the goals of DSM-III, we shall see how well it has met certain specific standards for judging the adequacy of a diagnostic system (based on Cantwell, 1980, and Spitzer and Cantwell, 1980.)

Goals

The goals of DSM-III are to provide a clinically useful, reliable set of diagnostic categories which will be valid for treatment and management decisions, acceptable to clinicians and researchers of different theoretical persuasions, and consistent with research findings. Terms which have outlived their usefulness should be discarded and new ones added, but major revisions should be avoided. The categories should be suitable for describing subjects in research studies while also serving an educational function for health professionals. Finally, the diagnoses should be comparable with the current International Classification of Diseases ICD-9.

Evaluation

We shall now present five standards for evaluating diagnostic classifications and see how DSM-III has fared.

RATIONALE. The rationale for singling out behavior as abnormal is typically embodied in a definition of psychopathology. In reality, there is no generally accepted definition, as our survey of models has shown. The authors of DSM-III do not pretend to resolve the knotty issue but are content merely to state their own criteria: clinically significant pain or impairment in one or more important areas of functioning with the inference that there is a behavioral, psychological, or biological dysfunction. In short, *distress* and *dysfunction* are basic.

There is one other point worth noting. The authors are careful to state that disorders, not individuals, are being classified. Thus, the manual never refers to "a schizophrenic" or "an alcoholic," as if the psychopathology were the person; instead it uses "a child with schizophrenia" or "an adult with alcoholic dependency." The point itself is simple but basic and easily lost sight of.

OBJECTIVITY OF DESCRIPTION. The diagnostic categories should be objectively described and operationally defined. There is now convincing evidence that reliability is directly related to behavioral specificity and declines as terms become more general, more inferential, and more theoretical. Thus, "Fights more frequently than age-mates" is more satisfactory than, "Is aggressive" or "Has destructive impulses." In respect to objectivity, DSM-III is quite behavior-specific and a significant improvement over its predecessor, DSM-II. To take only one example, Separation Anxiety Disorder is defined in terms of nine behavioral criteria, such as unrealistic worry about possible harm befalling major attachment figures, repeated nightmares involving the theme of separation, persistent reluctance or refusal to go to school in order to stay with major attachment figures. As additional aids, specific information is furnished as to age of onset, course, degree and kind of impairment, prevalence, sex ratio, familial pattern, and differential diagnosis.

While being applauded for their behavioral emphasis, the authors of DSM-III have also been scored for their failure to have their criteria conform to current research findings in given instances (Rutter and Shaffer, 1980). The diagnosis Reactive Attachment Disorder of Infancy, for example, states that the onset is always before 8 months "since attachments are formed by eight months if there has been adequate caretaking" (APA, 1980, p. 38). Such a statement ignores the fact that attachment is a process which develops over time, and the issue of when it is formed depends on what criteria one uses. In addition, it fails to recognize the marked individual differences among infants, which invalidate most absolute age criteria.

RELIABILITY. Realiability is concerned with the consistency of results obtained from using a diagnostic instrument. An instrument that would place the same child in different categories when used by two different clinicians, for example, would not be very useful. One criterion of reliability is the consistency with which a diagnostic instrument functions at two points in time, or *test-retest reliability*. More frequently, however, diagnostic systems utilize *interobserver agreement*, in which two experts are asked to evaluate the same child at the same point in time. In the field-testing of DSM-III, eighty-four clinicians evaluated 126 child and adolescent patients, two clinicians typically evaluating four cases, utilizing the same material such as case records, nursing notes, and family informants. The study was done in two phases, and, while the reliabilities in Phase I were quite satisfactory, those in Phase II were unaccountably lower. The overall conclusion is that the reliability of DSM-III is only fair. In light of the infrequency with which reliability studies of diagnostic classifications have been done in the past and the generally poor showing when they were conducted, the present results are promising and a step in the right direction.

VALIDITY. *Validity* is the extent to which a test measures what it claims to measure or, in this case, the extent to which a diagnostic system does, in fact, correctly classify disturbed children. The concept has proved a troublesome one and has spawned a variety of definitions. There is *content* or *face* validity, which is the degree to which the content of a diagnostic category has an obvious relation to what is being evaluated. In the case of Separation Anxiety Disorder, the three behavioral criteria mentioned make sense on the face of it. Ideally, the criteria should also be analyzed statistically to test whether they do, in fact, cluster together. *Predictive* validity compares current evaluations with some future criterion; for example, children diagnosed as schizophrenic in middle childhood should continue to be more disturbed as young adults than children diagnosed as having a school phobia. *Concurrent* validity compares the current evaluation with some other contemporary criterion; the diagnosis of a reading disability based on parental report could be compared with scores on a reading achievement test, for example. Note that the difference between predictive and concurrent validity concerns whether the outside criterion lies in the future or is current. *Construct* validity is the relationship between a diagnostic category and other variables which should be related to it theoretically; for example, children classified as violently antisocial should do poorly on measures of self-control, such as the ability to delay gratification. And, finally, *discriminative* validity is the extent to which clinical features are unique to the disorder in question and differentiate it from other similar disorders. It corresponds to the traditional clinical task of differential diagnosis.

Admittedly, DSM-III has only face validity. This is about as good a showing as reality allows, however. There are few independent criteria that can be used for predictive or concurrent validation studies, and many of the relations between diagnostic categories and other variables either have not been investigated or have yielded controversial findings. Practically speaking, the clinician cannot indefinitely postpone the task of diagnosing children until the desired validation studies have been done (Spitzer and Cantwell, 1980). Now that the pace of research on childhood psychopathology is accelerating, however, periodic revisions and updating in light of the results would be highly desirable. This would be one of the best ways for DSM-III to serve its espoused educational function.

COMPREHENSIVENESS. A diagnostic system should be comprehensive in its coverage of psychopathologies. In this respect, DSM-III is a significant improvement over DSM-II, containing twice as many categories for children and adolescents as its predecessor. The major areas of disturbance that DSM-III covers are intellectual (for example, mental retardation), behavioral (for example, conduct disorders), emotional (for example, anxiety disorders), physiological (for example, eating disorders), and pervasive and specific developmental disorders (for example, autism for the former, reading disabilities for the latter). Not that all the additions have been immune to criticism. Oppositional Disorder, defined in terms of disobedient, negativistic, and provocative opposition to authority figures for at least six months' duration, has been singled out as sounding more like "the kid down the block" than a psychopathologically disturbed one. At the same time there is no recognition of the fact that children can have mixtures of diagnoses—an adolescent can be both withdrawn and violently aggressive, for example—rather than coming in a single, neatly wrapped diagnostic package (Rutter and Shaffer, 1980).

A New Feature

A significant departure from the past is the use of a *multiaxial* classification system. Instead of being classified in terms of a single dimension as has been the custom, each child is classified along five dimensions. For many years clinicians have realized that diagnosis is multifaceted, so that a single label often fails to do justice to a child's disturbance. In addition, some of the diagnostic dimensions involve different frames of reference. It makes sense to ask if a child is autistic or schizophrenic because the question involves a discrimination between two kinds of psychopathologies. However, to ask if a child is mentally retarded or diabetic makes as little sense as to ask if he walks to school or carries his lunch. The multiaxial approach represents one solution to the problems of multiple psychopathologies and independent dimensions.

Axes I and II contain the classifications of all the mental disorders. Axis I includes the clinical syndromes, such as mental retardation, conduct disorders, infantile autism, anxiety disorders, and eating disorders. Axis II includes specific developmental disorders such as reading, arithmetic, language, and articulation disorders. This separation ensures that consideration is given to the less spectacular developmental disorders, which might be overlooked when the clinician concentrates on the presenting symptoms. Axis III includes any current physical disorder or condition which is potentially relevant to understanding or management, such as neurological damage or a chronic debilitating illness. Axes I through III comprise the official diagnosis.

The remaining axes are used in specific research and clinical settings. Axis IV, labeled Psychosocial Stressors, rates the severity of such stressors on a 7-point scale from None to Catastrophic (for example, multiple family deaths). The dimension is important, since a psychopathology which occurs in the absence of stress is more ominous than the same one occurring in the presence of great stress.

Axis V, Highest Level of Adaptive Functioning during Past Year, rates a child's social relations, functioning as a student or worker, and use of leisure time on a 7-point scale from Superior to Grossly Impaired. The axis has prognostic import, since individuals tend to return to their previous level of adaptive functioning after the psychopathological episode is over.

As was true of other criteria, applause for the multiaxial approach has not prevented criticism that research literature was ignored (see Rutter and Shaffer, 1980). Among psychosocial stressors, for example, chronic parental fighting is regarded as less stressful than death of a sibling, while the evidence indicates that it is more important to the production of psychopathology. And to limit the period of highest adaptive functioning to a year is arbitrary; it would have been better to use as the criterion the period before the onset of the psychopathological disturbance, letting the specific time vary according to the individual's history.

Critique

DSM-III has been justifiably praised for its assets and criticized for certain shortcomings. The increased specificity of its diagnostic criteria, its atheoretical, behavioral orientation, its added scope in regard to children and adolescence, and its venturing into a multiaxial approach are generally admired. Its definition of psychopathology and reliance on face validity are probably as good as reality allows, although far from satisfactory. Its reliability is marginal and needs improving. In certain instances it has been out of step with research findings in its diagnostic criteria; in addition, the wisdom of its choices for including and excluding specific categories has been questioned. Its encouragement of continued research and revision is commendable.

But DSM-III has generated more controversy than would seem warranted in light of this balancing of assets and liabilities. The basis of some of the more biting attacks is an assumption that DSM-III conforms to the medical model. In fact, it does not. While it classifies in terms of categories of disorders as is done in medicine, such classification is common in the natural sciences, where animals are separated from vegetables, felines from canines. In addition, the authors recognize that these categories should not be regarded as discrete, qualitatively different entities, since the issue of continuity and discontinuity among categories is an unsettled one. While the medical terminology of "symptom" and "diagnosis" are retained, they are consistently operationalized in behavioral terms. The implications that a symptom is a sign of some underlying disorder or that the majority of the diagnoses have an organic etiology are explicitly denied; symptoms are nothing more than behaviors, and etiology in the majority of cases is unknown.

However, the medical terminology remains, together with the fact that the manual is the product of physicians; with feelings running high among health care professionals, this is enough for DSM-III to stand accused of adhering to the medical model. Nor is the situation helped when individuals involved in DSM-III publish articles stating that its mental disorders are a subset of medical disorders (Schacht and Nathan, 1977). More is involved here than mere conceptual confusion, however; at stake are issues of territoriality (which profession or professions have the final authority over psychopathologically disturbed children?) and livelihood (which professions have the right to bill for their services directly?). If, indeed, mental disorders are a subset of medical disorders, then the medical profession in general—and psychiatrists in particular—preempt both territory and livelihood. No wonder feelings run high!

There are those who maintain that DSM-III should be evaluated solely in terms of its successes and failures in achieving its stated goals (Rutter and Shaffer, 1980). Its authors are in no way responsible for its misuse. As a descriptive classification, it says nothing concerning who should diagnose and treat, and this neutrality should exempt it from involvement in interprofessional squabbles. On the other hand, there are those who claim that DSM-III is part of a social context marked by interprofessional rivalries and emotionally charged legal battles. Whether intentionally or not, both its form and its content serve to extend the medical domain far beyond justifiable limits. What we have in these opposing views is a variation of the old question: To what extent is science answerable only to itself, and to what extent is it answerable to society? It is an issue each individual must wrestle with and decide on his or her own.

THE MULTIVARIATE STATISTICAL APPROACH

Until recently there has been a perfect inverse relation between reliability and utility in classification. The traditional diagnostic systems had low reliabilities, while the reliable categories, such as internalizer versus externalizer or neurotic versus psychotic, were too gross to be useful to the clinician. However, just as the authors of DSM-III have been concerned with improving the precision of their diagnostic categories, advocates of precision show promise of devising a more finely differentiated set of classifications.

Progress in science, so the argument goes, often involves a change from description to measurement and quantification. In the realm of diagnosis, quantification has often involved a multivariate statistical approach. (For a review of the studies, see Quay, 1979.) The basic format is simple. Collect specific behaviors used in describing psychopathologically disturbed children, eliminate the infrequent, redundant, and obscure ones, and subject the rest to statistical techniques designed to determine which are highly related. The statistical technique frequently employed is called *factor analysis* and the resulting cluster of related behavioral items are called factors. After examining the content of the interrelated items, the investigator assigns each factor a label. Such labels may resemble those used in traditional diagnosis, such as delinquent or hyperactive; however, they should not be regarded as equivalent until empirical evidence has shown them to be.

To illustrate the multivariate statistical approach we shall concentrate on the work of Achenbach, who is currently advancing it further than his predecessors (Achenbach, 1979; Edelbrock and Achenbach, 1980). Achenbach's first step was to collect descriptions of pathological behavior from psychiatric case histories and from the literature. Through a series of preliminary studies these were reduced to 118 items which formed the Child Behavior Checklist (CBCL). Examples of items are: the child argues a lot, complains of loneliness, does not eat well, runs away from home, has strange ideas. Another set of items concerned competencies and were used to construct additional scales, but they will not concern us now.

Next, the CBCL was filled out by parents of 1,800 children referred for mental health services, and the results were factor-analyzed. The factor analyses yielded both *narrow-band* or specific syndromes of behavior problems (such as Somatic Complaint, Depressed, Delinquent) and the *wide-band* or general syndromes of internalizing (problems primarily with the self) and externalizing (problems of conflict with the outside world). To give two illustrations of narrow-band syndromes: the Schizoid scale contained the behavioral items of clinging to adults, fretting, fear of school, auditory and visual hallucinations, nightmares, shy and timid, while the Delinquent scale contained the behavioral items of destroys own and others' things, disobedient in school, has bad friends, lies, cheats, runs away, sets fires, steals, truants, and swears. As so often happens in multivariate studies, the majority of the narrow-band scales could be subsumed under either the internalizing or externalizing scales.

It was also decided to analyze the data separately for boys and girls and for the age groups 4 to 5 years, 6 to 11 years, and 12 to 16 years in order to detect both sex and age differences in syndromes. It was found, for example, that, while 6- to 11-year-old boys and girls shared the syndromes of Delinquent, Aggressive, and Hyperactive, the girls had the additional syndromes of Sex Problems and Cruel; 12- to 16-year-olds shared the syndromes of Somatic Complaint and Schizoid, with the boys having the added syndromes of Uncommunicative, Immature, and Obsessive-Compulsive, and the girls having the added syndromes of Anxious-Obsessive and Depressed Withdrawal.

In order to obtain norms, the CBCL was next administered to 1,400 nonclinical children matched for age, sex, race, and socioeconomic status with the clinical population, and percentiles calculated for the scores in the various narrow- and wide-band syndromes. Utilizing these data, an individual child's score can be evaluated in terms of its deviation from the norm. Thus, a boy with a score of 1 on the Schizoid scale would be at a point equivalent to 69 percent of the population and therefore within normal limits; however, the same boy's score of 26 on the Aggressive scale would be higher than 99 percent of the population and may well be cause for concern. After scoring all eight or nine narrow-band scales (depending on the child's age and sex), one can obtain a profile indicating which scales are within normal limits and which exceed them. A hypothetical child might be within the normal limits for the internalizing scales of Schizoid, Depressed, Uncommunicative, Obsessive-Compulsive, and Somatic Complaint, while exceeding the norm in the externalizing scales of Delinquent, Aggressive, and Hyperactive.

The final statistical analysis was performed on the profiles of 2,683 boys and girls between 6 and 16 years of age in order to obtain empirically derived patterns of problems characterizing groups of disturbed children. A number of such patterns appeared for boys and girls at the various age levels; for example, boys and girls ages 6 to 11 had distinctive patterns for Somatic Complaint, Delinquent, and Hyperactive syndromes, the pattern being named after the highest scale in the three distinctively different profiles. In order to determine whether such patterns were meaningfully related to other psychological variables (a measure of construct validity), the profiles were correlated with the scales evaluating competence. Only one of the many interesting results is reported here. While other studies have found that internalizers do better in school performance than externalizers, the more refined profile analysis shows that this is only true of the Hyperactive profile type; the Delinquent externalizer does as well as the internalizers. Whether the profiles correlate meaningfully with other psychological variables remains to be seen. Even more relevant to a determination of their clinical utility, of course, will be the profiles' relationship to etiology and prognosis, with or without treatment.

Since using computers to generate syndromes is quite different from using clinicians, it is interesting to compare Achenbach's (1980) factors with the diagnostic categories of DSM-III. Overall, DSM-III is more differentiated in the sense of having more categories, but there is general agreement between the two approaches in regard to the kinds of psychopathologies such as aggressive, anxious, socially withdrawn, obsessive-compulsive, depressed, somatic complaints, and sex problems. However, the DSM-III has certain diagnostic categories not to be found among Achenbach's syndromes, while Achenbach uncovered syndromes of Immaturity, Cruelty, and Depressed, which are missing from the DSM-III's categories for children.

It is easy to understand the appeal of the statistical approach for those who value precision. Reliabilities are characteristically satisfactory whether measured in terms of interrater agreement or retesting over a short period of time, while the behavioral nature of the basic data gives them a palpability which the more inferential diagnostic systems lack. As an added bonus, the CBCL and similar instruments are great time-savers compared with the traditional diagnostic procedures.

Yet, one should not make the mistake of assuming that the combination of behavioral specificity and statistical manipulation guarantees either precision or relevance. To begin with, objectivity in behavioral evaluation is a matter of degree. While it is true that the statement "Is disobedient at home" is more objective than "Has a problem with authority figures," the former still requires a judgment. Thus, the same behavior which a mother might regard as disobedience in her son might be dismissed by the father as "just the way boys are." There is evidence that behavioral ratings, for example, depend on who does the rating and the situation in which the behavior occurs: parents, teachers, and professionals may all disagree in rating a particular child either because they evaluate the same behavior differently, or because the child behaves differently in different settings, or because of a combination of both factors (Achenbach, 1978). Finally, behavioral data vary according to the method used to collect them: direct observation might yield different information from a case history; ratings might differ from questionnaires. In sum, behavioral data are never independent of the perceiver, the setting, and the data-collecting technique, all of which introduce variability that affects precision.

As for factor analysis or any of the other statistical techniques which have been used, they cannot confer a precision which the original data lack, nor can they go beyond such data's limitations. An example of the latter is the frequent failure of the statistical approach to produce a cluster of behaviors corresponding to the severe child psychopathologies of autism and childhood schizophrenia. Because of their rarity, these psychopathologies may have few behavioral descriptions among the pool of items. It is a truism that a factor analysis can only produce what is put into it.

None of these limitations are serious in themselves, and they are minor compared with the problems involved in increasing the precision of traditional diagnosis. Yet the success of the statistical endeavor will depend on the answer to two questions. First, can the multivariate statistical approach produce a clinically useful system of classification? The diagnostic tradition runs deep and is used on an international basis. It would take a potent competitor, and one with convincing evidence of its superiority, to dislodge it. And this leads to the second question: How well can the multivariate statistical approach fulfill its promise of generating a host of meaningful relationships with other psychological variables and of improving our understanding of etiology and prognosis, with and without therapy? While such questions are difficult, the forces pressing for an alternative to traditional diagnosis are strong, and the coming decade may see a vigorous pursuit of their answers.

THE CLASSIFICATIONS

In our presentation of the classifications we shall draw upon both DSM-III and the so-called GAP Report (Group for the Advancement of Psychiatry, 1966). The latter has been popular among child clinicians and widely used. It is less behavioral and explicit than DSM-III, more theoretically oriented, and consequently, less reliable. However, it has features which make it a valuable complement to DSM-III. To begin with, the GAP Report contains two categories which are important in understanding childhood psychopathology—Healthy Responses and Developmental Crises—neither of which appears in DSM-III. The theoretical orientation of the GAP report serves to highlight issues especially in regard to neurosis which we wish to explore in detail. Also, the GAP Report retains certain traditional designations, such as Psychotic Disorders, which are more in keeping with our presentations than are the revisions of DSM-III. In sum, a combination of both the GAP Report and DSM-III will provide an overview of childhood psychopathologies that will be more relevant to our subsequent discussions than either one alone.

Healthy Responses

In previous discussions we were more concerned with delineating normal development than with defining health per se. The GAP Report sensitizes us to the importance of having a diagnostic category, Healthy Responses. In the past, clinicians have focused exclusively on the psychopathological elements in the child's personality, almost as if it were their professional obligation to ferret them out. Experience has shown that such a narrow focus, which fails to do justice to strengths and assets, distorts both the current picture and the prognosis. This matter of assets was touched on obliquely when it was noted that aggression in the context of sociability and friendship differs from aggression which isolates the child from his or her peers. Now, however, we can explicitly recognize the evaluation of health as central to the clinician's charge of deciding whether a child is disturbed and the degree of disturbance. (The issue of evaluating growth-promoting and growth-inhibiting behavior will be discussed again when we examine the neuroses in chapter 7.)

The GAP Report states that there is no single criterion for health; rather, a number of functions are involved. In *intellectual functioning*, health involves "adequate use of capacity, intact memory, reality-testing ability, age-appropriate thought processes, some degree of inquisitiveness, alertness, and imagination" (p. 220). Healthy *social functioning* involves an adequate balance between dependence on others and autonomy, a reasonably comfortable and appropriately loving relation with adults and other children, and an age-appropriate capacity to share and empathize with peers. The emphasis on age appropriateness makes an understanding of normal development essential. Healthy *emotional functioning* involves an adequate degree of emotional stability, some capacity for self-perspective, some degree of frustration tolerance, and sublimation potential, along with some capacity to master anxiety and cope with conflicting emotions. Healthy *personal and adaptive functioning* require a degree of flexibility, a drive toward mastery, an integrative capacity, a degree of self-awareness, the existence of a self-concept, and the capacity to use fantasy in play constructively.

Note that the definition makes frequent use of qualifying phrases such as "a certain degree of" or "some capacity for." As clinicians we would prefer more exact statements so that our evaluations would be less subjective. Such objective criteria for health lie in the future; the definition reflects current reality. On the positive side, the GAP Report does not present an idealized picture of the "normal, well-rounded child," with the implication that any deviation from such an ideal is suspect. Indeed, what is impressive about normal children is how much "deviance" they can take in stride!

Finally, the GAP Report emphasizes the importance of stage appropriateness—which they prefer to age appropriateness—of development. There should also be a general "smoothness" of development, as contrasted with alternating periods of exceptionally slow and rapid growth. And finally, there should not be excessive discrepancies in growth among the components of health, as is seen in the pseudomature 6-year-old whose adult behavior effectively blocks peer participation.

Developmental Crises

In line with earlier discussions of the empirical bridge, the GAP Report recognizes that there are inherent crises in normal development itself. It lists separation anxiety, which accompanies attachment in the first year of life; the subsequent variation of separation anxiety, that comes as the toddler turns away from the mother in order to explore the environment; the fearfulness that marks the transition from the preschool to the school-age periods; ritualistic behaviors such as excessive neatness and propriety, which are part of the conformity of middle childhood; and the search for identity that underlies some of the erratic behavior of the adolescent.

Situational crises are also part of normal development. These are events which are not inherent in the developmental process itself, but which the child may well encounter: a severe illness or accident, being transferred from a favored to an unfavored school because of integration, family disruption owing to the father being drafted or the mother returning to work, and so forth. In situational crises there are no ominous preludes to the event, such as a mother going to work because she finds caring for her children intolerable. Although the children may be upset, their overall development is not blocked, nor is their behavior excessively age-inappropriate. Once again, a knowledge of normal development is essential in evaluating the appropriateness of the behavior.

With situational crises, the bridge from normal development is complete. Now the psychopathologies themselves will be presented.

THE PSYCHOPATHOLOGIES

Reactive Disorders (GAP Report) or Adjustment Disorder (DSM-III)

Reactive disorders comprise the first class of psychopathologies to take us out of the realm of normal development while still partaking of some of the qualities of normality, particularly of situational crises. (The GAP Report, rather than DSM-III, will be used, since it is more specifically concerned with children.) As in a situational crisis, the child's behavior is in reaction to a specific event or set of events. In addition, the untoward behavior patterns have not become internalized; that is, they have not become relatively autonomous, tending to persist long after the precipitating event has passed. While not as "self-corrective" as situational crises, in which the natural intra- and interpersonal forces making for growth are usually sufficient to enable the child to achieve mastery, the majority of the reactive disorders tend to be transitory; appropriate advice to the parents or a few psychotherapeutic sessions with the child usually suffice in eliminating the troublesome behavior. In general, then, reactive disorders represent a more extreme version of situational crises; the reactions may block growth to a greater degree or involve the return of more developmentally inappropriate behaviors. Consequently the risk of the reactive disorder becoming a more serious form of psychopathology is greater than in the case of situation crises.

While certain situations may be potentially traumatic for most children, such as the loss of a loved parent, the GAP Report emphasizes the variability among children, so that an event which overwhelms one might be only temporarily distressing to another. The intensity of the reaction depends on the meaning of the experience to the children and their parents, their past experiences and original endowment, their level of development and adaptive resources. The behaviors themselves may vary depending on the developmental level of the child: an infant deprived of parenting may react with apathy or eating and sleeping disturbances; the preschooler may become aggressive or withdraw into self-stimulation such as thumb sucking or masturbation for solace; the early school-age child may start wetting or soiling or retreat into excessive daydreaming.

In certain instances, the children may seem to be severely disturbed only because they are living with severely disturbed parents and modeling parental behavior; thus a child's bizarre ideas, for example, that people are out to kill her or that it is unsafe to eat food away from home, may not be evidence of primitive, omnipotent thinking but a reflection of parental fears. The psychopathology that appears to be so serious is, in fact, reactive. Once again we see the importance of viewing a behavior in context.

Psychoneurotic Disorders* (GAP Report) or Anxiety Disorders (DSM-III)[1]

The GAP Report retains this time-honored classification and its conceptualization, while DSM-III prefers the purely descriptive label, Anxiety Disorders. Psychoneurotic disorders are conceptualized as resulting from internalized conflicts between the child and significant people in the environment, most frequently the parents. They tend to have their origin in the preschool years and, because of their internalized character, tend to be more chronic than reactive disorders. However, there is no marked personality disorganization and the child's reality testing is not grossly disturbed. There are a number of specific types of psychoneuroses.

ANXIETY TYPE (GAP REPORT) OR OVERANXIOUS DISORDER (DSM-III). The picture here is of intense, diffuse feelings of apprehension. The anxiety is not only stronger than in normal fears but also may be free-floating, in that the child knows neither what has produced the anxiety nor how to diminish it. By the same token, an anxiety neurosis is different from a panic reaction to a specific traumatic experience, which would ordinarily be classified as a reactive disorder.

PHOBIC TYPE* (GAP REPORT) OR PHOBIC DISORDERS (DSM-III). A phobia is an intense, persistent, irrational fear of an animate or inanimate object or of a situation. The list of phobias is extensive: spiders, school,* dirt, high places, germs, airplanes, and so on. Unlike free-floating anxiety, the anxiety here can be managed as long as the child can avoid the specific eliciting stimulus.

SEPARATION ANXIETY DISORDER (DSM-III). This disturbance is marked by excessive anxiety upon separation from major attachment figures, from home or other familiar surroundings; for example, the child may experience anxiety to the point of panic when sleeping overnight in a friend's home or attending camp. Children are unrealistically worried about what harm might befall the loved adult or themselves during separation.

CONVERSION TYPE (GAP REPORT) OR CONVERSION DISORDERS (DSM-III). In this disorder, conflicts are dealt with unconsciously through disturbances in bodily function. There may be disturbances in motor functions, such as tics or paralysis; in sensory perception, such

[1] An asterisk (*) indicates psychopathologies that will be discussed in chapters 4 through 12.

as blindness or deafness; or in awareness, as in convulsivelike phenomena. Certain instances of vomiting and hyperventilation may be evidence of a conversion reaction. Conversion reactions must be distinguished from symptoms of physical illness, one clue being that the dysfunction may follow the child's naive concepts of the body rather than anatomic lines of distribution.

OBSESSIVE-COMPULSIVE TYPE (GAP REPORT) OR OBSESSIVE-COMPULSIVE DISORDER (DSM-III). An obsession is a persistent, recurring idea, usually of an unpleasant nature, which the child is unable to control. A religious adolescent, for example, may be bedeviled by "dirty" words which intrude upon his thoughts during prayer time, while another may have recurrent thoughts of plunging a knife into her breast. Compulsions are persistent, irresistible, irrational behaviors. The classical example is the need to wash one's hands over and over in a futile attempt to counteract a feeling of being dirty.

DEPRESSIVE TYPE (GAP REPORT). Neurotic depression is more intense and persistent than the transitory feelings of depression in healthy children undergoing developmental or situational crises. There is a greater loss of self-esteem, more intense feelings of self-deprecation and guilt, along with a depressed mood. Eating and sleeping disturbances and even agitation may also be part of the picture.

Personality Disorders

While psychoneurotic disturbances affect only limited areas of the child's functioning, personality disorders represent ingrained traits which pervade a good deal of the child's functioning. From what we have learned about the development of control, we can understand why personality disorders are uncommon until the later school-age period when the organization of the child's personality begins to stabilize. The GAP Report and DSM-III essentially are in agreement on this classification.

There are a variety of personality disorders, the GAP Report and DSM-III differing somewhat in their categories. We shall follow the GAP Report since it specifically addresses children.

COMPULSIVE PERSONALITY AND ANXIOUS PERSONALITY. In these disorders, neurotic behaviors have become pervasive personality traits. Thus, the compulsive personality is excessively concerned with orderliness, cleanliness, and conformity, is relatively rigid and inflexible, and cannot relax. Ordinarily such a child performs well and may have a kind of pseudomaturity which adults may mistake for healthy childhood behavior. Children with an anxious personality are chronically tense and apprehensive over new situations and perceive their environment as threatening, although their anxiety is not as intense and crippling as in an anxiety neurosis. After an initial fearfulness, they are able to deal adequately with new situations.

HYSTERICAL PERSONALITY. These children, most of whom are girls, tend to be overly dramatic and flamboyant, affectively labile, dependent, and suggestible. While they may be coy and seductive, they tend to be repressed sexually and have difficulties establishing a sexual relationship. Conversion symptoms may occur in times of stress but are not characteristic.

OVERLY DEPENDENT PERSONALITY. Children in this category are chronically helpless and clinging, indicating their great difficulty in achieving autonomy and taking initiative. They may also be markedly controlling and passively aggressive, utilizing demandingness and helplessness as a means of tormenting and antagonizing adults. DSM-III specifically designates these latter children as having a Passive-Aggressive Personality Disorder.

OPPOSITIONAL PERSONALITY. These children express their aggressiveness by oppositional patterns generally of a passive nature, although some may be actively aggressive. Their persistent negativism, stubborness, dawdling, and procrastination covertly express their underlying hostility. If oppositional tendencies invade the learning process, blocking out, "failing to hear," or passively resisting the teacher's authority may lead to one form of learning disorder.*

OVERLY INHIBITED PERSONALITY. The overly inhibited child is excessively shy. Motor action and initiative are inhibited, there is a general constriction of personality functions including, at times, diminished speech or even elective mutism. Unlike isolated children, overly inhibited ones seem to long for a meaningful relationship but are too inhibited to achieve one. Neither are they overly dependent, functioning quite well under special circumstances in which they feel comfortable. Their inhibition may spread to the school situation, however, because of the assertive, competitive aspects of academic achievement, and result in a learning disorder.

OVERLY INDEPENDENT PERSONALITY. Children in this category are action-oriented although not hyperactive, with a strong desire to rush toward independence. While impatient to grow up, they do not react to adult constraints with aggressive or antisocial behavior. Their need to deny helplessness or dependence may drive them into overambitious activity, and they may, in certain instances, be overcompensating for fears of harm or injury or for sexual anxieties.

MISTRUSTFUL PERSONALITY. This rare disorder appears primarily during preadolescence or early adolescence. It is marked by intense suspiciousness and mistrust, along with rigidity of thinking. Projection is used as a defense, the malice the children perceive in others being rooted in their own hostility.

Tension-Discharge Disorders (GAP Report) or Conduct Disorders (DSM-III)

Children in this category directly act out their feelings or impulses toward others in an antisocial or destructive fashion. Many labels have been given to such children, including antisocial personality, psychopathic personality, and impulsive character, but the essential feature is the persistent violation of the rights of others or of major societal norms and rules. The GAP Report is more congruent with our discussion, in which we shall use the label acting-out behavior.* There are two varieties of tension-discharge or conduct disorder:

IMPULSE-RIDDEN PERSONALITY (GAP REPORT) OR UNDERSOCIALIZED, AGGRESSIVE TYPE (DSM-III). These children have great difficulty in controlling their aggressive and sexual impulses, which are acted out immediately and impulsively, often without regard for the consequences. Their relationships with adults or other children are shallow, and they have little anxiety or guilt. They tend to project their hostile feelings onto adults and society and to rationalize their own behavior. Stealing, fire-setting, vandalism, aggressive attack, and other antisocial acts may occur frequently. All children in this category are referred to in our discussions as psychopathic or sociopathic delinquents.*

NEUROTIC PERSONALITY DISORDER (GAP REPORT). While superficially resembling the impulse-ridden personality, children in this category have reached a higher level of personality development: relationships are warmer and more meaningful, self-control and conscience are stronger, as manifested in a greater amount of anxiety and guilt. Rather than acting out on the spur of the moment and engaging in a variety of antisocial acts, they behave in a repetitive manner suggestive of a specific conflict; for example, a child may steal every time a favored younger sibling receives special attention from parents and teachers. This category is discussed under the label neurotic delinquent.*

SOCIOSYNTONIC PERSONALITY DISORDER (GAP REPORT) OR SOCIALIZED, AGGRESSIVE TYPE (DSM-III). This category was created in recognition of the fact that aggressive and antisocial behavior may not result from poor impulse control but from conformity to familial or group standards which are deviant from those of society. For example, a boy may steal because his embittered, impoverished family believes that the poor have a right to take everything they can get from the rich. Thus, antisocial behavior arises from antisocial socialization. The GAP Report regards such children as having a personality disorder (Category III) rather than having a tension-discharge disorder. This disorder is labeled subcultural delinquent in our discussions.*

Attention-Deficit Disorder (DSM-III)

The essential feature is developmentally inappropriate inattention. The disorder has been variously called the Hyperkinetic Syndrome, the Hyperactive Child Syndrome,* or Minimal Brain Damage or Dysfunction.* The GAP Report regards hyperactivity primarily as a manifestation of chronic brain dysfunction, an idea which is more dated and less congruent with research findings than is the DSM-III classification. There are two subtypes of the disorder: attentional-deficit disorder *with* hyperactivity and attentional-deficit disorder *without* hyperactivity.

ATTENTIONAL-DEFICIT DISORDER WITH HYPERACTIVITY.* Hyperactivity in the young is manifested by gross motor activity such as excessive running or climbing; in older children it typically takes the form of extreme restlessness and fidgeting. Behavior has a haphazard, poorly organized quality.

ATTENTIONAL-DEFICIT DISORDER WITHOUT HYPERACTIVITY. The child has the inattention, distractability, and impulsivity of the former classification but does not have the excessive motor activity or restlessness.

Substance Abuse (DSM-III)

DSM-III has a special classification, Substance Abuse, or what we shall call drug abuse,* while the older GAP Report mentions it only infrequently. Abuse, as contrasted with use, is marked by a significant impairment of social or occupational functioning caused by a pattern of pathological use (such as a need for daily use, an inability to cut down or stop despite repeated effort or serious physical damage) lasting at least one month.

Sexual Deviation (GAP Report)

This category should be rarely employed and only when the personality disturbance is sufficiently chronic and pervasive as to dominate the individual's orientation toward social life. Behaviors which are considered perversions in adults may be part of normal development, while deviant sexual practices may serve nonsexual goals, such as the adolescent who unconsciously uses promiscuity to flout her parent's conservative and restrictive values. Of the many deviations, we shall be discussing homosexuality* (GAP Report) in detail. DSM-III divides this disturbance into ego-dystonic homosexuality, which is persistent, unwanted, and distressing; and gender-identity disorder of childhood, which is a persistent conviction that the child belongs to the opposite sex both physically and psychologically.

Disturbances Related to Bodily Functions

Both classifications address the disturbances related to bodily functions, the GAP Report in the form of specific symptoms, DSM-III as a special class of Physical Disorders. We shall only sample the list from DSM-III.

Among Eating Disorders DSM-III lists anorexia nervosa,* which is an intense fear of becoming obese eventuating in a weight loss of at least 25 percent of original body weight; bulimia or recurrent episodes of binge-eating accompanied by an awareness of the abnormality of the eating pattern, fear of being unable to stop eating voluntarily, and a depressed mood; and pica, in which nonnutritive substances such as sand, bugs, leaves, or hair are persistently eaten. Among Other Disorders with Physical Manifestations are listed functional enuresis,* or involuntary voiding of urine during the day or night after the child is 5 years of age; functional encopresis, or the repeated voluntary or involuntary passage of feces in inappropriate places after the child is 4 years of age; and sleep-terror disorder, or repeated episodes of abrupt awakening in a state of intense anxiety, which is relatively unresponsive to efforts of others to comfort the child.

Psychotic Disorders (GAP Report)

The GAP Report includes all the severe disturbances of childhood under the traditional classification of psychoses. DSM-III argues that, since severe disturbances are so distinctive and—especially in the case of autism—have so little counterpart in adult psychopathology, it would be misleading to include them all under a classification derived from adult psychopathology. While agreeing with DSM-III, we shall follow the GAP Report as a matter of convenience, with the caveat that the term psychotic only be interpreted as meaning a severe psychopathology.

In psychotic disorders there are marked, pervasive deviations in interpersonal relationships, thought, affect, perception, motility, speech, and individuation; for example, there may be severe and continued impairment of emotional relationships with others, associated with aloofness and a tendency toward preoccupation with inanimate objects; loss of speech or failure in its development; bizarre or stereotyped behavior; outbursts of intense, unpredictable panic; absence of a sense of personal identity; and a blunted, uneven, or fragmented intellectual development. The specific categories of psychoses are presented in order of their chronological appearance, since the nosological formulation is heavily predicated on developmental considerations.

The following constitute psychoses of infancy and early childhood.

EARLY INFANTILE AUTISM* (GAP REPORT) OR INFANTILE AUTISM (DSM-III). This disorder has its onset during the first thirty months of life. The child is extremely aloof, shows little apparent awareness of other human beings, and is preoccupied with inanimate objects. Speech is delayed, absent, or not used for communication. There is a strong need to maintain sameness and resist change, temper outbursts or acute anxiety resulting from alterations in routine. Stereotyped and bizarre motor patterns are frequent.

INTERACTIONAL PSYCHOTIC DISORDER (GAP REPORT). Many of these children have developed adequately in the first year or two of life but subsequently show unusual dependence upon the mother, evidenced by intense separation anxiety and clinging, together with other regressive behaviors including the giving up of communicative speech. This category includes symbiotic psychosis.*

The psychoses of later childhood include:

SCHIZOPHRENIFORM PSYCHOTIC DISORDER (GAP REPORT). This disturbance usually is not seen until the child is between 6 and 12 years of age. The clinical picture may include marked withdrawal, intense involvement in fantasy, low frustration tolerance. Intellectually there may be concretistic thinking, looseness of association, and a breakdown of reality testing. Bizarre behavior and stereotyped motor patterns such as whirling are frequently present. Certain children have sudden outbursts of either aggressive or self-mutilating behavior, inappropriate mood swings, and suicidal threats and attempts. True hallucinations are not common until the later school-age period. Onset may be gradual, or there may be a sudden, acute eruption marked by intense anxiety, uncontrollable phobias, marked withdrawal, and distorted reality testing. This disturbance will be discussed under the heading of *childhood schizophrenia*.*

The psychoses of adolescence include:

ACUTE CONFUSIONAL STATE (GAP REPORT). This disorder is characterized by a rather abrupt onset, with acute, intense anxiety, depressive trends, and confused thinking. The adolescent's sense of identity is disturbed, but there is not the kind of bizarre ideation that would indicate a breakdown of reality testing. The adolescent can also maintain meaningful emotional relationships and adaptive capacities, although both may be unstable. The prognosis for a relatively quick recovery is good.

SCHIZOPHRENIC DISORDER, ADULT TYPE* (GAP REPORT AND DSM-III). The traditional adult classifications of simple, catatonic, paranoid, and hebephrenic schizophrenia can be seen in adolescents.

Simple Schizophrenia (GAP Report) is characterized by withdrawal from involvement in interpersonal relations, abandonment of ambitions, apathy, dullness, scattered attention, daydreaming. Since they are generally quiet and placid and do not have florid symptomology, simple schizophrenics can manage to get along in a protected environment.

Hebephrenic Schizophrenia (GAP Report) or Disorganized Type (DSM-III) is characterized by giggling, grimacing, and absurd posturing, neologisms, and word salads (a jumbling of words and phrases in a meaningless manner), delusions and hallucinations. Because the behavior is both blatantly bizzare and disorganized, it conforms to the popular stereotype of being "crazy."

There are two types of Catatonic Schizophrenia (GAP and DSM-III). The first is marked by stupor, mutism, negativism, and/or waxy flexibility, in which the individuals may leave their limbs in positions imposed by another person for long periods of time as if they were a flexible, wax doll. The catatonic individual may be huddled in a painfully awkward position in a corner for long periods of time or may be standing rigid and immobile, staring blankly ahead. Catatonic excitement is marked by incessant, highly excited, driven activity, at times spilling over into violent behavior.

The Paranoid Schizophrenic (GAP and DSM-III) is characterized by persecutory delusions and hallucinations, at times jumbled and vague suspicions that others are "out to get" him or her, at times elaborately worked out, highly technical proofs of conspiracies. There may be delusions of grandiosity; for example, the individual believes he is Napoleon or Christ or some other famous figure. Hallucinations may consist of faces in the dark or voices which complement the individual's delusional systems.

Psychophysiologic Disorders (GAP Report) or Psychological Factors Affecting Physical Condition (DSM-III)

More popularly termed psychosomatic disorders, psychophysiological disorders result from the interaction between somatic and psychological components. Unlike conversion disorders, which involve the voluntary portion of the central nervous system, these involve the autonomic or involuntary portion. Psychophysiologic disorders may be precipitated and perpetuated by psychological stress. Unlike the simple physiologic concomitants of emotion involved in "fight or flight," psychophysiological disorders involve structural changes continuing to the point of being irreversible or even life-threatening. There is no specific personality type or interpersonal interaction characteristic of individual psychophysiological disorders, such as "the ulcer type" of child; rather diverse psychological as well as physiological factors play varying roles. The more common psychophysiological disorders are neurodermatitis, "tension" headaches, bronchial asthma, essential hypertension, peptic ulcer, and ulcerative colitis. Psychological factors may be minimally implicated in some disorders while playing a major role in others. It would therefore be a mistake to regard these disorders as exclusively psychogenic; rather the relative role of psychological and somatic factors must always be considered.

Brain Syndrome* (GAP Report) or Organic Brain Syndrome (DSM-III)

The disorders included here are caused by impairment of brain tissue, particularly that of the cerebral cortex. They are characterized by impairment of orientation and cognitive functions, such as judgment, discrimination, learning, and memory, as well as by lability of affect. In addition, there may be personality disturbances associated with the basic syndrome, such as psychotic or neurotic manifestations. Both the child's age and personality prior to the brain impairment are important in determining the kind and degree of disturbance as well as the prognosis in regard to recovery.

There are two categories of brain syndromes.

ACUTE BRAIN SYNDROME. In general, these disorders produce a delirium characterized by wildly agitated or confused behavior and hallucinatory experiences. However, the manifestations may be subtle disturbances in awareness or mildly stuporous states, withdrawal, irrational fears, and perceptual-motor difficulties which, while not persistent, may render the child more vulnerable to learning difficulties on entering school. The brain disorders are associated with intracranial infection, systemic infection, drug or poison intoxication, alcohol intoxication, trauma, certain types of convulsive disorders, and metabolic disturbances, among other causes.

CHRONIC BRAIN SYNDROME. These disorders result from relatively permanent, diffuse impairment of cerebral tissue function, produced by brain trauma, syphilis of the central nervous system, congenital cranial anomalies, convulsive disorders, among other causes. One syndrome seen in preschool and young school-age children with diffuse cerebral cortical damage is characterized by hyperactivity, distractibility, and impulsivity. Difficulties in perceptual-motor functioning, spatial orientation, and integration lead to problems in employing symbols as, for example, in reading and writing, as well as problems in abstract concept formation. The GAP Report describes the hyperactive child syndrome, whose relation to diffuse or minimal brain damage is more tenuous than the report indicates.

Mental Retardation (GAP Report and DSM-III)

Mental retardation involves both significantly subaverage general intellectual functioning and deficits in adaptive behavior. There has been a strong trend away from defining mental retardation exclusively in terms of intellectual functioning and from defining degrees of retardation in terms of absolute IQ scores; instead, the child's total pattern of adjustment must be considered. There are three major groups of retardates.

The biological group includes conditions of known etiologic factors affecting brain function, such as prenatal infections and toxic influences, birth trauma, metabolic disturbances, and congenital abnormalities such as Down's syndrome (mongolism).*

The environmental group includes retardation owing to sociocultural factors, such as inadequate intellectual stimulation in economically and educationally deprived families, and retardation resulting from psychological disturbances, such as severe anxiety or significant emotional deprivation.

The intermediate group includes retardation arising from both biological and environmental factors.

Developmental Deviations (GAP Report) or Specific Developmental Disorders (DSM-III)

Since individuals differ, we should expect children to vary both in their overall rates of development and in their progress through the components of personality delineated in chapter 2. The image of the well-rounded child is an ideal; most normal children are advanced in some areas, while lagging in others. However, beyond a certain difficult-to-define point, the range of normal variation is exceeded. The child may then be classified as having a developmental deviation, defined by the GAP Report as those deviations which "occur at a time, in a sequence or to a degree not expected for a given age level or stage of development" (p. 225). Biological factors such as heredity, constitution, or maturation play an important but not an exclusive etiological role, since environmental influences may also be involved. The child does not have the kinds of brain damage delineated in the section on brain syndrome nor is there the generalized developmental lag characteristic of the mentally retarded. Finally, the deviations are not predominantly physical in nature, such as those found in delayed growth or precocious puberty.

The two classificatory systems differ in the psychopathologies to be regarded as developmental deviations. The GAP Report adopts a functional approach. Some of the specific listings are: deviations in motor development, such as coordination and activity level (both hyperactivity and hypoactivity); deviations in sensory development, such as over- or underreactivity to ordinary sensory inputs; deviations in speech development, including both infantile speech and marked precocity; deviations in cognitive functions, or what we shall call learning disabilities*; deviations in affective development, as evidenced by emotional lability, overcontrol, or apathetic tendencies. DSM-III limits its categories to learning* and speech by including only reading,* arithmetic, language, and articulation disorders.

Our coverage of the GAP Report and DSM-III has not been exhaustive, since our aim has been to present an overview of the major diagnostic classifications of childhood psychopathologies. The original publications should be consulted for a comprehensive account as well as for richer descriptive pictures than have been presented here. However, we are now sufficiently acquainted with the nature and range of childhood psychopathologies to turn to the issue of their persistence over time.

LONGITUDINAL STUDIES

Since the best evidence concerning persistence comes from longitudinal studies, we need to learn about the methodological issues involved in collecting such data. In the process we shall gain a better understanding than we now have of what it means for a child to outgrow or not to outgrow disturbed behavior.

The Continuity of Behavior

The issue of the persistence of psychopathology is one aspect of the general problem of continuity of behavior, which lies at the heart of developmental psychology. The discussion of personality variables in chapter 2 demonstrated that continuity is not a simple matter of the constant recurrence of a specific behavior. Developmental forces reshape manifestations of the same variable so that, for example, the toddler's temper tantrum becomes the highly organized vengeance of rival street gangs. At the very least, manifest behaviors must be organized into *categories* relevant to psychopathology, and the developmental course of these categories charted.

Such a model is still too simple, however, because it only allows room for categories of pathological behavior to continue or to disappear over time. In reality, one kind of psychopathology may be replaced by another: an enuretic preschooler may become a fire setter in middle childhood; a truant from school may turn to drug abuse; or a psychotic adolescent may pull together and become an adequately functioning obsessive-compulsive neurotic. Thus, we must be on the lookout for *systematic relationships* among psychopathologies within the developmental context and, if possible, evaluate how such relationships affect the child's prognosis in terms of making it more favorable or unfavorable.

Finally, continuity must be evaluated with and without *therapeutic intervention.* As we shall see, certain psychopathologies are responsive to remedial measures, others are not. Understandably, the more severe the disturbance, the more difficult it is to alter its course.

Research Strategies

THE RETROSPECTIVE STRATEGY. A time-honored method of gathering developmental data is the *interview* in which a disturbed adult or the parents of a disturbed child are systematically questioned for historical information; the origins of the psychopathology are subsequently reconstructed from such data. In spite of its popularity among clinicians and researchers alike, much retrospective data are of questionable reliability and validity. In order for a parent to be a satisfactory informant, for example, he or she must accurately observe the behaviors a clinician will deem important (without foreknowledge of what behaviors these might be), preserve the observations in memory over a considerable period of time, and recall them intact on being questioned. Such an image befits a computer better than a parent, who is apt to distort information at all three stages even when the parent and child are psychologically sound—let alone if they are disturbed. While *retrospective data* may contain initial leads as to which intra- and interpersonal variables may be fruitful to study, they are currently considered an inadequate basis for understanding the origins and developmental course of childhood psychopathologies (Yarrow, Campbell, and Burton, 1970).

The reaction against retrospective data has spurred an interest in techniques which evaluate the child at two different points in time, Time 1 and Time 2. The intervals should be sufficiently long to capture general developmental trends, while the evaluations should be independently conducted by individuals who are more objective than parents. Two of the most popular strategies are the *follow-back* and the *follow-up* study, both of which eliminate a number of the deficiencies of retrospective data, although they have their own limitations.

THE FOLLOW-BACK STRATEGY. Like the retrospective approach, the follow-back study begins with a population of disturbed children or adults but obtains Time 1 data from records kept by observers other than parents: school records, teachers' assessments, child guidance case studies, court records, and so forth. A control group should also be selected, say, from the next name in the list of classmates or clinic patients, in order to narrow the variables relevant to the psychopathology being studied. For example, one might find that parental death, while hypothetically an important precursor of a given pathology, occurred no more frequently in disturbed children than in a control group.

In the follow-back study, not only can the investigator immediately focus on the target population, but the strategy also has a flexibility which allows the pursuit of new etiological leads as they emerge. As we shall soon see, the follow-up strategy has neither advantage. However, the strategy has a number of limitations. The *data* may be uneven in quality, some being comprehensive and reflecting a high degree of professional competence, others being skimpy and distorted by conceptual or personality biases. The data also tend to be gross—for example, number of arrests, decline in school grades, intact or broken family, number of job changes—lacking both the detail and the interrelatedness of variables to be found in an in-depth evaluation.

Other problems concern design and *population bias* in particular. Clinical populations may not be representative of disturbed children in general. To take one example: parents who seek professional help for a child with a school phobia may be different from those who do not, so findings from a clinical population cannot be generalized to all parents of phobic children. Or again, children who are arrested may not be a representative sample of all youthful offenders, since police officers have their own biases as to whom they arrest and whom they let go.

More important, reliance on child guidance and court records bias the data in terms of accentuating pathology and exaggerating relationships found at Time 1 and Time 2. A follow-back study, for example, indicated that 75 percent of alcoholics had been truants as compared with 26 percent of healthy individuals—a highly significant difference; yet, a follow-up study revealed that only 11 percent of truants became alcoholics as compared with 8 percent of the nontruant population which also became alcoholic. Thus, truancy can have a variety of outcomes, its particular association with alcoholism being too weak for predictive purposes. In general, follow-up studies which capture the variability of development show fewer relations among Time 1 and Time 2 variables than do follow-back studies which select especially disturbed individuals.

THE FOLLOW-UP STRATEGY. What could be a more ideal method of charting children's development than the follow-up strategy? The resulting longitudinal data should reveal which children develop what psychopathologies, together with the fate of the population with and without intervention. The children may be evaluated at Time 1 and Time 2 only, or at regular intervals as was done in the Berkeley Growth Study. Instead of being at the mercy of extant records as with follow-back studies, the investigator can insure that data will be gathered by well-trained investigators using the best available evaluative techniques.

Yet the follow-up study has a number of disadvantages. It is extremely *costly* in terms of time, money, and expenditure of effort. Investigators are bedeviled with the problem of *attrition;* not only do they lose track of subjects but they also may do so selectively, the most disturbed, unstable families or children tending to move around, move away, or be uncooperative. Thus, researchers may be faced with a dwindling number of people in the very population they are most interested in studying. Population *selectivity* is another problem. Since most psychopathologies are rare, large numbers of children must be evaluated at Time 1 to insure a reasonable number of disturbed ones at Time 2. As one solution, many investigators begin with a disturbed population or with a population at risk for developing a given psychopathology, such as infants of schizophrenic mothers, who have a greater likelihood of becoming schizophrenic than do infants from an unselected population. However, such selectivity may introduce the same population bias that we noted in the follow-back design.

Moreover, the follow-up study is *rigid.* Once having selected variables to study, the design does not allow the investigator to drop some and add others as results from relevant studies come in or as new theories and concepts come to the fore. Moreover, new measurement techniques may be devised which are superior to the ones in use but cannot be substituted for them.

One final problem with follow-up studies is the so-called *cohort effect;* one cannot assume that groups born at different times are equivalent, since the time of birth may significantly affect development. If one finds that 80-year-olds are more religious than 40-year-olds, one cannot conclude that people become more religious as they grow older, since the 80-year-olds may have been raised at a time when religion played a more significant role than it did forty years later. More to the point, children born in times of war or depression are not necessarily comparable to those born in times of peace and prosperity, just as children born before television grew up in a different environment than those born afterward. Thus, the results of a twenty-year longitudinal study may or may not be applicable to the current population of children.

It is easy to see how the cohort effect may confound the *cross-sectional* approach to gathering developmental data, which consists of studying different age groups at one point in time. Although these groups may be equated for all the variables thought to be important, such as intelligence, sex, and socioeconomic status, they cannot be equated for differential experiences which they might have had because of their time of birth. For example, the parent–child relationship of a group of 14-year-old boys who grew up during the Vietnam war might differ significantly from a group of 7-year-old boys who grew up after the war. Thus, obtained differences, say an increased incidence of antisocial behavior in the older boys, might be the result of the extended disruption of their family lives rather than any contemporary variables. To conclude from our hypothetical study that there is a developmental change whereby 7-year-old boys comply with paternal directives while 14-year-old boys rebel against them would be erroneous, since the latter group might have been equally compliant had they been reared in peacetime.

One solution to the confounding of developmental with cohort effects is the so-called *longitudinal, cross-sectional approach.* In this design children at different ages are studied as in the cross-sectional approach but are subsequently followed until the children in the younger groups are the same age as those in the next older groups; for example, groups of 3-, 6-, and 9-year-olds can be followed for three years, so that the 3-year-olds are now 6 and the 6-year-olds are 9. Such a design allows one to compare the age trends obtained cross-sectionally with longitudinal data. The saving in time is obvious; a longitudinal study which would have had to follow the 3-year-olds for six years can now be accomplished in half the time. As with any design, this one is not foolproof, since problems in equating groups and in selective loss of subjects remain. (For an example of the longitudinal, cross-sectional study, see Klausmeier and Allen, 1978.)

EVALUATION. While the follow-up and follow-back strategies are an improvement over the retrospective approach, neither is a panacea. Because of its flexibility, the follow-back strategy is most suited to generating hypotheses. Leads as to possible significant antecedents can subsequently be accepted or rejected as they are put to further tests. However, follow-up studies, because of their ability to monitor the child's development while it actually occurs, provide the most convincing data concerning change. This strategy also comes closest to testing causal relations among variables, although because it is basically naturalistic rather than experimental, it cannot provide the kind of manipulation and control of variables essential to the establishment of causation. (For a more detailed presentation of longitudinal strategies see Garmezy and Streitman, 1974.)

One final cautionary note: the design of follow-up and follow-back studies has only recently received the attention it deserves. Consequently, our review of longitudinal research will include studies of varying degrees of methodological sophistication and results with varying degrees of conclusiveness. While containing the most important leads as to the developmental course of childhood psychopathology, the findings reviewed should be regarded as tentative.

The Findings

First, the continuities among psychopathologies will be examined, including those that are behaviorally consistent or consistent within categories of behavior, and those that change from one classification of psychopathology to another. Then the discontinuities or the psychopathologies which the child "grows out of" or "grows into" by adulthood will be presented. The primary concern will be with long-range predictions from childhood into adulthood, although occasionally developmental trends within childhood itself will be dealt with. (This presentation is based on two reviews: Kohlberg, LaCrosse, and Ricks, 1972; and Robins, 1979.)

THE CONTINUITIES. The three deviations with the greatest degree of continuity from childhood to adulthood are the psychotic disorders, aggressive-antisocial or acting-out behavior, and severe mental retardation.

The *psychoses* of infancy and early childhood have a gloomy prognosis, although even here one-quarter to one-third of the children make an adequate adult adjustment with or without treatment. The deviant behavior of those who do not recover may well change while still remaining in the psychotic category; for example, an autistic preschooler may no longer evidence the classical signs as an adult but may be diagnosed as a simple or undifferentiated schizophrenic. More provocative is the finding that around one-quarter of the psychotics who fail to recover develop clear evidence of organic brain pathology, even though none was present earlier. Finally, the prognosis for schizophrenia in adolescence is equally as poor as it is for the early psychoses.

Poorly controlled, *acting-out* behavior after 6-years of age becomes predictive of subsequent aggressive-antisocial behavior in the adolescent period; specifically, disobeying the teacher, cheating, unpopularity because of fighting and quarreling, poor school work, and truanting are predictive of what is popularly called juvenile delinquency. Neurotic symptoms such as "nervousness," nail-biting, bed-wetting, and thumb-sucking are unrelated but not incompatible with becoming a delinquent, some of whom rate high on the anxiety-withdrawal dimension.

Aggressive-antisocial behavior in adolescence, in turn, is predictive of a host of acting-out behaviors affecting every area of the adult's life—criminality, vagrancy, excessive drinking, marital friction, promiscuity, and gambling. About half the children evidencing acting-out behavior will continue such behaviors into adulthood, although there is no way of predicting which children will do so. Robins (1979) concludes that "if one could successfully treat the antisocial behavior of childhood, the problems of adult crime, alcoholism, divorce, and chronic unemployment might be significantly diminished" (p. 509). The implicit irony is that effective treatment of serious antisocial behavior in childhood has yet to be devised.

An interesting example of continuity of disturbance but discontinuity of behavior is *adult schizophrenia,* which is characterized by emotional withdrawal, anxiety, and thought disturbances in the form of delusions and hallucinations. None of the characteristics are to be found in children destined to become schizophrenic as adults. The prevalent belief to the contrary, there is no evidence that the shy, withdrawn child is apt to develop schizophrenia—or any other adult psychopathology for that matter. On the contrary, the at-risk child evidences both acting-out and withdrawal behaviors and is characterized as unstable, irritable, aggressive, resistant to authority, seclusive, friendless, and given to daydreaming. The conceptual bridge between such behaviors and adult schizophrenia remains to be built (Ledingham, 1981).

School adjustment, which includes both academic achievement and attendance, is moderately related to adult adjustment, although, obviously, the specific behaviors involved are different. On the positive side, absence both of school retardation and serious truancy predict a high level of adult success in slum-dwelling children; on the negative side, the presence of these problems in similar populations predicts delinquency, problem drinking, and marriage to a delinquent mate. Sadly, truancy in both sexes predicts having children who will also be truant.

Kohlberg et al. (1972) note that school problems themselves are often the result of low IQ, distractability, and weak ability to restrain impulses, the latter two factors also being involved in acting-out behavior. Thus school becomes another setting in which poor self-control portends acting-out behavior in adulthood. These authors also note that IQ scores are better predictors of adult adjustment than any personality test, not because intelligence tests do such a good job but because personality tests do such a poor one!

The limited data on *sexual behavior* presents a mixed picture in regard to the continuity-discontinuity dimension. There is no evidence that the sexually deviant boy will grow up to become the adult who engages in sex crimes. Thus, there is discontinuity in regard to specific sexual behavior. However, to the extent that sexually deviant behavior is evidence of poor self-control and a tendency to act out, it is predictive of adult antisocial behaviors, which may include sex crimes along with other criminal, irresponsible behavior. Once again, self-control rather than sexuality per se becomes the predictive variable. The same findings hold true of girls, except that in addition to antisocial behavior the sexually deviant girl is also likely to become the hysterical woman. This relation between sexual problems and hysterically determined body dysfunctions has been noted from the time of the Greeks to Freud.

THE DISCONTINUITIES. Aside from the early psychoses and severe mental retardation, problem behavior in the toddler/preschool period tends not to be a good prognosticator of subsequent disturbances, although the evidence is not wholly consistent on this point. Such unpredictability is congruent with the fluidity of early development. Around 6 or 7 years of age predictability increases, children with many symptoms at one age tending to have many symptoms later as well.

In contrast with acting-out behavior, a wide range of *neurotic behaviors* tend to be "outgrown" by adulthood, since anxiety-withdrawal disorders have a good prognosis. Not only is the shy, withdrawn, inhibited child unlikely to become a neurotic adult, but adult adjustment is also likely to be as good as that of a random sample of the normal population. The only cloud in this sunny picture is the finding that preadolescent boys (aged 11 to 13) who are introverted, shy, and somber and preadolescent girls who are excessively modest, dependent, and finicky eaters tend to be maladjusted adults.

The findings from a recent follow-up study of 200 adults seen ten to fifteen years earlier at a child guidance clinic underscore and elaborate on the summary just presented. Except for the extreme deviation of psychoses and excessive antisocial behavior, there was little continuity between child and adult disturbances. Childhood neurosis, which comprised the largest category of children, did not portend severe maladjustment in adulthood, with or without therapy. It was easier to predict health than maladjustment, since the healthier children were likely to continue to be so while the children with severe problems might either remain disturbed or improve. Severity of disturbance, social class, and IQ were significantly related to the degree of adult maladjustment. Sex was another predictive variable, withdrawn girls and aggressive, antisocial boys rating low on adult adjustment. In regard to age, the data indicated that problems in the preadolescent period (11- to 12-year-olds) and very early in life (before age 5) foreshadowed later maladjustment. In general, children receiving outpatient therapy failed to show a better social adjustment than those equally disturbed children who received no therapy. (For further details and an extensive discussion of the problems involved in follow-up research, see Cass and Thomas, 1979).

NORMAL CHILDREN. Even psychotic and acting-out children who have the gloomiest prognosis are not all fated to become disturbed adults. But if disturbed children can "outgrow" their psychopathology, can normal children "grow into" disturbances as adults? The meager evidence suggests that this possibility exists. While the Berkeley Growth Study did not specifically address itself to the issue of psychopathology, it was concerned with the kind of adjustment children made as adults. One investigator found that a group of able, confident, well-adjusted children turned out to be brittle, restless, puzzled adults (MacFarlane, 1964). A more statistically elegant analysis of the same data uncovered a type of gregarious, vigorous, cheerful adolescent boy who became a tense, touchy, hostile man, as well as a type of bright, driving, relatively mature adolescent girl who grew to be an isolated, rigid, pushy, depressive woman (Block and Haan, 1971). When acting-out behavior is discussed in chapter 8, data will be presented indicating that children rated as extremely high on adjustment in early childhood can be rated very aggressive or withdrawn a few years later.

The thought that certain well-functioning children are at risk for becoming disturbed is a tantalizing one. Just what are the telltale signs indicating that all is not as well as it appears to be? And even if we know these signs, what are the implications of informing the parents that such a child is at risk and needs help, as our concern with prevention would require? Such questions are so far from being answered as to be almost hypothetical. However, the developmental approach requires an equal concern with "growing into" as with "outgrowing" psychopathology. It may even be that understanding the former will provide important clues to understanding the latter.

INCIDENCE VERSUS DURATION. Robins (1979) makes an important distinction between variables that predict the incidence or likelihood of occurrence of various childhood psychopathologies and those that predict their duration. Let us take a brief look at the former.

Low socioeconomic status and broken homes have frequently been found to be associated with the now-familiar constellation of antisocial behavior and underachievement in school, although they are not related to anxiety, psychoneurosis, and psychophysiological (psychosomatic) symptoms. Closer scrutiny has revealed that it is parental behavior rather than SES or broken homes per se which is highly correlated with psychopathology. Specifically, *antisocial parents* who quarrel, separate, and work at low-level occupations when they work at all, are apt to have acting-out, low-achieving children. Such parents are more frequently found in the lower classes and in broken homes. Finally, *large sibships* have also been found to be associated with both antisocial behavior and poor school achievement and adjustment.

Psychiatric illness in parents increases the incidence of psychopathology in children. While it is difficult to disentangle the contribution of genetic from environmental factors, the passing on of problems from one generation to the next occurs at a rate well beyond chance for hyperactivity, school problems, delinquency, schizophrenia, and mental retardation. Genetic factors have been most clearly established in the cases of the last two disturbances. However, the generational picture is complicated by the fact that disorders other than the one exhibited by the parents also appear in their children more frequently than in the general population. A schizophrenic mother, for example, is more apt to have not only a schizophrenic child but one with various kinds of antisocial, acting-out behaviors such as convictions for felony, alcoholism, and drug abuse. Why this should be is not clear.

The above information concerning incidence or likelihood of occurrence is essential to the clinician and researcher concerned with *prevention* of psychopathology. However, the variables predicting incidence do not predict the duration of the psychopathology once it has occurred; for example, the presence of childhood behavior problems is a more powerful predictor of adult disturbances than is family pathology. In our future discussions we shall meet other instances in which the intrapersonal context carries greater prognostic weight than the interpersonal and superordinate contexts. Information concerning duration of psychopathology is crucial to the issue of *treatment* when a decision must be reached regarding whether therapeutic intervention is warranted and, if so, what measures can be taken to shorten the natural course of the psychopathology.

CONCLUDING REMARKS

This overview of diagnostic categories and longitudinal studies helps us appreciate the special fund of information a professional must have in order to make knowledgeable statements concerning *diagnosis* and *prognosis* epitomized by the statement, "Most children act like this and your child will outgrow it," or its more ominous version, "The behavior is unusual and your child should receive special help." We now have at least a working idea of what the psychopathologies are, when they are apt to appear, and the chances of their continuing, changing into other psychopathologies, or disappearing with time.

We have also ventured in a preliminary way into the realm of *prevention* and *treatment*. The longitudinal data suggest that the major thrusts should be directed toward eliminating or ameliorating the early psychoses, severe acting-out behavior, and mental retardation. Ironically, these are the very disturbances which are only fitfully responsive to even the most heroic therapeutic efforts and can be prevented only in special instances.

Equally as troublesome as the inadequacy of therapeutic techniques for children who need help most is the ethical issue of providing psychotherapy for that large group of anxious-withdrawn children who are apt to "outgrow" such behavior without treatment. Certainly the conscientious professional cannot recommend remedial measures on the basis that they will forestall even greater and more intractable trouble in the future—one of the bedrock reason for treating children. Rather, the clinician must find other grounds for recommending treatment, such as a humanitarian concern that children should not suffer unduly, even if such suffering is temporary.

The longitudinal overview has also dispelled any notion we might have had that children are "easier" to treat than adults. As with adults, some children respond readily to treatment, others are highly resistive. The decision to become a professional helper should be made on the basis of wanting to help children and finding such help intrinsically rewarding, not on the basis of an expectation that somehow the task will be an easy one.

We are now ready for a detailed exploration of selected psychopathologies. As much as possible they will be taken in chronological order, using the information about normal development provided in chapter 2 to answer the question, How can this psychopathology be understood in terms of normal development gone awry? How deviations from normality at one point in time affect future development will also be discussed. This dual concern requires reconstructing the natural history of the psychopathology. Finally, the issue of the efficacy of psychotherapeutic measures in curtailing further deviance will be addressed. However, a systematic examination of psychotherapy will come only after our exploration of the psychopathologies themselves is concluded.

4 ▪ Severe Deviations in Infancy: The Undermining of Normal Development

What lies at the heart of human development in the first two years of life? The establishment of the bond of love, surely, and curiosity, and symbolic communication culminating in speech. And what if all were wrenched from their normal course? One would rightly predict severe psychopathology. In fact, a number of such psychopathologies have been described under the general category of psychoses. Here, only two will be discussed: autism and childhood schizophrenia. First, their behavioral manifestations and effects on subsequent development will be outlined. Then, the knotty and unanswered etiological question will be discussed, namely, What causes these deviant behaviors?

Since the role of intra- and interpersonal variables in producing autism and childhood schizophrenia is uncertain, it would be instructive to examine situations in which environmental deviations are extreme to see their effects on attachment, curiosity, and communication. What if human contact were reduced to a minimum, while the physical surroundings were monotonous and empty, as happens in certain institutions? Or, at the other extreme, what if the caretaker were brutal and physically abusive instead of sensitive and loving, as happens in child abuse? Gross developmental deviations would again be predicted, but would they resemble those found in autism and childhood schizophrenia? In searching for an answer to this question we shall learn a good deal about the similarities and differences among conditions that strike at the very foundations of normal development.

AUTISM

YOU ARE A CLINICAL CHILD PSYCHOLOGIST APPROACHING a group of disturbed preschoolers in a play yard. From a distance they look surprisingly like any healthy, intelligent youngsters. You particularly notice a little girl on a swing. Her face is pensive. She has an ethereal beauty. You go up to greet her and start a friendly conversation. She does not look at you, nor does she look away. Rather, she looks through you as if you did not exist. Face to face, and she looks through you. Later, if you were to put her on your lap, her body would not accommodate to yours, but she would sit as if you were a chair. If she needed you to do something, say, open a door, she would take your hand (rather than taking *you* by the hand) and bring it in contact with the doorknob. As a person you would not exist.

The initial encounter with autistic children can be a shattering experience. Other disturbed children might ignore you or defy you or call you names, or strike out or kick and bite, all of which are forms of relating. But to be impervious is different; it runs counter to the basic responsiveness of one human being to another.

In his classic paper, Kanner (1943) delineated the three essential features of early infantile autism. The first is extreme isolation and an inability to relate to people, as we have just seen. The second is a pathological need for sameness. This need applies both to the child's own behavior and to the environment. Often the child's activities are simple, such as sitting on the floor and rocking back and forth for long periods of time, or twirling his or her shoelaces, or running up and down a hall. Sometimes the activities resemble complex rituals, such as a 5½-year-old who takes a toy truck, turns it on its side, spins a wheel while making a humming noise, goes over to the window, looks out while drumming his fingers on the sill, and then returns to the truck, only to repeat the exact same sequence over and over. The need for environmental sameness can be expressed in a number of ways; for example, the child must have the exact same food and plate and utensils, or wear the same article of clothing, or have the same arrangement of furniture. The intensity of the need is evidenced not only by the rigidity of the behavior but also by the child's panic and rage when attempts are made to alter the environment even in minor ways, such as providing a different food or moving a chair to a different part of the room. (For an example of such rigidity in a laboratory study, see Ferster and DeMyer, 1962.)

The third characteristic of autism is either mutism or noncommunicative speech. The latter may include echolalia, phrases or sentences which are irrelevant to the situation (for example, while repeatedly flushing the toilet, an autistic girl suddenly said, "The hamburgers are in the refrigerator!"), extreme literalness (when taught to say "Please" to get a cookie, an autistic boy would use the word only when he wanted a cookie, as if "please" and "cookie" had become inseparably linked), and personal-pronoun reversals, typically the child referring to himself as "you" Kanner (1946–1947) presents evidence that, in certain instances, seemingly irrelevant remarks are meaningful from the child's point of view. A 5-year-old would frequently say "fifty-five," which seemed nonsensical until it was learned that his favorite grandmother was 55 years old and the number was his way of referring to her. Another autistic child said, "Don't throw the dog off the balcony," which again was irrelevant but referred to the fact that, three years previously, his mother had angrily said this when he was throwing a toy dog off the balcony. The first child was recalling a loving image which could comfort him; the second child was checking an impulse to throw something. Both children were not communicating because, instead of taking their listeners into account, they were living in and expressing a world of private meanings. Unless children can take the point of view of others, thereby relinquishing their egocentrism, they cannot communicate.

There are other behaviors which may be present, but are not essential to autism. Autistic children are frequently healthy and have good motor coordination. They seem to be intelligent, judging by their facial expression. They also may have excellent rote memory and may perform remarkable feats of remembering names or tunes or pictures. Finally, they are at home and content in the world of physical objects rather than in the interpersonal world. (For a current résumé, see Kernberg, 1979.)

Kanner's 1943 paper is a prime example of the *naturalistic tradition* as implemented by means of the *clinical eye.* The descriptions remain vivid and fresh and can be read with profit four decades after they were written. As any good naturalist should, Kanner also takes care to differentiate infantile autism from other conditions which might resemble it, schizophrenia in particular. But many clinicians share Kanner's keen eye for detail; what really distinguishes him is his ability to organize these richly detailed clinical pictures into categories of behavior that serve to define the psychopathology. Thus, the clinical eye nourished a conceptualizing intellect. If today we can say, "of course" there is aloneness, sameness, and mutism, it is because Kanner opened our eyes to the "obvious." After all, autism has probably been in existence for centuries and had gone unnoticed, just as the cognitive developments in the sensorimotor stage had before Piaget. Kanner's *descriptive classification* of early infantile autism remains a scientific achievement of the first order.

Subsequent research has added important new information concerning autism while generally confirming Kanner's three defining characteristics (Rutter, 1978). Although autistic behavior may be noted in early infancy, it can also appear after a period of up to thirty months of normal development. Oddly enough, its appearance is not necessarily associated with any particular precipitating event. The clinical impression of average or above average intelligence, based on the child's facial expression and feats of memory, has not been confirmed. Initially it was thought that the child's unrelatedness prevented the utilization of innate intelligence, but subsequent research found that retardation tends to persist over time when progress is made in social relations. Whether the thinking characteristic of retarded autistic children is peculiar to them or resembles that of comparably retarded, nonpsychotic children is not known. DeMyer (1976) found few meaningful differences in intellectual functioning between autistic and nonpsychotic subnormal 5- to 6-year-olds whose mean IQ scores were between 61 and 65. Admittedly, the findings are preliminary. Finally, autism can coexist with known organic brain pathologies. Out of 243 children who had been infected with congenital rubella (German measles) in utero, 10 had symptoms of autism along with organic defects such as visual, auditory, and neurological handicaps (Chess, 1971). In addition, both grand mal and psychomotor seizures develop in roughly one-quarter or more autistic children, compared with a 7 percent rate among children in general. Typically, the seizures do not appear until adolescence, and up until then there is no evidence of a neurological disorder.

That autism can coexist with both mental retardation and known organic brain pathologies complicates, rather than solves, the task of understanding etiology. It would be unwarranted to claim that either one causes autism, since the majority of mentally retarded and organically damaged children do not evidence the full-blown syndrome described by Kanner (although individual behaviors which constitute the syndrome—such as social isolation—might appear separately in specific cases). The discovery of coexisting pathology means that we must understand not only the etiology of "pure" cases of autism but also the special role mental deficiency and organic brain damage play in producing autism in given instances.

Developmental Course

One would correctly predict that so severe and pervasive a disturbance occurring so early in life would have ominous implications for future development. In summarizing eight follow-up studies of 474 autistic children, Lotter (1978) found that between two-thirds and three-quarters had poor outcomes, in that they continued to be severely disturbed, roughly 40 percent being institutionalized. The prognosis is worse than that of other severe childhood disturbances, such as borderline psychosis or mental deficiency. Speech, IQ scores, and severity of disturbance are the most potent predictors of future development—children who have not developed communicative speech by 5 years of age, who are untestable or have an IQ score below 60, and who are evaluated as being severely disturbed have the worst prognosis. On the other hand, socioeconomic status, mental illness in the family, age of onset of autism, and the development of seizures are unrelated to outcome.

It is also possible to sketch a more differentiated developmental picture than is found in outcome studies (Miller, 1974; Rutter, 1978). Based on retrospective accounts of infancy, the following behaviors are absent, delayed, or qualitatively impaired: eye contact, posturing anticipatory to being picked up, smiling in recognition of a familiar person, vocalization, stranger anxiety, interest in early games such as peekaboo, pointing, and response to sound. The infant's body may be rigid and therefore difficult to cuddle, or flaccid to the point of "collapsing" or "melting" into the mother's body.

Toddlers and preschoolers show few positive social responses. They do not follow or greet parents, or kiss and cuddle, or go to parents for comfort when hurt; but neither do they physically withdraw and avoid. Rather, they seem profoundly detached. Not only is language delayed, but babbling may also lack the richness and variety found in normal development. Understanding of language is also impaired; the child may follow a simple command if it is accompanied by a gesture, but not one that contains two ideas such as, "Go to your room and get your toy." There is no delight in "chatting" or in give-and-take conversation, and there is no infatuation with the magic of verbal communication. The child is deficient in social imitation (for example, waving bye-bye), in meaningful exploration of objects (being content to spin a wheel on a toy car or mouth it, for example), and in dramatic play such as "house" or "tea party." Play patterns tend to be limited and rigidly repeated.

In middle childhood the lack of social relatedness abates somewhat but the children tend to be friendless, noncooperative, and lacking in empathy. While no longer impervious, their social responses are odd and inappropriate. In a like manner, they do not speak in a communicative way but talk *to* rather than *with* a person. What they say is often confined to the immediate situation. (Of course, certain children remain mute or have no intelligible speech.) Activities continue to be ritualistic, with adherence to strict routines and marked distress at slight deviations. Special preoccupations might appear, such as memorizing timetables.

Adolescence is a time of dramatic developments. Seizures appear in about one-quarter to one-third of the children, predominantly those with IQ scores below 65. At the other extreme, Kanner et al. (1972) found that the period could be one of significant improvement. Certain adolescents seem to realize that their behavior is deviant and make a conscious effort to act in an appropriate manner. Between 5 and 15 percent of autistic children achieve a satisfactory social and occupational adjustment, either with or without therapy (Lotter, 1978). Typically, they cope with life by scrupulously living according to the rules of acceptable behavior. Their speech, for example, may resemble that of certain foreigners who use flawless English but still sound rather stilted. Work and play have the same quality of being learned by rote without the freedom to vary and improvise which comes with full understanding. Adequately functioning adults know the letter of the law, but the spirit eludes them. They can be devoid of empathy and, significantly, seem generally indifferent to sexuality. On the positive side, their slavish devotion to rules and regulations can fit nicely into the demands of a bureaucratic society.

One final point, which will become important in a subsequent section: while the majority of autistic children continue to be severely disturbed, they do not become classically schizophrenic in the sense of having delusions and hallucinations. Whether there is a basic difference between autism and schizophrenia is a hotly debated issue to which we shall return.

Underlying Causes

If some malevolent force from outer space—or outer television—compelled you to give a formula for making healthy babies autistic, what would you say? Probably something like this: "Make their major interests and pleasures aversive!" In the first weeks of life a multitude of factors conspire to make the adult human the most attractive and pleasurable stimulus in the infant's environment—the human voice quickly becomes preferred over all other sounds, the infant's range of vision is the distance from the nursing mother's breast to her face, and the patterning of that face, particularly the eyes, holds a special fascination; moreover the infant learns to adjust his or her body to that of the caretaker when held and to anticipate relief from distress when the caretaker comes into view. In addition, the need for variable stimulation lies at the heart of exploration of the environment, the infant being nicely constituted to seek ever more complex challenges as the simple ones are mastered. In autism, the very basis of cognitive and affective development is undermined so that avoidance and repetition replace approach and expansion.

In a most general way we have accounted for autism. Yet scientists are rarely satisfied with such generalities and continue to ask, "Yes, but why?" What has gone wrong to produce this negative image of normal development? At present the answers are legion, everything from blood platelets to social class being implicated. (For a review of these etiological hypotheses, see Prior, 1979; Schwartz and Johnson, 1981.)

Recent laboratory studies of etiology provide some of the best illustrations of the advantage of the *control of relevant variables* inherent in this research methodology. The discovery that a considerable number of autistic children might also be mentally retarded casts doubt upon previous research by raising the question, Which aspects of these children's behavior are the result of autism per se and which are shared with the general population of retardates? The question, in turn, is part of the quest to find the psychological defects or deficiencies specific to autism. It can be answered by adding a control group of nonautistic retardates matched for mental age with the low-functioning autistic children. A further question can also be raised: To what extent is the behavior of low-functioning autistic children shared with a younger, normal population? This is the issue of whether the observed behavior of the autistic group represents developmental delay or fixation, or whether it represents a qualitatively distinct behavior having no counterpart in normal development. This question can be answered by adding a control group of normal children whose chronological age is matched with the mental age of the autistic children. Thus, a study might be designed as shown in Table 4.1.

Table 4.1 Research Design Comparing Autistic, Mentally Retarded, and Normal Children

	Autistic Children	*Mental Retardates*	*Normal Children*
Chronological age	8	8	5
Mental age	5	5	5

One such study was conducted by Hermelin (1976), using 10- to 15-year-old autistic children with a mental age of about 5 years, matched with mental retardates with similar chronological and mental ages, and with normally developing 5-year-olds. In the first experiment, the children were presented with a card on which were two black rectangles, one large and one small. Then they were presented with a series of cue cards with either a large or small rectangle of the same size as the ones on the original card. The task was to match the rectangle on the cue card with the one on the original card. In this task the autistic children performed as well as the mentally retarded and normal children. Even when asked to match from memory by first showing and then removing the cue card, the autistic children performed as well as the normals and were superior to the retardates. Therefore, there is nothing faulty in their basic ability to discriminate size. However, when a series of five black rectangles of differing sizes were presented in random order and the children were asked to arrange them from smallest to largest, the autistic children's performance was inferior to that of both other groups. This is only one of many instances in which the autistic child is capable of responding appropriately to simple stimuli but is hamstrung when dealing with complex patterning or ordering of stimuli.

The control that the laboratory affords also allows the kind of highly refined exploration of a given psychological function that would be next to impossible using any other research methodology. Let us take memory for example, since one could hypothesize that the autistic children's difficulty in coping with the physical and social environment might be owing to a memory defect. The laboratory approach allows the investigator systematically to vary many parameters of memory: the kind of material to be remembered, such as meaningful or nonsense; the interval of time for remembering the material, from immediate recall to varying periods of delay; and the mode of presentation of the material to be remembered, such as visual or auditory. Even more important, a laboratory approach can separate a memory defect from a defect in the initial intake of information; for example, an apparent deficiency in the recall of a list of words may be because the autistic children were able to take in fewer words than the other groups. Only when there is evidence that the groups are similar in the amount of information they can initially process can one properly attribute an inferior recall to a memory deficiency.

Prior and Chen's study (1976) illustrates this last point. The investigators made sure that the autistic, mentally retarded, and normal groups were equally adept in the acquisition phase of the task before testing for recall. The study involved nine children in each group, all of whom had mental ages between 4½ and 5 years of age, with the autistic and retarded groups being approximately 10 years of age, the normal children around 4 years of age. The test material consisted of hollow blocks which varied in size, shape, and color. The blocks were presented two at a time, and the children were to guess which was the correct one. If they succeeded they would receive a bit of candy hidden in the hollow. To illustrate: for a given child a small white pyramid might be the correct choice. This block would be paired with other blocks, such as a large white cube or a small black cylinder. Each child had to solve a number of such puzzles. In the initial phase of their research, the investigators demonstrated that the autistic children were equally as adept as the other children in learning the correct choices. Only then did the researchers vary the time between presentation of pairs from 30 to 60 to 120 seconds in order to test the effect of the length of interval on memory. They found that, while delay did significantly affect performance—the longer time intervals making it more difficult for the children to remember the correct responses—it affected all groups of children equally. Mental age rather than autism was the significant determiner of memory.

One final general point: laboratory research with any severely disturbed population, such as autistic or retarded or hyperactive children, presents special problems which do not arise when studying less disturbed and normal children. It is essential that the investigator makes sure that the disturbed children attend to the task, that they are motivated to perform it, and that they understand its nature. Without such safeguards, there is the danger that an inferior performance would be interpreted in terms of a psychological deficit or deviation when it may represent nothing more than a disinterest in or a resistance to performing the task at hand.

ATTENTION AND PERCEPTION. Autistic children do well on standard tests of hearing and vision and are capable of sustained attention. Thus they are not like deaf children, although they are sometimes mistaken for deaf because of their unresponsiveness; nor are they like hyperactive children, who are continually distracted by irrelevant stimuli. Also, like normal children, they prefer looking at complex stimuli rather than simple ones. Since autistic children can see and hear and attend to the environment, some other process must have gone wrong.

Unlike normal toddlers, who can modulate their responses to environmental stimulation, autistic children may be *extreme* and *erratic* in their reactions. As infants they may be hyperirritable or too placid; as toddlers their bodies may be excessively rigid and their actions may have a driven quality, or they may be limp and inert like a sack of flour. They may scream in distress when a vacuum cleaner goes on but then at another time prefer a louder sound than a normal child. They may be impervious to the speech of the adult standing next to them while listening intensely to the sound of a garbage truck two blocks away. In a fit of rage a child may bite his arm and then look with detached wonder at the blood, showing no evidence of pain.

Some authors conceptualize this responsiveness in terms of a faulty *arousal mechanism*. (For a detailed presentation of the arousal hypothesis, see Schwartz and Johnson, 1981.) Others prefer to theorize in terms of an *imbalance between excitation and inhibition* in the brain (Miller, 1974). The insufficiently aroused child is comfortable assimilating only a small portion of available stimulation and gravitates toward simple activities which do not tax the meager supply of energy. If arousal or excitation is excessive, the child is readily overwhelmed by novel and complex stimuli; as a protection, many of the sights and sounds of the everyday environment are defensively blotted out through inattention or through clinging to the safety of simple repetitive activities. This latter hypothesis of hypersensitivity is the more popular one.

A different hypothesis is that autistic children have failed to make the transition from *proximal to distal receptors* in exploring the environment (Miller, 1974). Normal infants explore objects with their mouths (a proximal receptor) as well as their eyes (a distance receptor). Give a 1-year-old a new toy and you may observe her vacillating: "Shall I mouth it or look at it?" The mouth is a crude organ for exploration compared with the eye, as are the nose and the fingertips. If a child is primarily interested in how an object tastes or feels or smells, he or she will not readily discover how a spoon differs from a toy car or a baby doll. Yet the autistic child can be preoccupied with such sensory experiences of mouthing and smelling and feeling objects, while the sights and sounds of the environment are ignored. Consequently, the ability to cope with the complexities of objects is significantly weakened. In spite of its plausibility, the hypothesis concerning preference for proximal receptors has not been supported uniformly by subsequent research (Schwartz and Johnson, 1981).

Another hypothesized deficit is the autistic child's tendency to respond only to a limited number of cues in the environment, a condition called *stimulus overselectivity* (Lovaas, Koegel, and Schreibman, 1979). In one experiment, normal and autistic children were reinforced for responding to a complex stimulus consisting of a bright red light, white noise, and a touch on the child's leg. In subsequent presentations of the visual, auditory, and tactile stimuli alone the normal children responded equally to each component, while the autistic children responded only to one of the components. Again, normal children, after training, learned to discriminate between male and female dolls on the basis of a number of cues, including the figure's head, while the autistic children used only a few minor, unreliable cues such as shoes. Clearly stimulus overselectivity would greatly hamper learning the complex stimuli involved in speech as well as interfering with the associations involved in classical conditioning, so that, for instance, the mother (who is a complex stimulus) would not become associated with the pleasurable experiences involved in caretaking. The research on stimulus overselectivity has been criticized, however, as being equally applicable to mentally retarded children and therefore not specific to autism (Prior, 1979). At present the criticism has not been successfully answered, but the issue has not been definitively settled, either.

MEMORY. Autistic children's short-term memory is intact, both in regard to visual and auditory material; for example, their ability to repeat a series of digits is age appropriate. What is lacking is the ability to make use of patterning and meaning in order to enhance memory. Unlike the situation with normal children, recall is not facilitated when visual stimuli are presented in a pattern such as Red, Green, Red, Green, Red, Green, rather than being presented randomly. The same insensitivity to patterning applies to auditory stimuli as well (Hermelin, 1976). In like manner a list of words belonging to specific categories, such as animals and foodstuffs, is not remembered any better than a list drawn at random. Even sentences may not be recalled any better than random words.

Autistic children have been described as having an "echo-box" memory. Like an echo in nature, they respond to and reflect the physical properties of speech, such as the sound and even the intonation of the words. The fact that these sounds have meaning may not register.

IMITATION. The research evidence clearly points to a deficit in imitation in autistic children regardless of their mental age level. Lovaas et al. (1979) vividly describe autistic children's failure to imitate even after 1,000 trials of hearing a teacher say "Phone" and observing a model pick up the phone. The children would learn only part of the response, such as merely touching the phone, or they would pick it up regardless of when the teacher gave the command. When we recall that imitation, along with classical and operant conditioning, is one of the three basic principles of learning, we can appreciate the magnitude of this particular deficit.

LANGUAGE AND COGNITION. A number of hypotheses have been generated to account for the autistic child's speech and higher-order thinking (Miller, 1974). One is that the children can take in information but cannot relate it to past experience; to use Piaget's term they cannot *assimilate.* As we have seen, autistic children tend to echo rather than understand. One consequence is that thinking is concrete and situation-specific; for example, once a girl has learned that "ride" means leaving the house and getting into a particular car, she will be unable to grasp the general idea that "going for a ride" can mean leaving from any place in any car. Thus, children learn to speak by rote rather than understanding the principle behind what they have learned.

Another hypothesis addresses itself to the autistic child's difficulty with comprehending verbal and nonverbal *symbols* and using them to communicate. The basic idea that a sound or gesture can represent an object or activity does not fully register with the autistic child. Recall that the infant will not imitate bye-bye gestures, the toddler does not pretend to sweep the floor and set the table, and, finally, symbolic play is impoverished in the preschool period. Difficulty in using words, therefore, is just part of a general deficiency in grasping the idea that one kind of behavior can stand for, represent, or symbolize another.

A third hypothesis is that autistic children have difficulty in grasping *speech patterns* and *grammatical rules* for ordering words into sentences because they cannot process sequential information. We have seen how this difficulty adversely affects the autistic child's ability to order a series of rectangles according to increased size as well as the child's ability to recall meaningful verbal material.

Current studies of language are more closely related to normal development than was past research. The data suggest that autistic speech is not simply delayed speech or normal development in slow motion. Rather, autistic children seem to lack "something" from the beginning (Menyuk, 1978). Normal infants make remarkable progress in *discrimination* of speech sounds, *imitating* patterns and using them *communicatively.* Infants may be innately programmed to discriminate human speech from other sounds, for example, and their subsequent babbling will have the rhythm and melody of speech even though the content is meaningless. Equally important, they grasp the notion of communication via expressive sounds; as early as 1 to 2 months of age they can take turns vocalizing with their caretaker, and by the end of the year, they can vocalize to indicate needs and feelings as well as to socialize. Autistic children go through no comparable sequence. The human voice holds no special attraction (recall that the children are sometimes thought to be deaf because of their unresponsiveness), their babbling has unusual sounds and rhythms (even the speech of adequately functioning adults who were formerly autistic can have an odd sound to it), while their affective isolation precludes communication.

At a more advanced level, learning the standard *lexicon of language* presents special problems, both in regard to the meaning of words and the ordering of words into increasingly complex patterns. Some children have difficulty grasping prepositions such as "beside" or "in" and subsequently in grasping the sequencing of words; for example, "Put the cup in the shoe" could be interpreted as "Put the shoe in the cup." "I" and "you" present special problems since they have shifting referrents depending on the speaker rather than consistently designating a single person. Even high-functioning autistic children have difficulty in double classifications which involve two people doing two different things at the same time; for example, "I have a ball and am sitting down; you have a bat and are standing up." Each idea can be grasped separately but cannot be entertained simultaneously.

One sees a progression here in terms of complexity. The simplest rule is this: one word stands for one object, such as the word "chair" standing for the physical object. Relational words like "on" or "I" are difficult because they do not refer to a single object or person. Multiple classifications of a single object are baffling (for example, a "white chair" presents problems since other objects may be white without being chairs and chairs need not be white), while double classifications are more baffling still. The patterning of words to produce sentences, the ordering of phrases within sentences, and the relations among sentences produce even greater obstacles in terms of analyzing and integrating information (Menyuk, 1978).

INTERPERSONAL FACTORS. Many hypotheses in this area concern the mother who, for a variety of reasons, cannot provide the infant with warm, sensitive care (Miller, 1974). She may be cold, obsessive, and intellectual, or she herself may be disturbed—psychotic, depressed, or immature. Even some behaviorists have speculated in terms of parental failure to attend to and reinforce the infant's early social overtures because the parents are depressed or preoccupied with illness or other concerns. Another hypothesis is that the negative feelings of the caretaker are directed toward the infant and engender a feeling of helplessness; fearing total destruction if he or she acts, the infant seeks safety in inaction and insensitivity to external and internal stimulation. Finally, various patterns of parental and familial interaction have also been implicated; for example, parents can use the child in an attempt to solve their own unconscious conflicts, thus preventing the development of an individualized identity.

Note that the interpersonal hypotheses typically regard perceptual, cognitive, and linguistic dysfunctions as consequences of faulty caretaking. The underlying assumption is that caretaking mediates every facet of development. If caretaking is highly deviant, all other development will be distorted.

In an ingenious variation of the longitudinal approach, home movies of infants who subsequently became autistic were collected and studied in terms of the mother–infant interaction (Massie, 1980). Particular attention was paid to eye contact, touching, clinging, feeding, and vocalizing, behaviors presumed to mediate the bond of love. Certain interactions were marked by insensitive, intrusive stimulation, but in one case, attachment was disrupted for 4 months by maternal illness when the infant was 7 months of age. Of particular interest are cases of maternal failure to respond to the infant's smile, in one instance by gaze aversion, in another by staring blankly at the infant. One is reminded of Brackbill's (1958) classical study of reinforcement, in which she reports that, after being continually rewarded by the experimenter's smiling face, the infants showed a strong aversive reaction to the presentation of her nonsmiling face. More important, when she forced the infants to look at her instead of turning away, they defended themselves by the same kind of impervious "looking through" her that characterizes autistic children. This suggests that an autistic defense may be called into play under conditions which, to an adult, seem rather benign.

A rare fragment of longitudinal data on a *resistive* infant comes from a study of mother–infant interaction in twins (Kubicek, 1980). As it happened, in one case of fraternal twin brothers, one of the boys subsequently became autistic. Analysis of filmed interaction revealed that the future autistic infant failed to establish eye contact with his mother, his face was expressionless, his head was either turned away from her or held back with his gaze directed toward the ceiling. For most of the interaction his back was arched, his arms rigidly flexed or extended, and his hands were fisted, indicating a high level of overall body tension. In spite of the mother's continued attempts to accommodate, the infant avoided her approaches. By contrast, the mother and her normal infant were able to establish a mutually pleasurable interaction by sensitively responding to one another's cues. If even a sensitive mother's caretaking can be perceived as noxious by her infant, the subsequent development of extreme social aloneness can readily be understood.

ORGANIC HYPOTHESES. The role of genetic factors in autism is unclear, as are pre- and perinatal difficulties, neurological signs, EEGs, and seizures (Ornitz and Ritvo, 1976). There is preliminary evidence that perceptual difficulties may be the result of dysfunction of the central vestibular system (Ornitz, 1976), while the reticular activating system has been implicated in faulty arousal and cognitive defects (Achenbach, 1974). There is evidence of increase in blood serotonin (one of the neurotransmitters or "chemical messengers" responsible for communication between nerve cells), although the relation between this finding and the behavioral characteristics of autism is admittedly uncertain. (See Yuwiler, Geller, and Ritvo, 1976; for a comprehensive summary of organic factors, see Kernberg, 1979.)

EVALUATION. While evidence can be marshaled to support any one particular etiological hypothesis, in no instance is there that accumulation of positive findings, refutation of alternative explanations, and control for confounding factors which would allow one to choose among rival explanations. Such a situation is understandable in light of the difficulties involved in conducting research. Autism is rare, and the very nature of the disturbance mitigates against the child's understanding and cooperating with the procedures. Until recently there have not even been objective assessment instruments to insure that one population labeled "autistic" was indeed comparable to another one labeled "autistic." Fortunately, researchers can now use a checklist (Rimland, 1971) or a behavior rating scale (Ruttenberg, Kalish, Wenar, and Wolf, 1978).

Another difficulty with the current situation is the frequent assumption that a single key will unlock all the etiological mysteries: that understanding the peculiarities of language development, for example, will explain the lack of relatedness and pathological need for sameness. Often the conceptual links from single defect to comprehensive explanation are speculative at best and are not buttressed by research findings. The single-key approach also runs counter to normal development, where behavior is the result of the interaction of multiple variables.

One more comment: at present, organic explanations are more popular than interpersonal ones—and for good reason. Attachment is rugged; while caretaking may affect the kind of attachment, the bond itself develops under a wide variety of conditions; neither physical abuse nor extreme neglect produces autism. In addition, the interpersonal hypotheses often sound similar to those found in less severe psychological disturbances and many champions of a psychogenic explanation also admit to an organic vulnerability. Finally, the cold, intellectualized mother described in the clinical literature may be the product of having a child whose development is erratic and baffling. Instead of producing autism, such a mother may be protecting herself from the constant defeats she suffered in the past when she reached out with love and understanding (Escalona, 1948). The effects of the infant on its caretaker are too well established in normal development to be ignored in the case of autism. In sum, it is difficult to avoid the conclusion that autistic children are, in some unknown way, ill-equipped to cope with a normal environment.

Yet, admitting a constitutional vulnerability does not justify the neglect of caretaking variables, since autism might result from an interaction of organic and environmental factors. To date there are few empirical data concerning the conditions under which the infant is forced to avoid responding to the caretaker. Yet the few hints we have suggest that not only do grossly deviant patterns (such as intrusive, insensitive stimulation) produce temporary imperviousness on the infant's part, but so do very subtle deviations, particularly in regard to face-to-face contact (such as changing from a smiling to a somber face), which would seem rather insignificant to adults. Categorical statements that all autism is due solely to organic factors seem particularly premature at a time when our understanding of the variables influencing the establishment of the bond of love is both more detailed than it was in the past and expanding.

The Effects of Psychotherapy

The prognostic picture for autism is not significantly altered by psychotherapy. While some improvement may be made, heroic efforts are required to achieve it, progress is slow and fragile, and gains are easily lost (Miller, 1974). Even the behaviorally oriented therapists, who have been most vigorous and versatile in their remedial efforts—reporting successes in the areas of teaching language, increasing appropriate self-help and social behavior, and decreasing inappropriate behaviors such as self-mutilation and tantrums—write primarily in terms of improving the level of functioning rather than of "curing" autism in the sense of producing a child whose behavior falls within the normal range (Rincover and Koegel, 1977).

What meager comparative data exist suggests that psychotherapy is better than mere custodial care, but that, among psychotherapies, no one has an advantage provided that it is sensitively and expertly implemented. This generalization applies to psychoanalytically oriented psychotherapy, behavior modification, educational therapy, and activity therapy (Wenar and Ruttenberg, 1976). It may be that intrapersonal variables determine therapeutic progress to a greater degree than does choice of therapy. There is evidence, for example, that preschool autistic children are both more disturbed and able to make significantly greater gains than autistic children in middle childhood, regardless of the type of therapy (Wenar and Ruttenberg, 1976). Mental age could be another potent determiner of success (Prior, 1979).

The obstacles to therapeutic progress are formidable. Most psychotherapies require at least a minimum of cooperation, while therapeutic progress necessitates change. Yet the very nature of their psychopathology renders autistic children impervious or resistant to responding to the therapist, while causing them to react to any variation in the status quo with panic and rage. In addition, the concreteness of autistic children's thinking results in their learning only what they are specifically taught. They do not *generalize* readily, nor do they *grasp rules.* Teach an autistic boy that a block may be yellow or blue, and you may have to continue teaching him that it can also be red or green or black or white. The idea that a block can be any color comes slowly. To make the point in a different way: in treating neurotic children the therapist can be reasonably sure that the progress such children make during the session will generalize to home or school; with the autistic child such a transfer is far less likely to happen. To compound the problem, there is evidence that what the child learns does not really become part of the self but has to be constantly maintained by environmental stimulation and rewards. In technical terms, the child does not *internalize* advances in the way a normal child does.

One of the greatest impediments to therapy is the autistic child's lack of *initiative.* In charting the progress of a large number of autistic children, there is evidence of a predictable sequence: imperviousness and resistance followed by acceptance until the children finally begin to do things on their own. This sequence applies to their relationship to significant adults, their exploration of physical objects, their learning of social skills (Ruttenberg et al., 1978). It is often the shift from recipient to agent, from willingness to be taught to wanting to learn, which marks a crucial turning point in therapy and which is so difficult to achieve. Lovaas (1977), for example, after citing impressive evidence that mute autistic children can be taught to speak in simple sentences, goes on to state that a major stumbling block is their lack of motivation to practice on their own—so unlike normal toddlers, who are infatuated with talking and practicing not only with others but also by themselves.

Such obstacles not only help us understand the slow progress of autistic children but also sensitize us to the importance of generalization, grasping rules, internalization, and initiative to normal development, all of which happen so naturally that we tend to take them for granted. Thus, psychopathology can illuminate normal development as well as the other way around.

In addition, the study of one psychopathology can throw light on another, as will be evident in the examination of childhood schizophrenia.

CHILDHOOD SCHIZOPHRENIA

As autism is identified with Kanner, so childhood schizophrenia is identified with Bender, who has been working with schizophrenic children since 1935. In all these years she has not modified her basic premise that schizophrenia is an organic pathology of the central nervous system—an encephalopathy that involves the total organism. She has never searched for the single key that would explain schizophrenic behavior, since multiple dysfunctions are involved. Bender has also been a thoroughgoing developmentalist; while schizophrenia is a single entity, its expression differs as a function of the child's developmental level. A schizophrenic infant, for example, could not behave like a schizophrenic school-aged child because the infant lacks speech, cognitive sophistication, a complex network of interpersonal relations, and an explicit awareness of self.

If schizophrenia is a pathology which affects behavior at every level and in every area of integration (Bender, 1947), its manifestations are legion. The *EEGs* of schizophrenic children are dysrhythmic, although they cannot be interpreted as any specific cortical pattern disorder. Such a finding is congruent with the concept of schizophrenia as a diffuse and global impairment in functioning. The children may have faulty *vasovegetative functioning;* for example, they may flush and perspire easily or be colorless and have cold extremities; a simple fever may seem to produce a state of shock, although it vanishes in an hour or so. The *timing of physiological events* is out of joint, causing daily rhythms of sleeping, eating, and elimination to be erratic. Likewise, long-term growth and sexual maturation are erratic, so that the child is too large or too small, obese or underweight, while menstruation in girls and puberty in boys are precocious or delayed.

Disturbances in *motor behavior* and *postural responses* are particularly important. The toddler and preschooler are awkward and insecure in mastering the many motor skills of the period, from walking and climbing stairs to using swings and tricycles. However, the child is not retarded, since primitive behavior can alternate with precocious grace and coordination. A postural reflex which is specific to childhood schizophrenics is their tendency to whirl round and round if someone turns their head while they are standing with eyes closed and arms outstretched. Normal children over 6 will merely accept the head turning without rotating their body. In addition, the childhood schizophrenic will show an extreme bodily dependence on others, pressing close as if to melt into them. Bender interprets such behavior as the child's lack of a center of gravity in a physical sense and lack of a concept of self, both of which produce a desperate need to rely on others. Finally, schizophrenic children have difficulty defining the periphery of their body, as seen in their indifference to bodily secretions such as saliva, urine, and feces and in their neglect of hair and clothing.

Perceptual difficulties show the same mixture of primitive and mature performance that characterizes motility. In copying geometric designs these children use an excess of vortical movements; a child may begin copying a rectangle or diamond and then get carried away by whirling, circular motions. Figures tend to lose their boundaries—just as the child's body seems to have no fixed boundary—and are elaborated according to inner impulses to go any which way.

Finally there are a variety of *thought* and *language* disturbances. In the first few years of life there may be mutism. If schizophrenia occurs later the child's language may be fragmented, dissociated, and bizarre: "It's open in the front but closed behind. I'm open in the front but closed behind. Did you see me today? I think I was here but Mommy wasn't. They don't take it away from Mommy. My dollie won't mind. I won't mind. (Enumerates all the members of the family who won't mind.) I was there yesterday. Was I here today?"

While the pervasiveness of schizophrenia is apparent from the above catalogue, Bender claims that an individual child is not equally damaged in all areas. Quite the contrary. It is the unevenness of development—the juxtaposition of primitive and adequate functioning, of immaturity and precocity—which is so devastating, since it prevents such children from making coherent sense of themselves and their environment, while leaving them chronically vulnerable to intense anxiety. If they were consistently retarded in all areas, as are some mentally defective children, or if only a delimited group of functions were adversely affected, as in some brain damaged children, these children could learn to cope more effectively than they do.

The Developmental Picture

INFANCY. By conducting a prospective study, Fish (1971, 1976) was able to obtain important data on infants who subsequently became schizophrenic, thus avoiding the distortions of retrospective information from mothers and the meagerness of routine medical data. One population was drawn from a well-baby clinic serving a lower-class neighborhood high in social and psychiatric pathology; the other population consisted of infants of hospitalized, chronically schizophrenic mothers who were subsequently reared in permanent adoptive or foster homes. Of the twenty-four infants that were independently evaluated when they were 10 or 18 years of age, two were diagnosed as schizophrenic and four had severe personality disturbances bordering on schizophrenia.

As early as the first month, Fish found no fixed neurological defect, but rather disorders of timing, integration, and organization with marked acceleration and retardation succeeded one another. For example, in one baby gross motor development was 45 percent behind normal at 9 months and then, with no environmental change, accelerated so that he more than doubled his rate of growth in the next two months. The usual orderly sequence of postural development—from head to feet, from trunk out to extremities—may be disrupted so that an infant is able to stand (which appears around 10 to 11 months of age), but unable to roll over from back to stomach (which appears around 6 to 7 months), or can roll over but is unable to sit (which appears around 5 to 6 months). The same erratic sequencing is evident in the visual-motor sphere; thus an infant that can perform a difficult task fails an easier one. In addition, abilities which seemed well established are unaccountably lost. One preschizophrenic infant, Linda, could not transfer objects from hand to hand like a normal 6-month-old, even when she was 13 months of age. Instead of reaching for an object, she would wave her arms laterally like a 4-month-old; and instead of grasping objects, she would gingerly pat and poke their surfaces. All this while her manual dexterity per se was normal. With time her visual-motor performance became less retarded until by 2 years of age she was performing normally.

Abnormally quiet and lethargic infants tended to develop severe pathology but only one of the two schizophrenics showed this pattern. Paradoxically, visual and attentional responses were either normal or precocious. Again we see the disjointed nature of development—instead of being generally sleepy, low arousal in certain systems coexisted with high arousal and alertness in others.

Fish, like Bender, states that such erratic and unpredictable functioning prevents the schizophrenic child from developing a stable image of the self and of the physical and social environment. However, she also recognizes how baffling such behavior is to parents and, later, to teachers. While the evidence indicates a genetic basis to schizophrenia, the reaction of caretakers can either help the infant compensate for its disturbances or intensify them, e.g., by quickly losing interest in stimulating their unresponsive infant or becoming impatient and punitive in their bewilderment.

PRESCHOOL PERIOD. Onset of schizophrenia is most common in this period (Bender, 1947). Social and linguistic regression may be slow or abrupt, and anxiety level is high. As the child starts again to progress, development is distorted by the schizophrenic process. Emotional instability is evidenced by irritability, excitement, anxiety, unprovoked aggression and temper tantrums, fears, disturbed sleep, and preoccupation with body functions. There may also be a demanding, angry dependence on the mother and other adults. However, as is so characteristic of this psychopathology, physical growth and language development may be accelerated.

MIDDLE CHILDHOOD. In middle childhood the clinical picture differs depending on whether the children internalize their problem, in which case they are called *pseudoneurotic,* or externalize their problem and are called *pseudopsychopathic* (Bender, 1947). In the former, traditional neurotic symptoms such as anxiety, phobias, obsessions, and compulsions are present, along with evidence of severe thought disturbances such as hallucinations and delusions of persecution or bizarre preoccupations; for example, an 11-year-old girl was preoccupied with the question of whether her mother was really her mother, saying at times that she could not be because the "lady" who took her home from the clinic was bigger, taller, had bigger feet, a longer head, was blacker, and did not speak in the same voice. She also imagined people in the street were talking about her mother and accusing the girl of being mean to her mother. Pseudopsychopathic children have a number of typical acting-out symptoms such as stealing, fire-setting, truanting, and sexual acting out, but there is also the same underlying picture that characterizes the pseudoneurotic, such as distorted reality perception and intense anxiety. For example, a boy may feel that he must fight back because he is being persecuted, or he may hear voices commanding him to set fires. Fish (1976) emphasizes the erratic nature of cognitive functioning; there are isolated areas of intactness seen in the child's ability to do puzzles and to remember word definitions and associations, but such abilities do not become integrated into useful goal-directed activities. Thus, behavior is haphazard or stereotyped and fragmented.

PROGNOSIS. The *prognostic picture* is the same for childhood schizophrenia as for autism: the earlier the onset the more severe the disturbance in adulthood. In 34 percent of the early-onset group, organicity dominated the picture and the life course was one of deterioration, combined with schizophrenia; in 40 percent of the cases, there was a life history of schizophrenia uncomplicated by organicity; only 26 percent of the population was adjusting to the community with the aid of various therapeutic programs and/or tolerant family situations. By contrast, 46 percent of the children with later onset were adjusting to the community, although their condition was ambulatory and they needed supportive help from family, social agencies, and mental health facilities. Overall, while outcomes vary and while a remarkable percent of children made some kind of adjustment to adult life, Bender concludes that "childhood schizophrenia inevitably leads to adult schizophrenia" (Bender and Faretra, 1972, p. 52). As we shall see, the conclusion is quite a controversial one.

One final comment: Bender found that puberty is the most favorable period in many schizophrenic children's development. Spontaneous remissions occur, and some children may not only be symptom-free but also deny or be unable to remember their former behavior. (Unfortunately, disturbed behavior frequently returns in midadolesence.) Kanner made a similar observation concerning autistic children. Yet, in normal development, the pre- and early-adolescent periods are often regarded as the most stormy and disruptive. It may well be so, but its very disruptiveness may weaken old, maladaptive patterns in severely disturbed children and offer opportunities for growth which were previously unavailable. As one experienced therapist humorously remarked: "I love to treat preadolescents. Maturation cures them and I get the credit!"

Is All Schizophrenia One?

Is autism a distinct type of psychosis, or is there a single underlying schizophrenic process throughout childhood which may be expressed in autistic behavior during infancy? The issue is hotly debated. Note that only severe psychopathologies of childhood are dealt with here; children at risk for developing adult schizophrenia typically have a different developmental pattern, as we have seen in chapter 3.

There is evidence that autism differs from childhood schizophrenia. The clinical picture of the two psychopathologies is different from middle childhood on. Autism lacks the delusions and hallucinations, the loose associations, and the mood disturbances which characterize schizophrenia. The autistic child is a highly ritualized, very odd outsider; the schizophrenic child's behavior is florid, excessive, and bizarre. In their developmental courses, schizophrenia is marked by progressions and regressions, while autism is highly stable. There are important differences in context factors. Parents of autistic children tend to have average or above average intelligence and tend to have high SES, while parents of schizophrenic children tend to have below average intelligence and come from low SES. Schizophrenia in parents of autistic children is no higher than in the normal population, while it is elevated in parents of schizophrenic children. (For a detailed presentation, see Kolvin, Ounsted, Humphrey, and McNay, 1971; Kolvin, Ounsted, Richardson, and Garside, 1971.)

While the case is impressive, it is far from being proved, as each point has been rebutted with evidence to the contrary (Miller, 1974). Even in our brief review we have seen that Bender cites cases in which at least some autistic infants develop into schizophrenic children.

The issue is further complicated by the fact that Bender's is not the only conceptualization of childhood schizophrenia. Goldfarb (1970), who for many years has done some of the most rigorous studies of schizophrenia in middle childhood, claims that there are two distinct types of children—organic children in whom there is evidence of central nervous system dysfunction (as Bender maintains), and those whose disturbance is psychogenic (which Bender would not consider). In his studies, Goldfarb found parents of children in the latter group to be extremely uncertain, passive, and lacking in direction and assertiveness. There was also an absence of spontaneity and empathy. Goldfarb characterizes the constellation as "parental perplexity." The resulting lack of structure, amorphousness, and unpredictability of his environment terrifies the child and produces a heroic effort to avoid dealing with it by utilizing various psychotic manuevers.

The controversies we are dealing with could best be settled by prospective studies of young toddlers and preschoolers who were clearly diagnosed as autistic or schizophrenic and followed in a longitudinal study. In light of the low incidence of these disturbances, crucial data will be difficult to come by.

TWO MODELS OF DEVIATION. For our purposes, the most important aspect of the above controversy is that it involves two different models of deviant development. In autism, variable stimulation in general and the human caretaker in particular are aversive. Development is marked by slow mastery of and clinging to a limited repertoire of techniques for coping with the physical and social environment. Aloneness, sameness, mutism, or noncommunicative speech all suggest a pathology of extreme encapsulation. Bender's, by contrast, is a model of profound imbalance and instability—retardation, normality, and precocity can exist within and between psychological functions at one point in time, as well as characterizing development over time. If the autistic child is all too predictable, the schizophrenic is all too unpredictable.

Thus we have taken one step in our quest to understand psychopathology as normal development gone awry, since we now have two specific models of how this can happen. We have seen the bedrock foundation of normal development undermined: in autism, people and objects are aversive rather than sources of interest, delight, and relief from distress, while in schizophrenia, orderly organization no longer marks a given developmental level or the progress to higher levels.

PRIVATION

Opportunities to study firsthand the role of constitution and caretaking in producing infantile psychoses are exceedingly rare and will continue to be. Not so with the study of the effects of extremely bleak caretaking environments. The pioneering investigation in this area was done by Spitz (1945), who opened the door to numerous subsequent studies. As is well known, Spitz was a consultant to a foundling home whose infants were wasting away and dying, a condition called *marasmus.* He found that while the institution was hygienic and the infants were given a nourishing diet, they received only minimal stimulation from the social and physical environment, as well as from the gross motor activities of their own bodies. The caretaker–infant ratio was 1:8, and feeding and toileting were done in a routine, impersonal manner. There were no toys, while sheets hanging over the railing screened out the environment. Finally, a hollow worn in their mattresses prevented the infants from turning in any direction. A more isolated, sterile environment would be difficult to imagine. Spitz's famous prescription was "tender loving care." Once the infants received adequate mothering, marasmus disappeared.

Spitz showed that, far from being a sentimental luxury, mothering is essential to healthy psychological development and, in certain instances, to life itself. However, neither Spitz nor subsequent research prove that institutions per se hamper normal development. It is privation—the absence of appropriate stimulation—which is inimical to psychological growth, whether it be found in institutions or in the home. Indeed, Russia and Israel have shown that institutions can embody the best of care, and infants seem to thrive in these settings. Nor did Spitz show that caretaking must be done by the mother or a mother substitute. The effects of a single caretaker compared with multiple caretakers are being vigorously investigated, and while the findings are far from conclusive, it is clear that the number of caretakers does not tip the balance in favor of normality or severe psychopathology. (For a résumé of the research on institutionalization and on alternate child-rearing environments, see Hetherington and Parke, 1979.)

The Effects of Privation

We are now dealing with privation, or the lack of growth-promoting stimulation from the social and physical environment. This differs from deprivation, which is concerned with the loss of a loved one once the bond of love has been established. Loss will be our concern in the next chapter; lack is our concern here. (The DSM-III classification is Reactive Attachment Disorders of Infancy.)

One of the most detailed accounts of the effects of privation is presented by Province and Lipton (1962), who studied seventy-five infants intensively during the first year of life. While the institution was orderly and clean, as was the one Spitz studied, it was not as psychologically sterile. The cribs were not shielded, there were age-appropriate toys, a radio played music softly. Yet it was clearly impoverished. The ratio of caretaker to infant was 1:8 for eight hours of the day, 1:25 for the remaining sixteen. While most of the caretakers liked the infants and some even had favorites, the institutional policies and schedules limited caretaking to the bare essentials of feeding, bathing, and diapering. Motor activity was also limited, since the infants spent only four hours at most outside the crib, while visual and auditory stimulation was monotonously the same day after day.

In regard to the effects on development, there was a two- to five-month period of grace in which development proceeded normally. Then it began to deviate, primarily in the direction of retardation or failure of age-appropriate behavior to appear, although there were also some behaviors not typical of normal infants. As could be predicted, language and social ties, the functions most dependent on interpersonal interaction, were most adversely affected; motor development, with its strong maturational thrust, was least affected. But the effects were significant in all areas.

In the second half of the first year, the infants' behavior was characterized by an affective blandness and a lack of initiative. In relating to adults they were generally amiable and responded with mild pleasure. But there was no attachment to a single adult, no intense pleasure when one approached or distress at separation. Nor did the infants turn to adults for play and pleasure or for relief from distress. They were even deficient in techniques for warding off unpleasant stimuli; if they did not like an adult touching them, they would cry helplessly rather than trying to push the hand away. Precursors of this bland and impoverished responsiveness were observed as early as the second month of life when the infants failed to make the normal postural adjustment to being held and carried. The social smile appeared on schedule at age 3 to 4 months, but at times there was an intense and preoccupied looking at adults, which was striking and unusual. However, this preoccupation did not facilitate visual discrimination, since the infants did not respond differentially to a stranger and a familiar attendant or, indeed, to a face versus a mask.

We can readily understand the institutionalized infant's blandness in light of what we know about normal attachment. Why should the infant look to anyone to maximize pleasure and minimize pain when no one has provided the appropriate sensory stimulation, contingent reinforcement, and prompt relief from distress? Infrequent experience with caretakers hampers both discrimination and the pleasure of recognition. "People" are just that—an undifferentiated mass in which anyone can be substituted for anyone else. Likewise, the pervasive language delay—seen from the second month as a diminution in vocalization and, by the end of the first year, as a failure to use language to communicate and to develop simple words such as "mama"—is understandable in terms of the lack of verbal stimulation.

Reaction to toys had the same quality as reaction to people—blandness. Spontaneous play was meager, and there was little of the enterprising, experimental behavior seen in normal children. There was no toy preference, no distress at the loss of a toy or effort to regain it. The development of the object concept in Piaget's sense was markedly delayed. The infants were best in activities requiring imitation of adults and poorest in those requiring them to figure out a solution on their own.

Recall that the infants were not deprived of toys as they were of human contact. Why, then, did they not explore, especially if there is an intrinsic drive to do so? Provence and Lipton (1962) speculate that exploration languished because it lacked the generally vitalizing effect of sensitive caretaking. And here we have an instance of deviant development highlighting a relationship between variables which might be overlooked in normal development. It may be that the exploratory urge in normal infants is less autonomous than it has been pictured; instead, it must be reinforced by the caretaker, who mediates exploratory activity through the introduction of interesting objects, or by the generally vitalizing effect of affective ties to the caretaker.

As has been noted, motor development was less affected by lack of stimulation than other functions, although sitting, pulling to stand, and walking were all delayed. There were also unusual motor behaviors in the second six months—prolonged, affectless rocking on all fours and hand-waving or posturing. In addition, movement lacked the smoothness of performance seen in the normal infant; instead, it went by fits and starts, inactivity followed by sudden, jerky, poorly controlled activity.

Provence and Lipton frequently observed that the infants did not function in keeping with their capabilities. Motorically, the infants were able to approach, grasp, and manipulate objects, but from 6 months on they reached for toys less frequently than did normal infants. Their repertoire of sounds at 6 months was average for their age, but they did not communicate vocally or vocalize for their own entertainment. Maturationally, they were capable of stimulating and exploring their body and thereby defining their body image, but grasping their feet, sucking their thumb, poking their belly button, and all other normal body-oriented activities were strikingly absent. The lack of initiative in relation to people has already been described. Thus, neither the social environment nor the physical environment nor their own body was utilized as a source of stimulation and play or as comfort from distress.

What a striking contrast between the pervasive blandness of these infants and the imperviousness, repetitiousness, and resistance of the autistic child, or the disjointed, erratic behavior of the schizophrenic child—and incidentally, what a contrast to the mentally retarded child who makes maximum use of his or her limited potential! These seem to be basically normal infants in whom the vitality of growth has been sapped. True, some of their behavior is strange—the staring at adults, the mannerisms with the hands, the fitful outbursts of motor activity—but it generally does not puzzle the viewer. The lack of the vitalizing influence of sensitive caretaking seems to hold the key to understanding the infants' lack of initiative, their superficial, indiscriminate social responsiveness, and the retarded development of specific psychological functions.

Developmental Picture

Because they seem less disturbed than psychotic children, we would expect institutionalized children's development to be less deviant and the chances of reversing the damage to be greater. Such is the case. However, the total impact of privation depends on its duration and the kind of environment the child subsequently lives in; the child who goes from a bleak institution to a series of cold, rejecting foster homes will be more damaged than one who experiences consistent love and care in a single foster home.

Goldfarb (1945) conducted one of the classical studies of the subsequent development of institutionalized children. He compared two groups of early adolescents, one having spent the first three years in a bleak institution, the other having been placed in foster homes from birth. The children in the first group were placed in homes that had been selected for their warmth and affection. However, once there, the children's behavior changed from docile and bland to hyperactive, insatiable, and disorganized. As adolescents they were intellectually retarded, having particular difficulty in organizing a variety of stimuli meaningfully and in abstracting relationships. Their self-control was weak, as evidenced by uninhibited, unreflective behavior, poor concentration, and general unmanagability. Severe temper tantrums and even cruelty were present, with very little attendant anxiety or guilt. In school they disregarded rules, had difficulty sitting in one place, lacked organization. While extremely curious about the environment, they were unable to grasp its meaning, asking questions, for example, but paying little attention to the answers.

In relating to adults they were insatiable in their demands for attention and even for physical affection: one adolescent would sit on the foster mother's lap and hug and kiss her. However, they were also indiscriminate and had no deep attachment to anyone. If they had to go to another foster home, they showed no sign of being affected. Their insatiability could carry over into their food habits. When given an apple, a boy ran to the refrigerator for another before he had finished the one he had in his hand. When his foster mother suggested he finish the first apple, he began stamping his foot and screaming. In a domineering family requiring the child to control his activity and aggression, a boy became isolated and apathetic and developed peculiar grimaces and tics.

A more recent review (Rutter, 1979b) confirms the picture of institutionally reared preschoolers as lacking in deep attachments, clinging, overly friendly with strangers, and attention-seeking. Such behaviors continue into middle childhood. Institutional children as compared with normal controls also tend to be more attention-seeking, restless, disobedient, and unpopular in school. They approach the teacher and other children more but tend to relate in socially unacceptable ways, such as calling out in class and disregarding the teacher's directions. In addition, they have greater difficulty in concentrating on the task at hand. In terms of our developmental model, their work orientation has been undermined.

Goldfarb uses the phrase "primitivization of the total personality" to epitomize behavior which is unreflective, lacking in depth and sustained goal-striving, and immediately responsive to the impulse of the moment. The phrase is apt and helps differentiate the behavior of these children from the constricted, ritualized, isolated behavior of autistic children. While resembling Bender's pseudopsychopaths, children suffering privation have neither the florid and bizarre psychopathology, such as delusions and hallucinations, nor the islands for normal and precocious behavior.

Using the model of normal development, we can speculate as to the reasons for this deviant outcome. Recall that self-control depends on affectional ties, which first increase tolerance for delay and then reinforce socialization demands by the granting and withholding of love as the child complies or defies. If the bond of love is weak, so too will be the caretaker's rewards and punishment as well as the child's own guilt, which represents the internalization of parental disapproval and withdrawal of love. Self-control also depends on cognitive development, which enables the child to abstract generalizations from specific rules and to manage progressively complex anticipations of consequences. The institutionalized children's meager exploration of objects might well have retarded development during the sensorimotor stage (the object concept was late in appearing), while deficient language development subsequently hampered abstract thinking and complex reasoning. Finally, the monotonous, routinized, institutional environment may have hampered the development of the coping skills necessary to meet the complex and variable demands of living in a normal environment. Thus, both emotionally and intellectually, the adolescents become creatures of the moment, uncritically giving in to affectionate or angry or antisocial feelings and having little ability to sustain their involvement or profit from experience.

Reversibility

That institutionalized children are not fated to develop like those in Goldfarb's study is shown by the pioneering research of Skeels (1966). Again, there were two groups of infants being reared in an impoverished institutional environment, in this instance an orphanage. However, at 19 months of age, a group of thirteen toddlers were sent to an institution for the retarded, where each one was cared for by an adult who became particularly fond of him or her. In addition, this one-to-one relation was supplemented by frequent interactions with other adults in the environment.

Initially, the toddlers' average IQ score was 64, while the control group of twelve toddlers who remained in the orphanage had an average IQ score of 86. However, about eighteen months after the transfer, the "mentally retarded" experimental group now had an average IQ score of 92, while the control group's IQ score had declined to 61—a dramatic reversal of positions. Subsequently eleven of the toddlers were adopted and maintained their gains, while the two who were institutionalized suffered a decline. Most impressive of all were the results of a follow-up study when the experimental children were between 25 and 35 years of age. In general, their adult status was equivalent to that of children reared by natural parents in terms of education, occupation, and income. By contrast, the control group continued to function at a retarded level.

While the Skeels study proved that the adverse effects of a bleak environment are reversible, it also suggests that such dramatic results are not easily achieved. No less than a totally rehabilitative environment was required. Thus, the cost of reversing initial damage is high, although the cost of doing nothing is even higher, not only in terms of wasted human potential but in monetary terms as well: the control group cost the state five times as much as the experimental group!

CHILD ABUSE

Child abuse is one of the major causes of death of children in the United States (Alexander, 1976). If not killed, the abused child may sustain traumatic injuries to any part of the body: bruises, lacerations, burns, internal hemorrhages, fractured or broken bones, including the skull. The facts are shocking. Equally startling, the very existence of child abuse was hushed up until early in the 1960s. Since then attention has understandably been focused on protecting the child from further abuse, on remedial measures for parent and child alike, and on a search for causes in the hope of eventual prevention.

The search has proved difficult. The naive assumption that the abusing parent must be manifestly psychotic has not been borne out. Child abuse can occur within a variety of familial and socioeconomic contexts and at all ages from infancy through adolescence. In the following discussion of "the abusing parent" and "the abused child," it is important to remember that we are dealing with frequently described rather than universal characteristics. In individual instances, the picture might be quite different. Child abuse itself will be defined as nonaccidental physical injury or injuries resulting from acts on the part of adults responsible for the child's care.

Causes

Studies of child abuse nicely illustrate the point that deviant behavior is often the result of both contextual and intrapersonal factors. Social, familial, parental, and intrapersonal forces are all at work. Child abuse is not a bolt from the blue striking a normally developing child. If it were, it might be considered a medical problem no different from any other kind of traumatic injury. Rather, child abuse is one in a constellation of forces hindering normal development. It is these forces and their effect on development which we will try to understand. (For a more detailed discussion of etiology, see Parke and Collmer, 1975, and Belsky, 1980.)

THE SOCIAL CONTEXT. While child abuse occurs in all social classes, it probably is more prevalent among lower-class parents. Unemployment and job dissatisfaction run high in abusive families. (Incidentally, these same two factors are responsible for an increase in other forms of intrafamily violence such as wife-beating.) The abusive family tends to be socially isolated. Friendships are brief, ending in quarrels and bitterness, and there is a general distrust of others. However, their isolation is not completely voluntary, since the families can also be rebuffed by the community. Abusive parents also prevent their children from developing friendships and participating in normal educational and recreational activities outside the home, such as organized sports and informal parties. Finally, the family in which abuse occurs tends to have an above-average number of children.

There are also those who claim that child abuse is tacitly encouraged by American society, which condones aggression in general and punitiveness toward children in particular. The high level of violence in this country, as compared with other Western nations, is evidenced by the statistics on murder and the content of television programs alike, while the right of schools to use corporal punishment on disobedient children has been upheld by the highest court in the land—the U.S. Supreme Court—in *Ingraham* v. *Wright* (Belsky, 1980).

THE PARENTAL CONTEXT. A variety of personality traits and types has been attributed to abusive parents: they are described as less intelligent, and more hostile, impulsive, immature, self-centered, rigid, domineering, dependent, narcissistic, childlike, and passive than nonabusing parents. We can only conclude that there is no "abusive personality" but that a number of characteristics can undermine parental control to the point that abuse occurs.

Nevertheless, there may be certain commonalities among abusive parents. A frequently reported observation is that they were themselves abused as children, suggesting a vicious cycle by which abuse is passed from generation to generation. However, the better-controlled studies have cast doubt on this observation: intergenerational continuity may exist, but it is not universal or typical. Thus, being abused as a child is just one of many conditions which may predispose a parent to be abusive, although the majority of them are not. Abusing parents tend to have unrealistic notions concerning child development, which they enforce inconsistently and ineptly (Sameroff and Chandler, 1975). They may expect the infant to be toilet-trained much sooner than is reasonable, for example, and then combine unusual punitiveness in this area with indifference or even neglect in other areas, such as health or protection from physical dangers. Finally, there is evidence that in their current relations, abusive families tend to have fewer interactions than do matched controls, the mother displaying less affectionate and supportive behavior, while being more threatening and complaining. In addition, marital conflict and discord run high. It is possible, therefore, that the aggression inherent in parental discord will be displaced or "spill over" to the children (Belsky, 1980).

THE CHILD'S ROLE IN ABUSE. Interestingly, the child tends to be deviant before abuse occurs, the implication being that he or she is more difficult to care for and more likely to become the target for abuse than the normally developing sibling. Infants having low birth weight (due either to prematurity or intrauterine growth retardation) are disproportionately represented among abused children (Parke and Collmer, 1975). It may be that the prolonged separation of the mother from the neonate prevents the development of a strong bond of affection, and/or it may be that the need for special care places an intolerable stress on the mother. In addition to prematurity, mental retardation, physical handicaps, and congenital malformations are overrepresented in the abused population as is parental perception of the child's being "different" (Friedrich and Boriskin, 1976). While the reports of abusing parents that their child was difficult or unmanageable cannot be accepted at face value, there is suggestive evidence that they are correct in certain cases. Some abused children are reported to have a particularly irritating and grating cry and there is even some support for the claim that the child may be deliberately provocative; for example, nurses find certain abused children particularly difficult to care for and foster parents find some to be intolerable and ask that they be placed elsewhere.

None of the above three factors is sufficient in itself to account for physical abuse. There is a host of sorely beset parents who do not abuse their children; parents who were abused do not inevitably abuse their children, just as parents of deviant and difficult children manage to cope with the added stress of caretaking without resorting to physical violence. In all probability, it is the interaction of all three factors—perhaps in combination with other, still undiscovered factors—which eventuates in acts of violence. (See Belsky, 1980, for an elaboration of this theme of interaction among variables.)

The Abused Child

In their concern over detection and intervention, professionals have paid scant attention to abused children themselves. We know only the grossest features of their development—that they may be physically deviant before the abuse occurs, and that the abuse may eventuate in brain damage, mental retardation, and learning problems. There is also evidence that they are apathetic and joyless as well as aggressive and resistant, and that they have a high number of symptoms of psychological disturbance and low self-esteem (Martin and Breezley, 1977). Hypervigilance and pseudoadult behavior have also been noted. But what happens to the bond of love, to curiosity, to communication, the three foundations of normal development which are the foci of the present discussion? The questions are rarely asked, much less satisfactorily answered. However, there are suggestive findings from individual studies.

EARLY DEVELOPMENT. Martin and Kempe (1976) have written one of the few comprehensive treatments of the early development of the abused child, although, admittedly, the book is often speculative because of meager data. *Pregnancy* presages that special mixture of positive and negative feelings which will mark the parents' subsequent attitudes toward the child. The pregnancy itself is stressful: not only are there physical complications, but a number of mothers also report being beaten by their mate; there is twice the risk of prematurity and ten times the risk of a Caesarean section as in the normal population; mothers from lower SES have to contend with inadequate nutrition and medical care as well as the tensions in the home. Yet, the mother looks forward to the baby with an idealized expectation that somehow all of her problems will be solved and all of her needs will be met. Understandably, her deepest longing is that she will be given to, since she is too beset with problems to feel she has much to give.

Birth can only bring disappointment and resentment at having to care for the infant.

Subsequent child care by both parents is marked by inconsistency. The unrealistic expectations continue, at times in terms of socialization, at times in terms of expecting comfort, protection, and even entertainment from the child. The child is punished and isolated for normal behavior—crying, exploring, resisting diapering, masturbating. Yet discipline is capricious and determined by the parents' mood; behavior that is punished at one time is ignored or even encouraged and enjoyed at another.

The general atmosphere at home is joyless and tense. There are few games and little laughter. Parents argue and fight frequently. Violence and cruelty are part of the child's everyday life. To make matters worse, the social isolation of the family and the active discouragement of peer relations prevent the preschooler from forming relationships which could provide alternate models of living and compensatory sources of gratification.

While there are few well-documented accounts of the development of *attachment,* there are some interesting leads. (Our discussion follows George and Main, 1980.) Social and affective withdrawal is the most likely behavior pattern in *infancy.* The abused infant fails to initiate or respond to social contact, and affect tends to be shallow when it appears. Social signals are ambiguous, and parents do not know how to interpret, say, an ambivalent mixture of bidding for physical contact and anger. A strong emotional bond to specific individuals, particularly the parents, is lacking; the infant is more responsive to strangers than to the mother.

The abused 1- to 3-year-old approaches adult caretakers less frequently than the nonabused child, and the approaches themselves are oblique, such as taking small backward steps in the direction of the target person or coming toward such a person from behind. Overtures to peers are similarly marked by approach–avoidance behavior, such as a boy walking toward a playmate with his head turned to the side. Friendly social approaches from others tend to be avoided. While there is no difference between abused and nonabused children at this age in regard to peer aggression, the abused child shows more aggression toward parents and adult caretakers in the form of physical assaults, threats, and harassment.

Martin and Kempe (1976) offer some further clues as to the subsequent nature of attachment when they describe the joylessness and hypervigilance of the *preschooler,* both of which seem natural consequences of joyless, unpredictable caretaking. Since they have been punished according to parental mood, the children become adept at reading mood changes in adults. They seem constantly on guard, as if asking, "Where is the danger? What are the telltale signs that the adult is about to strike out at me?" When brought to the hospital after being abused, such behavior can become "frozen watchfulness," as the child sits quietly and immobile, surveying every move the staff makes. In order to cope with this fear of unpredictable violence, the child seems further to be asking, "What can I do in order to divert or distract or placate or please the threatening adult?" Consequently, the children are described as "chameleons in their adaptation to various people" (p. 107). Even when being given an intelligence test, for instance, they often look at the examiner for clues as to whether they are pleasing her or not; in certain instances they will change a correct response to an incorrect one if they fancy that the examiner showed some slight annoyance. Role reversal also can be observed in the hospital, the battered child bringing the parents magazines to read, straightening toys in the playroom, or dusting and cleaning up the examination room. However, abused children typically show little separation anxiety when their parents have to leave them in the hospital. During their subsequent stay they may show some of the indiscriminate relationships to adults which characterize institutionally reared children; for example, one 3½-year-old immediately went up to a woman doctor he had never seen before saying, "I like you," and followed her around the ward constantly asking her to play with him (p. 61).

Initiative suffers in a special way. The constant concern over doing what the parents want the child to do overwhelms self-reliance. Toddlers dare not turn their backs on parents and venture out independently but must always keep a wary eye on them. In addition, parents' unrealistic expectations concerning socialization subject the child to continual failure experiences. As a result, low self-esteem is one of the abused child's prominent characteristics by the preschool period.

The intellectual expansiveness which is part of initiative also suffers. The incidence of mental retardation and learning disorders is high in abused children. In part, this is the result of prematurity and organic brain damage resulting from physical abuse. But the deficiencies can also be psychogenic. "Learning, competency, exploration, initiative, autonomy are not valued in most abusive homes; indeed, they may be the basis for physical assault by the parents" (p. 193). Gross motor development and language seem particularly vulnerable in the preschool period. Recall that the normal toddler is all over the place and into everything; it may be just this natural expression of curiosity which the abusive parents find intolerable. In a like manner, language may suffer both because of inadequate verbal exchanges with parents and because the child may be hit for questioning, complaining, expressing feelings, or "sassing." The preschooler's talking, like the infant's crying, is regarded as an irritating intrusion. The above-mentioned sense of failure also undermines the child's motivation to learn and achieve.

What little evidence there is suggests that the *timing* of abuse is not as important as parental behavior and events surrounding the abuse. In a study of fifty children, there was no correlation between the age abuse occurred and various deviant behaviors; however, the degree of disturbance was significantly correlated with the perceived and actual stability of the home, whether biologic, foster, or adoptive (p. 106).

EFFECTS ON LATER DEVELOPMENT. Early reports tended to paint an ominous picture of the effects of abuse on the development of the child (Martin, Breezley, Conway, and Kempe, 1974). However, these studies often failed to control for the effects of low birth weight, neurological damage, and low socioeconomic status, each of which may have an adverse influence on development in and of itself. As the quality of studies improves, the detrimental effect of abuse has been found to be considerably less than originally described, except in those cases where it results in organic brain damage. One of the better studies (Elmer, Evans, and Reinhart, 1977) matched seventeen abused children, seventeen children injured by accident, and seventeen nontraumatized children in terms of age, race, sex, and socioeconomic status. Even by the end of the first year of life, differences between the two traumatized groups began to disappear. By the end of the eighth year, there were few significant differences between the abused and the control groups in terms of health, language, hearing, impulsivity, aggression, empathy, self-esteem, motor activity, school ability and achievement, and degree of disturbance. The authors conclude that the factor most responsible for the adverse outcomes was poverty and its "well-known companions: poor education, menial jobs, inadequate housing, poor health, and environmental violence" (p. 84). Martin et al. (1974) arrived at a similar conclusion concerning the importance of the environment; for example, after eliminating children with neurological damage, IQ scores were significantly related to the instability of the home (unemployment, high mobility, poor management, a chaotic social situation) rather than abuse per se.

It is important to note that the studies finding that abuse per se does not significantly affect many aspects of development have been conducted on lower class, often multi-problem families. We do not know whether abuse would also play a minor role in determining the future development of middle-class children. However, as things presently stand, we must conclude that—aside from its organic complications—physical abuse is not a major source of deviant development. In this respect it is quite different from privation. While professionals and the public alike are justifiably shocked and concerned about child abuse and its threat to organic intactness and to life itself, it seems less a unique problem than one facet of a generally noxious environment.

Remediation

Remediation tends to follow etiology in emphasizing the role of either the parents, society, or the child in abuse. (For a detailed presentation of intervention programs, see Belsky, 1978.)

Many remedial programs involve one or both parents. In an effort to supply the nurturant and caring relationships the parents might have missed in their own childhood, they can be seen in individual psychotherapy by a professional or they can have contact with a warm, sensitive lay person who has had experience raising children and who can act as a sympathetic friend and companion. There are also groups such as Parents Anonymous (modeled on Alcoholics Anonymous), which offer emotional support and counteract the parents' sense of isolation. Behavioral therapies help the parents develop alternative techniques for dealing with the child, which can supplant the pattern of excessive demands and neglect.

Those who view child abuse as a social problem advocate a number of programs of social action. Since there is evidence that lack of day-care facilities may be related to child abuse, increasing the number and availability of such facilities might reduce the caretaking pressures on the parent and lessen child abuse. Crisis nurseries have been established where parents can bring the child for a few hours when they have reached the limits of their endurance. A number of educational classes are being tried; some are concerned with general child care and are aimed at correcting the parents' misunderstanding of normal development, while some are geared specifically to managing the problems of low birth weight and physically handicapped children. As a preventive measure, it is suggested that parenting classes and supervised experiences with caring for children be widely available to teenagers, either to prepare them for the parenting role or to help them decide that they would rather forgo it. There are also advocates of heroic social action to eliminate the poverty and the widespread acceptance of violence—as evidenced by corporal punishment and television programming—which are assumed to foster child abuse.

For the children, there is medical care, play therapy, remedial classes to compensate for developmental delay, along with temporary or permanent institutional or foster-home placement. Behaviorally oriented therapy helps the child respond to parental anger in ways other than defiance, since there is evidence that this serves to escalate anger.

While all intervention programs claim a measure of success, it is too early to determine their relative effectiveness or their effectiveness over time. The ideal goal of preventing the abuse before it occurs is even further from realization.

A COMPARISON OF PSYCHOPATHOLOGIES

Let us now look at all four psychopathologies and see what they have taught us concerning deviant development.

First, there seems to be a fundamental difference between autism and schizophrenia on the one hand and privation and physical abuse on the other. In the former, the essential requirements for normal development are lacking—namely, that the infant be interested in and responsive to the social and physical environment and that changes within and between psychological functions proceed in a harmonious manner, regardless of their pace. In the latter, the ingredients for normal development are all there but are prevented from following their prescribed course by identifiable environmental events.

The above distinction makes the behavior of autistic and schizophrenic children seem baffling and bizarre because it runs counter to our expectations. We are constantly searching for insights which would bridge the gap between description and understanding: what this boy says is meaningless because he does not take his listener into account, that girl whirls around because her body image is diffuse, while excessive literalness causes a third child to refer to himself as "you," and so on. By contrast, it seems natural that a neglected child should languish and a brutalized one should be guarded. Another consequence of the undermining of normal development is that autistic and schizophrenic children are more difficult to treat than children suffering from privation or abuse. Therapeutic change is possible but painfully slow and requires heroic effort, since the children's capacity to internalize, integrate, generalize, and take initiative is so severely crippled.

Next, the characteristics of the psychopathologies differ. The autistic child's isolation and need for sameness is different from the erratic and florid behavior of the schizophrenic, which is itself in contrast to the blandness and subsequent primitivization of the child suffering from privation. Since physical abuse occurs in a variety of contexts, it has no single characteristic behavior; however, the fairly common pattern of apathy, aggressiveness, low self-esteem, and hypervigilance distinguishes this group from the other three. Thus, we can answer the question raised in the introduction to our discussion: the extreme environmental deviations of privation and abuse do not produce autism or schizophrenia. In terms of both behavioral manifestations and underlying processes, the psychopathologies seem to be distinct. Ironically, physical abuse, which has generated such great social concern, seems to be the least damaging of the four; even the multiple problems which beset the abused child and the abusing family do not seem to hamper development as much as privation (Martin and Kempe, 1976, p. 154). By implication, inconsistent and punitive attention is less damaging to development than neglect. It may be that the need to act and react is so basic that even noxious stimulation does not affect development as adversely as meager and monotonous stimulation.

In all the psychopathologies discussed so far, the normal loving, trusting relation between the infant and its caretaker has failed to develop. But what if the bond does develop and is then disrupted? What happens to normal anguish when separation is prolonged or permanent, as in the case of the death of a loved caretaker? Such questions lead us into the topic of the psychology of loss and depression, which will be discussed next.

5 ▪ Depression and the Consequences of Loss

Development would be easy to understand—but far less interesting—if it were linear or a matter of "more of the same": if children would become progressively more intelligent, self-controlled, conforming, empathetic, and so on, just as they become taller and heavier. In the very first chapter, however, we saw that such a linear model does not fit all the facts of development; instead, there are normal progressions and regressions, appearances, disappearances, and reappearances, as well as seemingly magical transformations.

What we discussed abstractly in the beginning can be concretely illustrated by the development of depression. The two periods in which the existence of depression is clearly recognized are infancy and late adolescence. The vast area of middle childhood is disputed territory. One can find claims that depression does not exist and, indeed, that it is developmentally impossible for it to exist during the period; there are equally strong counterclaims that it is present, and that the child's developmental status serves only to determine the form in which it is expressed. There is even disagreement over the existence of suicide in middle childhood, an issue one would think could be settled on purely empirical grounds (Pfeffer, Conte, Plutchik, and Jerrett, 1980). While the controversy over depression in middle childhood will not be resolved, it is important to remember that the appearance, disappearance, and reappearance of behavior is perfectly congruent with the developmental approach. A well-known illustration is the fact that newborn infants can walk soon after birth if properly held, that these movements cease only to return some eight to ten months later.

Having posed the developmental question in its most general form, we can now examine both the data on and the conceptualizations of depression from infancy to adulthood. For the most part, normal and pathological consequences of loss will be dealt with.

DEPRESSION IN INFANCY

In chapter 4 we saw that adequate mothering in infancy is not a sentimental luxury but an absolute necessity for both optimal physiological and psychological development. Being deprived of mothering after the bond of love is forged results in dramatically deviant behavior.

Anaclitic Depression

The classical studies of *maternal deprivation* were conducted by Spitz (1946) and Bowlby (1960). From the beginning, depression was observed as a response to a prolonged loss of contact with the mother. Typically, the infants were studied in settings such as hospitals or orphanages or foundling homes which lacked adequate substitute mothering, even though the infant's physiological needs might have been adequately met.

The descriptive picture of the infant's reaction to maternal deprivation is important to our understanding of depression. Bowlby (1960) labels the first stage *protest*. The infant is severely distressed, cries loudly, searches the surrounding area for the mother, shakes the bed, and rejects all substitute caretakers. Agitation and anxiety are both prominent and the phase can last anywhere from a few hours to a week or more. The next phase Bowlby labels *despair*. The infant becomes withdrawn and inactive, for example, lying in bed with face averted, ignoring adults. Attempts to initiate contact produce panic and screaming. Loss of appetite and weight as well as insomnia are present. The facial expression resembles that of a depressed adult. The final phase Bowlby labels *detachment*. The infant once again responds to caretakers, to food, to toys. However, the infant no longer acts as if he or she were attached to the mother, treating her like any other friendly stranger. Relationships are socially acceptable but lack depth of feeling.

It is important to note that in the very first year of life the child evidences both depressed affect and a constellation of behaviors and physiological reactions that are also indicators of depression. The entire pattern has much in common with depression in adults. Yet from the beginning, Spitz emphasized its psychological distinctiveness by labeling it *anaclitic depression*. The crucial factor is the actual loss of a much loved and needed caretaker. In adults, by contrast, depression is due to guilt—at least so claim the psychoanalysts. Guilt is loss of self-love; adults become their own parents, judging their behavior as "bad" and thereby recreating the anguish they felt when their parents called them "bad" and withdrew love. Since conscience has not developed in the infant, such guilt reactions are not possible.

It is also important to underscore the fact that *agitation* and irritability are reactions to loss. And so are *anger* and aggression—at this point seen in angry attacks on substitute caretakers. While subsequent discussions will focus on depression, it is also true that loss involves an element of striking out, at times as a direct expression of anger, at times as a defense against the anguish of loss.

One final point pertains to the conceptualization of anaclitic depression. While the typical explanation is in terms of the rupture of the affective bond between mother and infant, Bibring (1953) regards depression as an expression of *helplessness*. It is the awareness that the heroic efforts to regain the mother during the protest phase are of no avail. In the past such efforts have been effective and now they are not; the ensuing helplessness lies at the heart of despair.

Consequences of Maternal Deprivation

The concept of maternal deprivation had a tremendous impact upon the professional and academic community. Initial clinical studies indicated that it was at the root of numerous severe psychopathological conditions, among them schizophrenia, depression, and delinquency. Psychoanalytic theory in particular predicted such a relationship; if a loving bond between infant and mother is the cornerstone of all subsequent healthy development, then the rupture of this bond should produce a variety of severe psychological disturbances.

Yet many of the studies were flawed. To mention only a few shortcomings: a large number of studies reported findings only on disturbed adults, and there was no way of determining how many nondisturbed adults had had similar childhood experiences of maternal deprivation. In some instances, maternal deprivation was just the beginning of a long history of rejections as the child was shunted from one institution or one foster home to another. And in documenting the ravages of being reared in bleak institutions, it was impossible to disentangle the effects of maternal deprivation per se from innumerable other aversive influences in such settings. At the same time that the clinical evidence was being questioned, the concepts of "mothering" and of "deprivation" were also undergoing a searching analysis (Yarrow, 1964). As a result, we now have a more sophisticated conceptualization of maternal deprivation and require more definitive documentation of its effects than existed in the past. As often happens, the picture is no longer as clear as originally painted by Spitz and Bowlby.

Conceptualization of Mothering and Deprivation

Mothering is a complex of behaviors involving both the relief from distress and the sensual stimulation that psychoanalysts emphasize, along with the sensory, motor, and linguistic stimulation that cognitive theorists emphasize. Thus, the mother is a source of security and erotic pleasures while also being the infant's favorite plaything.

While these components of mothering are inexorably intertwined in nature, conceptually we can distinguish the affective relation between infant and mother from the cognitive stimulation the mother provides. It is also important to remember that attachment can take place between the infant and other caretakers, such as the father or grandparents, and is not exclusively to the mother. By the same token, the infant derives cognitive stimulation from a wide array of objects in the physical environment even though human beings are the most interesting. Thus, the current emphasis is on understanding the infant's total social and physical environment, rather than concentrating exclusively on the mother.

Finally, it is important to distinguish deprivation from privation. In the former, the affective bond has developed but is disrupted; in the latter, it has failed to develop.

With these points in mind, we are ready to examine the current status of short-term and long-term consequences of maternal deprivation.

Short-Term Effects of Maternal Deprivation

Spitz and Bowlby's original descriptions of reactions to maternal deprivation have stood the test of time and are still regarded as valid. (Our presentation follows Rutter, 1972, 1979b.) The characteristic behaviors appear after the child is 6 months old, because this is when attachment develops, and continue through the first three years of life. Not all infants show such behaviors, though, perhaps because of temperamental differences, perhaps because of prior experiences with separation. A host of other factors influence the responses to loss of mother. If the separation is of short duration, if the mother or other familiar figures can be with the infant periodically, if sensitive substitute care is available, then the distress-depression reaction is minimal; it is the extended stay in a strange, bleak, or socially insensitive environment with little or no contact with the mother or other familiar figures that is so devastating. Interestingly, the effect of the prior mother–infant relationship upon reactions to separation is uncertain; some investigators find that a good relationship enables the infant to tolerate the separation reasonably well, while others find that a poor relationship produces less disturbance, presumably because the infant has already experienced various forms of aversive or neglectful caretaking at home.

In sum, maternal deprivation is not an absolute evil to be avoided at all costs, as has sometimes been depicted in the professional and popular literature. Rather, the total interpersonal, intrapersonal, and temporal context must be taken into account. (Etaugh, 1980). Intense and prolonged distress-despair appear only under special circumstances and can be avoided under others.

Long-Term Effects of Maternal Deprivation

In discussing long-term consequences of maternal deprivation, we will follow Rutter's (1972) lead and separate the adverse effects resulting from deviant attachment from those resulting from lack of linguistic, sensory, and motor stimulation.

EFFECTS OF DEVIANT ATTACHMENT. Tracing the effects of early maternal deprivation on subsequent developments presents certain problems. Few psychologists subscribe to a single-trauma approach, which states that the disruption of the affective bond is a necessary and sufficient condition for producing severe psychopathology. Fortunately, human beings are not that precariously balanced on the edge of disaster. On the other hand, if maternal deprivation is just the first in a series of traumatic events—coming at the beginning of a long stay in a bleak institution, for example, or the first in a series of losses as the child goes from one foster home to another—there is little reason to attribute the resulting pathology exclusively to disrupted attachment.

There are two theoretical reasons for weighing maternal deprivation in infancy more heavily than subsequent deleterious experiences. The first is the widely held notion that traumatic experiences occurring early in development tend to be more damaging than those occurring subsequently. The clearest supporting evidence comes from animal research where traumatic events can systematically be introduced and their effects on development studied. The second assumption is that the infant's relation to the mother is central, and that attachment to her is the pivotal event in the infant's life. Incidentally, neither assumption has gone unchallenged. There have been objections to extrapolating from animal to human development and attempts to refute empirically the "myth" of early experience (Clarke and Clarke, 1977). Next, there is increasing recognition that the infant often attaches to a number of family members, particularly the father, and there is no reason to give the bond to the mother an exclusive status. However, both challenges are recent, and their implications for the effects of maternal deprivation have not been studied. For the present we can accept the assumption that prolonged distress-depression in the infancy-to-preschool period is a particularly noxious experience, although the final psychopathology may be due to the cumulative effects of subsequent distresses and deprivations.

Now let us look at the relation between maternal deprivation and the development of psychopathology in *middle childhood* and *adolescence.* In a comprehensive review Rutter (1972, 1979b) finds no evidence that deprivation, uncomplicated by other stresses, is related to subsequent psychopathology. While hospitalization may produce anaclitic depression in infancy, there is no evidence that, in and of itself, hospitalization is the prelude to psychological disturbances in later childhood. There is a relation between antisocial behavior and broken homes, but the rise in delinquency is greatest in homes broken by divorce rather than by death, the latter representing the more severe disruption of the affective tie to the parent. Since there is evidence that delinquency is related to parental disharmony and neglect even in intact homes, it seems that the nature of the family interaction is more important than the disruption of affective bonds by either divorce or death.

In sum, Rutter concludes that the evidence—meager and unsatisfactory as it is—suggests that it is a distorted relationship between parent and child rather than a bond disruption per se which is related to the subsequent development of psychopathology. Such a conclusion would not dismay the psychoanalysts, who often conceptualize maternal deprivation as any departure from an optimal relation between mother and child. In fact, their case reports are replete with instances of cold, insensitive mothering, anxious mothering, hostile mothering, guilt-ridden mothering, conflicted mothering. However, we are now in the realm of bad parenting, which is far removed from the privations and deprivations described by Spitz and Bowlby. We agree with Rutter that little is to be gained—except increasing confusion—by using a single term such as maternal deprivation to cover a number of distinct phenomena.

There is clearer evidence for the deleterious consequences of maternal *privation* for subsequent development in childhood and adolescence, particularly in regard to the "affectionless psychopath" (Rutter, 1972). This is a special kind of child who is deficient in empathy and guilt, characteristics which normally serve to check antisocial behavior before it happens or to punish such behavior if it does occur. Affectionless psychopaths typically do not act out because of uncontrolled anger or because antisocial behavior is an accepted way of life in their special subculture; rather, their pervasive unconcern for the feelings of others permits them to exploit or rob or injure as they please.

The conceptual link between maternal deprivation and the affectionless psychopath was made by Bowlby. Recall that the final stage of maternal deprivation is "restitution," in which the infant abandons the parental bond, which has been a source of such distress and despair, and relates on a socially acceptable but superficial basis. Carried to an extreme, detachment could lead to a superficial, manipulative pattern in which people are used and discarded solely in terms of the pleasures they provide the child. Rutter amends Bowlby's original observations, in that the affectionless psychopath seems to have suffered from a failure to *form* an attachment early in life rather than from a disruption of attachment.

The picture in regard to *adult psychopathology* is unclear. Gregory (1966), who conducted one of the more sophisticated studies, found no significant relation between the permanent loss of one or both parents, the age of first permanent parental loss, and a wide variety of psychotic and neurotic disturbances in adults, including depression. On the other hand, certain studies which concentrated exclusively on adult depression did find a relation between parental death and severe—not moderate—depression (Beck, Sethi, and Tuthill, 1963; Munro, 1966). Munro found no relation between severe depression and the patient's age at the time of parental death, while Beck et al. found a suggestive trend for severely depressed adults to suffer parental loss before 5 years of age. As so often happens, we are faced with data which are both contradictory and far from definitive. Perhaps it is best, therefore, to regard the hypothesized relation between early maternal loss and adult depression or other forms of severe adult psychopathology as not proven to date. A decision to either accept or reject the hypothesis would be premature.

DEPRESSION IN MIDDLE CHILDHOOD

Anaclitic depression provides a valid point of departure for discussing depression in the first few years of life. By contrast, the very existence of depression in middle childhood is disputed. (The diversity of viewpoints is well represented in Schulterbrandt and Raskin, 1977.) According to some authorities, the basic question is whether or not the adult behaviors characterizing depression can be observed in children. Other authorities object that such a criterion flies in the face of development by requiring a child to be a miniature adult; the behaviors defining depression must be consonant with the child's capacities to think and feel. Finally, there are those who regard the underlying causes of depression as the crucial element. In this approach, behavior becomes secondary, and indeed, everything from a stomachache to robbing a bank can be regarded as a disguised manifestation of depression.

One reason why confusion abounds is that empirical data are meager. There are a handful of clinical studies which, while important, serve more to raise problems than to resolve them (Gittelman-Klein, 1977). Thus, both conceptually and empirically we will be traveling on the sea of uncertainty, and we can expect no more than to explore the controversial issues. However, these controversies can be used to good purpose in the end by evaluating them in terms of our special developmental approach. (For a lively exchange of ideas, see Lefkowitz, and Burton, 1978; Costello, 1980; and Lefkowitz, 1980.)

The Adult Picture

Since adult depressive disorder has been the point of departure for discussing depression in middle childhood, we should be familiar with its behavioral characteristics and popular theories concerning its etiology (Calhoun, Acocella, and Goodstein, 1977).

BEHAVIORAL CHARACTERISTICS. Depressive disorder involves changes in four areas: affect, motivation, physical and motor functioning, and cognition.

While most normal adults have their ups and downs, individuals suffering from depressive disorder manifest characteristic *affective symptoms.* These include dejection, hopelessness, and/or loneliness. All pleasures vanish, whether they be social, vocational, or sexual.

Motivation declines during episodes of depression, and the depressed adult suffers a "paralysis of the will." At worst, the simplest activities, such as getting dressed or reading a book, become overwhelmingly burdensome. Initiative and new ventures are out of the question. While depressed persons become increasingly passive and dependent, they often berate themselves for their helplessness.

Changes in *physical and motor functioning* which accompany the depressed mood include loss of appetite, insomnia (especially waking early in the morning), loss of sexual responsiveness, and fatigability. In the case of retarded depressions, movements are slow and labored, the individual often sitting slumped over and inert. In an agitated depression, the individual is constantly in motion—restless, pacing, moaning, fidgeting.

Cognitive symptoms include immutable feelings of worthlessness, even in the face of manifest competencies and successes. Depressed individuals feel both helpless and hopeless, firmly convinced that neither they nor anyone else can bring about any change. They elevate the slightest imperfection to a major defect, and they constantly torture themselves with self-blame.

Depressions vary in severity. In neurotic depression the individual can continue to function in spite of depression; Abraham Lincoln is one famous example. Psychotic depression, however, is totally debilitating. The severity of the disturbance is manifested in delusions of sinfulness and worthlessness (for example, "I caused my mother to die," when the death was due to natural causes; "I caused Christ to suffer;" "My guts are rotting;" "My flesh stinks;" "I am dead"). Finally, depressive episodes can either be precipitated by a traumatic event or be without apparent cause. The former are called exogenous, the latter endogenous.

THEORIES. There are three relevant theories of depression. *Psychoanalytic theory* emphasizes loss of the loved parent. If the relationship has been basically healthy, the adult can go through the normal process of mourning and subsequently resume his or her life without untoward psychological consequences. With the depressed individual, however, the relationship has been a highly charged mixture of anger and dependence, typically originating in the first few years of life. The strong need for the mother's love forces the child to repress anger. In later years, the loss of the loved one, say, through death, causes the individual to turn that anger inward in the form of self-accusations or feelings of worthlessness: How could I be so terrible as to hate the one person I loved and needed?

Cognitive theory regards affect as the consequent of cognition. Depressed individuals perceive themselves, the world, and the future all in negative terms. Their distorted and illogical thinking leads to extreme and absolute judgments, overgeneralizations from single incidents, exaggerations, and personalizations. In sum, they view themselves and the significant aspects of their life in terms of being "a loser." Depressive affect is engendered by such a cognition and serves to reinforce the view of the self as worthless and deficient. (For a searching comparison of these two theories, see Abramson and Sackeim, 1977.)

In *behavioral theory,* the most seminal idea is that of learned helplessness. The individual who has learned that he or she cannot escape a noxious situation will give up trying to do so, even when the situation has changed so that escape is now possible. Laboratory findings have provided what may be analogues to the helpless-hopeless attitude of depressives even when effective means of changing for the better are available. (The concept of learned helplessness will be elaborated on in a subsequent section.)

Now we have three keys: Loss of a loved one, negative cognition, and learned helplessness. Our task is to see how each fits the development of depression in middle childhood. But first we should become familiar with the manifestations of depression during this period.

The Behavioral Picture in Middle Childhood

After reviewing clinical descriptions of *neurotic depression* in children, Kovacs and Beck (1977) concluded that many of the behaviors cluster in the same categories indicative of depression in adults: emotional (feels sad, cries, looks tearful); motivational (school work declines, shows no interest in play); physical (loss of appetite, vague somatic complaints); and cognitive (anticipates failure, says "I'm no good"). Freeman (1976) also describes manic depression of psychotic proportions in children, but only a few cases are cited and further documentation is needed. Admittedly, the findings are preliminary and not based on satisfactorily objective data, a limitation which Beck (Kovacs and Beck, 1977) recognizes and is trying to remedy. Until more definitive information is available, however, we can provisionally accept the existence of a syndrome of neurotic depression in children (Carlson and Cantwell, 1980).

The basic disagreement among experts concerns the issue of *masked depression*—children who do not necessarily present manifest signs but who, nevertheless, are judged as having a strong underlying depression. A remarkably varied catalogue of behaviors can mask depression: physical symptoms such as abdominal complaints, anorexia, migraine headaches, and encopresis; delinquent behavior and rebelliousness; obsessional activities; restlessness and hyperactivity; and affectionless, psychopathic behavior (Malmquist, 1972). Small wonder that behaviorally oriented psychologists cry, "Hold, enough!" (Gittleman-Klein, 1977).

The concept of masked depression creates all kinds of mischief. If a child is not acting or feeling depressed, on what basis can one infer depression? The answer is far from clear. Sometimes it is on the basis of a history of depression, sometimes on the basis of fantasies which resemble those of depressed children; more often, however, it is on the basis of the same etiological factors which are assumed to lead to depression—perceived loss of love and a negative self-image.

But the confusion does not stop here. If we accept the clinician's finding of a strong depressive element in a number of disturbances, there are three possible explanations, masking being only one. Another is that the same conditions produce both kinds of disturbances; for example, continual parental belittling leads both to a negative self-image and to intolerable anger, which forces the child repeatedly to run away from home. Finally, the depression may be a reaction to the psychological disturbance itself; for example, a boy with a chronic school phobia might gradually begin to despair about himself and his future.

We are not denying the possibility of a masked depression. As we have seen, a 1-year-old is capable of "masking" anaclitic depression by apparently normal behavior in the restitution phase. It is just that the category needs both greater conceptual clarification and more solid empirical verification than it presently has.

The Developmental Dimension

In contrast to anxiety, which has been extensively researched, the study of the affect of depression has been neglected. Little is known concerning its developmental course, and there are almost no clues regarding the distinction between normal sadness and the intense, prolonged, pervasive dysphoria that can be considered as pathological. We know that infants differ in regard to having a generally positive or negative mood, but such differences are not stable over a five-year period (Thomas and Chess, 1977). Thus, children do not seem to be moody "by nature." We also know that depressive swings are fairly characteristic of 5-year-old boys and 6-year-old girls (MacFarlane, Allen, and Honzik, 1954), suggesting that the normal problems involved in making the transition from the preschool period to middle childhood might engender a certain degree of depression, which should not be considered pathological. But these are only scraps of information. Our knowledge concerning the development of the motivational, physical, and cognitive changes which characterize the syndrome of depression is equally meager.

There are a few studies concerned with the precursors of pathological depression and with the effects of such depression on subsequent development. Caplan and Douglas (1969), utilizing a mood definition of depression, found a significantly higher incidence of parental deprivation in a depressed group of children between 10½ and 11½ years old than in a comparable group of disturbed children who were not suffering from a persistent sad mood. Parental deprivation included death, divorce, illness, and economic necessity, all of which significantly differentiated the groups. However, if the child was placed in a foster home after the parental death, the likelihood of depression increased. The results thus suggest that the impact of parental deprivation might be heightened by subsequent stresses.

In regard to depression's effects on subsequent development, there is some evidence of short-term continuity. Poznanski, Krahenbuhl, and Zrull (1976) found that five out of ten children diagnosed as depressed were still so diagnosed four to six years later when their mean age was 16.9 years. Not unexpectedly, environmental conditions, particularly loss of the father through divorce, were conducive to maintaining the depression. The evidence in regard to adult disturbances, however, fails to substantiate a clear relationship. Robins (1972, particularly p. 441) reports that adult depressives, unlike adult schizophrenics and psychopaths, are rarely known to child guidance clinics. While both Friedlander (1945) and Robins (1966) found a relation between depression in childhood and adult schizophrenia, the depression was just one of many symptoms of psychological disturbance.

Depression as a Reaction to Loss

While there is a real need to trace the developmental courses of depressive affect and the syndrome of depression, neither task is directly relevant to the developmental framework utilized here. When we turn to depression as a reaction to loss of a loved one and as a severe loss of self-confidence, however, we are on familiar ground. Depression now becomes a sign that the normal course of love and initiative have gone radically awry. We can, therefore, resume the inquiry into the consequences of loss, which was of central concern in discussing the infantile period.

LOSS OF LOVE THROUGH DEATH. The death of a loved parent would seem the middle-childhood counterpart to maternal deprivation in infancy, and the same questions can be asked concerning it: What is the expected reaction to death? What are the hallmarks of a deviant reaction? What are the developmental consequences of such a deviant reaction? Unfortunately, answers are either sketchy or nonexistent. Death, more than sex, has been the taboo topic in psychology, and children's reactions to it have been assiduously avoided as an area of research. However, this situation has begun to change in the last few years, so that we have some descriptive data to consider.

Immediately we are confronted with a surprising fact. Almost nothing is known concerning the *normal* reaction to parental death. There are clinical studies of children who are sufficiently disturbed to be brought for professional help, and there are cognitive studies of the concept of death utilizing children from intact families. There is no answer to our initial question, What is the expected reaction to death in middle childhood?

Before starting across the shifting sands of middle childhood, therefore, it will be helpful to anchor ourselves in infancy and adulthood—the two periods where there is reasonable agreement concerning normal reactions to loss. In infancy, as we have seen, anxiety is the expected reaction to the caretaker's departure, once the bond of love has been established. At this early age the infant cannot know whether the caretaker will return in a few minutes or never again. Thus, the anguish of separation is part of the love relation from the very beginning. What the child must subsequently learn to master is the irrevocable separation, which is death.

Adults master the death of a loved one through what Freud calls "the work of mourning." In addition to experiencing anguish, the adult must come to grips with Nevermore. This cannot be done all at once. Rather, the adult dwells on memories and plans involving the loved one and confronts them with the fact of irrevocable loss: "That's the park where she took the children to play." "This is her favorite dress." "Here is where we planned to go on vacation together." The process is piecemeal, so that bit by bit the adult can master a fact whose total impact is potentially overwhelming. Moreover, the mourning has an adaptive function. The realization of Nevermore diminishes the affective tie to the image of the dead person and enables the survivor to establish a bond of love with a new partner. Thus mourning, like separation anxiety, is an appropriate reaction to loss; unlike separation anxiety, however, it does not reinforce the bond of love but serves the adaptive function of loosening it and making other loving relationships possible.

MIDDLE-CHILDHOOD REACTION TO DEATH. One might expect that separation anxiety—in the sense of feeling "I need mother and she is not here"—continues to be manifest in times of stress throughout the preschool period and even into middle childhood; for example, when first going to preschool, when seriously hurt or ill, when frightened by a television program a baby-sitter is watching. However, it plays only a minor role in the child's life.

Death confronts the child with the fact that the loved parent will never return. Is the child sufficiently developed emotionally and cognitively to grasp the concept of irrevocable loss and to experience the adaptive process of mourning? The answer is either no or yes, depending on which authority one reads. Wolfenstein (1966), on the basis of studying forty-two children between 3½ and 19 years of age, claims that the child is incapable of handling the impact of irrevocable loss. Consequently, the typical picture is one of denial, in which the child acts as if nothing wrong has happened. Only in adolescence is it possible to face the loss and work it through by mourning. E. Furman (1974), on the basis of studying twenty-three children between 10 weeks and 13 years of age, claims that mourning is indeed possible, although it is not identical to the process described in adults.

Before examining the disagreement between two experts, let us distinguish the question, Can a child mourn? from Does a child mourn? The first is a developmental question which concerns capabilities. The second concerns manifest behavior; for example, it is possible that a child is capable of mourning but is prevented from doing so by environmental factors.

CAN A CHILD MOURN? Specifically, can a child *cognitively* grasp the irrevocability of death and affectively "dose" the pain of loss so that it can ultimately be mastered?

The concept *death* is cognitively complex. The child must understand the fact that death is a biologically determined event which is both inevitable and universal. This, in turn, requires an accurate differentiation of the animate from the inanimate and the ability to generalize to all animate objects, as well as to grasp the temporal implications of Nevermore. The child will be around 10 years of age before beginning to master such demanding concepts (Kastenbaum, 1974). However, interest in death is evident in the third or fourth year of life, and various investigators have charted the fascinating cognitive changes which take place. We will only be interested in the concept of irrevocability, since it is the one which is central to the issue of mourning.

The preschooler regards death as completely reversible, believing that an unlimited number of lives and deaths are possible; for example, a ball dies when the air is let out of it and lives when it is blown up again (Safier, 1964). Recall that conservation has not taken place, so that objects change their nature as they change in appearance. Certain investigators note how casually the preschooler treats questions about death—but why not, if it is so insubstantial? Note also the tendency to think in terms of specific objects dying, such as a ball or the moon; the preschooler is incapable of thinking in terms of abstractions such as, All animate things die. The preschooler also conceptualizes death in terms of attendant ceremonies such as burials, coffins, and graves—something is dead when it is buried (S. Anthony, 1972). In all this, we see the literal thinking of the preschooler in the preoperational stage of cognitive development: unable to grasp the relation between death and the inner workings of animate objects, the child believes what he or she sees. Irrevocability plays no role in the preschooler's thinking.

Incidentally, the myths preschoolers are told concerning death cater to their misunderstanding. If "Grandmother is asleep," why can't she awake? If she has "gone on a long trip," why can't she come back? If "God has taken her to heaven," why can't He send her back? Such myths fail to confront the child with a different conceptualization or challenge him or her to change, although Piaget would claim that the realistic explanation could not be grasped until the cognitive revolution of conservation had been achieved.

There is evidence that both the universality and irrevocability of death are beginning to be grasped around 6 years of age, coinciding with the appearance of the Piagetian stage of concrete operations (Kane, 1979). However, it is not until the end of middle childhood that the major aspects of death are fully understood. Within middle childhood itself unevennesses in development can result in the continuation of unrealistic ideas. Initially there is a belief that death is externally caused, for example, and only gradually does the child realize its intrinsic inevitability. One consequence of an external agent, such as a weapon or a germ, is the possibility that death can be avoided, say, by being careful. There is also evidence that the concept of irrevocability develops more slowly than the concept of universality; for example, in one study only 40 percent of fourth-graders had grasped the former concept while 73 percent had grasped the latter (White, Elsom, and Prawat, 1978).

The next question concerns the child's *emotional capability* to mourn. Wolfenstein (1966) claims children are not capable. Their emotional reactions are still too extreme, too all-or-none, to permit them to experience and master tolerable doses of pain. It is the potentially overwhelming nature of their feelings that necessitates the denial which is so characteristic of children. E. Furman (1974) claims that children do have the emotional capabilities. While both studies are innocent of objective data, Furman documents her findings in greater detail than does Wolfenstein. Lacking more stringent scientific criteria for choosing, we are forced to rely on the black swan principle, which states that the sighting of a single black swan disproves the hypothesis that all swans are white. Furman's data indicate that the capacity does indeed exist.

THE NATURE OF MOURNING. We have reached the point where we can assume that the child is both cognitively and emotionally capable of mourning, but the discrepancy in Wolfenstein's and Furman's findings is still perplexing. A more detailed presentation of the latter will suggest a reconciliation.

Furman points to the differences between adult and childhood mourning, in terms of both the content and the developmental status of the mourner. The loss of a parent means the loss of a special relationship which has no counterpart in the adult's loss of a partner or a child. The child is still dependent upon parents for love, tender care, guidance, security, stimulation, values. While friends and school are increasingly important, the home still serves as the "secure base" from which the child expands. The psychological situation is quite different when a spouse dies, since the adult relationship is more concerned with companionability and with sharing responsibilities, intimacy, vocational and recreational goals. The autonomous adult is also free to seek another mate, while the dependent child cannot seek a substitute parent.

In addition, the adult's personality, being more completely developed, can function more autonomously than can the child's. Consequently, with an adult, mourning can proceed to run its course relatively independent of environmental events. With a child, there is a delicate balance between forces—both internal and external, historical and contemporary—which can either allow mourning to take place or block it (R. A. Furman, 1973). Especially important is the presence of a sympathetic adult who will support children in expressing grief and help them face the painful encounters with memories and anticipations involving the lost parent. It is as if children need others in order to accomplish the "work of mourning," which adults can achieve on their own. Children require reassurance that the continuity of their lives will be maintained in spite of the disruption of death and that their needs will be met by a substitute adult. The relationship with the dead parent should have been primarily positive, and the child's current life should be free of major distresses aside from the death. Finally, as we have seen, the child should have a realistic understanding of the nature of death itself.

And how many forces conspire to prevent this favorable constellation from occurring. The mystique surrounding death often dictates that the child is either too young to understand what has happened or too sensitive and therefore must be protected from facing the event. The grieving spouse is often too concerned with his or her own mourning to give the child the needed emotional support, while the decline in large families mitigates against the availability of substitute adults. Even at the cognitive level death tends to be explained in terms of myths and fancies rather than in terms of facts. In addition, factors within the child make mourning difficult. These may be the dictates of cultural stereotyping, which say that big boys and girls don't cry—only babies cry. They may also be more deep-seated problems concerning anger with the parent, which death makes unbearable. Finally, there may be realistic stresses having nothing to do with the death—such as a severe illness or failing in school—but which make mourning an intolerable affective burden.

In light of the many contingencies involved in childhood mourning, it may be quite possible to study a population of disturbed children, such as Wolfenstein's group, and find no evidence of mourning—no sad feelings, little weeping, no preoccupation with thoughts of the loved one. Only indirectly is the reaction to loss expressed—a decline in school performance, periods of irritability, misbehavior in school, truanting, and stealing.

Subsequent Effects on Development

By now we know that the question, What effect does parental loss have on subsequent development? is too simple to be meaningful. There are few absolutely traumatic events which will distort development regardless of all other past and future events. So it is with death. While the loss itself may be painful, the repercussions depend on the total context—intrapersonal, interpersonal, and temporal—in which it takes place.

The literature underscores the point. Some studies show a relation between parental loss in childhood and depression in adulthood, while others do not (Bendiksen and Fulton, 1975; Markusen and Fulton, 1971). The disagreement is partly due to deficiencies in research design; retrospective studies often fail to control for a number of important variables or lack control groups. But the disagreement is partly due to the contingent nature of the effect of death. To illustrate: Hilgard, Newman, and Fisk (1960) found that the independence of the surviving parent was important in determining the subsequent mental health of the child. This was particularly true in the mother–daughter relationship. Girls who subsequently made a good adjustment as adults had mothers who were strong, responsible, hard-working, and even strict, rather than sweet and loving. The mother could also use the support of relatives, the church, or community resources after being widowed. By contrast, the women who did not make a good adjustment had mothers who became extremely dependent upon their children after the death of the husband, making separation particularly difficult or impossible. Consequently, the child had inadequate opportunities to develop the skills and assurance necessary for successful living as an independent adult.

Two other studies are worth reporting in detail. Bendiksen and Fulton (1975) reevaluated by means of a questionnaire, 250 33-year-olds whose family structure was categorized as bereaved, divorced, or intact when the children were in the ninth grade. Subjects from bereaved families reported more major illnesses and extreme emotional distress than the intact group, but so did the subjects from divorced families. However, the bereaved group was no different from the intact group in terms of number of divorces and arrests, suggesting that both their adaptation to marriage and their impulse control did not suffer from the early experience of parental loss. While health and happiness were affected by loss, the adults were making an adequate social adjustment. Finally, Adam (1973) found more suicidal ideation and attempted suicides in a population of 114 university students who had lost one or both parents prior to age 16 than in a matched control group. Like Hilgard et al., Adam found that the presence of a consistent, stable, nurturant adult and the ability to find substitutes for the lost relationship were protections against developing suicidal ideas. And, like Bendiksen and Fulton, he found that the effects of divorce or separation were the same as parental death. (For a critical résumé, see Crook and Eliot, 1980.)

Summing up the studies in middle childhood and comparing them with those in infancy, we see that subsequent events play an important role in determining the effect of parental death on future adjustment. Stability and continuity of care, along with the availability of satisfactory substitutes facilitate mastery; continued disruption and stress within the family impede mastery and incline the child toward future psychopathology. In infancy, parental death per se does not presage delinquency in middle childhood, and while parental death might be related to adult depression, the evidence is only suggestive at best. There is some evidence that parental death in middle childhood may increase the chances of suicidal ideation and attempts in adolescence, as well as negatively affecting the adult's health and happiness. Even here, context factors play a central role in the severity of the adolescent's disturbance, while adults make adequate personal and social adjustments. At all ages, the interpersonal context rather than parental death per se seems to be the crucial variable affecting future adjustment. In regard to the context of time the data do not support the critical-period hypothesis concerning infancy; rather, parental death seems to have more far-reaching consequences in middle childhood, when the child's personality is sufficiently structured so as to sustain the adverse affects of loss.

Since there is evidence that loss of parental love through divorce might have an equally potent effect on development as death, this topic will be examined again later.

Paternal Loss

The association of maternal loss with infancy is so strong that the mother–infant relationship has until recently monopolized the attention of investigators. The days of such a narrow focus are over, however, and the infant's multiple attachments, particularly to the father, are being studied. At present, the nature of the father–infant bond is being explored to determine how it resembles and differs from the mother–infant attachment. It may be, for example, that attachment to the mother is mediated primarily by tender care and moderate stimulation, while attachment to the father is mediated by excited play. When we have a clearer idea than we now do of the nature of fathering, we will be in a better position to predict the consequences of being deprived of it (see Parke, 1979).

The findings concerning father loss in middle childhood and adolescence have a familiar ring (Herzog and Sudia, 1973). There is no evidence that paternal death is the prelude to subsequent psychopathology. While paternal loss owing to divorce, desertion, and separation does have adverse consequences, such conditions are complicated by many added stresses, and there is no evidence that loss per se is prepotent. In fact, the same stresses in intact families are equally likely to produce subsequent psychological disturbances.

DEPRESSION IN ADOLESCENCE

There is general agreement that adolescents have developed to the point where they can become depressed as adults do. Emotionally, they are capable of experiencing intense sadness and of sustaining this experience over time. Cognitively, they can think in terms of generalizations and can project into the future. They can consciously evaluate their self and judge it as helpless or inept. In fact, moderate versions of the classical signs of depression may appear in adolescence as part of the expected turmoil of the period. The question is no longer, Can an adolescent be depressed? but, How can one tell normal from pathological depression? This diagnostic task of the clinician need not concern us here, however.

The *clinical picture* of depression undergoes an interesting development within the adolescent period. The adult manifestations rarely appear before age 16 or 17. Rather, the early adolescent's reluctance to express feelings openly, together with a tendency to deny negative and self-critical attitudes, result in a number of camouflages: boredom and restlessness, which disguise an underlying feeling of emptiness and isolation; difficulty in concentration with a special inability to absorb and retain information while studying, which is a disguised manifestation of general apathy; acting out in the form of temper tantrums, running away, and a variety of defiant behaviors, which protects the adolescent from facing feelings of being unloved and inadequate; exaggerated approaches to people, say, in the form of sexual promiscuity, to counteract the feeling of being unloved or unwanted; and exaggerated withdrawal from people to avoid the possibility of being rejected by them (I. B. Weiner, 1980).

The *reasons* for depression in adolescence are not new, since they involve actual or fantasied loss of a significant personal relation or of self-esteem (I. B. Weiner, 1980). However, the developmental context is different from what it was in middle childhood. In middle childhood, children have the basic security of knowing that they are an integral part of the family unit. By contrast, adolescents are faced with the task of giving up their place within the family and developing a new status as an independent adult. Even in healthy adolescence, therefore, one might expect some temporary depressive states when closeness to the family is taboo but mature sources of love have not been found as yet. Temporary loss of self-confidence might also be expected during the search for a vocation which would utilize the adolescent's competences. Thus, depression is more of an exaggeration of normal developments in adolescence, while in middle childhood it is a reaction to the disruption of normal expectations that parental love will always be available when needed.

Adolescent Suicide

Depression is a rather infrequent psychopathology among adolescents. It becomes ominous, however, as a frequent prelude to suicide, which is the fourth leading cause of death among 15- to 19-year-olds in the United States (I. B. Weiner, 1980, p. 458).

Suicide is not specific to the adolescent period, however; while quite rare, it can also occur in middle childhood. The typical clinical picture is one of great stress and unhappiness. Paulson and Stone (1974), for example, in their study of twelve suicidal children found that severe depression was the principal symptom, while breakdown of the family unit by separation, divorce, or death, hostility between parents, lack of friends, peer rejection, and sibling jealousy all culminate in total isolation from the social environment. Significantly, 50 percent of the families provided models of suicidal behavior, either through actual suicides, serious attempts, or constant rumination. While chronic family disharmony and fear of abandonment were the ultimate causes, the suicide attempt itself was perceived in a variety of ways—as a cry for help, as a magical means of changing the family for the better so that the child could return to it afterward, as a means of getting even with rejecting parents.

Such reports must be considered preliminary, however. While the picture is dramatic, it also resembles that found in other disturbed children who do not attempt suicide. Until more studies are done with comparison and control groups, the specific factors which precipitate suicide in middle childhood will remain uncertain. And until we understand more of the meaning of the suicidal act to the child, we will not understand how to account for it developmentally.

Theories and clinical studies of adolescent suicide abound, the latter resembling Paulson and Stone's findings regarding middle childhood. However, the data are such that they do not allow us to choose one theory over another as being more plausible, and the clinical studies generally lack a control group which would allow us to tease out the variables specific to suicide.

A notable exception is Jacobs's (1971) study of fifty 14- to 16-year-olds who attempted suicide. A control population of thirty-one subjects, matched for age, race, sex, and level of mother's education was obtained from a local high school. Through an intensive, multitechnique investigation, Jacobs was able to reconstruct a five-step model of suicidal attempts.

1. A long-standing history of problems from early childhood to the onset of adolescence. Such problems included parental divorce, death of a family member, serious illness, parental alcoholism, school failure. The control group had also experienced such problems, although not quite to the same extent; for example, 72 percent of the experimental group came from broken homes (parental loss, separation, divorce) as compared with 53 percent of the control group. No single event or combination of events separated those who attempted suicide from those who did not.

The importance of a control group is clear. Many clinical studies, lacking such a group, point to broken homes and parental disharmony as a prime cause of suicide. Jacobs's study suggests that familial problems should be regarded as a contributing factor rather than a necessary and sufficient condition.

2. An acceleration of problems in adolescence. Far more important than earlier childhood problems was the frequency of distressing events occurring within the last five years for the suicidal subjects; for example, 45 percent of the experimental subjects experienced a broken home while only 6 percent of the control group did. Termination of a serious romance was also much higher among the suicidal group, as were arrests and jail sentences.

3. The progressive failure to cope with the increase in problems leading to isolation from meaningful social relationships. Among coping mechanisms, the suicidal and control groups were equally rebellious in terms of becoming disobedient, sassy, and defiant. However, the suicidal adolescents engaged in much more withdrawal behavior, such as running away, long periods of silence, and a depressed mood. The isolation in regard to talking with parents was particularly striking; for example, while 70 percent of all suicide attempts took place in the home, only 20 percent of those who reported the attempt reported it to their parents. In one instance, an adolescent telephoned a friend who lived miles away, and he, in turn, telephoned the parents who were in the next room!

4. A dissolution of social relationships in the days and weeks preceding the attempt, leading to the feeling of hopelessness.

5. A justification of the suicidal act, giving the adolescent permission to make the attempt. This justification was reconstructed from 112 suicide notes of adolescents and adults attempting and completing suicide. The notes contain certain recurring themes, an example being that the problems are not of the adolescent's making but are long-

standing and insolvable so that death is the only solution. The authors of such notes also state that they know what they are doing, are sorry for their act, and beg indulgence. The motif of isolation and subsequent hopelessness is obvious.

Jacobs's research has its limitations. Its findings apply only to adolescents who attempt suicide; those who successfully complete the act might have a different psychological background. However, it does point to the futility of trying to relate suicide to a single factor; rather, problems, resources, and timing are all crucial variables. The occurrence of multiple problems during the adolescent stage in particular, and the adolescent's lack of inner resources and social supports to cope effectively with them, results in the suicidal attempt.

Jacobs's research also embodies the points we made about depression in general. The single-trauma hypothesis is untenable, even in regard to such a disruptive event as separation from or the death of a loved parent. The context of the event determines its effect. The intrapersonal context contains the child's coping mechanisms and vulnerabilities. The social context involves supports and stresses within the family and the broader context of peers and extrafamilial adults. The context of time involves both the child's developmental status when the loss occurs, as well as his or her history in regard to love and initiative and the events subsequent to the loss. Thus, loss of love serves as the focus of inquiry; in and of itself, it is not an adequate explanation of psychopathology.

LOSS BY DIVORCE

Death is not the only instance of loss of love. Illness or new job demands may take one or both parents away from the family; parents can become enmeshed in their own emotional problems, which divert them from attending to their children; they can enjoy infancy but be frightened of adolescence; they can become disappointed in or angry with their child. However, of all possible sources of loss, divorce is the most important. Statistically, divorce is on the rise, increasing 7 percent between 1975 and 1976 alone. In 1977, one out of every six children under 18 years of age was living in a single-parent home, caused primarily by divorce or separation (Everly, 1977). In addition, research findings from the previous section alert us to the possibility that divorce may be as detrimental as parental death.

Once again we must deal with inadequate research, but there are a sufficient number of studies to sketch in a developmental picture. As usual, we will be concerned with expected and extreme reactions to divorce at different ages, and the effects of such reactions on subsequent development (Rohrlich, Ranier, Berg-Cross, and Berg-Cross, 1977).

Infancy

There are meager data concerning the effects of divorce on infants, and much of the writings represent extrapolations from normal development; for example, if the mother is depressed by the divorce and cannot care for the infant, or if she becomes overly protective and prevents the toddler from asserting his or her independence, the child will suffer. While such extrapolations sound sensible, empirical testing is needed.

The Preschool Period

McDermott's (1968) research, while involving only sixteen normal 3- to 5-year-olds, contains unique observational data on preschool behavior before, during, and after the divorce. Even in this small sample, four patterns could be delineated. Three children were unchanged, indicating that they had coping mechanisms equal to the stress they were experiencing. In addition, they were well-adjusted, well-liked, and had parents who negotiated the divorce while still remaining on good terms. The largest group—eight in all—were labeled "sad-angry." Some became aggressive, possessive, noisy, restless, and disruptive of peer play. Others cried a good deal, sat alone, gave up activities, and complained of feeling sad. Three girls adapted to the divorce by taking on a "pseudo-adult" role, scolding and lecturing the other children, becoming overly concerned with neatness, health, and manners. The two children in the final "lost-and-detached" group were the most disturbed. One was insatiable in his demands for affection, was unwilling or unable to dress, and began losing all his possessions; the other was tearful, tense, totally self-absorbed, soiled and wet occasionally, began sucking her thumb and masturbating openly. Both children had had long-standing disturbances, and while both went into therapy, only the second was able to return to her prior level of adjustment. On the whole, the group returned to their predivorce level of adjustment in two to three months. Unfortunately, there was no long-term follow up.

Hetherington, Cox, and Cox (1978) provide a vivid account of the many difficulties faced by both parents and children. Ninety-six divorced and intact families were studied for a two-year period, beginning when the children were 4 years of age. Both divorced parents were beset by problems ranging from the management of household routines to a lowered self-esteem. Divorced men found it difficult to shop, cook, and do the laundry; such chores sometimes interfered with job performance. Their lives were further complicated by the economic stress of maintaining two households. Divorced women were less likely to eat with their children than mothers of intact families, bedtimes were more erratic, and the children were apt to be late for school. Intrapersonally, the intoxicating feeling of freedom after the divorce was followed by depression, anxiety, and apathy. Both divorced parents felt they were failures. Social life and the search for meaningful relations was difficult, since socialization is generally organized around couples. Both men and women spoke of intense feelings of loneliness; casual sexual encounters were unsatisfactory, and there was a need for fulfilling intimacy. The first year following the divorce represented the high point of negative reactions. While happiness, self-esteem, and feelings of competence increased steadily in the second year, they were still not as high as those of married couples.

Poor parenting was apparent in the two years following the divorce. Inconsistency of discipline resulted in a lack of control over the children, as compared with parents in intact families: mothers tried to control by being restrictive and giving commands; fathers tended to be permissive and indulgent. Parents made fewer maturity demands on their children, communicated less well with them, and showed less affection. Boys suffered more from poor parenting than did girls, suggesting that the effects of divorce are more severe and enduring for them.

For their part the children were likely to oppose their mothers and comply with their fathers. Boys were oppositional and aggressive, girls whining and complaining. The harassed mother had to deal with children who nagged and whined, were dependent one minute and ignored her the next. As with the parents, the first year after the divorce was the most difficult for the children and was followed by gradual improvement. On the other hand, one-third of the child's life was spent in mastering the problems involved in divorce. The overall picture is surely a far cry from the image of "creative divorce."

Middle Childhood

One of the most extensive studies involving 131 children from sixty divorced parents was conducted by Kelly and Wallerstein (Kelly and Wallerstein, 1976; Wallerstein and Kelly, 1976), who found children behaved differently depending on their age. The 7- and 8-year-olds reacted with pervasive sadness and were unable to do anything to relieve it. Boys in particular cried a good deal, were worried about their future, and missed their fathers. One-fourth of the children felt pressured to align with one parent, while bitter fighting between parents served to aggravate their conflict of loyalties.

As compared with the younger group, the 9- to 10-year-olds were better defended on the one hand and also better able to express their anger toward the parents on the other. They could seek support from others, deny or evade their troublesome feelings, or divert themselves with constructive activities. While there was an increase in demanding, aggressive behavior, the older children also felt lonely in reaction to their parents' preoccupation with their own problems. Equally pressured to align with one parent against the other, the children usually were able to resist. There was also a decline in schoolwork, which was corrected in four of the fifteen children in a year's time.

The children were followed up twelve to eighteen months later. Of those available, about half had returned to their predivorced level of functioning or had even reached a higher level. Eighteen were still struggling with the negative postdivorce reactions, while six were significantly worse.

Not all studies agree with Kelly and Wallerstein's findings (Rohrlich et al., 1977), but this is to be expected in the preliminary stages of inquiry.

Adolescence

Wallerstein and Kelly (1974) studied twenty-one children over the age of 13, the small number partially reflecting the fact that divorce is relatively rare in this period. All adolescents experienced a painful sense of betrayal, a feeling of loss and anger, along with loyalty conflicts. They were also concerned about the success of their own future marriages and about financial security. Their primary defense was distancing themselves from the family by increasing social activities and avoiding home. The protective maneuvers apparently were successful, since at a later date almost all were able to be supportive of and empathetic with their parents. Part of their healthy adjustment was the adoption of a realistic orientation toward the future.

While there were some pathological reactions, these occurred in the context of deviant family patterns prior to the divorce—an openly seductive mother who became excessively overprotective, jealous, and preoccupied with her boy's health after the divorce, for example. Both the aggressive acting out and the pseudomaturity noted in middle childhood were also found among adolescents.

Summary

The data, while limited, offer a rich descriptive picture of the nature of divorce and the child's reactions to it at different developmental stages. Hetherington et al. alert us to the multiple sources of stress, thereby placing divorce in its proper intra- and interpersonal context. The degree of disturbance seems to be a function of the general level of psychological health in the parents and in the child, while a certain number of children can either cope with the divorce without significant regression or even find it a growth-promoting experience. For the majority, however, divorce produces intense distress, depression, and anger. Subsequent regressive behavior is what one would expect at different ages: preschoolers lose control of bodily functions, while in middle childhood peer relations and schoolwork suffer.

The child's perception of the divorce changes. Rohrlich et al. claim that preschooler's egocentrism leads them to feel responsible for the divorce; unable to comprehend the true reasons for parental disharmony, preoperational children tend to view themselves as the cause of events in the external world. In early latency, children feel they must be loyal to one parent, while later they feel more ashamed and angry. Adolescents have the ability to detach themselves and appreciate the problems their parents have as individuals. Finally, there are changes in self-concerns, the school-age child worrying, Who will take care of me in the future? the adolescent worrying, How will this affect my ability to take care of my own marital and financial future?

The limited data make other generalizations chancy. The relation between age and length of disturbance is uncertain. McDermott reports recovery in preschoolers within two to three months, while Hetherington et al. report major behavioral disruptions throughout the first years, a finding more in keeping with Kelly and Wallerstein's study of middle childhood. In all probability, the length of the recovery period will turn out to be some combination of age, general level of adjustment, and degree of stress involved in the divorce itself. The finding that adolescents take divorce in stride better than other age groups is particularly interesting if verified by further research. Unlike younger children, becoming independent of the parents is a major goal for adolescents. While divorce forces them to face the problems of independence prematurely, the image of themselves as no longer being guided and loved by parents is a congruent rather than a terrifying one, as it has been previously.

COMPARISON OF LOSS BY DEATH AND DIVORCE

The studies cited thus far have indicated that, in regard to general adjustment, both bereavement and divorce were equally deleterious. However, more intensive studies suggest that the two kinds of losses may have qualitatively different consequences.

Felner, Stolberg, and Cowen (1975), in a study of school-age children, found that while both groups were significantly more disturbed than a control group, separation and divorce produced more acting-out symptoms such as restlessness, impulsivity, and obstinancy, while parental death produced more moody, withdrawn, unhappy symptoms. Hetherington (1972) found that while both groups of adolescent girls had heterosexual problems when compared with subjects from intact families, adolescent girls whose fathers had died were excessively shy and uncomfortable around males, while adolescent girls whose parents were divorced were inappropriately assertive or promiscuous. Subsequently, the daughters of divorcees married younger than daughters of widows; their husbands were immature, impulsive, and self-centered; the marriage tended to be unstable; and their general attitude was characterized as "Men are no damned good." Daughters of widows, by contrast, had an idealized image of men and married later to men who were self-controlled, nurturant, ambitious, and highly conventional to the point of being "extremely straight" (Hetherington and Parke, 1979).

Hetherington's research is an example of the *naturalistic tradition,* implemented by *objective procedures.* In essence, she utilized an "experiment in nature" by locating three groups of twenty-four adolescent girls: the first from families in which the father was absent because of divorce; the second in which the father had died; and the third group from intact families served as a control. She matched the groups for socioeconomic status (lower- and lower-middle class), race (white), ordinal position and siblings (firstborns with no male siblings). In the first two groups there were no other males living in the home. The matching helped eliminate the influence of confounding variables, including the one of having a father substitute or a brother in the home, both of whom might significantly affect the girls' attitudes and behavior toward males.

Two of the measures involved observation of ongoing behavior, one during a dance held at a recreational center, the other during an interview in the psychological laboratory. Observers were trained to observe and record the frequency of certain target behaviors during a 30-second or a 1-minute observational unit. Their reliability was calculated in terms of percentage of agreement as to the occurrence of specific behaviors. At the dance, for example, the inhibited daughters of widows were observed to remain in the cluster of girls on the dance floor, some spending over 90 percent of the evening hiding in the ladies' room. The assertive daughters of divorcees by contrast, spent time at the boys' end of the hall and asked male peers to dance. In the interview situation, the girls' nonverbal behavior was observed through a one-way mirror. Daughters of widows seated themselves at the most distant chair from the male interviewer, had little eye contact and a constricted body posture, with arms tensely folded and legs crossed, while daughters of divorcees sat close to the male interviewer, looked at him, and assumed a sprawling, open-body position with legs and arms apart.

Both mother and daughter were interviewed for a variety of relevant topics; for example, the daughter was asked about feminine interests, security around male peers, and conflict with the mother, while the mothers were asked about child-rearing practices and attitudes toward their daughter and spouse. The interviews were tape-recorded and rated by two judges, and the interrater reliabilities were calculated. Among the findings: the mothers did not differ in child-rearing practices, being equally loving, consistent, and permissive; they were equally feminine, equally rewarding of their daughters' sex-appropriate behaviors, and had equally positive attitudes toward men in general. However, the divorcees were anxious and unhappy, hostile toward their spouses, and had negative memories of marriage, while widows had a positive attitude toward marriage and toward their lost husbands.

Finally, mothers and daughters were administered a number of standardized tests assessing general personality, femininity, internal-external locus of control, and anxiety. The results were mainly negative, except that both groups of daughters without fathers felt more anxious than daughters from intact families.

Unlike Kanner, Hetherington did not rely on her own clinical eye but on objective techniques for gathering data. Her use of naturally occurring behavior was particularly ingenious, while her interpretation of the complex and multitudinous findings showed a high level of integrative ability. The picture of the two groups which she constructed from the many bits of data is both true to the statistical analyses and psychologically convincing.

It certainly seems reasonable to infer that loss by death and by divorce will have different consequences. Loss by death plays on feelings of guilt and lends itself to idealization of the lost parent. It generally occurs in the context of social sympathy and support. Divorce often is the climax of extreme parental disharmony and accusatory behavior; bitterness and disparagement are likely to continue afterward, aggravated by a lack of social support or even condemnation. The child sees the parents at their worst. Thus, there is neither parental love and discipline nor personal guilt to hold the child's resentment in check, while the parents serve as models of acting-out behavior.

LOSS OF INITIATIVE

Recently, interest in the etiology of depression has shifted from loss of love to helplessness and hopelessness—that overwhelming feeling that failure is inevitable, so effort is futile. In terms of our developmental model, helplessness represents initiative gone awry. Self-confident enterprise is replaced by a despairing image of the self as a failure or a "loser" to use Beck's term (Beck et al., 1963), along with a defeatist attitude toward anything new.

Just a reminder: we are no longer in the realm of being loved and being loveworthy; we are in the realm of competence, of being an effective agent. Being able to do things well is different from gaining parental approval for being a good boy or girl. As early as the first year of life there is evidence that controlling the physical and social environment is highly rewarding, and much of development itself can be viewed in terms of expanding areas of effective behavior. Feelings of being an effective agent are based on feedback from both the physical and the social environment. This feedback may be in terms of the toddler's successful attempt to reach a cookie by bringing a stool over to the kitchen counter, or it may be in terms of a coach saying "Good!" when a 10-year-old makes a basket. The implicit message is the same—"You are an effective agent"—and it is a powerful one.

How can such a powerful force be stifled and distorted into a view of the self as helpless?

By *poverty*, for one thing. Not that poverty is a homogeneous entity in which all people behave alike; there are diverse patterns of behavior among the poor and individual differences within those patterns. It is just that, among the very poor, there is a greater likelihood of finding a constellation of factors which discourage the development of initiative in the growing child. Early initiative flourishes in a physically and socially responsive environment. The overburdened, harassed caretaker concerned with the problems of subsistence in an overcrowded and disordered home has little time to provide either. Punishment may be administered haphazardly on the spur of the moment, leading the child to conclude that discipline is capricious. In school, there is the likelihood that positive efforts will be ignored and failures met with irritation and criticism; either overtly or covertly the message is that the child is stupid. The lives of adult models offer little hope that individual efforts will be rewarded; on the contrary, work is erratic and chances of advancement are infinitesimal. The families are not only vulnerable to job loss and financial stress but also to illness, desertion, divorce, and death. Thus, from infancy to adulthood, forces conspire to discourage initiative and inculcate an attitude of hopelessness. (For a more detailed discussion of the roots of apathy, helplessness, and ineffectuality, see Haggstrom, 1970. For a discussion of the effects of poverty on the child's self-concept from a learning-theory perspective, see E. J. Davis, 1972. For poignant anecdotal accounts of the hopelessness engendered by poverty, see Coles, 1971a, 1971b.)

Institutions can undermine initiative, as we have seen in our discussion of maternal deprivation. Again, this does not imply that all custodial institutions are the same. The sad fact, however, is that there are a number of custodial institutions whose meager staff is either too overworked or too disinterested to do anything but see that the children are dressed, fed, washed, and put to bed at the proper time. Activities are nonexistent, toys are locked away in the closet, even the television set is not turned on. Not only is there nothing to do, but docile compliance is also the only behavior which is rewarded. Exploration and play, along with resistance and defiance, are punished because they are disruptive. A complementary deterioration ensues; the motive to initiate activities declines along with the practice of the skills needed to implement them successfully. Both the desire and the ability are sacrificed.

Some of the most convincing documentation of the adverse effects of insensitive custodial care comes from research on mentally retarded children (Rosen, Clark, and Kivitz, 1977). One result of institutionalization is helplessness in handling demands beyond those of routine living. For example, one individual, while making an adequate social and vocational adjustment after being discharged, was totally incapable of meeting the special demands of moving to new quarters. In spite of having been given three months' notice, he made no effort to find new accommodations and at the last minute had to be rescued by a counselor from the institution. A somewhat different result is overdependence, in which the individual is always looking to others either to take care of him or to give him cues as to how he should act. In both helplessness and overdependence the loss of initiative is in excess of the realistic limitations of the individual's capabilities.

But a defeatist attitude is not limited to children in poverty settings; it can be engendered by *parental pressures* on children with adequate or superior abilities. Recall the "pace-setting" parent who fosters competence in the child—vital, involved, loving, always requiring that the child do his or her best but respecting the child's feelings and point of view. Substitute anger, irritation, coldness, or a derogatory attitude for warmth and respect, and you have the pushing parent of the failing child—a dyad so familiar to professional clinical child psychologists. "I drill him in spelling every night until I am blue in the face and again in the morning so I'm sure he knows every word. Then he goes and misses those very identical words on a test!" "I can't understand why he's so clumsy. I'm athletic, his brothers and sisters are athletic, and the whole family is athletic, and he can't hit a ball better than a 2-year-old. Sometimes I feel like digging a hole in the backyard and burying him alive." In some instances parental goals are unrealistically high in relation to ability (A mother called her daughter with an IQ of 120 "the dumb one" because her brother had an IQ of 146!); at times parental investments are tangential to the child's interests; and at times it is the sheer relentless pressure without compensating respect or praise that causes the child to balk. Incidentally, the parent's exasperation may unconsciously be reinforcing to the child and represent a way of retaliating against parents too powerful to oppose directly.

Clearly, many conditions—ranging from the realistic burdens of hard-core poverty to the insensitive pressuring of individual parents—can erode initiative. The child's world contracts rather than expands, self-reliance is replaced by the defeated self. While the damage may not be all-pervasive, the loss can affect significant areas of development.

However, H. E. Rie (1966) raises a searching question: In middle childhood, is the phenomenon of hopelessness and helplessness comparable to that seen in despondent adults? With adults, the negative evaluation represents the adults' passing harsh judgment upon themselves. It is also a generalized judgment: "I am worthless." And it is a judgment which extends indefinitely into time: "Nothing I do will ever be any good." Rie questions whether in middle childhood such a highly developed psychological pattern is possible. His point is well taken. Clinically, there is nothing in the literature on children comparable to the self-inflicted torture of a successful adult—say, a famous composer or an astronaut—who becomes mired in irrational hopelessness. And cognitively, the abilities to think in terms of generalities and realistically project into the future do not appear until adolescence.

There are some research data which indirectly support Rie's contentions. Judgments of self-worthiness become stable only around 10 to 11 years of age, and the discrepancy between the real image of the self and the ideal image ("Me as I am" versus "Me as I would like to be") increases between the fifth and eleventh grades. Along with the latter change goes a concomitant increase in guilt (Katz and Zigler, 1967). If self-esteem fluctuates in the early years of middle childhood, and if there is no great disparity between the actual and the ideal self, the conditions for generating a deeply felt and self-perpetuating sense of worthlessness do not appear to be favorable.

Once again we face the same problem as in the discussion of mourning, and the solution is the same. Clinical reports indicate that children's self-image is a depreciated one; they are not merely reacting to environmental judgments. In addition, their suffering is genuine. But, because the self is still developing, it lacks the autonomy, stability, and potency of the adult's. Thus their self-condemnation seems much more closely linked to reality than is the case with adults. Their negative evaluation may also be more specific, and certainly their projection into the future, where it exists, cannot carry the same weight of interminable hopelessness.

The points previously made about the status of self-control in middle childhood are now being made in terms of the status of self-evaluation. Self-evaluation, like autonomous self-control, is a developmental achievement. Only in middle childhood can the child conceptualize and symbolically represent the self, so that the self becomes an object of thought. Only in middle childhood can the child consciously pass judgment on that self in terms of adequacy of functioning and feel the pangs of self-condemnation. But the development is still in midstream compared with what it will be in adulthood. It is still more environmentally sensitive, more area-specific, and more tied to the present than it will eventually become.

Learned Helplessness

The laboratory has provided an interesting model for certain aspects of loss of initiative. (This presentation follows Seligman, 1975.) In one study a dog is strapped into a hammock and administered sixty-four electric shocks from which there is no escape. Twenty-four hours later he is put into a box and again shocked, except now he can escape by jumping over a barrier into an adjacent box. Dogs with no previous experience with inescapable shock quickly learn to jump the barrier to safety. However, approximately two-thirds of the dogs who had been shocked failed to escape. After an initial reaction of running around frantically they would lie down and whine, passively accepting the pain. The behavior is not limited to dogs: it has been found in cats, rats, fish, nonhuman primates, and people.

In all the studies subjects learn that noxious events occur independent of their own responses. Therefore, they no longer respond with an effort to avoid pain. Such nonresponsiveness is called *learned helplessness.* It has a complementary cognitive and motivational component. Cognitively, the individual learns that responding is futile, and this concomitantly reduces the motivation to respond. In terms of self-conceptualization, the individual is no longer an agent but the recipient of whatever pain happens to come along.

Seligman (1975, p. 104) draws a number of interesting parallels between extremes of learned helplessness and certain aspects of depression. The parallel between learned helplessness and the depressive sense of futility is obvious: powerlessness and helplessness are rooted in a perceived loss of control over gratification and relief from suffering. In both conditions there is a decline in the initiation of voluntary responses, seen in the depressives' motor sluggishness, their complaints concerning the difficulty in meeting even the routine demands of living, and the decline in the level of intellectual performance. There is a similar negative set in which individuals, no matter how capable, believe they are ineffectual, that they will continue to fail, and that they are losers. Recall that Beck et al. (1963) place this negative set at the heart of depression. In both conditions there is a diminution of sexual and aggressive behavior as well as a loss of appetite and weight.

There is some evidence that learned helplessness is a developmental phenomenon, being rarely found in kindergarten children and increasing at least up to the fifth grade (Rholes, Blackwell, Jordan, and Walters, 1980). Especially relevant to our interest in depression is the finding that only in fifth-graders does it begin to affect the child's mood. Investigators have speculated that one reason younger children are less susceptible to learned helplessness is that they do not view failure as implying stable limitations in their own ability to perform; for example, younger children do not relate their successes or failures to their ability to do a task, or if they do make the connection, it does not form the basis for a generalized expectation. Such findings and speculations are congruent with Rie's contention that self-judgments are still too unstable to generate a strong, pervasive conviction of worthlessness—or, in this instance, of helplessness.

Provocative as the concept is, many questions remain to be answered about learned helplessness. Certainly, giving up trying when one's efforts do not meet with success can be adaptive, just as the persistent exposure to punishment or pursuit of unrealistically high goals can be maladaptive. Learned helplessness falls somewhere between these two extremes, but little is known concerning the conditions which produce various adaptive and maladaptive variations in persistence and retreat.

In spite of some provocative data the developmental implications of learned helplessness have yet to be satisfactorily worked out and documented. In general it can be speculated that a nonresponsive or a capriciously, inconsistently responsive environment caters to its production—the neglected infant, the preschooler who is punished or loved according to the moods and whims of the parents, the school-age child whose best efforts are ignored or disparaged, the hard-core-poverty teenager who sees adults hired and fired for no discernible reason.

However, like many ideas derived from the laboratory, learned helplessness has the advantage of conceptual clarity, so that its proper explanatory range as well as its limitations can be delineated. Like all good concepts, it also unifies otherwise disparate behavioral phenomena. Finally, it has bridged the gap between clinical and laboratory research—a rare feat indeed. (For an extensive discussion of the concept, see "Learned Helplessness as a Model of Depression," special issue of the *Journal of Abnormal Psychology*, February 1978.)

Loss of Initiative as Psychopathology

Loss of initiative in middle childhood cannot be found in any of the accepted diagnostic categories of childhood psychopathology. Yet our developmental orientation requires that it be considered a psychopathology if it is sufficiently severe and chronic to block the progress in a major area of development—social, intellectual, scholastic, or vocational. Clinically, it seems as ominous as the neuroses in terms of hampering growth.

Because we are interested in depression, we are dealing with one variety of loss of initiative—the painful awareness of the self-as-ineffectual. It is possible that children defend themselves against this pain just as they protect themselves from experiencing anxiety through neurotic symptoms. Thus, the clinical picture may be one of studied indifference or acting-out behavior or somatic complaints or some other protective maneuver.

Is a severe loss of initiative always accompanied by pain? This is not known. The pain of perceived ineffectuality in children has not been investigated. It is possible that children who have had little chance to develop a strong sense of the self as an agent can come to regard themselves as ineffectual. Extremes of poverty or discrimination may lead to an acceptance of educational, vocational, or status hopelessness, which can be passed from one generation to another. Such a culturally determined loss of initiative would still be regarded as pathological even if the children did not suffer.

In sum, while painful self-devaluation is an essential component of depression, an extreme loss of initiative per se is pathological, whether or not it is accompanied by such pain.

SUMMARY

From the beginning love and anguish are joined. One sign of infant attachment to the mother is an anxious protest as she leaves. Anaclitic depression is the pathologically extreme reaction when separation is prolonged and no adequate substitute care is provided. Certain infants are immune for some unknown reason, but many succumb. The behavioral hallmarks are agitation and anxiety followed by extreme withdrawal and despair. Anger is present but only fitfully.

The infant response to loss of the loved adult is global because infants are still relatively undifferentiated psychologically. Their needs are few—for pleasurable and interesting stimulation and for relief from distress—although such needs are consuming. Infants are also at the mercy of the environment, since they are neither sufficiently practiced nor versatile to satisfy their need for interesting activities, and they are totally incapable of relieving physiological distress. Cognitively, they are trapped in the present, knowing only, "I need my loved caretaker and she or he is not here." They cannot understand the multiple reasons for the absence or its temporal limits when such limits exist, such as "Mommy can see you in a week." One way they cope with despair is by denying the bond of love; the parent is treated as just another adult, so that the anguish of prolonged separation may be bypassed.

In middle childhood children still suffer from the loss of the beloved parent, but their reaction is no longer global, since they are more differentiated. The bond of love itself has been elaborated, the parent now being a source of approval and disapproval of good and bad behavior, an appreciative audience for acquired skills, a recipient of affectionate overtures, a guide to managing interpersonal problems. Children also have a varied set of meaningful relationships with others, peers in particular, but also distant relatives and extrafamilial adults. They are more practiced and resourceful in pursuing their own activities and have a repertoire of coping devices and defense mechanisms at their disposal. Cognitively, they can grasp the nature of concrete reality.

Because of such change, the child's depression has all the features of adult depression: affective (crying, loneliness, etc.); cognitive (negative self-evaluation); motivational (avoidance, decreased interest); physical (appetite and sleep disturbance). Yet the behaviors are not as self-sustaining, intense, and all-embracing as they are in adults. The child is more reactive to the immediate situation than are adults and thinks more in terms of the present; these developmental limitations serve as a protection to being engulfed by pervasive depression. (The same point will be made in chapter 7 in regard to neuroses in children and adults.)

Anger more often accompanies bond disruption than it did previously. At times, acting out seems a direct consequence of loss and the loosening of parental controls which accompany loss; at times, acting out may serve to divert the child from the pain of loss. It is possible that depression predominates over anger in the case of parental death, while in divorce the relationship is reversed.

Mourning is an adaptive reaction to parental death, since it allows the child gradually to assimilate the reality of irrevocable loss, thus paving the way for developing new bonds with other adults. Cognitively, the child can grasp the irreversibility and universality of death (which the preschooler regards as temporary) but lacks the autonomy to mourn as adults do. A particularly bitter reality is that the child, unlike the adult, is not free to seek a new love to replace the one which was lost, the tendency to idealize the dead parent making it doubly difficult to find a substitute. Often a sympathetic adult is needed to help the child express feelings, to assure him or her that existing needs will be met and the continuity of life maintained. Since a host of intrapersonal, interpersonal, and cultural conditions conspire to prevent mourning, the feelings are repressed and may show up in the form of acting out, lower achievement in school, and irritable, moody, babyish behavior.

The adolescent is sufficiently developed psychologically to experience depressed mood and the syndrome of depression as adults do. Parental death and divorce prematurely force the issue of independence, which is an important developmental task of the period, rather than threatening to shatter the security of home, which younger children believe to be indispensable. While pathological depression is relatively rare in adolescence, it is still ominous as a possible prelude to suicide. Here the cumulative stress of multiple recent losses plus an exhaustion of coping mechanisms lead to progressive withdrawal and finally attempts at self-destruction.

While loss of love is painful throughout development, its total impact, as well as its effects on future development, are a function of context factors. In general, intrapersonal resources and interpersonal support can allow the child to master its distress and resume development if not unscarred, at least without extensive psychological crippling.

There is surprisingly little evidence of long-term detrimental effects of parental loss by death or divorce, however. Failure to establish a bond of love in infancy seems more pathogenic than loss per se, the former tending to produce an affectionless psychopath, the latter having no clearly established pathological consequences in middle childhood. While there is some evidence of a relation between severe depression in adults and parental loss, it is tenuous at best. There is some continuity between depression in middle childhood and adolescence, but this relationship does not extend into adulthood. Parental death and divorce are somewhat more frequent in adolescents who attempt suicide than in a control group, but these are only two of many stresses which become unbearable. There is also some suggestion that parental death or divorce during early adolescence is related to increased emotional distress and physical illness in the adult but does not affect social and marital adjustment.

While the evidence concerning the long-term effects of parental loss is unsatisfactory, it does indicate that even an event as stressful as death or divorce is not the necessary and sufficient condition for producing psychopathological consequences. The context of the event must be included. Realizing this, we can begin studying the relevant context variables to determine which ones are supportive and tide the child over so that growth can continue and which ones increase distress, thereby impeding or distorting growth. Given the inevitability of death and the increasing frequency of divorce, such knowledge will be of immense value in helping the child successfully cope with the distress of loss of love.

Depression also involves a painful loss of self-reliance—the pain being the essential link with depression. The self is no longer regarded as an effective agent; on the contrary, it is viewed as helpless and hopeless. A possible precursor of helplessness might be the infant's desperate but futile attempts to cause the mother's return in the protest preceding anaclitic depression. Another precursor may be observed in the toddler, in whom lack of stimulation or insensitively timed stimulation has sapped the motivation to utilize acquired skills. However, an explicitly depreciated self-image is not possible until middle childhood. Only then is the child cognitively capable of viewing the self as an object and judging it as a failure. Such judgments may be on the basis of negative labels applied by parents or by society, and the subsequent self-condemnation can be keenly felt. However, it is not until adolescence that the child is sufficiently autonomous to generate this condemnation on his or her own, sufficiently advanced cognitively to apply the judgment to the self in general, and sufficiently aware of the realistic dimensions of time to project the negative image into an infinite future. In short, only now is a general attitude of helplessness and hopelessness possible.

The study of loss of self-reliance and the development of painful self-devaluation have languished, perhaps because they lack the humanistic appeal of loss of love, perhaps because they figure only incidentally in the diagnoses of childhood psychopathology. In spite of such neglect, loss of initiative must play a central role in psychopathology conceptualized as a severe deviation from the course of normal development.

We will now shift our focus from loss to socialization. In the next chapter we shall see how the efforts of normal toddlers to establish their independence from socializing parents can go awry, as can the socializing parents' effort to teach toddlers to control their biological needs to eat and to urinate. This will be followed by a discussion of two psychopathological conditions in middle childhood: in the first, control becomes excessive and lays the groundwork for neurosis; and in the second, inadequate control produces antisocial acting out. The developmental model has alerted us to the fact that the shift from love to socialization is not an absolute one, since the two are interrelated; the discussion of psychopathology will amply illustrate the point.

6 ▪ The Toddler/Preschool Period: Psychopathologies of Initiative and Early Socialization

The toddler and preschool period is a time of increased expansiveness on the child's part and increased restrictions on the part of the socializing adults. It is natural that these two should go hand in hand: toddlers who are now physically able to explore vast new regions of the environment inadvertently damage valued household items and personal possessions, leave chaos in their wake, and occasionally endanger themselves. Unfettered initiative must be limited by "No" and "Don't." Socializing parents want to teach their toddlers control of unacceptable behavior, while the enterprising toddlers brazenly assert their autonomy. The ensuing battles are fought over the issue, Who is going to control whom? If all goes well, the toddlers will emerge as socialized preschoolers who can both control themselves and be assured of their autonomy. In short, they are both self-controlled and self-reliant.

In this chapter we will discuss certain pathological deviations from this normal development. While healthy toddlers literally and psychologically turn their back on the mother, a few are terrified of autonomy and react with a disturbance of psychotic proportions. Its specific name is *symbiotic psychosis.* On the other hand, the healthy need for self-assertion evidenced in oppositional behavior can be carried to an *extreme of negativism,* which disrupts relations with caretaking adults, while blocking the child's own growth.

While the requirements for self-control affect many aspects of the toddler's life, they are keenly felt when they intrude upon bodily functions. The young child lives close to his or her body, eating and elimination holding special pleasures and special fascinations. The socializing parents' demands can, therefore, trigger some of the most intense conflicts of early childhood. Such disturbances are sometimes referred to as habit disorders. We shall discuss two such disturbances—*eating disturbances* and *enuresis*—together with *obesity* and *anorexia nervosa,* which represent pathological indulgence in and avoidance of eating.

One final reminder: preschoolers are still in the process of learning and internalizing prohibitions. They are externally oriented, being cognitively and affectively bound to the immediate situation. Thus, their conflicts, angers, and fears are directly reactive to parental behavior. It is not until middle childhood that prohibitions become sufficiently internalized that children can be at odds with themselves and can punish themselves with anxiety and guilt for behavior which they themselves judge as bad. When this happens, neurotic disturbances make their appearance.

SYMBIOTIC PSYCHOSIS

Symbiotic psychosis was first described by Mahler (1952, 1965, 1972), who is still the principal authority on the subject. The term *symbiosis* comes from biology and means the mutual sustaining relation between two different organisms. It aptly describes the healthy mother–infant relationship as the bond of love—or, to use the psychoanalytic terminology, as an object relation—is being formed. Recall that initially the infant is not capable of distinguishing "me" from "not-me," so there is a fusion between the self and the mother; only toward the end of the first year is the mother's independent existence grasped. True to her psychoanalytic orientation, Mahler regards symbiosis, in which the mother sensitively cares for the infant and the infant utilizes the mother to structure his or her rapidly developing ego, as the bedrock foundation of healthy development. Consequently, when symbiosis fails to develop normally, the infant is vulnerable to severe psychological disturbances.

Mahler's thesis has its counterpart in objective studies of mother–infant interaction. Sensitively cared for infants are both emotionally secure and secure in their exploration of the environment. They also relinquish crying in favor of vocalizations that are the prelude to speech. Moreover the mother's responsiveness to their signals greatly enhances their feeling of controlling the environment through their behavior. Thus, infants gain the confidence, the experience, and the techniques for mastering the challenges in the toddler period ahead. In Mahler's terms, their fragile ego is strengthened by the mother's sensitive care (see Ainsworth, 1973).

Failure of symbiosis may be due to the mother's being depressed, inconsistent, intrusive, and so on, various specific patterns of caretaking having the same adverse effect on the mother–infant relationship. But failure may also be due to the infant's intrinsically fragile ego. In this case, even good mothering cannot strengthen the ego to the point of coping successfully with the challenges of the toddler and preschooler period. Mahler notes that the infant's fragile ego may go undetected, but there may also be telltale signs, such as the boy who gives up locomoting for months because he fell down when he first attempted walking.

Maturation, particularly of the motor apparatus, propels the toddler into the stage of development Mahler calls the *separation-indi-*

viduation phase. While the healthy toddler eagerly turns away from the mother in order to explore the environment alone, the vulnerable toddler reacts with extreme panic over routine separations, such as sickness, going to nursery school, or the birth of a sibling. There are also violent temper tantrums with shrieking, biting, and kicking, along with bizarre hallucinations and fragmented speech.

Mahler (1965) describes a typical case as follows: Steve had an uneventful infancy, but at 16 months of age, he became extremely anxious and had severe tantrums over even short separations from his mother. He was distressed night and day, imploring his mother not to leave, moaning pitifully. However, if the mother tried to take him in her arms, he would push her away vigorously. When he was brought to the clinic at 3½ years of age, he was clinging to his mother and shrieking in distress. He would alternately "melt into the mother's body" and then arch his back in an attempt to break away from her embrace. His speech was fragmented, at times echolalic, at times consisting of phrases from television advertisements. However, there was some appropriate behavior, such as saying hello to the new doctor.

Steve's mother was relentlessly intrusive: she directed his every activity, tickled him, kneeled over him when he lay on the floor, and talked to him incessantly. She lied to him, for example, telling him he could not go out of the office because the door was stuck shut. She stifled individuation by a total disregard for Steve's need to seek gratifications and experience frustrations on his own. In our terminology, she completely undermined his initiative.

While the core problem differs in autism and symbiosis—the former involves a fear of human contact and the latter a fear of separation-individuation—clinical histories of psychotic children reveal an overlap of the two conditions. Autistic withdrawal may precede the symbiotic picture in certain instances, while in others the symbiotic panic may produce a secondary autistic defensive organization involving mutism and a shutting out of the human environment (Mahler and Furer, 1968). As often happens, "classical" and "pure" cases help orient the clinician both descriptively and theoretically, while in actual practice children present a mixed picture, the nature of development itself making such complexity inevitable.

Mahler interprets the alternations between craving and resisting body contact as expressions of the child's desire to reestablish the original fusion of the symbiotic period and the consequent fear of losing the self completely if this were to happen. This ambivalence is the core problem. Along with remnants of appropriate speech, it also distinguishes "pure" cases of symbiotic psychosis from autism, where object relationships and appropriate speech patterns have never been established.

Symbiotic psychosis has not been sufficiently studied to trace its developmental course. Mahler (1972) describes a group of preadolescents who had received prolonged psychotherapy since early childhood. They were sufficiently recovered so that they could carry on age-appropriate life activities, although they were still struggling with severe neurotic or borderline psychotic problems. The type of therapy they received derived from Mahler's etiological theory. The therapist was a warm, supportive mother figure who gradually helped the child master the challenges of self-reliant living. The fact that the availability of such a mother figure was still indispensable to the children's functioning suggests that the basic problem of individuation was never resolved and a vulnerability to regression remained.

NEGATIVISM

Negativism has been as neglected in the clinical literature as in the literature on normal development. There are descriptive accounts of the forms negativism takes and some discussion of psychotherapy, but the questions which concern us most are rarely raised, much less adequately answered: Under what conditions does normal negativism become pathological? What developmental forces are responsible for the changes negativism undergoes? How does pathological negativism at one time affect subsequent development? Consequently, we have to deal in hints and speculations, clinical impressions and meager data. (This presentation will rely heavily on the classical article in the field by Levy, 1955. More recently, Anthony and Gilpin, 1976, devoted a series of chapters to the oppositional character. Material from these chapters will also be used.)

In extensiveness, pathological negativism can range from focal opposition expressed in a single symptom to a generalized oppositional character disorder. It also spans the developmental periods from toddlerhood through adolescence. Levy, for example, writes about therapy with negativistic 2-year-olds, while other clinicians describe it in middle childhood and especially in adolescence.

Development

While the manifestations of negativism have not been treated developmentally, the descriptions from Levy and Anthony can be arranged in a meaningful sequence. The *toddlers* Levy describes were resisting the mother's efforts to socialize eating and elimination. Even at this tender age they showed great versatility in their techniques. Some were manifestly willful. "I *should* move my bowels but I *won't*," as one toddler put it; or, from the exasperated mother's point of view, "I can't talk him out of anything; no matter what I do he persists in having his own way." But direct confrontations can be alloyed with passive maneuvers; food refusals can become pickiness or dawdling. Finally, there are purely passive techniques, such as mutism or pretending not to hear or to understand parental instructions or directions.

In *middle childhood* school and friends play a special role in negativism, as would be expected from the developmental model. The toddler's "I won't" becomes "I won't learn" in middle childhood, resulting in underachievement or school failure. Often, in such cases, academic achievement is overly valued by parents, who set high standards for the child; school failure represents the child's revenge. Levy observes that such parents need not be coldly intellectual; they can be quite warm and child-centered. Note that now a social institution—the school—has become the arena for acting out problems originating in the home. However, it is also possible that certain teachers or methods of teaching or even pervasive school atmospheres may provoke negativism independent of the home situation.

As the group increases its hold in middle childhood and *adolescence*, negativism can take on what might be called a derived status. The child can oppose not because he or she balks at an adult's authority but because of group expectations. The child by this time is internalizing group standards, just as parental standards were previously internalized to form the conscience. Redl (1976) refers to the "invisible group" within the child, which might be sitting right under the therapist's couch and (like the early conscience) might be more demanding and difficult to deal with than the visible group. It is this invisible group which makes the child think, "What would the gang say if I gave in to an adult so readily? While I have nothing personally against this particular adult, how could I face the gang if they found out I gave in to 'the enemy' without a struggle? Better oppose and be safe."

In adolescence, or even in middle childhood, the law becomes the coercive force and law enforcers become the coercive adults, especially for children of lower socioeconomic status. For those who are labeled juvenile delinquents the court is now the arena for acting out negativistic encounters. However, because the law becomes the new opponent, this does not mean that the old ones fade away. A vivid picture of excessive negativism from every developmental level is presented by D. C. Ross (1964) under the label of the "negatively organized child." A 15-year-old boy was brought to the clinic because he threatened to shoot his girlfriend's father after the father had forbidden her to see the boy. This was the climax of innumerable stormy oppositions to people in authority. At home no issue was too large or too small to become a battle of the wills—the tie he wore, the food he ate, the music he enjoyed, his disorderly clothes closet, his poor dental hygiene, his choice of friends and leisure-time activities. His parents relentlessly nagged, exhorted, pleaded, and scolded, which only succeeded in exasperating the boy. In spite of superior intelligence, he was failing in school, probably in retaliation against his intellectually ambitious parents. Home life was unbearable, and he spent as little time at home as possible. Fortunately, he excelled in athletics and enjoyed working on a friend's farm where he could do as he pleased. Aside from this, his response to most of the demands placed upon him was a defiant "I won't."

Research on negativistic children is sparse and findings are preliminary. Gilpin and Worland (1976) compared 5- to 7-year-old and 10- to 12-year-old negativistic boys with a matched control group of clinical cases. All of the boys' parents came from a deprived, chaotic background. Aside from negativism there were few significant differences between the experimental and control groups: for the younger boys, acting-out symptoms, such as temper tantrums and physical aggression predominated, with poor school performance playing a secondary role; for the older boys, the reverse was true. The mothers of the younger, negativistic boys were significantly more controlling, masculine, and aggressive than were the mothers in the control group. In addition they liked mischievous, tough boys who acted out, and they were argumentative with their sons. The fathers interacted with the younger, negativistic boys primarily in terms of discipline. Both parents agreed that it was "bad" for a child to be autonomous. Perhaps because the mother was such a strong figure and the father so distant, the younger boys perceived little difference in parental roles. In the older group of boys, there was no significant difference in maternal behavior in the experimental and control groups. However, the fathers were significantly more passive ("I get along with my boy because I give in to him.") and identified with their sons to a significantly greater degree ("He tells white lies, but that's normal. I do too."). They also related to their sons primarily in terms of discipline.

These tentative findings suggest that when negativism is one element in a psychopathological picture, parents play different roles at different ages, the mother being more important in early childhood, the father later. It also suggests that negativism in boys may result from a combination of strong control plus active or passive condoning of negativistic behavior—the aggressive mother liking a scrapper, the disciplining father extenuating or giving tacit consent to his son's oppositional behavior.

At a more molecular level, Forehand and his colleagues have undertaken an extensive research program concerned with the nature and elimination of negativism, or what they call noncompliant behavior. (For a summary of their findings, see A. O. Ross, 1981.) Since their research has utilized the behavioral model, they have concentrated on the conditions which elicit and maintain noncompliance in a clinical population. They found that noncompliant behavior is maintained by parental attention, which serves as a reinforcer even though such attention often takes the form of anger and punitiveness. Our preference is for interpreting their findings in terms of reinforcement of initiative. Toddlers are quite capable of learning that certain behaviors will uniformly exasperate or infuriate their parents, their control of parental reactions becoming more gratifying than the psychological and physical punishment they must endure in the process.

Even more interesting are Forehand's findings concerning the types of parental commands which are apt to elicit noncompliance. His so-called alpha commands are specific and clear. They include commands which have a clearly designated, explicitly stated objective, questions which involve a motoric response, and instructions to stop an ongoing behavior or not to begin a behavior which is about to take place. The so-called beta commands are vague and interrupted. They are difficult or impossible to obey, either because of their ambiguity or because the parent issues a new command before the child has a chance to comply. Beta commands are more characteristic of parents of noncompliant children than are alpha commands.

Forehand's research has primarily been with preschool and early school-age children and has added significantly to our understanding of the parental role in eliciting and maintaining negativistic behavior. Furthermore, these insights have been utilized by Forehand as the basis of his therapeutic program, which is discussed later.

Nature of Psychopathological Negativism

Negativism is part of the normal development of the self-as-agent. Levy (1955) adds that it protects the child against submissiveness; for example, when he asked a negativistic boy, "What would happen if you gave in to your mother just once?" the boy replied that the mother would make him do everything her way and would never let him do anything on his own. Thus, negativism can both enhance and protect the autonomy of the self.

While not originally aggressive, negativism can subsequently be used as a safer form of aggression than angry outbursts and direct attack either by children who are submissive and fearful or by children having to deal with strongly authoritarian adults. The passive forms of negativism, such as dawdling, pretending not to hear, mutism, and inattention, are favored by these children.

Finally, both Levy and Anthony concur in regarding authoritarian demands as one of the principal causes of pathological negativism. Such demands are multiform—for affection, achievement, neatness, self-control, cleanliness. As we have just seen, parents may also consciously or unconsciously reward, condone, or identify with the child's negativistic behavior.

The literature lacks a full-dressed discussion of the difference between normal and pathological negativism. While Anthony purposely evades an answer, Levy briefly distinguishes the two in terms of the excessiveness of the reaction—psychopathology is an exaggeration of normal behavior. Exaggeration, in turn, consists of intensity, pervasiveness, and persistence. Equally important, such exaggeration tends to block future development. Thus, Levy writes of the rigidity of personality and of the social isolation resulting from pathological negativism, both of which cut the child off from growth-promoting experiences with socializing adults and peers.

Note that psychopathology as exaggeration is not the same as psychopathology as age-inappropriate behavior. While psychopathological negativism may be age-inappropriate (for example, when an 8-year-old "acts like a 2-year-old"), it is also found both in the toddler and adolescent period, where negativism is age-appropriate. Consequently, the clinical child psychologist's job of distinguishing normal from pathological negativism in these two periods is a particularly difficult one.

Treatment

In the past, the treatment of negativism has been neglected. Predictably, psychodynamically oriented therapists prefer to explore the child's conscious and unconscious feelings toward family members, while atheoretical practitioners follow the commonsense advice of telling parents not to nag and coax, and to avoid being dictatorial, overprotective, overcorrecting and putting the child into a "give in or lose" situation (Bakwin and Bakwin, 1972).

Recently, however, Forehand and other behaviorally oriented therapists (Ross, 1981) have begun a systematic exploration of techniques designed to reduce excessive noncompliance. In order to alter both the elicitors and reinforcers, parents are taught to replace their vague, interrupted beta commands with specific alpha ones, to shift from punishing noncompliant behavior to rewarding compliance with praise, approval, and positive physical attention, and to employ a "time-out" procedure of isolating the child for a brief period after noncompliance. It is also helpful to teach parents the general principles of operant learning rather than providing them solely with techniques for handling specific problems. While the successes in the home do not generalize to the school, they do affect other behaviors within the home; for example, one girl who was reinforced for picking up her toys spontaneously began to keep her clothes tidy. Moreover, there is evidence that the compliance of untreated siblings undergoes the same positive change, since the mother alters her behavior to them as well.

REVIEW

Let us review symbiotic psychosis and negativism in terms of the models of deviant-development. Symbiotic psychosis is an example of age-inappropriate behavior. The toddler or preschooler who may have been developing with no signs of serious disturbance reexperiences separation anguish with the overwhelming intensity which marks its initial appearance in infancy. Negativism is an exaggeration of an age-appropriate behavior which blocks progress in important areas of development. While it may be inappropriate to a given age, it need not be. In symbiotic psychosis the toddler or preschooler regresses to the separation anguish of the infantile period; negativism represents a regression only when it is age-inappropriate. In symbiotic psychosis there is a failure of development (of normal symbiosis), and in negativism there is an exaggeration of normal development, both of which result in fixations.

In regard to the deviant development of initiative, symbiotic psychosis represents a basic undermining of self-reliant expansion, as the toddler or preschooler is trapped between the double terrors of independence from and closeness to the mother. Just as in the case of autism and childhood schizophrenia, the child is devastated because the basic foundations of normal development have been destroyed. Negativism is quite different, since normal development takes place but in an exaggerated form. However, why the exaggeration occurs is unclear: such children may be normally autonomous but are forced to protect themselves against intrusive, demanding parents; or they may be protecting their fragile autonomy from further erosion; or they may have an inflated sense of autonomy because their parents have encouraged and condoned it. Or—as so often happens—all three explanations may be valid.

FEEDING PROBLEMS

YOU KNOW, I WAS 32 YEARS OLD BEFORE it dawned on me that I didn't have to eat everything on my plate! I was alone in a restaurant, staring at a pile of turkey and dressing with gloppy brown gravy wondering how in heaven's name I was going to get all that food into my stomach. Then it hit me. This is just a lot of damned foolishness. I've been a good girl long enough. Now it's time to grow up.

On a more serious note, a young bachelor underwent psychoanalysis because of a number of fears, one being panic when eating out with a woman. He could tolerate business lunches but only felt really safe when cooking his meals and eating alone in his apartment. During therapy the following repressed material was uncovered:

MY MOTHER SAT AT THE HEAD OF THE table and served the family. (His father had died when he was 5 years old.) I remember that she would say to me, "Tell me when I've given you enough potatoes or peas," or something. But when I said, "That's fine," she would always take just a little more and plop it on my plate. It would make me furious, but I never could say anything to her.

He also reported the following dream:

MOTHER AND I WERE SITTING ON A PIER overlooking a marina of some sort and she was sewing. Suddenly, she put the needle through my eyelid and pulled it closed with the thread. I didn't dare move because that would tear my eyelid off. When I woke up I still felt terrified.

We will return to this young man's memory and his dream after discussing early eating disorders.

As adults, most of us would not regard eating as the emotional high-point of the day. It has its minor irritations and pleasures, which are quickly forgotten. Consequently, we tend to underestimate the significance of hunger and feeding in the life of the infant and toddler. We need the psychoanalysts to remind us of the importance of eating and of the interplay among somatic, psychic, and intimate interpersonal relations which it engenders. Physiological distress and relief from such distress are the most highly charged experiences of early infancy. The first ego, so the psychoanalysts maintain, is a body ego: the first dim notion of the self as good or bad depends upon the ratio of bodily pleasures to bodily distress. Likewise, the first view of intimacy as pleasurable and trustworthy or noxious and untrustworthy depends on the sensitivity and reliability of relieving physiological distress and maximizing physiological pleasures.

The Infantile Period

Now let us focus specifically on eating, using Anna Freud (1965) as a guide to our conceptualization. One of the earliest conflicts between the infant and the socializing caretaker centers on feeding. In the 1920s and 1930s, C. M. Davis (1929, 1935) conducted a series of studies to determine what infants would do if given complete freedom to choose the kind and quantity of nourishment they wished. One-week-old infants could choose among four formulas and orange juice throughout the nursing period, while 6-month-olds were presented with a wide variety of foods for periods of six months to a year. The results were both enlightening and amusing. All the children were healthy and well-nourished at the end of the study and there were no digestive disorders owing to the self-selection of food. However, there was a wide variation in the quantity eaten, including unpredictable food jags—three to four bananas at one meal, five to seven servings of potatoes, a full quart of milk in addition to a complete meal! Thus, infants "naturally" have strong but shifting food preferences and vary widely in the amount needed to satisfy them at any given feeding. Such variability is a far cry from the adult caretaker's concern that the infant eat a given quantity of food which contains a balanced diet. The erratic nature of the infant's hunger also conflicts with the adult's need for regularity and intrudes on the adult's realistic commitments to activities other than feeding. A certain amount of disharmony between infant and caretaker is inevitable and, Anna Freud notes, normal. If the mother is reasonably sensitive and flexible and the infant reasonably tractable and resilient, they manage to accommodate one another.

But many things can go wrong. The mother may be insensitive, depressed, inconsistent, neglectful, burdened by realistic problems; temperamentally the infant may be erratic, hypersensitive to distress, difficult to divert, or may transmit behavioral signals that are weak, undifferentiated, and difficult to read. Consequently, infants are frequently in a high state of distress. Note that, at this stage, infants react directly to the mother as her behavior impinges upon them, since they have not yet evolved a mental representation which can be sustained in her absence. Note also that their reactions to distress are primitive—crying, vomiting, unmodulated rage, refusal to eat, apathetic withdrawal—since the more sophisticated defenses and socially attuned coping devices have yet to develop.

The Toddler Period

This is a more relevant period than infancy, since an object relationship has been established and initiative is running high. Again, Anna Freud points to normal conflicts, such as the battle of the spoon in which toddlers insist on feeding themselves and the battle of wills over the amount and kind of food they will eat, and the manner in which they will eat it. As in the infantile period, psychopathology consists of extreme versions of normal confrontations, this time between the willful toddler and the socializing caretaker. The following quotations from mothers who have brought their toddlers to a child guidance clinic illustrate just how intense these confrontations can become:

> I'VE TRIED EVERYTHING. I WATCH TO SEE what he likes so I can give it to him next time, but next time he don't like it. I promise, "If you be good and eat, I'll get you a real puppy-dog all your own." But that don't work. Sometimes I get mad and say, "Damnit, you're gonna eat if I have to cram it down your throat." Then, sometimes I figure, "If he eats, he eats;

if he don't, he starves. I can't be bothered no more." But nothing works. It's picky, picky here and picky, picky there until I think I'm going out of my mind.

She won't eat nothing but sweets all the time. You know and I know that's no good. It's going to rot her teeth for sure when she gets her full set and she's going to be fat all over. One day I forced her to eat her hamburger and potatoes and she just vomited it back up. I never saw a child that stubborn. Like a mule.

Kanner (1977) estimates that a quarter of all toddlers and preschoolers have feeding difficulties. He believes the majority of problems are caused by parents who rigidly try to force the "correct diet" on the toddler or who are obsessively and coercively overprotective. Toddlers, in turn, may respond in a number of ways. At the most primitive level, they may gag and vomit or complain of stomachaches; at a more sophisticated level they may dawdle or become picky eaters; the more manipulative ones use eating to monopolize the parent's attention and dominate them, say by insisting on certain foods prepared in a given way, or by intentionally provoking and upsetting the parents.

Kanner maintains that, for therapy to be effective, the caretaker's attitude must change from one of concern with what the child is eating to concern for the child who is eating. Specific techniques such as rewarding desirable and ignoring undesirable behavior will not work because the toddler will perpetuate the battle. While the behavior therapists may well challenge his recommendations, Kanner's observation that the toddler will continue provocations on his or her own points to a significant advance over the infantile period. Not only is the toddler differentiated from the mother but he is also aware of her vulnerabilities, and can intentionally set about to defy, subvert, and upset her. Such social sensitivity and intentional behavior is in striking contrast to the infant's primitive repertoire of reactions. The confrontation is still between caretaker and child; it is the technique for managing the confrontation which has changed.

However, the toddler has not developed to the point of internalizing the requirements of socialization so that the requirements become self-perpetuating, as in the case of the 32-year-old woman and the young bachelor, whose eating problems introduced our discussion. Let us take a second look at these vignettes in light of what we have learned.

In the first vignette, the mother's mandate, "Eat everything on your plate," created anxiety and guilt over disobedience so strong that it resisted critical evaluation until adulthood. Yet the conflict between doing what she wanted or obeying her mother was readily available to the woman's consciousness, and the price paid for obedience was relatively minor. The young man faced a more serious dilemma. His rage is understandable. On the one hand, the mother implicitly said, "You are the decision maker; I will do what you say," but then she added, "What you decide does not matter; the ultimate power is mine." He felt betrayed. But why did he not protest? For fear of losing the mother's love symbolized, so the psychoanalysts would claim, by food. As his dream indicated, any attempt to break away from the mother's control would be self-destructive. There is both a binding and a blinding—he could not face the mother's subversive control, and he could not break away and become independent of her. The impasse continued into adulthood, where the demands for independence reactivated it and its attendant anxiety. We also can see that the young man's anxiety involved both kinds of eating problems we have discussed—the conflict over autonomy in the toddler period and the infantile equating of being fed with being cared for and protected against the terror of isolation and helplessness.

The two examples also teach us something about the developmental model of psychopathology. Eating disturbances may represent exaggerations of developmentally normal disharmonies between caretaker and child, as Anna Freud claims. Subsequent experience may undo the damage they cause, they may persist but only cause minor discomforts, or they can serve as the nucleus of a crippling anxiety. What determines the difference between these outcomes will be discussed in chapter 7 on neurosis.

Developmental Consequences

Objective data on developmental consequences of feeding disturbances are meager. Heinstein (1963) found a relation between feeding practices and maternal warmth in infancy and problem behaviors such as disturbing dreams, finicky eating, and nail-biting between 6 and 12 years of age; boys who were nursed for a long period by a cold mother were the most maladjusted children in the group. In general, personality damage seemed to occur when the intimacy of feeding was combined with coldness, oversolicitousness, or hostility.

In the realm of normal development, the Berkeley Growth Study (MacFarlane, Allen, and Honzik, 1954) uncovered two peak ages for food finickiness: between the first and sixth year of life, when 30 to 40 percent of the children evidenced the problem, and again around 12 years of age, when it was evidenced by approximately 20 percent of the children. In the early years, the finicky eaters came from disharmonious homes in which conflict and tension between parents were high. However, it was not related to a variety of personality variables. In 12-year-old boys finicky eating, by contrast, was related to irritability, overdependence, attention demanding, temper tantrums, lying, and poor appetite; in girls finicky eating was only related to insufficient appetite. The authors speculate that the 12-year-old boys are highly conflicted over their dependency upon the mother, wanting very much to break away and assert their masculinity but not being sufficiently secure to do so. Consequently, they vacillate between clinging and angry rejection. At a more general level, the study indicates significant sex differences in intrapersonal variables, and more important, it suggests that the same behavior problem might have different meanings depending on the developmental status of the child. The latter implication will be explored in greater detail as we discuss obesity.

OBESITY

The study of obesity both expands and deepens our understanding of eating disturbances as a developmental deviation.

Bruch (1973), who has studied eating disorders extensively, writes that initially she was looking for the single etiological factor underlying obesity. The more children she studied, the more she realized that it has multiple causes. Obesity can be physiologically determined, in which case the child may be psychologically sound or may develop problems in response to parental or peer disparagement. Richardson et al. (1961), for example, found that 11- and 12-year-olds ranked obesity as the most undesirable physical handicap, even more so than facial disfigurement or crippling. Bruch delineates two kinds of psychogenic causes. The first is reactive obesity, in which the child eats excessively after experiencing a trauma such as the death of a parent. Such cases are rare in childhood and typically represent an attempt to ward off depression. Next, there is developmental obesity, which is intimately linked with the child's personality. This category is of greatest interest here.

Numerous specific problems are included within the category of developmental obesity. While Bruch does not do so, it is possible to order many of the problems developmentally. The symbolic meaning of food as love and autonomy in the infant and toddler period has already been discussed. In addition, food may symbolize the girl's wish to be a man and possess a penis, her wish to become pregnant, or her fear of pregnancy during the oedipal stage (if one holds to the psychosexual theory) or the preschooler's conflict over her sex-role identity (if one holds to the social-learning theory). Such problems may resurface in adolescence when eating may also serve as a substitute for sexual gratification and a way to avoid adult responsibilities. Other meanings of food seem to span the entire developmental age range: eating as an expression of rage and hatred or as a way of gaining a sense of power and self-aggrandizement.

We should also remember that while the meaning of eating is changing, the child is becoming more complex psychologically. The toddler's reactions to conflicts with the socializing adult are more socially sensitive, sustained, and intentional than the infant's. Continuing the trend, conflicts which could only occur in the context of a direct confrontation between socializer and toddler can eventually take place within the child; for example, the adolescent's fear of sex, which leads to overeating, may be of her own making rather than the result of a frightening sexual encounter.

We have here a concrete illustration of the point made earlier concerning deviant behavior. The same behavior—obesity—can have multiple causes: physiological, reactive, developmental. And, within the developmental category, the same behavior can have different meanings depending on when it occurs. Finally, the deviant behavior can vary in seriousness as a function of the age appropriateness of its underlying cause. A 6-year-old girl who becomes obese because she resents the power and status granted to boys is not as disturbed as a 6-year-old boy who becomes obese because he is terrified that his mother will leave him and he will be helpless. Now we begin to see why the clinical child psychologist's task of determining etiology is so difficult—and also why it is so important.

Why Obesity?

If a variety of developmental conflicts underlie obesity, why do certain children "choose" to overeat rather than evidencing other kinds of deviant behaviors? In attempting to answer this question, Bruch (1973) makes her most intriguing contribution to understanding deviant development.

To begin with, Bruch maintains that the infant is not born with a hunger drive that is experientially distinct from other states of physiological arousal. Consequently, hunger as a distinctive inner cue has to be learned. This is a novel hypothesis. By now Piaget has accustomed us to the idea that the infant must learn the nature of the physical and social environment. What we must consider seriously is the possibility that the infant must also learn to differentiate the internal environment of needs and affects.

How does such learning take place? In a way analogous to learning the external environment—more specifically, by feedback. The infant learns to differentiate a rattle from a string of beads because each responds differentially to exploratory behaviors such as shaking and mouthing. Analogously, the infant learns to differentiate inner drives and affects by the differential responses of the caretaker. The sensitive mother is constantly on the alert for specific cues from the infant so she can come to say, "That's his hungry cry," "She's just fussy and needs her nap," or "He's really mad." As she responds appropriately—now feeding, now soothing, now diverting—the infant comes to distinguish more clearly among inner states of arousal.

But suppose the mother interprets all distress as hunger. Perhaps she is overindulgent, perhaps she cannot tolerate negative affect, perhaps she is rejecting and pops a bottle into the baby's mouth in the hope that the infant will be quiet and quit bothering her. When verbal labeling enters the developmental picture, such mothers continue the pattern by responding to all signs of distress with, "Oh, he's just hungry." Consequently, the child will fail to differentiate inner states, so that a variety of needs and affects are regarded as hunger. Instead of being angry or bored or frightened or sexually aroused, the child feels hungry and eats. The self is likewise impoverished. Instead of learning, "I am a person who has a rich variety of sensations, needs, and affects," the infant learns, "I am a person who is hungry."

Another possibility—which Bruch does not stress—is that the infant's behavior is undifferentiated and difficult for the mother to "read." We know that infants differ in the degree to which cries and facial expressions and body gestures express their various inner states. Even attentive mothers may have difficulty decoding certain infants' vague and baffling signals.

But Bruch claims there is a further complication. As the self is impoverished, initiative suffers. By imposing her interpretations and insisting on them, the mother robs the child of the desire to explore and experiment independently. Bruch cites the case of a 14-year-old whose mother went down on her knees to tie his shoes during the interview, who answered all questions directed to him, and who hovered anxiously over him. While such children may well learn techniques for tyrannizing their mothers or the entire family, they feel helpless in meeting the developmental demands outside the family circle. Characteristically, they are sedentary, avoiding self-assertive, competitive, and aggressive activities which require motoric involvement. In fact, physical inactivity seems as important as food intake in contributing to obesity. The father also contributes to the child's difficulties, at times being passively subservient to his wife, at times demanding that the child look and act and achieve in accordance with the father's own standards. Thus, both parents in their own ways try to impose their own needs and images on the child.

In sum, a diffuse body- and self-awareness plus a crippled sense of effectiveness are the psychological conditions underlying developmental obesity.

The Adolescent Picture

Adolescence plays into the vulnerabilities occurring during the first few years of life. The self is closely identified with the body, peers are intolerant of physical or behavioral deviations, the sexual drive must be managed, and independence from the family must begin. It is as if adolescence conspired to confront the obese child with developmental tasks he or she is least equipped to master. But Bruch insists that the adolescent can take all such difficulties in stride if self-image and self-confidence have not been damaged. It is the feeling of body- and self-diffuseness and helplessness in the face of impulses and demands for autonomy that may be devastating, both in terms of weight gain and emotional well-being.

Data on the developmental consequences of obesity which take into account both the physical and psychological components are meager. In a follow-up study, Bruch found that 40 percent of the children with severe adjustment problems continued to have them as adults; around one-third of the children were making a satisfactory adjustment as adults, some having lost weight, others remaining obese. The common element in this group was warm, accepting parents and absence of persecution for being fat.

As far as prognostic signs in middle childhood, Bruch lists severe inactivity associated with social isolation or withdrawal in the child and a family life marked by anxiety and discord with parents who are overpowering and pressuring.

Expansion of the Developmental Model

Certain etiological factors in obesity are familiar by now, particularly the overwhelming of initiative by intrusive parents. But Bruch adds a new perceptual-cognitive component. As a consequence, obesity becomes a developmental failure due to misinformation conveyed by the mother to the infant/toddler. It is a cognitive infantilization, so to speak, in that caretaking adults perpetuate the undifferentiated perception of drives and affects which characterize infancy.

ANOREXIA NERVOSA

While anorexia nervosa is primarily (but not exclusively) found in adolescent females, opinions concerning its origins are so diverse that it could be discussed at any developmental stage. It is introduced here rather than in the chapters concerning adolescence because of a number of similarities with obesity. Its proper niche in the developmental scheme of things awaits more definitive data than are now available.

Etiological confusion has been virtually guaranteed by diagnostic confusion—the same label being applied to different behaviors. Anorexia means loss of appetite, and loss of appetite can occur in a number of normal and psychopathological conditions. It may be part of the transitory aestheticism of adolescence; it can result from a traumatic event (for example, a 10-year-old boy became disgusted by food after a man tried to force him to perform fellatio); the child may have a phobia about food or a compulsive food avoidance. Furthermore, as we have seen, loss of appetite is one of the marks of severe depression, and it can also stem from a schizophrenic delusion (for example, the food is being poisoned by germs released by secret Russian agents).

More important, "loss of appetite" fails to capture the essence of the psychopathology of anorexia nervosa, which is a voluntary restriction of food and an active pursuit of thinness, usually with pride in control over eating. As a result, there is at least a 20 percent loss of body weight without organic cause (Sours, 1969). The startling feature is that, unlike ordinary dieting, the individual wastes away to a dangerous state of emaciation in pursuit of some ideal image of thinness. Not only is health endangered, but anorexia nervosa is also one of the few psychopathologies which can lead to death; studies have reported a fatality rate of between 3 and 25 percent (Bemis, 1978). Typically, there is denial of hunger although there may be periods of bulimia ("eating jags") followed by self-induced vomiting. As the condition advances, diets become increasingly restrictive; one girl would eat only two chicken livers a day, another ate only celery sticks and chewing gum for a year before her death (Bruch, 1973).

Among the secondary symptoms of anorexia nervosa, excessive activity is one of the most common (Sours, 1969). At times the intensity of the activity is masked by its socially acceptable form, such as doing homework or participating in sports; but an activity such as running up and down the driveway until exhausted or literally walking around in circles may have a deviant quality. Amenorrhea is another common secondary symptom, menstruation often ceasing prior to weight loss.

Since anorexia nervosa is the result of voluntary actions, one would think it would be relatively easy to divert the adolescent from her health-endangering and even life-threatening course. If the adolescent "chooses" to become thin, why can she not "choose" to eat again? These typically bright, middle-class girls seem strangely indifferent to their fate and stubbornly resist efforts to help them. In order to solve this puzzle, we must examine the source of their baffling behavior.

Etiological Concepts

Since we now know that the psychological significance of eating changes, we should not be surprised that etiological hypotheses emphasize now one, now another of its developmentally determined meanings. These hypotheses also differ in emphasis, attributing the disorder to motivational factors in the child (her drives and affects) or control mechanisms (her ego and her self-concept).

One of the earliest hypotheses, within the psychoanalytic framework, regards anxiety about the sexual drive as a basic factor—a plausible notion in light of the absence or significant diminution of sexual activity both at the physiological and psychological levels. In this view, the specific symptom of food rejection is due to a reactivation of a misunderstanding of sexuality dating back to the oedipal period; namely, that women become pregnant by eating. The adolescent's avoidance of food, therefore, results from her unconscious fear of oral impregnation.

The hypothesis is developmentally sound and nicely accounts for food avoidance. As we have seen, curiosity about sex flourishes before the preschooler is capable of understanding its mature form. When told that a baby is growing inside a pregnant woman, the child assimilates this information in terms she can understand—the mother must have eaten something. (Likewise, birth is understood in terms of defecation since this is how something inside the body gets out.) This misunderstanding occurs even if given correct and detailed information and even if the child can perfectly repeat the lesson she has learned. As is generally true of cognitive development, the child assimilates new information in terms which are most meaningful; things get inside the body by eating! "Impregnation," "uterus," "embryo," and "delivery" are concepts which will not be truly understood for years to come.

In spite of its soundness, continued clinical study of anorectics revealed that the oral impregnation hypothesis applied only to a limited number of adolescents. Psychoanalysts began to theorize that the rejection of food stems from damage much earlier, at the *oral stage* of psychosexual development (see Sours, 1969, for a résumé). The initial caretaking of the infant is marred by insensitivity usually taking the form of intrusive overprotectiveness or excessive control. The result is a hostile dependent relationship in which the exploited child cannot express her rage because of the fear that the mother will leave her alone and helpless. Other theorists, both within and outside the psychoanalytic tradition emphasize the devastating effect the mother's behavior has on the child's ego and identity, her self-assurance and self-respect.

The damage during the infant/toddler period is perpetuated by ingrained patterns of interaction which prevent the school-age child from correcting or compensating for it. The characteristic picture, surprisingly, is of attentive, concerned parents of a model child who is obedient, dependable, and considerate at home, and a popular, high-achiever at school. When one examines the picture more closely, however, one sees that the child is living out a parental image of proper behavior which permeates every facet of her life—her physical appearance (thinness being especially valued), the food she eats, the clothes she wears, her friends, her activities. Any sign of resistance or self-assertion would result in painful self-recrimination. How could she go against the wishes of parents who are so obviously concerned about her welfare? Her own misery is either banished from consciousness or borne in silence.

Bruch (1973) adds that not only does the child feel that her life and her self are not her own, but even her body is not her own. Gaining or losing weight, sickness or health are viewed not in terms of bodily pleasures and pains but in terms of pleasing or displeasing parents. Eating, in particular, has nothing to do with personal enjoyment but has everything to do with parental preferences and values.

Adolescence, with its heightened sexual drive and its mandate to establish an independent identity, is shattering to the anorectic, as it is to the obese child. She becomes increasingly preoccupied with restricting food intake and pursuing the unattainable goal of thinness. However, theorists disagree about the meaning of this preoccupation. Some regard it as a primitive means of establishing control over submerged hostility, particularly toward the mother who is the original source of food. Others regard it as a desperate struggle to gain self-respect by achieving an idealized image. We now begin to understand why the anorectic cannot merely "choose" to eat again: her basic feeling of being loved and valued, her autonomy and initiative, her self-respect—all of which lie at the core of the human experience—are at stake.

But still a puzzle remains. The developmental drama just described is not unique to severely disturbed adolescence. Why is its resolution acted out in terms of the body? Bruch (1973) again has the most provocative hypotheses, derived from her many years of studying the psychological meaning of the body. She claims that somatization is due to three factors, two of which have been discussed in relation to obesity: a feeling of helplessness and worthlessness, and an inability to discriminate hunger and satiety. The third factor, which involves the body image, is more variable and not as potent in obese children. Our body image is not an accurate representation of our features and physique but a composite made up of a multitude of experiences, among them being evaluations of our bodies by significant others (see Wenar, 1971). In the case of the anorectic, parental evaluations are so prepotent that the adolescent literally cannot see herself realistically. One patient had difficulty discriminating between two photographs of herself even though there was a seventy-pound difference in her weight. Another said she could see how emaciated her body was when looking in a mirror, but when she looked away she reverted to her belief that she was larger. Thus, the image of the body, which is a reasonably accurate psychological construction in normal development, borders on a somatic delusion in the anorectic. Perception is determined not by reality but by deeply felt needs. According to Bruch, the anorectic's vain pursuit of self-respect through food refusal is expressed in the vain pursuit of a body which literally is never perceived as sufficiently thin. Objective studies tend to confirm Bruch's hypothesis that anorectics significantly overestimate their physical dimensions (see Bemis, 1978).

ANOREXIA NERVOSA AND DEVIANT DEVELOPMENT. At the beginning of the discussion, we described the normal battles for control between toddlers and parents which produce preschoolers who are both self-reliant and self-controlled. Anorexia nervosa shows this normal process going tragically awry. The parents assume total control of the child and often use love and concern as their technique for doing so. Since they seem to be acting for the child's good, her rebellion results in guilt and shame. Autonomy is surrendered. With the crisis of adolescence, the girl evolves a pitiful caricature of autonomy by asserting control over her food intake. However, it is control without self-confidence, nagging doubts leading to increasingly restricted food intake in pursuit of an unattainable ideal of thinness. Note that the girl tries to resolve her problem by involving her body rather than directly confronting the people responsible for producing it. Yet, as she continues to fast she may well produce a belated control over her parents through their worried concern, their catering to her culinary eccentricities, their helplessness to change her. While the victory may finally be hers, it is won at the price of impoverishing her life and endangering her health.

Finally, anorexia nervosa illustrates self-destructive negativism, in contrast to healthy self-assertiveness. The anorectic's rejection of parental attempts to help are understandable. But therapists often encounter the same stubborn refusal both to eat and to cooperate. The resistance may be passive, such as taking two hours to eat a bowl of corn flakes and trying the therapist's patience to the limit, but it is, nonetheless, a powerful impediment to treatment.

THE FAMILY APPROACH. Recently, anorexia nervosa has been conceptualized in terms of family interaction. When previous investigators studied the parent–child relationship, the focus was on the child and the effects of parental behavior on her development. In the family approach, each member both affects and is affected by the behavior of every other member in a dynamic interplay of influences. Thus, the basic task is that of understanding patterns of interaction and the ways in which such patterns enhance or impede growth.

Minuchin and his coworkers (1975) describe four characteristic patterns of interaction in families of anorectic children.

1. *Enmeshment.* Members of the pathologically enmeshed family are highly involved and responsive to one another but in an intrusive way. They have no strong sense of individuality so that changes in one member or in the interaction of two members quickly reverberate throughout the entire family system. There is a lack of privacy, an exaggerated "togetherness." Minuchin and his group cite the example of a 15-year-old who complained that his mother always moved the furniture around when he was not at home—as if this were as much his business as hers. Enmeshed families have poorly differentiated perceptions of each other, and parents often speak of their children as a group. Roles and lines of authority are diffuse; children assume parental roles or one parent enlists a child's support in struggles with the other parent.

2. *Overprotectiveness.* Family members of psychosomatically ill children are overly concerned for each other's welfare. A sneeze can set off "a flurry of handkerchief offers," criticism must be cushioned by pacifying behavior. The family's exaggerated concern for the ill child retards the development of au-

tonomy and the child, in turn, feels responsible for protecting the family from distress.

3. *Rigidity.* Pathological families resist change. Particularly in periods of normal growth, such as adolescence, they intensify their efforts to retain their customary patterns. One consequence is that the child's illness is used as an excuse for avoiding problems accompanying change. Since attending to the child's illness diverts the family from facing conflicts, the illness is constantly reinforced.

4. *Lack of conflict resolution.* This final characteristic is the result of the first three, although its manifest forms differ. Some families deny conflict; others bicker in a diffuse, scattered, ineffectual way; some have a parent who is an avoider, such as a father who leaves the house every time a confrontation threatens. An honest facing up to conflicts is often bypassed by adherence to a strong religious or ethical code that provides a prefabricated answer to all interpersonal problems.

The picture of the family that emerges is congruent with the one presented by Bruch. However, Minuchin enlarges our understanding of how the child's illness supports the entire network of family relationships. He also expands our understanding of the various roles the child may play within the family pattern. *Triangulation* puts the child in the distressing position of siding with one parent against the other in a parental disagreement. In a *parent-child coalition,* the child does side with one parent; for example, a girl might staunchly defend her mother's being incapacitated by "sick headaches" while the father taunts her with pampering herself and "putting on an act." In *detouring,* the parents escape their conflicts by regarding the sick child as their only problem. Some require the child to reassure them that they are indeed concerned only with her welfare; others alternate between concern and exasperation over the child who is such a "burden" and "does not try to help herself."

Minuchin's ideas concerning etiology are also congruent with the ones already presented. The family of the future anorectic is overly concerned with diet, food fads, table manners. Their intrusiveness undermines the child's autonomy, and both her psychological and bodily functions are continually subject to their scrutiny. Adolescence is a particularly stressful time for the family. The child, sensing the stress, responds with a behavior such as dieting which is subsequently utilized as a detouring mechanism and is subtly reinforced by the family. As the symptom becomes enmeshed in the family pathology, it gradually escalates into a full-blown anorexia.

Treatment

Anorectics are difficult to treat successfully. While there may be an initial improvement in terms of eating and weight gain, less than half are making a satisfactory adjustment when follow-up studies are conducted. According to Bemis (1978), who has given us a detailed critique of treatment effectiveness, probing underlying motives by means of psychoanalysis is inappropriate because of the anorectic's hypersensitivity to intrusion. Bruch (1973) recommends a factual, noninterpretive approach to restore the patient's self-confidence. Behavioral therapies have achieved excellent initial results which often are not sustained over time. Minuchin (1975) reports that family therapy has an impressive, sustained success rate, but the technique is too new to allow an evaluation of its efficacy in a large number of cases treated by a diversity of therapists.

In light of what we have learned about

etiology, it seems reasonable to assume that therapies which alter the parental and familial setting of the anorectic will be more successful than those which try only to change the adolescent herself. It may well be that the relapses after initial improvement represent a reinstatement of old patterns of intrafamilial interactions that therapy bypassed.

Historical Perspective

In chapter 1 we saw that the quest to understand developmental psychopathology is itself constantly evolving. Some changes come from within the profession as new psychopathologies are delineated and new insights gained. Some result from social changes, such as those which forced professionals to attend to neglected mental health problems in the late 1960s. Some are due to the waxing and waning of psychopathologies themselves, anorexia nervosa being one that is on the rise (Bemis, 1978).

Many of these developmental trends are illustrated by the various attempts to understand the nature of anorexia nervosa. Freudian theory was initially concerned with understanding the sexual drive and particularly emphasized the role of the Oedipus complex in adult psychopathology. The theory of oral impregnation is illustrative of this early phase. However, as the original formulations proved inadequate to account for a number of psychopathologies and, interestingly, as there seemed to be a decline in the kind of hysterical patient Freud first analyzed, the theory expanded in two directions. First, the earlier stages of psychosexual development were explored and increasing importance was attached to sensitive caretaking in the oral stage and to individuation in the anal stage. The second direction was an investigation of control mechanisms, so that the theory became less drive-oriented and more ego-oriented. The hypothesis that anorexia nervosa is the ego's defense against rage at the mother for being an insensitive and domineering caretaker fits nicely into this expanded version of psychoanalytic theory.

Bruch epitomizes the current emphasis on the self and on cognition. She claims that not only does the anorectic learn to view the self as essentially helpless and depreciated, but also hunger and the physical appearance of the body are cognitively distorted because of experiences in the infant/toddler period. Minuchin represents one aspect of the current shift away from the child to various social contexts—in this instance, the family—a shift which was strongly reinforced by the social unrest of the 1960s.

It is too early for all these changes to be assimilated into a unified theory of anorexia nervosa, since the majority of investigators are busy exploring and deepening their own hypotheses. A juxtaposition of the various approaches to unraveling the mystery reveals overlaps and discrepancies, but there seems to be general agreement that the anorectic adolescent is robbed of initiative and individuality early in life by oversolicitous and/or overcontrolling parents. But why this common source of psychopathology should result in the specific behavioral syndrome of anorexia nervosa remains controversial.

ENURESIS

YOU ARE A CLINICAL CHILD PSYCHOLOGIST VISITING an Israeli kibbutz. The client is a 5-year-old boy who wets his bed at night. In Berkeley, California, where you practice, only 16 percent of children continue to wet their beds, and at this age, bedwetting ceases to be part of normal development, becoming instead, the psychopathology of enuresis. But you also know a number of other facts. While toilet training is benign and child-centered on the kibbutz, bedwetting is twice as prevalent here as in Berkeley. Finally, the client, like other kibbutz children, is psychologically healthier than his Berkeley counterpart in that he rarely has tantrums or fears or eating and sleeping problems.

What do you decide? That the little fellow is generally coming along all right, that bedwetting at his age is not all that deviant in the kibbutz, and that paying undue attention might prolong it? Or is bedwetting one way that 5-year-olds have of saying "Something's troubling me!" and indeed, at this age, is deviant behavior the only way 5-year-olds can send such a message? If so, you would want to investigate the situation further to find what has gone wrong.

Such decisions are never easy. Fortunately, you know one more fact which will help you decide. We will discuss it in time, but right now we will use the example to illustrate the child clinician's problem of shifting criteria of disturbance to fit different social contexts. As enuresis becomes more prevalent does it lose its status as a symptom? Surely we would not say that of malnutrition, illiteracy, or gang violence, all of which are very prevalent in certain cultures and classes. But is bedwetting as serious as those conditions? At what point do we say, "This is just the way these children are brought up," and at what point do we say, "This is deviant development"? The problem of distinguishing differences from deviations is central for clinicians who choose to work with inner-city Blacks or American Indians or Chicanos, as well as those who go to foreign countries.

The Nature of Enuresis

In summarizing the findings concerning enuresis itself it is worthwhile to look at the kinds of questions a child clinician might ask not only about enuresis but about any disturbance. (Except where indicated, the information is taken from Shaffer, 1977.)

1. How is enuresis defined? Nocturnal enuresis is the involuntary discharge of urine during sleep after 5 years of age.

2. Is it a simple or complex symptom? Complex. In primary enuresis the child has never been trained to be dry at night. In secondary enuresis there is a relapse after a period of dryness. The two types represent two kinds of developmental deviations, one in which development fails to take place (fixation) and another in which development occurs but the child returns to a previous stage (regression).

3. Is there a developmental pattern? Clearly. It consists of a gradual decline in incidence from 20 percent of 4- to 5-year-olds to 2 to 3 percent of 14-year-olds (Lovibond and Coote, 1970). There is also some evidence (Essen and Peckham, 1976) that in 5- to 7-year-olds enuresis is associated with a general developmental delay that affects both walking and talking, whereas in 11-year-olds, it is associated with behavior problems at home and in school. Mothers of 8½-year-old enuretic boys are masculine and emasculate their sons as do fathers, although to a lesser degree. Thus, enuresis may be related to the achievement of masculinity in middle childhood (Achenbach and Lewis, 1971). Not only does incidence change over time, then, but so also might the importance of etiological factors.

4. Is there a genetic component? Yes. Enuresis runs in families, so that some children are more prone to become enuretic than others, depending on whether or not their siblings are enuretic.

5. Is there an organic component? Yes. Urinary infection, small functional bladder capacity, and low threshold of responsiveness

of the bladder may be associated with bed-wetting. Also, retarded neuromuscular maturity evidenced by poor fine- and gross-motor coordination may hamper achievement of bladder control (Kaffman and Elizur, 1977).

6. Are context factors important? Yes.

Do cultural and socioeconomic status contribute? Yes. Social disadvantage and low socioeconomic status are associated with a high incidence of enuresis.

Are family factors important? Yes. Parental indifference to the child's physical and psychological well-being, family breakup through death or divorce, separation from the mother for at least one month, the birth of a sibling, and moving to a new home all increase the incidence of enuresis.

Are there any other contexts? Yes. Institutional and foster care as well as hospitalization and surgery are apt to increase the incidence of enuresis.

7. Are intrapersonal factors important? Yes. Enuresis can be associated with both personality characteristics and psychiatric symptoms. Enuretic 4-year-olds have a higher number of symptomatic behaviors (temper tantrums, fears, eating problems, etc.) which indicates that they are more generally disturbed than are nonenuretic children, although no single kind of disturbance predominates (Kaffman and Elizur, 1977). Enuretics aged 5 to 7 and 11 show more problems at home (trouble concentrating, social isolation, worry, destructiveness, victim of bullying, etc.) and more adjustment problems in school than nonenuretics (Essen and Peckham, 1976). While statistically significant, the findings do not warrant the generalization that all enuretic children are disturbed since many clearly are not. In sum, enuresis may be the only disturbed behavior or it may be one of many signs of disturbance.

Are there sex differences? Not so much in the preschool years but increasingly so in middle childhood when more boys than girls have the problem.

8. Is it related to specific socialization practices? Specific nighttime training is not related to enuresis. The age at which toilet training is started may be. Recent evidence (Kaffman and Elizur, 1977) suggesting that "late" training (in other words, after 20 months) increases the incidence of enuresis is contrary to the view of many child-care experts who emphasize permissiveness. Coercion appears to be related to enuresis, but more definitive data are needed.

9. Have the interrelationships among etiological factors been established? No. No one variable is critical or found only in enuretic children (Kaffman and Elizur, 1977). It is up to the child clinician to be cognizant of the variables and evaluate the contribution of each to an individual case.

10. Is there a treatment of choice? Yes. It is the "bell and pad" method, in which the child's urine activates a bell, which in turn causes the child to awaken and cease urinating. Then the child gets up to urinate or is helped by the parents. Repetition of the procedure night after night causes the stimulus of bladder distention preceding urination to elicit the response of awakening. This procedure arrests bed-wetting in 75 percent of the cases, although 41 percent relapse within six months of treatment. While learning theorists are still debating the mechanism involved, the behavioral approach seems to be superior to psychotherapy and counseling. (For a more extensive review see Doleys, 1977.)

(The same questions can be applied to fecal soiling, or encopresis. However, the literature on this psychopathology is not sufficiently rich or developmentally oriented to be discussed. A good review is offered in Hersov, 1977.)

A Developmental Study

The kibbutz example that opened the discussion of enuresis is based on one of the few longitudinal studies of enuresis (Kaffman and Elizur, 1977). In the kibbutz, four to six infants are reared by a trained caretaker, or metapelet (plural, metaplot) in a communal children's house. Each child spends four hours daily with his or her parents. Generally speaking, the children's development and the parent–child relationships are similar to those in traditional Western families. From the standpoint of research, the advantage of the kibbutz is that it controls toilet training, which, as has been noted, is generally benign and child-centered. In the study reported by Kaffman and Elizur, 153 children were assessed on a number of physiological, inter- and intrapersonal variables from infancy to 8 years of age. They regard enuresis as beginning at 4 rather than 5 years of age, which DSM-III gives as the age at onset

While the investigators found the usual genetic and physiological predisposing factors in the 4-year-old enuretics (enuretic siblings, smaller functional bladder capacity, impaired motor coordination), the personality and interpersonal factors are of greater interest. The enuretic children had a significantly greater number of behavior symptoms than the nonenuretic ones, suggesting that they were generally more disturbed. Within this general context, two high-risk personality patterns could be distinguished. Around 30 percent of the children were "hyperactive," aggressive, and negativistic in response to discipline, had low frustration tolerance, and resisted adjusting to new situations. How difficult it must have been for these children to sit or stand still when being potty-trained! A smaller group of enuretics were dependent, unassertive, had low achievement and mastery motivation, and masturbated frequently, perhaps to compensate for their lack of realistic pleasures arising from the interpersonal and physical environment. In contrast, the nonenuretic children were self-reliant, independent, and adaptable, and they had a high level of achievement motivation. They also showed a negative response to wetness and urine contact, in contrast to their enuretic counterparts, who showed no such reaction. The authors note that the two sets of high-risk traits did not characterize all enuretics; like obesity, bed-wetting can be a single symptom, part of a personality pattern, or one element in a picture of severe emotional disturbance.

In the interpersonal sphere, the clearest relation was between parental disinterest and enuresis; while there was some correlation to both emotional coldness and indulgent infantalization, it was not statistically significant. In addition, temporary separation from the parents was the only stress related to increased bed-wetting, for the kibbutz children took in stride the stresses of a sibling's birth, hospitalization, and even war. Interestingly, absence of the metapelet produced no such reaction, suggesting that the parent–child relationship was central. While not statistically significant, a relationship between bed-wetting and the metapelet's behavior was suggested; permissiveness, low achievement demands, and insecurity tended to be related to enuresis, whereas structured, directive, and goal-oriented toilet training in the context of a loving relationship enhanced early bladder control.

The authors draw some general conclusions from the data. For low-risk children the timing of toilet training does not matter. In the high-risk group, delayed training increases the likelihood of enuresis. The motorically active, resistive, and aggressive infant is difficult enough to socialize, but the difficulties are compounded during the "terrible twos and threes." In the interpersonal realm, a permissive attitude, combined with noninvolvement or uncertainty, tends to perpetuate bed-wetting since there is neither sufficient challenge nor sufficient support for the child to take this particular step toward maturity. Such a finding is congruent with studies of normal development that show that a child's competence is maximized when parental affection is combined with challenges and an expectation of achievement. Overall, the children's personality characteristics were more highly correlated with enuresis than were interpersonal variables.

The Problem of Prognosis

Let us now return to the decision concerning whether or not to recommend therapy for the 5-year-old Israeli boy. In their longitudinal study, Kaffman and Elizur found that 50 percent of enuretic children were identified as "problem children" when they were 6 to 8 years of age, in contrast to 12 percent of nonenuretics. Learning problems and scholastic underachievement were the most frequent symptoms, although some of the children also lacked self-confidence and felt ashamed, guilty, or depressed. While some children "outgrow" enuresis, the behavior problems of others increase (Essen and Peckham, 1976). The importance of the point cannot be overemphasized. Looking at a graph showing the progressive decline of enuresis, one would opt for the prediction that the child would "outgrow" his problem. But longitudinal studies which include intra- and interpersonal variables alert the clinician to the possibility that enuresis in some 4-year-olds may be the first sign of problems which will persist and perhaps escalate.

Unfortunately, Kaffman and Elizur did not analyze their data to discover why certain enuretic children are at risk. The kind of shaming which might well be responsible for their negative self-image in this country is minimal in the kibbutz where the attitude is one of acceptance of bed-wetting. It may be that the child's aggressiveness or dependence and the uneasy permissiveness of caretakers continue to hamper the child in subsequent socialization and in achievement of the self-discipline necessary for making a successful school adjustment.

There is one final point to be made concerning the relation between psychopathology and development. The children who were not enuretic at 4 years of age evidenced a significant amount of fearfulness at 3 years of age. They showed diverse fears during the day and were especially frightened about going to sleep or would awaken crying for their caretakers. It is possible that such behaviors were a sign of the stress of toilet training, and that even in a benign setting the conflict between autonomy and losing parental love can take its toll on healthy children. The finding also underscores the limitations of using the symptom approach exclusively when defining psychopathology. A child clinician must decide when a disturbance is part of healthy growth (as in the fearful 3-year-old) and when it is the first sign of trouble to come (as in the enuretic 5-year-old). Longitudinal studies are all too rare in this regard. Until more data have accumulated, the clinician has no choice other than to evaluate the various etiological variables along with the child's general development and rely upon the guidelines resulting from accumulated experience.

REFLECTIONS ON THE DEVELOPMENTAL MODEL AND ON INITIATIVE

We have learned a number of clinically useful lessons about the importance of contexts in understanding psychopathological behavior. First there is the *organic* context, which includes the genetic and physiological factors in enuresis and obesity, as well as the vaguely defined biological vulnerability in symbiotic psychosis. Then there is the *intrapersonal* context. Symbiotic psychosis (like autism and childhood schizophrenia) engulfs the child; however, anorexia nervosa and enuresis may be reactions to a specific trauma, or the primary psychopathology, or one manifestation of another psychopathology such as antisocial acting out or depression. Failure to take the intrapersonal context into account can result in inappropriate recommendations for therapy and is responsible for a good deal of confusion in the research literature. In the *interpersonal* context, parental behavior has consistently emerged as a potent determinant of psychopathology; only in enuresis is there a suggestion that it may be less influential than the child's temperament. Pathogenic patterns of family interaction have been delineated for anorexia nervosa, and we suspect this approach could readily be extended to negativism and enuresis, where the roles of the mother and father in relation to the child have been tentatively explored. The *superordinate* context of socioeconomic status and culture holds some surprises: anorexia nervosa is found primarily in the well-fed middle class, while enuresis flourishes both in disadvantaged American slum children and their well-cared-for counterparts in the kibbutz. The formula "poverty engenders psychopathology" proves far too simple to account for the psychopathology of toddlers—as it will again in the case of delinquents (chapter 8).

Then, there is the all-important context of *time*. The same psychopathological behavior may have different meanings depending on when it occurs in the developmental sequence: witness the changing meanings of eating, as well as the 4-year-old enuretic with a general developmental lag in walking, talking, and coordination as compared with the 8-year-old enuretic concerned about his masculine identity. There are also hints that the potential contribution of parents to psychopathology changes with time, the mother being more important initially, the father in middle childhood. Time poses the knottiest questions for the clinician: When is a disturbance temporary (as in the fearful 3-year-old who will be dry during the night a year later), and when is it the first sign of trouble to come (as in the enuretic 4-year-old)? Or again, when is disturbed behavior age-appropriate (such as the 5-year-old who gorges herself because of some unrealistic sexual anxiety), and when is it a regression to a previous developmental stage (such as the 5-year-old who gorges himself because of a sudden terror over being separated from his mother)? Research furnishes far too few guides to answering these questions; much of the time the clinician must rely on skill and experience.

We have also learned about different *models* of deviant development. One model involves failure to progress as expected: the mother–infant symbiosis does not develop; drives and affects are not differentiated as specific states of high arousal; control of bladder and bowels is not achieved. This, of course, is the *fixation* model of psychopathology. A variation of the fixation model involves an exaggeration of normal development—negativism and feeding problems being the prime examples—if such exaggerations are prolonged and block further growth. The second model is *regression*, the clearest examples being secondary enuresis, fear of oral impregnation, and the separation anxiety in symbiotic psychosis.

Finally, we have learned about the *deviant development of initiative* and early socialization. Self-reliant enterprise can be totally undermined by a mother–infant interaction which traps the toddler between the terror of autonomy and the terror of a return to infantile dependence. In all the eating disorders the self-as-agent is usurped by parental *intrusive-*

ness, at times in the form of naked domination, at times in the form of solicitous concern for the child's welfare. While the enterprising component of initiative may suffer in the sedentary obese child, it may be accentuated in the anorectic. Even the child's perception of drives and affects can be distorted by parental usurption of the self-as-agent.

In both negativism and enuresis there is the suggestion that parents can directly or indirectly encourage excessive opposition and that overpermissiveness combined with detachment or insecurity hamper the development of control of urination. Parental rewarding of sickness also figures prominently in the family-interaction approach to anorexia nervosa. Thus, parental *reinforcement* and *laxness* appear as etiological factors in deviant development, although they are not as fully documented as parental intrusiveness.

Exploration of the issue of deviant socialization as a source of psychopathology has just begun and will continue as we turn to middle childhood and adolescence. We will find that both excessive control and inadequate control can work mischief, while the scene of action will shift from the child's body to the child in conflict with society or with himself. It is this latter conflict which will now be discussed.

7 ▪ Neuroses and Excessive Self-Control

In the course of being psychoanalyzed, a middle-aged man recalls, "When I acted up as a kid my grandmother would scold me, saying, 'You're too young to have nerves!' For a long time after that I kept wondering, 'Am I old enough now?'—like having nerves was one of the signs of being grown up."

Grandmother, unknowingly, was a good Freudian. According to psychoanalytic theory, psychoneurosis or neurosis is a developmental achievement. Not that infants and preschoolers cannot suffer—as we have seen, they can; but they are not sufficiently sophisticated psychologically to have a classical neurosis until middle childhood.

However, Freud's concept of neurosis has always been a controversial one. His ideas concerning unconscious motivation, infantile sexuality, and the relation between adult psychopathology and childhood trauma were greeted with incredulity, shock, and derision by members of the professional community. While many of his concepts are now regarded as plausible or obvious, the psychoanalytic formulation of neurosis is currently under attack from two directions. As could be expected, behaviorally oriented psychologists regard the formulation as both incorrect and needlessly complex. Quite unexpectedly, DSM-III dropped the classification of neurosis completely, preferring diagnoses which would be purely descriptive and have no etiological connotations. Unfortunately, interest in childhood neuroses is currently in the doldrums and research is particularly sparse, so programmatic statements and polemics flourish, while there is little substantive progress in understanding.

In light of the many controversies centering around neurosis, this chapter will proceed in the following manner. First, we shall look at behavioral descriptions of types of neurosis. These are noncontroversial and must be accounted for by any theory which is concerned with etiology. This descriptive introduction will be followed by a brief discussion of the reasons why DSM-III abandoned the classification of neurosis. Then, because of our interest in diverse models of psychopathology, we shall examine and compare psychoanalytic theory and a conceptualization from within the behavioral camp. Finally, in a review of the research on the neuroses we shall focus on one of the most important of these disorders—school phobias. (For more detailed coverage of the topic, see Adams, 1979.)

THE DESCRIPTIVE PICTURE

Anxiety Neurosis

Anxiety neurosis is characterized by unvarnished fear, which erupts in repeated attacks of panicky feelings. In some cases the anxiety is described as free-floating, in that the children neither know what causes it nor do they have any consistently effective means of alleviating it. In varying degrees children with an anxiety neurosis suffer from "nervousness," irritability, restlessness, insomnia, indecisiveness, and feelings of inadequacy. Inevitably there are autonomic concomitants, such as diarrhea, dilation of the pupils, dizziness, dryness of mouth, nausea, palpitations, sweating, and trembling.

Adams (1979) cites the case of a 9-year-old girl who was much closer to her alcoholic father than to her neurotic mother. The father described her as "nervous and high-strung" like her mother. She would become upset when the mother berated the father for his lack of business success, and since the mother claimed she was a better Christian than the father, the child also worried that her father would not go to heaven. On the other hand she was fearful that the father might murder her mother when he came home drunk and belligerent. She also worried about the father's inability to provide her with candy, clothes, and material possessions, was afraid to go to sleep, and was concerned that nobody liked her. While she was initially a good student, her schoolwork declined as she became increasingly unable to concentrate in class. The girl's anxiety was not the free-floating kind but was constantly triggered by the reality of the family situation and by her own imaginings. In other instances, children's anxiety is far in excess of realistic provocations and is due more to intrapersonal factors.

Phobic Neurosis

Once called anxiety hysteria, phobic neurosis is marked by a persistent, intense, irrational fear of an animate or inanimate object or of a situation. The list of phobias is legion, including spiders, enclosed places, germs, heights, and even phobophobia or a fear of phobias! Phobias should be distinguished from fears which may be developmentally appropriate (see chapter 2) or which represent a realistic reaction to a traumatic experience (such as being in an automobile accident). The hallmark of a phobia is that the fear is out of proportion to the reality of the situation. It cannot be explained or reasoned away. It is beyond voluntary control, unadaptive, and neither age- nor stage-specific. It persists over an extended period of time and leads to avoidance of the feared situations (Miller, Barrett, and Hampe, 1974).

The Hysterical Neuroses

Hysterical children often share three characteristics. First is an enchanted world view in which magical or primitive ideas are more potent than they are in age-mates. Religious beliefs or superstitions, for example, may be more vividly experienced and believed with more conviction. Next is an extreme expression of emotions. The children are overly dramatic, like ham actors, at the same time being self-centered rather than concerned with the feelings of others. Finally, there is an increased suggestibility. Hysterical children tend readily to pick up the symptoms of relatives and schoolmates, being copycats rather than empathizers (Adams, 1979). In all three characteristics runs the theme of immaturity and egocentrism, which becomes increasingly inappropriate as adolescence approaches. At the same time, the hysteric's self-dramatization tends to elicit responses such as, "Things can't be all that bad," or "Act your age," rather than reactions of sympathy and concern.

Conversion hysteria is marked by disturbed sensorimotor functions, such as paralyses or anaesthesias of the arms or legs, functional blindness or deafness, and tics. It is crucial that all such symptoms be of psychological rather than physiological origin. One striking concomitant of these physical symptoms is a lack of anxiety concerning them; in fact, the child may seem quite comfortable with playing an acceptable sick role. This unconcern is called *la belle indifférence.* From the time of the Greeks to present-day Freudians, the "imaginary" physical symptoms of hysteria have been attributed to frustrated sexual needs.

Dissociative hysteria is marked by three characteristics: disturbances in consciousness, such as trances, stupor, or pseudodelirium; personality disorganization, as evidenced in depersonalization and multiple personalities; and odd motor expressions, such as sleepwalking, aimless running and pacing, or catalepsy (a condition in which the limbs keep any position they are placed in). There are two popular images of the dissociative hysteric. One is the individual with multiple personalities or with a split personality, which the media frequently mislabels as schizophrenia rather than hysteria. The other is the rural adolescent girl at a revival meeting, who suddenly has visions of religious figures, is unaware of her surroundings, writhes on the floor speaking in tongues and shouting she has been saved, while later having total amnesia for the entire episode.

Depressive Neurosis

This category has already been covered in our discussion of depression in middle childhood. In brief, the criteria are a dysphoric mood and loss of interest or pleasure in most of the usual activities and pastimes, together with poor appetite, insomnia, agitation, fatigue, feelings of worthlessness, diminution in concentration, and recurrent thoughts of death.

Obsessive-Compulsive Neurosis

The obsessive-compulsive neurosis is marked by intrusive ideas (obsessions) and impulses (compulsions) that seem to arise from sources over which the child has no control, are irresistible, and often recognized as irrational. Sometimes the neurosis appears to be an exaggeration of the usual ritualistic behavior of childhood; however, unlike ordinary rituals or routines, these engender intense anxiety or guilt when interfered with and consume an inordinate amount of time. The child recognizes the senseless nature of the behavior but is unable to change it. While handwashing is the most familiar example, other neurotic behaviors concern safety—such as continually checking the doors to make sure they are locked—or involve repeatedly counting to a particular number or touching objects a given number of times.

In certain children, obsessive-compulsive behavior has a more bizarre quality than those just depicted. Adams (1979) describes an 11-year-old who felt obliged to step on imaginary dots on the floor. He would not feel temporarily free of the compulsion until he had performed the ritual three times. He thought the dots might be fecal in nature, although he realized they were not really there, and was preoccupied with the idea that some of the toxin from the dots would enter his body through his anus. Subsequently his obsessive worries about germs, feces, and bodily harm nearly led him to a psychotic state.

Mixed Neuroses

While clinicians are constantly concerned with ordering psychopathologies into categories, children themselves fail to come in neatly packaged classifications. Most evidence a mixture of psychopathologies. The classification of mixed neuroses recognizes the fact that a variety of neurotic manifestations can be found in a given child.

CURRENT STATUS OF THE DIAGNOSIS

The controversy concerning the etiology of neuroses has affected the classification of the psychopathology itself. Because of the pervasive Freudian influence, neurosis had come to be identified not only with the behavioral manifestations of the psychopathology but also with the psychoanalytic interpretation. As this interpretation came to be increasingly questioned and as other etiological accounts—particularly the behavioral— gained in popularity, various attempts have been made to find a classification which would be strictly descriptive.

The solution of DSM-III was to discard the term neurosis altogether and substitute the more neutral term *disorder* (APA, 1980). Thus, a phobic neurosis becomes a phobic disorder, an obsessive-compulsive neurosis becomes an obsessive-compulsive disorder, and so on. The emphasis is on the purely descriptive characteristics of neurotic behavior: the presence of anxiety; the unacceptable, alien nature of the symptoms; the relative intactness of reality testing; the enduring nature of the disturbance; and the fact that the symptoms do not actively violate social norms. No longer united by an etiological account, the traditional neurotic subtypes are no longer united in a single category but are dispersed among other categories; thus, the traditional conversion hysteria is grouped with other conditions such as hypochondriasis and psychogenic pain disorders, in which the symptoms, while suggesting a physical disorder, have no demonstrable organic basis. Such disturbances are called Somatoform Disorders. Neurotic depression becomes absorbed into the general category of Affective Disorders, while phobias and obsessive-compulsive disturbances are considered two varieties of Anxiety Disorder.

As discussed in chapter 3, there is no agreement as to the optimal way of classifying childhood psychopathologies. Some of the current classifications are descriptive, others are tied closely to theories, while still others rely on statistical techniques to generate behavioral categories. In light of the uncertain etiology of all childhood psychopathologies, however, there is a clear advantage to having DSM-III confine itself to the descriptive approach. In this way a number of possible etiologies can be included, while there is no danger that its users will confuse the soundness of a clinical description with the validity of a particular etiological theory. The descriptions themselves can also serve as a common behavioral base from which research—both theoretical and atheoretical—can emanate.

THE PSYCHOANALYTIC THEORY OF NEUROSIS

The presentation of psychoanalytic theory will be divided into three sections. The first will discuss concepts which can be evaluated in terms of general developmental theory. The next section will deal with concepts concerning the nature of neurotic symptoms which, while congruent with general developmental theory, have not become part of it. The final section deals with concepts specific to the psychoanalytic theory, since they derive from the psychosexual theory of development.

Freud never directly studied a child. His insights into the nature of neurotic behavior were derived from his therapy with disturbed adults. His single venture into child psychoanalysis—the famous case of a phobic boy named Hans—was conducted on the basis of reports from the boy's father. Subsequently, the direct study of normal and disturbed children became one of the most vigorous branches of the psychoanalytic movement. While new discoveries did not alter Freud's basic model, they did produce important additions and qualifications. It is this more comprehensive view of early development that will be discussed. (This presentation will follow Nagera, 1966; see also, Shapiro, 1973.)

Psychoanalytic Theory and General Child Development

Conflict lies at the heart of the psychoanalytic theory of neurosis. In fact, Freudian theory has been called a theory of conflict. If this is a caricature, it is a good one, since the resulting distortion highlights a prominent feature of psychoanalytic physiognomy. In essence, the psychoanalysts conceptualize the development of self-control in terms of a conflict between what infants, toddlers, and preschoolers want to do and what socializing adults require them to do. Let us summarize the developmental picture.

In the *oral* period, the conflict is between infants' need for immediate physiological gratification—to eat, to sleep, and to be awake when biological rhythms dictate—and the caregivers' desire or ability to meet such needs. Note that in no sense is the conflict "in" the infants; it is strictly between infants and caregivers. Yet, as early as the end of the first year, infants evidence the ability to delay or inhibit immediate gratification. In the *anal* period, the conflict is initially between the toddlers' wish to defecate whenever and wherever they please and the socializing adults' requirement for delay. By the end of toilet training the conflict has become internalized, toddlers now instructing themselves as to when and where they can defecate. The same paradigm holds for curiosity, where the conflict is between parental prohibitions and the desire to examine an attractive object. Eventually, children can selectively inhibit their exploratory behavior even when the parent is not present. Finally, in the *oedipal* stage, once again the conflict is initially external, the threatening father opposing the boy's desire to possess the mother. By identification with the father the conflict becomes internal with the boy now censuring his own erotic feelings.

The conflicts described by the child psychoanalyst are inferred from observable behavior, and the hypothesized transition of such conflicts from an external to an internal locus is an acceptable developmental principle. The transition to a large degree reflects the child's increasing ability to represent actions by symbols, which both guide and control behavior. The initial symbols are simple, fragile, and situational, such as the toddler saying no when reaching toward an electric outlet; later they become a complex weighing of pros and cons, such as the adolescent's struggle over whether to start drinking with the gang.

The next component of neurosis is *anxiety*. Affect, like conflict, lies at the heart of psychoanalytic theory. Especially in early childhood, the purely intellectual comprehension of prohibitions would not be sufficiently potent to counteract children's desire to do what they want when they want to do it. It is the threat of parental punishment and withdrawal of parental love that provide an affect charge sufficiently strong to lead to the inhibition of socially unacceptable behavior. Returning to the conflict model, we now see that the conflict is between the desire to and the fear of gratifying strongly motivated behaviors.

With the introduction of anxiety the situation becomes more complicated. Anxiety is not only a deterrent; if sufficiently strong, it is exceedingly painful and can set into motion a whole array of maneuvers designed to protect the child from experiencing its distress. These maneuvers are called *defense mechanisms*. Let us briefly review the important ones. The basic defense is *repression*, in which children avoid an erotic or aggressive impulse with its accompanying ideation by banishing them both from consciousness; for example, instead of feeling angry and wanting to hit her baby brother, a girl now honestly believes that she has no such thought and feeling. Often repression does not offer sufficient protection against anxiety and further defenses must be marshaled. In the present discussion we will be concerned with only three: *reaction formation*, in which the child thinks and feels the opposite of the forbidden impulse; *displacement*, in which the object of the impulse is changed to one which does not arouse anxiety; and *projection*, in which the child's impulses and attendant ideas are attributed to another. To illustrate using the girl who wants to hit her baby brother: in reaction formation, she will feel great fondness for her brother; in displacement she will angrily kick a chair she accidentally bumped into; and in projection she will bitterly complain about the way older girls in school are always picking on her.

These are the basic ingredients of a neurotic conflict. Yet the little girl who kicks the chair instead of hitting her baby brother is in no way neurotic. In fact, according to Nagera (1966), observations of preschool children reveal extreme versions of normal anxieties and defenses—an excessive fear of spiders, for example, or an intense disgust of messiness. What is more, such extreme reactions need not be the precursors of a subsequent neurosis because of the fluid nature of early development. If this is so, if both the mechanisms and the behaviors characteristic of neurosis are present before middle childhood, why is neurosis considered a developmental achievement of that period? The answer must be in terms of a quantitative rather than a qualitative change. Only by middle childhood is that self-censoring faculty, the conscience, sufficiently strong and consistent to sustain deviant patterns of behavior which persist over time and are relatively impervious to environmental efforts to alter them. The toddler's or preschooler's conscience is fragile and fragmentary: it operates in this situation, but not in that; it is here today and gone tomorrow. The anxieties and defenses which it engenders have the same insubstantial quality. By contrast, a neurosis requires a stable internal guide to the social acceptability or unacceptability of behavior.

So far there is nothing in the psychoanalytic theory of neurosis which would put it beyond the pale of tenable developmental concepts. In part this is because the more controversial conceptualizations specific to psychoanalytic theory have intentionally been avoided: the *id,* which is both the source of asocial sexual and aggressive impulses and the repository of repressed impulses; the *superego,* which is the conscience; and the *ego,* which is responsible for erecting defenses. We shall soon see that there are a number of objections to these concepts. Yet, it would be a mistake to reject the developmentally defensible aspects of psychoanalytic theory just because one cannot accept the partitioning of personality into id, ego, and superego.

Presenting the developmental aspects of the psychoanalytic theory has led to the conclusion that neurosis is deviant socialization: it is self-control gone awry in the direction of excess. The checks on unfettered expression of impulses that are inherent in socialization arouse disproportionate anxiety over transgression. The psychoanalytic answer to the question of why self-control becomes excessive, however, is a complicated one which must be postponed until the presentation of the theory of neurosis is completed.

The Nature of Neurotic Symptoms

Next come concepts which, while not part of general developmental theory, are congruent with it. Psychoanalytic theory states that neurotic symptoms have a symbolic meaning, which differs from the manifest content of the behavior. Freud was fascinated by the question of meaning: What does a dream mean? The peekaboo play of a 2-year-old? The delusion of a paranoid adult, who believes his guts are turning to stone? The slip of the tongue of a gracious hostess who says to a departing guest, "I'm so glad to see you go"? The simplest answer—and one which many behaviorists prefer—is that behavior means what it says: a child who is terrified of spiders has probably been bitten by one or has been frightened by a picture of them or is imitating a parent who fears them. Undoubtedly this can happen, as the Freudians recognize. However, such a simple, realistic explanation cannot account for all of the bizarre, irrational features of psychopathological behavior. Freud thought that the meaning of a symptom had to be decoded, and—typically—he looked to development for the key, particularly the development of thinking.

In chapter 2 we saw that Freud and Piaget agree that an acccurate grasp of reality is a developmental achievement. During the first half-dozen years of life much thinking does not conform to reality. Recall, for example, how the tendency to think in literal terms—to believe what one sees and hears—results in all kinds of misconceptions: that a gesture could cause a distant physical object to move, or a cry could magically make an absent mother appear; that there was more clay when a ball of clay was flattened out into a pancake; that a little girl could grow up to be a man if she changed her hairstyle and the way she dressed; that breaking four cups accidentally was worse than breaking one on purpose.

Freud's special name for early ideation was *primary-process thinking.* "Primary process" is the primitive need to maximize pleasure and avoid pain. Once again we see Freud's emphasis on affects and motivation, this time in the realm of ideation. In normal life daydreams partake of this need-determined quality, in that we suddenly suspend realistic thinking and indulge ourselves in sexual escapades or grandiose achievements or vengeful triumphs over enemies. Hallucinations are another form of need-determined ideation: just as the thirsty man in the desert can hallucinate an oasis, a psychotic adult with pent-up hostility can hallucinate a voice commanding him to kill the president of the United States. The Freudian emphasis on need-determined thinking, in contrast to Piaget's purely cognitive theory, has not become part of general developmental theory, however.

One example of primitive thinking relevant to neurosis is what Freud called *symbolization* (Meissner, Mack, and Semrad, 1975, pp. 501–502). Here a concrete object is used to represent or substitute for another tabooed object or idea on the basis of a common element. A familiar example is the phallic symbol, in which an elongated object such as a knife or fountain pen symbolizes a penis; in a like manner, containers such as a vase or a box can symbolize the vagina. While there may be a few common symbols, symbolization is highly idiosyncratic: a car may mean masculine power to one boy, destructiveness to another.

The second feature of symptom formation concerns conflict resolution. From his study of neurotic symptoms, Freud concluded that the symptom represented a compromise in which both warring factors—the asocial sexual or aggressive impulses and the righteous conscience—were partially gratified. Thus, for example, the prudish censor regards himself as the protector of public morality while at the same time viewing pornographic pictures. While not a part of developmental theory, conflict resolution by compromise is a plausible and congruent concept.

Illustration

The way that the basic components combine to produce a specific neurosis can be illustrated by a phobia. The case in point is a 7-year-old girl who was terrified of spiders, which she feared would bite her. Psychoanalytically oriented play therapy revealed that the basic neurotic conflict was between a desire to express anger toward her mother and her primitive conscience's mandate that she be a good girl. Her self-condemnation as "bad" engendered anxiety, and—as is typical of phobias—a triple defense was set into play. First came repression, so that the girl could banish the angry thoughts and feelings from consciousness. Next came projection, in which the mother was seen as angry at the girl. Finally came displacement, in which a relatively innocuous object was invested with exaggerated destructive powers. Why a spider? Remember that there is never a pat answer to questions of symbolization, since the meaning can be highly idiosyncratic. In this instance the girl, having heard of the deadly bite of the black widow spider, equated both the quality of hostile attack and blackness with her mother, who made a great deal over the versatility of her "basic black" dress. Finally, the phobia represented a compromise: since she did not express her anger directly, her conscience was satisfied that she was a good girl; however, her fearful preoccupation caused her mother great embarassment and concern, while robbing her of the pride she took in being a perfect parent. Certainly, inducing chronic worry and undermining self-esteem can be as destructive as an angry outburst.

Neurosis and the Psychosexual Stages of Development

We now come to that facet of the theory of neurosis which is based on psychosexual development. We are therefore no longer in the realm of generally accepted or potentially acceptable developmental concepts. As a partial answer to the baffling question of why one neurotic symptom develops rather than another (the so-called choice of neurosis), psychoanalysts postulate relations between specific symptoms and specific stages of psychosexual development.

The Oedipus complex and the anal stage are the source of two prominent groups of symptoms—hysterical and obsessive-compulsive.

HYSTERICAL SYMPTOMS. Three varieties of hysterical symptoms will be dealt with. In *anxiety hysteria,* the child is unaware of the cause of anxiety because the forbidden sexual or hostile impulse has been repressed. However, repression is not successful and the impulse threatens to return to consciousness. Hence the recurrent waves of panic and the persistent "nervousness."

A *phobia* represents one method of mastering the helplessness evidenced in anxiety hysteria. As we have seen, projection and displacement focus the anxiety on an external source. The child now has something to be afraid of and ways of avoiding the frightening object or situation. The content of the phobia represents variations on the oedipal themes of sex and aggression, the variations being legion—biting animals, automobile accidents, and fires can be feared because of their violence, for instance, while "slimy" snakes, egg yolks, and the physical closeness of a confined space can be feared because of their erotic connotations.

Another defensive maneuver involves bodily functions. The resulting symptoms are called a *conversion reaction,* following Freud's notion that a psychological conflict is converted into a somatic malfunction. One example in the motor area is a persistent tic. As always, direct expression of a forbidden impulse is blocked by repression, but instead of utilizing projection as in a phobia, the child utilizes the body as a vehicle for acting out a disguised version of the conflict. The particular motor activity may well have a symbolic meaning: blinking, for instance, may result from anxiety over the impulse to look at sexual organs; head-shaking or grimacing may symbolize angry defiance.

OBSESSIVE AND COMPULSIVE SYMPTOMS. While obsessive and compulsive symptoms, like hysterical ones, may originate in an inability to resolve the Oedipus complex successfully, in this neurosis the child regresses to the anal level. Recall that the conflict here is between conformity and rebellious self-assertion, and that in normal development the defense of reaction formation enables the child to make the transition from fascination with feces, dirt, and messiness to cleanliness, orderliness, and obedience. In the neurotic school-age child, the anal conflict returns in a highly charged repetitive manner. In a hand-washing compulsion, for example, the child can never dispel the nagging feeling that his or her hands are not absolutely and totally clean; rituals to insure safety, such as checking locks on doors at night, can never satisfy the child that the house is absolutely burglarproof. The technical terms for such attempts to nullify the guilt over unconscious hostile impulses is *undoing*—a kind of perpetual but ineffectual attempt to assure oneself that badness never existed. A final defense is *isolation,* in which a thought is cut off from associated thoughts and from affect. Consequently, ideas of doing repulsive or destructive or forbidden things can return in the form of obsessions. Separated from their affective charge, they remain at the level of ideation and are relatively safe. In certain instances obsessional thoughts can lead to compulsive acts in an attempt to nullify or undo them. Thus, a boy who was obsessed with the idea that his penis was damaged (an unmastered castration anxiety) was driven to obsessive masturbation in a futile attempt to prove this was not so. In sum, then, regression to the anal phase and the defenses of reaction formation, undoing, and isolation are the mechanisms responsible for obsessive and compulsive behaviors.

Determinants of Normal versus Neurotic Development

While psychosexual theory may tell us what neurosis is likely to develop, it still does not answer the question of why a child becomes neurotic instead of continuing to develop normally. The classical answer proposed by Freud was in terms of *excessive* or *insufficient gratification* of libidinal and/or aggressive impulses at the various psychosexual stages. The infant who is indulged in oral gratification will have difficulty giving up these pleasures and will have a strong tendency to return to them when subsequent developments prove difficult; in a like manner, the infant who receives only meager gratification will continue to long for the missing pleasures, such longings becoming a regressive undertow in subsequent development. In the anal stage, excessive attention to toileting or rigid, hostile, inconsistent demands make for undue fixation at this level; in the oedipal phase, either the seductive or the cold parent makes resolution difficult. The greater the total regressive pull, the less likely the child will master later developmental conflicts.

However, subsequent observations of normal and disturbed children have introduced new elements, so that the current answer to our question, Why neuroses? is in the terms of the *balance of forces*, some making for psychopathology on the one hand, some for healthy development on the other (Nagera, 1966). Freud's classical formulation is still considered valid but incomplete.

What are the additional sources of vulnerability? Some are *constitutional* and *maturational*. Certain infants experience anxiety more intensely than others and are persistently disrupted by its effects. The maturation of impulses and control can also be out of phase, so that the latter far outstrips the former, and the child becomes an overcontrolled, pseudomature "little adult." In such a child, sexual and aggressive impulses remain an alien, potentially disruptive force. Other vulnerabilities are *experiential*, failure to receive sensitive care in infancy being particularly important. The institutionalized child is the most frequently cited example, although severe and prolonged illness or depression in the primary caregiver can have a similar effect if little substitute attention and affection are forthcoming. No matter what the circumstances, inadequate mothering in the first two years increases vulnerability to subsequent psychological disturbances.

As for assets—constitution and maturation can be aligned on the side of health as well as on the side of vulnerabilities. Certain infants are innately rugged and resilient, either experiencing less intense anxiety or readily taking it in stride. Later on, they tend to grapple with and master difficulties and frustrations rather than having to retreat and protect themselves. Psychosexual development itself is maturationally determined, according to psychoanalytic theory, so there is always a strong force propelling the child on to the next stage and protecting him or her from becoming mired in the conflicts of the current one. In middle childhood, family entanglements become less intense, while concomitantly the development of friendships, achievement in school, positive relations with teachers, coaches, and other adult models all strengthen the child's ability to deal with conflicts constructively. The physiological maturation of adolescence can be another potent force pushing for adult heterosexuality and counteracting the tendency to become passive and/or bisexual. Even a neurotic conflict can itself become a constructive force in the child's developing personality. Take, for example, the boy who handles his hostility toward a younger sibling by the reaction formation of being especially concerned with the plight of relatively weak and helpless youngsters; this, in turn, can lead to an interest in helping physically handicapped and mentally retarded children, and eventually to a successful vocation in one of the helping professions. As Anna Freud (1965) puts it, one can never be sure whether a therapist is eliminating a neurosis or "nipping a budding physicist in the bud."

THE FLUIDITY OF CHILDHOOD NEUROSIS. Observations of normal and disturbed children have revealed another important characteristic of childhood neurosis. Unlike their adult counterparts, which are remarkably fixed and persistent, childhood neuroses tend to be fluid. An adult may be terrified of riding in an elevator all of his or her mature years, but children are usually not similarly hamstrung by their disturbances. In part, this is because the child is changing more rapidly than the adult and patterns of self-control and self-censoring are not as fixed. In part, this is because the child's personality is less differentiated, so that conflicts from many different psychosexual stages can more easily surface at one time or another. And, in part, this is because the child is more highly reactive to environmental events than is the adult, so that favorable or untoward happenings weigh more heavily in relieving or accentuating their neurotic disturbances.

This concept of fluidity has important implications concerning the *intrapsychic* aspects of the psychoanalytic theory. Those who misunderstand the theory describe it as claiming that all problems are due to internal conflicts between the id and the superego, leaving no room for realistic difficulties which exist between the child and the environment. Now we see that this interpretation is wrong on two counts. First, it is not until middle childhood that a purely intrapsychic conflict is possible, and second, all through middle childhood and adolescence, environmental influences continue to play a role in the fate of the neurosis. Only in adulthood is personality sufficiently formed to sustain a relatively self-perpetuating neurosis.

DIAGNOSTIC IMPLICATIONS. The picture of the malleable child in whom forces for growth contend with forces for fixation and regression makes diagnosis a heroic undertaking. First of all, behavior per se cannot be used as evidence of disturbance. An irrational fear may indicate a neurosis, or it may be a temporary reactivation of a normal anxiety, such as separation anxiety, resulting from stresses inherent in growth or in realistic life problems. What is more, if a symptom such as a phobia suddenly disappears, it may be because the child has resolved the underlying conflict, or the symptom may soon be replaced by another such as a compulsion or a psychosomatic stomachache. Consequently, psychoanalytic diagnosis involves a comprehensive evaluation of the child's psychological development, the current status of impulse expression and control, and significant interpersonal transactions, with an eye to delineating the assets and liabilities both in the child and in the environment (A. Freud, 1965). Especially in the realm of neurosis, the seemingly simple question, "Is this child disturbed?" admits of no simple answer. The psychoanalytically oriented clinician might well envy his or her behavioral counterpart, who seems to cut the Gordian knot of convoluted diagnosis by proclaiming, "The symptom *is* the neurosis"—in effect, the manifest behavior is all that needs concern one.

But this is only one of the many contrasts between the psychoanalytic and the behavioral approach to understanding neurosis. It is time to explore such contrasts in detail.

THE BEHAVIORAL APPROACH

One problem in presenting the behavioral theory of neurosis is that there is no single, agreed-upon behavioral theory; as was evident in chapter 1, there are extremists and moderates, purists and revisionists (see Mahoney, Kazdin, and Lesswing, 1974). Psychoanalysts are similarly divided among themselves. How large a gap there is between the psychoanalytic and behavioral theories, therefore, depends on which variation one chooses to present.

The two issues dividing behaviorists are: (1) whether the basic data of psychology must be palpable environment events and overt behaviors or whether "mentalistic" concepts, particularly cognitive ones, may be introduced, provided they are operationally defined and increase explanatory potency; and (2) whether the three principles of learning are adequate to account for all learned behavior or whether additional theories must be added. This schism will be elaborated on shortly. However, it is important to understand that even radical behaviorists such as Skinner recognize that humans have a rich inner life of thoughts, wishes, and fantasies; their objection is that there is no satisfactory means of studying such phenomena objectively. Mental events are excluded not because they do not exist but because they cannot be brought into the realm of objective scrutiny.

Specific Objections to Psychoanalytic Theory

Behaviorally oriented psychologists variously object to the psychoanalysts' emphasis on *inner* determinants of behavior, *underlying* causes of neurosis, and *inferred* psychological constructs. Some of their specific objections will be presented briefly.

DRIVES. The basic psychoanalytic assumption that much of behavior is motivated by sexual and aggressive drives is regarded as unwarranted by behaviorally oriented psychologists. "Drive" is one of those unobservable inferences which is regarded as superfluous; all that is needed is sexual and aggressive behavior. If drive goes, so does the contention that the child is relentlessly driven to obtain direct or indirect sexual and aggressive gratification. And, if this goes, so does the image of development as a struggle between the asocial demands for immediate gratification and the requirements to delay, moderate, and disguise gratification in order that society exist.

What behaviorists substitute for drive is what one can observe—specific behaviors in specific situations. While Freud was correct in stating that stimulating areas of the body is a source of great pleasure—or, to use behavioral terminology, is highly reinforcing—the amount of gratification and frustration the child experiences depends upon whether significant adults ignore, encourage, or prohibit such pleasure-seeking behaviors; it is not a function of a need to obtain a fixed amount of pleasure. Even more hotly contested is the notion of a fixed quantity of aggression which must find direct or indirect outlet, the behaviorists countering that the amount of aggression a child displays is a function of the environment's responses to such behavior.

INFERRED CONCEPTS. Behaviorists regard the psychoanalytic structural concepts such as ego, id, and the unconscious as unnecessary to explain behavior. They also claim that psychoanalysts tend to reify psychological processes and indulge in circular explanations. Thus, the id, ego, and superego become like actors in a drama, the beleaguered but reasonable ego trying to settle the interminable battle between the villianous id and the prudish superego. Circularity enters when a given behavior is explained in terms of these three entities: thus, a boy successfully solves his Oedipus complex "because" he has a strong ego. And how do we know his ego is strong? Because it would have to be to solve such a complex!

While both criticisms are justified in terms of actual use—or misuse—of the concepts, the defects are not intrinsic. The ego, for example, is defined in terms of a cluster of psychological processes: attending, remembering, reality testing, controlling motility, defending against anxiety, and integrating. The processes are clustered because they serve a common purpose, which can broadly be defined as adaptation to reality and homeostatic regulation of tensions. Thus, the ego is not a "thing" by nature, even though the temptation to think of it that way is strong. In a like manner, successful or unsuccessful conflict resolution must be accounted for in terms of the specific processes involved; for example, our hypothetical boy resolved his Oedipus complex successfully because he was secure in the love his parents showed him, he could identify with a strong father, he was not anxiety-prone, nor were there undue stresses in terms of sickness or death, etc.

"PRIVATE EVENTS": THE CONTROVERSIAL AREA. Behaviorists are united in their objection to Freud's mentalism—the freedom with which he speculated about images, thoughts, and fantasies. Such a psychology runs counter to the behavioral emphasis on objectivity. References to mental events, if introduced at all, must be done cautiously, with great care to point to the behavior which necessitates their introduction. Recently, however, there has been a dissatisfaction with the gingerly treatment of images, thoughts, and fantasies, along with a vigorous attempt to give cognitive variables the status they deserve. The impetus for doing so did not come directly from the works of Piaget as much as from behavior therapists who discovered that their results could not be fully accounted for if cognitive variables were excluded, while their repertoire of therapeutic techniques could be enriched by utilizing such variables (Mahoney, 1977). Mahoney (1974) argues persuasively that behaviorists' past neglect of the study of private events has deterred them from understanding the very behavior they wished to explain. At the simplest level, a stimulus cannot uniformly be defined in terms of its objective characteristics, since it can arouse different internal symbolic responses; an oncoming snowstorm may mean, "Great! Now I can go skiing," to one person, and "I'll probably skid and have an auto accident," to another. These two individuals' subsequent behavior is understandable only in light of their mediating symbolic responses.

Bandura (1969) summarizes numerous studies showing the important role mediating symbols play in a variety of behaviors. Memory was improved by instructing subjects to associate two unrelated words with a distinctive image; for example, recalling "dog-bicycle" was facilitated if the subject imagined a dog riding a bicycle. Instructions to "Think *T*" aroused an autonomic response in subjects who had previous been shocked every time they were presented with and asked to pronounce the letter *T*. Instructions to imagine lifting different weights were followed by muscle contractions proportional to the imagined weights.

The explanation of private events also divides behaviorists. Purists such as Skinner insist that only the locus changes when one moves from overt to covert behavior; the conceptual framework and the learning principles remain unchanged. When a boy says, "That's good," to himself after receiving all As on his report card, he is merely transferring reinforcement from the external to the internal environment; when a girl says, "I'm going to try harder next time," she is merely setting a standard of achievement for herself which had formerly been rewarded or modeled on others. Even complex thinking and planning can be accounted for by the chaining of prior, simpler symbolic activities just as, say, expert piano playing results from building up increasingly complex motor skills.

Other, equally dedicated behaviorists claim the theoretical model must be expanded to accommodate the nature and complexity of symbolic behavior. Bandura (1969) inserts an "internal information-processing" system between stimulus and response which involves attending to stimuli, encoding the information, storing it either momentarily or permanently, and, ultimately retrieving the stored information when it is needed to guide future behavior. (See also Mahoney, 1974.) The details of information processing need not concern us; what is important is that it is a complicated process, each of its components involving its own incompletely understood complexities. Note also that four distinct psychological processes are united under a single label which is a descriptive shorthand, not an explanation. In addition, the explanations of how information processing works, while not agreed upon, go beyond the laws of conditioning and imitation. The break with the purists is obvious.

Glancing back briefly at the discussion of "inferred concepts," we see that the uniting of diverse processes under the heading of "information processing" is no different from the uniting of diverse processes under the heading of the "ego." The justification for the union is that the separate functions serve a common goal—to enable individuals to understand the environment in the case of information processing, to enable them to adapt to reality and maintain homeostasis in the case of the ego. While the cognitive revisionists might object that the "ego" is a poor choice of constructs, since information processing is simpler, more amenable to experimental investigation, and so forth, they cannot object to the strategy of introducing constructs per se when this simplifies the task of understanding complex behavior.

The Behavioral Theory of Neurosis

If the behavioral account of etiology is thin compared to the psychoanalytic, this is due to history more than to inherent inadequacies of the theory. The lion's share of interest and the greatest vitality and creativity have been in the realm of behavior therapy. Etiology has been treated something like a stepchild. However, therapeutic success can in no way be offered as proof of the correctness of the etiological hypotheses behaviorists do present. One cannot assume that conditions responsible for changing behavior were responsible for producing that behavior. To illustrate: certain disturbances can be more easily treated than others. Phobias, for example, can be eliminated more readily than compulsive rituals. Consequently, the literature is filled with reports of how phobias were cured using quite diverse therapeutic techniques, each having its own rationale. The overall picture is a hodgepodge of etiological speculations, no one of which can be given more weight than the rest because each can only point to therapeutic effectiveness as proof.

In behaviorists' discussions of psychopathology, one may not find a heading labeled "neurosis" or any other traditional diagnostic category, for that matter. They do not believe people "have" neuroses in the sense that they "have" physical illnesses. A disturbed person evidences certain behaviors which either society or the individual involved chooses to place in a special category. But such categorization in no way makes the behavior different, nor does it necessitate the introduction of any new psychological principles. On the contrary, all human behavior obeys the same principles of learning. (Incidentally, Freud repeatedly made this point concerning the continuity of normal and psychopathological behavior, although he had his own explanations in mind rather than the laws of learning when he did so.)

As a gentle reminder of the primacy of behavior, traditional diagnostic categories tend to be replaced by behaviorally oriented ones. A. O. Ross (1979), for example, discussed psychopathology in terms of deficient behavior (such as early infantile autism, learning difficulties, and mental subnormality) and excess behavior (such as aggressive behavior, withdrawn behavior, and psychotic disorders). Bandura (1968) uses the term "inappropriate stimulus control of behavior" for those cases in which formerly innocuous or inappropriate stimuli come to elicit intense and aversive emotional reactions. His term includes the neuroses already discussed—intolerable anxiety, phobias, obsessive-compulsive reactions, and somatic complaints.

CONDITIONING OF INAPPROPRIATE RESPONSES. In discussing the behavioral viewpoint Bandura's (1968) presentation will be followed. (While Bandura's more recent work, "Social Learning Theory," 1977, significantly expands the cognitive domain of the behavioral approach, the implications for a theory of neurosis has not been spelled out in detail. Therefore, the older work is more suited to this discussion.) Bandura would agree with the Freudians that the response which lies at the heart of neuroses is frequently anxiety. Anxiety-flight, just as anger-fight, can be adaptive when it is a reaction to realistic threat; when the response is inappropriate, however, when no real danger exists, the behaviorists regard it as psychopathological.

Traditional learning principles can account for the various ways in which innocuous and inappropriate stimuli come to elicit aversive emotional responses. The most familiar principle is aversive classical conditioning, in which a formerly neutral stimulus (the Conditioned Stimulus), occurring in conjunction with a stimulus (the Unconditioned Stimulus) which elicits an unpleasant affective response (the Unconditioned Response), itself comes to elicit that unpleasant response (the Conditioned Response). The classical case is of 11-month-old Albert who, after being exposed to a number of pairings of a white rat (CS) with a loud, frightening noise (US) became frightened by the sight of the rat alone (CR). A variation in this same model is higher-order conditioning in which a stimulus, once conditioned, serves as the basis for further aversive conditioning when paired with neutral stimuli. In an experimental situation, names of persons or nations or even nonsense syllables which had been associated with words having negative connotations, such as "bitter" or "ugly," subsequently tended to be viewed as unpleasant. In realistic situations, a child who hears that sex is "dirty" may develop a disgust for sexual behavior even without engaging in it.

A negative affective response may also be acquired by vicarious classical conditioning. Here the mere observing of another person responding with pain or anxiety to a previously innocuous stimulus—say a buzzer which always preceded a shock—will subsequently produce an aversive response in the observer when the innocuous stimulus is presented. On this basis a girl whose parents are afraid of being burglarized can come to fear every creak of the stairs after bedtime, as her parents do.

In addition to such familiar mechanisms for learning a new response, Bandura notes that inappropriate behavior can result when irrelevant aspects of a complex social stimulus are attended to and generalizations made on the basis of what, in reality, are noncontingent relationships. He cites the example of a woman who wrote to "Dear Abby," warning other women that men who wear bow ties can never be trusted!

STIMULUS GENERALIZATION. Once established, inappropriate behavior can spread by stimulus generalization. The classical example is, once again, little Albert, who after being conditioned to fear a white rat, subsequently was afraid of a number of white, furry objects. However, stimulus generalization in an 11-year-old is bound to be more complex than it is in an 11-month-old. Semantically related cues can take precedence over the sheer physical similarity of words; for example, subjects conditioned to "hare" will generalize to "rabbit" rather than to "hair." Generalization can also occur to categories of objects; for example, a subject who receives a shock when a rural word such as "barn" is presented will also have an aversive reaction to other rural words.

While these are promising leads they represent only the initial stage of applying learning principles to symbolic behavior. The same reservation holds in regard to social situations. Behaviorists recognize that people emit highly complex patterns of verbal and nonverbal cues, and there is at present no way of predicting the course of generalization from one person to another. Thus, when a 6-year-old girl goes to school for the first time, one cannot predict whether she will generalize the anger she feels toward her mother on to her teacher, or whether she will perceive the teacher as a "nonmother" adult and respond appropriately. Only after the reaction occurs can it be explained.

REINFORCEMENT OF AVOIDANCE RESPONSES. The final component in the behavioral explanation of neurosis is the reinforcement of responses which enable the individual to avoid the conditioned aversive stimuli. Like psychoanalysts, behavioral theorists regard anxiety as an unusually potent motivator; any behavior which reduces or eliminates it will be reinforced. A wide array of such behaviors can be conceptualized as avoidance responses. There is "place avoidance," in which the individual avoids a noxious stimulus in the environment; a child who is frightened by spiders avoids going down to the basement which is hung with cobwebs, for example. More important for our discussion is "response inhibition." If an act is habitually punished, both the behavior itself and its cognitive representation come to elicit anxiety. In order to prevent such anxiety from occurring, not only the behavior but also its cognitive representation can be avoided. In other words, the child avoids both doing and thinking about doing a forbidden act. This, of course, is exactly the same process as repression. The difference is that behaviorists regard as superfluous the psychoanalytic assumption that the "ego" represses the forbidden idea into the "unconscious," where it continues to exist and press for expression. In fact, the entire gamut of defense mechanisms are congruent with learning theory as long as they are regarded as learned avoidance responses rather than protective devices initiated by the ego.

Such is the potency of fear that even irrelevant behavior which is in progress when a reinforcing event occurs will itself be reinforced. This is one basis on which superstitions and compulsive rituals derive their power. If eating reduces anxiety, for instance, the individual may gradually insist on a special kind of food cooked in exactly the same way, placed on the same part of the plate, and eaten in exactly the same order, as more and more irrelevant behavior become conditioned reinforcers.

Specific Neurotic Behaviors

As noted, behavioral psychologists have primarily been interested in using learning principles to change neurotic behavior; in regard to etiology they often have been satisfied with speculative accounts. One misses the close meshing of theory and experimental data which the behaviorists themselves advocate, while certain classes of neurosis such as conversion symptoms and obsessions have received scant attention.

The behaviorist's etiological account of *phobias* is the most convincing, the mechanisms of aversive and vicarious classical conditioning being well supported by laboratory studies on both animals and humans (Bandura, 1968). Behaviorists add that, once learned, the reaction of the social environment is a potent factor perpetuating the phobia. While a child might originally develop a fear of insects by modeling a parent, the subsequent attention received from the parent, either positive or negative, may further reinforce the phobic response. In general, the social reverberations of disturbed behavior play an important role in maintaining it.

Compulsive rituals, as we have seen, can result from the reinforcement of irrelevant behavior. They can also result from symbolic mediation. To illustrate: during toilet training, "dirty" may become a stimulus whose aversive consequences can be reduced by washing one's hands. On learning that sex is also "dirty," an adolescent may reduce the anxiety engendered by sexual thoughts and activities by taking a shower. If the anxiety becomes pervasive, not only will washing increase but also a host of behaviors designed to avoid dirt and insure cleanliness—public toilets, public parks with dog feces, and specks of film on restaurant silverware may all be labeled "dirty" and avoided, while efforts to keep the body and house and possessions immaculate increase. Even though the individual avoids ("represses") sexual activities and thoughts, the environment is replete with sexual and "dirty" stimuli, which could perpetuate the compulsive rituals.

It is now easier to understand the behaviorist's objection to psychoanalytic accounts of etiology. It is not that such accounts are complex—they are needlessly complex. The involved process of repression, projection, displacement, and so forth, add nothing to the explanatory power of basic learning principles, while making the task of experimental verification next to impossible to accomplish. By the same token, there is no reason to search for underlying causes in unresolved Oedipus complexes or intrafamilial conflicts—a frightening spider is a frightening spider, not a symbol for an angry mother.

A NOTE ON "NEEDLESS COMPLEXITY." It is difficult to evaluate the behaviorist's charge that psychoanalytic theory is needlessly complex when the behavioral movement itself is in such an expansive state. Bandura (1977) has enlarged the cognitive domain to include images, memory, expectancies, and problem solving, along with a variant of initiative which he calls self-efficacy. In the realm of behavior therapy a similar expansion is taking place. (For a résumé, see Graziano, 1978.) Simple reinforcement and modeling procedures have been supplemented by sophisticated verbal techniques designed to increase self-control, self-esteem, assertiveness, and rational thinking. This therapeutic expansiveness may require a concomitant theoretical expansion beyond the learning principles of conditioning and imitation and certain behaviorists are now searching for a suitable theoretical model (Mahoney, Kazdin, and Lesswing, 1974). How complex this model will be cannot be predicted at this point. However, we can look at one aspect of the current scene which is particularly relevant to this discussion, namely, verbal behavior.

While behavior therapists are increasingly relying on verbal exchanges with the client, the use to which words are put is generally simple and straightforward with scant attention paid to the study of words per se. Words are the vehicle for effecting change, not the focus of inquiry. Freud, by contrast, was fascinated by the symbolic nature of words, particularly their more intricate manifestations in puns, double meanings, and, most of all, in metaphors. When someone says, "I'm happy as a lark," or when someone sings, "That man has a heart like a rock cast in the sea," not only do we "get the message," but we get it in a particularly vivid manner. If a lark can represent happiness and a rock indifference, then certainly a poisonous spider can represent a hostile mother. Freud's hypothesis that metaphorical thinking lies at the heart of neurosis is a tenable one which behaviorists will have to grapple with sooner or later. Whether they will produce a simpler, more empirically based model than Freud's remains to be seen. (For a review of the burgeoning research, see Ortony, Reynolds, and Arter, 1978.)

The issue of "needless complexity" can be summed up by pulling together several strands from the previous discussion. The behaviorists' charge cannot be accepted until they show that they can provide a simpler, experimentally verified account of the descriptive clinical data. In certain instances, notably phobias, they have presented a convincing alternative in which theory and laboratory data dovetail nicely. In other areas, their account is sketchy and programmatic; namely, neurotic behaviors other than phobias, cognition, and symbolization. Whether the introduction of information processing as an organizing concept will fill the cognitive gap remains to be seen. But even information processing partakes of some of the complexity of psychoanalytic concepts, and its applicability to neurotic behavior has not been convincingly demonstrated.

The current involvement in therapy has forced behaviorists to confront the study of "private events" head on. In a sense they are in the same position of having to conceptualize their clinical observations as Freud was when he embarked on his psychotherapeutic ventures. Since the two schools of thought are finally grappling with similar data, we will one day have a chance to judge whether the behaviorists' explanations justify their criticism of needless complexity or whether their model will be equally complex while, we may hope, being better buttressed by laboratory findings.

INTEGRATION AND EVALUATION

Ideally, the choice between two different explanations in science should go to the one which provides the more satisfactory account of behavior, that is, the theory which subsumes the larger proportion of the phenomena studied and has the greater predictive power. A choice between the psychoanalytic and behavioral approaches in terms of breadth of explanation and accuracy of prediction is not possible at present. In addition, the contenders do not even agree upon what data should be regarded as crucial to making such a choice—the complex, ongoing behavior of children in psychoanalytically oriented psychotherapy and in natural settings such as home or preschool, or the responses of children in a carefully controlled laboratory setting. Moreover, the discussion in chapter 1 has taught us that methodology alone cannot be the basis of the decision, the clinical eye (favored by the psychoanalysts) having advanced understanding of psychopathology as much as the controlled laboratory study (favored by the behaviorists). Luckily, it is our task not to choose between theories but to utilize them to further our basic goal of viewing psychopathology as normal development gone awry.

First let us look at areas of agreement. Both behavioral and psychoanalytically oriented psychologists agree that while anxiety holds the key to understanding much neurotic behavior, there is no qualitative difference between the anxiety which leads to appropriate, adaptive behavior and that which leads to inappropriate, maladaptive behavior—both kinds of behavior obey the same laws. Adherents of both schools agree that the child can adopt parental fears either by identification (psychoanalytic theory) or modeling (behavioral theory) and that, once initiated, such fears can be sustained by attention from significant figures in the environment. Both agree that the socialization process, with its inevitable conflicts generated by the desire to do the forbidden, is a source of anxiety. Both agree that anxiety, in turn, motivates various avoidance techniques, defense mechanisms being prominent ones. There also seems to be substantative agreement concerning the nature of anxiety neurosis, in that both the instigation to perform a forbidden act and the need to avoid conscious recognition of that act are strong, resulting in a high level of anxiety with no awareness of its source.

In their explanations of other neurotic symptoms the two approaches diverge widely. Principles of conditioning clearly apply to the formation of certain symptoms—a fact which psychoanalysts, for some unaccountable reason, persist in ignoring. On the other hand, it seems unwise to discard the psychoanalysts' findings concerning the specific defensive maneuvers which underlie specific neurotic symptoms. Their reconstruction is plausible, and their record of insights into human behavior is too good to dismiss their explanation as unnecessary. Without more definitive data on symptom formation, a dual theory of etiology seems appropriate. There is no virtue in parsimony if it involves the sacrifice of tenable hypotheses.

On two other counts where the theories diverge, the psychoanalytic has more to offer than the behavioral. While the behaviorists write as if all aversive stimuli were equipotential, the psychoanalysts claim—and rightly so—that forbidden feelings toward parents (as delineated in the psychosexual stages) are particularly threatening to the child, motivate the most complex defensive maneuvers in order to deny or disguise them, and are most resistant to being recognized. In its pathogenic potential, a child's fear of shouting "I hate you" at the parents far outweighs, say, a fear of being bitten by dogs.

Even more important for our purposes is the fact that the psychoanalytic theory is a thoroughgoing developmental one; the behaviorists only fitfully introduce a development component. One facet of the psychoanalytic theory of development is the increasing autonomy of the child, so that by middle childhood, psychopathological patterns of behavior can be sustained relatively independent of environmental influences and often in spite of environmental pressures to change them. More important, the psychosexual theory provides specific hypotheses concerning the kinds of experiences, the timing of those experiences, and the interrelationship among those experiences that are crucial determinants of normal or pathological development. To reject this store of developmental hypotheses—regardless of one's position concerning the theory of psychosexual development per se—would significantly impoverish our understanding.

An important variation on this theme of development concerns the irrational aspect of neurotic behavior. While there may well be continuity between normal and disturbed behavior, one reason for distinguishing the two is that the latter is unreasonable in the sense of being maladaptive and inappropriate. Behaviorists tend to explain irrationality in terms of learning irrational behaviors from the environment. Bandura (1969), for example, cites the case of a schizophrenic who believed that "disagreements" meant "constipation" because her mother told all of her children that they were constipated and gave them an enema every time they disagreed with her. The other behavioral explanation of irrationality is in terms of fortuitous or irrelevant contingencies being reinforced—

a bracelet becomes a good-luck charm if it is worn when a child does well on a series of examinations. For the psychoanalysts, as for Piaget, irrationality is part and parcel of the developmental process itself. Children, especially young children, do not merely reflect their social environment; they interpret it. The younger the child, the more apt he or she is to have a distorted understanding of reality, even if parents send out reasonable messages. Currently, the weight of both clinical and experimental evidence supports the Freud-Piaget position, which has been both more explicit and more detailed concerning the nature of early irrationality than that of the behaviorists.

In sum, the psychoanalysts claim that the combination of high affective involvement with parents in the toddler and preschool period, together with a tendency to distort the reality of social interactions, is a fertile breeding ground for neurosis. The claim is developmentally defensible, and while it is not the only clue to the irrationality of neurotic behavior, it is still the most important one.

The issue of conflicting models will be discussed briefly again after the research findings on the neuroses and on school phobias have been presented.

RESEARCH ON THE NEUROSES

Neurosis as Internalization

Behaviorally, the neuroses share a number of characteristics: a high level of anxiety (except in the case of *la belle indifférence*), which interferes with optimal functioning; less distortion of reality and grossly maladaptive behavior than is present in the psychoses; no major etiological role played by organic factors; and suffering primarily turned inward on the self. (The presentation of research findings follows Schwartz and Johnson, 1981.)

This last aspect of neuroses—turning suffering inward—has been amply demonstrated by factor-analytic studies of psychopathological behavior in children. Typical of such studies is Achenbach's factor analysis of a 91-item symptom checklist using 600 male and female psychiatric patients as subjects (Achenbach, 1966). The first principal factor was a bipolar one, which he labeled internalization–externalization. Among internalizing symptoms he included phobias, worrying, stomachaches, withdrawal, nausea, vomiting, compulsions, insomnia, seclusiveness, depression, crying—all indicating a distressed child. Externalizing symptoms included disobedience, stealing, lying, fighting, destructiveness, inadequate guilt feelings, swearing, temper tantrums, running away, and vandalism—all indicating a child in conflict with the environment. Indirectly the data support the thesis that neurosis is due, in part, to excessive self-control, the anxiety and guilt which is inherent in socialization becoming extreme.

Constitutional Factors

Eysenck (1960) has been one of the most persistent champions of the hypothesis that there is a constitutional-genetic component in neurosis. This hypothesis was based on a statistical analysis of disturbed behavior that yielded a factor which Eysenck labeled "neuroticism" and subsequently proved to be related to emotional reactions which were labile, intense, and easily aroused. Genetic studies also suggested that identical twins show a greater degree of similarity with regard to neuroticism than fraternal twins. Finally, there are clinical reports claiming that some infants are more prone to experiencing anxiety and have more difficulty in coping with it than others.

Eysenck's empirical data have not gone unchallenged, while he himself recognizes and emphasizes the role of environmental factors in producing neuroses. A conservative conclusion would be that there might be a genetic or constitutional predisposition to becoming neurotic but environmental influences are the major determinants.

The Family

Among environmental influences, one might expect that family interactions would predominate. Yet investigators have been unable to isolate interactions, particularly between mother and child, that would distinguish neurotic behavior from other kinds of disturbances or, in some instances, from normal behavior. There have been some provocative findings from individual studies, but they are still tentative (Schwartz and Johnson, 1981). There is some evidence that neurotic children come from homes in which a higher proportion of parents have similar types of neurotic symptoms when compared with the general population and where there is more marital dissatisfaction and conflict. There is also some evidence that neurosis in children is associated with an intermediate degree of parental control administered by relatively critical and nonnurturing parents. Especially with boys, there may be a pattern of an overly close but warm relationship with the mother and a distant relationship with a critical, nonaccepting father. (For a more detailed presentation of the research, as well as for a methodological critique, see Hetherington and Martin, 1979.)

The meager yield of positive findings may be partly because the family approach to understanding neurosis has not generated the kind of intensive investigatory efforts as has schizophrenia. The older studies also did not have the advantage of the more recent conceptualizations, such as the family as a system, or of more sophisticated techniques for obtaining information concerning family interaction. As things stand, discovering the contribution of family interactions to the production of neurotic behavior is one of the most important pieces of unfinished business confronting the research-oriented clinician.

Phobias

There is no evidence that phobic children have particular personality characteristics, such as intellectual giftedness or retardation, an unrealistically high or low self-image, or irresponsibility. However, compared with the general population, they do evidence a variety of problem behaviors, such as aggression, hyperactivity, withdrawal, sensitivity, academic disability, immaturity, and irritability (Miller et al., 1974). Thus, a phobia tends not to be an isolated problem in an otherwise normally functioning child but may well be accompanied by a number of other difficulties.

Hysteria

The societal context seems to play an important role in regard to the incidence of hysteria. Once prevalent among the middle class in Victorian times, it gradually declined, perhaps as attitudes toward sex became less repressive. At present, childhood hysteria is rare but seems to occur most frequently among children from rural backgrounds or from those of lower educational and socioeconomic status, where, it is speculated, both repressive attitudes toward sex and superstition continue to contribute to its development (Proctor, 1958).

Hysteria occurs in both male and female children, even though it is most prevalent among adult females. While of average or above-average intelligence, children with conversion reactions tend to be underachievers and to display other problems such as anxiety, depression, poor peer relations, and overdependence. The psychopathology is often preceded by some precipitating event. While mothers tend to be overprotective and fathers ineffectual, and while parents serve as models for or reinforce the child's somatic complaints, such a pattern of parental behaviors can in no sense be regarded as specific to hysteria. (For details, see Schwartz and Johnson, 1981.)

Obsessive-Compulsive Neurosis

Children with obsessive-compulsive neurosis tend to be of above-average intelligence, to have a rigid moral code accompanied by marked guilt feelings, and to have an active fantasy life. Other problems such as phobias and aggression toward parents are often present. There are some data indicating an increased incidence of physical illness and of obsessive-compulsive behavior in the parents. There is also some evidence supporting the clinical observation that, at least in the more severe cases, the condition may be related to psychosis (Schwartz and Johnson, 1981).

Generally speaking, the neuroses have been sadly neglected by researchers. While there is much speculation and a rich body of descriptive material, there are few well-controlled studies which would significantly advance our understanding or aid in choosing one etiological explanation over another. One might hope that research on anxiety, which lies at the heart of neurotic behavior and is a simpler concept, would have fared better. However, after reviewing the evidence, Ross concludes that, "the current state of research-based knowledge about anxiety in children is thus one of considerable ignorance" (A. O. Ross, 1980, p. 148).

Of all the neuroses, only school phobia has received a modicum of the attention it deserves from researchers and clinicians alike. In addition, it is one of the most common and crippling of childhood neuroses, the child both suffering and failing to learn the school-related cognitive and social skills so important to his or her development. Therefore, this psychopathology will be presented in detail.

SCHOOL PHOBIA

Description

A youngster with a school phobia is a pitiful sight. On a school morning, for example, a boy might sit at the breakfast table pale and silent, his eyes tearful, listlessly pushing a spoon around his bowl of oatmeal. If he forces himself to eat a spoonful and take a gulp of milk in response to parental coaxing, it is with great effort. Soon he says he has to go to the bathroom either to throw up or to have a bowel movement, which he might or might not do. As the time approaches for him to catch the school bus he becomes increasingly agitated, pleading, crying, or shouting accusations at his mother. In no way can such distress be mistaken for malingering or attention getting; rather, it has all the behavioral and physiological characteristics of intense fear. However, if the child is allowed to stay at home he is relieved and may resume his usual activities.

School phobia—defined as an irrational dread of some aspect of the school situation, accompanied by physiological symptoms of anxiety or panic when attendance is imminent and resulting in a partial or total inability to go to school—may be one of the most frequently occurring neuroses because compulsory school attendance makes its anxiety well nigh inescapable. Although the data are contradictory, there is no clear evidence of a sex difference, suggesting that this psychopathology does not conform to the usual pattern of boys outnumbering girls. Studies report either no difference in socioeconomic status or a predominance of middle-class children. School-phobic children have normal intelligence, do well academically, and do not dislike school. Some studies describe them as unusually conscientious and as setting high standards of achievement for themselves. School phobias occur in schoolchildren of all ages; reported peak frequencies range from 10 to 13 years of age; however, there have been few attempts to study the disturbance within a developmental framework. (For a more detailed presentation, see Herbert, 1974, and Kelly, 1973. See also Graziano, DeGiovanni, and Garcia, 1979.)

Etiology

School phobias can originate in diverse sources and can occur in different intra- and interpersonal contexts. Three frequently mentioned etiologies are fear of separation from the mother, lack of self-confidence, and an unrealistically high self-image which magnifies any threat of failure. In the self-reports of school-phobic children, for example, the most frequent fear is that harm will befall the mother in the child's absence, followed by a fear of being ridiculed and the fear of failure in school. However, reasons can overlap and change, while a number of children have no idea why they are afraid. Finally, a distinction has been made between a school phobia that occurs in a fairly sound personality and a healthy family setting and a school phobia that is part of a more pervasive disturbance within the child and his or her family (Herbert, 1974).

The diverse interpersonal relations have been organized into three patterns: an overindulgent mother and an inadequate father, dominated by a willful, stubborn, demanding child at home who is timid and inhibited in social situations away from home; a strict, controlling, demanding mother, a passive father, and a passive, obedient child at home who is often timid and fearful away from home but who may become stubborn and rebellious at puberty; and a firm, controlling father, an overindulgent mother closely bound to and dominated by a willful, demanding child who is alert, friendly and outgoing away from home (Hersov, 1960).

In one of the few studies comparing school-phobic with other neurotic children (Waldron, Shrier, Stone, and Tobin, 1975), the former were found to have significantly more separation anxiety, to be more dependent and depressed, to have unrealistically high self-expectations, and to be preoccupied with mistreatment from adults outside the family. Their greater difficulties in adjusting to school antedated the appearance of the school phobia itself. The most frequent pattern of interaction was a hostile-dependent relationship between mother and child; here, the child's hostility was disguised as a concern for the destruction which might happen upon separation (for example, accidents, sickness, death), while the interaction itself was marked by intrusive overconcern, irritation, and/or badgering on the mother's part, passive defiance, babyish demanding, whining, and/or resistance on the child's. The next most frequent pattern involved the child's exaggerated fear of failure or teasing at school resulting from low self-esteem and lack of autonomy. There were overlaps between patterns, and both parents and children had more signs of disturbance than were found in the comparison group of neurotics. Incidentally, the fact that the child's fear may concern the parents rather than the school has led certain authorities to prefer the more general term *school refusal* to school phobia.

The above findings suggest that certain school phobias involve separation anxiety and a low degree of autonomy. In terms of our conceptual scheme, the basic problem is one of initiative which, in certain instances, is undermined by the mother but which, in other instances, is weakened by unknown factors. The pattern here reminds us of the one we met in discussing psychopathologies of the toddler period, where there was a complementary relation between the ability to separate from the mother and a feeling of confidence in one's ability to cope with new challenges. However, speculation is tentative at this point because the data are meager and because a number of cases of school phobia seem not to be the result of problems of separation and autonomy.

As we have already noted, little attempt has been made to place school phobia within a *developmental context*. However, there is some evidence that separation anxiety predominates in younger children, while in older children the problem is specific to school and is characterized more by depression and withdrawal (Kelly, 1973). Such a progression would make sense developmentally in terms of the increasing autonomy and self-evaluation of the school-age period. One can speculate that the same parental overdependence underlying separation anxiety in the younger child might subsequently produce feelings of personal inadequacy in meeting the demands of school as school itself increasingly comes to resemble the adult world in terms of its work requirements and peer orientation. Older children may suffer either from a chronic sense of inadequacy or an overevaluation of their abilities, an unrealistically high standard of achievement rendering them vulnerable to overreacting to ordinary failures and setbacks.

While this speculation integrates a certain amount of the data, by no means does it cover the entire etiological, developmental picture. Much more must be learned about school phobias before a comprehensive account will be possible.

Psychoanalytic and Behavioral Models

A psychoanalytic reconstruction of the school phobia would run as follows: initially there is a hostile-dependent relation between mother and child. The child's unacceptable destructive impulse, "I wish my mother were dead," is repressed and returns to consciousness in the disguised form, "I am terrified that she will die," which, in turn, is displaced onto the school situation in the form of, "If I go to school, something terrible will happen to my mother." If the repression is complete, however, the child will have no idea of the source of the terror. Other traumatic events akin to the destructive wish may also trigger an outcropping of anxiety, such as a death in the immediate family or a prolonged illness of the mother. Note that in this psychoanalytic formulation it is not essential for the mother to be concerned about school; rather, school will unconsciously be seized upon by the child as a means of avoiding the terror of being angry with the mother.

On the other hand, it can also happen that a disturbed mother subtly communicates to her child that school is a dangerous place—a communication which might, in turn, play into her dependent, dominated child's fear of never being able to master challenges. The ensuing phobia can be readily explained in terms of the learning principles of modeling and conditioning (in that the stimulus, school, is associated with the response of anxiety), while keeping the child home serves to reinforce the phobic behavior itself. The behavioral approach could also account for phobias resulting from realistic events at school, such as bullying and failures; in such instances, there might have been a repeated association of peers with painful experiences or of failures with various forms of punishment from parents.

Do the findings concerning school phobias allow us to choose one model over the other? Unfortunately not. While the psychoanalysts might point to Waldron's data concerning a hostile-dependent relation between mother and child, they would be the first to admit that such findings in no way validate their theory; instead, they rely primarily on intensive therapy or interviewing as sources of information. The behaviorists could likewise point to findings suggesting that the conditioning, modeling, and reinforcement of anxiety would be highly likely in the case of school phobias. Yet, their account is also inferential, in that it states how the anxiety could be generated and maintained rather than providing data showing that this was indeed what happened (A. O. Ross, 1980, p. 148).

Prognosis and Therapy

Not only are school phobias rarely studied in a developmental context, but many prognostic studies also fail to relate age, intrapersonal, and interpersonal variables or even severity and chronicity of disturbance to outcome. Among these studies short-term prognosis is generally reported as good, 83 percent of phobic children returning to full school attendance (Roberts, 1975). Many of these reports fail to consider subsequent relapses or the appearance of other school problems, however. The long-range outlook is not so bright; around half the population have significant adjustment problems. The results of Roberts's well-designed investigation are more optimistic, indicating that only 25 percent of school phobics had symptoms which created difficulties in attaining a reasonably stable and age-appropriate role; the remaining 75 percent, while not symptom-free, were making adequate adjustments. Since this investigation followed the children longer than many other more pessimistic studies, one might infer that children progressively "outgrow" their difficulties with age; however, Roberts could locate less than half her original group, so her data might contain a disproportionate number of respondents who were getting along well.

One of Roberts's most important findings was that age, sex, chronicity, acuteness of onset, and a wide range of intrapersonal and parental characteristics—with the exception of a psychotic illness in the mother—failed to predict adult outcome. There was some suggestion that initial degree of pathology paralleled the goodness of outcome, and that children with pathological mothers and passive fathers made the poorest adjustment. The most potent prognostic sign was the successful and continued resolution of the symptom itself as evidenced by resuming school on a regular basis with a positive attitude and few subsequent difficulties in regard to school attendance. Such findings would delight those behaviorists who maintain that the symptom is the pathology, although the child's general level of adjustment cannot totally be discounted as a contributing factor to outcome.

THERAPY. School phobia is one of the psychopathologies which readily responds to therapeutic intervention; psychoanalysis and psychoanalytically oriented psychotherapy, behavior modification, cognitive therapy emphasizing the transitory nature of the symptom and the child's ability to overcome it, the ventilation of hostility—all have high rates of cure, as do medication and placebos (Kelly, 1973). A controversial issue cutting across specific psychotherapies concerns the amount of pressure placed on the child to return to school, some therapists regarding an immediate return as essential even if some force must be applied, others recommending timing the return in keeping with therapeutic progress. However, there is general agreement that the child should return as soon as possible, even if only for a brief period.

Relative Effectiveness of Different Therapies

With diverse therapies claiming to cure phobias, the question naturally arises as to which is the most effective. In light of the dismal state of research on the neuroses, it is gratifying to report that one of the few model studies in all the therapeutic literature is addressed to answering this question. The study serves as a model for many reasons. The children were evaluated objectively by individuals other than the therapist, thus eliminating the unconscious biases which might creep in when therapists evaluate their own work. The groups of children receiving different treatment were carefully matched at the beginning to ensure that one was not better adjusted, more intelligent, and so forth than the other. Even more important, the therapists themselves were matched in terms of skill, so the outcomes would reflect the kind of therapy rather than the expertness with which it was implemented. The therapeutic goals were agreed upon, so that improvement in both groups conformed to the same behavioral criteria and was therefore comparable. Finally, the test of therapeutic effectiveness was made at the end of a follow-up period, since there is evidence that immediate improvement tends to wash out with time.

This model study was conducted by Miller, Barrett, Hampe, and Noble (1972), who compared the relative effectiveness of a behavioral therapy (reciprocal inhibition), a psychoanalytically oriented play therapy, and a control group of children on a waiting list who received no therapy. All sixty-seven subjects were phobic, the ones in treatment receiving one-hour sessions three times a week for eight weeks. All children were evaluated at the end of a six-week follow-up period. There was no evidence that either therapy was more effective, which might have been, in part, because the actual behavior of the therapists from the two different schools was quite similar! There was a diminution of symptoms in all three groups. Whether the two therapy groups improved more than the nontreated control group depended on who evaluated them, parents reporting significantly greater improvement, a noninvolved clinician finding none. Age proved to be a significant variable, 6- to 10-year-olds showing greater improvement with therapy than the controls, 11- to 15-year-olds failing to show such a difference. Similar results concerning the relative effectiveness of behavioral and psychoanalytically oriented psychotherapy have been found with adults (Sloane, Staples, Cristol, Yorkston, and Shipple, 1975).

In light of the fact that poorly designed studies of therapeutic effectiveness have been so misleading in the past, our preference is to conclude that, at present, there is no treatment of choice for childhood neuroses. Our conclusion is also congruent with reviews of outcome studies indicating that no one therapeutic approach has been shown to be superior to the others (Bergin and Lamberts, 1978).

Subsequent Developments

In the review of longitudinal studies in chapter 3, we found that there could be continuity of specific deviant behaviors from childhood into adulthood, continuity in terms of general severity of disturbance, and discontinuity of development—with either disturbed children becoming adequately adjusted adults or adequately functioning children becoming disturbed adults. We also saw that there was a surprising discontinuity in regard to neurotic behavior. True, there was some continuity of symptoms—for example, a small percent of hysterical children became hysterical adults—and some continuity of severity, in that children with a large number of neurotic symptoms tended to have various kinds of disturbances as adults. But on the whole a sizable number of neurotic children tended to become adequately adjusted adults, regardless of whether or not they received treatment.

But now we come to a dilemma. In spite of the many reports of success, there is no evidence that treatment as compared with no treatment makes any difference in prognosis. "Life" or "growth" seems to be as effective as any professional therapist (Roberts, 1975). How, then, can a clinician in good conscience treat a child for a disturbance which the child would probably "outgrow" with time? This dilemma, which strikes at the very heart of the therapeutic enterprise with children, will be examined in depth in chapter 14.

8 ▪ Acting-Out Behavior—Inadequate Self-Control

YOU ARE A CLINICAL CHILD PSYCHOLOGIST. YOU ARRIVE AT YOUR OFFICE AT EIGHT IN THE morning. Mark Redfleish is already waiting. He says, "Hi, Doc! Dad dropped me off on his way to work." He is a lively, assured 11-year-old, nice looking, well built but small for his age. An all-American-type boy. Except that, for the past two years, he has been breaking into, ransacking, and robbing houses in the wealthy suburb where he lives. At first he threw the stolen silverware and hi-fi sets into a nearby lake. Then he established connections with a man who bought the loot with no questions asked. After a robbery was discovered, Mark would show up and offer to help put the house back in order. His manner was one of sincere concern, and he asked for no favors in return. He was finally caught because a careless remark revealed that he knew an item had been stolen before the owner had mentioned it to anyone outside the family.

Mark is bright, enterprising, and capable beyond his years. But he is also a daredevil and a loner. He loves to ride his motorbike at full speed over a downhill path through the woods, making it jump over small crevices and creeks, doing a "pop-a-wheely" by riding only on the back wheel, turning sharply at the end of the ride in a cloud of dust. At school he was the youngest boy to smoke marijuana and drink alcohol. He charmed his way into being taught how to drive a car and then bribed the caretaker's son into letting him use the jeep to ride on the back roads on the far side of the lake. Yet he is not a show-off or a braggart, nor is he responding to dares. Rather he is obeying an inner restlessness.

Other boys are sporadically attracted by Mark's daring and helpfulness, but friendships are short-lived. He enjoys luring younger boys into joining him in venturing into forbidden places—a beer-and-wine carryout, an adult bookstore, an abandoned quarry—because he likes being in command. In school he is restless and inattentive, except in shop, where his interests and skills make him the top student. He is a master of the sincere lie—looking the teacher straight in the face. One of them said, "I just can't reach him with anything. I could beat him or plead with him or take him on my lap and cuddle him, and it just wouldn't matter."

Mark's father, a successful surgeon, has little time for his family during the week but enjoys being with his son on weekends, going hunting and ice-skating in the winter, fishing and sailing in the summer. In his eyes, Mark could do no wrong. Even the robberies were extenuated: "Wild colts make good horses," was what he told you. Mark's mother is basically a kind and loving woman but lacking in resources. Early on she perceived Mark's disregard for her prohibitions concerning dangerous objects and activities, and she did not know what to do about his constant lying. But more than anything else, his sheer energy exhausted her patience. Affection and reasoning gave way to angry shouts and finally to whippings with a strap. Mark was determined not to cry; he sensed that, if she could not hurt him, she would be powerless.

At ten o'clock you see Angelo Ruccio, another 11-year-old, for the second time. He will be brought by his parole officer, since the judge has said that either he gets psychological help or he would be confined in the juvenile correctional center. "That's like playing tennis with both hands tied behind your back," you think, but it is far better than having the boy sent to a punitive, ineptly run institution. The judge was lenient because Angie was the only member of his gang to get caught breaking into and robbing a corner grocery store. He was caught because he was obviously a not-too-bright follower who was doing what he was told.

Yet his loyalty to the gang far outweighs any sense of wrongdoing. And for good reason. School has been an endless series of humiliations and failures. He was passed primarily because he was not a troublemaker, and his teachers became tired of yelling at him for making mistakes and handing in sloppy homework. His family is large and poor, and while they fight a good deal, they also have a sense of loyalty. The father is a laborer who is hired and fired according to the state of the economy. He is a bitter man who demands respect from his children but sees no reason for them to be good citizens in a society which has treated him so shabbily. To his mother—a meek, careworn woman—Angie is another mouth to feed, and while she prays to the Virgin every night to help her children, she wonders where she will get the strength to see her through another day.

So it is the gang that gives Angie a sense of belonging, of sharing, of being valued. While his slowness makes him the goat, the leader has taken a liking to him, and Angie's fondest dream is one day to become a leader himself. That will be a tough dream to shatter, and right now you do not know what you can put in its place.

You have been seeing Richard Hammer, a 10-year-old, for half a year, and he is making good progress. Rick's father owns a successful chain of hardware stores. He knows how to succeed and how to enjoy life. He has a large house with a swimming pool, a yacht, and a private plane. He also has a large family who shares in the pleasures success has brought. In this zestful, expansive atmosphere, Rick was out of place—"the runt of the lot," his father called him. He was a sensitive and shy youngster, more an onlooker than a participant. His vulnerability touched his mother's heart, and she hovered over him with a special mixture of protectiveness and good-hearted shaming, which alternately delighted and embarrassed Rick—and made him feel all the more inadequate. Rick was a serious student who did well in school and had a close friendship with a boy who, like himself, was a bright, quiet outsider.

All seemed to be going well until Rick's mother,

while looking for an old lamp in the attic, came upon a box filled with various tools which her husband told her had been missing from one of his stores. When she confronted the family with her discovery, Rick began to cry and beg forgiveness. It was readily granted, and the matter seemed to be settled. A few weeks later, however, the mother found some money clips and three gold pen-and-pencil sets at the bottom of Rick's underwear drawer. They were poorly concealed, "as if he wanted me to find them," she said. The parents decided that their son needed help.

In therapy Rick at first did not know why he had an irresistible urge to take things. As it turned out, he had had the compulsion for four or five years but had always taken small items—a box of nails, a cheap pair of earrings. The more serious thefts began around the time the oldest sibling became engaged. The wedding became the center of everyone's attention, including the mother. Gradually Rick began talking about feeling angry and cheated. You begin to suspect that stealing was in part an expression of that anger, in part a bid for attention, in part a symbolic compensation for his feeling of being deprived of love.

CHILDREN WITH INADEQUATE SELF-CONTROL

The lesson is familiar—the same pathological behavior may have different origins. In this case, the lesson is particularly important in light of the consequences of antisocial behavior, as we shall see. Studies of groups of antisocial adolescents have yielded three types: the psychopathic or sociopathic, the subcultural, and the neurotic. While only the first type will be dealt with here, it will be instructive briefly to compare it with the other two. (For a more extensive presentation, see Clarizio and McCoy, 1976).

The Psychopathic or Sociopathic Delinquent

Traditionally regarded as the most severe disturbance of the three, the psychopathic pattern is marked by active, antisocial aggressiveness. Fighting, disruptiveness, destructiveness, temper tantrums, irresponsibility, disobedience, and attention seeking are characteristic behaviors, along with a history of physical aggression and defiance of authority. Psychopaths are impulsive, fail to learn from experience, and are deficient in guilt feelings and anxiety. Their difficulty in accepting any authority brings them into constant conflict with the school and the law. Their disregard for social values is evidenced in stealing, lying, drinking, and sexual misbehaviors. Finally, their relations with both family and peers are shallow.

Since psychopaths are the purest example of inadequate self-control, we will be studying them in detail. Note that Mark is a special case. He is more like an embryonic "con man" because he is more controlled and socially adroit than the blatantly antisocial psychopath. But the irresistible impulse to action, combined with a disregard for social and moral values, an unconcern for the feelings of others, an absence of guilt, and an inability to form a close relation with parents and peers are sufficient to include him in the category.

The Subcultural Delinquent

Subcultural delinquents have not developed in a deviant manner but have been socialized with a deviant set of values. Typically they come from a stable lower-class home in a deteriorated urban area. As was the case with Angie, these children have little chance to learn the accepted values of society. The gang—with its emphasis on physical prowess and the ability to outwit others, its rebelliousness toward authority, and its desire for excitement—becomes central in their lives. Unlike psychopaths, subcultural delinquents are fiercely loyal to peers; while they are relatively unconcerned over their antisocial acts, their failure to live up to the standards of the gang produces guilt. Subcultural delinquents are considered the least disturbed of the three types, since it is primarily the content of their socialization that is deviant.

Some sociologists have concluded that since they are reasonably sound psychologically, the cultural delinquents' problems are rooted in a faulty society and social action is the remedy. Various theories have been proposed. The anomie theory states that lower-class people have the same values and goals as do middle-class individuals but are deprived of the means of achieving them. In their frustration they turn to deviant means. The term *anomie* itself refers to their state of being detached and dispirited. Other theorists have claimed that the lower class has a culture all its own whose values—such as being smart, tough, and daring—differ from those in the middle class. Neither theory is without its difficulties, and attempts at empirical validation have yielded equivocal results (see Achenbach, 1974).

The Neurotic Delinquent

The children here are no different from other neurotics, except that—like Rick—they engage in antisocial acts. In general, they are shy, self-conscious, hypersensitive, unhappy, guilty, worried—all the signs of excessive socialization. Why they go against the grain and act out rather than consistently internalizing their problems is an unsolved mystery.

Cautionary Remarks

Classifying delinquents according to types does not mean that they are qualitatively different from other children. There is evidence that half of the nondelinquent adolescents admit to having engaged in antisocial behavior such as truanting, petty theft, buying and drinking liquor, intentionally damaging property, and violating game laws (Clarizio and McCoy, 1976). Thus, a certain amount of acting out against society is to be expected as part of the normal growth process. Within the family, outbursts of temper, stubbornness, and defiance may also be part of the normal turmoil of early adolescence. Individual delinquents often present a mixed picture: a psychopathic delinquent may engage in gang activities, for example. Finally, antisocial behavior is compatible with other disturbances: a mentally defective boy may steal because he has not fully grasped the prohibition, while vicious aggression can be part of a psychotic disintegration.

In discussing autism and anorexia nervosa it was important to distinguish "pure" cases from those confounded by other disturbances. In antisocial behavior there is yet another source of confusion: "juvenile delinquency" is a legal term for all youths who have committed antisocial acts as defined by law and who have been caught. Not only does the legal definition vary from state to state, but it may also be at variance with psychological criteria of disturbance. We have just seen that antisocial behavior may be part of normal development as well as being a feature of other kinds of disturbances, while even pure cases may have diverse roots. Psychological studies and therapeutic interventions which uncritically accept the legal designation of juvenile delinquents are apt to produce confused and contradictory results.

Additional Findings

Research on differentiated groups of delinquents is comparatively meager. There is evidence that instead of being overreactive, the psychopath may have a relatively underreactive autonomic nervous system and the aggressive, thrill-seeking behavior may be an attempt to relieve boredom (Quay, 1979).

Findings concerning the family context are sparse (Hetherington and Martin, 1979). For the psychopathic delinquent, parental rejection of boys runs high, and while aggression is restricted in the home, it is encouraged on the outside; for girls there is no clear pattern of parental dominance, little parental control, and inconsistent discipline. There is some evidence that the mother is dominant in the families of neurotic delinquents, while the father is dominant in the other two types. Parents of neurotic delinquents seem high on ambivalence: they are punitive, restrictive, and anxious about aggression on the one hand but have a stable, happy marriage, uphold conventional values, and are distressed by their child's antisocial activities. Some studies picture the families of cultural delinquents as stable and relatively normal; other studies find parents to be rejecting and permissive with sons, while exercising little control over their daughters. Jenkins (1973) claims that the children do not want for affection but rather lack effective supervision, control, and adequate parental models to emulate. Certainly, more substantial data need to be obtained before we can have a clear picture of the relation of family patterns to different kinds of delinquencies.

One interesting finding is that female delinquency seems to be increasing, and there is a shift from the traditional "feminine" crimes of sexual delinquency, running away, and incorrigibility to the more "masculine" crimes of auto theft, burglary, assault, and vandalism. Incidentally here is another illustration of changing social attitudes—this time in regard to women—affecting the incidence and manifestation of psychopathological behavior. Such developments may also affect the generalizability of longitudinal data.

(For a general review of the literature on delinquents as a group, see Peterson and Becker, 1965.)

INADEQUATE SELF-CONTROL AND ACTING-OUT BEHAVIOR

Self-control is essential to socialization. A 4-year-old may not attack a 2-year-old sibling in a rage, masturbate in the supermarket, or try out a new toy hammer on the hi-fi set. Honesty, truthfulness, respect for the rights and property of others, obedience to the authority first of parents, then of teachers, and finally of the law are required. The requirements are essential because toddlers and preschoolers have a strong desire for immediate gratification of their aggressive, sexual, and exploratory urges, and they tend to be greedy, egocentric, selfish, and self-seeking. The reasons why adequate self-control fails to develop or to function properly will be explored in this chapter.

Behaviors resulting from inadequate self-control are termed *acting out*, which includes aggression, temper tantrums, lying, stealing, truancy, vandalism, fire setting, disobedience, and bullying. Note that some of the behaviors, such as aggression and temper tantrums, have a high-intensity, impulsive quality; others, such as lying and stealing, may be of low intensity and premeditated. But they all involve a breach of socially accepted behavior.

For the first time in our discussions the *societal* context rivals the home and the school in importance: the 12-year-old who is caught cutting up all the clothes in her mother's closet or clogging the school toilets with sanitary napkins is in a different social situation from the one who is arrested for shoplifting. Getting into trouble with the law may involve the child in juvenile court and correctional institutions, both of which may have a special impact on the child's future. For this reason we need to examine the social-legal context in detail.

The Development of Normal Control

At this point a review of the variables involved in the development of normal self-control is in order. First there are ones which give an *affective* charge to socializing directives—the bond of affection that makes the child educable, and later, sympathy and empathy, which counteract self-centeredness. Then there are a host of *intellectual* and *cognitive* variables. At the most basic level, the child must be able to remember the socializing message and recall it at appropriate times. Increased intellectual sophistication enables the child to progress from simple directives ("Don't touch that vase") to generalizations ("Everything in the living room is off limits") to conditional statements ("Don't take anything that belongs to somebody else unless you ask them first"). The development of *language* significantly facilitates the process of delaying and guiding action in accordance with socially accepted values. Concomitantly the child becomes increasingly practiced in making decisions and taking responsibility for actions. A dependable, trustworthy *environment* also aids the child in postponing immediate gratification, as does the ability to find substitute gratifications or alternative means of achieving a goal.

The development of *conscience* and *ego ideals* plays a part in countering impulsivity and egocentrism. Cognitively, moral judgment progresses from a concern with immediate rewards and punishments for specific acts to the morality of shared standards, rights, and duties, while the ego ideal changes from superficial and exaggerated images of glamour and success to realistic, socially oriented images. The affects involved in the conscience and ego ideal are self-satisfaction and self-esteem on the one hand, guilt, shame, and inferiority on the other.

In the interpersonal sphere both *parents* and *peers* play an important role in the development of self-control. In general, the optimal family setting includes affection and consistency, age-appropriate requirements for self-control and autonomy, help in understanding consequences of one's actions, and explicitness as to values. Peers counter egocentrism by forcing accommodations and by valuing proven worth over pedigree.

Clearly, an impressive array of factors contribute to self-control. Now let us see what blocks and undermines its development. In this presentation a number of longitudinal studies will be explored, and then acting-out behavior in middle childhood will be examined in detail. The questions we shall be asking are: How well do the variables just enumerated account for the behavior of pathologically disturbed children? and What development model is most appropriate?

THE PRESCHOOL PERIOD

We will start with the hypothesis that many instances of acting out in the preschool period represent *developmental lags.* In the case of temper tantrums, we expect infants to react to frustrations with rage. During the "terrible twos," willful toddlers are also apt to strike out in anger when they do not have their way, but now they can intentionally try to hurt. By 5 to 6 years of age the incidence of severe explosions should be rare (MacFarlane, Allen, and Honzik, 1954). Their persistence suggests both that the child is not making appropriate progress in achieving self-control and that he or she will be ill equipped to adjust to the demands of school successfully.

The hypothesis of a developmental lag

also holds for stealing and lying. Let us examine the former. For the toddler every attractive object is fair game for exploration; it is the socializing adult who divides the world into things that are "OK" and things that are "no-no's." Prohibitions based on property rights are particularly difficult for the toddler to grasp. There is nothing in an object itself which proclaims its status as "mine" or "yours," so other cues must be utilized such as location ("mine" comes out of the big box by the bed I sleep in) or frequency of use (the fire engine big brother plays with all the time is a "not-mine"). Concurrently the toddler must learn that it is wrong to take objects which do not belong to him or her. While taking property peaks at 3 years of age (MacFarlane et al., 1954), this should not be regarded as stealing, since the idea of property rights has not registered. Only after the meaning of prohibitions has been grasped and intentional transgression has occurred does "taking" become "stealing."

And so it goes for lying. A mark of early thinking is a failure to differentiate the physical world from the psychological world of thoughts, feelings, and wishes. The 3-year-old boy who quite literally believes there is a wolf under his bed at night also quite literally may believe that his big sister started a fight, when he himself was to blame. Only after objective and subjective reality have been differentiated can the concept of lying become meaningful. By 6 years of age the child should have grasped the basic meaning of stealing and lying, although the understanding of both will continue to develop.

Now suppose a mother came to you as a clinician and said, "My 4-year-old is always lying to me." Suppose further that you found out these were mainly face-saving lies. Would you reassure the mother that "most children her age tell such lies, and there is nothing to worry about?" Not all all. The chance that there is nothing to worry about does not negate the importance of exploring context variables. In regard to the little girl, you would at least want to know if this is the only sign of disturbance. The clinician should look not only for other symptoms but also for evidence of a generalized developmental lag. For example, does the girl habitually shun peers and play alone? Is her play repetitive? Is she withdrawn whenever she goes outside the protection of the home? Does she prefer to be only with her mother? The context of the mother's complaint is equally important. Does it arise from a lack of information concerning normal development, or does the mother talk about the child with the kind of controlled exasperation which suggests that lying just provides an excuse for expressing an underlying resentment? You might also ask about the father and the general pattern of family interaction before deciding that information coupled with reassurance is all that is needed. While the developmental approach helps put behavior in perspective, it does not supply categorical answers.

One final clinical example. A 19-year-old mother is complaining about her 3-year-old.

HE DON'T DO NOTHING BUT BAD [THINGS]. If he don't like what I make him [to eat], he throw it on the floor. I tell him I'm going to take a strap to him, and he just yells back at me, "Shut up, you old mother fucker," and I whip him with all I got and he still don't cry until he have to. . . . He pees in the closet every time he takes a mind to, and he takes his BMs and rubs them in his hair right while I'm looking at him. . . . Now he's taken to getting up in the middle of the night and turning on the bathwater with the stopper in so there's water all over the place. . . . If somebody don't straighten him out soon, I'm going to kill him!

At first glance the boy's behavior would seem to be primitive and uncontrolled. However, note that he smears feces in front of his mother and gets up in the middle of the night to flood the bathroom, both of which suggest purposeful behavior. As it turns out, he knows quite well what he is doing. The mother is unmarried, childish, already worn down by poverty and lovelessness. Both emotionally and intellectually she was unprepared to be a mother at 16 years of age and felt burdened and resentful toward the baby. Fortunately for the boy, his grandmother was able to care for him, although only fitfully and grudgingly. The attention the boy received from his mother was primarily angry shouts and whippings. He was a resilient child, and in the toddler period he not only grasped the connection between doing "bad" things and exasperating his mother but also began to use it for all it was worth. The negative attention he gained from the mother was better than neglect, while her distress was his revenge.

Is Acting-Out Behavior "Outgrown"?

Data to answer this question come from Kohn's (1977) five-year longitudinal study of 1,232 lower- and middle-class preschoolers. Kohn developed two scales, one entitled Interest-Participation versus Apathy-Withdrawal, the other entitled Cooperation-Compliance versus Anger-Defiance. It is the latter which interests us. Items at the Anger-Defiance extreme include "child expresses open defiance against teacher's rules and regulations," "child is hostile or aggressive with other children (teases, taunts, bullies, etc.)." The children's behavior was evaluated by their teachers.

High anger and apathy scores in the preschool period were more predictive of overall evaluations of disturbance and need for psychological treatment in the fourth grade than were social class, race, ethnicity, and broken homes. In fact, sex was the only demographic variable of any predictive potency; boys became more disturbed than girls. Incidentally, both sexes tended to become more disturbed and to achieve less as they progressed through school; boys showed the greatest change in the first and second grades, and girls became more apathetic during the first three grades but showed no consistent pattern of change in aggressiveness. Kohn notes that there is no evidence that the emphasis on "feminine" values of obedience and docility caused boys to become disturbed; rather, schooling accentuated the behavioral problems already present.

While aggressiveness was the most stable behavior over the five-year period, the significant correlation of 0.36 was sufficiently low to indicate that a good deal of change was also taking place. Analysis of the data revealed that 59 percent of the preschoolers scoring high in Aggressiveness were no longer disturbed in the fourth grade; moreover, 14 percent of the highest-scoring aggressive children were subsequently among the healthiest fourth graders, while 13 percent and 16 percent respectively of the preschoolers scoring highest on Interest and Cooperation were now rated either extremely aggressive or extremely apathetic.

The findings are both significant and sobering in light of the current emphasis on early detection and remediation of psychological disturbances. Kohn rightfully points out that his scales are a giant step forward in detecting high-risk preschoolers. But he also admits that predictability becomes increasingly inaccurate with the passage of time. As they stand, his data mean that an intervention program at the preschool level would be wasted on 59 percent of the aggressive children who would "spontaneously outgrow" their problem, while missing the 29 percent of extremely well-adjusted preschoolers who subsequently would become disturbed. Parenthetically, telling the parents of a well-functioning preschooler that their child needs psychological help has built-in dilemmas. Would a preventive program be worth the time and money involved? The question has no easy answer. In part, it depends on how readily the early difficulties could be remedied and how serious the consequences if they were not. If a year of psychological help would save 40 percent of the children from severe academic underachievement and eventual delinquency, a preventive program would clearly be called for. As the time-and-money cost of change goes up and the severity of the ultimate disturbance declines, the need for early intervention becomes less clear. While no one would quarrel with the idea of preventive mental health, some of the problems involved in its implementation are concretely illustrated by Kohn's data.

Etiological Considerations

Both *temperament* and *parental behavior* have been frequently implicated as etiological agents in acting-out behavior. In their well-known study of temperament, Thomas, Chess, and Birch (1968) documented an impression parents have long had that some infants are easy to care for, while others are difficult. The latter are irregular in physiological functions—such as the sleep-wake cycle, eating, and elimination—intense and negative in mood, and nonadaptable in that caretakers have difficulty in changing their behavior in a desired direction. One suspects they have special problems in achieving self-control owing to their irregularity and the frequency with which they are engulfed by negative affect. Such characteristics certainly make the job of socialization particularly trying for the parent.

Longitudinal data indicate that, indeed, difficult infants have a significantly greater number of psychological disturbances in the preschool years than the rest of the population studied. However, the disturbances are primarily mild to moderate in degree and involve not only acting-out behaviors (temper tantrums, bossiness, protective lying, stealing) but also worry, anxiety when separated from the mother, and sensitivity to teasing. Thus, while a certain temperament may predispose an infant to mild or moderate psychological problems, it is not specifically related to acting-out behavior in the preschool period. (For a critique of the concept, see Bates, 1980.)

There is also evidence that interpersonal variables affect self-control in the preschool years. In general, aggression increases if the parents are either severely punitive or permissive. Acting-out behavior also increases if discipline is inconsistent, one parent being restrictive, the other lax. Identification with a dominant, hostile parent is facilitated when there is disharmony between the parents and when both parents are cold; if either disharmony decreases or the nondominant parent is warm, hostile identification also decreases. These findings apply to both normal and disturbed preschoolers and usually are more striking for boys than for girls. (For a more detailed account of the research, see Hetherington and Martin, 1979.) Peer interactions can also play an important role either in reinforcing the aggressive preschooler or in turning the passive, nonassertive child into an actively aggressive one (Patterson, Littman, and Bricker, 1967).

MIDDLE CHILDHOOD AND ADOLESCENCE

Early in our discussion we discovered that children evidencing neurotic behavior in middle childhood stood a good chance of achieving normal adjustment once they reached adulthood. Such fortunate malleability of behavior does not apply to acting out. Longitudinal studies of aggression, of disturbed children and of normal children who subsequently become disturbed, all document its fixed nature. It will be worthwhile to examine these studies in detail. (For a summary of studies of adolescence, see Gold and Petronio, 1980.)

Longitudinal Studies: Aggression

Olweus's (1979) review of sixteen longitudinal studies of aggression in males sets the stage. While not concerned with psychopathology, these studies do trace the course of a behavior which lies at the heart of self-control. Olweus concludes that there is a substantial degree of stability of aggression over time; indeed, it seems to be as stable as intelligence. Since there is a tendency for the most aggressive boys to drop out of longitudinal studies, the available data may even underestimate the degree of stability.

Olweus was able to summarize the findings with a simple formula: the younger the subject and the longer the interval of time, the less the stability. Thus, for example, over the same interval of time, a 2-year-old's aggressive behavior will vary more than that of a 10-year-old; and at any given age, predictability decreases with the passage of time. By the time the boy is 8 or 9, there is a substantial correlation with aggressive patterns ten to fourteen years later; by 12 to 13 years of age, the stability is even higher for the next 10 years and, as we shall see, has considerable predictive capacity for later antisocial aggression.

The stability of aggressive behavior in the face of environmental variation and influence designed to change it leads Olweus to conclude that it is a relatively consistent reaction tendency or motivational system within the individual. Far from reacting to environmental provocation, highly aggressive children may actively seek out situations in which to express their need. Learning theorists who prefer viewing aggression as environmentally elicited and sustained would challenge such an interpretation, and definitive tests of these discrepant viewpoints are lacking. Whatever the reason, the data themselves indicate that the control of aggression has a significant impact on future development.

Olweus offers two cautionary statements, however. Aggression should not be regarded as a simple trait which is expressed regardless of the situation, and its stability should not be interpreted as an inevitability. As always we are talking in relative not absolute terms—of characteristics not caricatures, of probabilities not fate.

Olweus (1978) also conducted a model study of aggression as manifested in bullying behavior. He shares Hetherington's versatility in utilizing *objective* procedures in a *naturalistic* setting but, unlike Hetherington (see chapter 5) is more concerned with systematically exploring hypotheses concerning correlates of the behavior under investigation.

Olweus was scrupulous in selecting his population of bullies. First he interviewed sixth-grade teachers who, because the study was conducted in Sweden, had known the children for three years, asking them to select and describe any bullies in the class. A bully was defined as a boy who fairly often oppressed or harassed someone else either physically or mentally. The same question was asked of a shop teacher who taught two or three classes to the children, while the children themselves made peer ratings of boys who started fights. A year later, when the boys were in a new school with a new teacher, the teacher was again asked to select bullies. The agreement among these four sources of information was high, indicating that the bullying behavior was consistent over situations and over time. The objective techniques and findings of the study will be described in terms of our own developmental model.

The *superordinate* context of school size and class size was examined by demographic data on the number of children in each. Socioeconomic status was determined by the parents' income and education. There was no relation to bullying in spite of the popular notion that such behavior flourishes in large classes and large schools and that it is predominently a lower-class phenomenon. The *interpersonal* context in the classroom was explored by questioning the teacher about the overall quality of the class, peer relations, attitudes toward homework, as well as the teacher's own feelings about teaching this particular class. A standardized attitude inventory tapping peer relations and attitudes toward the teacher and toward homework, was administered to a total of 247 boys in various schools. A special technique called *sociometric choices* was also used as a measure of popularity. In this instance, the boys and girls were asked to select the four classmates they would prefer to spend their breaks with. The children with the highest number of choices were regarded as the most popular. Peer ratings concerning fighting which were utilized in selecting bullies, were also included. None of the schoolwork and teacher variables related to bullying. However, peer relations did prove to be important; bullies were both very aggressive and relatively popular. Thus, hypotheses that classroom atmosphere and social isolation are correlates of bullying were not supported.

A number of *intrapersonal* variables were explored. Grades were used as an index of academic achievement. The teacher filled out a checklist of fourteen characteristics relevant to physical appearance and strength. To assess personality characteristics, the boys and their mothers performed a *Q sort,* which is a special technique that involves placing fifty-seven items in seven different piles ranging from "applies very well to me (my son)" to "applies very poorly to me (my son)": for example, "Generally I (my son) am (is) fairly sure of myself (himself)"; "I (my son) prefer(s) to get out of the way when someone is picking on me (him)." Finally, characterizations were extracted from the sixth-grade teachers' description of the bullies. Except for being stronger than the average boy, the bullies were not physically deviant, nor were their grades below average. While more aggressive and having a more positive attitude toward violence than the average boy, bullies were secure, unafraid, and evaluated themselves and their behavior positively.

In general, the hypothesis that bullying is a reaction to a host of variables—social isolation, low academic achievement, physical deviations, crowded classrooms, and so forth—received little support; neither did the hypothesis that bullying is accompanied by personality problems such as a negative self-image, anxiety, and guilt. Olweus's study is not only a revelation; it is in every respect an exemplary piece of research.

Longitudinal Studies: Psychopathological Development

In the 1950s, Robins (1966) compared 491 adults who had been seen at a child guidance center thirty years previously with a control group of 100 normal children matched for age, sex, IQ scores, race, and SES. Children with IQs below 80 were eliminated. The population was predominantly male children of American-born Protestant parents of low socioeconomic status. Family disruption was high, with only one-third of the children living with both parents. Approximately one-quarter to one-third of the fathers drank excessively and failed to provide financial support, while almost half of the mothers were severely nervous, mentally ill, or feeble-minded.

The continuity of antisocial behavior was striking—45 percent of the clinic group having five or more antisocial symptoms as adults, as compared with 4 percent of the control group. Conversely, the absence of antisocial behavior in childhood made the appearance of adult sociopathy extremely unlikely. Children referred for problems other than antisocial behavior—temper tantrums, irritability, fears, shyness, insomnia, tics—tended to be diagnosed as hysterics, alcoholics, or psychotics somewhat more frequently than the control group, but the differences were not as striking as with antisocial behavior; in fact, antisocial children were equally liable to become psychotic adults as were children referred for other behavior.

Antisocial—or what Robins calls sociopathic—behavior occurred solely in males, beginning early in the boy's schooling. However, age of onset did not predict adult status when severity of antisocial behavior was held constant; thus, there is no evidence that early onset is particularly ominous. Theft, incorrigibility, running away, associating with bad companions, sexual activities, and staying out late were prominent reasons for referral. Most children were discipline problems in school—62 percent never graduated from grammar school—and were variously described as aggressive, reckless, impulsive, slovenly, enuretic, lacking guilt, and lying without cause. Almost four out of five appeared in juvenile court, and around half were sent to correctional institutions. Antisocial behavior was directed toward parents and teachers, businesses and strangers. Approximately half of the future sociopaths had fathers who were themselves sociopathic or alcoholic, while two-thirds came from broken homes.

As adults, almost every sociopath had marital problems and a poor work history and had been financially dependent on social agents or relatives. Three-fourths had multiple arrests and prison terms. They were impulsive, sexually promiscuous, vagrant, belligerent, and socially isolated.

Of greatest interest to us are Robins's findings concerning the predictive potential of childhood variables. The single best predictor was the *degree of antisocial behavior* as evidenced by the number of symptoms, the number of episodes, and the seriousness of the behaviors as measured by appearance in juvenile court and being sent to a correctional institution. Surprisingly, many variables frequently reported as childhood characteristics of adult sociopaths were not predictive when the level of the child's antisocial behavior was taken into account—parental deprivation and rejection, being a school dropout, poverty, foster home or orphanage placement, and antisocial behavior on the part of the mother.

Sex, age, class, and ethnic values determined the *kind* of deviancy, not the deviancy itself: for example, antisocial acts among women were confined to sexual and maternal areas and the Irish children were more likely to develop alcoholism than other ethnic groups. Nor does "bad company" predict future sociopathy. Rather than the good boy being led astray by the availability of delinquent gangs, the antisocial child seeks out other children on the basis of common interests—a point which Olweus made about normally aggressive children.

For boys who had fewer than six antisocial symptoms and therefore were not deeply enmeshed in antisocial behavior, it was the fathers who played the central role in determining their fate. More than two-thirds of such boys had fathers who were themselves sociopaths or alcoholics. These children were likely to live in lower-class neighborhoods, receive little or inconsistent discipline, or be sent to a correctional institution by a juvenile court wishing to remove them from the home environment. However, sociopathic behavior in middle-class fathers had the same detrimental effect upon predelinquent middle-class sons.

For the boys with six or more antisocial symptoms, lack of discipline or inconsistent discipline was important in determining which ones would and would not become adult sociopaths. The pioneering Cambridge-Somerville Youth Study (McCord and McCord, 1969), which followed 253 11-year-old boys from a densely populated, economically deteriorated urban setting for a period of sixteen years, produced a similar finding concerning discipline and modeling. In general, parental warmth and family cohesiveness were related to a low incidence of criminal behavior; quarrelsome and neglecting homes, lax or inconsistent discipline (either between or within parents) was related to a high incidence of criminal behavior. Interestingly, punitive discipline consistently applied checked subsequent criminal behavior. If the father was cruel, neglectful, erratic, or lax in discipline, if he was absent, and if he was a criminal himself, the chance of criminal behavior increased. Such findings fit nicely into our discussion of the importance of warmth, consistency of socialization, and modeling in the development of self-control.

One final point: in reviewing all the predictive variables, eleven involved characteristics of the child or the severity of his antisocial behavior; only two involved parental behavior, one involved family size, and two involved social institutions (juvenile court and correctional institutions). Thus, the child's current behavior predicts his future better than any context variable. This is too provocative a finding to let pass; we shall return to it after presenting the final longitudinal study.

Longitudinal Studies: Pathological Development in a Normal Population

In 1970, Lefkowitz, Eron, Walder, and Huesmann (1977) reevaluated 427 19-year-olds who had initially been studied in 1959 as third-graders. Unlike Robins's population, this one was predominantly middle class, all had finished twelve grades of school, there was an equal number of boys and girls, and the setting was a semirural county. Peer and parental ratings, personality tests, and self-report questionnaires were used to evaluate aggression that is "desirable neither for the individual nor society." The investigators were particularly interested in instigations to aggression—parental rejection, lack of parental nurturance, parental disharmony, and television violence—in parental punishment as a reinforcer of aggression, and in identification both with the parents and with the child's own sex role.

The intriguing overall finding was that while parental instigators were related to contemporary aggression, they were not predictive; identification variables, on the other hand, were. Specifically, when the children were third-graders, parental rejection was significantly related to aggression in both sexes, as were lack of nurturance and low school achievement in the case of boys, but none of these instigators was predictive.

Punishment was related to neither present nor future aggression.

Parenthetically, the research literature contains another example of this baffling discrepancy between contemporary and predictive variables. On the basis of extensive research, the Gluecks developed criteria which can differentiate delinquents from nondelinquents. The criteria have generally been confirmed by other investigators; for example, delinquency, alcoholism, and emotional disturbance in the parents, a crowded and disorderly home, parental indifference or hostility toward the boy, lax or unsuitable discipline (see Peterson and Becker, 1965). Yet these criteria as measured in a population of 6-year-old boys failed successfully to predict their delinquency at 15 to 17 years of age (Voss, 1963).

Returning to the Lefkowitz study, low identification with parents turned out to be the most potent predictor of aggression for both sexes. Boys who identified with their mothers and preferred girls' games were subsequently low on aggression; girls who identified with their fathers were likewise low, although their sex typing as revealed in game preference was not predictive. On the other hand, parental religiosity was predictive of low aggression for girls but not for boys. Thus, it seems that the boys' identification with culturally defined, nonaggressive, "feminine" values and the girls' identification with nonaggressive religious values mitigated their growing up to be violent.

Among sociocultural variables, the parents' upward mobility was strongly predictive of aggression for both sexes but particularly for boys. Upward mobility may well place special pressures on the child and involve special frustrations in the parent–child relationship. While violence in the suburbs may not be as prevalent as violence in the slums, it does exist as a serious problem, and the overly ambitious father may undermine self-control in his son, just as his psychopathic counterpart in low SES families does.

Lefkowtiz's findings concerning the effect of television violence on aggression are of special interest in light of the controversial nature of the subject. It has been argued that viewing violent television has no lasting effects on actual behavior and that the correlation may well be due to the aggressive child's preference for such violent programs. Because Lefkowitz evaluated his subjects at different points in time, he was better able to resolve the dilemma regarding direction of effect inherent in correlational data obtained at one point in time. He found compelling evidence that watching violent television programs in the early years was a probable causative influence on a boy's later aggressiveness (Lefkowitz et al., 1977). Television violence was certainly not the only cause, but it was a potent one that operated independently of other influences on subsequent aggression, including IQ scores. The effect of television violence on girls was less pronounced and in the opposite direction, perhaps because girls are socialized to express aggression in fantasy rather than in action and because there are few aggressive female models on television.

Finally, like Robins, Lefkowitz found that the level of aggression in the third grade predicted subsequent aggression in both boys and girls better than any other variable.

Longitudinal Studies: Evaluation

All studies reviewed, including Kohn's, underscore the persistence of aggressive and antisocial behavior, particularly in boys, whether the population studied was normal or disturbed, lower or middle class. But more intriguing and perplexing is the finding that the child's current status in regard to aggression or antisocial behavior is more predictive of future acting out than any context variables. Many variables which have been regarded as crucial to deviant development—lack of parental love, neglect, cruel or inconsistent discipline, broken homes, gang membership, poverty—may be related to the child's current level of control but either have no effect on or do not play the determining role in his or her future status. Of course, context factors are not irrelevant. Parental identification seems particularly important, although it functions differently in different classes: for the lower-class boy not heavily involved in sociopathic behavior, having a sociopathic or alcoholic father is devastating, while for the middle-class boy, identifying with the mother (and, presumably, with nonaggressive "feminine" values) serves as a protection against subsequent violent acting out. Neglect or inconsistent parental discipline predicts continued difficulties for the lower-class boy already caught up in a pattern of serious antisocial acting out, while the religiosity of the middle-class family protects the girl from becoming an aggressive adult. Social mobility is positively related to future aggression in middle-class children, while being seen by the juvenile court and being in a correctional institution serve the same function for lower-class children.

But why the weak showing of context variables? As we have seen, Olweus regards aggression as a reaction tendency or motive system within the child, illustrating his thesis by his study of sixth-grade bullies (Olweus, 1978). Even Lefkowitz, who is in the tradition of social-learning theory, regards aggression as a trait a child learns early in life and one that is perpetuated probably because of the success it brings. Certainly, our image of the child-as-agent explicitly recognizes the strong tendency for the child to take the initiative in fulfilling his or her needs. If this is true of intellectual stimulation and social attention, for example, it could also be true for the expression of aggression. But postulating traits and introducing initiative beg the question of etiology; nor do they explain why aggression persists when so many neurotic behaviors do not. Developmentalists naturally look for origins early in life, but as Olweus has shown, the younger the child the less stable is aggressive behavior. Our examination of temperament and interpersonal variables in the preschool period also provided no convincing evidence that they set the pattern for future acting out.

To summarize, we can understand how lack of parental affection and consistency of socialization can undermine self-control at any given point. Such findings are in keeping with our developmental model. We can also understand why identification is a better predictor than contemporaneous parental behavior, since it involves the child's internalization of parental characteristics and therefore should be enduring. Yet, we leave our discussion of longitudinal data with the feeling that a key element responsible for the self-perpetuating nature of aggression and antisocial acting out has eluded us.

One point should be borne in mind. The studies by Robins and Lefkowitz et al. provide the first illustration of a point previously made concerning longitudinal data: as children change, so does the society in which they live. Consequently, a longitudinal study done at one point in time may no longer be totally applicable to one done at a later date. Specifically, Lefkowitz found a new variable contributing to adult violence which was unknown in the 1920s when Robins's data were first recorded—television violence. Thus technology, along with changing social values and class structures, can limit the applicability of longitudinal data. How to solve the problem of conducting long-term studies while allowing for broad changes in the social context is one of the basic challenges of longitudinal research.

THE ANATOMY OF ACTING-OUT BEHAVIOR

Fritz Redl's writings will serve as our guide to understanding acting out (Redl and Wineman, 1951). Redl presents a detailed account of five 8- to 10-year-old boys who received milieu therapy in a residential home called Pioneer House for fifteen to nineteen months. Five other boys were also observed for one to three months. They all were healthy, had normal intelligence, and were of lower socioeconomic status. Their behaviors included destructiveness, hyperaggressiveness, stealing, running away from home, truancy from school, temper tantrums, lying, "sassing" adults, and profanity; however, they were not so disturbed that they could not function in the community, since they attended public school and used neighborhood recreational facilities.

The boys had no positive, sustained relation with any adult. Their parents were brutal, neglectful, or self-absorbed; their homes were broken by divorce and desertion; and they had been shuttled between foster homes and institutions. They were in special classes at school or had been expelled. They ran with a delinquent gang or were lone wolves, committing impulsive delinquent acts. Thus, there was a total absence of positive experiences in the home, the school, and with peers.

Some of Redl's vivid descriptions of the boys' behavior are primarily illustrative of low self-control; others offer clues as to etiology.

Illustrations of Poor Self-Control

POOR CONTROL OF INNER IMPULSES. The boys at Pioneer House had little ability to modulate or contain high states of arousal. Even mild frustrations would produce strong, disruptive affective reactions: a door which accidentally jammed was immediately kicked and pounded and cursed with furious rage; a slight mishap during an enjoyable game would throw the group into wild outbursts of bickering, fighting, and griping. Neither anxiety nor guilt could be tolerated. The former would so quickly lead either to total flight or ferocious attack and diffuse destruction that the boys literally were only fleetingly aware of their fearfulness; for example, one boy reacted to his fear at bedtime by emitting high banshee wails, striking and cursing his pillow, and attacking other boys with a combination of vicious aggression and erotic teasing. While guilt feelings were infrequent, they had an equally disorganizing effect. Finally, the boys could manage neither the discouragement of failure nor the joy of success. Some were so sensitized to failure that they would not try even a potentially pleasurable activity; others reacted to their mistakes and limitations—no matter how tactfully handled by the staff—by sulking, tearful rage, or depressed fury. Success quickly spilled over into excited bravado and provocative depreciation of others.

OVERREACTION TO EXTERNAL STIMULI. Weak control was also evidenced by low resistance to environmental lures. As might be expected, lures to delinquent acts proved irresistible for the boys; a bit of loose change lying unnoticed on a desk was apt to be stolen, even if the boy had no prior intention of stealing. But the behavior did not have to be delinquent; it might just as well be mischievous or playful. One boy could not resist picking up and throwing a plastic knife on display in a store; the group could not resist wildly jumping up and down and breaking the springs on a mattress in a new bedroom where they were spending the night during Easter vacation. For these boys, it was as if to see was to act.

But of all perceived environmental lures, excitement was the most irresistible. The mere sight of a boy throwing clothes or banging his fork ferociously against his plate or jumping back and forth on the furniture would trigger similar behavior in the onlooker. Redl calls this spread of excitement *contagion.* The exposure to even mildly excited group moods was apt to undermine control. Thus, when one boy escalated a game of sailing cards idly across the room to heaving several cards around, the other joined in until "the air was thick with checkers, cards, pieces of candy, all in motion." Redl aptly describes the behavior as group psychological intoxication.

DEVELOPMENTAL IMPLICATIONS. Throughout his discussion, Redl points to the normal counterparts of acting-out behavior. His theme is that all these signs of weak self-control would be developmentally appropriate for younger children. His point is well taken: one can readily imagine toddlers and preschoolers going into a rage when frustrated or sulking after failure or dashing heedlessly into the street at the sound of the ice-cream truck; and the phenomenon of contagion is well known to any preschool teacher desperately trying to bring her little savages back under control after a game of tag has escalated to the point of intoxication. Thus, the model of poor self-control as a developmental delay is appropriate.

Etiological Factors

MEMORY. The prerequisite for socialization is that the toddler or preschooler remembers the situational behaviors which elicited positive or negative responses from the socializing adult. Having been punished for trying to poke a finger into the electric socket, the toddler is able to recall the punishment on the next exploration of electric sockets and inhibit the action. One of Redl's most provocative observations is that the boys at Pioneer House literally did not seem to remember past experiences; for example, the boys would insist on taking a favorite toy or gadget to school in spite of having such toys broken or destroyed time and time again in a playground battle. There was never a flicker of awareness of the relation between bringing the gadget to school and its certain destruction. Most puzzling of all was the boys' failure to remember pleasant experiences. When the staff tried to reexpose them to activities and games they had enjoyed, the boys would at first deny they had ever done anything like that before or, when they did remember, deny that it was fun.

When memory and recognition go, so does anticipation. There is nothing at the beginning of a sequence of behaviors to signal, "This will lead to punishment" or "This will lead to pleasure." The result is the common observation that psychopaths fail to learn from experience. Redl notes that they do not learn from the experience of others, either; the fact that one boy was seriously injured by a car when skating in the street did nothing to deter the others, who merely said, "That dumb jerk don't know what's going on, anyway." If each behavior sequence is experienced anew, the child cannot evoke the increasingly complex and abstract guides which are essential to self-control. Of course, this is an exaggeration in order to make a point: a child totally unable to learn from experience would be too dangerously impulsive to function in society. Here we are dealing with a deficiency in learning.

We can only speculate about the reasons for such baffling behavior. It is not the result of a memory defect, since the boys had learned all too well certain lessons from their traumatic past, such as "No adult is to be trusted." Consequently, every adult, no matter how loving and well intentioned, immediately activated the signal, "Danger ahead." It may be that, aside from certain traumatic experiences they dared not ignore, the boys developed a massive resistance to recall. Remembering per se could so quickly lead back to past nightmares that they protected themselves by living in the present as much as possible. Memory also depends on repetition, and repetition requires consistency of events. And it is environmental consistency which was so lacking for these boys. Shifted from home to foster placement to institution, their socialization may have changed with the values and idiosyncracies of the setting, as well as with the mood of the socializing adults. Thus, the boys' subsequent failure to anticipate consequences may reflect the haphazardness of those consequences in the past.

Support for our speculation comes from the finding that parents of sociopaths are inconsistent in their discipline and in their general behavior, for example, alternating between punitiveness and indifference (Peterson and Becker, 1965). Minuchin (1967) vividly describes the impermanence and unpredictability of the home environment of certain disadvantaged children. Meals have no set time, place, or order, a mother preparing four individual dinners one day according to her children's wishes and then preparing nothing the next day. Care is divided among mother, aunts, grandmothers, and siblings who sometimes shower the child with attention and sometimes totally neglect him or her. Adult responses are relatively random, being dependent upon the mood of the moment. Even the physical environment is impermanent, so that a toy or a piece of candy will not be where it was left an hour ago; in fact, the chances are good that someone will have come along and taken it. In such an environment it is understandable why children learn to live in and for the present.

Of course, this is speculation. Only future research can solve the mystery of why children who are capable of remembering fail to do so.

PERSPECTIVE. The boys in Pioneer House were pathologically weak in assessing social reality. They did not stop to consider the feelings and motives of others or to predict how others might react toward them. This same insensitivity was also evidenced in relation to the group code and social norms of proper behavior. One boy, for example, went around bragging that he was going to get a haircut, when he should have known that any evidence of special treatment would throw the group into a jealous rage—which it did; another boy took off his pants in a public park because he had gotten them wet and they itched.

This insensitivity to the thoughts, feelings, and actions of others was included in the discussion of *social perspective* (chapter 2). One of the pivotal developments between the preschool period and middle childhood is decentering, that is, shifting from cognitive egocentrism—in which the world is viewed primarily from the child's own vantage point—to cognitive perspectivism—in which a situation can be seen from the diverse views of the individuals involved. Objective studies tend to confirm Redl's clinical impression that delinquents are deficient in social-perspective taking. Chandler (1973) found chronically delinquent 11- to 13-year-old boys significantly deficient in role-taking skills as compared with a control group matched for SES and ethnic background. In this instance, perspective taking involved the realization that a latecomer viewing the final cartoon in a sequence (for example, a father observing his son's alarm at a knock on the door) would have no basis for interpreting it in the same way as a person who had viewed the entire sequence (in this instance, pictures showing the boy accidentally breaking a window with a baseball). In a like manner, Jurkovic and

Prentice (1977) found that 15½-year-old psychopathic delinquents and, to a lesser degree, neurotic delinquents were inferior to subcultural delinquents and normal controls in role-taking skills. In this experiment, the boy takes five cents from under one box or ten cents from under another. He is not observed by the experimenter, but he must predict which box the experimenter will choose. A high level of role taking would be, "I know he will think I'll be greedy and take the dime, so I'll fool him and take the nickel"; lower levels would be merely taking the dime, either because it was more money, or because the child infers that the adult would want the dime. Results of these studies are usually interpreted in terms of a developmental lag, since the delinquent's perspective taking resembles that of a 4- to 6-year-old (Selman and Byrne, 1974).

Let us return once more to Pioneer House using perspective taking as a concrete illustration of the "guiding and controlling function of thought" (chapter 2). If the boys immediately translate feeling into action, thinking can serve neither function. On the other hand, the question, "How will others perceive and react to what I do?" of necessity serves to check action. The answer to the question changes as the child is progressively capable of grasping the values, motives, and intentions of others and, ultimately, of simultaneously being aware of his own perspective and the perspective of others. As this guiding function advances, behavior becomes more socially adaptive. The unfortunate braggart who was to have his hair cut should have been able to think, "I want to lord it over the others—but this is just the thing that will drive them wild, because they can't stand the idea of someone getting anything special." Once having decentered, he now would be in a position to act in a socially appropriate manner. However, as Redl cautions, knowing what is right is not equivalent to doing what is right. The boys at Pioneer House often were not able to decenter; other types of acting-out children—such as Mark—know but cannot resist the force of their impulses.

As was the case with memory, we do not know what is responsible for the lag in social-perspective taking. In normal development, parents, dramatic play, and confrontation with cognitive discrepancies in peer interaction are all involved. It would be difficult to imagine the parents of the Pioneer House boys sensitizing them to the feelings of others; in addition, the boys' own failure to develop stable peer relations might have been particularly detrimental to the ability to decenter. Since peers, like any other group, cannot tolerate impulsivity and egocentrism, the boys might have been caught in a vicious circle: their inability to cooperate prevented them from having access to the very experiences that could have helped them advance in their social awareness.

While the development of social perspective is generating a lively research interest (Shantz, 1975), the study of empathy, defined as the ability to feel what another is feeling, is meager and unsatisfactory. There is some evidence that empathy in 7-year-old boys is related to low aggression in school, but there is little objective evidence corroborating the clinician's observations that children such as Mark may be quite adept in social-perspective taking but have no guilt or—more important—no concern for the distress they cause others.

The Pioneer House boys not only lacked perspective on others, they lacked perspective on themselves. Redl describes it as "the evaporation of self-contributed links in the causal chain" (Redl and Wineman, 1951, p. 128). Children literally would not remember, even after a short time, their own share in provoking a fight or a chaotic scene. They forgot not only their feeling, motivations, and intentions but also their surface behavior, such as being the first one to throw a stone, thus beginning a free-for-all, or mishandling a favorite toy so that it eventually broke.

We are now in an area different from social perspective (which involves understanding how others perceive the self); we are in the realm of self-observation. The psychoanalysts write of the "observing ego" when dealing with the ability to be a spectator in relation to one's own thoughts and actions. Piaget (1967) sketches the development of the ability of children to reflect on their own thinking. Egocentric preschoolers believe that something is true, immediately comprehended, and universally accepted because they say or think it. It is only as this belief is challenged by social encounters that they can, in middle childhood, begin to challenge themselves as to what they mean and why they believe it to be true. This "inner social discussion" is the beginning of reflection or the ability to examine one's own thoughts. Why reflection fails to develop in acting-out boys is not known, although Minuchin et al. (1967) speculate that "fast and externally geared resolution of cognitive-affective stress that becomes the dominant coping style" inhibits cultivation of reflection (p. 198).

INITIATIVE. Instead of being expansive and seeking new challenges, the boys at Pioneer House were frightened of newness. Perhaps because their environment had been both unpredictable and punitive, newness had become equated with danger. In place of normal exploration, their examination of a new object was characterized by "panicky haste, nervous incompleteness and a flustered jumpiness" or a "frenzy of aggressive handling and poking around" (Redl and Wineman, 1951, p. 119). Goal-directed behavior was well-nigh impossible. At times they denied newness, as when one boy insisted that, "This place ain't different; I been here lots of times before" when he was being taken on a trip, or when another boy claimed that he saw his uncle driving a number of different trucks when he went for a ride. Such a fear of newness prevented the boys from diversifying their behavioral repertoire and further entrapped them in their repetitive patterns of acting out.

But initiative was lacking in an even more important way, namely, in the boys' inability to generate constructive activities or alternate coping devices. As Redl properly notes, normal school-age children, when left to their own devices, can call up memories of past interests or pleasures and proceed to pursue them. Normal children also have a variety of techniques to help them tolerate the tension of delayed gratification: they can take their minds off the unavailable goal by thinking of or actually doing other things, or they can use the "sour-grapes" technique of depreciating the desired goal, or they can reward themselves for having delayed so long or punish themselves for starting to yield to temptation, or they can transform the desired object into an abstract, less tempting image, or they can even go to sleep (Mischel, 1978). But all these devices must be generated, and it is just this generative ability which acting-out children lack. When they have nothing to do, they literally can think of nothing to do; when faced with frustration, they literally have no alternative to acting out their anger.

Twenty-five years after Redl stressed the importance of generating alternatives to boredom and frustration, psychologists began exploring the phenomenon under the label of *interpersonal problem solving*. While interpersonal problem solving can be simply defined as the analysis and resolution of problems involving other people, there is a certain amount of disagreement as to the specific functions involved. This discussion will follow the conceptualization of Spivack, Platt, and Shure (1976). They postulate the following components: an initial sensitivity to human problems, an ability to imagine alternative courses of action, an ability to conceptualize the means to solve the problem, sensitivity to consequences, and understanding cause and effects in human relations.

Of all the components, generating alternatives and means–end thinking proved the most important in this research. In the preschool period, generating alternative solutions to problems such as, What could you do if your sister were playing with a toy you wanted? was the single most significant predictor of interpersonal behavior in a classroom setting. Children who were deficient were rated by their teachers as being high on acting out or inhibition; for example, they were disruptive, disrespectful, and defiant; they could not wait or take turns; or they needed to be close to the teacher. In middle childhood, alternative thinking was still related to classroom adjustment, although not as strongly as it was previously, while means–end thinking emerged as an equally important correlate. For instance, when presented with the problem of a boy's feeling lonely after moving to a new neighborhood, the well-adjusted child could think not only of different solutions but also of ways to implement the solutions and overcome the obstacles involved, such as saying, "It would be easy if he found someone who liked to play soccer like he does, but he'd better not go to a kid's house at suppertime or his mother will be plenty mad!" Again, both impulsive and inhibited children were deficient in these two cognitive skills. It is interesting to note that the capacity to think in means–end terms was a developmental achievement, since it did not emerge until middle childhood. The data on adolescence were meager but suggested that means–end thinking and alternative thinking continued to be correlated with adjustment. The new component involved thinking of consequences or weighing the pros and cons of potential action: "If I do X, then someone else will do Y and that will be good (or bad)." Thus the developing child is able to utilize progressively advanced cognitive skills to solve interpersonal problems. Incidentally, such problem solving is not closely related to measured IQ.

Spivak et al. also have data on the kinds of parenting which facilitated interpersonal problem solving. The mother focused on the child's own thinking ("Tell me what happened." "Why did it happen?" "What did you feel?" "How do you think the other child felt?" and so forth) and supported the child's attempts at solutions, though not always approving of the solution itself. In the process the parent served as a model of problem-evaluation, solution-attempting behavior. There was an interesting sex difference, however, the mother being effective only in relation to her daughter's problem-solving skills; wherever the son learned his, it was not at his mother's knee. Problem solving was discouraged by ignoring or disparaging the child ("Don't be a baby"), by absolutistic directives ("Stop crying and go outside and hit him back"), or by depreciating the child's alternatives ("That's the silliest thing I've ever heard of"). Under such conditions social problem-solving skills atrophied from sheer lack of use.

Returning now to the Pioneer House boys, we can better appreciate how impoverished they were in terms of their repertoire of solutions to interpersonal problems. While Redl states that they were unable to utilize their past to provide alternative courses of action in the present, he might also agree that their past was barren soil for the cultivation of problem-solving skills.

CONSCIENCE. As could be predicted, the lack of love, of models, and of tutelage produced a defective conscience in the Pioneer House boys. While not completely absent, their conscience was fragmented and inefficient.

There was a certain amount of acceptance of delinquent mores, along with pride in being tough, smart, and daring. (Recall that delinquents often do not come in pure types, so that psychopaths can also have characteristics of cultural delinquents.) There were fragments of middle-class values, which were isolated vestiges from the past; for example, one boy would suddenly berate another for swearing. Inefficiency was evidenced by the lack of anticipatory guilt; when it appeared, guilt typically followed a transgression. Guilt also seemed specific to the individual making the original demands for good behavior; for example, after stealing, a boy might feel ashamed in his mother's presence, but only in that one setting and only in relation to that one incident. Such situationalism nicely illustrates our point concerning the importance of generalizing rules for proper behavior in the development of self-control.

Objective evidence of delayed moral development in psychopaths comes from Jurkovic and Prentice's study (1977), which showed them lagging behind neurotic and subcultural delinquents as well as normal controls on Kohlberg's scale of moral development. Compared to the other groups, they were more likely to think in terms of Preconventional Morality and less likely to think in terms of Conventional Morality. This means that they were concerned primarily with avoiding punishment, with giving in order to get in return, and with deferring to the power of the maker of rules; they were less concerned with living up to family or group expectations regardless of the immediate consequences to themselves and with conforming to the "good-boy" image of being nice, conforming to rules, doing one's best, maintaining order, and respecting authority. An interesting aside is that the other three groups did not differ in their moral judgments in spite of different histories of delinquent behavior, proving that knowing what is right does not necessarily lead to doing what is right. (The complex relation between moral judgment and moral behavior is discussed in Jurkovic, 1980.)

THE "DELINQUENT EGO." The behaviors examined so far could fit into a model of developmental delays of various types and to varying degrees. However, the delay is not pervasive, since many functions are intact or even highly developed. The problem is that they are used to maintain and justify impulsive behavior rather than to enhance self-control. Redl cites many examples of what he calls "the delinquent ego." The boys were past masters of the "He did it first" and "Everyone else does it" technique for justifying their impulsivity. Other techniques included: "He had it coming to him," "I did it to save face with the others," "He's a no-good so-and-so himself," "But I made it up with him afterwards," and "Nobody likes me; they're always picking on me." Such defenses sound suspiciously like those that parents of healthy preadolescents have to deal with.

Initiative that was so lacking in many areas was fully deployed in supporting delinquent gratifications. A boy would seek out other children with similar impulses in order to gain support for his behavior, often abandoning the relationship after the deed was done. Or he would skillfully provoke another boy into starting some disruptive behavior so he could join in as a blameless participant. Or the group would readily champion the cause of one of its members not so much from genuine concern as from a desire to find an excuse to rebel.

In contrast to their usual imperviousness to adults, the children displayed a remarkable sensitivity when they were cornered. They knew precisely what modulation in the tone of voice meant that the adult would do nothing about their delinquent behavior and when it meant the adult had run out of patience. (Remember that the adults were therapeutic staff members who were trying to remain on an even keel with the boys.) They knew the staff's whims and weaknesses, sensing the kind of argument which would appease or divert them and knowing when cajoling or affection seeking would throw them off guard. They knew how to act cute in public, to wheedle things out of a suspicious storekeeper, to convince a guard that they were "good kids." As we have noted, they remembered all too well that people could not be trusted and were constantly on guard against anticipated harm or against forming a positive attachment. To protect themselves from the latter, they provoked rejection (for example, by making impossible demands) or anger. Thus they avoided one more betrayal by "proving" that the staff was no different from all the other adults they had known.

Incidentally, this contrast between developmentally delayed and normal behavior has an interesting counterpart in the experimental literature. (For a more detailed presentation, see Achenbach, 1974). Initial evidence indicated that psychopaths might be different from normal individuals, since they did not learn from noxious experiences; for example, in learning a "mental maze" they made proportionally more shocked than nonshocked errors, showed smaller galvanic skin responses (GSR) to a buzzer which had repeatedly been paired with an uncomfortable shock, and preferred frightening activities over onerous ones. Thus, they seemed to be deficient in normal anxiety. However, subsequent research revealed that their reaction depended on the kind of punishment involved: true, when learning a maze they were relatively unaffected by physical punishment or social censure such as being told they were wrong in a disapproving voice; but when deprived of money their maze performance was slightly better than that of normal subjects, while their GSR was the same! Instead of being incapable of experiencing anxiety, psychopaths have a different set of values. When these values are threatened, they, like the Pioneer House boys, react the same as normals.

To end on a clinical note, let us return to Mark whose case opened this discussion. Like the con man he might well become, Mark is high on interpersonal skills and evidences little of the blatant impulsivity of the Pioneer House boys. Yet he is equally unable to resist the impulse to lie, steal, cheat, and seek excitement while being relatively untroubled by guilt. He can cognitively view a situation from the perspective of others but has little empathy and affective involvement with them. In the nontechnical sense of the word he is totally egocentric. What is not known is whether Mark and the boys from Pioneer House are on a continuum—whether the charming psychopath has the same kind of "delinquent ego" as the impulsive psychopath, only more highly cultivated and better able to hold motor activity in check. Regardless of how the issue is ultimately settled, there is no doubt that inadequate socialization and weak self-control can be manifested in diverse forms.

Redl's *naturalistic* research is a prime example of the *clinical eye* nourishing a conceptualizing mind. Unlike the majority of clinicians, who are content with collecting vivid anecdotes, Redl was constantly asking, Why? In this, he differed from Kanner, who was primarily asking, What? That Redl was able to tease out so many variables involved in acting-out behavior and to place them in a developmental context is an achievement of the first order. His technique of observing children for prolonged periods in natural settings is also very much in keeping with the current emphasis on ecological validity, even though the research was conducted forty years ago.

Yet Redl's research also illustrates the limitations of naturalistic research utilizing the clinical eye. There is no concern for reliability, which would serve as a check for observer bias and increase the likelihood that the data are accessible to the scientific community. More important is the question of generalizability. Redl's observations were made on ten boys at most. What can one infer from such a small sample? Did Redl capture the essence of all impulsive psychopathy or did he merely illuminate the psychological workings of a limited subpopulation? His ecological approach also prevented him from determining which of the many variables he delineated are essential and which are peripheral or even noncontributory to delinquency. More controlled studies, which could manipulate variables, would be required to answer such questions. Thus, Redl's research is best regarded as hypothesis generating; while of great value, his findings need further testing either in the laboratory or through objective techniques in naturalistic settings.

NONDELINQUENT ACTING OUT

Acting out need not be antisocial. Poor control can be manifested in behaviors which are of concern to parents and teachers but not to society at large. These will be called *conduct disorders.* (Our discussion will follow Wolff, 1977.) Conduct disorders usually include disobedience; quarreling and fighting; temper tantrums; high-strung, overreactive behavior; and difficulties with attention and concentration. Factor-analytic studies indicate that conduct disorders are distinct from other kinds of psychopathologies. Again, however, we must remember that disturbed children do not necessarily fit neatly into a single diagnostic category, and conduct disorders are frequently associated with other disturbances: they often go with delinquency, learning disabilities, and school failures, with psychosis, and with organic brain pathology. Finally, conduct disorders are found predominantly in boys and tend to be associated with lower socioeconomic status and large families. Developmentally, they are common in preschool children, decline during the early school years, and rise again in adolescence.

Etiology

The usual litany of etiological factors has been invoked to account for conduct disorders. Organic brain pathology may generally weaken self-control as may temperamental traits of high-activity level, intensity of reaction, and a low threshold of responsiveness. Parental rejection, punitiveness, and threats, inconsistent parenting, and disharmony between parents may be correlates. The bond of love is weak, parental guides are either inadequate or conflicting, frustration runs high, and adequate models are lacking—all of which may well undermine the development of self-control. Father absence in lower-class boys may result in an overconcern with masculinity and aggressive acting out as a reaction to the threat of a mother-dominated household. Divorce is likely to lead to aggressive behavior in boys, while death of the father is likely to lead to neurotic problems. Parental permissiveness for aggressive behavior between siblings as well as peer reinforcement of aggression also play a role in producing conduct disorder.

Because they tend to be intellectually dull and impulsive, children with conduct disorders may do poorly academically and be discipline problems in school. The school itself may make its own contribution to their problem, although what aspects are responsible—the method of teaching, techniques for maintaining discipline, the social interaction between teacher and pupil or among teachers themselves—has not been determined. Finally, television, as we have seen, has been strongly implicated in aggressive acting out.

Prognostically, nondelinquent conduct disorders during early and middle school years often lead to delinquency at adolescence, especially when they are associated with school failure. Poorly controlled aggression in boys, whether it takes the form of antisocial behavior or conduct disorders, is strongly associated with adult sociopathy.

Evaluation of the Developmental Model

Our developmental model has served us well. The intrapersonal variables comprising self-control and the interpersonal variables responsible for its development have generally provided plausible explanations of the clinical data. In some instances, the clinical data have enriched our understanding. The study of interpersonal problem solving in particular has given us a much more detailed account of the process than we had when we merely referred to the ability to find alternative means of reaching a goal. While little new was added in regard to social cognition, we now have a better appreciation of it as a supplement to the usual material on conscience development. The one variable which was slighted, if not exactly omitted, was self-observation, which deserves to be more fully studied in its own right. Finally, most of the clinical and research data on psychopathic behavior could be conceptualized in terms of a developmental lag or fixation.

THE JUVENILE COURT

The social context plays an important role in the life of antisocial acting-out children. Society has chosen the legal system to serve the dual function of protecting life and property while helping the child become a productive citizen. The responsible legal agent is the juvenile court, which from its inception has been unable to live up to its high aspirations. (The presentation will follow Orlando and Black, 1975.)

In the mid-nineteenth century, reformers were concerned that children were tried and sentenced as adults and were subsequently maltreated and brutalized. By the turn of the century, the juvenile court system was initiated with the purpose of assisting rather than punishing the child. The judge was to function as a good parent for those children whose natural parents had failed to provide them with the proper care and guidance. Due process was not necessary, since the judge, as "state parent," was charged with determining how children became delinquent and what could save them from their downward career. "Salvation" replaced "punishment." In spite of such lofty ideals, little was done to accomplish the goal of "salvation." Children remained in the poorhouse or jail, the new institutions which were built were punitive, and maltreatment of children continued. Thus, children received neither the legal protection offered adults nor the treatment they were entitled to.

In the *Gault* case (*In re Gault,* 1967), the U.S. Supreme Court altered the paternalistic role of the juvenile court by introducing due process. Children now have a right to legal counsel, and the state can intervene with treatment only after they are proved guilty. Another development involves an increased differentiation of antisocial acts. Under the old system, juvenile delinquency included everything from property crimes to habitual use of vile language in public places, patronizing public poolrooms, smoking cigarettes, and sleeping in alleys. Now many states have a dual classification; *juvenile delinquency* includes only acts which, if committed by an adult, would be a violation of the criminal law; *children in need of supervision* includes those who are habitually truant, persistently disobey reasonable commands of their guardians, or violate laws applicable only to children. The legal term for behavior that would not be criminal if committed by adults is *status offense.* Many legislatures prohibit placement of children classified as "in need of supervision" in the same institutions as delinquents.

In spite of the procedural improvements since the *Gault* case, the juvenile court is beset with problems. The sheer magnitude of its task is staggering. In 1970, for example, the juvenile court system handed over a million cases of juvenile delinquency—not including traffic violations—involving 2.8 percent of the population between the ages of 10 and 17 (Knopf, 1979). Next, criminal behavior has multiple roots that extend beyond the family to weakened traditional socializing institutions such as the school and the church, the failure of the educational system to meet the academic and vocational needs of youth, the inability of society to provide meaningful work and relevant medical, social, and psychological services to large segments of the population, and the lack of youth and community involvement in making policies which directly affect them. To expect the juvenile court to remedy all such problems is wishful indeed.

To make matters worse, the state has woefully underfunded its juvenile courts, probation staffs are inadequate, and resources to help the child are scarce. The forces for law and order and the concern for crime in the streets are often far stronger than the forces favoring the child's rehabilitation. Even the nice distinction between juvenile delinquents and children in need of supervision does not seem to be having its desired effect, since the latter tend to be treated in the same way as the former. In sum, the court is hobbled in its attempt both to understand children and to fulfill the charge of caring for and guiding them.

One of the objections to the juvenile court system concerns the stigma of being labeled a delinquent. Society reacts negatively to young people so labeled, and this, in turn, reinforces their negative self-image, convinces them that they cannot be part of normal society, and leads them to further delinquency. This is an example of a self-fulfilling prophecy: a person who is treated like a criminal will become one. However, Orlando and Black caution that the stigma of labeling is far from proved, and there is as much evidence disconfirming as supporting it. In light of what we have learned about the psychological and social origins of antisocial acting out, it seems unlikely that labeling per se could be as potent as some people claim.

There is more convincing evidence that the label of delinquent does affect young people's economic future, since they are less apt than nondelinquents to be hired, to hold membership in labor unions, and to participate in union apprenticeship training, while occupational licensing practices may also prevent them from pursuing certain careers. Thus, delinquency may be perpetuated because legitimate sources of financial stability are not available. In fact, the vocational arena mirrors the legal dilemma: on the one hand, there is the desire to protect society (in this case, employers) from hiring someone who might surreptitiously rob them, but there is also the desire to give the delinquent a chance to go straight by holding down a job.

Orlando and Black speak for those who hold a generally pessimistic view: "It would probably be better for all concerned if young delinquents were not detected, apprehended or institutionalized. Too many of them get worse in our care" (1975, p. 370). They recommend that children in need of supervision, including status offenders, no longer come under the juvenile court's jurisdiction but be referred to community agencies for help with their problems at home and in school. In addition, the court itself should have access to social and psychological services to help it both understand the needs of the individual delinquent and formulate specific, appropriate treatment plans.

Whether recommendation to improve the lot of delinquents will be heeded is difficult to say. A number of groups made significant advances as a result of the social unrest of the 1950s and 1960s, Blacks and women being the most prominent. Yet criminals and juvenile delinquents seem to have gained relatively little. To borrow a phrase from Redl, they are still "the children nobody wants." (See also Rubin, 1977. For an overview of the social-legal context, see Children and the Law, *Journal of Clinical Child Psychology*, 1978.)

TREATMENT

If Orlando and Black's recommendations were implemented and psychologists were uniformly consulted in regard to treatment, what could they offer? Ironically, the prevailing opinion until recently was that "Nothing works," since attempts to change delinquent behavior were usually unsuccessful. The most prominent and discouraging report was the so-called Cambridge-Somerville Youth Study conducted by the McCords. In this study two groups of boys between 5 and 13 years of age were matched for age, family background, home environment, and risk for delinquency. The experimental group received counseling twice a month, tutoring, medical or psychiatric attention, were sent to summer camp and brought into contact with community groups such as the Boy Scouts and YMCA. The control group received no special attention. Thirty years later 506 experimental and control subjects were reevaluated (McCord, 1978). Not only were there few differences between groups in terms of court convictions for criminal behavior, but the treatment group did not fare as well as the control—they were more likely to commit a second crime, to be alcoholics, to have serious mental illnesses and stress-related diseases, to have occupations with lower prestige, and to find their work less satisfying. Ironically, many of the men had quite positive memories of the McCords' work and perceived the program as having helped them. (This last finding illustrates the limitation of relying on self-reports as the sole criterion of therapeutic improvement.)

The negative reports concerning therapeutic effectiveness have been particularly discouraging in light of the findings that adult delinquency is one of the few psychopathologies which can be spotted in childhood, and effective treatment would vastly diminish the problems of adult crime, alcoholism, divorce, and chronic unemployment. Fortunately, psychologists have been unwilling to admit defeat, and there are currently a number of therapeutic programs claiming success. While not specifically addressed to adolescents and juvenile delinquents, a review of programs that work suggests some general guidelines (Gendreau and Ross, 1979). Multiple methods are more effective than single methods: in the behavioral realm, a versatile use of role playing, modeling, peer reinforcement, and a token economy is to be preferred over the exclusive reliance on a single technique. Since delinquents vary widely, the therapy and the personality of the therapist should be matched to the problem and personality of the delinquent; too often the population has been regarded as homogeneous and the same remedial measure has been applied to all. Finally, sufficient time should be allowed for the treatment to prove its effectiveness; some "classical" studies, for example, consist of only one treatment contact per month. The review implies that one reason why therapy has not worked is that it has not been properly done—a rejoinder that is often made to the criticism that rehabilitation programs in general have been ineffective.

There is also speculation that the thread running through successful programs with adolescents is the enhancement of the delinquent's movement toward independent and respectable adult status (Gold and Petronio, 1980). This can be done in the school by means of special classes which permit individual and group decision making by the juvenile delinquents while avoiding placing them in a depreciated role in relation to nondelinquent peers. Comprehensive vocational programs enhance the adolescents' status as workers not only by finding them jobs but also by helping them keep the jobs and even upgrade employment by additional training. Family contracts, in which parents and adolescents negotiate what rewards will be given for which behaviors, may well change the parent–child relationship in the direction of increased autonomy for the adolescent. Supportive and accepting psychotherapy that enhances the adolescent's feeling of being an autonomous, worthwhile individual has also proved effective.

While such a lively interest in helping acting-out children is encouraging, none of the approaches has had sustained beneficial effects for large numbers of such children and youth over long spans of time. However, they do allow us to conclude this discussion on a note of cautious optimism.

With the conclusion of our discussion of the psychopathologies of deviant self-control, we are ready to take up the psychopathologies of the child-as-worker. This will involve a shift of focus to the school setting, since it is not by chance that we speak of school work and home work. As we have just seen, the acting-out child often does poorly in school and is being ill prepared to assume the role of adult worker. In light of the child's background, it is easy to understand why the requirements for acceptable classroom behavior are difficult to meet. But there is another group of children who, in terms of both intellectual endowment and family background, have every reason to succeed. Yet, they fail to learn. It is this baffling group which we shall study next.

9 ▪ Learning Disabilities

YOU ARE A CLINICAL CHILD PSYCHOLOGIST. IT HAS BEEN A ROUGH DAY. THE CLIMAX WAS A phone call to the principal of Wyckwyrc Junior High School. It is the kind of suburban school in which children from two-swimming-pool families do not speak to children from one-swimming-pool families. The call had been about Jon Hastings, a 16-year-old with a long history of school failures. The intelligence test showed him to be bright enough to do college work, and yet he is only in the eighth grade. He is articulate, has a talent for making miniature rockets and speedboats, and a real flair for drawing cartoons. Yet the written word is Jon's nemesis. He reads laboriously one word at the time, while his writing is even more painfully slow. Because of repeated failures and because he is now a social misfit with peers, he has begun cutting up in class and talking back to the teacher. More unusual, he is in danger of getting hooked on drugs, so you are more concerned about him than other learning-disabled children.

You had phoned the principal to suggest ways of bypassing Jon's reading disability. Since he is sufficiently bright to absorb most of the lecture material, could he be given oral examinations every now and then? If he were taught how to type, could he type instead of writing his examinations? Would the principal consider introducing special classes for all the learning-disabled children?

The principal was suave and ingratiating and a compendium of the resistances you have run up against in the past. He "understood your concern" but asked that you "look at the situation from my point of view." The school had "tried everything possible to no avail," "the boy is incorrigible," "you can't help a child unless the child wants help," and finally—you could feel this one coming, since you had heard it so often—"I can't give one student a favor without giving a favor to all of them. I'd have half the mothers in my office next day demanding something extra to pull their child's grades up." You had always doubted the validity of this "special-favor" objection but had never found an effective way of countering it. Stalling for time you had asked if you could come and talk with the principal. He was most gracious. He would be happy to tell you about the school and have a student show you around—which was not at all what you had in mind.

A few years back an insightful but poorly educated mother had remarked, "When I get frustrations I come here and bring them to you. When you get frustrations, where do you put them?" The question comes back at times like these.

TYPES OF LEARNING DISABILITIES

In chapter 2 on normal development, we saw how the inherently curious infant becomes the academically achieving student. While the drive to explore is potent, curiosity thrives on stimulation from the social and physical environment during infancy and the preschool period, verbal stimulation being particularly important in our present concern with learning disabilities. With school comes the requirement to learn and the beginning of the child-as-worker. Parental values concerning the importance of education and achievement will encourage maximization of the child's potential. Teachers wrestle with the problem of whether traditional or progressive education will best enhance the child's desire to master academic material. Peers serve to reinforce academic learning, although the study of their influences has been relatively neglected. Because the child is complex by this age, progress will be affected by work habits and freedom from distracting anxieties and angers, which are typically rooted in the family circle.

What can go wrong with this development? In the most extreme cases, biological and/or environmental factors render some children incapable of understanding the world in all its complexity, and they find academic subjects particularly perplexing. These children, the mentally retarded, do not learn at a normal rate because they lack the necessary intellectual endowment (see chapter 11). Other children suffer from being members of a social outgroup and from the physiological and psychological effects of poverty. Such children are not necessarily retarded but have spent their early years in an environment whose very fabric makes it difficult for them to adapt successfully to the requirements of middle-class education.

The third case is the *learning-disabled* child, who is intelligent enough to do better, whose family and cultural background are congruent with academic achievement, who has no gross physiological defect that would obviously impede learning, and who is reasonably free from crippling psychological problems arising from sources outside of the learning situation. Yet the child does poorly, perhaps in reading or in spelling or in arithmetic or in all three. Why? The answer should be simple. Unlike autistic, hyperactive, or severely retarded children, learning-disabled children are both willing and able to cooperate with researchers, while their parents and teachers are eager to help find the source of their difficulties. Why, then, does the etiological question go unanswered, and why are the voluminous research findings fragmented, contradictory, and inconclusive?

At the heart of the mystery lies the fundamental question, How do children learn basic academic skills? Until the normal process is understood it is difficult to know what has gone awry. We will concentrate on reading because it is the pivotal academic skill, it has been the most extensively investigated learning disability, and it has the most elegant theory of normal development.

READING DISABILITY

A reading disability is usually defined as a failure to learn to read or make appropriate progress in reading in spite of at least normal intelligence and adequate instruction. The reading-disabled child has no gross neurological defect, although most definitions also include presumptive evidence of neurological involvement. The child's hearing, vision, and motivation to learn are adequate. The reading disability is not a secondary consequence of a severe emotional disturbance, such as autism, or a depressive reaction to a traumatic event, such as the death of a parent. The term *dyslexia* is frequently used instead of reading disability. (For a comprehensive review of the literature, see Meier, 1978.)

The Developmental Picture

Our presentation of the development of reading skills will closely follow Gibson and Levin (1975), which is one of the few attempts to integrate theoretical and empirical findings into a developmental framework. In order to understand the theory, we must first discuss certain linguistic, perceptual, and cognitive developments which precede learning to read.

THE DEVELOPMENT OF SPEECH. Before learning to read, children learn to talk. The toddler discovers that those interesting but meaningless sounds are verbal symbols conveying meaningful messages. Subsequently, toddlers themself master the art of speaking to the point where they can use words to express ideas and to communicate. In order to do this they must grasp the basic rules of grammar which dictate how the words must be ordered into sequences appropriate to the language. The challenge of reading consists of learning that if interesting but meaningless visual stimuli are properly sequenced, they can convey the same symbolic meaning as speech.

PERCEPTUAL DEVELOPMENT. E. J. Gibson (1969) maintains that human beings are innately constructed so as to extract information from stimuli emanating from objects, places, and events in the environment. The infant's eye is not a camera passively and accurately taking pictures of mother, bottle, crib, and so forth. Rather, the eye is an active seeker in search of invariant information in the vast flux of stimuli which constitutes the infant's perceptual environment. The infant can take in only a fragment of the information in the stimulus flux, however, and is only gradually capable of perceptions that are both richly detailed and highly organized. The following developmental trends are particularly relevant to reading.

First, the developing infant learns *distinctive features* of people and objects so that, for example, mother becomes perceptually distinct from bottle and blanket and also distinct from father and grandmother. As applied to reading, perceptual development enables the child to make increasingly fine discriminations among letters. An adult looking at the Arabic alphabet for the first time may have the same trouble discriminating distinctive features as a youngster looking at the Roman alphabet: one little line makes the difference between an *E* and an *F*, an *O* and a *Q*, an *n* and an *h*. As perception becomes increasingly specific and detailed, these fine distinctions become increasingly apparent.

Equally important, the developing infant must learn that distinctive features are *invariant* over a number of transformations—mother remains mother when she is the groggy, disheveled breakfast companion who has been kept awake all night by the infant's fussiness and when she is the well-groomed matron showing the baby off to friends. Again, applied to reading, the child must learn that the letter *A* remains the same whether it is scribbled or printed, capitalized or lowercased.

Next, the developing infant must learn *higher order relations:* the distinctive features that characterize individual people, objects, and events can be subsumed under a more comprehensive unit that embraces a complex set of relations. When viewing the human face, for instance, infants first perceive separate features which are spatially related, so that they look from eyes to hairline to mouth without being able to integrate these fragments into a complex whole. Subsequently, not only can they take in all the features, but such features also become subsumed under the larger unit of "face." Likewise, the child who is taught to read one word at a time comes to cluster words in more complex units; *in, the,* and *house*—at first laboriously perceived one word at a time—can be taken in at a glance as the phrase *in the house.*

As perception becomes both more finely detailed and more highly organized, information processing becomes more efficient. Attention is optimized as irrelevances and distractions are ignored and the child focuses on essential information. To cite only one study, Nodine and Steuerle (1973) recorded the eye movement of kindergarten, first-, and third-grade children when the children were trying to determine whether two letters were the same or different. The older children could decide on the basis of a few cross-comparisons because they immediately focused on the essential features; the kindergarten children spent a much longer time and made a larger number of cross-comparisons involving relevant and irrelevant features before coming to a decision. Extrapolating to sentences, knowing the rules for ordering words is more efficient than trying to understand the sentence by reading one word at a time.

But learning to extract meaning from a printed page involves more than perceptual development, which, after all, is limited to the discovery of invariants in the stimulus flux—the distinguishable properties of tangible things, the orderly relations among elements, and the predictable relations between events. From such perceptual developments children evolve general strategies for organization, problem solving, and remembering, which they can bring to a given situation rather than extracting from it.

Take memory, for example. Many people do not realize that remembering involves strategies. Just as the eye is not a camera, the brain is not a tape recorder passively registering and storing events that can be accurately played back at some future date. In fact, remembering per se is a developmental achievement. It requires a particular set—namely, attending to stimuli for the purpose of subsequent recall—plus strategies such as rehearsal to insure that the stimuli will, in fact, be recalled. There is evidence that such purposeful remembering is not a feature of the developmental picture until after the preschool years. One study (Appel, Cooper, McCarrell, Sims-Knight, Yussen, and Flavell, 1972) found that for preschoolers and first-graders, there was no significant difference in recall whether the children were told to memorize a set of items for future recall or whether they were merely told to look at a similar set of items. However, even when children grasp the concept of purposeful recall, their repertoire of strategies is meager and inefficient; for example, they will merely name the objects to be remembered or point to them. With time, however, more sophisticated and effective strategies enter. (For a comprehensive treatment of memory, see Kail, 1979.)

LEARNING TO READ

We are now ready for the developmental reconstruction of learning to read. Three periods will be dealt with: the prereading skills period characteristic of children in kindergarten and first grade; the initial period, which lasts until the fourth or fifth grade; and the period of skilled reading, which continues throughout the rest of childhood.

Prereading Skills

Children aged 5 to 6 grasp the idea that the squiggles on the printed page are a special kind of visual stimuli. They have been fascinated by their own spontaneous scribbling since they were 18-month-old toddlers. The fascination seems to be intrinsic, toddlers needing no reward other than the interest in watching their tracings. As they develop through the preschool period, their initially aimless scribbles become more varied, systematic, and articulated. Subsequently, well-marked units that look like words appear and, even later, approximations to real letters or even a sprinkling of letters themselves. While a few children go on to ask questions about spelling and then to learning how to read, this is not typical; children who copy letters and words usually can read very little of what they have produced.

As so often happens in development, perception precedes production—just as in learning to talk, comprehension precedes the ability to speak. Even 3-year-olds can distinguish letters or words from pictures of objects, regardless of whether they can name or read the former. Assuming they come from an environment which offers ample opportunities to explore reading matter, 5-year-olds can make fine distinctions between actual script and artificial printed or written characters. Gibson and Levin (1975) regard this development as a case of pure perceptual learning, children on their own learning the characteristic features of writing even though they do not know the name of any given letter. Adults cannot have taught them this discrimination, because adults themselves are not exactly sure of the features which characterize printed letters.

While kindergarten children are quite good at discriminating individual letters, they make many errors in regard to groups of letters; for example, they can correctly choose a *G* out of a series of similar letters such as *C*, *Q*, and *O* but often mistake *CQ* for *OQ* or *CO* or *QC*. Still unable to perceive *patterns of letters*, children must deal with each one individually, which results in an inefficient performance, as we saw in the discussion of perceptual learning. Incidentally, beginning first-graders do not even perceive the boundaries of written words, pointing to a letter or to an entire line of print when asked to point to a word. Thus, the idea that print, like speech, is divided into words, and that words are derived from special patterning of letters, has yet to be learned.

Although *reversals* (such as *saw* for *was*) account for more than half of the errors kindergarten children make in identifying single letters, there is no evidence that such errors are the basis for reading disabilities, since by the third grade they are rare even among poor readers. However, poor third-grade readers still have difficulty matching words or strings of letters, although, again, reversals do not predominate. And here is the first clue as to what perceptual difficulties are important and unimportant in producing a reading disability: single-letter reversals do not matter greatly, but difficulties in perceiving regularities in the patterning of letters, and the consequent jumbling of letters, may well impede progress.

Finally, there is evidence that knowledge of *letter names* is a good predictor of reading achievement. Why this should be is not clear, since such knowledge is not essential to discriminating individual letters, nor is it very helpful in learning how letters are actually sounded when they appear in words. The relation may be a general one, in that children who know letter names are more interested in language and reading than others.

While understanding the spoken word will eventually prove a great facilitator to reading the written word, it has one drawback. Spoken words are learned whole and it never occurs to the preschooler that they are composed of basic sound elements. Evidence for this lack of understanding comes from preschoolers' insensitivity to rhymes. Read them the sequence *cat, bat, fat* and ask them if "bicycle" belongs with these words, and they are apt to answer yes. While units of sound can be ignored when learning to speak, units of words—letters—cannot be ignored when learning to read, nor can the child ignore the relation between letters and sounds. Since written English has a phonetic basis, the child must learn to match the speech stream to the written code. Learning to *abstract component sounds* facilitates reading, as evidenced by the correlation between success in rhyming tasks and reading achievement in the first grade.

The Initial Period

One might regard the second period as the *mastery of the mechanics* of reading, if one is careful not to derogate this into meaning mastery of its simple, nonintellectual aspects. The preceding section contains convincing evidence that reading is never simple and mechanical but challenges the child's perceptual and cognitive abilities to their utmost. However, in the second stage, the child must pay conscious attention to the reading process per se, to the task of knowing what a word or phrase or sentence actually is. Only subsequently are such units grasped with less effort, leaving the child free to concentrate on meaning. The analogy to learning to play the piano is apt. Initially the child must concentrate on understanding each note and relating it to a particular location on the keyboard. Next, the child begins to learn patterns among notes: if a piece is in the key of C, certain sequences of notes and certain chords are highly likely; if the piece is in the key of G, a different sequence and set of chords are highly likely. With practice, the fingers begin automatically to play the notes the eye perceives, and the child is freed to concentrate on playing themes and melodies as units. At this point mechanics are secondary and the music comes to the fore.

One approach to understanding how children learn to read is to observe them in the process of learning rather than to atomize reading and study its components. When this approach is used with first-graders, a significant finding emerges: initial attempts at reading are strongly influenced by *language*, regardless of the skill of the reader. Language and its rules for acceptable structure are familiar to the child, while the printed word is new and relatively unknown; consequently, the pull to "read" something which is grammatically acceptable is strong and can override the requirement to interpret the written word accurately. When children make an error in reading, such an error usually involves substituting a word which is meaningful in the context of the sentence; for example, "Spot can help me" is read, "Spot can see me." If children produce a meaningful sentence they tend to disregard the error, although they occasionally might go back for another look. However, when they produce an ungrammatical sentence they are likely to go back and correct the error if they are good readers. Poor readers tend to accept the meaningless sentence, even though they do not make more errors or different kinds of errors. Is this a cognitive failure in that the meaninglessness does not register? Probably not, since these children have a good grasp of meaningful statements. Is it a motivational failure in that these children are not sufficiently concerned with accuracy or lack that crucial self-monitoring ability that would enable them to listen to what they are saying and judge its correctness? We do not know, but the question deserves study.

In sum, an early reading strategy seems to be, "When in doubt, substitute any word that makes sense." This is followed by a stage in which children look at the troublesome word and say nothing. They have grasped the idea that what they read must be related to the text, but since they cannot decode the text, they keep silent. The earlier that children enter this no-response phase, the more successful they will be as readers at the end of the first grade. Errors are based on graphic similarity showing that the children are focused on the written word regardless of whether it makes sense or not. At this stage, children realize that reading aloud is not the same as speaking with a book in front of them; instead, what they say must be determined by what is printed. Only subsequently are children capable of simultaneously obeying two directions: "This must make sense in terms of what you know about meaningful sentences," and "This must be true to the graphic information contained in the printed text."

How can this obedience to two directives be achieved? Gibson and Levin (1975) state that no single approach holds the key, and that a multilevel approach involving *sentences, words,* and *letters* is essential. Reading sentences is important, since it conveys meaningful information, which, after all, is the essence of reading. In mastering sentences, children can apply both their knowledge of grammatical structure and of semantics or meaningfulness. Thus, when a sentence begins, "John hit the ball with his ______," knowledge of grammar will tell them that the next word will be a thing, and knowledge of semantics will tell them that this thing is more likely to be a *bat* than a *bathtub.*

In mastering words children do not have such ready-made skills but must develop new ones. These skills involve spelling-to-sound correspondences and rules regulating the patterning of letters within words. Learning to segment words, such as *Sunday* or *forget,* also is a strategy that helps children grasp the notion of analyzing words into syllables. The old battle between learning to read by phonics (sounding individual letters) or by the whole-word approach is futile because it is based on the false premise that a single method is best.

In regard to learning to read words, there is evidence that as early as kindergarten, children recall more words presented as meaningful patterns (for example, having similar spelling such as *tap* and *nap*) than words that are unrelated (for example, *tap* and *rub*). Thus, *rulelike internal structures* facilitate learning more than do the sight-word or the letter-by-letter, paired-associate approach. Just as children had to grasp the grammatical rules for organizing words into sentences when learning to speak, they now must grasp the orthographic rules of spelling which order letters within words. These are the rules which make words more than an arbitrary string of letters. One set of rules, for example, involves monosyllable words in which either the initial letter (*rat, bat, cat*), the medial letter (*bad, bid, bed*), or the final letter (*bad, bag, ban*) is varied. The ability to process letters in clusters and to grasp relations among them distinguish the good readers from the poor, just as the ability to discriminate groups of letters distinguished the two kinds of readers in the prereading skills period.

Finally, by the fourth grade, *eye-movement* behaviors have stabilized. Reading does not consist of continuous, smooth eye movements but a series of fixations with little jumping movements in between. These quick movements between fixations are called *saccadic*, and they serve to direct the fovea of the eye (which is the point of highest visual acuity) to the letters or words the child wants to look at. In addition to this forward pattern there are also regression movements, which are saccadic movements to parts of the text which have already been perused.

There are a number of interesting findings concerning eye movement. Developmentally, fixation frequency, duration of pauses, and number of regressions markedly decrease between the first and fourth grades. Thus, the child is able to take in more of the text at a faster rate with fewer instances of returning to previously read material. The increase in efficiency is obvious. While reading continues to improve beyond the fourth grade, the change is not in the pattern of eye movement but in the ability to process and comprehend increasingly difficult reading material.

Even more interesting for our purposes is the finding that good readers differ from poor readers in almost all measures of eye movement. Not only do good readers make fewer fixations or pause more briefly between fixations, but their eye movement is more adaptive to the ease or difficulty of the material being read. Poor readers have to fixate more often for longer periods of time, must return to refocus on prior material, and maintain the same pattern regardless of the difficulty or ease of the text.

Finally, efforts to improve reading by teaching poor readers to move their eyes like good readers have proved futile. The reason for this failure should be clear by now. As was already mentioned, the mechanics of reading should not be equated with the mechanical aspects of reading such as eye movement. Skilled readers have efficient eye movements because they have grasped the regularities and patterns which enable them to become more efficient in perceiving the printed text. Their eye movement is merely an index of this increased efficiency. Poor readers must still labor to get from one word or cluster of words to another.

Skilled Reading

Previously it was stated that mastery of mechanics allows children to concentrate on meaning. Now this idea can be restated more accurately. The desire for meaningfulness is there from the beginning; in fact, it is so strong that children will improvise their own meaning when they cannot comprehend the text. The rude awakening is the realization that meaning must correspond to the written words. We have also seen how children begin to bridge the gap between the spoken and written word both by grasping certain rules for ordering letters to make words and by grasping rules for clustering words.

This last development, which has been described but not adequately accounted for, deserves elaboration. Just as orthography can be regarded as the rules for ordering letters within words so that they will be spelled correctly, *grammar* can be regarded as a set of rules for ordering words into comprehensible sentences. Another way of saying the same thing is that grammar provides a context for ordering individual words. The sentence, "He ______ the ball," requires a verb, which means that all other classes of words are automatically eliminated. How much more difficult reading would be if there were no predictable orders, so that an adjective or adverb or noun would be as likely to occur as a verb. Then we truly would have to read one word at a time, since there would be no way of anticipating what would come next.

Using grammatical structure for meaningful ordering of words is not an all-or-nothing strategy, however. Even slow readers in the second grade are better at reading words in a sentence than at reading unrelated lists of words. Thus, it is not literally true that slow readers read one word at a time; it is just that proficient readers make more use of grammatical structure, and this use increases with age.

Incidentally, since it seems that poor readers are deficient in so many areas it is something of a relief to learn that, at least in regard to scanning ability—that is, the ability to detect whether a given word is present in a grammatical or in a scrambled sentence—poor readers from the second to sixth grades are as quick and accurate in their response as are good readers. Their problem is not in recognizing words (just as, at a younger age, it was not in recognizing letters), but in ordering them.

However, we still have a way to travel. All the organizational developments described so far are necessary but not sufficient conditions for the extraction of meaning, which, after all, lies at the heart of reading. Unfortunately, both the research literature on and the conceptualization of meaning are far from definitive, so the developmental picture must become a sketchy one.

At this high intellectual level, organization is not a matter of letters within words or words within sentences but of selection of information. When confronted with, say, a paragraph, the reader must be able to select the critical and relevant information. To regard all bits of information as equally important would be as inefficient as reading word by word was previously. In fact, readers who have mastered all the mechanics may still be deficient in comprehension because they have not learned to select. While factors both in the reader and in the text which influence selectivity have been studied, summarizing them would add little to our understanding of the differences between good and poor readers.

Finally, for the meaning of a written passage to register, higher cognitive functions must come into play; so it is no accident that Gibson and Levin introduce a purely cognitive construct at this point—namely, *schema*. Schema as used here are organized bodies of information. A paragraph on the care and feeding of dogs makes sense because it can be assimilated into a body of organized information concerning dogs. If the child could not integrate the message from the written text into a body of relevant knowledge, very little of its content would be comprehended. As with selectivity, however, the various conceptualizations of comprehension and the research they have generated add little to our understanding of reading disabilities.

PERCEPTUAL-COGNITION APPROACH

Gibson and Levin (1975) have made one of the most comprehensive attempts to place the literature about reading into a developmental framework. Theirs is a *perceptual-cognition* approach, which stresses the importance of structural variables—at first the patterning of individual letters, then the orthographic rules which determine the patterning of letters within words, and finally the grammatical rules governing the patterning of words in a sentence. While they explicitly recognize the importance of motivational, interpersonal, and academic variables, these are not their primary concern. Predictably they regard a deficit in serial ordering or in perceiving invariant relations among stimulus events to be an essential determinant of reading disabilities.

Gibson and Levin help put one generalization about the development of reading into proper perspective—namely, that reading difficulties tend to be perceptual in the early stages and conceptual and verbal subsequently. The danger in this generalization is that it might be interpreted as meaning that initially the child is functioning at a low intellectual level, merely learning to associate one letter or one word with another in a mechanical way. Clearly, perception is not such a mindless process but involves the same search for rules and order that characterizes higher level thinking. Another danger is that the perceptual-conceptual generalization will be interpreted in an all-or-nothing manner. The developmental picture supports a notion of relative emphasis. From the beginning children read for meaning—they want to make sense of the words on the printed page. Their lack of skill forces them to attend to letters and words, so in this sense perceptual factors come to the fore. Once letters and words are mastered, children are free to concentrate on the substance of what they are reading and on comprehending the increasingly complex ideas contained in the written text.

If Gibson and Levin are to be faulted, it is in their failure to present a satisfactory conceptualization of meaning itself. They are strong on structure but not on content. Structure will tell a child that a noun will complete the sentence ("The boy hit the ______."), but only meaning will tell him that *ball* is a more likely word than *ice cream.* However, the fault lies not with Gibson and Levin as much as with developmental psychologists, who have only recently begun to give the concept of meaning the attention it deserves.

The perceptual-cognition approach is only one of many ways to account for reading disabilities. We shall examine some of the others briefly. (For a detailed presentation, see Meier, 1978.)

NEUROLOGICAL THEORIES

While reading disability, by definition, is not caused by gross neurological damage, there have been repeated attempts to relate it to more subtle neurological dysfunctions. As early as 1925, Orton speculated that dyslexia resulted from a failure to establish hemispheric dominance between the two halves of the brain, a hypothesis which has been revived and revised in light of recent research on *laterality.* (This presentation follows Kinsbourne and Hiscock, 1978, and Naylor, 1980.)

Research on brain-damaged patients and on normal subjects has indicated that the left cerebral hemisphere is functionally specialized for certain kinds of language processing, such as letters, syllables, numbers, and words, while the right cerebral hemisphere is specialized for nonverbal, visual-spatial processing, such as face recognition, as well as for nonverbal stimuli such as music, emotional tone, and intonation patterns. The *progressive lateralization hypothesis* makes the reasonable assumption that, as the highly complex language of the adult develops from a nonlinguistic neonatal state, the cerebrum undergoes a similar development from functional symmetry to left hemisphere specialization. The failure to develop lateralization constitutes the neurological basis for dyslexia.

A traditional index of lateralization has been hand preference in performing tasks, since each hand is controlled by the opposite cerebral hemisphere. In fact, a number of investigators reported a high incidence of left-handedness or ambidexterity in dyslexic children. Eye and foot preferences have also been used as indices of lateralization. A more recent technique called *dichotic listening* involves the simultaneous presentation of competing sounds in the two ears. Superiority in detecting right-ear sound is presumed to reflect left-hemisphere representation of language.

In spite of the plausibility of and initial empirical support for the lateralization hypothesis, the bulk of the research shows that there are no important differences between normal and reading-disabled children in regard to handedness or eye preference. Dichotic listening studies have similarly failed to yield confirmatory data. In part, the contradictory findings have been due to methodological problems along with situational and experiential factors which can alter asymmetry of perception. (See Kinsbourne and Hiscock, 1978, for details.) Until the psychological processes involved in reading are more convincingly related to hemispheric functioning, there is no basis for regarding the lateralization hypothesis as tenable.

Nor has the developmental hypothesis fared any better. Far from being functionally equipotential, current research indicates that the infant's cerebral hemispheres are specialized. Anatomically, the neonate's temporal speech region is usually larger on the left side than on the right; patterns of electrical activity recorded off the infant's brain indicate asymmetries in response to speech and music; a right-handed preference has been shown in 3-month-old babies (infants retaining objects in the right hand significantly longer than in the left, for example); and there is right-ear advantage for speech and left-ear advantage for music in infants as young as 50 postnatal days. Thus, it appears that brain functions are lateralized from birth and that language does not become increasingly lateralized as the child matures.

A more unfortunate development than the lateralization hypothesis has been the linkage of learning disabilities with minimum brain damage and hyperactivity. The search for neurological correlates has led to the assumption that subtle dysfunction of the central nervous system undermines both the processes involved in reading, such as perception, learning, conceptualization, and memory, and the control of attention, impulses, and motor functioning. The linkage has been unfortunate because the concept of minimal brain dysfunction itself is fraught with conceptual ambiguities and unsubstantiated assumptions. While it is true that certain learning-disabled children may be hyperactive, the association is far from inevitable; in addition, the assumption of an underlying central nervous system dysfunction is totally unwarranted, since the behavioral picture can have psychogenic origins.

The interchangeable use of learning disabilities, minimal brain damage, and hyperactivity has created confusion in the research literature, making it difficult to know what population the results can be generalized to, while rendering replication an almost hopeless task. The consequences for clinical practice have been equally untoward, since learning problems require psychoeducational intervention, while hyperactivity requires treatment with stimulant drugs, which are ineffective in improving general scholastic achievement. (See H. E. Rie, 1980a, pp. 12–

13. For an historical background to the present situation, see Kessler, 1980.)

Undoubtedly certain reading disabilities have correlates in brain functioning. What such correlates are will become clearer only as progress is made in understanding both the nature of reading and the functioning of the brain.

MOTOR THEORIES

While Gibson and Levin's conceptualizations are plausible and congruent with research findings, they pay scant attention to research indicating that visual-motor coordination in kindergarten children is one of the better predictors of reading ability by the end of the second grade (de Hirsch, Jansky, and Langford, 1966).

Intuitively Gibson and Levin may seem to be justified in their stand. Learning to read does seem to be a cerebral activity, more a task for eye and brain than for bone and muscle. But intuition can be misleading. We tend to forget how close children live to their bodies during the first five years of life. Piaget labeled the initial state of cognitive development *sensorimotor* in recognition of the fact that motor activity lies at the heart of early cognitive development. Throughout the toddler period the body continues to be a vehicle for exploring objects and physical space as well as for problem solving (Wenar, 1971). Early in development our mind is in our body as well as in our brain.

But we are dealing here with something more than the body as a vehicle for cognitive development. Bender (1957) theorizes in terms of the body's maturational schedule. If this is faulty, the proper integration of visual and motor activities fails to take place, and the child is significantly hampered in a number of developments, learning to read being one. Bender also devised one of the most popular measures of visual-motor coordination, the Bender Visual Motor Gestalt Test (Bender, 1962), which requires the child to copy a series of abstract patterns.

Kephart (1968) is also a strong defender of the importance of motor development per se in learning to read. His emphasis is not so much on the development of specific skills, such as throwing a ball or hopping on one foot, as on the basic sense of body intactness as revealed in overall coordination, balance, and laterality. According to his reconstruction, early development consists of an initial disorganized state of motor behavior and perception followed by a sequencing from motor to motor-perceptual to perceptual-motor stages.

COMPARISON OF THEORIES

While not denying the importance of all the etiological factors discussed so far, it is clear that Gibson and Levin present the most convincing case for their perceptual-cognitive approach. Bender is more global and programmatic in her theorizing, while her evidence is less rigorous. Kephart's reconstruction of early development runs counter to recent studies of infants and toddlers showing motor activity to be organized rather than disorganized in many instances and intimately related to perceptual and cognitive development from infancy on (Appleton, Clifton, and Goldberg, 1975).

A review of the research (Meier, 1978) suggests that visual perception per se and visual-motor coordination have been overemphasized, while auditory and visual discrimination and long- or short-term visual memory are not basic to dyslexia. The correlation between the Bender test and reading disabilities may be because the test also measures conceptual development, which may be more closely related to reading than visual-motor coordination. The evidence is far from definitive, but it does not support the developmental hypothesis that perceptual disorders are important in early reading disabilities while conceptual disorders assume importance later. Concluding that the importance of visual perception and visual-motor coordination have been overemphasized, however, does not mean that such factors are unimportant; in certain kinds of dyslexia they may play a crucial role. In turn, this suggests that dyslexia should be renamed *the dyslexias* in recognition of the diversity of etiologies.

It is also clear that higher order processes are coming to the fore as etiological agents in reading disabilities. Language in particular seems vitally important. Dyslexic children, when compared with nondisabled readers, have less verbal facility, less knowledge of words and of syntax, less ability to use words categorically, and to organize words into meaningful expressions. In fact, the child with a developmental speech and language disorder is generally learning disabled, since not only is reading likely to suffer but spelling and writing as well (Beadle, 1979). In addition, the reading-disabled child does poorly on various aspects of processing semantic information, such as verbal short-term memory, rapid naming, and verbal association learning.

Another facet of the trend toward studying higher order processes is an emphasis on strategies. In certain instances there has been an interesting reversal of causal relation between perception and reading. The evidence suggests that the good reader has learned strategies for searching out invariant and distinctive features of letters, words, and numbers and transfers these skills to perceptual problems, such as finding a given geometrical shape which is embedded in a larger design and thereby camouflaged. Rather than perception underlying reading, cognitive strategies facilitate or impede both.

The current research emphasis is of interest at a more general level. It suggests that the traditional approach of analyzing behavior into its basic component units and then studying how these units are combined to produce a complex skill may not be a valid model for the learning process. The human may be biased from the beginning to search for overall rules and regularities, utilizing perceptual information primarily as clues to what such rules and regularities might be. The processing of information may be more important than specific input at the perceptual level.

OTHER INTRAPERSONAL FACTORS

In our presentation of intrapersonal factors personality and motivation—which also play a role in reading—have been neglected. De Hirsch et al. (1966) found that ego strength and work attitudes in kindergarten children are predictive of reading ability at the end of the second grade. The ability to concentrate on a task, to persist in the face of frustrations and distractions arising from within (such as anger or excitement), or from the environment (such as playful peers or intriguing toys) are important assets from the start. Being motivational, they do not cause learning to take place, but they do provide a congenial setting in which to utilize the assets at the child's disposal. Phrased negatively, disinterest and distractibility can prevent the child from having the task orientation essential to learning how to read.

Incidentally, children do not have to be taught to read, since some teach themselves. In Smith (1973), Torrey reports a fascinating case study of John, a 5-year-old Black child who did just that. Like many other such children who have been studied, John came from the lower class rather than from a professional, middle-class home. He took the initiative in learning, apparently making use of television commercials and labels on tin cans to bridge the gap between spoken and written words. He also enjoyed writing and spent a good deal of time printing words and numbers. Socially he was something of a loner: he was close to his mother and related easily to adults but had difficulty with the more aggressive aspects of peer interaction. Reading was a source of great pride, and he delighted in showing off his ability to read better than his brothers. There was no evidence that he received help, for both his mother and grandmother reported how surprised they were with his accomplishment. His tested verbal ability was no more than average, and he had perhaps even below-average cultural stimulation in regard to reading. Although he did not speak standard English, this rarely interfered with his ability to read it correctly. Torrey infers that John learned to read because, rather than being bothered with sounding individual letters or words, he asked the key question, "What does the print say?" thus directly bridging the gap between speaking and reading.

SUBSEQUENT DEVELOPMENT OF CHILDREN WITH READING DISABILITIES

The short-term outcome for the reading-disabled child is poor in regard to academic progress: only a minority are in age-appropriate grades, while the majority have a history of "rampant grade repetition." (Our presentation follows Helper, 1980.) Deficits in learning skills persist into adolescence, and academic achievement remains deficient. Equally persistent are deficits in attention and information processing, functions which underlie reading. Of special interest is the finding that the adolescent evidences behavior problems only when hyperactivity accompanies the reading disability; in and of itself, reading disabilities do not presage conflict with others, such as parents, teachers, and community authorities. Progress in reading tends to be slow and below normal expectations into adulthood. The remainder of the adult picture is uncertain. However, there is some evidence that if the child is intelligent, has parents in a profession, and attends a school or university with a reading clinic, the prognosis for academic and vocational success is very good—although the feeling that reading is difficult might persist into adulthood. The fate of the child's personal and social adjustment is unknown.

Remediation

There is no treatment of choice for reading disabilities. Predictably, Gibson and Levin favor programs directly addressed to perceptual and cognitive difficulties the child has in mastering the written text. While advocating a comprehensive remedial program, Frostig (1972) concentrates on perceptual and visual-motor training, such as eye-motor coordination (as involved in drawing continuous straight, curved, or angled lines between boundaries of various widths), discriminating reversals and rotations of figures, and figure-ground perception. Kephart (1968) includes motor tasks along with perceptual and visual-motor ones, for example, teaching balance by having the child walk the length of a beam or facilitating laterality by having the child stand on a board that rocks back and forth as weight is shifted from one side to another.

Other programs address themselves to facilitating the learning of reading per se rather than to remedying the presumed deficiencies that underlie the disability. Some involve breaking down standard instructions into smaller steps and presenting the material at a slower pace than with nondisabled readers. An automated talking typewriter has been used to make the learning process more intriguing. Phonetic alphabets have been tried in an attempt to aid reading by reducing the discrepancy between letter and sound in the traditional alphabet. Other programs attempt to facilitate reading by utilizing the child's strongest learning modality under the assumption that some children are primarily visual learners, others auditory, and still others tactile-kinesthetic; for example, the Braille technique has been used with severely dyslexic teenagers in the hopes that the kinesthetic cues will provide new pathways to learning. (For research supporting the idea that different strategies should be utilized for teaching boys and girls, see Townes, Turpin, Martin, and Goldstein, 1980.)

The most famous controversy in regard to reading involves the phonics versus the whole-word approach to teaching. While not remedial programs per se, they have been implicated in the production of reading disabilities, since it has been argued that proper teaching would significantly reduce the dysfunction. The phonic camp advocates teaching the child how to sound individual letters and then how to blend the sounds to produce words; for example, *kkk-aaa-ttt* would congeal to produce *cat*. The whole-word camp advocates teaching the child to recognize the overall patterning of words; for example, the child would learn that the constellation of letters *cat* is the word *cat*. Opponents of the phonics method point out that there is no uniform correspondence between letters and sounds in English, and there is no way of blending sounds together to produce a word unless the child has a pretty good idea of what the word is going to be in the first place. Opponents of the whole-word approach point out that the system provides no means of generalizing from one word to another and burdens the child with having to learn hundreds of isolated units. The battle has been long and bitter at times but there is no evidence that it has had any appreciable effect on eliminating reading disabilities.

Since all remedial programs report a certain amount of success but none has proven superiority, the clinician's choice is a pragmatic one of finding the technique which is best for a particular child in light of a comprehensive individual diagnosis. (For an account of comprehensive diagnosis, see Clarizio and McCoy, 1976. For a detailed presentation of remediation, see Meier, 1978.)

THE COMPLEXITY OF READING DISABILITIES

We now have a better appreciation of the complexity of reading disabilities and can briefly touch upon some of the problems which must be faced by researchers and clinicians alike. (For details, see Torgensen, 1975.)

Because of the variety of etiologies implicated in reading disabilities, children in the same category may have a wide array of difficulties. A researcher investigating one variable, for example, visual-motor coordination, may find only a weak relation to reading disability because by chance alone only a small subgroup of the population has this particular problem. Or a lack of verbal facility may be strikingly demonstrated in one population and absent in another, again because of chance sampling biases.

An analogous problem confronts the diagnostician and, by implication, the therapist. Labeling a child reading disabled is just the beginning of the diagnostic task, since the child must be administered a battery of psychological tests in order to specify the source of the difficulty. In addition, the child's medical history, socioeconomic status, home environment, and educational experiences must all be evaluated for their contribution to the problem. While we have ignored these factors for the purpose of simplifying the etiological problem, the clinician can afford no such luxury. In light of its complexity, therefore, it seems desirable to use reading disability as a general category to be followed by a listing of specific areas of vulnerability; for example, reading disability associated with an unstimulating home environment and difficulty in grasping sequential visual and auditory patterns. Such a diagnosis would also contain valuable leads as to remediation.

Since reading disability is multidetermined, it would seem logical to assess it by means of a battery of specialized tests in order to pinpoint the relevant dysfunction(s). Such assessment instruments are being devised (Doehring and Hoshko, 1977; Senf and Comrey, 1975.) Senf and Comrey are conducting the SCREEN Early Identification Project, which evaluates self-concept and school adjustment, visual skills, auditory skills, figure copying, and basic knowledge. Statistical techniques are available for determining the relative contribution of each test to the total disability score and the clustering together of measures. Such techniques are invaluable in deciding which functions are essential, which peripheral, and which noncontributory to reading disabilities, as well as in simplifying what may well be an unmanageably lengthy series of tests.

The promise of multifaceted evaluation is not without its problems, which to date have defied solution. Let us start with a relatively simple one which will be of special interest to clinicians. Huelsman (1970) found that as a group, poor readers in the fourth grade had low scores on the information, arithmetic, and coding subtests of the Wechsler Intelligence Scale for Children (WISC), a standard intelligence test. However, when individual test protocols were examined, not a single child had significantly low scores in all three areas, and 64 percent were not significantly deficient in any of the areas! Group results are a composite which may be representative of few of the individuals within the group. Clinicians who usually deal with individual children may be misled in evaluating how typical or atypical a given WISC protocol is when they rely on group results for guides. Incidently, theoreticians could also fall into the same trap of trying to account for a pattern of test scores which in reality characterizes few children.

Another roadblock in the path of understanding reading disabilities by means of multifunction assessment is that neither the functions themselves nor the instruments for measuring them are simple. So far we have glibly talked of perception, memory, integration, and strategies. Yet each is complex and there is no general agreement as to how it operates. Certainly, perceiving a *p* and a *b* is different from perceiving a line of printed text; immediately recalling six digits is different from remembering the contents of a paragraph a day later. To diagnose a reading disability as owing to a "perceptual problem" and to recommend "perceptual training" turns out to be only a little better than diagnosing the child as having a "reading disability."

The same point can be made in terms of

another variable not mentioned in this discussion. An essential element in learning to read is that of equating a known auditory symbol (for example, the spoken word *dog*) with a particular pattern of visual stimuli (in this instance, the written word *d-o-g*). This requires the child to perceive the equivalence of stimuli presented in different sense modalities, a process called *intersensory integration*. There is evidence, however, that, at least in auditory-visual intersensory integration, the problem may lie not in transfer but in a basic inability to code sequentially presented stimuli (Blank, Weider, and Bridger, 1968). Specifically, there is a difference in perceiving a pattern of light simultaneously and grasping this same pattern when a single light flashes; for example, seeing a row of four lights with a space between the second and third is different from seeing a single light going flash, flash, pause, flash, flash. The latter requires children to retain and construct the pattern mentally so they can have it in mind while comparing it with patterns from another modality. Children who can perceive patterns presented simultaneously cannot necessarily construct and retain patterns from a single stimulus. Obviously, those who cannot grasp the original sequential pattern cannot adequately transfer the pattern to another modality. What appeared to be a perceptual problem turns out to be a conceptual one.

It has been maintained that the study of the *process* of learning to read per se has been sadly neglected (Torgensen, 1975). Instead of charging off in all directions in pursuit of components, researchers could better spend their time studying how children actually go about mastering the challenge of reading. This approach has been bolstered by the success of psycholinguistic research, in which important insights have been gained from observing and recording the speech of children in the process of learning to talk. At present there is no way of deciding what research strategy will be the more fruitful; it may be that a combination of strategies including both the total process and its components is needed.

LEARNING DISABILITIES: PERSONALITY AND INTERPERSONAL FACTORS

Thus far the discussion has concentrated on "pure" cases of reading disabilities, although, in reality, reading and learning disabilities are found in conjunction with a wide array of psychopathologies—severe emotional disturbances, mental retardation, organic brain pathology—as well as in conjunction with cultural deprivation. At this point we will examine some of the personality and interpersonal variables implicated in learning disabilities, as well as some of the psychogenic roots, within the framework of the organically intact middle-class child. We will focus on learning disabilities instead of reading disabilities because, with a single exception, there is no evidence that reading disabilities have a specific psychogenic etiology.

It seems only reasonable to assume that the learning-disabled (LD) child will have a *negative self-image* as a consequence of being seen as a failure by teachers and peers as well as parents and siblings. Being reminded daily that one is doing poorly in a work situation from which there is no escape would probably undermine the self-esteem of adults as well as children. The LD child's negative self-image is established by 9 years of age and increases with age. More ominous is the evidence that by the time the child reaches adolescence, the expectations of parents and teachers are even more negative than those of the children themselves (Bryan and Pearl, 1979). Even when teachers and parents are understanding, however, the special help the child needs is often not available or, if available, is not uniformly successful. (For a sobering account of one special-educational program, see Koppitz, 1971.)

Social relations are also adversely affected by learning disabilities. (Our presentation follows Serafica and Harway, 1979.) LD children are less popular than other groups from the first grade through grammar school, and there is some suggestion that because they are more frequently rejected as work or play partners, LD girls are less popular than LD boys. To compound the problem, both parents and teachers perceive the LD child as having less social success, and there is evidence that teachers have a less positive attitude toward LD children than toward their classmates. LD children, on the other hand, tend to rate themselves significantly higher in social status than they actually are, their misinterpretation perhaps being defensive.

On the positive side, nonacademic talents such as athletic ability or good looks may enhance the LD child's attractiveness to peers. Moreover, the LD child is neither friendless nor an isolate. The latter finding points up the importance of studying the effects of the entire social network on the LD child. Rather than prematurely assuming that the lack of popularity is damaging, one should inquire as to whether the LD child's friendships are sufficiently rewarding to make the child feel socially acceptable.

There are two major explanations for the relatively low social status of the LD child. The first is that the LD child, in the face of frustrations, anxieties, and failures, acts in ways which alienate or antagonize peers and adults, or that the LD child is perceived and even labeled as being different and is consequently rejected by peers. The other explanation is that the same cognitive deficiencies which are responsible for problems in the academic sphere affect the social sphere as well, rendering the child less capable of perceiving and successfully coping with the challenges of peer acceptance. The explanations are not mutually exclusive, and evidence for both can be marshaled.

A high level of *affective arousal* may hamper concentration on school subjects. Such arousal may be due to specific affects such as anger or anxiety or to general restlessness, agitation, or excitement. Defenses against experiencing these disturbing affective states can also hamper learning. Children may withdraw into the protection of fantasy and be "off in another world" when they should be attending to class work. Or they may become excessively inhibited and, in an effort to avoid all excitement, shy away from the moderate stress involved in recitation, asking questions, or even mastering new information. As an example of this last defense, a 10-year-old with superior intelligence strongly resisted learning long division because, as he said, "I can't stand not knowing the answer right away." The tension of having to go through a succession of operations before arriving at an answer was a source of great distress to this child, who was trying desperately to have everything under immediate control at all times.

The clinical literature provides evidence that learning disabilities may be tied to *interpersonal* and *intrapersonal difficulties* (Kessler, 1966). However, there is no evidence that any specific problem or constellation of problems underlie them. Instead, a host of difficulties originating in the family may spill into the academic setting.

School is the prelude to the *adult world of work*, a setting in which esteem-worthiness matters more than loveworthiness and the child's productivity takes precedence over family evaluations. Under certain circumstances children may have a severe conflict over taking this step toward maturity. They may have a close, infantilizing relation with a mother, who—consciously or unconsciously—is threatened by their independence. Such a mother may assume responsibilities which rightfully should be the child's such as making sure they know their lessons. She may even usurp affective reactions, agonizing over a coming examination, loudly protesting a failing grade. The children fail both because their self-confidence is constantly being undermined and because closeness to the mother is still gratifying. For the boys the problem is further aggravated if the father does not provide a model of an achieving male in his work. Modeling may also be important in the classroom. In America, where grammar school teachers are apt to be female, the proportion of males to females having learning disabilities is 3 to 1; in Germany, where the teacher is apt to be male, the proportion is reversed.

For certain children the competitive *achievement orientation* of school may be a source of anxiety. Psychoanalysts have been particularly sensitive to the competitive tensions between father and son and between mother and daughter, as well as to the trace of hostility implicit in any competitive situation. Handled correctly, these can prove a spur to achievement; however, they can be mismanaged so as to frighten the child unduly. A powerful, successful parent may inadvertently intimidate the child, who believes that it is safer to fail than to compete with such a formidable rival. For children who are afraid of expressing anger, the destructive implications of competition become exaggerated. "For me to win you must lose" takes on the quality of a fight to the death.

Anger can block achievement in a subtle way. Recall that in the socializing bargain toddlers and preschoolers give up asocial pleasures and conform to parental standards of behavior because they receive love in return. In the school years certain pressuring parents can make achievement the sole basis for relating positively to their children who, in turn, come to feel manipulated and cheated. Their revenge, usually unconscious, is to fail in school, thereby keeping parents in a state of helpless exasperation while depriving them of realizing an ambition which obviously means more to the parents than to the children themselves. Adolescents may even jeopardize their own vocational future in a self-defeating effort to punish parents by being failures.

Finally, *curiosity* itself can become a source of anxiety. The toddlers' and preschoolers' very openness to new experiences leads them into taboo areas. Sexual curiosity is the classic example cited by psychoanalysts, but the category has been broadened to include any closely guarded family secret, such as the fact that the child was adopted or illegitimate or that the parent has cancer. When children innocently touch upon the taboo topic, the parental reaction of distress not only frightens them but also makes them judge themselves as "bad." Subsequently, "finding out" becomes equated with "finding out something distressing" and the children defend themselves by inhibiting curiosity. In healthy children the inhibition can be confined to a given area, but under circumstances which have never been clearly delineated, the inhibition can generalize to curiosity about academic subjects as well.

And, of all subjects, reading poses the greatest threat. Reading, unlike arithmetic and spelling, deals with ideas. The highly sensitized child, not knowing what ideas he or she might happen upon and fearing reexposure to the taboo topic, retreats to the safety of avoiding learning how to read. By comparison, arithmetic, with its manipulation of impersonal quantities and spelling, with its rote memorization, are safe to learn.

Remediation

Since the treatment of children with reading disabilities has already been discussed, only two comments relevant to treating the LD children will be made, with particular reference to the concomitant psychological problems.

Research has shown that LD children may have a number of behavioral problems which interfere with their meeting the demands of the traditional elementary school classroom. Specifically, LD children may be overactive, inattentive, impulsive, and distractable. Certain of these behaviors can be reduced by drugs and behavior modification. However, teaching the child to sit still is not tantamount to the child's being able to learn. On the contrary, the evidence indicates that academic performance is unaffected. Consequently, the therapist should regard hyperactivity and attentional deficits as secondary and concentrate on improving skills. Such direct remediation often has the effect of decreasing disruptive behavior.

Aggressiveness, on the other hand, is another matter, since it predicts future maladjustment, especially in combination with low academic achievement. Rather than regarding the behavior problem as secondary, therefore, it should be dealt with directly, along with remedial programs for the learning disability itself (Routh, 1979).

Up until now learning disability has been presented as a complex dysfunction requiring heroic remedial efforts. The picture is not wholely accurate. There is evidence that communication with children and parents about the meaning of LD is associated with children having higher self-esteem than when they are told nothing. It seems reasonable that presenting a realistic picture of the dysfunction should reduce ambiguities and misunderstandings on the parents' part. It might also help check the dour anticipations which exceed those of the LD child himself. Moreover, teachers, especially those in regular classrooms who tend to have a negative attitude toward LD children, might also be helped to become more supportive through a discussion of the nature of the children's learning problem and some of its social and emotional concomitants (Serafica and Harway, 1979).

While seeking answers to the knottier issues concerning the nature, remedy, and prevention of learning disabilities, the clinician should not lose sight of simple remedial measures. There is much to learn, but there is also a good deal that is known. The sharing of this knowledge with concerned parents and teachers may itself relieve some of the distress that places an added burden on the LD child.

Charting the developmental course of various psychopathologies has frequently taken us into the adolescent period. Now it is time to examine adolescence in its own right by discussing three of the disturbances specifically identified with it: schizophrenia, drug abuse, and homosexuality. As always, we shall be trying to understand these three conditions as normal development gone awry. In addition, we shall be concerned with evaluating their status as psychological disturbances. While schizophrenia is clearly a psychopathology, there is a question as to when recreational drug use becomes psychopathological drug abuse, while homosexuality is viewed by some solely as an alternate lifestyle to heterosexuality. Before confronting the issues concerning how and whether normal development has gone awry, it will be necessary to sketch the current view of the normal adolescent phase, where marked changes in its image have important implications for the clinician.

10 ▪ Psychopathologies of the Adolescent Transition

Adolescence marks the transition from childhood to adulthood. The body itself sets the stage with physical changes more rapid than those of any other developmental period except infancy, with hormonal changes during puberty, and with the advent of adult sexuality. (This overview will follow Rutter, 1979a.) Society follows suit by requiring the adolescent to relinquish dependence upon the family and assume responsibility for making decisions regarding those dual foci of adulthood, love and work. The transition is facilitated by the increasingly important role peer relations play and by the newfound cognitive sophistication which enables the adolescent both to envision future possibilties and to expand the situation-specific self-examination of middle childhood into the overarching question, Who am I?

Until recently the image of adolescent transition has been one of turmoil, the inherent instability of the period being epitomized by G. Stanley Hall's phrase "storm and stress," coined in his classic turn-of-the-century study. Psychoanalysts, in a similar vein, characterize the period as marking the return of primitive impulses and unresolved conflicts from the early stages of psychosexual development while, according to Erikson, a weakened ego struggles to master an identity crisis and role diffusion. And, as if this were not enough, the more recent literature emphasizes the distress brought about by the generation gap and by alienation.

However, it is becoming increasingly clear that the image of adolescent turmoil is applicable primarily to the more visible and the more disturbed minority of adolescents. Most adolescents make the transition without significant emotional problems. While peer relations deepen and bickering with parents over everyday issues such as clothing and hair style increases, the parent–adolescent relationship is generally harmonious, lines of communication remain open, and adolescents continue to share parental values and to turn to parents for guidance on matters of major concern. In a like manner, the search for identity goes on unaccompanied by crises, although there may be an increased anxiety about the future.

The revised picture should not be taken to mean either that adolescence is a uniformly serene period or that it has little import developmentally. Moodiness, depression, and self-depreciation reach a peak in adolescence, even though such feelings characterize only a minority of this age group. Certain psychopathologies also show a sharp rise in adolescence: suicide and suicide attempts, alcoholism, drug abuse, schizophrenia, anorexia nervosa, and depression. However, the overall rate of psychopathology increases only slightly, since other disturbances such as hyperactivity are on the decline. Interestingly, disturbances are less clearly associated with family discord and disruption or with school problems than they were during earlier childhood, although the question as to what such disturbances are due to has not been satisfactorily answered.

Adolescence also leaves its imprint on future development. In the Berkeley Growth Study the status of normal adolescents was predictive of their mental health at 30 years of age. As we have seen, a certain number of autistic children will develop epileptic seizures for the first time during adolescence, while others will begin their successful effort to lead a normal social life. And, as in middle childhood, neurotic disturbances tend to disappear with time, while psychotic disturbances tend to persist.

For clinicians the changed picture means that they cannot so readily dismiss deviant behavior with the reassurance that "most adolescents act like that and he or she will outgrow it." The situation is much too complex. Longitudinal data suggest that neither turmoil nor tranquility should be regarded as normal. Instead, as with childhood neurosis, the path of development is determined by the balance between stresses and resources. (For details, see Livson and Peskin, 1980.) Two examples, one from a normal, the other from an at-risk population, illustrate this. One study showed that well-adjusted 30-year-old women who were independent and self-confident and controlled their tempers during preadolescence became dependent and had low self-confidence and explosive tempers during adolescence. The important point is that these women had the personal resources and cognitive sophistication to experience and master a degree of turmoil during adolescence. In the second study, preschizophrenic girls were found to display a pattern of extreme conscientiousness, industry, and responsibility in adolescence, while their normal controls were more nervous, restless, and worried. While the clinician's task of evaluating disturbance would be immeasurably simplified if there were absolute guideposts to psychopathology for all adolescents, here, as with other age groups, the clinician must deal with complexities and contingencies.

Erikson's concept of *identity* integrates many of the diverse strands of adolescent transition as well as providing specific leads as to assets and liabilities. (For a summary of research on identity, see Marcia, 1980.) Identity involves both inner continuity and interpersonal mutuality. It is a coming to terms with oneself and finding one's place in society. Adolescence is marked by an identity crisis because it is a "necessary turning point, a crucial moment" (Erikson, 1968, p. 16), in which the adolescent must master the tripartite challenge of finding a fulfilling vocation, sexual role, and ideology or risk stagnation and regression. The adolescent faces the task of achieving an identity with the accumulated resources and vulnerabilities from the past—trust, autonomy, initiative, and industry on the positive side; mistrust, shame, doubt, guilt, and inferiority on the negative side. Cognitively the adolescent is capable of a more sophisticated level of self-exploration and a more realistic grasp of the options that society offers so that choices and decisions now have an air of commitment, of "playing for keeps," which was absent from middle childhood.

In light of the formidable nature of their undertaking, society grants adolescents a *moratorium,* a period for exploration and experimentation during which they are exempt from carrying the full responsibilities of adulthood. Adolescent exploration might include championing ideologies which society abjures and engaging in behaviors which society condems or regards as delinquent, as exemplified by the activist movement and the "do your own thing" philosophy of the 1960s. Whether such behaviors are normal or deviant depends not so much on their manifest content as on whether they serve to advance the adolescent quest or whether they represent a kind of self-defeating defiance that is as detrimental to the individual as to society.

While the concept of identity will not integrate all the material we shall discuss, it will provide markers serving to orient us in our own search to answer the question, Why should particular psychopathologies flourish in adolescence?

SCHIZOPHRENIA

Unlike drug abuse and homosexuality, schizophrenia is unquestionably a psychopathology and a severe one. Schizophrenics are deviant in the way they relate to the social environment, in the way they think, and in what they say. From the discussion of cognition in chapter 2 we can understand why these deviations go hand in hand. Both cognitive development and communication require that children constantly modify their early distortions of reality and their egocentric orientation so that they can think in terms of shared meanings and attune their speech to their listeners. Such modifications take place in the context of interpersonal transactions. If the basic social bond is tenuous, thinking and communicating are in danger of going markedly awry.

Exactly what sets this disastrous process in motion is not known, but there are a number of tenable explanations, which will be discussed shortly. The developmental picture itself is gradually being pieced together from two sources of data—follow-back studies of schizophrenic adolescents and prospective studies of children at risk of becoming schizophrenic. In reviewing these studies, the basic developmental question will be kept in mind: Why should the incidence of schizophrenia almost quadruple between 18 and 24 years of age?

But first a descriptive account of schizophrenia itself. (Our discussion will follow Calhoun, 1977, and I. B. Weiner, 1980.)

Description

DISORDERS OF THOUGHT. Certain disturbances involve the process of thinking itself rather than the content of thought: "It's like someone poured molasses into my thinking machinery. I've got to work and work to get from one idea to another, and sometimes the whole thing just stops running." "My mind keeps going in all directions at once. I don't know what's going to pop up next. That's why I'm so scared. My mind's going haywire."

These two adolescents are describing the collapse of directed attention, which is essential to orderly thinking. One result is *blocking,* which may be clinically manifested by long pauses before the adolescent can answer a question. Such sluggishness is different from the defiant silence or purposeful negativism of the psychopath or the frozen fearfulness of the neurotic. At the other extreme is *fragmentation,* in which tangentially related or even unrelated ideas constantly intrude and disrupt the adolescent's train of thought.

The content of thinking is disturbed in a number of ways. We shall describe only a few. *Delusions* and *hallucinations* represent an extreme loss of reality contact. The former include delusions of grandeur (for example, an adolescent boy picked up a book he had never read, briefly flipped through the pages from beginning to end, and announced, "I know everything that's in this book.") and delusions of persecution (for example, a young girl was certain a neighborhood gang was planning to capture, rape, and torture her "like Patty Hearst"). Hallucinations are often auditory (for example, hearing voices), visual ones being infrequent. Perception of bodily sensations and functions can also be radically distorted (for example, the body is emitting a foul odor, there are roaches eating the brain, or feces will come out of the mouth if the adolescent speaks).

Another kind of thought disturbance is *perseveration,* in which the adolescent dwells on a single idea. At the opposite extreme is *overinclusiveness* in which ideas flit from one tangential association to another. ("Jody said he wanted to sleep with me and I said two's company and three's a crowd, and that's what this intercourse bit is all about. But I'm not about to have it. I got too much going—coming and going. I've come a long way, baby. You can see it in my eyes. They're sometimes brown and sometimes green depending on the light. But I'm all the time light. None of this 'Black is beautiful' crap for me.")

SOCIAL ISOLATION. The social withdrawal of schizophrenics can be evidenced in a variety of ways. They may be oblivious to others, puzzled or confused by things happening around them, excessively preoccupied with their own thoughts. Their affect might be blunted, or they might be touchy and hypersensitive, subject to inappropriate outburts of anger or to silly laughter. Isolation from peers is particularly important. At times such isolation may be masked by a superficial conformity which is lacking in any personal meaning or emotional investment in others.

DISORDERS OF MOTOR BEHAVIOR. Here one finds facial grimaces, odd postures and movements such as persistent rocking while standing or sitting, long periods of immobility, bizarre repetitive actions such as incessantly rubbing the forehead or angrily slapping the wrist or scratching the skin in spite of producing open, bleeding sores.

Theories of Schizophrenia

Etiological theories of schizophrenia abound, the heredity-environment issue in particular being hotly debated. (For a comprehensive account of theories, see Garmezy, 1974a.)

THE GENETIC THEORY. While the incidence of schizophrenia in the general population is less than 1 percent, the child of one schizophrenic parent has a 16.4 percent chance of becoming schizophrenic, the child of two schizophrenic parents a 39 percent chance—evidence strongly suggesting a genetic factor. Suggesting, but certainly not proving, since environmental influences need to be controlled. More definitive data come from adoptive studies where children of schizophrenic parents are adopted at birth and thus have the genetic endowment of one family while being reared by nonschizophrenic parents. Such studies have shown an elevated incidence of schizophrenia in the adopted children. While one might think that such data settle the issue of the inheritance of schizophrenia, we shall soon see that this is not the case.

But granting a genetic component still leaves the question of transmission unanswered. The *monogenetic-biochemical* theory holds that a single gene is responsible for the specific metabolic dysfunction that, in turn, produces the behavioral manifestations of schizophrenia. The *diathesis-stress* hypothesis states that only a predisposition to schizophrenia is inherited; its actual appearance is contingent upon the kind and amount of environmental stress the individual encounters.

INDIVIDUALLY ORIENTED THEORIES. Learning theorists maintain that being raised by schizophrenic parents provides ample opportunity for the child to learn such behavior by imitation and reinforcement. It is also possible that disturbed parents do not reward responses to the usual social stimuli, so that the child responds increasingly to inappropriate, idiosyncratic cues. The resulting bizarre behavior may succeed in attracting attention, thereby being socially reinforced and personally reinforcing. The psychoanalytic theory emphasizes the schizophrenic's regression to the infantile period, in which the ego and environment are not clearly differentiated and bizarre (primary-process) ideation abounds. Such regression is due to fixation at the early stages of psychosexual development, subsequent trauma, or a combination of both. Finally, certain theories regard anxiety as the key to understanding schizophrenia. Such anxiety may be either experientially engendered or the result of a faulty physiological mechanism of arousal and reduction. Whatever its origins, anxiety forces the individual to become increasingly withdrawn from reality as a protection against its attendant terrors. (For an elaboration of these theories, see Garmezy, 1974a.)

FAMILY THEORIES. We will concentrate on the family context, since some of the most important contributions to understanding psychopathology have resulted from the intensive scrutiny of schizophrenic families. The three major theories focus on three different aspects of family interaction, which in turn are related to three different characteristics of schizophrenia. (The presentation follows Mishler and Waxler, 1965.)

Gregory Bateson traces the origin of schizophrenia to a particularly vicious pattern of parental *communication* called the *double bind,* which traps the child between two negative injunctions. The often cited example is of a mother who stiffened when her schizophrenic son impulsively put his arm around her shoulder but, when he withdrew, reproached him with, "Don't you love me anymore?" This "damned if you do and damned if you don't" dilemma is compounded by a prohibition against escaping from the family and a further prohibition against calling the parent's attention to his or her incongruous messages.

The only way out of the intolerable dilemma of repeated exposure to the double bind is to shatter the bond of communication itself. Rather than trying to convey meaning, schizophrenics purposefully attempt to avoid conveying meaning. In so doing they also avoid defining their relationships to others—

those implicit messages which say, "I am a person who has information (or who needs help or can say amusing things or is sexually aroused.)" Making it impossible for the ordinary listener to understand them and their ideas is the schizophrenics' intent, escape, and protection.

Lyman Wynne locates the psychopathology not in communication but in the *structure* of the family as a whole. The drifting or scattered thinking of the schizophrenic represents the internalization of a diffuse or fragmented family structure. Amorphous patterns of interaction are marked by vague ideas, by blurring of meaning, and by irrelevancies. Note the following responses of a mother being interviewed for her schizophrenic child's developmental history.

PSYCHOLOGIST: Was it a difficult delivery, or did everything go OK?

MOTHER: I know just what you mean. And I can say for certain that I'm not one of those women you read about where they are so brave and natural childbirth is just the greatest thing in their life. (Laughs) Believe me, when the time comes, I want the works when it comes to care.

PSYCHOLOGIST: But did everything go OK?

MOTHER: Well, there was this Dr. Wisekoff that I never liked, and he said all kinds of doom and gloom things, but I told my husband I was the one who had the baby and I was the one who ought to know, so my husband got into this big fight and didn't pay the bill for a whole year, and the doctor threatened to hire one of these collection agencies, and what that was all about, don't ask me—just don't ask me.

PSYCHOLOGIST: I see, but I'm still not sure . . .

MOTHER: (interrupting) But that's just what I mean.

Later the psychologist, who was just beginning his clinical internship, told his supervisor that he wanted to shake the mother and yell at the top of his lungs: "But was the delivery difficult or easy!" One can only imagine how difficult it would be for a child to grow up surrounded by such diffuseness, accompanied by a total obliviousness to the diffuseness itself.

Like amorphous thinking, fragmented thinking can be traced to parental communication. In this case, parental communication is marked by digression from topic to topic, non sequitur reasoning and extraneous, illogical, or contradictory comments. In fragmented thinking itself, attention can be focused for brief moments but bits and pieces of memories become intermixed with current stimuli. The technical name for this abrupt shift from one topic to another is *overinclusive* thinking. We saw an example of overinclusiveness when we first described the thought disturbances in schizophrenia. Affectively, the adolescent is alert and anxious rather than flat and impoverished as is the case with amorphous communication (Singer, Wynne, and Toohey, 1978). Wynne further maintains that amorphousness and fragmentation combined with intrusiveness are responsible for the schizophrenic's difficulty in maintaining focused attention. The ability to keep one's mind "on the track" does not develop naturally but is nurtured by continued exposure to ideas which are clearly expressed and follow a logical sequence. When the child's own thinking is constantly interrupted, when attempts to define reality are countered with ambiguities, when the entire structure of family interactions lacks clarity and continuity, the capacity for focused attention atrophies, leaving the child vulnerable to pathological thinking.

Wynne delineates other faults in the family structure. The family members cannot maintain an appropriate psychological distance, detached impersonality unpredictably alternating with highly personal remarks and confrontations. However, there is a concerted effort to act as if there were a strong sense of unity which results in what Wynne calls *pseudo-mutuality.* There are great pressures to maintain a facade of harmony, the child being allowed neither to deviate from nor question a prescribed role. Beneath this facade lie pervasive feelings of futility and meaninglessness.

In such an environment, children are prevented from developing their own identity as well as from testing reality. They learn to "go through the motions" of a family-prescribed role rather than discovering their potentialities and limitations through actual reality encounters. The enveloping web of family cohesiveness also prevents them from having outside contacts which might serve to counter the influences in the home. Adolescence, with its societal demands for independence from the family, self-direction, and flexibility can be devastating. A schizophrenic reaction may be one solution to the dilemma of being unable to remain completely within the family while being unable to establish an adult identity.

Our final theorist, Theodore Lidz, deals less in terms of total family structure than Wynne and more in terms of *roles and functions.* In the healthy family, maternal and paternal roles are clearly delineated as are generational or parent–child roles, while parents transmit to their children useful ways of adapting to the demands of society. There is also role reciprocity which requires the acceptance of each member's role, values, and goals.

In the schizophrenic family, roles are blurred and parents use children to serve their own egocentric needs. Lidz delineated two kinds of distorted patterns. In the *skewed family,* more commonly found with schizophrenic boys than girls, the mother is overprotective, intrusive, dominating, and seductive, while the father is passive and weak. Because of her tenuous emotional equilibrium, the mother perceives events according to her own needs and insists that her son do likewise. The adolescent boy becomes increasingly fearful of being engulfed by his mother but moves toward autonomy produce unbearable guilt. In the *schismatic family,* more characteristic of schizophrenic girls than boys, there is continuing overt conflict between the parents, each depreciating the other to their children and often competing for the children's loyalty. The mother has little self-esteem and security and is constantly being undermined by her husband's contempt; the father is insecure in his masculinity, is in constant need of admiration, and uses domination as a substitute for strength of character. Disappointed in his wife, the father turns to his daughter to fill his emotional needs. His behavior may be highly inconsistent, alternating between tyrannical tempers and seductiveness or even maternal tenderness. The daughter is caught in a bind, since pleasing one parent alienates the other. The mother, who disparages herself, is a poor model of mature femininity, while the father, who disparages women, is an equally poor model of adult masculinity.

Recently, Lidz (1973) has stressed the role of egocentrism in the etiology of schizophrenia. Parents relate to the child in terms of their own needs and conflicts, while the child comes to view his or her self in these terms, instead of in terms of a separate individuality. Like Wynne, Lidz maintains that adolescence, with its demands for autonomy, places the child in an intolerable situation. The solution is to escape by relinquishing reality contact in favor of prior modes of egocentric thought. Here Lidz explicitly follows Piaget in delineating these early forms of egocentrism: the inability of infants to differentiate themselves from others, and the magical notion of preschoolers that they control the physical and social environment or, contrariwise, that all events in the environment are related to them. Such magical notions are the basis for delusions and hallucinations. Adolescence introduces its special egocentrism characterized by attributing unlimited power to one's own thought. In normal development this may be evidenced by idealistic solutions to the world's problems or soul-searching discussions concerning the meaning of life, with little or no need to integrate ideas with reality. Such integration takes place gradually through constant confrontations with and assimilation of the realities of the adult world. It is just such confrontations that the future schizophrenics, with their strong ties to unrealistic family images, are unable to experience. Because of their egocentrism, the usual self-consciousness of the period can become delusionary (for example, "*Time* magazine had a write-up about gays which did everything but come out and say that's what I am"), as can the adolescents' idealistic expansiveness (for example, "I could clear up all this nuclear arms race if I could just get to the president and tell him my idea, but they won't let me.")

RESEARCH. Reviewers disagree as to how family theories have fared when tested by objective research. Doane presents quite a favorable evaluation (Doane, 1978; Wynne, Toohey, and Doane, 1979). The data show that, in normal families, parents are in coalition rather than in conflict, and their authority is greater than their children's; the family shares similar values, is supportive, functions effectively in solving problems, and is both clearly and flexibly organized. The families of disturbed children are characterized by marital discord, with the child being drawn into cross-generational coalitions; by an absence of closeness and shared values; by impared task effectiveness; and by rigid patterns of interaction. However, it is not clear what specific patterns distinguish families of schizophrenic children. Communication deviance increases along with the severity of the child's pathology, fragmentation being correlated with a good premorbid history, amorphousness with a poor premorbid history.

In a rejoinder to Doane, Jacob and Grounds (1978) maintain that none of her conclusions are justified by the available data. One reason for such disagreement between experts is the newness of the research itself: the problems of operationalizing the concepts, of devising reliable and valid instruments, and of designing crucial tests of hypotheses are far from being solved. However, there is no disagreement in regard to the importance of the concepts themselves and their potential for clarifying the etiology of schizophrenia.

THE HEREDITY–ENVIRONMENT CONTROVERSY. While we are on the subject of research let us return to the matter of obtaining definitive data on the heredity–environment controversy. One of the most sophisticated studies was conducted by Rosenthal, Wender, Kety, Schulsinger, Welner, and Rieder (1975), who examined 258 adults in four groups: adoptees who had a schizophrenic or manic-depressive biological parent; adoptees whose biological parents had no known psychiatric illness; adoptees whose biological parents had no known psychotic disturbance but were reared by persons with these disorders; and non-adoptees reared by a schizophrenic or manic-depressive parent. Subjects were given a 3- to 5-hour psychiatric interview, in which they were asked about various aspects of their life with their adoptive parents. The information concerning the parent–child relationship was subsequently evaluated in terms of its positive or negative quality, and a correlation was done between this child-rearing variable and the degree of adult disturbance. The results showed that rearing patterns had only a modest effect on individuals with a genetic background for schizophrenia but an appreciable effect on persons without such a background. Thus, the genetic background appreciably although not totally neutralizes the impact of child rearing with respect to psychopathological disorders; only when the genetic background is normal does child rearing have its maximum effect.

To which the family theorists might answer, "Not proven!" Recall of childhood events is notoriously unreliable in general, and one characteristic of schizophrenic families is the parents' efforts to blind the child to the reality of family life. In addition, parents who engender schizophrenia do not themselves have to be schizophrenic, although they are often described as disturbed. In fact, there is some evidence (Doane, 1978) that patterns of communication are more highly correlated with schizophrenia in the child than is the categorization of parents as schizophrenic or not. Until the genetic camp finds ways to control for the hypothesized pathogenic family interactions, its case will remain unproven.

And so the controversy goes on. While we might be sympathetic to the family theorist's objection, the evidence for a genetic component in schizophrenia is too impressive to be dismissed (Gottesman, 1978). For their part, many family theorists accept the concept of a genetic predisposition while maintaining that, in certain instances, familial variables are sufficiently potent to produce schizophrenia even when the genetic vulnerability is absent. At present, the diathesis-stress hypothesis seems the most sensible resolution to the heredity–environment tug-of-war. The genetic component predisposes the child to schizophrenia, while various family patterns become one of many possible stresses leading to its actual appearance.

Developmental Studies

PROCESS VERSUS REACTIVE SCHIZOPHRENIA. A critical developmental variable is the premorbid adjustment of the schizophrenic adolescent. In certain cases, labeled *process* schizophrenia, there is a long history of deviance, while in other cases, called *reactive* schizophrenia, the disturbance appears abruptly, often in reaction to a specific traumatic event. The distinction has important prognostic implications, process schizophrenics having longer hospitalizations and less favorable chances of recovery than reactive schizophrenics. It will be worthwhile examining the contrasting developmental pictures in some detail. (See Kantor, Wallner, and Winder, 1953. For a general discussion, see "Premorbid Adjustment and Schizophrenic Heterogeneity," *Schizophrenia Bulletin*, 1977.)

In process schizophrenia there is the likelihood of a severely disturbed parent in addition to chronic schizophrenia in relatives; in the reactive cases, parents tend to be neurotic and psychosis in relatives tends to be acute. A higher percentage of process than reactive schizophrenics tend to be below average in intelligence. The first five years of the process schizophrenic's life are marked by psychological trauma, long and severe physical illness, and "odd" behavior, while the reactive schizophrenic enjoys good psychological and physical health. The middle years are characterized by difficulties at school, failure to get along well with peers, stubborn, quarrelsome, and antagonistic behavior for the process schizophrenic, with a personality change in adolescence involving withdrawal and retreat into fantasy. The reactive schizophrenic tends to be shy, quiet, and introverted, to be ignored rather than actively rejected by peers, and to make an adequate school adjustment. Adolescence merely exaggerates the tendency to withdraw under stress (J. D. Roff, 1974).

RETROSPECTIVE STUDIES. A number of etiological studies have not been specifically cast in the mold of process versus reactive schizophrenia. In the ones to be discussed, the childhood characteristics of adolescent and adult schizophrenics have been reconstructed through interviews or public records, such as those from child guidance clinics, schools, or juvenile courts (Offord and Cross, 1969). Two of the major findings are: there is no one type of preschizophrenic personality, and the majority of patients evidenced no severe childhood disturbances suggesting that they would be reactive schizophrenics subsequently. The first point needs to be elaborated.

The stereotype of the preschizophrenic is that of the "shut-in" child—aloof, peculiar, friendless, living to and in himself or herself. The image is valid (although shyness alone is predictive neither of schizophrenia nor of any other adult disturbance), but is only one of many valid images. The preschizophrenic child is just as likely to be psychopathic as evidenced by stealing, lying, truanting, running away from home. However, there are some differences: acting-out behavior is not as serious as that of the psychopath's and tends to take place within the family rather than in the community. Instead of gravitating to gangs, the future schizophrenic tends to have poor peer relations because of aggressiveness and quarrelsomeness. To complicate the picture even further, there can be a combination of psychopathic with neurotic behaviors such as worrying, excessive dependence, nail-biting, and depression. School retardation, an increased incidence of mental illness in the family, and early hospitalization for severe psychopathology are characteristic of these "stormy" preschizophrenic children.

One of the most detailed pictures of the preschizophrenic child comes from Watt and Lubensky's (1976) analysis of the tenth-grade homeroom teachers' annual comments on fifty-four children who became adult schizophrenics. Between one-third and one-half were sufficiently deviant for their behavior to be described. There were important sex differences, however. The boys were negativistic, egocentric, unpleasant, antisocial, and scholastic underachievers. The girls were primarily quiet, introverted, but also egocentric (as contrasted with being considerate). The authors epitomize the childrens' deviance as emotional immaturity; they would cry on the slightest provocation, were overshadowed by older siblings, were insensitive to the feelings of others, had temper outbursts, were self-conscious, and were delayed in physical and scholastic skills. While the IQ of the disturbed group was significantly lower than that of matched classmates, it did not differ significantly from that of their siblings. Intellectual functioning was stable over time rather than showing a progressive deterioration prior to the onset of schizophrenia. The authors concluded that there was no evidence that low intelligence per se is a significant etiological factor in schizophrenia.

CHILDREN AT RISK. Every solution creates its own problems. The limitations of reconstructive data can be overcome to a degree by longitudinal studies. However, this strategy has its own difficulties, not the least of which is locating a population (Garmezy, 1974b). Since schizophrenia occurs in less than 1 percent of the population, one would have to follow 1,000 randomly selected infants in the hope of obtaining only 10 schizophrenic adolescents. It would facilitate research considerably if one could locate a group of infants or children at risk for developing schizophrenia. The most popular solution is to study children of schizophrenic parents: regardless of whether one holds a genetic or environmental position, the chances of such children becoming schizophrenic are significantly increased.

One word of caution before we review the literature: while a certain proportion of the at-risk children do grow up to be severely disturbed, they are not necessarily schizophrenic. The most valid generalization is that severely disturbed parents tend to have children with a variety of psychological disturbances (although such an outcome is by no means inevitable), rather than there being a close correspondence between the disturbances of parents and children.

The developmental picture can be pieced together from a number of sources. There is a heightened rate of infant and child mortality in children of schizophrenic mothers (Garmezy, 1974a). The mothers of high-risk children who subsequently become severely disturbed experience more emotional stress during pregnancy than do the mothers of high-risk children who do not become severely disturbed; birth is relatively difficult, labor longer and marked by more complications; such mothers are also more disturbed, are hospitalized earlier, and tend to be married to mentally ill mates. Disturbed high-risk children not only suffer loss of the mother at an earlier age but also do not have a substitute mother (B. R. Mednick, 1973). However, at 30 months of age, the high-risk toddlers do not differ from those born to women with other psychopathologies or to nondisturbed women of low SES in regard to perceptual-motor, cognitive, affective, and social functioning. They are by no means healthy toddlers, since they have high levels of illness, fearfulness, negative mood, retardation, and social maladaptiveness; but there is nothing which sets them apart from other toddlers exposed to a variety of deviant environments (Sameroff and Zax, 1978). Cognitive and attentional impairments found in 1-, 3-, and 5-year-old children of schizophrenic mothers are no longer present in 6-year-olds (Garmezy, 1978). What data there are indicate no difference in child-rearing attitudes and behavior between parents of high-risk children who do and do not subsequently become severely disturbed.

Middle childhood is marked by the now-familiar findings of behavior problems, low achievement in school, and poor peer relations. Teachers characterize the children as disruptive, inattentive, disrespectful, low on initiative, withdrawn, easily angered. As was the case in infancy, such behaviors do not seem to be specific to children of schizophrenic mothers, since they characterize children of depressed mothers as well (Garmezy, 1978). However, within the high-risk group itself there is some evidence that by adolescence the deviant behaviors are much more in evidence in the children who become severely disturbed (Mednick et al., 1975). As compared with children of neurotic mothers, children of schizophrenic mothers evidence more acting-out behavior such as stealing, temper tantrums, and destructiveness, along with more digestive and sleep disturbances. In general, it is the degree rather than the specific kind of maternal disturbance that seems to be the crucial factor.

In addition to the behavior problems in high-risk adolescents who become severely disturbed, there is also evidence of a thought disturbance which takes the form of irrelevant associations. Given the word *chair* for example, the adolescent is apt to say something like, "table, top, leg, girl, pretty, sky." Such "drifting" seems closely akin to the overinclusiveness which characterizes schizophrenic thinking (Mednick et al., 1975). The factors accompanying the actual schizophrenic breakdown and hospitalization are: parental psychosis present in the first seven years of the adolescent's life, increase in life stresses—including acute deterioration and rehospitalization of the parent—and a prevailing sense of social incompetence, along with changes in affective level and frustration tolerance. The first finding is particularly interesting from the developmental point of view but again does not seem specific to schizophrenia: generally speaking, children are particularly vulnerable to the negative consequences of having severely disturbed parents during their early years (Garmezy, 1974a). Finally, there is a personality change from acting out to withdrawn behavior, particularly in those adolescents who become chronic schizophrenics as adults (J. D. Roff, 1974).

The course of schizophrenia itself is varied, although there is no agreement as to the expected proportions of recovered, improved, and chronically ill individuals (Zubin, 1978). One can find, for example, that one-third to one-fourth of the schizophrenics make a full recovery, a figure which becomes doubly impressive when one considers that, until recently, the prognosis was regarded as quite poor. While the outcome is somewhat worse than for other disorders, pessimism or therapeutic defeatism are not warranted (Strauss, Kokes, Carpenter, and Ritzler, 1978).

PHYSIOLOGICAL REACTIVITY. S. A. Mednick, who pioneered the prospective study of high-risk children, found that physiological reactivity was one of the most potent variables differentiating adolescents who would become severely disturbed from adolescents who would not. (Mednick et al., 1975). Specifically, for the adolescents who became disturbed, the latency of the galvanic skin response (GSR) was shorter, did not habituate, and resisted extinction, while the rate of recovery was unusually rapid. Mednick interprets his data as indicating that the autonomic nervous system responds too quickly and too persistently rather than responding at a moderate rate and subsequently tapering off with continued exposure to stress. Thus, the individual is "rapidly, exaggeratedly and untiringly emotionally reactive" (p. 232). One way of escaping from this distressing state is by thinking situationally irrelevant thoughts. Because of the GSR's rapid recovery rate, such thoughts will be immediately rewarded and will tend to become habitual.

While Mednick postulates a physiological predisposition to develop schizophrenia, he also states that the autonomic system is responding to noxious stimuli from the environment. Thus, a predisposed individual might well avoid becoming disturbed in a benign, nonstressful setting.

COMMENTS. Adolescent schizophrenia is reminiscent of infantile autism: in both psychopathologies specific etiological variables are being isolated, but their interaction is poorly understood. With schizophrenia, of course, there is the added complication of fifteen years of development, during which time these same variables may well vary in potency. One can only admire the dedication of the many investigators who have accepted the challenge of unraveling the etiological mystery and are conducting some of the most extensive, demanding, sophisticated research in all of childhood psychopathology.

Yet in its current state, the literature is fragmented—to borrow a term from the description of schizophrenia itself. It is difficult to tell what is compatible, what is complementary, and what is contradictory in regard both to theories and data. To take just one example: the family theorists' picture of the preschizophrenic child tightly locked into a prescribed role of uncritical compliance is quite different from the picture of the "stormy" preschizophrenic in a broken home with a neglectful mother.

The literature also seems to account for severe disturbances in general better than for the specific characteristics of schizophrenia. Certainly a formidable list of high-risk factors have been isolated: a genetic predisposition, obstetrical complications, disturbances in autonomic functioning, poor adjustment to peers and to school, psychopathological parents, a broken home or maternal death, a highly deviant family structure (Strauss, Kokes, Klorman, and Sacksteder, 1977). While the diathesis-stress hypothesis is the most tenable one extant, it is a general frame of reference within which the real work of teasing out interactions among genetic and environmental variables must take place. Much work is needed to link the distinguishing features of schizophrenia with the specific developmental status of the adolescent.

Owing to the fragmented nature of the field there is no satisfactory *developmental model* for adolescent schizophrenia. S. A. Mednick postulates an initial-defect model that may deflect development from its normal course at the very beginning. Utilizing Piaget's stages of egocentric thinking, Lidz proposes a regression model to account for certain thought disorders. Data showing preschizophrenics to be emotionally immature in middle childhood suggest fixation rather than regression. Aspects of family theory, along with learning theory, suggest that bizarre patterns of thinking are modeled on parental behavior and need not represent either fixations or regressions. And finally, conceptualizing schizophrenia as a solution to an intolerable situation suggests that it might be a new development unrelated to the past; for example, the decision to shatter communication and obscure one's self-definition may have no counterpart in normal or preschizophrenic development.

To conclude that many kinds of deviations are involved in a disturbance as severe as schizophrenia is probably correct but far too general. The challenge is to come to grips with specifics and to narrow down possible etiologies to necessary and sufficient ones.

The Invulnerables

Bleuler (1974) followed 184 children of 206 schizophrenic parents and found that approximately 72 percent were functioning normally. The percentage is higher than is usually reported (which ranges between 35 and 50 percent) perhaps owing to the uncertainty of the definition of normality, perhaps because, as a family psychiatrist, Bleuler came to know his patients more thoroughly than most researchers know their subjects. But the mystery of normal functioning has deepened with the discovery of high-risk children who are making exceptionally good adjustments. Some have schizophrenic parents, some come from poverty backgrounds, and their home environment would seem inimical to normal development; for example, one 8-year-old girl's father was in jail, her mother was severely depressed and unable to see even to her children's basic needs for food, while her four siblings were either retarded or predelinquent school dropouts.

While the study of these invulnerable children has only recently begun, certain of their characteristics have been delineated (Pines, 1979). Socially they are well liked by peers, while they are at ease with adults and adept at capturing adults' interest. They rate high on initiative. They actively try to master their environment and have a sense of their own power; for example, when asked why he was eating when both his mother and his two older sisters feared the food was poisoned, a 7-year-old replied, "I'm not dead yet, am I?" Not only can they manage their own home life in the face of parental neglect or brutality, but they are also helpful to others. They maintain their autonomy both in terms of their physical environment and their attitude toward their family. Physically, they may seek out a private space, such as a corner in the basement, which can serve as a retreat. Psychologically, they can detach themselves from the surrounding chaos, viewing it objectively, realistically, and even sympathetically while not identifying with it or being overwhelmed by it. They are achievement-oriented, doing well in what they undertake both in school and outside of it. Some are exceptionally creative. Interestingly, the vast majority of invulnerables are boys, perhaps because the traditional feminine role of passivity and compliance makes the girls more vulnerable to parental influences. However, invulnerability might have its developmental hazards: the very detachment which is essential during early and middle childhood may hinder the adolescent in establishing a sustained intimate relationship (E. J. Anthony, 1974).

Invulnerability has been easier to describe than to understand. It might be a matter of genetics or constitution or environment or a happy combination of all three. The quest for understanding is particularly exciting, since it involves two related variables which lie at the heart of normal and deviant development: initiative and the ability to be strengthened rather than undermined by stress. (For a discussion of the role adolescent stress plays in the development of a healthy adult, see Livson and Peskin, 1980.)

Therapy

PSYCHOSOCIAL AND BEHAVIORAL THERAPIES. First, some of the major therapies used with schizophrenics will be briefly discussed (Mosher and Keith, 1977).

In *individual psychotherapy* the emphasis is on establishing a positive relationship and interpreting reality in order to counteract the schizophrenic's isolation and faulty reality testing. Therapists must be versatile in finding ways of presenting themselves as warm and trustworthy, but they must also be able to understand and interpret the adolescent's mistrust, resistance, touchiness, and metaphorical communications. In interpreting reality, they must be careful not to antagonize the adolescent and jeopardize the positive relationship (I. B. Weiner, 1970). *Group psychotherapy* capitalizes on the individual's ability to receive support, understanding, and constructive advice from interacting with individuals who have similar problems, under the leadership of an experienced therapist. Some groups emphasize facilitation of insight into personal and interpersonal problems; most group work with schizophrenics, however, tends to be oriented toward providing support, offering an opportunity to form friendships, as well as developing social skills which enhance a positive adaptation to reality. *Family therapy* aims at correcting the deviations presumably responsible for engendering and maintaining the schizophrenia by promoting clear communication, developing constructive techniques for coping with stress, substituting constructive for destructive role alignments.

The desire to help schizophrenics has produced heroic efforts to change the total environment. In *milieu therapy*, treatment becomes a twenty-four-hour affair, all individuals who interact with the schizophrenic being actively involved in implementing a therapeutic program. There is evidence that acute and chronic schizophrenics require somewhat different programs. The former respond best in an accepting, supportive, low-keyed environment oriented toward solving practical, down-to-earth problems. Chronic patients do better in a highly organized environment focused on changing specific behaviors (Mosher and Keith, 1977). *Rehabilitation* programs try to reintegrate the formerly hospitalized patient into the community by combining emotional support with vocational rehabilitation aimed at raising the level of independent functioning. The programs can be implemented in different settings, such as day-care centers or half-way houses, which provide a protective buffer from the stresses of living in the community. Such extrafamilial resources are particularly important for those schizophrenics who are sufficiently recovered to leave the hospital but who cannot or should not return to their own families.

The picture in regard to relative effectiveness is far from clear owing to conflicting findings and methodological flaws in comparative studies (Mosher and Keith, 1977). In general, however, it seems that therapy becomes increasingly effective as it embraces more of the schizophrenic's social environment. Thus the effectiveness of individual and group therapy is controversial, while family, milieu, and rehabilitation therapies have a more positive record of success.

Behavior modification has been utilized extensively with adult schizophrenics (Redd, Porterfield, and Andersen, 1979). The basic techniques of modeling and contingent reinforcement have been applied with admirable versatility to change such behaviors as mutism, delusions and hallucinations, abstract reasoning, apathy, and withdrawal. Token economies, in which patients receive a token for appropriate behavior which can be redeemed for a reward such as cigarettes, candy, or a special privilege, have been particularly effective in hospital settings.

One of the most exhaustive and well-controlled studies of effectiveness was conducted by Paul and Lentz (1977). The patients were severely debilitated, chronic schizophrenics who had been hospitalized for an average of seventeen years. A token economy, in which progressively more complex, socially acceptable behavior was immediately rewarded, was compared with a milieu program in which patients were organized into self-governing decision-making groups, the staff serving a facilitating, supportive function. The behavioral program proved consistently superior over the four years of the study. When the programs were terminated, twenty-seven of the original twenty-eight schizophrenics in the behavioral program could be placed in a shelter-care facility in the community, while only nineteen of the patients from the milieu program could be so placed. Although the study is impressive, it was begun before it was known that chronic schizophrenics do best in a highly structured milieu; requiring that they function as autonomous decision makers may have put milieu therapy at a disadvantage.

In sum, none of the comparative data are sufficiently conclusive to state that there is a treatment of choice for adolescent schizophrenia. However, our coverage of therapies serves to introduce two other approaches which have not been discussed up till now—prevention and psychopharmacology.

PREVENTIVE MENTAL HEALTH. E. J. Anthony (1977) has described one of the most extensive prevention programs with at-risk children. Four kinds of interventions are involved. (1) *Compensatory* intervention, implemented by warm, interested paraprofessionals, aims at strengthening self-confidence and enhancing both initiative and reality contact through tutoring, camping, big-brother relationships, recreational and creative activities. (2) *Classical* interventions consist of traditional individual and group psychotherapy. (3) *Cathartic* interventions, conducted only in the acute, tumultuous phase of the parent's illness, encourages the expression of fear, shame, guilt, anger, and depression. (4) *Corrective* intervention is used to counteract magical thinking by helping the child differentiate his or her self from the physical and social environment and by "demystification," for example, helping a boy master his bewilderment in the face of his mother's belief that the food is poisoned and people in the street are plotting her death. A preliminary analysis of relative effectiveness suggests that classical intervention may be the most effective, catharsis the least. However, the tentative nature of the findings should be emphasized. (For a description of other preventive programs, see Garmezy, 1974a, and S. A. Mednick and Witkin-Lanoil, 1977.)

Anthony's program is our first encounter

with a mental health program aimed at intervening and helping children at risk before the actual appearance of the psychopathology. This approach will be discussed in detail in chapter 14.

PSYCHOPHARMACOLOGY. Psychopharmacology as a major treatment modality has not been frequently used with any of the psychopathologies previously discussed. (For a general discussion of psychopharmacology, see Conners and Werry, 1979.) Currently drugs are widely used in the treatment of severely disturbed adults, but their effectiveness with adolescence has not been as thoroughly documented. Tranquilizers seem to serve a useful role in the management of psychotic adolescents, making them less withdrawn, less overactive, less anxious, and more tractable. While tranquilizers are not truly antipsychotic in the sense of ameliorating schizophrenic behavior per se, they do make the individual more amenable to other forms of therapeutic intervention. The superiority of any particular compound over the others has not been demonstrated, so a discussion of their various chemical compositions and physiological effects is not warranted. (For a comprehensive review, see Winsberg and Yepes, 1978.) There is also no firm evidence that antianxiety drugs have any usefulness in psychoses (Rapoport, Mikkelsen, and Werry, 1978).

DRUG ABUSE

YOU ARE A CLINICAL CHILD PSYCHOLOGIST. THE TIME IS 11:42 on a Saturday night. You get out of bed to answer the phone. It is Mitzi, the younger sister of your client Ada. She says Ada is high (on drugs) and has just hit her mother, knocking her down on the kitchen floor and bloodying her nose. You say you will be right over and hurriedly dress. Your husband grumbles about having "one hell of a family life, to say nothing of a sex life," adding, "I hope you charge them double for overtime." The last remark is ironic. Ada's mother has not paid you in two years. A widow, whose husband's jewelry business was going bankrupt at his death, she is a borderline psychotic barely able to keep herself together, much less manage her four children. As you are about to leave, your husband says, "How about me coming with you," but you refuse. The family lives in a deteriorating middle-class neighborhood, which is relatively safe.

When you arrive, the household is surprisingly quiet. Mitzi meets you at the door. She is a miracle—a mature, sensible, assured 14-year-old. She says her mother is upstairs resting. You will talk with her later. Ada is lying on the living room sofa. She is a strikingly beautiful 17-year-old, her voluptuous figure spilling over her tight, low-cut dress. "I'll sleep with anything," she had once told you, "man, woman, horse, dog, or pig." Then she had added with mock suffering, "But I'm really not bad; I'm just terribly, terribly lonely."

Ada has a brilliant, facile mind, and listening to her, you often cannot tell fact from fantasy, true feeling from mock sincerity. You are sure she frequently rode on a motorcycle with various gangs of delinquents, committed minor thefts, and then delighted in avoiding arrest either by crying or by being seductive with the police. "Pigs" is her favorite expression of contempt, which she applies to everyone—family, peers, teachers, the world in general. In spite of her obvious provocativeness, she constantly sees herself as unfairly victimized. Her one genuine desire is to graduate from high school (her father had been awed by education and "learning"), yet her uncontrollable restlessness in class has caused her to fail continually. Right now she is asleep on the sofa, snoring slightly—or perhaps she is pretending to sleep to avoid talking to you.

You try to decide what to do. Ada has a 22-year-old brother. (A second brother stays in his room much of the time, immobilized by fears and depression.) A high school dropout, he has already amassed a good deal of money by charming elderly people into buying expensive, unnecessary, defective hearing aids. Although Ada violently dislikes him, he is quite fond of her. Tomorrow you will phone to see if he will pay for a boarding school, so that Ada can realize her ambition of completing high school while receiving psychotherapy. If he agrees, you will have to talk Ada into accepting the idea. Mitzi will help, and Ada's mother would be glad to get her out of the house. If that fails, you will have to try to find some other resource, as you have been doing for over two years. While some would call this supportive psychotherapy, you think of it more in terms of "rolling with the punches."

Clearly Ada is not a normal, well-adjusted adolescent. But many cases of adolescent drug use are considerably less clear-cut. Often the clinician must decide whether to regard drug use as part of a pattern of normal development or as a symptom of maladjustment. Making this determination necessitates evaluating all of the contexts, which are even more numerous than those of juvenile delinquency: to the intrapersonal, interpersonal, and societal we must add the physiological and historical contexts as well. The last is particularly important, since history offers scant support for equating drug use with deviant behavior.

Historical Context

Most cultures have used alcohol: mead was possibly used around 8000 B.C. in the Paleolithic era, the biblical Noah became drunk, and the Indians who met Columbus had their own "home brew." Certain drugs were indigenous to particular areas: nicotine was native to the Americas, as was the peyote cactus, which provided a natural source of hallucinogenic drugs; in Europe, mild doses of poisons such as belladonna were used to alter consciousness; and the Arabs and Chinese used tea and chocolate as sources of caffeine. Drugs have been used in religious ceremonies, to medicate, to counteract fatigue, to increase fierceness in battle, as well as for recreation. Cultures have applied different sanctions to drugs, one drug having multiple uses, for example, while another is strongly prohibited.

In modern times, there were more opiate addicts in the United States at the turn of the century than there are now, many being women using opiate-based patent medicines to treat various physical complaints. Some physicians considered opium as a cure for alcoholism, while heroin was regarded as less harmful still, medical journals stressing its nonaddictive properties. It was after the Harrison Narcotics Act of 1914, banning opiates, that the number of women addicts decreased, while male addicts turned increasingly to crime in order to obtain the now-illegal drugs. (For details, see Achenbach, 1974. For a comprehensive review of the literature, see Dupont, Goldstein, and O'Donnell, 1979, and Lettieri, Sayers, and Pearson, 1980.)

The current drug scene is as much a patchwork as its historical context. By far the most lethal forms of drug abuse are alcoholism and smoking, yet legal sanctions against them are relatively benign. Public and professional concern over the mental health of alcoholics in no way matches the concern over drug abuse, and few people have suggested that smoking be considered pathologically self-destructive.

The capriciousness of its history raises the question of whether drug abuse among adolescents can rightly be regarded as a psychopathology or whether it is a reflection of the degree of social turmoil at a particular time; perhaps the current concern, like the hippie movement and the student protests, is merely a facet of the social unrest of the late 1960s. The developmental approach raises a second question: Why does drug abuse appear on the developmental scene specifically at adolescence rather than earlier or later? Before attempting to answer these questions we must become acquainted with the nature of drug abuse and the findings in regard to context variables. First, a description of the diverse types of drugs and the reasons for taking them will be presented.

Classification of Drugs

Our coverage of drugs will be selective. Caffeine (coffee, Coca-Cola, NoDoz), nicotine (cigarettes and cigars), tranquilizers (Valium, Miltown), antidepressants (Elavil), and miscellaneous drugs such as nonprescription sedatives, antihistamines, and glue will be omitted. Selectivity within categories will also be maintained, the concern being with the physiological and psychological effects of the drug under scrutiny. (For a comprehensive drug chart, see Calhoun et al., 1977.) All the drugs are *psychoactive* in that they affect the central nervous system in such a way as to produce alterations in subjective feeling states.

CANNABIS. This classification includes marijuana ("grass," "pot," "joint") and hashish ("hash"), small doses of which produce relaxation and euphoria. With intermediate doses there is the illusion of thinking more clearly, although judgment and memory become impaired, while heavy doses induce hallucinations, delusions, and thought disorders. Cannabis is used to get high, to escape, to relax.

HALLUCINOGENS. This category includes PCP—phencyclidine ("angel dust")—lysergic acid diethylamide—LSD ("acid," "sugar")—and mescaline (peyote), which produce visual imagery and increased sensory awareness, as well as anxiety and nausea. They may also cause panic in unprepared individuals and sometimes precipitate or intensify an already-existing psychosis. Curiosity, consciousness expansion, and seeking for meaning are typical reasons for use.

NARCOTICS. Opium, heroin ("horse," "H"), methadone, morphine and even cough syrups belong in this category. All are central nervous system depressants that produce relief from pain, euphoria, and impaired intellectual functioning and motor coordination. They are usually taken to get high and as an escape.

STIMULANTS. There are two principle stimulants: amphetamines ("speed," "uppers," "pep pills"), which include Benzedrine ("bennies") and Dexedrine ("dexies"), and cocaine ("coke," "sugar," "snow"). Both are central nervous system stimulants that increase alertness and produce euphoria, along with insommnia and loss of appetite. They are taken for stimulation, to get high, and to relieve fatigue.

BARBITURATES. This category includes Nembutal ("yellow jackets"), Seconal ("red devils"), Quaalude ("ludes"), and Doriden ("goofers"). All these are central nervous system depressants inducing relaxation and sleep, slowing down reaction time, impairing judgment and coordination, weakening emotional control; sometimes they also produce euphoria. They are taken to relax and sleep or to get high.

ALCOHOL. Whiskey, gin, beer, and wine ("booze," "hooch") are all central nervous system depressants inducing relaxation and drowsiness, while interfering with reaction time, coordination, judgment, and emotional control. Alcohol is drunk to relax, to escape tensions and inhibitions, and to get high.

Complexities of Drug Abuse

Drugs vary in psychological and physical dependence potential, narcotics, barbiturates, and alcohol being high on both, stimulants being high on psychological and low on physical dependence, cannabis and hallucinogens being moderate to low on psychological dependence while entailing no physical dependence. In addition, physical tolerance affects the course of drug taking; the body seems to become sensitized to marijuana so that the individual requires less of the drug to achieve a high with time, while opiates produce high tolerance resulting in an ever-increasing need for larger quantities. Note that tolerance and dependence (or addiction) may vary independently; tolerance develops rapidly for most hallucinogens, although they are not physically addictive. Both factors affect the lengths to which the adolescent must go to maintain a habit, as well as the degree of difficulty in breaking it.

In addition to the differential legal risks involved in maintaining various drug habits, there are differential risks in regard to physical consequences. The long-term effects of marijuana use have been disputed by scientists: for example, prolonged, heavy use lowers the male sex hormone, testosterone, but there is no clear evidence of impaired sexual functioning; or again, chronic use impairs one part of the body's immune system, but there is no clearly established clinical effect of such impairment. However, its acute effects in impairing both classroom learning and driving skill remove marijuana use from the category of a harmless pastime (Peterson, 1980). The long-term effects of LSD are similarly in doubt. By contrast, chronic heroin use may be devastating. Loss of appetite leads to malnutrition and susceptibility to disease; carelessness concerning injection techniques and the sterility of needles may result in tetanus, blood poisoning, and hepatitis; too large a dose may result in a coma and death. Overdoses of barbiturates cause accidental deaths as well as suicides, while withdrawal from both barbiturates and alcohol is harrowing, dangerous, and potentially fatal. In most instances, adverse effects come about by habitual use of high dosages, both of which indicate drug abuse rather than casual or recreational use.

But the situation is not that simple, since many individuals are multiple drug users (Robins, 1980). At times drugs are combined to heighten their effect, such as the "speedball," which is a vicious combination of cocaine and heroin. Sometimes one drug will be used to offset the negative features of another; for example, a depressant such as a barbiturate can be used to counteract the "crash" which comes when the effect of amphetamines wear off.

ESCALATION. A final complication is the risk of escalation. While marijuana may be a relatively benign drug, for example, it may also be the first step along the path leading to more potent and dangerous ones. However, the evidence concerning escalation is far from clear. Both cross-sectional and longitudinal studies indicate that use of illicit drugs begins in the early teens, peaks around 22 to 23 years of age, and declines to a very low level afterward (Kandel, 1978). Thus, a simple escalation model, which assumes that a process once set in motion has a built-in propensity to accelerate, receives little empirical support.

When escalation does take place, it follows a predictable pattern: from beer or wine to cigarettes or hard liquor to marijuana to other illicit drugs. Legal drugs are a necessary intermediate between nonuse and marijuana (Kandel, 1978). A high proportion of adolescents who try marijuana will go on to experiment with other illicit drugs, one study showing that 25 percent of adolescents using only marijuana at the beginning of the school year were experimenting with harder drugs six months later. This does not mean that they became habitual users, however. There may be cultural and historical determinants of the choice of hard drugs themselves, ghetto Blacks turning to cocaine, heroin, barbiturates, and hallucinogens in turn, while high school populations in general tend to go from stimulants and barbiturates to hallucinogens to narcotics.

There is also evidence that different determinants may be involved at each stage of escalation (Kandel, Kessler, and Margulies, 1978). Adolescents who begin to drink have engaged in a number of minor delinquent activities, enjoy high levels of sociability with peers, and are exposed to peers and parents who drink. The transition to marijuana use is preceded by involvement with peers who use marijuana, by a belief and value system that favors or condones marijuana use, and by participation in the same minor forms of deviant behaviors which precede involvement with hard liquor. While parental and peer models of illicit drug use also precede the transition to the use of hard drugs, depression and lack of closeness to parents are equally important.

Thus the influence of peers, while the most potent determiner of drug use, changes in nature: in the early stages a general sociability or group membership makes the adolescent susceptible to using drugs, while in the final stage a single best friend plays an important role. Parental behavior is also influential in leading the adolescent to experiment with hard liquor, the model they present being more important than their beliefs and values. In the final stage, it is the quality of the parent–child relationship which matters, warmth and closeness shielding the adolescent from involvement in more serious drugs. The intrapersonal variables change from values and beliefs condoning drug use to feelings of despair as the adolescent moves into involvement with hard drugs.

This understanding of the stages of escalation protects us from making simplistic statements such as, "In adolescence, peers become more important than parents." Recall that the revised image of the period, presented at the beginning of the discussion, also corrects such a one-sided emphasis. Parents are as influential as peers in the final, crucial stage of drug involvement, their warmth and closeness being particularly important—characteristics, incidentally, which are associated with the early parent–child relationships and which we might have thought the adolescent had outgrown. The developmental progression is of more than academic interest; locating individuals within the sequence furnishes important leads as to the focus of psychotherapy, since peers are particularly influential in the early stages, while the transition to hard drugs adds the element of negative self-esteem and alienation from the family.

Escalation can also refer to an increase in drug-engendered criminal activity and/or negative motivational syndromes, such as a profound indifference to one's personal fate and the requirements of constructive social living. While the data are not conclusive, longitudinal studies suggest that such deviant behavior tends to precede drug use. In regard to criminality, one study showed that delinquency, particularly crimes against property, anteceded the use of drugs (Johnston, Bachman, and O'Malley, 1977). While there was a relation between the seriousness of the crime and the seriousness of the drug used, changes in the latter were not paralleled by changes in the former. The authors speculate that the association between drugs and crime might be due to the adolescent's social environment or personality characteristics; for example, delinquents tend to become part of a deviant peer group which approves of drug use, while both delinquency and drug use appeal to adolescents who are already "deviance prone." The authors are also careful to state that their conclusions do not apply to addicts, nor do they deny that criminal behavior might increase in order to support the habit. Other data indicate clearly that narcotic addiction increases the frequency of income-generating crime (McGlothlin, 1979).

In a like manner, negative motivational states are likely to precede drug use, or both kinds of deviant behavior may result from other factors (Kandel, 1978). To cite one example: among high school students, a reduction in aspiration for college tended to precede rather than follow the initiation into illicit drugs other than marijuana. However, as with criminal behavior, such findings do not preclude an increase in deviant behavior following addiction, since regular use of heroin, amphetamines, and barbiturates has been shown to lead to adjustment problems such as alcoholism, violence, unemployment, and marital breakup (Robins, 1979).

In one instance the fear that drug use will cause severe psychopathology is justified: The "speed freak" who injects amphetamine into his veins for three to four days readily engages in paranoid and violent behavior. The psychosis seems to be drug-induced rather than the drug triggering a latent paranoia. In fact, this is the only drug-induced psychosis which is behaviorally identical to a "functional" psychosis (Bootzin and Acocella, 1980). Aside from this instance, the evidence linking drugs to psychopathology is not clear.

INTRAPERSONAL VARIABLES. Personality variables have been studied primarily in relation to marijuana use (R. Jessor, 1979). One of the most consistent findings is that prospective users rate higher on expectation for independence and lower on academic aspirations and motivations than do prospective nonusers. They tend to be nonconformists, unconventional, and rebellious, although not necessarily aggressive, while placing a low value on achievement and having low expectations of being able to gain achievement satisfaction. Another characteristic is that users, as compared with nonusers, tend to be more open to experience, more aesthetically oriented, more interested in creativity, play, novelty, and spontaneity. On the negative side there is some tendency for future users to have depressive moods.

CONTEXT VARIABLES. The influence of parents and peers has already been discussed, the latter being the most potent predictor of drug involvement. Low grades and high frequency of school absences have consistently been found to precede involvement in marijuana use in high school. Poor performance seems to be a matter of motivation, since, both in terms of intelligence and aptitude, future users are as gifted intellectually as nonusers. A study of servicemen in Vietnam documents the impact of the sociocultural context on older adolescents and young adults (Kandel, 1978). The easy availability and superior quality of drugs, especially heroin, both accelerated the timing of initiation and increased the number of users of marijuana and narcotics. However, it was the soldier who was already predisposed to use drugs who was most strongly affected by the situational lures rather than the drug's availability equalizing use among men from different social and behavioral backgrounds.

METHODOLOGICAL NOTE. Longitudinal data help clarify antecedent-consequent relations in regard to low academic achievement, rebelliousness, depression, and criminal activity, all of which tend to precede drug use. In addition, longitudinal studies of normal populations present quite a different picture from studies of extreme segments of the drug-using population, such as individuals in special treatment facilities for addicts or prisoners. The pessimistic findings from the latter type of study run the risk of being regarded as typical of all drug users, especially in times of great public concern. Kandel (1978), on the other hand, paints a more benign picture, stating, for example, that few unfavorable outcomes of marijuana use have been identified and that, in certain instances, drugs may serve an adaptive function such as forestalling depression. However, she also recognizes that longitudinal data from normal populations may be spuriously positive, since the most severely isolated, defeated, and disturbed individuals are likely to be difficult or impossible to locate. While few studies involve a truly representative population of drug users, the ones that have been summarized here come closer to the mark than those based on extreme subgroups.

We are now in a position to answer the first question raised at the beginning of the discussion. It is easy to understand why drug abuse can be regarded both as one aspect of adolescent rebellion and as a serious disturbance. It can be both. It can reflect nothing more than the desire to be independent and a chafing at being shackled with schoolwork; but a persistent use of hard drugs may be motivated by despair and a regressive longing for parental love, and it may increase criminal and other maladaptive behavior, as well as being a threat to health or to life itself.

Why Adolescence?

In order to answer the second question concerning the appearance of drug use in adolescence, a study by Jessor and Jessor (1977) will be discussed in detail. The study has a developmental conceptual framework which places drug use in the context of a number of important intrapersonal and interpersonal variables.

CONCEPTUAL FRAMEWORK. According to the Jessors, highly prized roles and rewards vary with age in our society. The adolescent, especially the early adolescent, has limited access to the valued goals of adulthood, such as autonomy, prestige, sex, mobility—and even working for pay. In addition, age norms ignore individual differences in the desire and readiness to pursue adult goals. Consequently, certain adolescents who are ready to make the transition are constantly frustrated and tantalized by the perceived attractiveness of mature status.

Furthermore, the Jessors state, the transition from a less mature to a more mature adult status is marked by problem behavior, which they define as behavior which is undesirable by the norms of conventional society. It should in no way be regarded as deviant or psychopathological. Many problem behaviors, such as drinking and sexual intercourse, will be regarded as acceptable and will be encouraged when the adolescent is old enough to be considered an adult. In essence, the Jessors regard adolescence as a period in which departure from accepted norms is not only to be expected but also may be a sign of healthy development. Their particular term for an adolescent's readiness to engage in problem behavior is *transition proneness*.

VARIABLES STUDIED. Jessor and Jessor regard behavior as a result of interactions between the individual's personality and the perceived environment.

Three categories of variables are included within the *personality* domain. The motivational-instigational structure includes the value placed on academic achievement, on independence, and on peer affection (in the sense of being popular). The personal-belief structure includes social criticism (the acceptance or rejection of the values and practices of society at large in such areas as social justice, economic opportunity, militarism, the environment); alienation (a sense of the meaningless of one's life and isolation from others); and self-esteem and locus of control (a belief that one is in command of one's destiny or the belief that one's fate depends on external forces). The personal-control structure includes attitudinal tolerance toward deviance or the degree of "wrongness" the individual attributes to trangressions such as lying, stealing, vandalism; religiosity or involvement with religious beliefs and activities; and the relation of positive to negative meanings attached to the same problem behavior (for example, sexual intercourse could be evaluated positively as making the adolescent feel wanted or negatively as spoiling the relationship). Personal beliefs are more general or distal, while personal controls are more specific or proximal.

The *perceived environment* is divided into a distal and a proximal structure. The former includes support and controls from parents and friends, the compatibility between parents' and friends' expectations, and their relative influence on the adolescent. The proximal variables include parents' and friends' approval of problem behavior and friends' modeling of problem behavior.

Finally, two categories of behaviors were studied: problem behaviors and conventional behaviors. *Problem behaviors* include marijuana use, sexual intercourse, activist protest, drinking, and general deviance such as stealing, lying, property destruction, disruptive behavior, and aggression. *Conventional behaviors* include academic performance and church attendance, both of which are viewed as reflecting conformity to societal values.

All variables were studied by means of an annual questionnaire submitted to 432 high school and 205 college students every year for a four-year period. This longitudinal design enabled the authors to investigate the factors related to beginning drug use at different ages. The population was drawn from a small, university-dominated city known for its attractive natural setting and comfortable standard of living. The authors claim that, while the population is hardly typical, the findings are generally congruent with those from studies with more representative populations.

NORMATIVE FINDINGS. Certain normative findings are of interest. All problem behaviors, except activism, were age-related, the rates typically increasing from the beginning of high school to the end of college. One exception was problem drinking, which declined during the college years. Next, marijuana use and nonvirginity were sufficiently prevalent to be regarded as statistically normative in college, two-thirds of the students reporting the former. Finally, sex differences were small in problem behaviors, which in the past have usually shown a predominance of males. (We are once again reminded of the importance of the historical context of research.)

The interrelationships among problem behaviors is also important. In high school, the degree of interrelatedness was high, except for activism. Thus, a marijuana user was likely to be a problem drinker and a nonvirgin and to engage in delinquentlike behaviors. The opposite is also true; for example, being an abstainer was associated with almost no engagement in other problem behaviors. Like Kandel, these authors note that becoming a drinker may well be the developmental precursor of other behavioral problems. A similar but much weaker pattern of interrelatedness was found among college students.

CORRELATES OF DRUG USE. In the personality realm, personal control variables proved to be most highly correlated with drug use, in both high school and college—specifically, tolerance of deviance, viewing drug use as more positive than negative, and religiosity, which was negatively related. Among high school students, motivational-instigational factors such as academic achievement and the need for peer affection (both of which were negatively related) and the valuing of independence over achievement were second in importance, while the personal-belief structure of social criticism was third. For the college population, social criticism, along with alienation (for females), were significant correlates, while the motivational variables were no longer significant. It may be that where drug use is relatively low, as in high school, a wide variety of personality variables must be engaged in order to tip the balance in its favor; where it is prevalent, as in college, drug use may become more a matter of going along with what others are doing.

Jessor and Jessor epitomize the personality dimension underlying their findings in terms of conventionality–unconventionality. The adolescent who does not use drugs is likely to value academic achievement; to be unconcerned with independence from the family, accepting of the social status quo, and involved in a religion; and to regard transgressions as having more negative than positive consequences. The individual with high proneness to problem behavior in general and drug use in particular has the opposite characteristics.

Among perceived environmental variables, proximal ones were far more important in determining drug use than distal ones for both high school and college students. Friends' approval and modeling of problem behavior, along with parental approval (or lack of disapproval), were all significant correlates. The pattern of distal variables was somewhat different for the two groups. For high school students, parental support and control were negatively related to drug use, while these variables were no longer important for college students.

The Jessors also analyzed their data in terms of the relative contribution of each variable to problem behavior and drug use. In general, both personality and environmental variables always appeared as major contributors, underlying the authors' thesis that behavior is a product of both intrapersonal and context variables. The specific variables contributing most to marijuana use were having friends who serve as models for problem behavior, a critical attitude toward society, and a tolerance of deviant behavior. The social-criticism variable distinguished marijuana use from the other problem behaviors studied.

Summarizing the results of the study of all problem behaviors, the authors present a complex but coherent picture. The transition-prone high school adolescent values independence more than academic achievement, is critical of society and its institutions, is tolerant toward transgressions, and views the use of drugs and sex positively. Parents are perceived as not disapproving of problem behavior; their influence is less than that of friends, while friends and peers serve as models for problem behavior. The reverse of this cluster is characteristic of conventional high school adolescents. Finally, this cluster of variables can be used to predict the onset of drug use, especially for females. The results for college marijuana users are similar although less clear.

General developmental trends are congruent with the above picture. Among personality variables, valuing of independence increases from high school through college while religiosity and alienation decrease; valuing of academic achievement declines in high school but levels off in college, while criticism of society and tolerance of deviation increase in high school but similarly level off in college. Predictably, high school is, in general, a time of more pervasive personality change than is college. Perceived environmental changes complement the ones in personality; friends as models of problem behavior, friends' support, and parental approval of problem behavior all increase. In regard to behaviors, use of marijuana increases while church attendance decreases. General deviant behavior (delinquent or predelinquent) increases in high school but levels off in college.

One final note: self-esteem, alienation, and internal locus of control had little to do with problem behavior. Thus, marijuana users felt no more inferior or alone or helpless than nonusers. In spite of the importance of peers, popularity was unrelated to the presence or absence of problem behavior. Actual grade-point averages were independent of problem behavior, perhaps because they are closely tied to intellectual ability rather than to attitudes. And, finally, socieconomic status was unrelated to problem behavior.

DRUG USE AND ADOLESCENCE. The Jessors have taught us a good deal about marijuana use in adolescence. Especially in high school it may well be only one in a constellation of behaviors which might include drinking, sexual intercourse, and delinquency. Concomitantly, there is a developmental pattern in which the valuing of independence progressively increases while the valuing of academic achievement declines; tolerance of unconventional behavior increases while acceptance of the conventional ideology in regard to society and religion declines; the influence of the family declines while a peer orientation and a utilization of peers as models increases. Within this developmental pattern there are individual differences in transition proneness or the adolescent's readiness to change.

The Jessors also supply an explicit answer to the question, Why does drug use enter the developmental picture during adolescence? They view the changes described above as part of the normal transition from the status of being a child to the status of being an adult. "Problem behavior may be viewed, at least in part, as an aspect of growing up" (p. 238). We are reminded of the terrible twos—which have humorously been referred to as the first adolescence—in which behavior which is difficult to manage and socially disruptive is part of normal development.

Yet, the Jessors' interpretation of their data cannot be accepted without reservations. First of all, they studied only marijuana users and not addicts and serious drug users who, as we have just learned, might well be psychologically disturbed. And they present no evidence that the behaviors which were delinquent correlates of drug use represented the kinds of minor transgressions many adolescents engage in rather than being a manifestation of serious lapses in self-control. Their most reassuring finding is that, although marijuana use increased in college, delinquent behavior leveled off; there is also no evidence that marijuana use, as distinct from marijuana abuse, is associated with maladjustment or psychopathology (R. Jessor, 1979).

These reservations are not criticism of the Jessors, who do not share our interest in psychopathology and who also recognize that certain transition-prone adolescents may well be disturbed. Rather, the reservations serve as a reminder that their study only partially answers the clinician's concern with separating normal from disturbed adolescents. In searching for an appropriate developmental model to guide us in making this distinction, reference to the terrible twos and the discussion of negativism may be helpful. In chapter 6 we saw that an exaggeration of normal problem behavior which threatens to jeopardize future growth could be regarded as psychopathological. The same principle could be applied here. When rebellion, defiance, and antisocial behaviors become ends in themselves rather than means for promoting autonomy, adolescents may be in a state not of transition but of stagnation. Or again, if problem behaviors seem primarily directed against the parents—if adolescents seem to be going out of their way to defy and upset parents, if unconsciously they are behaving like a "bad child" in order to prolong their status as a child—then we begin to suspect that fixation rather than transition is calling the tune.

Erikson's writings on identity are useful at this point. In keeping with the Jessors he states that youth often goes to extremes during the moratorium in order to test the "rock bottom of some truth" before committing themselves to a particular way of life (1968, p. 236). These extremes may include not only rebelliousness but also deviant, delinquent, and self-destructive behaviors. It is only when such tendencies defeat the purpose of the moratorium by fixating the adolescent or necessitating a permanent retreat to primitive behavior that they become psychopathological. Take for example a *negative identity,* which in many ways is the adolescent counterpart of the toddler's negativism. Here the adolescent perversely identifies with all the roles that have been presented as undesirable or dangerous in the past; in despair of realizing the unattainable positive roles, the adolescents become "the last thing in the world" the parent would want them to be. If, in addition, authorities such as judges or mental health workers also label them as "delinquents" or "addicts" or "psychopaths" or "alcoholics," adolescents will make sure they become what the community has called them, thus abandoning the freedom of choice essential to a constructive outcome to the moratorium. (For a conceptualization of adolescent delinquency in terms of negative identity, see Gold and Petronio, 1980.) In a like manner, the depression and moodiness of the normal adolescent is different from the *despair* evidenced in the abandonment of the desire to grow, expand, and find new meanings in life, just as the devaluing of academic achievement differs from a *work paralysis,* which suffocates even recreational and avocational activities in a pall of futility, and just as an antireligious stance differs from an immobilizing *confusion of values.* Thus, the difference between normality and deviance is a quantitative one, psychopathology not only being more extreme but (and this is the essence) representing a retreat from the struggle to establish an identity rather than a progression—no matter how painful to the adolescent and to society—along the way to reaching that goal.

The Eriksonian reconcilation has been helpful, but there is still a dearth of specific guidelines as to when growth-promoting defiance of convention shades into self-defeating deviance. When experts disagree as to what is normal problem behavior and what is maladjustment, clinicians are forced to rely on their own experience and the accumulated experience of colleagues.

Treatment

Drug abuse comprises such heterogeneous behaviors that we cannot expect a single treatment modality to be appropriate to them all. Unfortunately, no specific treatment or combination of treatments has been successful in eliminating drug abuse, much less proving itself to be the treatment of choice (Achenbach, 1974).

Drugs which produce a physical dependency, such as alcohol and heroin, require a detoxification program under medical management. The physiological and psychological withdrawal reactions may be treated with tranquilizers, while vitamins and a high-carbohydrate diet combat the effects of poor nourishment. In the case of heroin addiction, methadone—a synthetic opiatelike drug—can be substituted. It blocks the craving for heroin, can be taken orally rather than intravenously, and has a longer-lasting effect. Moreover, since it is legally available, it eliminates the necessity of engaging in criminal activities in order to support the habit. However, methadone maintenance involves substituting one drug for another and does not alter a life-style which may involve criminal activities and the use of other drugs such as alcohol and barbiturates.

Individual treatment of drug abuse has been unsuccessful, whether it is psychotherapeutically or behaviorally oriented. The former often requires a willingness to change and the formation of a positive relationship between client and therapist, both of which may be lacking in the drug abuser. The latter often involves pairing of a noxious stimulus, such as a nausea-inducing chemical or a painful electric shock, with the drug, and its effectiveness has not been clearly established (Callner, 1975). Psychotherapy combined with medical treatment fails to help the majority of addicts, although those who are older and are in the upper socioeconomic group relapse less frequently. Transcendental meditation, an Indian form of meditation and thought control, seems to have had some success, but its faddish nature does not augur well for its future.

Group approaches to treatment have met with some success, although satisfactory evaluative data are often lacking. Alcoholics Anonymous capitalizes on group support. Each new member is assigned an exalcoholic who is available at any time to give advice and to help the member resist the temptation to drink. During regularly held meetings, members confess and recovered alcoholics give inspirational speeches. There is a strong religious element, members being encouraged to rely on the healing power of God.

Various total living environments have also been tried. Some are modeled after Synanon and are run by exaddicts. The structure is that of an autocratic family, the new members first being given menial household chores but gradually being allowed to do more responsible work as they can abstain from taking drugs. Group therapy sessions allow emotional catharsis, while the staff constantly tries to instill spiritual values which will lead to self-reliance. The Synanon approach strives to create new social roles for its members who remain within the organization. Other approaches also utilize the principles of the therapeutic living arrangement but eventually try to help its members make the transition back to the community.

The only ray of hope in this dark picture comes from Robins's study of Vietnam veterans (Robins, Davis, and Nurco, 1974). She found a 95 percent remission rate for narcotics addicts after their discharge in the United States. While it is reassuring to learn that heroin addiction is not necessarily permanent, we are also left wondering how the dramatic change in living involved in shifting from a wartime to a peacetime existence could be replicated or even simulated in any known therapeutic setting.

HOMOSEXUALITY

The classification of psychopathologies has its own developmental history. The same social ferment in the 1960s which forced the recognition of poverty as a mental health problem (as well as an economic one) was instrumental in eliminating homosexuality from the American Psychiatric Association's list of psychopathologies in 1974. It was replaced by "sexual-orientation disturbances" in people who are "disturbed by, in conflict with, or wish to change" their homosexual orientation. However, the issue concerning homosexuality as psychopathology was hotly debated, and there were strong objections to the final decision. For our purposes, the controversy serves to organize the discussion around the question, Is there any basis from a developmental point of view for regarding homosexuality as a psychopathological deviation, or is it better regarded as an alternate style of sexual behavior on a par with heterosexuality?

Before starting, it will be wise to repeat a lesson already learned: a given psychopathology can occur in conjunction with other psychopathologies while not being causally related to them. A homosexual adult might be neurotic or psychopathic or schizophrenic simply because he or she has multiple problems; there is no reason to assume that a deviant choice of a sexual partner is the core problem. Moreover, intrapersonal factors determine how disruptive homosexuality itself might be. In certain instances a strong urge to engage in homosexual behavior may precipitate a terrifying panic; in other cases, a homosexual relation may be regarded as acceptable and fulfilling; in still other cases, for an exceptionally withdrawn, isolated individual, a homosexual attachment may be the one human contact preventing a general personality deterioration.

Definition

This is not the first time we have been confronted with a lack of agreement concerning definition. Definitions of homosexuality tend to fall along an overt–covert continuum with or without a frequency/duration variable ranging from few to many experiences and from brief to sustained relationships. The simplest definition of homosexuality is sexual behavior between people of the same sex. More differentiated definitions add the elements of frequency of sexual behavior and number of partners in a given time span. At a more covert level, homosexuality has been defined as a desire for same-sex contact and/or conscious sexual arousal from thinking about or seeing persons of the same sex. In such instances, the individuals may or may not engage in homosexual behavior because fear or moral scruples prevent them. Some definitions locate homosexuality in the self-image and require that individuals consider themselves to be homosexual regardless of their actual behavior. Finally, there are latent homosexuals, whose desires are either unconscious or who will turn to homosexual behavior only when heterosexual outlets are unavailable, such as in prison. When diverse behaviors are subsumed under a common label, one can expect a contradictory and confused literature.

In spite of varying definitions, there is general agreement concerning certain characteristics of homosexuality. The landmark research of Kinsey, Pomeroy, and Martin (1948) showed that, rather than being dichotomous, there is a continuum of behavior from heterosexual to homosexual. The Kinsey study found, for example, that 37 percent of adult males had one homosexual experience to orgasm since adolescence, 18 percent had as much homosexual as heterosexual experience, and 13 percent had homosexual impulses, which they did not act on. The incidence of homosexuality in women was lower, being only 13 percent. The estimate of individuals who are exclusively homosexual in terms of persistent and exclusive behavior ranges between 2 and 5 percent (West, 1967). Homosexuals vary as widely as heterosexuals in behavior and personality, the effeminate male and the tough female representing only a small minority. Nor can homosexuals be classified in terms of their assuming an "active" or a "passive" role in their sexual relations; both males and females alternate between the roles. Homosexuality is distinct from *transvestism,* which involves obtaining sexual gratification through dressing in the clothes of the opposite sex. While some transvestites may be homosexuals they typically masturbate in private. Homosexuality should also be distinguished from *transsexualism*, which is a gender identification with the opposite sex; for example, from early childhood a boy may be convinced that he really is a girl and has been assigned the wrong body. It is the transsexual who typically seeks sex reassignment through surgery and sex hormones. Most transvestites and transsexuals are male. (For further discussion, see Bootzin and Acocella, 1980.)

MULTIPLE DIMENSIONS OF SEX. A number of dimensions of sexuality will be relevant to our discussion. There is both variability within and complex relations among these dimensions.

First, there is *anatomic sex differentiation.* Variability ranges from distinct differentiation into male or female at one extreme to hermaphroditism (in which a single individual has both male and female reproductive organs) at the other extreme and includes instances in which the external genitalia appear to be at variance with the internal reproductive system owing to a physiological anomaly; for example, a malformation of the infant's penis may result in his being called a girl (Money and Ehrhardt, 1972). Then there is *gender identity* or the self-classification as male or female which develops in the toddler and preschool period. It is not unusual for children during this period to believe that they can change their gender identity merely by changing their appearance. And while cultures may prescribe distinct *sex roles,* individuals combine all degrees of masculinity and femininity in their behavior, as we shall soon see. Then there is *erotic preference,* which involves the ideal choice of a sexual object. Finally, there is the capacity to enjoy and sustain a *love relationship* over time. Erotic preferences are numerous—they can involve not only the same or the opposite sex but also children, animals, and inanimate objects such as clothes—while a love relationship can last from a year to a lifetime.

Just to give a sample of the complex interrelations which exist among these varying dimensions, an infant who is physiologically a girl can be raised as a boy because of an anomaly of external genitals, while a preschool boy with no anomalies can become convinced that he is really a girl—a conviction which might last into his adult years and eventuate in his seeking a sex change. A woman may submit to intercourse with her husband as required by her sex role while ideally preferring a homosexual partner, while prisoners or sailors might engage in homosexual behavior not from preference but because only males are available.

MULTIPLE ROOTS. As with so many psychopathologies, homosexuality is alleged to have multiple roots, although all etiological hypotheses lack convincing empirical support. (For a more extensive discussion of etiology, see Thompson and McCandless, 1976.)

In regard to *genetic* influences there has been one study which found concordance for homosexual behavior among identical twins and not among fraternal twins, but it has failed to meet the scientific tests of replicability by other researchers. *Hormonal influences* have also been implicated as a physiological cause of homosexuality. Some hypotheses involve *early brain differentiation* (Money, 1970). Embryologically, humans are morphologically female and will continue to develop as females unless androgen is released at specific times in development. It is tempting to speculate, therefore, that in the case of homosexuality, something has gone wrong with this masculinizing process. Other hypotheses concern differences in *circulating sex hormones* in adult homosexuals and heterosexuals. To date there is no definitive evidence to support either hypothesis, although occasional positive findings hint that hormonal factors might play a role in certain cases of homosexuality. (For a general discussion of physiological factors in homosexuality and other sexual deviations, see Money and Higham, 1976, and West, 1977.)

Among context variables, parents as socializing agents are thought to play a major role in a child's sexual development, both in terms of rewarding appropriate and punishing inappropriate behavior and in terms of serving as models of masculinity and femininity. In middle childhood and adolescence, peers become increasingly important in terms of channeling sexual activities, ridiculing the sissy and (to a much lesser extent) the tomboy who defy the sex-role stereotypes. However, there is some evidence that, as early as 3 years of age, same-sex peers are preferred over opposite-sex peers, and even a hint that a decidedly effeminate boy will be criticized and ostracized. In school there is evidence that teachers are partial to girls and to the traditionally feminine values of compliance, docility, and motoric quietude. Consequently, the boy with feminine attributes might be rewarded by his female teacher and use her as a bulwark against the teasing of his peers. (For a further discussion of parents, peers, and school, see Thompson and McCandless, 1976.)

CONCEPTUALIZATIONS. In chapter 2 we learned that there were two quite different conceptions of sexual development. The first is in terms of sex role and involves the learning of behaviors and feelings which society regards as appropriate for the male and the female. This conceptualization is favored by social-learning theorists, who account for sexual development in terms of reinforcement by and imitation of socializing agents. The psychoanalytic theory views sexual development in terms of eroticized intimacy, which begins in infancy and goes through the special transformations that comprise the psychosexual stages. Psychoanalysts are concerned with understanding the love relations that exist between and among individuals. Their term for this relation is *object choice*.

Sex role and object choice are not only conceptually distinct but behaviorally distinct as well. To illustrate, let us look at a study of fetally androgenized girls—girls whose mother received injections of testosterone during pregnancy and who were born with normal internal female reproduction systems but had an enlarged clitoris resembling a penis and labial folds fused to resemble a scrotum (Money and Ehrhardt, 1972). Although given corrective surgery and reared as girls, their behavior was quite tomboyish. They enjoyed vigorous athletics, such as ball games. They were competitive with boys on the boys' own turf (although they were not physically aggressive). They preferred utilitarian clothing, such as slacks and shorts, to dresses and adornments and engaged in little rehearsal of the maternal role, such as doll play in early life or baby-sitting in adolescence. They were assertive in their attitude toward sexuality and achievement and more or less ignored groups of girls but sought out and established themselves in the dominance hierarchy of males. However, there was not an unusual incidence of lesbianism among these girls, who chose a male sexual partner both in real life and in fantasy.

This is only one instance in which sex-role behavior cannot be equated with object choice. In adults, transvestism can accompany all degrees of heterosexual and homosexual preferences. Certain heterosexual men are aroused by the sight and touch of female clothing, especially underwear, which they put on in order to increase the pleasure of their heterosexual foreplay and intercourse. Thus, feminine sex-role behavior can serve a masculine sexual preference.

In reviewing the literature on homosexuality, consequently, the distinction between sex role and object choice must be kept in mind, so we do not assume that findings concerning one automatically apply to the other. Incidentally, the literature often implies that the difference is a theoretical one involving the psychoanalytic and social-learning theories rather than an actual distinction between two aspects of sexuality.

Intrapersonal Variables

THE EROTIC DIMENSION. Freud's "shocking discovery" of infantile sexuality has been amply documented. In some societies a parent may masturbate a fretful preschooler in order to soothe him, girls are thought to be ready for sexual amusement by 4 to 5 years of age, and in middle childhood, genital manipulation and erotic pleasures are regarded as normal child's play by parents. Note that this is not pretend play but has the same goal of producing erotic sensations as does postpubertal sexuality.

Such cross-cultural data add credence to adult recollections of early sexual interests and behavior. One of the most extensive studies was conducted by Saghir and Robins (1973), who interviewed eighty-nine adult male and fifty-seven adult female homosexuals and a control group of forty unmarried heterosexual men and forty-four unmarried heterosexual woman. The group was largely urban and middle class, which might affect the generalizability of the findings.

Saghir and Robins studied three aspects of the sexual response: *romantic emotional attachment*, which is an intense feeling of closeness and affection quite different from friendship or the child's feelings toward the parents; *cognitive rehearsal*, which involves fantasies and imagery of a romantic or sexual nature; and *sexual arousal*, which is a pleasurable reaction to genital or nongenital physical contact. In general, homosexuals developed emotional attachments earlier than did heterosexuals and experienced more sexual rather than platonic feelings. For example, 78 percent of homosexuals recalled homosexual emotional attachments before 14 years of age, compared to 49 percent of heterosexuals' recall of heterosexual emotional attachments. Platonic relationships predominated in both groups (that is, wanting to be near and do things for the other person), although 49 percent of homosexuals reported fantasizing physical contact (hugging, kissing, genital contact) compared to 11 percent of the heterosexuals. Also noteworthy is the finding that the same proportion of adult homosexuals as heterosexuals had heterosexual emotional attachments before 14 years of age, but these attachments tended to be more transient and less frequent in homosexuals. In general, the homosexuals had more overlap with heterosexual behavior than did heterosexuals with homosexual behavior, although such heterosexual behavior lacked the element of intense involvement and intrinsic motivation.

Cognitive rehearsal and sexual arousal both began earlier for the homosexual than for the heterosexual; for example, approximately three-quarters of the adult homosexuals were sexually aroused by homosexual stimuli before 14 years of age, while approximately the same percent of heterosexuals were aroused by heterosexual stimuli between 14 and 19 years of age. Moreover, the earliest contact of homosexuals was genital, while the heterosexuals engaged in nongenital behavior such as kissing and hugging. Finally, more homosexuals than heterosexuals reported masturbating at an early age and masturbated more frequently. The pattern of heterosexual dating and intercourse was similar for both groups, although the homosexuals were not as intensely involved and their interest declined rather than increased with age. Incidentally, this element of intensity of involvement also characterized heterosexual development: the mutual, same-sex masturbation occurring in 20 to 50 percent of future heterosexuals had a playful, experimental quality which was not recognized or acknowledged as homosexual by the participants (Saghir and Robins, 1973).

The above pattern of development applied to both male and female homosexuals. There were a few differences: a large proportion of women and none of the men reported early romantic attachments to same-sex school teachers, their responses tended to be more platonic, and their early relationship tended to be nongenital. Such differences conform to the preadolescent-adolescent picture of the male being more genitally oriented, the female more romantically inclined. Heterosexual involvements were similar for both male and female homosexuals.

Saghir and Robins's data are impressive in revealing how early homosexuality can develop: before 14 years of age a pattern of intense romantic involvement, fantasies, erotic arousal, and (at least with males) genital stimulation—in sum, many of the features of mature eroticized intimacy—may be established. Since the data are retrospective rather than prospective we do not know how often the preadolescent pattern is continued into adulthood; in fact, other studies have even failed to corroborate Saghir and Robins's evidence of earlier sexual maturity in male homosexuals (West, 1977). A conservative conclusion, then, is that adult homosexuality may have—but does not necessarily have to have—its origins in the preadolescent period. One clinically relevant finding is that homosexuals were more guilty and fearful than heterosexuals, especially during the preadolescent and adolescent periods, when such feelings characterized half the population.

PERSONALITY CHARACTERISTICS. Saghir and Robins (1973) also studied cross-gender behavior, that is, effeminacy in boys and tomboyishness in girls. Effeminacy included a preference for playing with girls, for housework, and for doll play, along with an avoidance of boys, athletics, and competitive, aggressive activities. The tomboy avoided domestic activities and was disinterested in being with and learning from her mother, preferring instead to play with boys and masculine-oriented toys like guns, trucks, and footballs. Approximately two-thirds of both male and female adult homosexuals reported such cross-gender behavior in their preadolescent or adolescent years. Since tomboyishness is more prevalent than effeminacy, and since its incidence far exceeds that of adult lesbianism, the chances of its being "outgrown" are greater. However, as the data under discussion suggest, tomboyish behavior might also be the prelude to adult homosexuality.

While most children engaged in some effeminate or tomboyish behavior in the preadolescent and adolescent period, Saghir and Robins suggest that for the future homosexual such behavior was more extensive, persistent, and—especially for males—socially handicapping in regard to isolating the boy from his peers. On the whole, however, effeminacy and tomboyishness did not significantly affect most of the behaviors discussed in the previous section, such as romantic attachment and sexual arousal. The implication is that adult homosexuality must be more than simply the eroticization of cross-gender behavior, since a third of the population who did not evidence such behavior became homosexual adults. Once again we have evidence that sex role and object choice may pursue independent developmental paths.

A survey of a representative sample of 411 adolescents puts the above findings into the context of the adolescent period (Sorensen, 1973). To begin with, homosexual experiences were comparatively rare; 5 percent of boys 13 to 15 years old, 17 percent of boys 16 to 19 years, and 6 percent of girls at both ages reporting one or more such experiences. Approximately 40 percent of adolescent boys and girls agreed that homosexuality was acceptable if both partners wanted it. Their tolerance was part of a more general attitude of "being yourself and doing your own thing" coupled with a rejection of preassigned roles. They regarded homosexuality as one of the many forms of exaggerated behavior characteristic of the period; as such, it was neither to be ridiculed nor awarded high status. In spite of this tolerance the majority of adolescents regarded homosexuality as abnormal and unnatural, rejected it for themselves, and would be upset if their children turned out to be homosexual. At least at the time of this survey, therefore, there was no evidence that tolerance for homosexuality went along with attraction to it.

Interpersonal Variables

PARENTAL RELATIONS. There is surprising agreement among retrospective studies of normal and disturbed male homosexuals concerning parental relations. The relation with the mother is overly intense, mothers being variously described as seductive, overprotective, dominating, restrictive, and tending to demasculinize the son. Fathers have been variously described as detached, inaccessible, ineffectual, critical, hostile, and brutal. (See, for example, Evans, 1969.) One of the few longitudinal studies found that lower-class adolescents who were either homosexuals or actively pursuing a feminine identity had a background of frequent father absence, and rejection, hatred, or neglect when the father was there. Both parents frequently made disparaging comparisons of their deviant son with siblings or other boys (McCord, McCord, and Verden, 1962).

Naturally, the above pattern of parental relationships does not characterize all homosexuals, nor is it exclusive to homosexuality. As has so frequently been concluded in discussing other psychopathologies, the necessary and sufficient conditions for producing homosexuality are yet to be discovered. However, the findings concerning the father are consistent with studies of normal development, in which a warm, nurturant, and dominant father has been found to foster the development of a masculine identity (Thompson and McCandless, 1976).

There have been fewer studies of lesbians, and the meager findings concerning parental relations are contradictory. The father is variously described as rejecting, negative, and ineffectual or as possessive and seductive, while Saghir and Robins's (1973) data indicate a close and involved relationship. The data on the mother–child relationship are equally inconsistent and confusing.

It would be helpful if we could have a closer look at the early childhood of homosexuals rather than relying so heavily on the recall of adults. Green's (1976) study of effeminacy in boys is relevant but not exactly suited to our need for two reasons: the meager follow-up data indicate that only a little more than half of effeminate boys (fourteen out of twenty-six cases) became sexually deviant and even fewer became homosexual. Next, the criteria for effeminacy were derived from studies of transsexual adults and represent an extreme of behavior not typical of the retrospective reports of homosexual adults. However, the research at least gives an inkling of what the developmental process might be in a limited segment of the adult homosexual population.

In the study, forty-eight boys referred to a child guidance clinic for effeminacy were matched with a group of noneffeminate boys whose parents volunteered to participate in the study. The modal age was 9 years, and the parents in both groups were highly educated. The criteria for inclusion were persistent cross-dressing (wearing women's clothes), relating poorly to boys but well to girls, preferring dolls to cars and trucks, playing the role of mother or other females in fantasy games, avoiding participation in rough-and-tumble play and sports, and an unusual interest in play-acting. Interviews revealed that many of the boys would like to be girls physically as well as psychologically. (For a more detailed account of the study, see Green, 1974.) This extreme pattern of effeminacy emerged in the preschool period for the majority of the boys, once again reminding us how early sex identity can appear in development.

Of most interest to us is the developmental reconstruction of effeminacy derived from the data. The mother regards the infant male as unusually attractive, and since she has few other avenues for channeling her feelings of caring and love, she devotes considerable attention to her boy. As the toddler begins to explore, the mother's clothes and accessories are readily available. The mother regards such exploration as cute and reinforces it. The father is not often present, but he too either regards his son's early play with feminine objects as funny or cute, or he does not object. As the boy begins to establish peer relations, girls are primarily available. Boys are experienced as "too rough" and meet with parental disapproval. The boy also may temperamentally be more docile than aggressive, so that he finds girls more companionable. As the boy participates increasingly in domestic activities, the father becomes progressively alienated, since he had looked forward to having a more vigorous son. Sensing his father's dissatisfaction, the boy withdraws even further from him. By the time he enters school, his strongly feminine interests alienate him further from male peers and lead him to seek the comfort of girl companions. The mother continues to respond positively to the boy's interest in cross-dressing or, at best, dismisses it as inconsequential. The father, who now feels he has failed in providing an adequate masculine image, defends himself by regarding the boy's behavior as unimportant: "All boys go through that, and he'll outgrow it." Finally, an adult outside of the family confronts the parents with the boy's increasingly feminine behavior and social alienation at school, and the parents bring the child to a clinic for consultation.

The reconstruction relies heavily on learning theory and, to a lesser degree, innate temperamental differences. It sounds eminently plausible. What is not known is how far it can be generalized and how specific it is to homosexuality rather than to disturbances such as transvestism and transsexuality.

PEER RELATIONS. The meager data on peer relations suggest that effeminate boys tend to be social isolates and are teased for being sissies. This may well be one consequence of their preference for feminine activities and interests, along with their fear and avoidance of masculine activities and companionship. Certain adult homosexuals recall how bitterly unhappy they were over being teased, which was a source of greater distress than effeminacy itself. One of the few longitudinal studies corroborates the retrospective data by indicating that poor peer relations in childhood are more characteristic of adult homosexuals than adult heterosexuals (M. Roff, 1966).

While documentation is lacking, there is no a priori reason for believing that the peer relations of noneffeminate future homosexuals differ from peer relations of future heterosexuals. Also, in general, tomboyishness is more acceptable in girls than effeminacy is in boys, but again, there are few data directly relevant to the early peer relations of future lesbians.

Homosexuality: A Psychopathology?

Let us now return to the question of whether homosexuality should be regarded as a deviant or merely a different kind of development.

In regard to children, the most honest answer is that we do not know enough to decide the issue one way or the other. The meager evidence suggests that some adult homosexuality is rooted in middle childhood and adolescence, but the data that would enable us to examine the development of homosexuality are lacking, so we cannot judge whether it is deviant or not.

The clearest findings concern interpersonal relations, and these do look ominous. The combination of an overprotective, domineering mother and a distant, disparaging father plus the possibility of poor same-sex peer relations in middle childhood cannot be dismissed as merely a different developmental pattern. That it may not be the necessary and sufficient condition for producing homosexuality is beside the point; it is sufficiently discrepant in its own right. This concern is buttressed by developmental data indicating that a negative father–son relationship may adversely affect academic achievement, peer relations, leadership, responsibility, self-confidence, and general adjustment (Biller and Davids, 1973).

However, the issue of difference versus deviance does not end here. As we discovered early in the discussion, continuity cannot be assumed between childhood and adult disturbances: disturbed children can grow up to be adequately functioning adults, and disturbed adults can have been adequately functioning children. If the homosexual adult makes a satisfactory adjustment in the areas of love, work, recreation, friendship, self-reliance, then childhood experiences will lose their ominous overtones.

By far the most relevant data come from Bell and Weinberg's (1978) study of 979 homosexual adults and 425 matched heterosexuals in the San Francisco Bay Area. Unlike other studies, which treat homosexuals as a group, these investigators divided their population into five empirically derived subgroups. (1) The Close-Coupled homosexuals would correspond to the "happily married" heterosexuals. They were living with a same-sex partner, had few sexual problems, engaged in relatively little cruising (that is, seeking contacts for the sole purpose of a temporary sexual outlet) but were not worried when they did, had few difficulties in finding and maintaining affection from their partners, were sexually active, and had few regrets about being homosexual. (2) The Open-Coupled, while also living with a special sexual partner, were not happy in the arrangement. They tended to seek sexual satisfactions outside the relationship through cruising but were worried about this activity. While they were quite active sexually they were concerned about their partner's or their own responsiveness to sexual requests. They also tended to regret their homosexuality. (3) The Functionals come closest to the image of the "swinging single": they scored high on the number of sexual partners and level of sexual activity, low on concern over their homosexuality. (4) Like the Functionals, the Dysfunctionals also had a high level of sexual activity and many partners but had a number of sexual problems in regard to their adequacy and regretted being homosexual. They most closely conform to the stereotype of the tormented homosexual, being poorly adjusted not only sexually but socially and psychologically as well. (5) Finally, the Asexuals were not "coupled" and rated low on sexual activity, number of partners, and amount of cruising. They had more sexual problems than the group as a whole, more regrets over their homosexuality, and were less exclusively homosexual than the group as a whole. They lead lonely, solitary, withdrawn lives.

Since Bell and Weinberg did not similarly classify their heterosexual group, no comparison of categories is possible. However, as they stand, the categories clearly refute any stereotype of "the homosexual" as well as the idea that homosexuals somehow have different kinds of relationships with their sexual partners. Certainly, heterosexuals also are happily or unhappily married, happy or unhappy swinging singles, or isolates.

While the categories were applicable to men and women, interesting differences were found. The lesbian was more apt to be involved in a quasi-marriage requiring a high degree of fidelity (that is, there were many Close-Couples); lacking this, they tended to find their homosexuality problematical, since they did not enjoy brief, varied sexual relations (that is, there were few Functionals). Males were less satisfied with quasi-marriages (there were more Open- than Close-Couples) but could enjoy the pleasures of being "swinging singles" (or Functionals).

The homosexual's psychological adjustment was related to sex and category. Generally speaking, lesbians were as well adjusted as their heterosexual counterparts while the homosexual male was less well adjusted. On the positive side, the homosexual male and, to a less extent, the lesbian experienced more happiness and exuberance than the heterosexuals. Among categories, the Dysfunctionals, Asexuals, and to a less extent, the Open-Coupled males accounted largely for the greater degree of maladjustment in homosexuals. Signs of lowered adjustment included psychosomatic symptoms, lowered self-acceptance, loneliness, increased worry, depression, tension, paranoia, and suicidal feelings. The Close-Couple and Functional males were generally as well adjusted as their heterosexual counterparts except, interestingly, for heightened loneliness and tension in the latter.

About half the males and two-thirds of the females had no regret concerning being homosexual. Those who were unhappy listed as reasons social rejection, restrictive opportunities for social participation, not being able to have children, and loneliness.

The work histories of male homosexuals were no different from those of male heterosexuals in terms of number of jobs held and job satisfaction. Approximately one-quarter felt restricted, but 11 percent found their homosexuality to be an advantage in obtaining a job. Lesbians had more job changes than female heterosexuals, but there was no difference in job satisfaction. There were no differences between homosexuals and heterosexuals in regard to having close friends, but the pattern of friendships differed, homosexuals being less favorably impressed with the opposite sex than heterosexuals and having fewer opposite-sex friends.

In sum, Bell and Weinberg's data clearly show that adult homosexuality per se should not be equated with psychopathology, although it increases the likelihood that specific categories of males will be less well-adjusted than heterosexual males in general. These findings are illuminating, but they are not totally satisfying for our purposes. One of our major concerns has been the development of love, and in this area the psychosexual theory has proven the best guide. Freud recognized that homosexuality has no necessary connection with mental illness (Bootzin and Acocella, 1980), but he did maintain that it necessarily limits the ability to establish and maintain a relationship that is mutually satisfying both psychologically and sexually. And it is on just this critical issue of the ability to love maturely that data are incomplete.

Bell and Weinberg's study suggests that Freud was wrong in assuming a necessary limitation in the ability to love maturely. The impression of some Close-Couples is that they had achieved a stable, mature, mutually satisfactory relationship. But does homosexuality decrease the likelihood that such a relationship can be established? We do not know. Approximately 10 percent of males and 30 percent of females in Bell and Weinberg's report could be classified as Close-Couples, but comparable data on their heterosexual controls are lacking.

Finally, there is the issue of parenthood. Certain homosexuals were unhappy because they were unable to have children, which suggests an important limitation, a lack of fulfillment in their lives. It should not be inferred that homosexuals cannot be good parents—they may well be—nor should it be inferred that all heterosexual couples who choose not to have children are necessarily unfulfilled. But in the overall evaluation of homosexuality, we should know its implications in regard to the desire to become parents and the ability to be good parents. From our perspective, the fate of the abilities to love and to parent lie more at the heart of the "homosexual issue" than any concern about mental illness or general adjustment.

IS SOCIETY TO BLAME? A strong case has been made that the homosexual's psychological disturbance is the result of the prejudice and discrimination built into the religious and legal fabric of our society, as well as the ridicule and contempt homosexuals encounter in their daily lives. As we have just seen, such prejudicial treatment can begin in middle childhood for effeminate boys. If homosexuals were treated as human beings who differ only in their sexual preferences, the argument goes, then they would be as well adjusted as heterosexuals.

Certainly, prejudice and discrimination could well be primary roots of the homosexual's disturbance. In this respect he or she is much like the juvenile delinquent, the mentally retarded, the psychotic, and a host of other individuals who have suffered from being labeled mentally ill or emotionally disturbed. Our society has been unjustifiably punitive and shamefully remiss in its attitude toward and treatment of those members who are regarded as deviant.

Yet, recognizing the role of society is not the same as regarding it as the sole etiological agent. With children, this single-cause hypothesis seems particularly unconvincing. The literature contains hints that other than social forces are at work. True, some effeminate boys in the Saghir and Robins study reported that being teased was a source of bitter unhappiness but their effeminacy was not. However, the pattern of a possessive mother and a distant, punitive father does not seem to be a result of social forces. And there are also reports (West, 1967) of adults feeling angry at being tied so close to their mothers, at being babied and restricted, at being forced into feminine activities and hindered in making dates. Here homosexuality seems definitely to have gone against the grain and have resulted from pressure on the child to fulfill parental needs. Such a pattern of family dynamics is familiar to the clinician and may well exist independent of social forces.

In sum, although we cannot fail to recognize the importance of the social context, there is inadequate evidence that it is the sole etiological agent in producing increased maladjustment in certain homosexual adults. Unless such evidence is forthcoming, the multideterminant model is preferred.

The Developmental Model

The paucity of data on homosexuality is a handicap in deciding upon an appropriate developmental model. The only finding which fits with prior discussions involves the future lesbian's preadolescent romantic attraction to a female teacher, since adolescent "crushes" on teachers are not uncommon in girls who subsequently make a heterosexual adjustment. In the lesbian's case, the attraction is sufficiently compelling to block further development in regard to an object choice. Here, then, is the same fixation model which was applicable in the discussion of negativism—an exaggeration of normal development which blocks further progress.

Nor has either of the conceptualizations of sexuality proved helpful in the quest for a developmental model. Learning sex roles by means of reinforcement and modeling adequately accounts for Green's reconstruction of the development of certain effeminate boys; on the other hand, these same two learning principles do not readily account for the fact that tomboyish girls, whose behavior is more or less acceptable, have less of a chance of becoming lesbians than effeminate boys, whose behavior is severely punished, have of becoming adult homosexuals. In general, explanations in terms of social-learning theory are post hoc and lack empirical support.

In pyschoanalytic theory, homosexuality is viewed as the result of fixations at various stages of psychosexual development. After describing the many intra- and interpersonal factors which might eventuate in the same-sex object choice, Anna Freud concludes that "the balance between heterosexuality and homosexuality during the whole period of childhood is so precarious, and the scales are so readily tipped in one direction or the other by a multitude of influences, that the opinion still holds good that 'a person's final sexual attitude is not decided until after puberty' " (1965, p. 1970). While we might agree to the principle of multideterminants, the statement is again too programmatic and too laden with contingencies to be helpful. However, Anna Freud's speculation that object choice is more open to change before adolescence than afterwards does provide us with some reason for discussing homosexuality at this age.

The question as to whether homosexuality is a psychopathology cannot be answered categorically. There is evidence that homosexuality does not preclude the development of a mature love relationship and that it may not be incompatible with good parenting, although evidence for the latter is preliminary. There is also evidence that, throughout childhood and into adulthood, society's punitive treatment causes needless suffering. Yet, there are other instances in which future homosexuals grow up in an exploiting and neglectful family to become adults who are resentful of their treatment, unfulfilled sexually, and dissatisfied with their lot. In such instances, homosexuality can be considered as deviant development. The challenge is to determine the forces which make the difference between the groups, so that the former can be given the social acceptance it deserves while the latter can be given the psychotherapeutic help it needs.

Thus far, these discussions have implicitly assumed that the developing child is not significantly deviant either intellectually or physiologically. The assumption has not always proved correct; in certain instance of autism, for example, both mental retardation and organic brain pathology have been shown to be present. However, the etiological import of intellectual and organic deviations has had to be demonstrated. The procedure will now be reversed, and mental retardation or a lack of organic intactness will be assumed, so that we may ask, What developmental deviations—if any—ensue?

11 ▪ The Developmental Consequences of Mental Retardation

We shall use the American Association on Mental Deficiency's definition of mental retardation, which is: significantly subaverage general intellectual functioning existing concurrently with deficits in adaptive behavior and manifested during the developmental period. It is an interesting definition which deserves to be examined in detail. But first we shall sample a few of the conditions which may result in mental retardation (MR).

ETIOLOGY

A number of *genetic anomalies* can be accompanied by MR, the best known being Down's syndrome (mongolism). Children with this anomaly have three number 21 chromosomes instead of the normal two. Hence, the condition is also called "trisomy 21." These children have distinctive physical features: almond-shaped eyes that slant upward; a flat nasal bridge; a relatively small mouth with a furrowed tongue that tends to protrude intermittently in infancy; small, abnormally shaped and positioned teeth; small, square hands with a short first finger and a single crease running across the palm. Their IQs vary widely from profound to mild retardation, although the modal mental age of school-age children is approximately that of a $3\frac{1}{2}$- to 5-year-old.

Phenylketonuria (PKU) is caused by a specific recessive gene. The affected infant lacks certain liver enzymes necessary for metabolizing the amino acid phenylalanine. Instead, phenylalanine accumulates and is converted to phenylpyruvic acid, a toxic substance that damages the brain. Although not totally satisfactory, screening methods based on the newborn's blood plasma can detect PKU, and a special phenylalanine-restricted diet can prevent retardation. The successfully treated child's intelligence is within the average range but somewhat lower than the intellectual level of the family.

A host of *pre- and postnatal* factors can damage the central nervous system and result in MR. Rubella (German measles) contracted by the mother during the first trimester of pregnancy can cause a number of impairments, MR being one. Syphilis is another cause of MR as well as of fetal death. Exposure to massive doses of radiation in the first few months of pregnancy, chronic alcoholism, age (35 years or older), and severe emotional stress throughout pregnancy are among the numerous maternal factors which increase the risk of MR in the infant. Prematurity and prenatal asphyxia (oxygen deprivation during or immediately after delivery) are hazards at birth. Postnatal sources of mental subnormality are head injuries (most commonly resulting from automobile accidents and child abuse), encephalitis and meningitis (inflammations of the brain resulting from infections by bacteria, viruses, or tuberculosis organisms), particularly if they occur during infancy.

Clinical disorders associated with MR include cerebral palsy, seizure disorders (epilepsy), lead and mercury poisoning from chemical pollutants ingested by the child (for example, by eating lead-based paint or shellfish that have absorbed methyl mercury from industrial waste).

The foregoing list is intended solely to provide a quick overview of genetic and physical etiologies. In each instance the relation to MR, the degree of retardation, and the percent of affected children vary widely; it would be erroneous to conclude, for example, that all children with cerebral palsy or with seizures are also retarded, since a considerable portion are not. (A detailed account of the complex relation between etiology and mental retardation can be found in Robinson and Robinson, 1976.)

Social factors play an important role in mental subnormality. Children's IQ scores tend to be positively correlated with the socioeconomic status of their families, the effect becoming progressively more manifest as the child grows older. Social class even affects the long-range prognosis of some of the pre- and postnatal sources of MR listed above. Sameroff and Chandler (1975) conclude that social status tends to reduce or amplify intellectual deficits in high-risk infants. In advantaged families infants who suffer perinatal complications generally show no or small residual effects in follow-up studies, while infants from lower-class homes with identical medical histories show significant retardation subsequently. They conclude that: "Social and economic status appear to have much stronger influence on the course of development than perinatal history" (p. 209).

Psychosocial disadvantage includes children typically, but not necessarily, functioning at a mildly retarded level but with no clear cerebral pathology. The family is impoverished, MR always occurring in its immediate members and often in the larger family circle. Another label is "cultural-familial MR," reflecting the assumption that both genetic and environmental factors play a role in its production (Achenbach, 1974). There are many reasons for the connection between poverty and retardation. All the pre- and postnatal risk factors previously discussed are more prevalent among the poor, while health care is grossly inadequate. Families tend to be large, the home may be disorganized and lacking in the kind of personal attention and physical objects such as books and "readiness" games which promote intellectual growth and prepare the young child for school. Parents may feel overwhelmed by problems of everyday living, lonely, and discouraged, preferring the child to be passive and conforming.

It is important to avoid stereotypes of "the poor," since there is a great diversity of behaviors among them; nor should we infer that brutality, neglect, disorganization, and other conditions inimical to intellectual growth are unknown in middle- and upper-class families. It is just that among the poor, such conditions can be found with greater frequency.

Finally, MR can be due to *severe emotional disturbances.* Whether it is possible or desirable to differentiate conditions in which the emotional problem underlies retardation from conditions in which retardation underlies emotional problems is a controversial issue still being debated by experts. The chicken-and-egg etiological puzzle remains to be solved not only by researchers but by the clinician faced with the problem of evaluating and diagnosing an individual child. In both instances, the solution has yet to be found.

THE INTELLECTUAL DEFICIT

Returning now to the definition of mental retardation, we see that the first criterion involves "significantly subaverage general intellectual functioning," typically as measured by a standardized intelligence test, such as the Stanford-Binet or the Wechsler Intelligence Scale for Children. Numerically, an IQ score that is more than two standard deviations below the mean is regarded as a significant deviation from average intelligence. Depending on the test, such a score is between 67 and 69. IQ scores are also used to make finer classifications within the retarded range, although the nomenclature varies. For purposes of this discussion, IQ scores in the range of 52 to 69 would classify a child as mildly retarded, 36 to 51 as moderately retarded, 20 to 35 as severely retarded, and below 20 as profoundly retarded. For educational purposes, children with IQs between 55 and 80 are classified as educable, those with IQs between 35 and 55 are classified as trainable, while those with IQs below 35 are classified as custodial.

Far more important than the classification of retardation is the attempt to understand the nature of the underlying intellectual deficit. Some of the research on learning and memory deficits in MR children will be reviewed. (Our presentation follows Robinson and Robinson, 1976.)

The Learning Process

Learning in MR children is slow and inefficient for a number of reasons:

ATTENTION TO RELEVANT CUES. In the basic research paradigm, which is called *discrimination learning,* the child is presented with a succession of stimuli, two or three at a time—say, objects differing in color, shape, and size—and on the basis of being told that a choice is either right or wrong, the child must learn to choose the correct stimulus—say, the red object. To illustrate: A girl is presented with a red circle and a blue square; guessing that "circle" is the correct response, she chooses the first figure and is told she made a correct choice. Next time a green circle and a blue triangle are presented and she is told her choice of the circle is incorrect. She must now change her hypothesis. If she remembers the original circle was also red, she strongly suspects "red" to be the solution, which she verifies when another red object is shown. If she does not remember, she must adopt another hypothesis such as "triangle" or "green."

The learning curve for children of normal intelligence rises quickly at first and then levels off. For retarded children, choices are no better than chance for a number of trials, followed by rapid improvement.

Further investigation reveals that MR children often do not attend to relevant aspects of the situation; they are not asking themselves, Is it color? or shape? or size? On the contrary, they have a strong initial preference for position which they persist in using in spite of being told that their choice is frequently incorrect. Once they can break this irrelevant set, they learn rapidly. By the same token, if given a task in which position is the relevant cue—for example, the correct object is the first one—they learn as fast as or faster than normal children. In a special sense they are not slow learners but slow to catch on.

The retardate's preference for position responses has its counterpart in normal development, since position habits have been observed to interfere with discrimination learning in 1-year-olds. Such habits no longer seem to affect discrimination learning in the toddler and preschooler, although the evidence is not conclusive on this point. If the retardate's preference does in fact represent a fixation, it is one which goes back to earliest childhood and may significantly interfere with subsequent learning. (For a review of the studies see Reese and Lipsitt, 1970.)

PROBLEM SOLVING. The same failure to generate relevant hypotheses that mars discrimination learning affects more complex problem solving. The classical twenty-questions task has been modified so that, in the simplest case, only one question is sufficient to supply the information necessary to make a correct choice. Even here, retarded children ask noncritical questions as frequently as critical ones. Once the information is supplied, they can utilize it effectively, however.

MEDIATIONAL STRATEGIES. The research paradigm here is paired-associate learning. Initially two stimuli are presented and subsequently, only the first is shown, with the child being asked to recall the second. Paired-associate learning can be facilitated if the child ties the two stimuli together in a meaningful manner; for example, *sun* and *bird* are more readily associated if related by, "the sun shines on the bird." The term for such facilitating cues is *mediational strategies*. While college students spontaneously generate mediational strategies, young children and retardates do not. If retarded children are either provided with mediators or even instructed to generate them, their learning is significantly improved. However, if the experimenter no longer instructs the children, they may fail to continue utilizing mediators on their own. Training them to "get into the habit" has met with only limited success, being effective primarily with the mildly retarded. Thus, it is not that MR children are deficient in and cannot utilize higher-level strategies; for some unknown reason, they fail spontaneously to utilize the abilities they possess.

GENERALIZATION. While MR children can be trained to do a specific problem successfully, they characteristically do not generalize to similar problems. It is as if each task is a new one which must be mastered in its own right. The impediment to learning is obvious.

Memory

Remembering is not like opening the shutter of a camera and allowing impressions to register on the brain passively; no less than learning, remembering is an active process.

Among other things, it depends on *spontaneous rehearsal,* which is clearly evident by the third grade in nonretardates. In older children a typical strategy is cumulative rehearsal, in which each new item is rehearsed along with all the prior ones; for example, in remembering a series of numbers a child may think, "six, six-three, six-three-eight," and so forth. Research indicates that MR children are deficient in rehearsal. If they are trained, their performance improves, but frequently they will not spontaneously use such aids. As with learning, they fail to do what they are capable of doing. And again, as with learning, this failure has its counterpart in normal development, since first-graders also make no use of their ability to rehearse (Flavell, 1977, pp. 195–201).

Remembering is also improved if incoming information is organized in a meaningful manner. Present the average child with, say, a list comprised of three categories of words arranged in random order, and the child will tend to recall them by categories; for example, the words following "dog" will tend to be other animal words in the list, those following "apple" will be the other food words, etc. This process of grouping is called *clustering.* Both retarded and young children of normal intelligence show little evidence of clustering. While retardates can be taught to do so, once again they fail to utilize this aid spontaneously.

Certain aspects of memory are intact in retardates, as is the case with certain aspects of learning. Long-term memory, as contrasted with short-term or immediate memory, is as good as it is in children with average intelligence if the degree of original learning is the same. And forgetting is no more rapid than in nonretardates.

A pervasive problem in both memory and learning, therefore, is the failure of MR children to grasp the principal that, regardless of the task, having a plan is superior to having no plan. They passively respond to each stimulus as it comes their way, and what they are taught in one situation stays welded to that situation alone. In short, they do not "plan to have a plan."

The *controlled-laboratory* methodology has furnished the majority of insights into the nature of mental retardation. These insights are all the more valuable because they run counter to common sense, such as retardates are nothing more than slow learners, or they do not use higher-order learning strategies because they are too unintelligent to generate them. With so many studies to choose from we have decided to present one on problem solving (Spitz and Nadler, 1974), since this particular function will not be covered in our other presentations on methodology.

The study is a simplified version of the twenty-questions game. The basic strategy in this game is to ask questions which will eliminate as many wrong answers as possible, while avoiding redundant questions which would add no new information. Thus, if one had to guess which of ten objects an experimenter was thinking of, half of which were animals and half of which were food, the most potent first question would be, Is it an animal? which would immediately eliminate half the objects. If the experimenter said no, and the subject then asked, Is it a dog? the question would be redundant, since it supplies no new information. Since the twenty-questions game is too sophisticated for many retardates, a procedure was devised in which only one bit of information was needed for the correct response.

The subjects were presented with three cards. In the corner of one was a small picture of a cat, in the corner of the next was a small picture of a dog and in the corner of the third was a small picture of a bird. The three cards each had three holes in identical positions, two on the top, one between them on the bottom. In the dog card, the hole on the top left was blank, the hole on the top right had a circle in it, the hole on the bottom had an X. The bird card had the same pattern except the bottom hole had a circle rather than an X. On the cat card, all three holes were covered, but each one could be opened by pushing one of three levers corresponding to the three holes. The problem was to find out whether the pattern on the cat card was like the one on the dog card or the one on the bird card. Since the top two holes on these cards were the same, uncovering the top two holes on the cat card would only produce redundant information. It was the bottom lever which would uncover the crucial bit of information. In the research proper a series of seven such problems was presented, with varying designs and crucial holes. A response was scored correct if the subject pushed the correct lever and gave the correct verbal response.

The subjects were thirty-eight institutionalized and noninstitutionalized retardates, whose mean chronological age (CA) was 15 years and mean mental age (MA) was 9.5 years. The control group consisted of twenty subjects those mean CA was 8 years and mean MA was 9 years. The investigators were careful to exclude subjects who failed to understand the nature of the task in a lengthy preliminary explanation.

As for results: only seven of the thirty-eight retardates learned how to solve the problem, significantly fewer than the normal controls. Further analysis indicated that the retardates' errors were often a result of position preferences, such as having a bias toward pressing the upper left lever. More interesting was the finding that when, by chance, the retardates pressed the correct lever they were capable of utilizing the information to match the cat card with the corresponding pattern on the dog or bird card. However, they could not use this experience to generate a rule which they would apply on subsequent trials. This schism between being able to utilize strategies when provided but being unable to generate them spontaneously is one of the baffling mysteries lying at the heart of mental retardation. It presents one of the major challenges to future researchers.

Looking back over these findings concerning intellectual deficits we are struck by the complementary interplay between normal and deviant development. The question, Why do retardates fail to advance? is countered by the question, Why do nonretardates succeed? If retardates continue to use position as a strategy in discrimination learning, why do preschoolers gradually abandon it in favor of strategies which take note of objects' characteristics? If retardates fail to use rehearsal to improve memory, how do nonretardates come to use it?

We do not know the answer either for normal or deviant development. In regard to rehearsal in nonretardates, for example, there are hypotheses but no scientific documentation. It may be that preschoolers are not sufficiently foresightful or planful to realize that they should do something special with the material they are to remember; it may be that they use a simpler, less effortful but less effective strategy; or, it may be that until the strategy is mastered to the point that it becomes almost second nature, it is too attention-demanding in its own right to be used in a memory task (Flavell, 1977, pp. 194–205).

Certainly, in studying retardates we have arrived at new insights into normal children. We tend to take learning in such children for granted—to assume that they will "naturally" go about learning in the right way, that they will automatically see the relevant cues and search for the relevant information. We also assume that once having hit upon a successful problem-solving strategy, they will "naturally" continue using it. Now we realize that what we have assumed requires an explanation. Nothing happens "naturally." How children learn is as much a puzzle as how they fail to learn.

ADAPTIVE BEHAVIOR

Recall that the definition of mental retardation specifically includes adaptive behavior as well as measured intelligence. Intellectual level and adaptation are undoubtedly related; however, the correlation is not so high that the latter can accurately be inferred from the former. In certain instances the correlation may be quite low. Inner-city or rural-poverty children can make perfectly adequate adjustments to their environments while failing in school. The so-called six-hour retarded child should certainly not be stereotyped on the basis of an IQ score as being capable of making only a marginal adjustment in all situations. To do so runs the risk both of underestimating and of failing to develop the potential in a significant number of children.

In order for adaptive behavior to be a useful concept, however, it first had to be defined in terms of specific behaviors, and then instruments had to be developed to assess it. (For a detailed discussion of both issues, see Coulter and Morrow, 1978.)

In the majority of instances, adaptive behavior is defined in terms of two skills: independent functioning and responsible social relationships. The former includes the ability to meet basic physical needs such as eating, toileting, and dressing, and the ability to function as an integral member of the community in terms of communicating adequately, handling money, traveling, etc. The latter includes cooperative interactions, initiative, caring for personal belongings, etc. The conceptualization also includes both a developmental and a cultural component, in recognition of the fact that adaptive behavior changes with age and varies with the social context.

Assessment

The AAMD Adaptive Behavior Scale (Nihira, Foster, Shellhaas, and Leland, 1974), which operationalizes the concept of adaptive behavior, is constructed along developmental lines. The items which follow have been selected and, at times, modified in order to delineate developmental trends in various areas.

I. Independent functioning
  A. Eating
    Use of utensils: from "feeds self with fingers or must be fed" to "uses knife and fork correctly and neatly"
    Drinking: from "does not drink from cup unassisted" to "drinks without spilling, holding glass in one hand"
  B. Toilet use
    Toilet training: from "is not toilet-trained at all" to "never has accidents"
  C. Cleanliness
    Bathing: from "makes no attempt to wash or dry self" to "prepares and completes bathing unaided"
  D. Dressing and undressing
    Dressing: from "must be dressed completely" to "completely dresses self"
  E. Travel
    Sense of direction: from "gets lost whenever leaving own living area" to "goes several blocks from home without becoming lost"

II. Physical development
  A. Sensory development
    Vision: from "no vision at all" to "no difficulty seeing"
  B. Motor development
    Body balance: from "unable to sit and stand without support" to "stands on tiptoe for ten seconds"

III. Economic activity
  A. Money handling and budgeting
    Money handling: from "does not use money" to "uses banking facilities independently"
  B. Shopping skills
    Errands: from "cannot be sent on errands" to "goes to several shops and specifies different items"
    Purchasing: from "does no shopping" to "buys all own clothes"

IV. Language development
  A. Expression
    Writing: from "cannot write or print" to "writes sensible letters"
    Sentences: from "speaks in primitive phrases or is nonverbal" to "sometimes uses complex sentences containing 'because,' 'but,' etc."
  B. Comprehension
    Reading: from "recognizes fewer than ten words" to "reads books suitable for children 9 years or older"

V. Numbers and time
  A. Numbers: from "has no understanding" to "does simple addition and subtraction"

VI. Domestic activity
  A. Kitchen
    Food preparation: from "does not prepare food" to "prepares an adequately complete meal"

VII. Vocational activity
  A. Job complexity: from "performs no work at all" to "performs a job requiring use of tools or machinery"

VIII. Self-direction
  A. Initiative: from "will not engage in assigned activities" to "initiates most of own activities"
  B. Perseverance
    Attention: from "will not pay attention for five minutes" to "will pay attention for more than fifteen minutes; e.g., playing games, reading"

IX. Responsibility
  A. General responsibility: from "unable to carry out responsibility at all" to "very conscientious, makes special effort, assigned activities always performed"

X. Socialization
  A. Cooperation: from "never helps oth-

ers" to "offers assistance to others"

B. Participation in group activities: from "does not participate" to "initiates group activities, is a leader and organizer"

The second part of the scale, which is not developmentally organized, concerns maladaptive behavior, such as violent, rebellious, and antisocial behavior; withdrawal; stereotyped behavior, odd mannerisms, and eccentric habits; self-abuse; hyperactive tendencies; sexually aberrant behavior; attention demanding; feelings of persecution; hypochondriacal tendencies; and emotional instability.

It is clear that the same behaviors in the first part will indicate different levels of adaptiveness depending on the age of the child. Thus, a 3-year-old who feeds himself or herself with a spoon with considerable messiness, drinks unassisted, indicates toilet accidents and needs, speaks in two-to-three-word sentences, and interacts with others in simple play activities would be mildly retarded, while a 12-year-old would be profoundly retarded.

The scale also individualizes children in terms of strengths and weaknesses in the ten domains. One 8-year-old might be well developed physically and reasonably able to feed, toilet, and dress himself, while being low in language development, restless, and in need of constant direction. Another 8-year-old may have a severe motor handicap which hampers her ability to care for her needs, while expressing herself well, understanding what others say to her, and showing a good deal of initiative and perseverance. Such differentiated information is helpful in planning remedial programs tailored to individual needs. Interestingly, the manual that accompanies the scale recommends that, in general, the therapist should concentrate on areas of strength first rather than trying to change areas of weakness. The chances of success are greater, and the child's motivation to change is apt to be stronger.

Finally, Leland (1978) cautions that stereotyping children in terms of their Adaptive Behavior Scale score is no better than stereotyping them in terms of an IQ score. Mental retardation covers a wide range of disabilities and dysfunctions, and we should not expect every child to conform to the same developmental pattern and sequencing; a child with a speech impediment, poor motor coordination, and a history of severe physical illness might take a different route to reaching a given level of adaptiveness than a physically intact child with the same degree of intellectual impairment. Thus, the Adaptive Behavior Scale score must always be placed in the now familiar intrapersonal, interpersonal, social, and cultural contexts.

Factor-Analytic Studies and Developmental Trends

A number of factor-analytic studies of the Adaptive Behavior Scale have been done. (For a review of the findings see Nihira, 1978.) In general, they show that Part I contains three factors—Personal Self-Sufficiency, Community Self-Sufficiency, and Personal-Social Responsibility—while Part II yields Acting-Out Aggression and Withdrawal factors. Nihira's study of 3,354 institutionalized subjects between 4 and 69 years of age adds a developmental perspective to the factors in Part I (Nihira, 1976).

Personal Self-Sufficiency is found at all ages and involves the ability to satisfy immediate personal needs such as eating, toileting, and dressing. Community Self-Sufficiency involves independence beyond immediate needs, along with self-sufficiency in relation to others; for example, using money, traveling, shopping, and communicating adequately. Personal-Social Responsibility involves initiative and perseverance, the ability to undertake a task on one's own and see it through to completion. These last two factors emerge around 10 years of age and are either weak or nonexistent in younger children. They also represent higher level behavior than the mere satisfaction of immediate needs.

Developmental trends differ according to the degree of retardation. In general the greater the retardation, the less rapid the development during childhood and the lower the final level of adaptation. For Personal Self-Sufficiency, for example, 90 percent of total growth is achieved by 10 to 12 years of age in the mildly retarded groups, while the severely retarded groups achieve the same percent of growth between 16 and 18 years of age. Only the profoundly retarded continue to grow throughout the life cycle, although their rate is the slowest and their level the lowest of all the groups.

For the mildly retarded children there is a rapid increase in Personal Self-Sufficiency during childhood which is gradually replaced by an accelerated growth in Community Self-Sufficiency during adolescence, a trend which seems to be congruent with development in nonretardates. In moderately retarded children, Community Self-Sufficiency grows more slowly, equaling Personal Self-Sufficiency by adolescence but never rising above it subsequently. In the severely retarded, Community Self-Sufficiency is consistently lower than Personal Self-Sufficiency throughout the life span, indicating that in an institutionalized population competence in caring for immediate physical needs is the area of highest achievement.

The Process of Adaptation

The development of assessment instruments represents a major advance in describing adaptive behavior and in charting its developmental course. However, this is only the first step. What remains to be discovered are the reasons why adaptive behavior lags and why it develops as it does. There is nothing comparable to the impressive body of literature on the causes of deficient thinking in retardates. How are initiative and negativism manifested in the retarded toddler, and how are they responded to? How does the preschooler go about playing and establishing a relationship with peers? How are socialization requirements internalized and moral guides understood? How do friendships and vocational goals develop in middle childhood and adolescence? In seeking answers to these kinds of specific questions we want to know how the behavior of the retardate differs from that of the adequately endowed child.

An example of the kind of inquiry we have in mind is Serafica and Cichetti's (1976) comparison of attachment and exploratory behavior in twelve Down's syndrome and twelve normal 33-month-old toddlers. (See also Emde, Katz, and Thorpe, 1978). In general, the similarities between groups outweighed the few differences. In regard to attachment, the only difference was a decrease in separation anxiety in the Down's syndrome children as evidenced by less frequent crying at the mother's departure from the experimental room. However, there was no evidence that such behavior was due either to a developmental lag or a difference in strength of attachment. Rather, the authors speculate that being alone in a strange room may have been less threatening either because the children's limited intellect made them less sensitive to cues denoting novelty or because of a generalized lower reactivity to stimuli. Both groups explored the environment but used different modes, the normal children favoring fine-motor manipulation, the Down's syndrome children gross-motor manipulation. In general, the normal children used a more active and differentiated manner in interacting with novel stimuli.

If such a study were done longitudinally, we could see the effects of low separation anxiety on subsequent social relations with the mother and adults in general. We could also determine whether the less differentiated exploration of the environment was one of the roots of a generally low level of intellectual functioning. The preference for gross-motor activity may also delay the development of self-help skills such as buttoning clothes and tying shoes, which increasingly require fine-motor coordination.

Investigators have only begun to apply the advances in studying personal-social development in nonretardates to MR children. An intensive program of research along these lines might well add a new dimension to our understanding of mental retardation.

PERSONALITY DEVIANCE

Not only intellectual limitations but emotional problems may also interfere with adaptation. While there is no such thing as a typically retarded child, since variability of personality is the rule, having to cope with the demands of a complex society generally increases the likelihood of maladaptive behavior, so that behavior problems are more frequent in the retarded than among normal children (Rutter, 1971). Most of the information which follows comes from studies of mildly retarded school-age children and adolescents. (For a detailed presentation, see Robinson and Robinson, 1976.)

MR children and adolescents usually show higher levels of *anxiety* than do nonretarded individuals of the same age. Such anxiety plays a dual role in regard to academic performance. Its energizing properties can facilitate the performance of simple tasks, enabling retarded children to do well on simple arithmetical computations, for example. It is on complex tasks, such as concept formation, that anxiety disrupts effective intellectual functioning. And it is just such complex thinking which is increasingly required in school. Thus, from both an intellectual and an emotional point of view, the retarded child tends to be increasingly handicapped in regard to having a successful experience in school.

Repeated experiences of failure, in turn, take their toll on *initiative*. MR children are less curious and venturesome, less prone to accept challenges and enjoy mastery for its own sake, than are children with normal intelligence. Thus, the failure spontaneously to utilize what they have been taught, which characterizes their intellectual functioning, has its counterpart in a pervasive passivity in the personality realm. In addition, MR children tend to develop a generalized expectation of failure, unlike other children who can take failure in stride and try to do better next time. Retarded children are apt to utilize a number of nonconstructive self-protective techniques, such as avoiding the failure situation, reconciling themselves to a low rate of success, making up unrealistic excuses, or substituting stereotyped responses for active effort and involvement; for example, on an intelligence test, the first failure may trip off an immediate "I don't know" or a shrug in response to all subsequent items. While following the same progression as normal children, the MR child lags behind them in the ability to postpone immediate gratification in favor of achieving long-term goals.

A related consequence of repeated failure is a distrust of one's own resources and a turning to the environment for cues on how to proceed. This special kind of dependency is called *outer directedness*. In and of itself, outer directedness is not deviant; in fact, it is adaptive when one has reached the limits of one's abilities, as well as being the basis of learning by imitation. It is just that in the retarded, outer directedness may be carried to the extreme of excessive reliance on others for direction. A related pattern of behavior is the retarded child's tendency to be conforming and cooperative rather than competitive and self-assertive. Again it is not the behavior but its excessive use that is maladaptive.

We now see that the MR child has a dual handicap, one intellectual, the other motivational. The problem may further be compounded in institutional settings where docility and conformity to a drab routine are rewarded, while assertiveness and initiative are punished. The challenge to researchers is to disentangle basic intellectual handicaps from those which result from motivational and environment influences. The therapeutic challenge is to find ways in which our society can accommodate to the realistic limitations while maximizing the assets of the MR child, which in turn will result in a more balanced mixture of successes and failures than presently exists. It is helpful to remind ourselves that in certain societies MR is not stigmatized or even viewed as a problem which needs correcting. Our achievement-oriented society might profit from such examples of acceptance.

DOWN'S SYNDROME CHILDREN

While impressive advances have been made in understanding the intellectual deficits and the adaptive behavior of retardates, developmental studies which relate these intrapersonal variables to the context variables of family and class are quite rare. Instead of summarizing the general literature, therefore, we have chosen to present in detail a single study which has a developmental orientation.

Overview

Until recently, Down's syndrome (DS) would seem to be an ideal form of retardation to study because of its simple, clear-cut etiology—a chromosome anomaly—and a predictable constellation of personality traits, the typical child being affable, docile, affectionate, mischievous, stubborn, and having a talent for mimicry. However, the current picture is far from simple. Down's syndrome can result from a number of chromosome abnormalities (Robinson and Robinson, 1976), each of which might or might not have a differential effect on development. At the same time numerous exceptions have been discovered to the "typical" behaviors. Research findings have been confusing because of a tendency to deal with the "DS child" without systematically controlling for such important variables as age, degree of retardation, sex, complication due to organic brain pathology and severe physical illnesses, social class, and type of care in the family and institution. In addition, findings have been variously interpreted depending on whether the DS child was compared with normal children or with other kinds of retarded children with or without organic brain pathology. Consequently, the descriptive and developmental picture is more tentative than it was in the days when the condition was originally described and explored. (Our discussion will follow D. Gibson, 1978.)

INTELLIGENCE. A generally accepted view is that in infancy there is only a very mild developmental lag, although laboratory studies suggest that standard tests might be too gross to detect more subtle defects in functioning that may be present. The favorable early developmental picture is followed by a precipitous but phasic decline in intellectual functioning. While mental age never keeps pace with chronological age as it does with children of normal intelligence, there is a growth spurt to approximately 18 months between the first and fourth year of life, followed by a plateau in mental growth for approximately one year; between approximately 5 and 9 years of age there is another spurt, bringing the child's mental age to 31 months; again there is a plateau until a final spurt between 11 and 13 years of age, which increases the mental age to 40 months. Most children do not evidence the third spurt, so their measured intelligence is like that of a 2½-year-old, although this does not mean that their total functioning is at this level. In terms of what is known of cognitive development this degree of retardation means that DS children will have particular difficulty with symbolic thinking, concept formation, and abstraction. Here as with other characteristics, however, variability is the rule, and one can find DS children who are both profoundly and mildly retarded.

According to D. Gibson (1978), biological factors seem to be preeminent in determining the picture of intellectual growth and decline. Aside from gross neglect and abuse, environmental factors seem to play a minor role. However, they cannot be altogether discounted, since there is evidence of an improvement in intellectual status with improved health and nutritional care and the introduction of special education. The superiority of home-reared over institutionalized DS children might also be taken as evidence for the importance of environment, the majority of the former group being in the moderately retarded range (IQ scores between 40 and 54), the majority of the latter having IQs below 35 (Robinson and Robinson, 1976).

The specific reasons for the intellectual decline are not known. Some speculate that the lowered level of responsivity to stimuli results in a kind of self-perpetuating sensory deprivation, which encapsulates the central nervous system and prevents its normal development. Others argue that the central nervous system itself is in some way defective and fails to grow.

SOCIAL SKILLS. Social skills have a good deal in common with adaptive behavior, many of the items in the adaptive behavior scale being taken from scales measuring social maturity. Unlike intelligence, social age (SA) continues to grow throughout childhood and early adolescence in DS children. Thus, a 15-year-old might have an MA of 4 years and an SA of 7 years. However, SA declines to approximate MA in adolescence and adulthood. The most favorable developmental picture is found in children with an affable personality, relatively good intelligence, few secondary physical complications such as organic brain pathology, who also receive good physical and psychological care. Typically, the DS child fares best in the self-help areas such as feeding, dressing, and toileting—skills requiring simple, mechanical abilities. The child does poorly in areas requiring conceptual ability and foresight, which in turn are essential to vocational independence, communication, and travel in the community. It may be that the intellectual decline ultimately blocks progress in adaptive behavior, or it may be that a common etiological variable affects both. At their worst, the older DS individuals become restless, aggressive, stubborn, and destructive, as do other severely retarded adults.

PERSONALITY. One reason why the positive stereotype of the DS child lasted so long is that contradictory behaviors were dismissed as exceptions to the rule! In a like manner, the developmental picture was epitomized in terms of the placid infant, who becomes the outgoing child, who then becomes the sullen adolescent facing premature aging and marked behavioral deterioration in early adulthood. While the variability of personality is now recognized, there has been no satisfactory way of conceptualizing it.

One solution has been to reconceptualize behavior in terms of types: the lively, good-natured, affectionate, docile, cheerful child versus the shy, reticent, apathetic, destructive, noisy, and negativistic one. In general, typologies conform to the introversion–extraversion model. Advocates of the typological approach tend to favor a physiological explanation of behavior as well as hypothesizing that subsequent pathology represents extremes of the tendency either to act out or to withdraw. However, typologies still fail to encompass the variations in observed behaviors, while the connection to constitutional and psychobiological variables has yet to be demonstrated. Gibson concludes that, "the empirical research has provided no firm grounds either for accepting or rejecting the classical personality stereotype for DS" (1978, p. 123). There is some evidence that positive prognostic signs include a relatively high intelligence with only a modest decline with age, good physical and psychological care, and being female—variables which, with the exception of sex, we have already encountered.

PSYCHOPATHOLOGY. Estimates of frank psychopathology have ranged from none to 60 percent depending on the nature of the population sampled—the degree of the defect, the child's general health and care received, the length of time in the institution, the presence of organic brain damage, the general developmental history. Once again, the theme of variability should be underscored. Generally speaking, however, psychopathology is less common and acute in younger DS children than in other moderately to seriously retarded children, the frequency perhaps increasing as adulthood approaches. The kind of psychopathology is not different than that for other retarded groups—hyperactivity, impulse disorders, and attention deficits being prominent. Later, DS adults seem to have more catatonic states, depression, and senile dementia, perhaps based on progressive neuropathology. Explanations range from an organic etiology (both intellectual and personality deterioration resulting from some yet to be discovered neurophysiological and metabolic mechanisms) to interpersonal (parents' initial hopes turning to disappointment and despair as the child's behavior progressively declines with age) to a combination of both. Speculation far outstrips evidence, which is meager and inconclusive.

The Developmental Study

Carr (1975) periodically evaluated thirty-nine home-reared and six boarded-out DS children from the time they were 1.5 months until they were 48 months of age. A control group of forty-two normal children was matched for age, sex, and social class. In keeping with the summary just presented, the DS childrens' initial IQ was somewhat lower than that of the normal controls (that is, a score of 80 compared with a score of 100) but declined in the subsequent months until it was around 40 for the home-reared and 20 for the boarded-out children at twenty-four months of age. The mean score of the boarded-out children was significantly below that of home-reared children, and the mean score of DS girls was significantly above that of boys.

EVERYDAY PROBLEMS. Carr's data contain many instances in which the specific nature of the infant's and toddler's retardation affected development. In regard to *feeding*, the infants were less alert and eager for food, had weaker sucking reflexes, and were sleepier than the normal controls. The mothers did not feed on demand simply because the infants were so undemanding—rarely crying and having to be awakened in certain instances—and fewer infants were breast-fed because of the difficulty involved in getting them to suck. Understandably, the mothers were more anxious over feeding than were mothers of normal infants. "He never cried so I had to wake him every four hours. It was terrible. I used to spend an hour giving him two ounces of milk. He just wouldn't suck" (p. 43).

Not only was bottle-feeding the rule, but DS children also remained dependent on the bottle owing to their lag in motor development. At 12 months they were like an 8-month-old, lacking the control of grasping necessary for self-feeding. More mothers of DS than normal children reacted with concern over feeding, forcing or encouraging the toddler or saving the food until later. However, the majority of DS mothers, like their normal counterparts, were unconcerned about the toddler's eating habits. "I don't worry. The dog has it, so there is no waste" (p. 44). They also showed confidence in the child's ability to judge what he or she needed.

While the 4-year-old DS preschoolers lagged behind the controls in self-feeding, two-thirds were capable of eating ordinary family meals, and feeding was no longer a problem to most of the mothers. Here, we see the infant "outgrowing" a problem and maternal concern diminishing. But it is also important to remember that mastery of self-feeding requires low-level skills, which the DS child can acquire. Thus, feeding differs from other adaptive behaviors which demand greater sophistication, such as going about the neighborhood and community or shopping.

In contrast to feeding, *sleeping* was a problem for neither group throughout the duration of the study. More DS children slept in their parents' bedroom, possibly because their parents felt they were still babies. Fewer DS children wanted cuddly toys at bedtime, perhaps because they were less apt to imagine terrors in the dark, perhaps because their coarse, thick skin resulted in less satisfaction from cuddling.

As could be predicted from their lag in motor development, DS children were less adept at *dressing* themselves at 15 months and at 4 years of age and were less helpful to their mothers during dressing.

Toilet training showed the opposite development from feeding, in that the DS children "grew into" deviant behavior. At 15 months there was no difference between groups in terms of the age at which training was started and in terms of maternal attitudes; by 4 years of age the DS children were significantly retarded in all aspects of toileting—they wet their beds and wet or dirtied their pants more and were less adept at self-care. Unlike early feeding, differences in toilet training did not differentially affect the mother's attitudes in spite of the fact that the DS children had many more accidents.

From a comparison of feeding and toileting we might infer that developmental delays may either be perceived by the mother as a problem or accepted as a fact. It would be interesting to know whether complicating emotional problems appear only under the former conditions.

Combining walking, eating, dressing, and toileting at 4 years of age into a single measure of independence, Carr found that between one-half and one-third of DS children needed little more looking after than the normal controls. This relatively advanced adaptive behavior compared with their measured IQ is in keeping with the findings presented in the previous section. Furthermore, there was evidence that interpersonal factors played an important role in determining the independence of the brighter DS children, but had little effect on the most retarded.

Crying in 15-month-old DS children also showed the imprint of their developmental delay. While there was no difference between groups in frequency, the DS children were more likely to cry because of physical upset such as hunger, tiredness, or pain, while normal children were more likely to cry for "psychological" reasons such as boredom, being teased, or not getting what they wanted. The difference is understandable, since mentally the DS children were more like 9-month-olds. The two groups of mothers comforted appropriately, either physically picking up or rocking the DS children or diverting the normal children with toys or a change of scenery. They differed significantly only in that mothers would not let their DS children cry as long as mothers of normal children. It is not clear whether this represents maternal overconcern or a realistic reaction to the children's immaturity.

In an interview, over half of the mothers in both groups spoke of difficulties they had encountered in the first 15 months of their children's lives. The control mothers mentioned sleeping problems, while mothers of DS children emphasized feeding problems. Most striking, however, was the distress of the latter over the condition of their retarded children, their disappointment, resentment, and worry. Some spoke of being unable to adjust to the shock of having a DS child or were concerned about the child's future social acceptance or anticipated increasing difficulties.

BEHAVIOR PROBLEMS AND DISCIPLINE. The DS children's placid infancy extended into the toddler period, during which time they had significantly fewer *temper tantrums* than did normal children. By 4 years of age, however, the difference had disappeared. At 15 months the instigations to anger differed, normal children reacting to not getting their way, DS children to being coerced. By 4 years of age the differences in instigators had disappeared. The mothers did not differ significantly in their methods of coping with tantrums at any age.

Getting into mischief—taking things out of the cupboard, knocking objects over, fiddling with light switches and plugs, putting things down the toilet—again showed a trend heavily influenced by the DS children's delayed development. While they were less mischievous at 15 months than the controls, this may have been because they were less mobile, none of them being able to walk. By 4 years of age, DS children had surpassed the controls in "naughtiness," as if they were belatedly going through the phase which their normal counterparts had left behind. They were also more housebound, so that their mothers were more aware of their behavior than that of normal children who, for example, might be playing in a mud puddle in the garden.

At 4 years of age there were few significant differences between DS and control children in regard to *aggressiveness*. There was a tendency for DS children to retaliate less in a fight and for their mothers to remove them or distract them from a quarrel rather than encouraging them to stand up for themselves or to settle the matter on their own; however, such differences were not striking.

Ninety percent of children in both groups were said to be happy, so the incidence of *distress and upset* was low. While the DS children did not live up to their stereotype of being unusually happy children, retarded development did not result in an increase in unhappiness at 4 years of age. Half of all the children were described as easy children with only five DS and six controls being regarded as problems. The types of problems were similar in both groups, namely, oppositional behavior, rudeness, attention seeking, mischievousness.

Maternal discipline of DS children changed from being more permissive and child-centered, more comforting and less punitive when the child was 15 months old to being comparable to the control mothers in terms of the amount of smacking and the handling of tempers. This increased toughness might have been due to the children's increased tantrums and naughtiness, as well as their being perceived as less fragile than they were at 15 months. Carr notes in passing that other studies suggest that this trend continues until mothers of DS children become stricter than those of normal children. On the other hand, mothers of DS children bribed and rewarded less on the theory that the children would not understand what the rewards were for, especially if they were promised rather than immediately administered. In a like manner, mothers preferred to smack the children rather than sending them to bed, because they believed the children could not remember the reason for the punishment for any length of time and would begin playing or wrecking the room. In sum, the mother's evaluation of her child's mental abilities biased her toward the immediately effective approach of smacking.

One final note: while the DS children were more vulnerable to various childhood illnesses and tended to become more seriously ill than the controls, their mothers did not rate them as more sickly and fragile. Whether this represents a constructive optimism on the mother's part or a defense against facing a painful reality is not known.

CONTEXT VARIABLES. The DS child did not seriously disrupt *family life*, at least in the early years. Contacts with friends, relatives, and casual acquaintances continued as before. Only 21 percent of the mothers described themselves as lonely, especially if they did not receive psychological support from relatives and friends, although there is no way of telling how much their own behavior contributed to their isolation.

The majority of children in both groups enjoyed *school*. Both groups of mothers regarded peer contacts as the main benefit, followed by learning self-help skills for the DS group, handicrafts for the control group. Since the DS group was in school for a full rather than half day, they had more *peer contact* than did the controls. At home both groups participated equally in the play of their siblings and their siblings' friends, the DS children often taking the part of pupil or patient in games of school and hospital. The one significant difference was that the DS children had far fewer friends of their own who came to play.

While *social class* impacted upon many maternal behaviors, it affected both groups in similar ways.

LONGITUDINAL COMPARISONS. In what ways did behaviors when the children were 15 months of age affect behaviors at 4 years of age? No significant relations were found for feeding in the DS group; for both groups, children who helped with dressing at 15 months were more likely to dress themselves completely at 4 years; and in both groups the tendency to have temper tantrums was stable over time. A good deal of consistency was found in parental life: the same mothers were working, the same fathers were participating in child care, parents were going out or staying at home as frequently and expressing the same degrees of contentment with their lot. The overall picture, then, is of parents continuing to behave "in character," of family styles being preserved and of children being influenced in the same manner by early experiences.

The principal difference between groups

was in regard to toilet training. Both groups conformed to the familiar pattern—children who were started early and whose mothers were concerned about progress were more reliably trained than those who started late and whose mothers were unconcerned. However, the difference was that the controls showed no evidence of adverse effects from early training while, for the DS children, such training was associated with temper tantrums. Thus, the DS mother had to choose between having either a clean child or an easily manageable one.

Comments

Carr's study provides us with a number of insights into the complexity of the early development of DS children. There were many areas of overlap with a nonretarded population, and in regard to sleeping, crying, and tantrums, the DS families were at a slight advantage. If clinicians focus on differences, it is only because differences are their special concern, both in terms of understanding and remedying them. And, undoubtedly, the DS children did evidence special problems—feeding problems in infancy and, later, problems in regard to toileting, dressing, getting into mischief, and health. We saw how they could grow out of their feeding difficulties and grow into trouble making and learned that their mothers were in a no-win situation in regard to toilet training, having to choose between cleanliness and manageability. As for the DS mothers, they took all the developmental deviations in stride with the exception of early feeding. However, they were markedly worried over the future, anticipating—probably realistically—that the most difficult problems were yet to come.

Carr's study also makes us wish there were comparable data on middle childhood and adolescence when school and the expectation of independence place special demands for adaptation. It would be interesting to know how such demands could best be handled so as not to burden the DS child and distress the parents unduly. Always there is the nagging question of how much emotional problems are due to ineptness in meeting the DS child's special needs and how much they are part of the same neurophysiological factors responsible for the progressive intellectual decline.

Before dealing with prevention and remediation, let us see what MR has taught us in terms of the search for developmental models.

Developmental Models

The exploration of intellectual and adaptive deviations of the MR child has revealed a variety of models of deviant development. In certain instances retardates seem to be hampered by a slow *rate* of growth; for example, the growth of community self-sufficiency in moderately retarded children, or the DS child's mischievousness at 4 years of age when normal counterparts have passed through this stage. The *pattern* of growth may also be different; recall the spurts and plateaus in the DS children's mental age, which contrasts with the relatively continuous change in the normal population. There may be growth failures or *fixations,* such as the utilization of position in discrimination learning or the failure to rehearse as an aid to remembering. There is the *exaggeration* of normal behavior as evidenced in the retardate's outer-directedness and reliance on external cues. Finally, we come to a possibility that has not been raised since the discussion of autism, namely that the children evidence behaviors which have very little counterpart in normal development. In the intellectual sphere there is a controversy as to whether certain kinds of thinking in retarded children are *qualitatively* different from that found in normal children. Achenbach (1974) argues against the qualitative difference hypothesis, citing the findings that the pattern of items passed and failed on the Stanford-Binet and the performance on certain Piagetian tasks is similar in retardates (without organic brain pathology) and normal children matched for mental age. Moreover, other characteristics of MR, such as rigidity and perseveration, have been shown to result from institutionalization. There is also evidence that retarded and nonretarded individuals go through the same Piagetian stages in the same order but at differing rates of progress (Weisz and Zigler, 1979). Whether all the cognitive deficiencies in MR can be subsumed under the quantitative model, however, remains to be seen. (See Robinson and Robinson, 1976, for a brief discussion. For a more detailed presentation, see Zigler and Balla, in press.)

We are also confronted with a new deviation, which is both intriguing and puzzling. Recall that there is evidence that the DS infant is attached to the mother but lacks the separation anxiety found in normal toddlers. Here is a situation in which one element in a complex pattern of behavior is missing. Does this mean that the developmental course of attachment will be deviant? We do not know. The consequences may be positive in that the children may be loving toward their mothers but not unduly concerned about being away from her, say, when going to school for the first time. On the other hand, attachment might subsequently lack a certain depth and be too readily relinquished. In the latter case such a development would be more likely regarded as deviant. Longitudinal data on the course of attachment would help decide the issue.

REMEDIAL AND PREVENTIVE PROGRAMS

One aspect of programs for the mentally retarded that is of special interest is the involvement of all branches of the federal government. (For an extended discussion of remedial and preventive programs, see Robinson and Robinson, 1976.) This involvement was spearheaded in the 1960s by a sympathetic president—John F. Kennedy—backed by a powerful pressure group composed of parents of MR children. The year 1965 was significant for the movement: the Elementary and Secondary Education Act (ESEA) provided special programs of assistance to disadvantaged and handicapped children, as well as new centers for innovative instructional material and for research; Project Head Start was aimed at preventing the intellectual ravages of socioeconomic deprivation, especially at the preschool level; and federal funds were provided for research and demonstration centers, as well as for educating MR children in residential schools. In 1966 the powerful Bureau of Education for the Handicapped was created, followed by the National Center on Educational Media and Materials for the Handicapped in 1969. By the end of the decade, some 15,000 to 17,000 new teachers for the retarded were being graduated each year, while approximately 80 percent of the 936,000 identified retarded children were receiving special instruction in the public schools. By 1973, $879 million were allocated for programs serving the retarded, with states spending on an average of 3 percent of their budget for special education. Such concern and funding at the national and state levels was unprecedented in this country.

In the 1970s the judiciary placed its stamp on the field of mental retardation—as it did on so many other aspects of public life—by explicating the rights of retarded individuals.

The stage had been set in the 1954 *Brown* v. *Board of Education of Topeka* decision, when the U.S. Supreme Court ruled that the principle of "separate but equal facilities" was unacceptable. Up until 1972, however, more than half the states excluded children with low IQ scores from the educational system, while three-quarters of the states were legally able to place children without parental permission. Both practices were declared illegal. The court also required a periodic reevaluation of all retarded children every two years and notification of parents before changing an educational assignment. Other decisions further strengthened the rights of the retarded as well as other handicapped children.

Such governmental involvement has done much to eliminate the neglect of the retarded and the shocking cruelty that characterized their treatment all too often. (Some institutions still retain, as historical relics, the rooms in which MR children were chained to the walls. See Blatt and Kaplan, 1966.) At present the trend is toward a broad array of programs, rather than a reliance on institutions, and participation not only by the schools but by parents and the community as well. However, no amount of federal support can solve the professional's problem of devising remedial and preventive programs and of evaluating relative effectiveness.

Comparing the heartening progress in the area of mental retardation with the lack of progress in the area of juvenile delinquency provides an object lesson in the politics of remediation. The "children nobody wants" languish, not because their need is less but because the government is not pressed by a well-organized group of concerned citizens and shows only fitful interest in their plight. This is also our first encounter with one of the many forces which have caused the clinical child psychologist to enter the political arena. Politics has been described as "one part idealism and ninety-nine parts power," and traditionally clinicians have been ill-equipped to survive in the political mainstream. As they become increasingly involved in the state and federal government, they must assume roles for which their education has not prepared them, although one day such training may be part of the curriculum.

Special Education

Children with IQ scores between 55 and 80 are classified by most school systems as educably mentally retarded (EMR) and are expected to perform at least at a third-grade level and occasionally as high as a sixth-grade level by the time they finish school. The trainably mentally retarded (TMR) with IQ scores between 35 and 55 are taught to function in a restricted environment because they are not expected to master traditional academic skills.

In special education classes, EMR pupils are taught academic subjects as tools to enhance social competence and occupational skills. Small classes with individualized attention are recommended. Between 6 and 10 years of age the EMR child, whose MA is between 3 and 6 years, is given the kind of readiness programs usually found in kindergartens; the emphasis is on language enrichment and self-confidence, along with good health, work, and play habits. EMR children between 9 and 13 years of age, whose MA is about 6 to 9 years, can master the basic academic skills involved in the three R's. At the junior and senior levels the applied emphasis continues; for example, reading the newspaper and job application forms, making change. Occupational education stresses appropriate work habits such as punctuality and following directives, since most vocational failures are due to poor adjustment rather than low mental ability. After formal schooling, sheltered workshops and vocational rehabilitation centers help the mildly retarded adjust to our complex society.

The curriculum for TMRs emphasizes self-care and communication skills, work habits, following directions, and rudimentary social participation. Reading instruction, for example, is likely to include recognizing signs such as "Stop," "Men," and "Women," while arithmetic is limited to making change. The majority of these children do not achieve social or economic independence as adults, although they can engage in useful work and adjust well in the protective setting of the family.

MAINSTREAMING. One unanswered question is whether MR children are best educated in special classes or in regular classrooms where teachers are trained to meet their particular educational needs. In keeping with the social fervor of the times, special classes have been labeled another form of "discrimination" and "segregation." The claim has been buttressed by poorly designed studies showing that MR children in special classes fare worse than those in regular classes. Such studies ignored the fact that children were often placed in special classes because they were doing poorly or were so disruptive that it was impossible for the teacher to handle them in the regular classroom.

In reality, we know very little about the relative merits of special classes as compared with mainstreaming, that is, placing MR (and other handicapped) children in regular classes. As we might have expected, the few good studies which have been done indicate that there are advantages and disadvantages to each (Robinson and Robinson, 1976). Keeping in mind the tentativeness of the data, the evidence suggests that children with IQ scores above 75 to 80 do better academically in a regular class, while EMRs do better in a special class. Specifically, EMR children tend to have a more positive self-image than if they are in regular classes, perhaps because they use other MR children as the reference group rather than comparing themselves with normal children. Their social adjustment also tends to be better, since they are apt to be social isolates in regular classrooms. However, the picture is not a simple one: in urban settings, retarded children in regular classes are rated high in peer acceptance, while they are rated low in suburban areas where, presumably, more status is given to academic achievement.

Let us return for a moment to the theme of the clinician in the political arena. The studies of mainstreaming indicate how important it is for clinicians to keep their critical (as well as their clinical) wits about them. It is difficult to argue another viewpoint when words such as "segregation" and "discrimination" are being bandied about. However, the clinician's main concern is insuring that the retardate receives the best of care and the most expert attention. A child who is deprived of these is indeed being discriminated against. Whether such goals can best be achieved through mainstreaming or special classes or some combination of the two should be decided on the basis of well-conducted evaluations of the two settings. The clinician does little service to the retarded child, or to society, by echoing slogans or failing to call attention to evidence which runs counter to current opinion.

Psychotherapy

Until recently, MR children were deemed unsuited for psychotherapy because of their limited comprehension and verbal ability, poor impulse control, and passivity in problem-solving situations (LaVietes, 1978). Typically, "environmental manipulation" was recommended in terms of consulting with parents and teachers and exploring resources in the community. While such counseling still plays a prominent role in remediation, a number of therapeutic techniques have been adapted to the special needs of the MR child. Nonverbal techniques such as play and art therapy can serve the dual function of tension release and self-expression. Verbal techniques can be used for reassurance, support, discussion, and advice, as well as for clarifying and interpreting feelings. Group therapies have become the most popular variant of psychotherapy; some take the form of discussions, others revolve around activities such as play, handicrafts, movies, or trips, while still others focus on the reflection and interpretation of feelings. Parent groups offer the opportunity for discussion in a setting of shared problems and mutual concern.

By far the most successful and widely used therapeutic technique is behavior modification, employing the operant principles of changing undesirable behaviors by altering the specific consequences which reinforce them and by reinforcing new, more socially acceptable responses. This technique has been used to encourage a wide array of behaviors: self-help behaviors (toileting, feeding, dressing), work-oriented behaviors (productivity, task completion), social behaviors (cooperation, group activities), nonacademic classroom behaviors (attending, taking turns, talking at appropriate times), academic learning (arithmetic, sight vocabulary), attention getting, aggressive, and self-injurious behaviors. An important fringe benefit is that parents can actively participate in the therapeutic program in the home setting. Equally important, behavior modification, more than any other single therapeutic technique, has been responsible for changing the prevailing attitude of helplessness among professional and nonprofessional caretakers. While data on relative effectiveness of various psychotherapies are meager, behavior modification has provided the clearest evidence that the behavior of MR children can be changed.

Prevention

The diversity of preventive programs reflects the diverse etiologies of MR itself. A number are medically oriented—such as genetic counseling, therapeutic abortions, elimination of defect-producing illnesses, compulsory tests for phenylketonuria—and as such lie beyond the province of this discussion. More relevant are the compensatory educational programs, especially those involving preschool children. Project Head Start is perhaps the best known, but there are also specialized programs for stimulating premature and blind infants (Robinson and Robinson, 1976). Some programs concentrate on enhancing specific skills such as speaking or reading; others try to increase readiness for formal schooling, while still others are concerned with the child's social and emotional development. Prevention in general will be examined in more detail in chapter 14. At this point, however, one of the more ambitious and successful programs—the so-called Milwaukee Project—will be presented (Heber, 1978).

Since a mother's IQ score is one of the best predictors of her child's IQ, forty mentally retarded mothers (with IQ scores less than 75) and their infants were assigned either to an experimental or a control group. The program for the experimental mothers emphasized educational and vocational rehabilitation along with home and child-care training. The infants received an intense, personalized program in an infant center every day from nine in the morning until four in the afternoon, five days a week on a year-round basis for a period of six years. Initially attention was given to facilitating perceptual and motor skills, providing opportunities for exploring the environment, stimulating cognitive and language development, and meeting social-emotional needs by providing a consistent, one-to-one relation with a teacher. In the preschool period, the emphasis shifted to language-cognition which was gradually broken down into the three traditional academic areas of reading, language, and math/problem solving. By this time, ten to twelve children were grouped together with three teachers in a modified open-classroom setting consisting of three learning and three free-choice areas. The latter offered opportunities for science, art, music, and gross-motor activities. The program is best characterized as having a cognitive-language orientation along with individualized instruction. It also emphasized the social and emotional development of the children since their motivation—their desire to use their skills—was regarded as essential to their achievement.

While mother and child were evaluated throughout the six-year period, the real test of the program's success was whether the gains would be sustained three years after the children had entered the public school system. By 6 years of age, the mean IQ of the experimental group was 120.7 compared with the control group's mean IQ of 87.2. In the three-year follow-up, the experimental group's mean IQ had dropped, although the children continued to perform in the normal range; the control group performed at the borderline mental defective level. At 8 years of age, for example, one-third of the control group tested below an IQ of 75, the traditional score for placement in special classes for the mentally retarded, while the lowest IQ in the experimental group belonged to two children who scored 88.

The project was most successful in preparing the mothers for employment, since their record of job stability, work performance, and income was distinctly superior to that of the control mothers. Certain behaviors and attitudes in dealing with their children also changed; for example, they showed a greater tendency than the control mothers to engage in verbally informative behaviors and to encourage reciprocal communication.

In spite of such gains, significant conflicts remained between mother and child as well as between mother, the school, and the community. Children who were fed at the intervention center now went hungry to school while mothers responded to minor school adjustment problems with beatings or threats to send the child away. Teachers blamed the mothers for failing to answer notes which were sent home, not realizing that the mother was unable to read or did not understand the request, while mothers too readily assumed a passive attitude of "the school knows best" and did not protest an unfair decision. As for the children, the experimental group showed the same number of social or behavioral difficulties in school as did the controls, although they were more verbal in their confrontations with teachers and classmates. Heber (1978) speculates that "parent-school incompatibilities and disrupted family living environments will continue to erode the high hopes engendered by our experimental childrens' performance at the end of our intervention effort. Nevertheless, the performance of our experimental children three years into follow-up is such that it is difficult to conceive of their ever dropping to the performance standards of the control group" (p. 61).

We can learn much from the Milwaukee Project. The first lesson is that children of retarded mothers are not fated to become retarded themselves. Prevention can break the vicious cycle. But we also learn that the effort required is an heroic one. In the early years of Head Start and other intervention programs there was an optimistic attitude that a summer or a year of a specialized program would "inoculate" the child against future intellectual decline and academic failure. When it was discovered that initial gains tended to wash out in the first three years of school, disillusionment set in. Looking back, we now can see how naive it was to assume that preschoolers would be sufficiently autonomous to maintain an interest in learning in the face of discouraging factors both at home and in the schools. (It would be difficult to imagine most adults being so self-motivated.) Consequently, efforts are being made to involve a number of people in the preventive program. Mothers in poverty settings, for example, are taught how to stimulate and relate to their children and may, in turn, become teachers of other similarly impoverished mothers.

Yet, the mothers themselves may be burdened by multiple problems which need attention—not only problems of low income but possibly problems involving nutrition and health care, marital and familial relations, limited education and vocational skills. Thus, the people charged with implementing preventive programs may find themselves tangled in the web of a total living environment and having to decide, arbitrarily, where to draw the line in terms of problems attended to and ones neglected. However, it is just this awareness of the importance of the child's total environment which was responsible for the shift from an individually oriented to a community mental health approach. The Milwaukee Project has afforded us our first glimpse of the significance as well as the magnitude of its undertaking. (For a detailed presentation and evaluation of preventive programs, see Chilman, 1973, and Horowitz and Paden, 1973.)

12 ▪ Deviations from Physiological Intactness: Blindness and Brain Damage

Throughout life, but particularly during childhood, the body is the stage on which some of the most significant developmental dramas are enacted. We have already explored the importance of eating and elimination in the normal and psychopathological development of children who are physically healthy. If children are chronically ill, we might rightly suspect that they must contend with special stresses and problems. They may be able to take such stresses in stride and even be stronger because of them. But they may also be taxed beyond their ability to cope successfully. For example, there is evidence that among 10- to 12-year-old children with chronic handicapping physical conditions, such as asthma, diabetes, heart disease, polio, and orthopedic deformities, twice as many (11.5 percent) have psychopathological disturbances compared to children in the general population (Rutter, 1977).

By the same token, we might expect children with severe visual, hearing, and speech disabilities to be at risk for developing psychological disturbances, not only because many developmental tasks are now more difficult to master but also because of the reactions of rejection, derision, or overprotection they elicit from others. Note again that physical disabilities are not being equated with psychopathology. Given the proper help and care, blind children, for example, can be as well adjusted as sighted children. The point is that such special help and care may not be available, thereby increasing the likelihood of deviant development.

Rather than discussing the entire field of physiological deviations, we shall concentrate on blindness and brain damage. The former has been chosen because of a study which raises precisely the question we have been asking: What is the effect of a given deviation from normality—in this case, blindness from birth—on development? Organic brain damage is of interest because, of all physiological deviations, it is most clearly and strongly associated with psychopathological development. (For a discussion of the effects of chronic illness and physical disabilities, see Suran and Rizzo, 1979.)

BLINDNESS: A MODEL STUDY

Fraiberg (1977) conducted a longitudinal study of ten blind infants who were otherwise physiologically and intellectually intact. While concentrating on "pure" cases, she explicitly recognized that in many instances blindness may be accompanied by other neurological defects and/or mental retardation, so her results cannot uncritically be generalized to all blind infants. Although Fraiberg studied a number of early developments, we shall consider only the development of attachment, initiative, and the representation of the self in language and play.

Attachment

At 18 months, nine of the ten infants were attached.

> THEY SET OUT ON EXCURSIONS AROUND the house, returned to touch base with mother, set out again for another trip, pausing sometimes to say "mama" or "hi," waiting for the reassuring voice to come back. They were wary of strangers, took a dim view of the research team, but put up gamely with our presence and our occasional testing nonsense. Without needing invitation or prompting they gave embraces to mother and father, or lovingly fingered their faces, and almost never favored our observers with such treatment. The absence of the mother for a few minutes or a few hours produced distress and turning away from the ministrations of substitute care-givers. (p. 114)

Yet the route leading to attachment was quite different from that taken by the sighted child and it is fascinating to follow Fraiberg's reconstruction of the deviant process.

THE SOCIAL SMILE. In sighted children, the human face and subsequently the face of caretakers become the primary (although not exclusive) elicitors of the smiling response by 6 months of age. The blind child smiles frequently at the voice of the mother and other familiar persons, but only tickling regularly elicits the smile. Lacking the visual stimulus of the human face, the social smile continues to be irregular and never comes to complete fruition.

PREFERENTIAL RESPONSIVENESS. Lacking vision, the mother-infant bond must take place within what Fraiberg calls the "tactile-auditory-kinesthetic dialogue," with the hands and ears serving the exploratory function of eyes. Observation of the infant's hands gives the more detailed picture of the development of discrimination of the mother. In earliest infancy, there are only chance encounters, which become tactile-seeking and, by 5 months, intentional exploration. "The blind child's hands send and receive messages in an archaic language: 'Are you there? . . . I am here' " (p. 120). Between 5 and 8 months the baby's hands begin extensive exploration of the face of the mother, father, and other familiar persons, while only briefly scanning the faces of less familiar adults. This discrimination and recognition of familiar adults corresponds, in time, to the same development in sighted children. Fraiberg speculates that the process might be due to maturation of the brain in combination with the growing affectional tie to caretakers.

STRANGER ANXIETY. In nine of the ten blind children, stranger anxiety emerges during the same period as it does with sighted children—between seven and fifteen months of age. The babies react to attempts to hold them with struggling, straining away, and crying. A stranger's voice alone elicits "quieting" or a cessation of activity or vocalization without signs of distress. "Quieting" has also been observed in sighted children, but whether or not it is an aspect of stranger anxiety is a matter of debate.

SEPARATION ANXIETY. Blind infants lag significantly behind their sighted counterparts in grasping the independent existence of the mother, one of the essential preludes to separation anxiety. Since Fraiberg closely follows Piaget's theory of the development of the *object concept* or the independent existence of objects and people, it would be helpful to review certain relevant features of his theory. (For a detailed account of the development of the object concept, see Flavell, 1977.)

Piaget, along with many other developmental psychologists, assumes that during the first weeks of life infants do not differentiate themselves—particularly their visual and motor activities—from the external world. Since there is no distinction between "me" and "not-me," objects and people have no existence independent of the infants' actions and perceptions of them; if a rattle falls from their hand or a bauble is removed from sight, there is no evidence that they realize that the object is still there in the external world. Out of sight is not only out of mind, it is out of existence. In the second quarter of the first year, however, one can observe a brief searching for a vanished object; if a spoon falls off a high chair tray, infants will look over the side instead of staring blankly at the point from which it vanished. It is the next development—Stage 4—during the last quarter of the first year, that is most relevant to our discussion. For the first time, infants grasp the idea of the independent existence of objects; for example, hide a toy behind a screen and they will retrieve it. Objects and people are "out there," even when not perceived. However, infants still have not totally divested the external world of subjective elements. If an infant retrieves an object from behind screen A and it is then hidden behind screen B in full sight of the infant, the infant will continue looking for the object behind screen A, where it was originally found, while showing no interest in screen B! The idea that an object's existence depends upon the infant's actions lingers on. It will take another year before infants thoroughly understand the fact that the objective world exists completely independent of their perceptions of or actions upon it. At this point, a toddler can see a ball roll under one side of the couch, walk over and wait for it to appear from the other side. The ball now has "a life of its own," as do all the things and people in the environment.

Around 8 months, the sighted child has advanced to Stage 4 in regard to the mother. Vision itself facilitates this achievement by providing a picture identity of the mother and by uniting her voice and touch with that picture. Blind infants are faced with the task of inferring that the mother's voice they hear out of their reach belongs to the same constellation of auditory-tactile-kinesthetic experiences of the mother when she is in direct contact with them. Thus, they must integrate the "proximal mother" of tactile contact with the "distal mother" of her voice alone. At 8 months there is no evidence that the infants Fraiberg studied could do so; while they smile or vocalize or become excited at the sound of the mother's voice, their hands do not reach out to touch or embrace her. In a like manner, a favorite sound toy would not be reached for when only the sound is made within easy range of the infants' hands.

Between 10 and 16 months blind babies demonstrate proximity-seeking behaviors toward the mother's voice. "Mother" is no longer a voice but a voice with the same substantial and differentiated features as characterize her during direct contact. Thus, she has become an object in space with an independent existence. Fraiberg rightly notes that this development is a cognitive achievement—an inference that "voices alone" must partake of identifying tactual qualities even when such qualities are not perceived. Blind infants have taken a giant step toward conquering their own private outer space.

By the same token, the link to separation anxiety has been established, for separation anxiety requires that the infant grasp the notion of separateness (Stage 4). Again we can appreciate the advantage of sight in facilitating the idea of "mother present" and "mother absent." Vision is continuous and the sighted infant can track the mother in her comings and goings. Sound is discontinuous so that "no mother's voice" does not necessarily mean "mother absent." The special problems of sightlessness delays the development of separation anxiety until the end of the first year instead of the third quarter of that year, as is the case with sighted infants.

Even at the end of the first year, however, the blind infant is only at Stage 4 (as is the sighted infant when separation anxiety appears) and still has not totally divested the external world of subjective elements. To illustrate with one of Fraiberg's observations: Karen is playing with her mother while they are sitting in a chair but then leaves to explore another part of the room. When she hears her mother get up and go out of the room she becomes very distressed, crawls back to the now-vacant chair and clings to it. Like the child who continues to believe a toy is still behind screen A because this is where he or she last acted upon it, Karen returns to the scene of her last interaction with her mother under the faulty assumption that the mother still must be there.

As with the sighted child, separation anxiety diminishes markedly when the infant has both the cognitive ability and motor skills to follow the mother's voice and footsteps. However, it is only toward the end of the second year that the blind toddler fully grasps the idea that the mother has a totally independent existence and therefore might be in any part of the house at any given point in time. The development of speech is a boon in regard to keeping in touch at a distance; instead of having to walk from room to room, the simple word "Mama" and a simple reply suffices.

THE DEVELOPMENTAL MODEL. Since blind children ultimately establish a normal attachment, should they be considered in our discussion of deviant development just because they traveled a deviant route? One could argue the point either way. Yet blindness must surely be considered a vulnerability which significantly increases the likelihood that the normal process will be disrupted. It is noteworthy that Fraiberg's research was conducted in conjunction with an intervention program, in which parents were given comfort, support, and hope to counteract their initial hopelessness and grief, were encouraged to maximize tactile intimacy and vocal contact, were taught to read the alien sign vocabulary of body language, were prepared for delays and deviations as well as given an explanation for them. It was within this context of emotional support, intellectual understanding, and effective coping techniques that attachment eventually developed. Had the environment been less sensitive and responsive, attachment might well have been delayed even further or possibly distorted by insecurity. Indirect evidence for this speculation comes from Fraiberg's observation that, even among these babies, prolonged separation for a matter of hours or days elicited a terror born of helplessness rarely observed among normally developing sighted infants.

Initiative

Fraiberg's study can further instruct us concerning the development of initiative. The delay in developing the object concept discussed above also affects gross-motor development—not the mechanisms for crawling and walking, which have a high maturational loading, but the utilization of these mechanisms. Toddlers do not do what they are capable of doing in regard to locomotion. And why is this? Because, before Stage 4 is achieved, there are no environmental lures, nothing to locomote *to*. Blind babies, for example, have been observed rocking back and forth on all fours. They are all ready to go but have no place to go. Until the baby can reach for a sound cue only, thereby demonstrating the utilization of this cue to reconstruct a tangible object or person, there is no incentive to creep or cruise or walk.

Fraiberg's study adds a specific cognitive dimension to our understanding of the early development of initiative which has escaped us until now. Toddlers, for example, are "all over the place and into everything" not only because of their enterprising spirit but also because their cognitive development has resulted in a differentiation of "me" from "not-me," while object permanence confronts them with an infinitely alluring environment. It also helps us understand that crawling and walking, typically regarded as maturational developments, contain an important cognitive component which guarantees that infants and toddlers will do what they are motorically capable of doing. Thus, Fraiberg's research nicely illustrates the way in which the study of normal and deviant development can complement and mutually enhance one another.

Self-Representation

Fraiberg observed a peculiar lag in an otherwise bright, verbal 3-year-old named Kathy: she would not refer to herself as "I," nor would she engage in pretend play with a doll. We have run across the former difficulty in discussing autism. The problem with first person pronouns is that they shift relative to the speaker: I am "I" to me but "you" to you; "my" eyes to me are "your" eyes from your perspective. Thus, the correct usage requires preschoolers to "get out of their skin," to see themselves as others see them, and to see others as they see themselves. Only then can they realize that each person has an "I" that relegates everyone else's status to "you." This is a cognitive achievement, not a matter of learning grammatical rules. Kathy, whose language development was otherwise quite good, could correctly point to facial features or comply with the request to "Show me Mommy's nose" but could not respond to the mother's request, "Where is my nose?" She did not refer to herself as "me" but used "her" or "Kathy"; for example, she said, "Give it to her" when she meant, "Give it to me."

Nor could she use a doll to play out sequences of pretend activities. When told to give a doll a bath, she herself got into the tub of water; suggestions to wash the dolly's hair met with no response. Yet, Kathy could pretend; in the tub she mimicked her mother giving her a bath and, later, curled up in a sink (which she recognized as such) and pretended to be going to bed. As with personal pronouns she could not "get out of her own skin" and project herself into the person of a doll.

We are reminded of the sociopaths who lacked an "observing ego" and were so carried away by the impulse of the moment that they could not reflect upon and monitor their own behavior. Kathy had a more fundamental problem, however, in that she could not get out of her own body and view her body-self objectively. Fraiberg speculates that blindness presents a tremendous obstacle to developing an objective view of one's body. As sighted infants look now at one hand, now at another, they begin to develop a picture of their hands; as they look into a mirror again and again, it dawns on them that it is their own reflection. Consequently they can construct a visual picture of their body and know how this body looks from the outside as well as how it feels from the inside. (See Wenar, 1971, for a further discussion of the development of the body image.) They also have a picture of themselves to place among their visual images of people around them. Such a representation greatly facilitates the ability to observe the body-self and to view it from the perspective of others.

Blind infants have only poor substitutes for visual pictures. Exploring their body surfaces with their hands results in crude and fragmentary information, while they might never have a chance to hear their own voice unless it happens to be recorded and played back. Fraiberg frankly admits that she is unable to reconstruct the process by which blind toddlers arrive at an objective view of their body. But Kathy did construct such a view. It took her two years and eight months longer than the sighted child with whom she was compared, but by 58 months of age she had mastered the use of personal pronouns, she could project her self into her doll in the form of imaginary play, and she had even invented an imaginary companion, Zeen, whom she invited to tea and later blamed for spilling macaroni all over the kitchen floor after she herself was caught in the act. Other blind children are not so fortunate, and a very large number of blind school-age children do not have "I" or any self-reference pronouns in their vocabulary.

Fraiberg's speculations about the development of self-representation are based on work involving only two children and are therefore tentative. Nonetheless, they are provocative because they suggest a relation between self-representation, pronoun use, and play that might have otherwise escaped us. Such speculations illuminate not only the development of the blind toddler and preschooler but of the sighted child as well.

Taken as a whole, Fraiberg's research is one of the best illustrations of the way in which the study of normal and deviant development can enhance one another. We can only wish that the fields of mental retardation and organic brain pathology were replete with similar investigations. Instead, all too often we are forced to contend with that timeless, changeless, mythical creature, "the child."

Fraiberg's research, the last of the examples of the *naturalistic approach* implemented by the clinical eye, has a number of distinctive features. Unlike Kanner and Redl, Fraiberg did not rely solely on her own clinical and research skills but enlisted the aid of many of the most prominent investigators of infant development. In her "laboratory without walls" Piaget and his student Décarie served as consultants for the development of the object concept, Spitz and Ainsworth for attachment, Lennenberg for linguistic development, while Escalone and Wolff acted in a general advisory capacity.

Fraiberg's data were also more objective than Kanner's and Redl's. She made considerable use of videotapes, which not only provided a permanent record of ongoing behavior that could be scrutinized by any investigator, but which could also be slowed down to reveal behavioral subtleties that might escape even the most sensitive member of the research team. Moreover, in the narrative descriptions of ongoing behavior, she made sure that each observer systematically recorded information on specific developmental and interactional categories. This insured that the same data would be available on all infants so that the infants could be compared with one another as well as with a sighted population. There were even standardized situations to test particular developments; for example, after the children were allowed to play with sound and soundless toys, the toys were gently removed in order to observe how the infant learned that the toy still existed even when not handled.

Yet, these objective procedures were primarily aids for the investigators, who had the ultimate responsibility for teasing out meaningful developmental patterns. It was Fraiberg and her colleagues who organized the otherwise overwhelmingly complex behavioral data into categories relevant to infant development: attachment, locomotion, language, manual exploration, self- and object-differentiation. And it was Fraiberg and her colleagues who raised the questions which became central to the project. Why did some blind infants become autistic-like in their behavior, while others made an adequate adaptation? Why were the autistic-like infants unable to locomote when other aspects of motor development such as rolling over and sitting without support appeared on schedule? How were the infant's signals read or not read by the mother, and what cues could the infant utilize to develop a concept of mother? Finally, Fraiberg and her colleagues were responsible for generating, by some mysterious process, the explanation which could best account for the data.

In regard to this last point, Fraiberg makes an interesting comment. When her proposed study was being evaluated for possible funding, she was criticized as "having too many chiefs and not enough Indians." Yet, she strongly defended her reliance on experts when exploring an area which had been almost totally neglected. It was not only that experts are more knowledgeable than novices, but they have another quality as well—they do not have to make the data fit preconceived ideas. Spitz and Piaget, for example, were particularly challenged by puzzling infant behavior which forced them to revise or expand their current thinking. It is this pleasure in puzzles and delight in novelty which Fraiberg believed could be found more in experienced than in inexperienced investigators. In her concern for openness to new ideas, she was also following Darwin's dictum that in naturalistic research one should pay special attention to observations which do not conform to one's current hypotheses or explanations.

By combining the excitement of discovery with the rigor of disciplined thinking and data collection, Fraiberg has produced a research program of rare quality and one which has significantly advanced our understanding of psychopathological development.

BRAIN DAMAGE

A visitor to a remote Bohemian town was impressed by the fact that, at the stroke of five every evening, the artillery sergeant lowered the flag and ordered his squad to fire a cannon. His curiosity impelled him to inquire as to how the sergeant knew when it was precisely five o'clock. The sergeant informed him that this particular town boasted of one of the best clockmakers in all of Europe, so each morning when he passed the clockmaker's shop he reset his watch. In this manner he was sure the cannon was fired exactly on time. Still not satisfied, the visitor went to the clockmaker and inquired as to how his clocks could be so precise in a town with almost no communication with the outside world. "I have a special advantage," the clockmaker replied. "There is a most remarkable artillery sergeant living here. Every evening at precisely five o'clock the garrison gun goes off, so I reset all my clocks when I hear its sound." (For further details of this charming anecdote, as well as a critique of the concept of brain damage, see Birch, 1964, pp. 3–12.)

The Problem

In order to determine whether dysfunctions of the brain are related to deviant behavior, it is essential to have independent and reliable assessments of both brain and behavior. This essential condition is rarely met. As in the anecdote of the sergeant and the clockmaker, psychologists, impressed by the precision of certain diagnostic procedures in medical science, assume that evidence of a damaged or malfunctioning brain can be clearly established, while physicians, impressed by the reliability of certain psychological tests, assume that the behavioral disturbances are objectively documented. Neither is correct. The resulting confusion is predictable.

In order to place the literature on brain damage in proper perspective it will be necessary first to understand some of the complex problems inherent in trying to build a bridge between brain and behavior. Next, some of the literature on manifest brain dysfunctions will be examined before turning to the more controversial concepts of minimal brain damage and hyperactivity.

THE PROBLEM OF DEFINITION. "Brain damage," like "mental retardation," can be defined in a number of different ways. A strictly neurological definition concerns itself with the nature, site, and size of damage to the brain. A behavioral definition is concerned with the functions impaired by the damage: motor and communication disorders, sensory and perceptual deficits, intellectual impairment, convulsive disorders, and so on. Brain damage can also be conceptualized in terms of a wide array of etiological factors, such as traumatic injury, anoxia, encephalitis, epilepsy, cerebral palsy, and lead poisoning, to name a few. Each approach is valid, but the complex interrelations among them have yet to be worked out. Therefore, it is important for us to realize at the outset that "the brain-damaged child" is an abstraction which glosses over crucial distinctions among children. The diagnosis "brain damage" is meaningless without reference to etiology and, more important, to the specific psychological functions which have been impaired and the nature of the impairment itself.

Moreover, there is a *quantitative versus qualitative* controversy among experts. Those championing the former claim that behavioral deviations are a function of the sheer amount of brain damage. At one extreme of the quantitative continuum lies massive damage which can result in death; at the other extreme lies minimal brain dysfunction and its presumed psychological correlates, including hyperactivity. The qualitative viewpoint, by contrast, argues that in light of the well-known localization of brain functions, the effects of damage depend on the site and size of the damage as well as the age at which it occurs. The controversy is far from settled. (For a more detailed account of the points presented in this and subsequent sections, see Werry, 1979.)

THE PROBLEM WITH ASSESSMENT. Because of the delicacy, inaccessibility, and complexity of the brain, most assessments are indirect and inferential. In addition, there are "silent" sections of the brain which have no externally measurable functions. Consequently, diagnostic techniques may fail to detect substantial brain damage, and conversely, positive diagnostic signs can occur in the absence of brain damage.

While *autopsy* is the surest technique for establishing brain damage, it is not helpful in diagnosing a living child. Diagnosis of brain damage frequently relies on the child's *history*, which may be highly unreliable. *Neurological examinations* can detect major degrees of brain damage with a high degree of accuracy when the lesion involves nonsilent areas of the brain; however, neurological findings may be normal in children with head injuries, encephalitis, and epilepsy. The examination can also be ambiguous and rely on the so-called *equivocal* or *soft* neurological signs, whose reliability and significance have been seriously questioned. The *electroencephalogram* (EEG), like the neurological examination, may reveal brain damage but may also fall in that uncertain area between normality and established pathology. Finally, *psychological tests* may provide some evidence suggestive of brain damage, but they are neither sufficiently reliable nor valid to be used as the sole criterion for diagnosis.

One might hope that the various assessment techniques described above might complement one another, so that ambiguity in one would be clarified by certainty in another. While multiple assessment is desirable and can pay off in terms of increased certainty of diagnosis, such an outcome is by no means guaranteed. All too often a battery of tests contains little more than redundant ambiguities. While the judgment that "diagnosis of brain damage or dysfunction in the majority of children with behavior disorders is no more than an enlightened guess" (Werry, 1979, p. 98) may be too severe, it stands as a healthy corrective to the idea that "brain damage" is a firmly established diagnosis.

THE PROBLEM WITH TIMING. The Kennard principle states that it is better to have your brain lesion early—if you can arrange it. Indeed, there is evidence of greater "sparing" of psychological functions if the damage occurs early in development rather than late. Recently, however, the principle has been challenged as being overly simple (Schneider, 1979). An unusually thorough study of children who had localized head injuries found no relation between age and the presence or absence of psychopathology. The age range was from the preschool period through adolescence (Shaffer, Chadwick, and Rutter, 1975).

Whether early lesions are more or less disruptive of subsequent behavior than similar lesions sustained at maturity depends on a number of factors. (Our discussion follows Teuber, 1975.) Most obviously, the effects on behavior depend on the site and size of the lesion, some parts of the brain showing resilience after early lesion, other parts showing less or none at all. Next, the effects of lesions depend on the nature of the particular psychological function being studied. Finally, time itself is the most important variable, since some deficits take time to recede after early lesions, whereas others take time to appear. Thus, no conclusions can be drawn from assessments made at only one point in time.

Teuber speculates that different regions of the brain have different "commitments" to specialized functioning early in development and therefore have different degrees of ability to take over the function of a damaged region. Moreover, in taking over such a function, a price may be paid: the "adopted" function may not be quite as highly developed as it would have been in the original region, while functions appropriate to the undamaged region may suffer. To illustrate, Teuber cites a study of fifty children who had brain damage in infancy either to the right or to the left cerebral hemisphere. The children were examined between 8 and 18 years of age, their normal siblings serving as controls. Language development, which is usually the province of the left hemisphere, can "escape" and be assumed by a potential language zone in the right hemisphere; that is, the right hemisphere is not totally "committed" to its specialties and can assume another function. However, a price is paid, in that the usual functions of the right hemisphere—dealing with visuospatial problems such as copying a design with blocks or fitting jigsaw-type pieces together—suffer. Moreover, there is suggestive evidence that the "right-hemisphere" language is subtly impaired in terms of higher functions such as comprehension. By contrast, the left hemisphere cannot as readily assume the visuospatial functions of a damaged right hemisphere because it is early "committed" to language and language-related activities.

This complex pattern of commitment or adaptability is, in turn, affected by the context of time. Certain right-hemisphere functions are severely affected whether the damage occurs early or late, since the left hemisphere cannot take them over; with certain language functions, however, later damage to the left hemisphere is more deleterious, since the right hemisphere becomes progressively inefficient in assuming the language function.

Incidentally, we might draw a parallel between the Kennard principle and the concept of a critical period in development. In chapter 1 we noted that while there was some supportive evidence, there was also sufficient contradictory data to question the concept as a general guide to the relation between time and development. A single formula seems far too simple to capture the complexity of normal and psychopathological development.

THE PROBLEM OF CAUSALITY. Correlation does not prove causation, as we all know. Yet, when a study shows a correlation between psychopathological behavior and brain damage, we tend to assume that the latter is the cause. The assumption is naive and may be misleading. Brain damage occurs within the same intrapersonal and interpersonal contexts as all the psychopathologies discussed so far. Such context factors may significantly affect the child's reaction to brain damage or in certain instances be more potent in determining future behavior than brain damage itself.

Let us take two examples. Suppose we find a correlation between brain damage and the now-familiar pattern of acting out in school, evidenced by inattention, disobedience, truanting, and underachievement. In all probability a sizable number of the children will also come from homes characterized by parental disharmony, emotionally disturbed or irresponsible parents, and a large number of siblings—conditions which increase the likelihood of acting-out behavior in organically intact children. Thus, the onus would be on the organicist to show that the presence of brain damage significantly affected our understanding of etiology, our prognosis, and our therapeutic interventions. Next, let us return to the study of children with head injuries (Shaffer et al., 1975). The authors reconstruct the etiology of deviant behavior in terms of an interaction between organic and psychological factors. Children from unhappy or uncaring homes are especially likely to be accident-prone, so that the brain injury itself may have been psychologically determined. Once it occurs, the injury may then increase the child's vulnerability to the noxious influences in the environment, while having a further negative effect on family cohesiveness and happiness. In such a complex interweaving of factors, it might be practically impossible to isolate the contribution of brain injury to the child's disturbance; however, to assume that the organic brain pathology was solely responsible for the child's emotional disturbance would be naive. In reality, few causal links between brain damage and psychopathological behavior have been clearly established.

If we have lingered over the problems involved in building a bridge from brain to behavior, it is because of the tendency to assume that the bridge is solidly in place. When minimal brain damage and hyperactivity are discussed, it will be evident that the assumption has particularly unfortunate consequences both for diagnosis and for treatment. Before turning to these two controversial concepts, however, let us survey the development of children who are known to be brain-damaged.

The Developmental Outlook

As we have just learned, "brain damage" covers such a variety of pathological conditions that generalizations are chancy. However, three generalizations do seem to be warranted. First, clearly established brain damage increases the risk of subsequent psychopathology. However, there is no one-to-one relation between brain damage on the one hand and specific kinds of psychopathological behavior on the other; for example, there is no such thing as an "epileptic personality." Finally, intrapersonal and interpersonal factors significantly affect both the severity of the psychopathological behavior and its prognosis. These points can be illustrated by two of the better studies of brain-damaged children, one cross-sectional, the other longitudinal.

In an unusually comprehensive research project (Rutter, 1977), 99 children between 5 and 14 years of age with cerebral palsy, epilepsy, or some other clearly established brain disorder were compared with 189 children from the general population of 10- and 11-year-olds and 139 10- to 12-year-olds with disorders not involving the brain, such as asthma, diabetes, and heart disease. This last group, called Other Physical Handicaps, was to control for the effects of physical illness per se on personality. While the rate of psychological disturbance in the Other Physical Handicaps group was 11.5 percent (which was almost twice that of the normal population), the rate of disturbance in the brain-damaged group was 34.3 percent of the population. There was also suggestive evidence that both the severity and nature of the neurological condition influenced the risk of psychopathology; for example, children with extensive damage were more at risk than children with moderate damage, and children with psychomotor seizures were more at risk than those with other kinds of epilepsy.

Most of the brain-damaged children showed the same mixture of emotional and conduct disorders as was found in children without brain damage. For example, restlessness, a symptom often thought to be associated with brain damage, was somewhat more common in the Brain-Damaged group, but the difference was slight and of little practical importance. "It may be concluded that the behavioral stereotype of the brain-damaged children must be firmly rejected" (p. 11). Context factors played an important role in determining the adjustment of the brain-damaged child. Low socioeconomic status, broken homes, and neurotic disturbances in the mother were more common environmental influences that greatly increased the risk of psychopathological behavior.

Our second study concerns a longitudinal evaluation of anoxic infants when they were 3 and 7 years of age (Corah, Anthony, Painter, Stern, and Thurston, 1965; Graham, Ernhart, Thurston, and Craft, 1962). In the first phase, 116 anoxic and 159 normal 3-year-olds were assessed in terms of their cognitive and personality development. Anoxic children did significantly poorer than the controls on all tests of cognitive functioning, including the Stanford-Binet, a vocabulary test, and a concept test. There was significantly greater impairment in conceptual ability than in vocabulary skill, while perceptual-motor functioning (such as is needed to copy simple designs correctly) was unimpaired. While the anoxic group was evaluated less favorably than the control group in terms of overall personality development, the only specific variable differentiating the groups was distractability. Characteristics such as impulsivity, demandingness, infantilism, negativism, and fearfulness, while somewhat more prominent in the anoxic group, were not statistically significant. In general, the differences in personality were not as striking as those in cognitive development.

By 7 years of age, when 134 normal and 101 anoxic infants were located, the pattern was reversed. The overall difference in intelligence was no longer significant, although the anoxics evidenced a significant deficit in vocabulary (which the authors interpreted as a continuation of the children's difficulty with conceptual and abstract thinking) and perceptual-motor ability. However, the most striking differences between groups was in the area of social competence. The most discriminating technique was the Vineland Social Maturity Scale, which indicated that the anoxics were more dependent than the controls. Evaluations by psychologists, psychiatrists, and parents indicated that anoxic children were more impulsive and distractible (recall they were also more distractible as 3-year-olds), had difficulty communicating their ideas in spite of adequate verbal ability, were less socially sensitive, and had less emotional control. In their communication, for example, they would use words and gestures excessively and inappropriately, while in their social interaction they were obtuse to the demands of others and ignored the effects of their behavior on others. Interestingly, there were no significant differences between groups in terms of teachers' ratings, indicating that the children's behavior in school was different from their behavior at home and with professionals.

In light of our concern with prognosis it is worth noting that there was no predictability from infant behavior to behavior at 7 years of age. The finding is not surprising because, except in cases of extreme damage, predictions from infancy are notoriously inexact. While there were a number of significant correlations between behaviors at 3 and 7 years of age, the order of the relations was fairly low and subject to error. Thus, some consistency of behavior was uncovered, but it was not striking.

One final point: the differences between

groups, even when significant, were minimal. In some of the discriminating measures, the differences were smaller than sex or SES differences. There was no evidence for an all-or-none effect with the anoxic children having one cluster of personality characteristics not to be found in the control children. On the contrary, there was a great deal of overlap between groups, indicating that for most measures the children's behavior could not be distinguished.

We learn two important lessons from this study. The first is a variation on a theme we have encountered before: behavioral correlates of brain damage are a function of when one evaluates the children, since they are apt to "grow out of" certain deficits (such as a lower IQ score) and "grow into" others (such as a deficit in social competence). The second lesson is that, while anoxia increases the risk for subsequent deviant behavior, a significant number of such infants will be developing normally when they enter school.

Unfortunately, the study does not provide us with those nice insights into the reasons for the changing developmental picture that we found in Fraiberg's study of the blind or Carr's study of Down's syndrome children. Did the distractability and lowered conceptual ability seen at 3 years of age progressively interfere with the preschoolers' ability to become self-sufficient, to control their behavior and speech, to monitor and accommodate to the behavior of others? Did parents become increasingly irritated with or overprotective of their children? Were the children increasingly rejected by peers? All such questions concerning the processes underlying the documented change can only be answered by future research.

However, we do have one clue concerning the conditions under which infants with a variety of organic brain pathologies either "outgrow" or fail to "outgrow" their initial deficits. After reviewing the evidence concerning factors placing the fetus and neonate at risk for poor developmental outcomes, Sameroff and Chandler (1975) conclude that socioeconomic status—or, more specifically, the quality of caretaking associated with SES—plays a major role either in perpetuating or dissipating the effects of reproductive risk in general and anoxia in particular. Infants born into an environment which will pay scant attention to their physical and emotional needs are apt to show intellectual deficits and personality deviations; those who receive proper care are apt to be no different or only minimally different from their healthy counterparts by middle childhood. In general, the caretaking context exercises a more potent influence on development then does anoxia, and the same conditions which facilitate or impede the development of the intact infant similarly affect the brain-damaged one.

MINIMAL BRAIN DYSFUNCTION AND HYPERACTIVITY

Definition

Minimal brain damage or minimal brain dysfunction (MBD) syndrome refers to children of near average or higher intelligence in whom deviations of central nervous system functioning are manifested by various symptoms, the most characteristic being hyperactivity, perceptual-motor impairment, emotional lability, coordination deficits, disorders of attention, memory, thinking, and speech, impulsivity, and specific learning disabilities. (Our discussion will follow H. E. Rie, 1980a.) Since the child may have average or above intelligence and since the signs of disturbed functioning are subtle, he or she may be regarded as merely "lazy" or "nervous." Etiological factors implicated in MBD include genetic influences, temperament, brain damage, perinatal stress, lead poisoning, food additives, and early sensory deprivation, among others, but none of the evidence is definitive.

The definition has an appealing plausibility. It makes sense to postulate that (1) there are degrees of brain dysfunction; (2) minimal CNS dysfunction is difficult to detect; and that (3) such dysfunctions selectively affect specific psychological functions. Furthermore, it seems reasonable to assume that organically caused psychological dysfunctions should be responsive to medication. Undoubtedly there are children in whom this constellation of events occurs. However, whether it occurs frequently is open to serious question and there is concern that it might not occur in the majority of children diagnosed as MBD and treated with drugs. As we shall now see, the evidence supporting the definition of MBD is either flimsy or controversial.

The Assessment of MBD

If clear-cut instances of brain damage are difficult to detect, how much more problematical are instances of presumed MBD, which elude the traditional neurological assessment techniques. Since the majority of MBD children have no evidence of gross, demonstrable neurological impairment, the diagnosis must depend on the so-called soft signs of CNS dysfunction. Rutter (1977) lists three groups of such signs. The first group involves developmental delays in functions, such as speech, motor coordination, or perception. Being developmental in nature, lack of skill in the various functions is normal in young children, and their clinical significance depends on the degree of impairment in relation to the child's mental and chronological age. There is also evidence that these signs tend to disappear with age (Rie, Rie, Stewart, and Rettemnier, 1978). Unfortunately, there is no way to determine whether such signs are indicative of brain damage rather than a maturational delay or intellectual retardation not related to CNS damage. The second group of soft signs involve nystagmus and strabismus, which also may be due to either neurological or nonneurological causes. The third group consists of slight abnormalities that are often minor examples of classical neurological signs, such as slight asymmetries of tone or reflex. The difficulty in detecting these abnormalities adversely affects the reliability of the assessment.

Rutter (1977) concludes that soft signs are an unsatisfactory guide to the presence of brain damage in the individual patient, although they may be of some value in the study of groups. Descriptively, they are useful as reflections of the child's functioning in areas such as speech, coordination, and perception, but they cannot be assumed to be evidence of brain damage, since they may be due to other causes. Only when there are developmental data comparing MBD children with a normal population, on the one hand, and various kinds of organically intact disturbed children, on the other, will we know which soft signs are outgrown at what age and which are specific to MBD children.

Even if the neurological assessment is questionable, there is always a possibility that the *psychological functions* presumed to be adversely affected can be adequately assessed. Unfortunately, the picture continues to be muddled. To begin with, the specific symptoms purported to be indicative of MBD are a mixed lot (H. E. Rie, 1980a). Some, such as "athetoid, tremulous or rigid movements of the hand" seem clearly to be the consequence of organic brain dysfunction. However, such symptoms are not the hallmark of MBD and would identify only a minority of

MBD children. The other symptoms may be either organic or psychogenic in origin, with no means of differentiating one from the other. Hyperactivity, as we shall soon see, is a prime example of an etiologically ambiguous symptom, as are other supposed physical characteristics of MBD children, such as excessive drooling at a young age, enuresis, and uneven, spotty performance on intelligence tests. Thus the ambiguity of soft neurological signs has its counterpart in the ambiguity of specific behavioral indices of MBD.

Nor is there evidence that these specific symptoms cluster together to form a complex of behaviors, since a number of factor-analytic studies fail to confirm the existence of an MBD syndrome (Weiss, 1980). Typically, there is a low degree of interrelatedness among organic measures (such as neurological and EEG findings) and behavioral ones (such as cognitive deficits and emotional lability), while strictly psychological variables such as hyperactivity, distractibility, and emotional lability also fail to show the predicted cohesiveness. Generally speaking, factor-analytic studies produce a number of unrelated dysfunctions.

Note that, unlike the situation with autism, subsequent research is disconfirming rather than confirming the existence of a clinical entity of MBD. Yet the children so diagnosed are undoubtedly disturbed and require a comprehensive assessment, including a careful history, an evaluation of intrapersonal factors (such as specific cognitive functions and personality variables) and of context variables (such as family and school), along with a neurological examination (Weiss, 1980; Wohl, 1980). Instead of the global diagnosis of MBD, however, specific areas of dysfunction should be delineated, such as "poor visual-motor coordination and short attention span when dealing with numerical problems"; and, instead of assuming an organic substratum, the entire gamut of etiological possibilities from neurological to intrapersonal to interpersonal should be explored.

The Developmental Dimension

THE DEVELOPMENTAL MODEL. While the literature on MBD is replete with descriptions of presumably characteristic behaviors, little attempt has been made to place these behaviors in a developmental context. Do they represent psychopathologies of timing, once having been developmentally appropriate but no longer so? Or are they qualitatively different, with little or no place in normal development? Lacking a complete examination of the issue and data specifically analyzed from a developmental perspective, we must rely on hints and suggestions.

In a critical review of the evidence (Rie and Rie, 1980) the term most frequently used to account for various kinds of deviant behavior was "lag." A brief summary of the relevant discussions follows.

The literature on *motor control and coordination* is a prime example of the logic underlying MDB. Since certain classic neurologic disorders, such as cerebral palsy, are clearly associated with gross motor impairment, then minor motor impairment such as clumsiness may well indicate minimum brain dysfunction. However, the evidence by no means bears out the latter relationship (Lucas, 1980). There are wide individual differences in motor skills among children at any given age, as well as wide variations in the rates of motor development. Thus, dyscoordination may well be due to a developmental lag. Some children will catch up in time, others will remain innately clumsy. In either case there is no reason to assume MBD. Naturally, such a conclusion does not rule out the possibility that in given instances clumsiness might have a neurological basis.

MBD may be associated with *cognitive* difficulties involved in taking in, remembering, organizing, and retrieving information. Although the data are not conclusive, such difficulties may be conceptualized in terms of a developmental lag in information processing (E. D. Rie, 1980b). The issue concerning the nature of the *language disorder* is not settled, most of the evidence pointing to delayed development in MBD children, although some evidence suggests deviant language systems (P. S. Weiner, 1980). There is no evidence to support the notion of an "MBD *personality*"; since MBD is turning out to be a term applied to a heterogeneous rather than to a homogeneous group of children, there is no reason to expect shared personality characteristics among them. It has been speculated that certain characteristics of MBD children might represent elaborations of initial temperamental differences, particularly the so-called difficult infant, whose biological functions such as sleeping and feeding are irregular, who avoids or is distressed by new experiences, who is slow to adapt to new situations, and who is given to fussing and crying (Berry and Cook, 1980). The implication is that certain MBD children lag in their personality development, continuing to evidence variations on their initial "difficult" temperament.

THE DEVELOPMENTAL PICTURE. The general forces shaping development are the same with MBD as with intact children—a sensitive, supportive environment ameliorating or suppressing the consequences of CNS impairment, a disordered, barren, or nonsupportive environment perpetuating and even magnifying its consequences. Even in untoward settings, however, a large number of high-risk children will develop normally. It is as if the human organism has been programmed to produce normal developmental outcomes under all but the most adverse circumstances—a phenomenon nicely epitomized as "the self-righting tendencies of Homo sapiens" (Werner, 1980, p. 28).

HYPERACTIVITY

The same logic used with other behavioral manifestations of MBD has been applied to hyperactivity—namely, if established neurological damage such as that caused by encephalitis can result in incessant motor activity or "organic drivenness," then more moderate versions of such drivenness must be due to more moderate damage to the brain—with the same highly questionable results. All the objections raised to MBD apply equally to hyperactivity, or as it is sometimes called, hyperkinesis.

Definition

Hyperactivity as a *symptom* is defined as chronic, sustained, and excessive motor activity. It tends to be most pronounced in motorically restrictive settings, such as the classroom or in "free-field" situations where the child has a choice of activities, while in one-to-one situations it is apt to be reduced or to disappear altogether (Werry, 1979). In addition, the same child might or might not be considered hyperactive, depending on the tolerance of adults for motoric behavior. In order to reduce this subjective element in evaluation, objective measurement techniques have been utilized, such as attaching a device to the child's leg which will record the amount of activity, or recording how frequently the child crosses lines on a gridded playroom floor. When such measures are used, hyperactive children do not differ from normal children in the amount of motor activity; rather, their activity seems to be more purposeless and nonfunctional. The implication is that the basic defect may lie in control of attention rather than in motor control (Kenny, 1980).

The Hyperactive Syndrome

Experts disagree as to the existence of a hyperactive syndrome. Some claim that the syndrome has been clearly established and includes short attention span, impulsiveness, irritability, clumsiness, poor schoolwork, antisocial behavior, along with soft neurological signs, mild EEG abnormalities, mild abnormalities of perceptual and cognitive functions, minor physical anomalies, and perhaps abnormal birth histories (Werry, 1979). Such hyperactive children are clearly differentiated from normal and anxious-withdrawn children. Other authorities (Kenny, 1980) are equally positive in stating that systematic studies have failed to uncover evidence of such a syndrome. The evidence itself must be controversial in order to allow for such disagreements. A conservative conclusion is that "pure" cases of the hyperactive syndrome may be found among clinical populations of children, but that there may also be many instances in which the component behaviors do not cluster as predicted.

However, all experts agree that there is a good deal of overlap between hyperactivity on the one hand and learning disabilities and antisocial behavior on the other (Belmont, 1980; Werry, 1979). Certainly it makes sense to assume that the child with adequate intelligence who is restless and has difficulty concentrating in class may also have a learning problem, although the direction of causation could be argued either way: that hyperactivity leads to the learning problem, or that having a learning problem and being confined to a classroom setting might cause the child to feel pressured, imprisoned, and anxious, which in turn would produce motor restlessness. It also makes sense to assume that poor motor control might also be part of a general pattern of poor self-control, although, again, it is impossible to decide the direction of causality.

Etiology

There is good evidence that hyperactive behavior in no way warrants the assumption of MBD. The neurological examination, the EEG, and the medical history may be negative; most studies of soft signs, for example, show that nearly 40 percent of the hyperkinetic population have no abnormal findings. On the other hand, positive findings may include nonspecific factors such as birth anomalies, which increase the infant's vulnerability to a number of deviant conditions aside from hyperactivity. This is not to deny the possibility that in certain instances hyperactivity may be due to MBD; the point is that organic etiology cannot be assumed.

For the present, hyperactivity, like MBD in general, is best regarded as having numerous roots—some organic, some psychological—operating alone or in concert to produce the deviant behavior. On the organic side, genetic factors and MBD might produce a predisposition to hyperkinetic behavior. Hyperactivity may be due to a developmental lag which the child may outgrow after a period of delay. Hyperactivity may also be part of the agitation that accompanies anxiety or the failure to achieve a stable system of self-control. Special problems with learning in school may be accompanied by hyperactivity whether such problems are due to organic or psychological factors or a combination of both. Finally, the familiar context factors of poor health care and nutrition, substandard housing and schooling, parental disharmony and familial instability may also cause or contribute significantly to the production of hyperactivity.

The Developmental Dimension

Ross and Ross (1976) are among the few authorities to place hyperactivity within a developmental framework. It is important to note at the outset that they present a composite description of the hyperactive child, a compendium of the problems and difficulties encountered from infancy through adulthood. Thus, their picture is an extreme one. In reality, there are individual differences among hyperactive children, as well as differences in degrees of hyperactivity.

INFANCY. Irregularity characterizes the physiological and psychological functioning of hyperactive infants. They may have minor physical anomalies such as widely spaced eyes, no ear lobes, a curved fifth finger, a wide gap between the first and second toe, very fine hair that cannot be combed. Adults and peers may react negatively to their somewhat asymmetrical features, while certain professionals use the label, "funny-looking kid." The infants may be calm one minute and then yell and appear almost apoplectic the next, their cry having a shrill, piercing quality "like a siren" or "like an animal in acute distress" rather than resembling the cry of normal infants. They do not fall asleep quickly or at regular times; there are only brief periods of quiet sleep, the infants being easily awakened with a startled reaction.

Infants usually show normal progress in growth and general development but exhibit advanced motor activity, often climbing out of their crib in the first year of life and sometimes wearing out the mattress with constant rocking. Thus, their activity level is far above average. One important consequence is that the mother has difficulty nursing her squirming, wriggling, twisting child. The infant's personality is often described in negative terms, such as irritable, demanding, unsatisfied, and rarely smiling.

It is easy to understand how the above constellation of behaviors would be detrimental to a harmonious mother–infant interaction. Even an attentive mother might be bewildered by the infant's irregularity, frustrated by the difficulty in feeding, disappointed by the rarity of the social smile, and irritated by the negative personality traits. In turn, the infant is deprived of the security and growth-promoting stimulation which derive from a mutually satisfying interaction. However, Ross and Ross note that causation may run in the opposite direction, a rejecting, punitive or indifferent mother producing a fretful, restless, erratically functioning infant. Many years ago, Province and Lipton (1962) noted that physiologically intact infants reared in a rather bleak institution began to show behavioral signs of "neurological damage." (See also Werry, 1979, p. 117.)

Preschool. Preschoolers, more than infants, are a serious management problem for the parents because they are more mobile, fearless, and do not learn from experience. One boy, for example, climbed out of a second-story window onto a tree, removed all the books from a large bookcase and threw them out of the window, and uprooted a number of new plants in the garden—all in the space of a week's time. The irregular mood and light sleep characteristic of infancy persist. These children have low frustration tolerance and a short attention span, and their temper tantrums are unusually intense. Their physical growth and development continue to be normal, although their running may have an unusual "driven" quality. Their adeptness at getting into and out of locked and closed rooms, emptying drawers, and opening bottles increases their vulnerability to accidents and accidental poisoning.

The hyperactivity of such preschoolers adversely affects the development of self-control and social relations. As they are relatively unresponsive to physical punishment, reasoning, and persuasion, the foundations of self-control cannot be firmly established. In structured social groups they tend to be aggressive and destructive, thereby alienating peers. Moreover, they seem unaware of others' feelings and of the fact that their behavior may be hurting or annoying them. Structured activities in a preschool setting also elicit restless, irrelevant behavior and poor conduct. It is not unusual for them to be shunted from one preschool to another in the hopes of finding one that will tolerate their behavior. In the process, their self-esteem begins to decline, especially if they have a successful sibling, and they may begin to develop techniques for gaining negative attention, such as teasing, name-calling, or showing off.

Fortunately, hyperactive preschoolers get along well in relatively unstructured situations. (We have already noted the influence of situational variables on hyperactivity.) In free play, for example, their activity level and social behavior do not differ from that of normal children. They also can relate well in a one-to-one situation and a strange situation. Thus, a parent bringing a hyperactive child to a guidance clinic may be dismayed to find the child acting normal.

The hyperactive child's delay in language nicely illustrates how diverse variables interact to generate a network of psychopathological behaviors. The weary and exasperated mother may only infrequently engage in social talk with her hyperactive infant, thus setting the stage for a subsequent verbal deficiency. As we have seen, words play a number of important functions. They enhance cognitive development, since symbols for objects can be more readily and versatilely manipulated than objects themselves. Verbalization also serves as a check on action, since manipulating symbols can now take the place of manipulating objects. Since the hyperactive child is slow in making the transition to verbal symbols, touching continues to occupy a dominant place in transactions with the social and physical environment. Such behavior is apt to antagonize peers who dislike being held and grabbed, as well as increasing the likelihood that the child will handle and break valued household objects, thereby antagonizing parents. Thus, the preschooler is not "merely" lagging in language; rather, the deficit reverberates to many other aspects of life.

MIDDLE CHILDHOOD. Hyperactive children are now less of a problem at home, primarily because they spend less time in the house. The Jekyll-and-Hyde quality of their behavior continues, normal periods alternating with periods of disruptive, distractible behavior. They have trouble sitting at the table throughout a meal, their attempts to help may end in disaster, and their actions may have a precipitous quality which dooms them to failure. Their low self-esteem and hopelessness, engendered by hostility and rejection from parents and peers, may result in feelings of unhappiness or depression.

Peer interactions continue to suffer. The hyperactive children's clumsiness and inability to sustain attention prevent them from playing games properly, while their tendency to be easily distracted and their poor emotional control result in their being labeled a quitter, a crybaby, or a poor sport. Even more unfortunate is the tendency for peers, like adults, to react negatively to children with high activity levels; thus, even when the children are friendly and helpful, they are likely to be rejected. Such punishment for socially acceptable behavior makes it difficult for the hyperactive child to master the rules of social interaction.

In school, the teacher may complain that such children cannot stay in their seats, finish their work on time, keep their minds on their work, refrain from calling out, and inhibit aggression. These children seldom follow oral directions accurately and make errors because they do not stop to think. Since they may also settle down for a brief period and become obedient and industrious, the teacher believes they could control themselves all the time "if they really tried." The teacher's resentment is picked up by other children, so that the hyperactive child's self-esteem continues its downward spiral, and school itself becomes a daily agony. It is not surprising that the combination of defects in attention and problem solving, on the one hand, and a sense of failure and lack of motivation, on the other, result in poor academic achievement; the hyperactive child repeats grades and functions below potential in basic academic subjects. It is also not surprising that aggressiveness and antisocial behavior increase.

ADOLESCENCE. Although the high levels of activity associated with hyperkinesis decrease, adolescents do not outgrow their difficulties. On the contrary, they enter this period with problems arising from many sources: a poor self-image, rejection by parents and siblings, a lack of social skills, poor school performance in spite of adequate intelligence, and a strong tendency to be nonconforming and to engage in antisocial behavior. With these handicaps they must face the normal adolescent challenges of physiological changes and sexual adjustment, of peer acceptance, and of the choice of a vocation.

The hyperactive adolescent is still more restless, distractible, and emotionally labile than are peers. Underachievement, poor self-esteem, and depression constitute major problems. Antisocial behavior now becomes a concern not only of parents and school, but also of society, leading to police contacts and court referrals for a significant number of hyperactive adolescents. Ross and Ross regard adolescence as a more difficult period for the hyperactive group than middle childhood.

ADULTHOOD. Data on the adult fate of hyperactive children are meager, unsatisfactory, and contradictory (Helper, 1980). One study found eight of fourteen adults had been institutionalized for psychosis, delinquency, criminal behavior, or retardation. Interestingly, only three of the subjects retained signs or symptoms related to hyperactivity itself. Another study found all twenty subjects to be working full time or in college, with none having been imprisoned or institutionalized, although four were diagnosed as sociopathic. While the data tend to be optimistic rather than pessimistic, adult disturbances are sufficiently common for hyperactive children to be regarded as a group which is at risk.

STABILITY OVER TIME. This composite developmental picture should not be interpreted as meaning that hyperactivity is a stable phenomenon from infancy to adulthood. Longitudinal data suggest considerable variability in developmental patterns. (Our illustrations are based on the data reported by Battle and Lacey, 1972.) Hyperactivity fluctuates during childhood for girls; while it is more stable for boys in adjacent age periods, such as the infancy and preschool periods, it is not stable over longer time spans, such as from infancy to middle childhood. Boys who are hyperactive during middle childhood tend to have anxieties over their intellectual competence as adults, while boys who are hyperactive in earlier periods do not. In a like manner, girls who are hyperactive during middle childhood have low standards of academic achievement as adults, while there is no such relation in earlier periods. Sex significantly affects the developmental pattern, hyperactive girls tending to be accepted by peers, hyperactive boys rejected by them. Sex also influences maternal behavior, mothers being critical, disapproving, unaffectionate, and severe in their punishment of their hyperactive sons, but not of their hyperactive daughters. Thus, a host of interacting variables determine the developmental course of hyperactivity, while the preliminary nature of the data makes prediction of future adjustment of hyperactive children highly uncertain.

THE DEVELOPMENTAL MODEL. While hyperactivity may prevent a number of variables from following their normal course, it is not clear which model is appropriate for conceptualizing the developmental deviation. There is some speculation that the hyperactive infant is just an extreme version of the temperamentally difficult infant, but there is no evidence to support such speculation. In fact, Ross and Ross (1976) rightly state that there is no evidence supporting the assumption that hyperactivity per se is nothing but an extreme of normal activity. In addition, they cite behaviors which seem to be qualitatively different from those of normal infants and toddlers—the piercing cry, the light, irregular sleep, and the special "driven" quality to locomotion. The authors thus raise the possibility that hyperactivity is like autism, in that certain behaviors have little counterpart in normal development and do not readily fit into a model of fixation.

Attention Deficits

The hyperactive child's scattered attention has already been noted. Here the empirical ground is firmer than it was in regard to activity level, thanks to the controlled laboratory studies of Douglas and her colleagues. Douglas and Peters (1980) clearly regard hyperactivity as the product of an *attentional deficit* that affects a wide range of tasks, from simple reaction time to complex problem solving requiring self-directed and self-sustained efforts. Since attention is multifaceted, it is logical to ask what aspects have gone awry. Douglas disagrees with the idea that such children are distractible, in the sense that their attention is readily "captured" by every extraneous stimulus in the environment. Studies which have introduced various kinds of distractions show that hyperactive children perform as well as normals. In one study, for example, the children were required to read with a telephone ringing, lights flashing, and the sound of a calculating machine. Expressed formally, hyperactive children are not deficient in the *selective* aspect of attention, that is, in the ability to filter out irrelevant environmental stimuli in order to focus upon those which are specifically relevant to the task at hand.

The hyperactive child's basic deficit, Douglas argues, is in *sustaining* attention. Sustained attention has a motivational and a cognitive component. Motivationally, it is contingent upon the child's *level of arousal*. Both underarousal (as in intense boredom) and overarousal (as in high states of excitement or anxiety) interfere with sustained attention, which flourishes at the level of arousal known as alert wakefulness. It is just this optimal level which hyperactive children have difficulty in maintaining. Frequently they are underaroused, and what has been described as distractibility is an avid seeking of stimulation to avoid the pain of sensory deprivation. (Recall that a similar theory has been advanced to account for the acting-out behavior of certain impulse-ridden delinquents.) At times, however, they can become hyperaroused by stimulation a normal child could readily take in stride.

Two of the purest measures of sustained attention are: *reaction time*, in which a warning signal (such as a buzzer) is followed by a preparatory interval terminated by a stimulus (such as a light) to which the subject has been instructed to respond as quickly as possible (for example, by pressing a lever), and *continuous-performance tests*, in which letters appear on a screen one at a time, the child having been instructed to respond to a given letter (such as *X*) only when another letter (such as *A*) precedes it. Not only are hyperactive children generally inferior to normal controls on these simple tasks, but their performance also deteriorates with time. Equally interesting, they show clear evidence of *impulsivity* on the continuous-performance task; for example, they respond to the preceding letter rather than to the target letter, or they respond to nonsignificant letters.

Douglas's studies illustrate the advantage of programmatic research in which a series of investigations successively test interrelated hypotheses. A single study, rather than being isolated, provides salient leads as to which variable to control next or which one to alter during the actual conduct of a study. In the process, the investigator can develop a special astuteness by pursuing various facets of a complex psychological variable.

We shall focus on Douglas's program in its initial phase when she was concerned with the function of attention. Conceptually she noted that the selective aspect of attention could be differentiated from its sustaining aspect, even though some of the research literature had merged the two by maintaining that hyperactive children had difficulty sustaining selective attention (Douglas and Peters, 1980). The control inherent in the *laboratory* approach allowed her to study each aspect separately to see whether it was functioning in a normal or a deviant manner. The population of children she used was between 6 and 12 years of age, hyperactivity having been the major complaint for several years. Children were excluded whose behavior seemed to be due to emotional problems, who were neurotic, psychotic, or retarded, who had specific learning disabilities, who had been diagnosed as brain-damaged, or whose histories suggested brain injury.

To test the hypothesis concerning selectivity, researchers administered Color Distraction Tests to twenty hyperactive and twenty control children matched for age, sex, and IQ scores (Campbell, Douglas, and Morgenstern, 1971). (As we have seen, distractibility is used as a measure of selective attention.) The initial card contained pictures of red apples, green lettuce, blue grapes, and yellow bananas, and the subjects were instructed to name the colors. The first distractor consisted of the same pictures of fruit with a number of black and white pictures of familiar objects, which the subject was instructed to ignore while naming the color of the fruit. The second distractor consisted of the same fruit but with contradictory colors; for example, bananas were either blue, red, or green, but not yellow, and the subject was instructed to name the color the fruit should be. In all three conditions, speed of color-naming was recorded. An interference score was derived from the difference between the speed of naming the colors in the initial condition and in the two distracting conditions. There was no significant difference between the scores of the hyperactive and normal children under either the initial condition or the two conditions of distraction. Therefore there was no evidence of increased distractability in the hyperactivity group.

In testing the hypothesis concerning sustained attention (Sykes, Douglas, and Morgenstern, 1973), twenty hyperactive and twenty control children were matched for age, sex, and IQ scores. A Choice Reaction Time Task was used to measure attention for brief periods. In this task subjects were required to press one of two buttons corresponding to one of two stimuli appearing on a screen; for example, either a circle or a triangle would appear, and the child had to press one of two buttons also marked with a circle or a triangle. In this task there was no difference between groups, indicating that attention for brief periods was intact in hyperactive children.

In the Continuous Performance Task (Visual Mode), twelve letters appeared one at a time at 1.5 second intervals on a screen, the child being instructed to press a button when the letter *X* was preceded by the letter *A*. While the letters were presented in random order, there were fifteen such *A-X* pairs in a run of 100 letters. In the Auditory Mode version of the procedure, the stimuli were presented by a recording of a female voice. In both versions of the tasks, the performance of the hyperactive group was significantly inferior to that of the control as measured by the number of errors, indicating a difficulty in sustaining attention for such children.

As was noted in the presentation of studies of autistic children, the laboratory not only allows for a refinement of differentiation (in this instance, selective versus sustained attention) but also for a systematic manipulation of variables (in this instance attention for auditory and visual material) which would be next to impossible with any other research methodology.

Before leaving Douglas's research project we would like to underscore her concern with the "inconsistent and ill-defined methods" used in selecting and labeling subjects (Douglas and Peters, 1980). Minimum brain dysfunction, learning disability, and hyperactivity are frequently used vaguely and even interchangeably in the research literature. Thus it is difficult or impossible to know to what population the findings apply. The same problem exists in research with other populations of disturbed children. Conceptual clarity and adherence to explicit criteria for placing children in a given group are essential to progress in research.

Douglas speculates that there is a constitutional predisposition toward poorly modulated arousal, impaired ability to sustain attention, and impulsivity. This triple handicap, in turn, adversely affects the development of higher cognitive processes, which require sustained attention by their very nature. It is not by accident that we tell a child to stop and think; in fact, Douglas epitomizes the basic defect in hyperactive children as an inability to stop, look, listen—and think. These abilities presuppose a certain cognitive development which can be described as a shift from *exploration* to *search strategies*. The argument runs as follows:

In the very young child attention is controlled by the compelling features of stimuli, such as their intensity, change, novelty, complexity, or unexpectedness. Thus, the infant is attracted to bright colors, moving objects, variable sounds, unexpected appearances. Exploratory strategies are typically spontaneous, unorganized, and short-lived. While learning both the properties and functions of objects and becoming more sophisticated in problem-solving skills, the infant becomes capable of search strategies which are deliberate, goal-oriented, organized, and logical. Thus, instead of being attracted to a brightly colored "thing," the infant now begins to look for an object such as a stick in order to reach an inaccessible cookie on the table. "What is *x*?" is replaced by "What properties does *x* have which will help me solve the task at hand?" The development of search strategies also marks a change from an *impulsive* to a *reflective cognitive style*. In the former, the child responds rapidly and with many errors in problem-solving situations; in the latter, the child responds slowly but accurately (Wright and Vliestra, 1975).

While hyperactive children do not lack search strategies, they are deficient in them as compared with normal children. This deficiency is evidenced in solving both perceptual and logical problems. In the Matching Familiar Figures Test, for example, the child is required to choose from a group of similar pictures the one which is identical to a standard picture, such as a man or a house. Hyperactive children perform in an impulsive manner, failing systematically to compare the standard with the entire array of pictures or failing to check back and forth between the standard and the array. Thus, their basic weakness in attentional and inhibitional skills make them respond prematurely and incorrectly. In a twenty-questions task, the child must decide which of an array of pictures the examiner is thinking of by asking a limited number of questions. Children with good search strategies would see that one question, such as "Is it a fruit?" would eliminate a number of pictures at once. Hyperactive children, in contrast, are likely to approach the task in a random fashion, with no task-relevant rule in mind, or they are liable to guess or focus too narrowly on a particular picture.

One final point: not only do hyperactive children have inefficient strategies, but the advantage of having a strategy to begin with also does not occur to many of them. Tutors, for example, may complain that the children are unaware of their own role as problem solvers; they do not realize that they must make a deliberate effort instead of having the solution "just come" to them. (Earlier, we noted a similar deficiency in mentally retarded children.) Translated into our own terminology, the hyperactive child fails to show sufficient initiative in problem-solving tasks.

In sum, Douglas postulates that a basic deficiency in the ability to modulate arousal, sustain attention, and control impulses leads to a subsequent impairment in these children's ability to assume and maintain a problem-solving set and limits their ability to generate effective problem-solving strategies. Since the progression from exploration to search strategies is a developmental achievement, we can assume that the hyperactive child is suffering from a developmental lag. Parenthetically, Douglas also recognizes that repeated failure in problem solving undermines the hyperactive child's feeling of competence, makes such tasks noxious, and further compounds the basic deficiency.

Treatment

PHARMACOTHERAPY. Paradoxical as it might seem, stimulants are the treatment of choice for hyperactivity; the three major groups are amphetamines, methylphenidate (Ritalin), and pemoline. A review of stimulant treatment shows that approximately 75 percent of the children improved (Barkley, 1977). However, it is important to note the kinds of behaviors that changed, as well as those that were not affected.

In line with the view that hyperactivity is the result of an attentional defect, many of the positive results concern a normalization of attention-concentration. In a laboratory setting, children were less impulsive and more planful on tasks requiring deliberation, made fewer errors of omission in tasks requiring sustained attention, evidenced fewer task-irrelevant behaviors, and in general were more goal-directed, more coordinated, and less impulsive when medicated. Their reaction time also increased when rapid responses were required. Among cognitive functions, perception, memory, concept attainment, and cognitive style were also improved. In the classroom, teachers rated children as less noisy and disruptive, more task-oriented, and more appropriate in their social behavior. On the playground, there was an increase in appropriate activity. Rather than either "speeding up" or "slowing down" behavior, therefore, the overall effect of the drugs is one of making behavior more appropriate to the situation. It is as if the child's self-regulating, adaptive mechanisms could come to the fore once he or she was no longer buffeted about by the reaction of the moment. Generally, an elevated positive mood accompanies medication, although negative affects such as depression, fearfulness, and withdrawal have also been observed. One cautionary note: the long-term effects of medication are unclear, since insufficient data are available. While some experts claim that no harmful effects have been demonstrated, others prefer to reserve judgment until more definitive evidence is available.

Since not all children improve with medication, it would be highly desirable to be able to predict those who would respond positively and negatively. Unfortunately, prediction is not possible at present. There is some evidence that soft neurological signs and the degree of inattention are the best predictors, although both are still unsatisfactory. Older children and those who experience good parenting also show some tendency to respond favorably. Interestingly, degree of hyperactivity as rated by parents, teachers, or clinicians is not predictive.

A number of important variables are not affected by stimulants, however: general cognitive level as measured by intelligence tests, complex learning, language skill, problem-solving ability, and academic achievement. It is as if stimulants make hyperactive children more amenable to learning, but they obviously cannot provide the academic knowledge which the children had failed to acquire, nor can they magically raise the overall level of their thinking. There is also no evidence that medication in and of itself significantly improves the long-term prognosis. In light of what we have learned, we can see why this is so. There is no reason to assume that medication will automatically raise children's self-esteem or provide them with the social skills needed to be accepted by peers, nor do patterns of family interaction necessarily change for the better as a child improves. (Certain families may need to perceive the child as psychopathologically disturbed.) In short, stimulants serve an important purpose by setting the stage for the therapeutic work which may still have to be done.

This résumé of the advantages and limitations of medication also serves as a useful background for understanding the reservations certain professionals have voiced concerning the use of drugs with hyperactive children. Like any treatment, pharmacotherapy should be administered with a high degree of professional competence. The child's problems should be carefully evaluated, while the kind and dosage of medication should be constantly monitored. The decision to discontinue medication should likewise be made only after comprehensively assessing the child's functioning at home, in the school, and with peers. Since there are few objective guides, all these decisions are a matter of clinical judgment. (See Kinsbourne and Caplan, 1979; hyperactivity is discussed under the heading Impulsive Extremes.) There is often a temptation to cut short this time-consuming procedure. At its worst, medication can be regarded as a quick cure-all or as a means of making the child more tractable and less burdensome to parents and teachers. Thus, medication can be overprescribed or wrongly prescribed, while compliant behavior on the child's part can be equated with cure. The illusion that life's problems can be solved by taking a pill is a seductive one, and one which can operate to the disadvantage of the child who is its victim. (For a detailed discussion of medication, see Conners and Werry, 1979.)

OTHER TREATMENT APPROACHES. *Behavior therapists* have been the most versatile in applying their techniques to remedying many of the problems attendant upon hyperactivity and in documenting their successes. The techniques themselves have varied greatly: the traditional ones emphasize reinforcing desirable behavior while ignoring or punishing undesirable behavior, whereas the newer, cognitively ones emphasize self-instruction in order to increase self-control (Douglas, 1980). Not only teachers but parents as well have been instructed in the use of behavioral techniques in order to increase the scope of the child's therapeutic environment. Behavior therapy has been successfully used to induce children to sit still and pay attention, to reduce their disruptive behaviors in class, and to improve performance on a variety of school tasks. They also have been employed to deal with behavior problems in the home.

While reports of success are impressive, most involve short-term management. The problems of generalizing success across settings and sustaining them over time remain to be solved. There are other "psychological" problems with behavioral therapy. Like patients who discontinue taking medicine as soon as they feel better, parents and teachers may discontinue their carefully worked out treatment program when the children become less hyperactive, but before they have sufficient self-control to do without environmental support. And as with medication, decreasing hyperactivity may be regarded as the sole therapeutic goal, while the child's learning and personality problems are ignored. In spite of such limitations, behavioral therapy is the psychotherapeutic treatment of choice.

Parent counseling is employed to educate parents concerning the nature of hyperactivity, to relieve the guilt they often feel, as well as to deal with their frustrations and disappointment; *parental training* instructs parents in the specific behavioral skills of observation, pinpointing behaviors to be changed, data taking, and devising strategies of reinforcement, punishment, and extinction. The advantages of parental training are that the therapeutic principles can be readily grasped, the parents can immediately become involved in changing specific behaviors, while the charting of these changes provides concrete evidence of change, thereby reinforcing the parent as well as the child. If behavioral techniques are also being used at school, parental training has the additional advantage of providing parent and teacher with a common language and a common base for coordinating their remedial efforts.

Family therapy has been used not directly to remedy the hyperactivity but to work through the problems which might have been generated by having a hyperactive child. Such children may have become a "scapegoat" on whom family members displace many of their own problems, or they may be used as a "negative bond" to hold a wavering marriage together. Helping families to become aware of and to change such patterns of interaction relieves the hyperactive member of the burden of rejection and discrimination.

Educational intervention involves the same controversy over special classes versus mainstreaming which we met in discussing mental retardation. There is also disagreement over whether hyperactive children are overstimulated and therefore need a barren work area free of distraction, or whether they are understimulated and therefore need stimuli with a high demand value, such as rock music, flashing lights, and caged mice. There is more evidence to support the latter than the former point of view. A variation on this theme of optimal learning environment involves the controversy over structured versus open classrooms. The meager data are inconclusive and addressed only to hyperactive behavior; there are no data concerning the effects of the two kinds of classrooms on academic achievement. (For a more detailed presentation of various treatment approaches, see Routh and Mesibov, 1980.)

MULTIPLE INTERVENTIONS. Because hyperactivity has multiple etiologies and may involve disturbances in a number of intra- and interpersonal areas, multimodal treatment tailored to the needs of the individual child seems the most appropriate approach to remediation. Medication, behavioral treatment, remedial education, parental counseling, and family therapy all should be utilized as needed. Consequently, the proper treatment of the hyperactive child requires a special cooperative effort on the part of the pediatrician, the school, and the mental health professional (Kenny and Burka, 1980).

YOU ARE A CLINICAL CHILD PSYCHOLOGIST. A PEDIATRICIAN has referred a hyperactive 8-year-old, and you have completed your evaluation. You are now planning your treatment strategy. The mother has told you that the pediatrician has placed her child on a special diet rather than on medication to control his hyperactivity. You know that the research on the efficacy of this diet is inconclusive, but bringing this up with the mother would put her in a conflict between the two professionals responsible for helping her child. You might discuss the decision with the pediatrician at some later date when both of you have more time—if indeed such a day ever comes. Your immediate concern is with informing the pediatrician of your findings and of the treatment program you have in mind.

You next make an appointment to see the mother again in order to explain the findings and treatment plans to her. You also will start working on the family problems centering around having a hyperactive 8-year-old and three younger siblings. While well intentioned, the parents have become increasingly exasperated with the boy and have escalated their punitive behavior. Your initial conference will center around the two great principles of behavioral therapy—ignore the negative and reward the positive (thus reversing the present family pattern) and focus on specific behaviors (which will immediately involve the parents in the constructive task of observing and recording the child's behavior and its social consequences).

You know the psychologist at the boy's grammar school. She is young, unsure of herself, and overworked. While conscientious, she does not seem particularly resourceful. Since the mother took the boy to the pediatrician initially because the school had found him "unmanageable," you suspect that his teacher has also reached the end of her rope. Yet, you will contact the school psychologist and see what can be done. The fact that other professionals are now involved might be a relief to the teacher and serve as an opening wedge to exploring other ways of dealing with the boy's management problems.

Since the boy is significantly below grade level in reading, he definitely will need more help in this area than is available in the schools. You know an excellent woman in remedial reading, but she is something of a prima donna who does not "believe in medication," regards special diets as "a hoax," and resents the "MDs who have no business making all the decisions and all the money off of children with educational problems." While she is infinitely patient with children, she is difficult and confronting with her colleagues. It would be easier on you to refer the child to a less talented but more cooperative reading specialist. For the moment you do not know which to choose.

You now have three names on your calendar and a question mark for the fourth. All will require a lengthy contact just to devise the remedial program. Implementing the program will require additional contacts in the future. All of this will take time, and time is always precious. And then there is the matter of billing. To charge the parents for all the time you will have to spend on the phone would confront them with a bill which would work a real hardship on their family budget. But you yourself cannot afford to charge them only for their direct contacts with you. You decide on a compromise—to charge for some of your time but not all, knowing that the decision will mean a financial sacrifice on your part.

While the ideal of skilled specialists meeting the multiple needs of the hyperactive child is an attractive one, its realization is exceedingly difficult. The sheer logistics of communication among specialists, as well as the added time involved, are problems in their own right. In addition, professionals differ in their degree of skill as well as in their willingness to cooperate with other professionals. They may be divided on the issue of medication and of behavioral therapy, each of which is apt to be strongly championed by some and equally strongly opposed by others. And the question of who has the ultimate responsibility for the child's welfare—which is the question of ultimate authority and power—can be a touchy one. Professionals are people with their own vested interests, vanities, personal and financial aspirations. To weld them into a cooperative team is a major undertaking.

We have now finished examining psychopathology from a developmental perspective. Two matters remain to be discussed. The first is *assessment* which is important to clinician and researcher alike. Assessment techniques of uncertain merit increase the chances that error will distort the evaluation of children's current psychological status, the history of their disturbance, and their prognosis. The rampant diagnosis of minimal brain dysfunction and hyperactivity together with the readiness with which stimulant drugs are prescribed as therapy testify to the practical dangers of using inadequate assessment techniques. The researcher is equally dependent upon assessment techniques as a reliable and valid means of assigning children to one group or another. Giving diverse children a common label, such as "autistic" or "juvenile delinquent," is bound to produce a bewildering array of contradictory research findings as investigators dip into now one, now another combination of psychopathologies comprising the heterogeneous population.

The issue of treatment has been touched upon in discussing a number of psychopathologies, but now it is time for a more complete presentation of *remediation* and *prevention*. We shall not only examine some of the major psychotherapeutic approaches to remediation but also see the expansion of the clinical arena from the office and the mental health clinic into the community and the nation. We will again raise a question which troubled us after examining the findings from longitudinal studies: How can a clinician ethically offer treatment for a child whose problem is apt to be outgrown? The question is even more serious than we anticipated, however, since the effectiveness of all psychotherapies has been challenged. If research indicates that there is no difference in adjustment between children who do and do not receive therapy, the entire remedial venture is in jeopardy. Just how black the picture is can be decided only after a review of the evidence.

13 ▪ Psychological Assessment

We have repeatedly seen that in order to be understood, behavior must be evaluated in context. The context of time is crucial and includes not only the child's current age but past history as well. Within this temporal framework both intra- and interpersonal factors must be considered: a severely retarded 8-year-old who steals because she has not fully grasped the principle of property rights is different from an 8-year-old of average intelligence who steals in order to be accepted by her friends; schizophrenic behavior in a child whose parents are also schizophrenic may not represent as severe a disturbance as the same behavior in a child with psychologically intact parents. Our goal has been a scientific one, namely, to understand all variables relevant to the production of psychopathological behavior.

Clinicians, however, vary in their need to evaluate psychopathological behavior in terms of all relevant contexts. In part, this variability is a function of different theoretical allegiances. Psychoanalytically oriented clinicians strive for a comprehensive understanding not only of present and past but also of conscious and unconscious determinants of behavior. Trait psychologists are satisfied with assessing the relatively permanent predisposition of individuals to behave in a certain way, such as aggressively, anxiously, or dependently. Clinicians with a systems orientation concentrate on current patterns of interpersonal interactions, particularly in the family. Behaviorally oriented clinicians focus on specific patterns of behavior in specific settings, while nondirective clinicians reduce assessment to a bare minimum.

A complementary constraint on comprehensive assessment arises from the clinician's primary role as a help-giver. Characteristically, he or she wants to understand a problem in terms that are congruent with a particular school of therapy and to devise and implement remedial plans as quickly as possible. "Why should anyone bother with a detailed exploration of the past," they may argue, "if this particular therapy is only concerned with altering current patterns of behavior?" One might think that there would be a complementary relation between understanding and helping: the more we understand, the better we are able to help. However, such is not the case. Our increased understanding of the sociopath and of autism has outstripped our ability to remedy these conditions, while the flowering of behavior therapies has not been paralleled by comparable advances in understanding the etiology of the psychopathologies that are successfully treated.

The present discussion will begin with the clinician who seeks a comprehensive understanding of the child's psychopathology, noting how those with different goals, particularly behavioral clinicians, would abbreviate and alter the procedure. This strategy allows the widest scope in presenting assessment techniques, as well as affording a glimpse into the assessment process at its most complex. Coverage of specific techniques will be selective, and knowledge of the construction, reliability, and validity of major psychological tests, commensurate with that gained in an introductory course in psychology, is assumed. (For an extensive coverage of assessment, see Palmer, 1970. A briefer treatment can be found in Knopf, 1979, chap. 5. For an introductory text covering psychological tests, see Lefrançois, 1980, chap. 15.)

THE ASSESSMENT PROCESS

Clinicians never assume that within the space of a few hours they will be able to understand the nature and origin of the problems which bring a particular child to their attention. They realize that they are viewing parents and child under special circumstances that both limit and bias the data they will obtain: the child who is frightened by a clinic waiting room may not be a generally fearful child, just as one who is hyperactive in school may be a model of cooperation when taking an intelligence test; parents may have their own misperceptions and blind spots in regard to their child's behavior, along with varying degrees of willingness to reveal information about themselves and their child. Thus, an initial session is only the first step toward understanding.

In attempting to assimilate and integrate the massive amount of data they collect, clinicians implicitly proceed like hypothesis-testing scientists. No single bit of behavior is definitive, but each is suggestive. As these bits accumulate, certain initial hunches tend to be confirmed and others discarded. By the end of the assessment process, the clinician can make some statements concerning the child's problem with a reasonable degree of assurance; other assessments will be tentative and qualified; and a number of questions will remain unanswered.

To illustrate this hypothesis-testing process briefly: Tom is a 10-year-old boy referred for a learning problem; specifically, he is lazy, failing reading and arithmetic, and beginning to be disruptive in class. Upon being introduced to the psychologist in the waiting room, Tom is unusually friendly and communicative. Most children are cautious initially, and rightly so. The psychologist mentally notes

Tom's behavior and wonders what it might represent. Perhaps this is a basically healthy boy whose problems have been exaggerated; perhaps he has been too close to adults at the expense of becoming alienated from peers; perhaps he is a charming sociopath; perhaps his social skills are a defense against some unknown fear. During the interview the boy continues to impress the psychologist as a bright, alert, open youngster.

However, Tom's behavior begins to change on the intelligence tests: he tends to say "I don't know" too readily when items become difficult; he quickly destroys a puzzle he had put together incorrectly as if trying to cover up his mistake; and he uses his conversational skills to divert attention away from the test material. When encouraged to respond to difficult items, it is clear that he does not know the correct answer.

At this point he seems neither a sociopath nor fearful nor prematurely adult; both his enjoyment of people and his openness seem genuine. Yet, the test adds a significant bit of data: he has only average intelligence. The psychologist then speculates, "If his sociability misled me into thinking he was intellectually bright, his parents and teachers might have also been misled into setting unrealistically high goals and pressuring him to achieve them." This hypothesis naturally would have to be checked by interviewing the parents and a telephone call to the teacher. It also raises further questions, such as the effects of being regarded as lazy on the boy's self-image, which could be explored by further assessment. In regard to diagnosis, the clinician is tentatively thinking in terms of a developmental deviation, in that the boy's problem seems to result from a significant discrepancy between his social and intellectual development. Another possibility is that the boy has a learning disability which had undermined his confidence on a variety of intellectual tasks.

Hypotheses are never generated out of the blue; rather, clinicians use a variety of sources: their preferred theoretical framework, the clinical and research literature relevant to the problem at hand, accumulated knowledge passed on from seasoned clinicians to novitiates, as well as their own experience. In this instance, the hypothesis generated by the discrepancy between Tom's social and intellectual development derived from a discussion of a similar case with his supervisor during the clinician's student days; the question concerning Tom's self-image came from the clinician's interest in the self-concept. Equally valid questions could be raised concerning the effects of Tom's failure on the family dynamics or on his status with teachers and peers at school. As we shall subsequently see, the very openness of the clinical process is a source of concern to certain psychologists, who would like to see assessment become less of an art and more of a science.

INITIAL SOURCES OF DATA

Referrals

The first data concerning the child come from the referral, which usually contains information about the problem as perceived by concerned adults, its duration and onset, its effects on the child and on others, and what measures, if any, have been taken to remedy it. Parents and teachers are the major sources of referrals.

The fact that children are not self-referred, as are most adults, has an important psychological implication. There is a great deal of difference between seeking help and being told one needs help. The child may or may not feel the need, may or may not understand why he or she is being brought to the clinic. Parents may either fail to tell them why or give them reasons which they do not understand or agree with. After establishing some rapport, the clinician should clarify why the child is there, what the assessment procedures are, and why they are being done.

Observation

The clinician's assessment begins on first seeing the parents and child. Their appearance and interactions provide clues as to family characteristics and the relationships among its members. First impressions furnish information concerning the family's social class and general level of harmony or disharmony, as well as its stylistic characteristics—reserved, demonstrative, authoritarian, intellectual, or whatever. Specific patterns of interactions are almost limitless: the mother may immediately launch into a long list of complaints, while her husband sits meekly in the background and her child pretends not to hear; or a father, with forced enthusiasm, may paint a falsely positive picture of "what a good time you're going to have" when the child is alone with the clinician; or the parent may turn uncertainly to the child and ask, "You really want to go to the playroom, don't you?" leaving the child unsure whether or not there is a choice in the matter.

Once with the child, the clinican systematically gathers certain kinds of information. The *overall impression* of the child's personality is always important: "an all-American boy"; "he already has the worried look of an old man, as if he does not know what it is like to be a child"; "a perfect little lady, a real showpiece for her mother"; "he has that sullen look, like he is constantly spoiling for a fight"; "a direct, honest, no-nonsense preadolescent girl, somewhat on the tomboy side." Such impressions help define the child's social-stimulus value, which may be a potent elicitor of positive or negative reactions from others. However, they should not be regarded as indicative of the child's self-image, which may be at odds with manifest appearance and behavior.

The child's *body* and *body language* provide important clues to physiological intactness as well as to personality variables. Significant departures from the norms of height and weight may indicate a medical problem or, more important, may cause the child to be teased and rejected by peers. From middle childhood on, the body image is an important component of the self-image; physical deformities or abnormalities and premature or delayed sexual development may be highly charged with psychological significance. The body can be read for more subtle signs of disturbance: bruises and scars suggest accident proneness or abuse; needle marks on the arm suggest drug abuse; squinting or putting the face close to the pencil when drawing or writing suggests a visual defect; frequently asking the examiner to repeat a question suggests an auditory defect; a slight tremor or awkwardness in handling a pencil suggests a problem in fine-motor coordination. While avoiding a medical diagnosis on the basis of psychological assessment, the clinician can describe the suspect behavior and recommend a medical examination. In their own right, the observations may be relevant to the personality problem or to the learning disability which brought the child for professional help.

Body language includes a wide array of expressive behaviors. Psychological tension is often embodied in physical tension: a strained facial expression, a forced laugh, a tense posture when sitting, pressured speech or stuttering, "nervous gestures" such as nail-biting, continually swinging the leg back and forth when seated, tics, general motor restlessness. A monotonous voice, slouched posture, masklike face, and slow movements suggest depression or withdrawal. Activity level is important to note, since some children are naturally placid, others naturally energetic. It is important for the clinician to distinguish the placid child from the inhibited one, and the energetic child from the hyperactive or acting-out one.

Finally, the child's *relationship* to the clinician furnishes an important clue as to his or her perception of adults. It is natural for children to be reserved initially, since in reality the clinician is a stranger. However, as they discover that the clinician is interested, friendly, and benign, they should become relaxed, cooperative, and communicative, although still reluctant to talk about sensitive topics. Certain children never warm up; they sit as far back in their chair as possible, speak in an almost inaudible monotone, rarely look at the examiner or else watch intently, as if he or she were a kind of monster who might strike out at any minute. Some children turn the examination into a power struggle: when the examiner asks questions they cannot answer, such children ask the examiner questions or try to find a topic such as television or movies or sports which they know more about than the examiner. Provocative children begin to "test the limits," mischievously peeking when told to close their eyes or destroying a puzzle when told to leave it intact. In general, the clinician is always asking, "Is the child distorting the kind of adult I am, and if so, why and in what way?"

But a relationship involves two people, the clinician as well as the child. Clinicians are not standard stimuli; they have their own styles of behaving, as well as their own talents and vulnerabilities. It is essential, therefore, that clinicians understand their own individual characteristics and include this understanding in their evaluation of the child. They may naturally be effusive or confronting or self-contained or intellectual, and such characteristics may naturally turn some children off or appeal to others. Knowing their own vulnerabilities, clinicians can see that they are becoming impatient with a whining child or angry with a provocative one or frightened by a hyperactive one and can then make sure that such reactions do not further undermine the child's self-control. While professionals can be expected to be objective about themselves as well as knowledgeable and resourceful in relating to children, they cannot be expected to transcend their own personalities.

Generally speaking, observation as used by many clinicians may be nearer an art than a science because the procedures are unstandardized and the target behaviors so wide ranging. However, observation per se is not unscientific. Behavioral clinicians, for example, bring to assessment the structure and reliability that the more open-ended approach lacks.

The Interview

Information concerning the child and the family comes primarily from interviewing the parents. Typically, the interview begins with an account of the present problem. Next, a detailed history, technically known as a *case history,* is obtained in order to explore the antecedent conditions which might have contributed to the present difficulties. Among the topics covered are the child's prenatal history, birth history, and early development. Was the pregnancy planned? What was the mother's physical and emotional condition during pregnancy? Were there complications during or after delivery? What was the infant's weight? Were there any problems with sleeping, eating, or toileting? When did the child sit up, crawl, walk, and begin to speak? The subsequent adjustment of the child within the family and with peers is explored, along with social and academic adjustment at school. Parents might be asked how their daughter got along with her mother and father, what her relationship with her siblings was like, whether she had friends and was popular, whether she liked sports and had hobbies, how she got along in class, what grades she received, and whether she seemed to be working up to her potential. For teenagers, information is obtained concerning sexual development and work history, as well as possible drug and alcohol use and delinquent behavior. The clinician also inquires about major illnesses and injuries. To complete the picture, the parents may be asked about their own marital and occupational adjustment, their specific goals, satisfactions, and dissatisfactions, and their relation to their own parents.

How clinicians integrate the historical material depends on their conceptual frame of reference. A social-learning theorist would attend to patterns of reward and punishment, as well as to the models provided by parents and peers. A psychoanalytically oriented clinician would emphasize the child's progress through the classical psychosexual stages. However, sensitive clinicians, whatever their orientation, use the interview to form an impression of the parents as well as to gather data. It is not only what the parent says, but also how he or she says it which provide clues as to the kind of person the parent is—warm, childish, despairing, domineering, overwhelmed, self-centered, and so on.

But what about the studies showing the unreliability of parental histories? While disqualifying parents as sources of accurate information concerning many aspects of development, the studies do not render their histories useless, because it is still important for the clinician to know the parents' perception of the facts. Whether or not the child was a "difficult" infant and a "bad" toddler may not be as important as the parents' perception or memory of the child as difficult and bad. However, the argument that it is the parents' perceptions which matter has its limitations. If a mother says, "My boy was doing all right in school until he had that bad accident on his bike," it would be important to know that the trouble actually started a year before the accident when she and her husband were on the verge of getting a divorce because of his extramarital affair. The mother's account suggests an organic etiology, while the actual sequence suggests a psychogenic one. Incidentally, the mother may not be trying to deceive the clinician and may firmly believe the accuracy of her account. The clinician must realize that in cases where accuracy matters, interview data should be verified, say, by medical or school records. In many instances, however, accuracy is impossible to establish.

There is one final aspect to the interview. In the process of interviewing, the clinician is beginning to know the parents, while the parents are also beginning to know the clinician. It is important that clinicians explain the nature and purposes of clinical procedures and the available services. Clinicians should establish their credibility as interested, concerned, competent professionals. They should also be able to deal with the suspicions, defensiveness, and hostilities which parents feel toward them. Since there is no hard and fast line between assessment and therapy, skilled interviewers can use this initial contact to lay the groundwork for the trust and respect that will be so crucial in future contacts with the parents.

Children are also interviewed concerning their view of themselves, their problems, and their relations with family and peers. It is not unusual for children to give rather limited responses to inquiries, however, partly because they do not understand the nature and purpose of a psychological evaluation (even after the clinician has explained it), partly because they are reluctant to talk about personal problems with a strange adult, and partly because most children are untutored in the skill of conceptualizing and communicating feelings and problems.

In an effort to bypass such obstacles, a *play interview* may be conducted with preschoolers and those in the early years of middle childhood. Children may be presented with a dollhouse and a doll family and encouraged to do anything they like. Theoretically, as the children play, they begin to express the problems they are having within the family. However, it takes a great deal of skill to decode such fantasies and to differentiate typical and age-appropriate themes from personalized, deeply felt ones; for example, a baby falling out of the crib may or may not be an expression of a hostile wish toward a younger sibling; but if the baby falls out of the crib, lands on the street, and is run over twice by an automobile, the clinician can be more confident of the interpretation!

PSYCHOLOGICAL TESTS

Of all professionals dealing with psychopathologically disturbed children, psychologists have been most concerned with developing assessment techniques which can be objectively administered and scored, which have norms based on clearly defined populations, and which have established reliability and validity. (The standard reference for tests is Buros, 1978.)

Intelligence Tests

The two most widely used intelligence tests for children are the Stanford-Binet and the Wechsler Intelligence Scale for Children or WISC. The most recent revision of the former is the Stanford-Binet, Form L-M (Terman and Merrill, 1973). Through its many revisions, the format of the Stanford-Binet has remained the same. It consists of six items located at mental age levels 2 through 14, with subsequent items going from average adult to superior adult. The content of the items varies widely, from building a tower of blocks, to copying a circle, to defining words, to repeating digits, to explaining why certain statements are absurd. No effort is made to have comparable items at the various mental age levels. The scoring allows for the computation of the child's mental age and intelligence quotient.

The most recent revision of the WISC is the WISC-R (Wechsler, 1974), which—like its predecessors—consists of twelve subtests, the items in each arranged according to increasing difficulty. Six of the tests—Information, Similarities, Arithmetic, Vocabulary, Comprehension, and Digit Span—comprise the Verbal Scale, because they require facility in utilizing verbal symbols. The remaining six—Picture Completion, Picture Arrangement, Block Design, Object Assembly, Coding, and Mazes—comprise the Performance Scale, because they involve concrete material such as pictures, blocks, and jigsaw puzzles. Note that "verbal" and "performance" refer to the form in which the task is presented, not the level of thinking required; certain performance subtests require higher-level thinking than certain verbal subtests. Scoring yields a Verbal IQ and Performance IQ, as well as a Full-Scale IQ.

While the IQ score is important, it is only one of many pieces of information gained from an intelligence test. The discrepancy between the Verbal and Performance IQs on the WISC-R furnishes clues as to the child's differential ability to handle the two kinds of tasks: the child who has a Full-Scale IQ of 100, a Verbal IQ of 120 and a Performance IQ of 80 is quite different from a child with the same overall IQ but with a Verbal IQ of 80 and a Performance IQ of 120. The second child may be particularly penalized in school, where the manipulation of verbal symbols becomes increasingly important. Analysis of successes and failures on individual items may provide further clues to intellectual strengths and weaknesses. A child may do well on problems involving rote learning and the accumulation of facts, but poorly on ones requiring reasoning and judgment; an otherwise bright child may be weak in visual-motor coordination, which, in turn, might make learning to write difficult.

An intelligence test furnishes important clues as to the child's *style of thinking,* regardless of IQ. Note the responses of two equally bright 8-year-olds to the question, "What should you do when you lose a ball that belongs to someone else?" "I'd get him another one." "I'd pay money for it. I'd look for it. I'd give him another ball." (The examiner asks her to choose one of the possibilities.) "I'd try to find it. If I couldn't, I'd give him money for it because I might not have the kind of ball he wants." Both answers receive the same high score, but one is clear, simple, and to the point, while the other is needlessly cluttered with alternatives.

Styles of thinking are closely related to psychological health or disturbance. Intelligence is not some kind of disembodied skill existing apart from the rest of the child's personality. On the contrary, a psychologically sound child tends to think clearly, an impulse-ridden child tends to think impulsively, an obsessive child (like the one we have just quoted) tends to think in terms of a series of alternatives which, in turn, may hamstring the ability to act. And, surely, a schizophrenic child tends to think bizarrely, as is revealed in this rambling, fantasy-saturated answer to the simple question, "Why should a promise be kept?" "If you don't keep a promise you get into trouble; you go to court; like teenagers give up promises; they're usually armed, guys who run around the forest and woods, the woods near the house. We go there to catch frogs, and we always have to have older people go with us because of the teenagers with guns and knives. A child drowned there not long ago. If you don't keep a promise they start a gang and drown you."

For clinicians, an intelligence test has a rich yield of *observational data.* To begin with, they can see how a given child copes with the challenge of solving intellectual problems. For some children, intellectual challenges are their "thing," and they work for the sheer pleasure of working. Others do what they are told in a joyless, dutiful manner; solving the problems is a burden, a chore. For still others, the tests are a chance to show off or just one more in a long series of humiliating failures. The clinician also notes whether motivation changes as the type of problem changes; it is not unusual, for example, for children who dislike verbal items to enjoy performance material, perhaps because the latter are less school-like and more gamelike. Such information concerning motivation may be helpful in planning remedial work for children with a learning problem, for example, since the therapist might want to approach them through their natural areas of interest rather than confronting them immediately with disagreeable tasks.

The intelligence test also allows the clinician to evaluate the child's *work habits.* Some children are task-oriented and self-motivated; they need almost no encouragement or help from the examiner. Others are uncertain and insecure, giving up readily unless encouraged or prodded, constantly seeking reassurance that they are doing well, or asking to know whether their response was right or wrong.

The clinician can note how children respond to the stress of failure: do they take it in stride, try to excuse themselves or rationalize their failures, try to cover up mistakes, or become increasingly angry or discouraged? Finally, the tests yield information concerning the child's capacity for self-monitoring, which is the ability to evaluate the quality of the responses. Some children seem to be implicitly asking, "Is that really correct?" or "Is that the best I can do?" while others seem to have little ability to judge when they are right or wrong, an incorrect response being given with the same air of uncritical assurance as a correct one. Earlier, this same deficiency in the ability to stand apart from themselves, as it were, and observe what they were doing was noted in certain impulse-ridden, mentally retarded, and hyperactive children.

In sum, it is for good reason that intelligence tests are so frequently administered as part of the assessment procedures. The IQ score itself is related to many aspects of the child's life—success in school, vocational choice, peer relations; and IQ is a better predictor of future adjustment than any score on a personality test. In addition, the test provides data concerning general areas of strength and weakness, the kind and degree of impairment of specific intellectual functions such as immediate recall or abstract reasoning, the child's coping techniques, work habits, and motivation, stylistic characteristics of thinking that may well be related to personality variables, and the presence of distorted thinking, which might indicate either organic brain pathology or psychosis (see Kaufman, 1979).

Yet, care must be taken that an intelligence test is used appropriately and that results are properly understood. As *IQ* became a household term, so did the misconception that the score represents an unalterable intellectual potential existing independent of background and experience. In order to counteract this belief that IQ is destiny, many clinicians do not report the score to parents. Rather, they talk in terms of categories of intelligence, such as average, below average, superior. Then, taking into account the child's background and experience so as to correct for their possible biasing effects on the test score, they go on to describe strengths and weaknesses, which in turn may lead to a discussion of remedial plans.

Infant intelligence testing requires special skill in accommodation so as to elicit an optimal performance. The examiner must know how to intrigue the infant with the test material, allow for distractions, temporarily become a comforting caretaker in response to fretting, postpone testing when distress becomes too great—in short, the good examiner must have the sensitivity, flexibility, and warmth of a good parent. Infant intelligence tests also require special ingenuity in their construction, since the kinds of items appropriate for older children are for the most part inappropriate for infants; a vocabulary test, for example, which is a mainstay in other individual intelligence tests, is meaningless in an infant test.

One of the best constructed standardized infant tests is the Bayley Scales of Infant Development, which evaluates development between 2 and 30 months of age (Bayley, 1969). The Mental Scale evaluates the infant's vocal and verbal behavior, memory, generalization, classification, and simple problem-solving ability, among other things; the Motor Scale evaluates gross-motor and fine-motor coordination and skills; and the Infant Behavior Record assesses the infant's social relations, responsiveness to objects, activity level, interests, emotions, and tendency to approach or withdraw from stimulation.

Younger infants may be examined by means of the Brazelton Neonatal Behavioral Assessment Scale (Brazelton, 1963), which was designed to measure the infant's available responses to the environment. Of particular interest are measures of self-regulatory behavior, such as infants' ability to modulate their state of arousal in order to be receptive to incoming stimulation, along with the activities infants use to quiet themselves. Thus, among other things, the scale measures infants' ability to maintain an optimal alertness without becoming distressed and disorganized by physiological stimuli from within or by stimuli from the social and physical environment.

While the emphasis on early detection of future psychological disturbances has accelerated interest in infant testing, such assessment is generally unrelated to IQ in middle childhood and adulthood and is best regarded as an evaluation of the infant's current status. However, low-scoring infants on the Bayley Scales may still be scoring low in the preschool period, particularly if the infant is also from a lower socioeconomic class. Thus the examiner has at least some clues about which infants may be at risk. (For a review of infant assessment, see Self and Horowitz, 1979.)

Brief intelligence tests have been devised to estimate the child's intelligence in less time than it takes to administer and score the Stanford-Binet and the WISC. The Peabody Picture Vocabulary Test (PPVT) requires the child to identify which of four pictures corresponds to a given word (Dunn, 1965). The words themselves are graded in difficulty. The test takes approximately 15 minutes and is designed for children between 2½ and 18 years of age. Brief tests are useful as screening devices and are helpful in ascertaining the child's general level of intellectual functioning. However, they should not be used as a substitute for the more comprehensive intelligence test when a precise and detailed evaluation of intelligence is required.

Group intelligence tests such as the Otis-Lennon Mental Ability Test (Otis and Lennon, 1967) are especially suited for administration in school settings. (For a comprehensive discussion of intelligence testing, see Sattler, 1982.)

Personality Tests

PERSONALITY INVENTORIES. Personality inventories consist of a series of statements to be judged as characteristic or not characteristic of an individual. The judgment is usually in terms of true-false. While adults most often fill out their own inventories, children's inventories are usually filled out by an adult who knows the child well, typically the mother.

The Personality Inventory for Children (PIC) is one of the most comprehensive (Wirt, Lachar, Klinedinst, and Seat, 1977). Its purpose is to provide a "comprehensive and clinically relevant personality description of individuals primarily in the range from six to sixteen years of age" (p. 1). The inventory consists of 600 true-false items and twelve scales, some of which evaluate intrapersonal variables—specifically, Adjustment, Somatic Concerns, Depression, Delinquency, Withdrawal, Anxiety, Psychosis, Hyperactivity, Social Skills, Achievement, and Intellectual Screening (intelligence); others evaluate interpersonal and historical variables—specifically, Family Relations and Development. In creating the inventory, the authors included a particular scale if they felt it would be useful to the practicing clinician; the choice was not based on any theory of personality development. The authors also relied on past empirical research, which showed that the majority of inventories yielded two personality dimensions: *internalizing* behavior, such as anxiety, depression, and somatic concerns; and *externalizing* behavior, such as delinquency and hyperactivity.

Items were culled from files of child guidance clinics, books on developmental psychology and child psychiatry, and the authors' experience with normal and disturbed children. Half of the scales were constructed on a rational basis; that is, three of four judges agreed that an item belonged in a given scale. The remaining scales were derived statistically by using a correlational technique. The validities of the scales were primarily (but not exclusively) evaluated by comparing the scores of children specifically diagnosed as delinquent, psychotic, hyperactive, and underachieving with the scores of a control group of 2,390 normal children between 6 and 16 years of age; thus, if the Delinquency scale was valid, children diagnosed as delinquent should score significantly higher than normal children on this scale. The control group also enabled the authors to establish cutoff scores, above or below which a given child's score could no longer be considered in the normal range. Finally, the authors devised three additional scales to determine if the informant was being unusually defensive or untruthful.

Further statistical analysis revealed meaningful clusters of items within each scale and provided information as to which of these clusters were the most potent indices of the characteristic tapped by the scale. To give one example: the Withdrawal scale was found to be composed of items indicating social and physical isolation, shyness and fear of strangers, isolation from peers and uncommunicativeness, emotional distance, distrust, and isolated intellectual pursuits. Among the most potent individual items in the Withdrawal scale were, "My child stays in his (her) room for hours" and "I often wonder if my child is lonely."

The authors have also explored interrelations among scales: an elevated Withdrawal scale may also be accompanied by an elevated Depression and Psychosis scale; Delinquency is somewhat related to Family Relations; Achievement is primarily related to cognitive scales such as Intellectual Screening and secondarily to psychosocial adjustment as measured by Psychosis and Social Skills; while Anxiety overlaps considerably with Depression and to a lesser extent with Somatic Complaints and Social Skills. Such clusterings are congruent with previous discussions of the specific psychopathologies.

Surprisingly, statistical analyses revealed no age trends of any practical significance in the normal population, except for intellectual screening. Studies using similar scales have also failed to uncover significant age trends. Why this should be so remains to be discovered. Certainly such findings fly in the face of the generally accepted picture of the preadolescent-adolescent period as one of increased emotional instability compared with the calm of middle childhood.

On the whole, the PIC shows how useful and fruitful an empirical, atheoretical approach to assessment can be. The authors regard it as an objective intake or screening device, leaving it to the clinician to decide how much additional information is needed before formulating a diagnosis and treatment plan. In spite of its objective format, the authors also state that the PIC should not be used by untrained, nonprofessional personnel. It is one thing to know how clearly diagnosed children score on the various scales; it is quite another to understand the profiles obtained from a population of clinical children whose individual members often have unusual mixtures of intra- and interpersonal variables rather than falling into clear-cut diagnostic categories. In addition, the number of potential profiles that can be derived from twelve scales is astronomical, and considerable work is currently being done on profile analysis. Thus, the clinician interpreting a given profile must be aware of the proper procedure for doing so and must keep abreast of the accumulating literature on profile analysis.

PROJECTIVE TECHNIQUES. In all the assessment instruments discussed so far the stimulus material is as clear and unambiguous as possible. Intelligence tests ask questions such as, "Why should a promise be kept?" and "Who discovered America?" Items on personality inventories cannot always be so straightforward, but the goal of clarity is the same. Projective techniques take the opposite tack by utilizing ambiguous or unstructured material; either the stimulus has no meaning, such as an inkblot, or it has a number of different meanings, such as a picture that is to be used as the basis of a story. Theoretically, the particular meaning attributed to the unstructured material is a reflection of the individual's particular personality. The term *projection* does not carry the connotation of a defense mechanism designed to protect the individual from facing frightening and unacceptable impulses; rather, it is a more general term that connotes a reading of personally meaningful material into an unstructured situation, the material itself being both positive and negative, conscious and unconscious. However, the disguised nature of the responses allows the individual to express ideas that would be too threatening to talk about directly; for example, a girl who is frightened of opposing her mother may feel free to tell a story about a daughter being angry with and defying her mother.

The *Rorschach test* is a series of ten inkblots, which the child views one at a time after being instructed to tell the examiner everything the blots look like. The child's responses are recorded and subsequently scored and interpreted in terms of a number of personality variables. We shall briefly mention only three: intellectual characteristics, personality structure, and specific perceptions and affects.

Rorschach responses reflect three different kinds of thinking: abstract, global thinking—the need to "get it all together" and achieve a comprehensive overview or understanding; concrete, down-to-earth involvement with practical issues in the here-and-now; and concern with minutia and a need for preciseness in the smallest detail. No one kind of thinking is ideal since healthy adaptation requires all three; a successful Girl Scout camping trip entails an overall plan, a realistic grasp of what food and equipment will be needed, and maps that are accurate to the last detail. However, individuals differ in the kind of thinking most characteristic of them. Psychopathological conditions produce exaggerations of the three types of thinking: a psychotic adolescent boy in a manic phase may have grandiose ideas of his intellectual prowess, such as believing that he knows everything in the world there is to know; an anxious individual may cling desperately to the mundane requirements of a day-to-day existence, any slight deviation from a routine being viewed as a potential danger; while a compulsive girl may waste her energies on trivia such as making sure that her shoes are arranged in a perfectly straight line, that there is not a speck of dust on any of the furniture, that her clothes are immaculately clean.

The Rorschach also reveals the kind and degree of emotional responsiveness (roughly translated as extraversion), inner resources and fantasy life (roughly translated as introversion), and rational self-control an individual has. As with the intellectual characteristics, all three elements are present in healthy individuals, but different ones predominate; some individuals have outgoing, expressive, convivial, and colorful personalities; others are reflective, intellectual, and "deep"; while still others are unemotional, self-controlled, and straight-laced. The Rorschach furnishes valuable information as to when such normal personality characteristics become extreme to a pathological degree: the reactive individual may become an impulse-ridden or violently acting-out one; inwardness may become pathological isolation and paranoid suspiciousness; while the self-contained individual may become so massively inhibited that any affect is perceived as a terrifying threat.

The content of the individual's responses provides clues to specific affects and perceptions of human relationships. The exuberance of the response, "the Eiffel Tower with fireworks going off all around" contrasts with the dysphoric affect in the response to the same card, "the inside of a mouth with food that is in varying stages of decay." In a like manner, "two waiters ready to serve dinner" puts men in a subservient but positive role, which contrasts with the destructiveness implicit in the response to the same card, "two cannibals getting ready to boil a missionary in a pot."

The question of the validity of the Rorschach has bedeviled psychologists since it gained popularity some forty years ago. Psychometricians have been dismayed by its poor performance, some recommending it be banished altogether, while some practicing clinicians regard it as indispensable in revealing information no other technique can match. A review of research (Klopfer and Taulbee, 1976) suggests that there have been a sufficient number of positive findings to reassure the clinician and a sufficient number of negative ones to gladden the hearts of nihilistic psychometricians. The decision to use the Rorschach, therefore, becomes one of personal preference. (See Exner, 1978. For a developmental interpretation of age norms, see Ames, Rodell, Métraux, and Walker, 1974, and Ames, Métraux, and Walker, 1971.)

The *Thematic Apperception Test* (TAT) consists of thirty pictures, although only around ten are used for a given individual. The instructions are to tell a story identifying the people in the picture, explaining their thoughts and feelings, and describing their past, present, and future. The examiner records the story and asks questions concerning elements that may have been omitted. Some pictures are for males, others for females, and still others are for both sexes, but all are purposefully ambiguous; for example, a figure sitting on the floor leaning against a couch may be male or female, may be exhausted or depressed or suicidal or merely resting. Some cards contain single figures. Others suggest interpersonal situations, such as the nuclear family, same- and opposite-sex parent–child interactions, and same- and opposite-sex adult relations.

Unlike the Rorschach, the TAT has no standard scoring procedure. However, most systems assume that the heroes of the stories represent various aspects of the individual's self-concept, although not necessarily the conscious view of the self. Thus, special attention is paid to the hero's needs, interests, traits, and competence. In the interpersonal sphere, themes concerning parents and the family unit are of special interest, stories being analyzed for the way parents are viewed and the hero's interaction with parental figures. Stories also reveal the nature and strength of the affect accompanying the various themes, along with the effectiveness of coping devices in dealing with the problems generated in the stories.

Let us return to Tom, the 10-year-old boy with the learning problem. The clinican was wondering whether the pressure to meet impossible academic goals had affected Tom's self-image and relations with his parents. Here one of Tom's TAT stories will be used to illustrate the process of analysis. However, a word of caution before starting: no one story—just like no one bit of behavior—is significant in itself; it is merely suggestive. Only as themes occur repeatedly and can be fitted together into some cohesive entity does the clinician have confidence in the interpretation of the data. A single story is being presented only because of limitations of space. The inferences drawn are repeated in other stories as well.

The card depicts a boy looking at a violin,

which is on a table in front of him. His expression is ambiguous. The following is Tom's story.

> WELL, THERE IS A LITTLE BOY, AND HIS mother told him to practice the violin, and he don't want to practice the violin, so he just sits there staring at it. After a while he fell asleep, and he has a dream and—now I have to think up a dream. He dreamed he was the greatest violinist in the world, and fame and success brought him riches and happiness. He bought his mother beautiful things, and his father—he bought him nice things and everything he wanted. He enjoyed living in such luxury. I don't want to end it yet. These are hard to figure out. He had a special violin, and no other violin could he play because this was the only one that ever worked for him, because there was only one that could play the right tunes. It seemed like magic that it played all right. He kept it by his bedside because if he lost the violin he would lose his wealth and everything. It was almost like magic. Finally, there came a time when his rival realized he could only play that one violin, and he sent some bandits to break up his violin and ruin his career. Just as the bandits were going to break the violin in half, he woke up.

This particular picture often elicits stories concerning responsibility and achievement; in terms of our conceptual scheme, the stories concern work. Tom's opening sentence contains the familiar theme of a child having to do something he does not want to do because his mother says he must. However, Tom's method of coping with this conflict is quite unusual—he escapes into a dream. It is as if telling a story about being pressured to work was not sufficiently safe, and Tom needs the twice-removed protection of a fantasy within a fantasy. The dream itself is richly imaginative, suggesting a creative potential in Tom. And what a contrast between the initial picture of the boy who is incapable of resolving the conflict of imposed duty, and the grandiose, world-famous, supremely rich, and happy achiever. The achievement is not solely egocentric, since it also enables the boy to give the parents everything they wanted. But, interestingly, Tom is not able to end on this theme of magical, compensatory fulfillment. Instead of bringing security, grandiose achievement is accompanied by a state of heightened vulnerability, since a competitive rival sets out to destroy him. And once again Tom cannot cope with the situation he creates, this time the anxiety over the competitive aspects of achievement. The boy in the story wakes up as one might from a nightmare in which anxiety has reached an intolerable level.

We can infer that Tom's situation of trying to meet unrealistic expectations has affected his view of himself in relation to his parents. Out of his impotence he has generated a compensatory image of grandiose success, which both allows him to fulfill parental expectations and to be on the giving end in regard to his parents. In its own right, this exaggerated image and reversal of parent–child roles could not be considered a healthy resolution. In addition, the wishful image cannot be sustained because of the destructive competitiveness Tom perceives to be an integral part of achievement. Thus, there is an impasse at both the reality and the fantasy levels. In sum, the pressures of unattainable goals has engendered a feeling of helplessness and a concern over loveworthiness on the one hand and a fear of competitiveness and achievement on the other. However, Tom has the great assets of a lively imagination and an openness in expressing ideas in a disguised form when they are too painful to face directly. One would expect that he would be a good risk for psychotherapy and that he would make significant progress.

In general, the TAT has fared better in reliability and validity studies than has the Rorschach. Not only does it differentiate various psychopathological groups, such as psychotics and delinquents, but it has also stimulated interest in studying a number of the needs which it taps, the achievement need being the outstanding example. (For further information concerning validity studies, see Klopfer and Taulbee, 1976.)

OTHER PROJECTIVE TECHNIQUES. The Children's Apperception Test (CAT) was designed on the premise that children will more readily identify with and therefore tell more meaningful stories about animal than about human figures (Bellak, 1954). The scenes depicted derive from Freud's psychosexual theory of development, such as a lion king sitting on a throne and a little mouse peeking out of a hole in the wall. The fact that the original premise has not been confirmed has relegated the CAT to the status of an ancillary technique: a child who tells meager stories on the TAT may possibly respond more freely to the CAT.

Of the many *drawing techniques*, the Draw-A-Person Test (DAP) is one of the most widely used. According to Machover's (1949) procedure, the child is first asked to draw a person, then to draw a person of the opposite sex. Next, a series of questions follows, such as "What is the person doing?" "How old is he(she)?" "What does the person like and dislike?"—although such questions have not become part of a standard procedure. Theoretically, the child's drawing is a projection of both the self-image and body image. Various characteristics of the drawing are interpreted in terms of psychological variables—a small figure indicating inferiority, faint lines suggesting anxiety or an amorphous identity, an overly large head indicating excessive intellectualization—while the answers to the questions are interpreted thematically, so that a figure who is "just standing there" suggests passivity, while one who is a cheerleader suggests activity and exhibitionism. The figure may represent either the self or the idealized self; Tom, for example, may have drawn either a very small or a very large male figure. While its popularity attests to its clinical utility, the DAP only rarely has met the test of validation (see Klopfer and Taulbee, 1976).

Other Psychological Tests

ACHIEVEMENT TESTS. An assessment of academic achievement is important in deciding whether a child has a learning disability and in evaluating the effectiveness of a remedial program; low academic achievement may also contribute to the development of a behavior problem. As with intelligence tests, there are individual, group, and short forms of achievement tests. Again, as with intelligence tests, individually administered achievement tests allow the clinician to make behavioral observations of the child and to analyze the nature of the child's failures, both of which may provide helpful clues as to motivational and academic problems; for example, a boy who gives up without trying is different from one who fails after trying his best, just as a girl who fails multiplication problems because of careless mistakes is different from another who fails because she has not grasped the basic process of multiplying. Typically, achievement tests are of the pencil-and-paper variety and cover reading, spelling, arithmetic, social studies, and science.

In many instances, a global measure of achievement in the principal school subjects suffices to answer the clinician's questions and the Wide-Range Achievement Test (WRAT) may be used (Jastak and Jastak, 1965). The WRAT provides tests for reading, spelling, and arithmetic, covers an age range from 5 years to adulthood, and can be administered in twenty to thirty minutes. Its reliability is high, as are correlations between WRAT scores and those on other tests measuring achievement in the same school subjects. When the clinician is particularly interested in evaluating a child's reading, the Gray Oral Reading Tests (Gray, 1963) is a time-honored and useful instrument.

Among group-administered achievement tests, both the Iowa Test of Basic Skills (Lindquist and Hieronymus, 1955–1956), designed to assess vocabulary, reading comprehension, work-study skills, and arithmetic in children in grades three through nine, and the Stanford Achievement Test (Kelley, Madden, Gardner and Rudman, 1964), which has five batteries of tests for children from first through ninth grade covering word and paragraph meaning, science and social studies concepts, spelling, language, and arithmetic concepts, have satisfactory reliability and validity and are widely used.

ABILITIES TESTS. A different approach to assessing learning disabilities is that of evaluating the abilities directly related to academic achievement rather than achievement per se. An example of such an approach is the Illinois Test of Psycholinguistic Abilities (ITPA) (Kirk, McCarthy, and Kirk, 1968). The scale is made up of twelve subtests sampling variables theoretically involved in language communication. Only a portion of the test will be described.

Certain subtests evaluate simple abilities, such as auditory and visual reception or auditory sequential memory as measured by the ability to repeat an increasingly long series of digits. Vocal association uses analogy statements, such as "A dog has hair; a fish has ———," to tap the ability to relate concepts presented orally; the ability to express concepts readily, or verbal expression, is evaluated by showing a child familiar objects and instructing him or her to "Tell me all about this." The ITPA can be administered to children from 2 to 10 years of age. Research on its ability to diagnose reading disorders has yielded both positive and negative findings, and like many other assessment instruments its clinical utility has outstripped its proven validity.

TESTS FOR ORGANIC BRAIN DAMAGE. Since we know that there is no one-to-one relation between brain damage and deviant behavior and since the manifestations of brain damage may range from a slight deficit in sensorimotor abilities to a pervasive disruption of every aspect of a child's intellectual and personality functioning, it follows that there can be no single diagnostic test either of organic brain damage or minimal brain dysfunction. No assessment technique can consistently and satisfactorily differentiate the organically damaged from the organically intact child. (For an evaluative review, see Wohl, 1980.)

If brain damage potentially affects a variety of functions, then a battery of tests casting a wide psychological net would seem to provide a reasonable strategy for capturing the elusive diagnosis. One of the more promising efforts along this line is the Reitan-Indiana Neuropsychological Battery for Children (Reitan, 1964), an adaptation of the Halstead Neuropsychological Battery for Children, which is applicable to children 9 through 14 years of age. The diversity of the tests may be seen in the following sampling. The Category Test requires the child to abstract principles based on variables such as size, color, number, and position from visually presented material. In the Tactual Performance Test, the blindfolded child is required to fit variously shaped blocks into a form board with the preferred, nonpreferred, and both hands and then, with blindfold, blocks, and form board removed, to draw a diagram of the board. This test evaluates memory and spatial location, both of which may be adversely affected by organicity. In Trailmaking B, the child is given a piece of paper on which twenty-five circles are scattered about; the circles are randomly numbered from 1 to 13 and randomly lettered from A through L. The child's task is to connect alternate numbers and letters, that is, to go from A to 1 to B to 2 and so on. The score is the time taken and the child is penalized for errors. Among other things, Trailmaking B is a test of flexibility of thinking, a facility which may be impaired in certain kinds of organic brain damage.

Tests of individual functions are more widely used than time-consuming batteries, but their popularity is rarely buttressed by solid evidence of diagnostic accuracy. A frequently used means of evaluating *perceptual motor coordination* is the Bender Gestalt Test for Young Children (Koppitz, 1964), consisting of nine figures which are presented one at a time for the child to copy; for example, a row of dots, a juxtaposed circle and diamond, two wavy lines intersecting. As a test of *memory* the Graham-Kendall Memory for Designs Test requires the child to reproduce from memory fifteen figures similar to those on the Bender (Graham and Kendall, 1960).

MULTIPLE ASSESSMENT. The System of Multicultural Pluralistic Assessment (SOMPA) is a promising attempt at multiple assessment in a single instrument (Mercer, 1977). There are nine sets of measures, each appropriate to three assessment models. The medical model includes a health-history inventory, along with measures of vision, hearing, weight-height, physical dexterity, and visual-motor coordination. The social-systems model evaluates adaptive behavior, such as the ability to assume responsible roles in the family, school, and community; the ability to participate in peer activities; and the ability to care for one's own needs. Finally, there is a measure of intelligence, either the WISC-R or the Wechsler Preschool and Primary Scale of Intelligence (WPPSI). The pluralistic model, which assumes that opportunities to learn and test-taking experience vary widely according to SES, provides for an estimate of learning potential that takes these sociocultural differences into account. Thus it is especially valuable in assessing children whose racial or ethnic heritage differs from that of the Anglo-American majority.

BEHAVIORAL ASSESSMENT

As we have noted, the scientist's quest for comprehensive understanding of psychopathology differs from the clinician's pragmatic goal of obtaining information relevant to implementing a particular kind of remediation. The most recent example of tailoring inquiry to a therapeutic procedure is behavioral assessment. Since behavior therapy focuses on the current situation, assessment aims at obtaining a specific account of a child's problem behaviors along with their immediate antecedents and consequences. (See Ross, 1980, chap. 6. For a more extended discussion, see Evans and Nelson, 1977.)

Behavioral assessment utilizes many traditional diagnostic procedures but the emphasis differs. In obtaining *referral information* the clinician focuses on the question of who has seen what behaviors in which situations. The answers provide initial clues as to the behaviors considered troublesome, the settings in which they are manifested, and the individuals who observe them.

The *behavioral interview* primarily aims at obtaining behavior-specific accounts of the problem and the environmental factors that may be maintaining it. The behavioral clinician also inquires into attempts to change the troublesome behavior and the results obtained. Adults directly involved with the child's problem, such as parents, teachers, and relatives, are interviewed. Generally speaking, obtaining historical information is minimized, since the clinician is only incidentally interested in reconstructing etiology. However, such information is sought to the extent to which it may throw light on the current situation.

Some of the main features of the behavioral interview deserve to be presented in detail. To begin with, general descriptions of the child, such as "nervous," "bad," "lazy," must be translated into specific behaviors. Because of their generality, the exact behavioral referents of such descriptions are obscure; in addition, the same behavior can be interpreted differently—one parent labeling it "restless," another "active"—just as different behaviors may carry identical labels—"nervous" meaning hyperactive to one parent, fearful to another. Next, the interviewer inquires concerning *antecedents* or a description of the situations in which the problem behavior occurs. Again, specificity is of the essence: "Sue-Anne starts yelling when we're eating" is not as helpful as, "Sue-Anne starts yelling when her pa and me are at supper, and he tells her 'Eat all your corn' or 'Help clear the table' or 'Do the dishes' or some other (dinner) chore." Next, the clinician inquires as to events which occur immediately following the problem behavior, namely, its *consequences*. Here, as in every aspect of the interview, behavioral specificity is sought in terms of exactly who is present and what is done: "After Sue-Anne starts yelling, her pa smacks her, and she just keeps on until sometime he can't stand the noise and leaves the house and I don't see him the rest of the evening."

Certain ancillary information is helpful. The clinician may obtain an initial inventory of potential reinforcers to be used in therapy by asking what the child enjoys, such as favorite foods, recreational activities, pastimes. The parents may be asked what behavior they would wish to have as a replacement for the present objectionable ones. The clinician may assess the amount of time the parent has to participate in a therapeutic program if one were deemed desirable, and evaluate the parent's ability and willingness to do so. Finally, the child may be interviewed to obtain his or her perception of the problems as well as a list of likes and dislikes.

The interviewer's emphasis on specific behavior in no way eliminates the problems inherent in conducting any clinical interview. Parents are personally involved rather than objective reporters; for example, in the preceding illustration, the mother may have cited only the father's behavior as an antecedent and omitted her own out of defensiveness or vindictiveness toward her husband or dislike of the clinician—or out of honest obliviousness. Thus, the behavioral clinician must be as skilled as any other in establishing rapport, constructively handling negative feelings, judging the accuracy of the information, and when it is suspect, finding ways of eliciting a more realistic account without antagonizing or alienating the parent.

Psychological tests are used sparingly; personality tests which reveal underlying attitudes, motivations, and perceptions of self and others are regarded as useless. Preference is for *behavior checklists,* which are typically composed of a listing of behavior problems, such as disobedience, attention seeking, social withdrawal, truancy from school. The adult who knows the child best checks the characteristic items. Some checklists also include positive items, while others are environmentally oriented, requiring the parent to designate the setting and social consequences for each of the problem behaviors.

BEHAVIORAL OBSERVATION. The behavioral approach has made a unique contribution to the assessment process by adapting the technique of naturalistic observation—previously used primarily for research purposes—to assessment goals and placing it at the heart of the process. It is easy to understand this emphasis on direct observation, since abnormal behavior is assumed to develop and to be maintained by environmental stimuli, while behavior modification corrects problem behaviors by altering the environmental conditions maintaining them.

On the basis of information obtained from the referral, checklist, and interview, the clinician identifies the target behaviors to be observed. These behaviors are, in effect, the operational definition of the child's problem, "bad" becoming translated into "yelling at her father during supper" in our example. While behavioral clinicians are always sensitive to the individuality of the child, they have found sufficient commonality among certain problems to have developed standard *behavior codes* for particular settings. Disruptive behaviors in the classroom, for instance, frequently fall within categories such as the child being out of his or her chair without permission, touching, grabbing, or destroying another child's property, vocalizing, speaking or noisemaking without permission, aggressiveness, and failure to do the assignment.

The behavioral clinician's next task is to determine the frequency of the target behavior in order to establish a *baseline* for its natural occurrence against which to evaluate the effectiveness of the therapeutic intervention. Observations are scheduled for the specific periods in which the problem behavior is most likely to happen. Depending on the natural occurrence of the target behavior, the period may last half an hour to an entire day, while observations may be made daily or only on particular days. Our obstreperous little girl, for example, only needs to be observed for about thirty minutes every day at suppertime, provided both parents are present.

There are a number of different methods for quantifying behavior observations. *Frequency* involves counting the number of times the target behavior occurs within a specific period. Frequency divided by time yields a measure called *response rate;* for example, a disruptive boy may leave his seat without permission five times in a fifty-minute class period so his response rate would be 5/50 or .10. In *interval recording* an observer has a data sheet divided into small time units, such as twenty seconds; aided by a timing device such as a stopwatch attached to a clipboard, the observer indicates whether the target behavior occurred in a given unit. Frequently, a *time-sampling* method is used in which the observer observes the child's behavior for twenty seconds and spends the next ten seconds recording the target behaviors which occurred in that twenty-second interval. This sequence is repeated for the duration of the observational period. Typically, only the presence or absence of target behavior is recorded. Some data are lost if a behavior occurs more than once during an interval, but such losses are often unimportant. Interval recording is usually more practicable than the frequency method when the observer wishes to record a number of behaviors. Finally, *duration* consists of measuring the interval of time between the onset and termination of the target behavior. This method is appropriate when decreasing the time spent in a particular behavior, such as head-banging, is a therapeutic goal.

In addition to being used to determine the frequency or duration of target behavior, observation provides information concerning antecedent and consequence events. However, this aspect of data gathering has not been formalized into specific procedures. Often the data are in descriptive or narrative form rather than being quantified. As always, the observer is aware of the setting-specific nature of the relationships observed and is alert to the possibility that the setting may significantly alter the functional meaning of behavior; for example, a mother's reprimand may tend to decrease provocative behavior when mother and child are alone, but it may increase such behavior when the father comes home, especially if he sides with the child.

Theoretically the baseline phase should continue until the target behavior has become stable. Because of the variability of human behavior, such an ideal is often difficult to achieve. The general consensus is that there should be a minimal baseline period of one week of data collection. (For a comparison of traditional and behavioral assessment, see Ciminero, 1977.)

THE RELIABILITY OF OBSERVATIONAL DATA. Everyone would agree that Sue-Anne's "badness" is nearer the behavioral level than is Tom's concept of himself as helpless. As personality characteristics become increasingly inferential, they become increasingly difficult to evaluate in terms of reliability and validity. This is one reason why achievement tests, which can be correlated with school grades in similar subjects, are more readily validated than projective tests, whose behavioral referents may be obscure. How would you go about determining whether Tom "really" felt helpless, for example? Note, however, that we are dealing with *levels* of inferences from behavior, not with inferential versus noninferential personality characteristics. Behavioral checklists contain primarily inferential descriptions rather than being composed of behaviors that are "out there" for everyone to see. Even experts can disagree as to whether a child is "hyperactive" or merely "lively," "withdrawn" or merely "self-contained," "aggressive" or merely "attention seeking." Thus behavior assessment reduces but does not eliminate the problem of the reliability of behavioral observation.

But what about reliability after personality characteristics have been operationalized? Certainly Sue-Anne's yelling is "out there" for anyone to see—and hear! In this particular instance the issue of reliability may be irrelevant. But for most problems the target behavior is not so clear; on the contrary, naturally occurring behavior may well be equivocal, while its variability makes interpretation and inference inevitable.

Researchers utilizing naturalistic observation have found it necessary to train observers in order to insure reliability. Typically, two or more trainees observe, record, and score the behavior of the same child. Disagreements are discussed and reconciled. Additional observations are made and scored until agreement between observers is at least 80 to 85 percent. Even after training is completed, it is highly desirable to "recalibrate" the observers periodically by repeating the training procedures. Such intensive training further attests to the fact that problem behavior is not "out there"; the emperor's new clothes notwithstanding, the untrained eye is an inaccurate observational instrument.

Behavioral clinicians rarely have the time or the personnel to train for accurate observation. Consequently, they must rely on untrained adults, such as parents and teachers. The expected decline in reliability has been documented (Achenbach and Edelbrock, 1978). In general, a given individual is consistent with himself over a period of one week to one month; even after six months, consistency is marginal but adequate. However, the agreement between two different observers at the same point in time is marginal to unsatisfactory: thus, one parent does not agree with another; nor does one teacher or even one professional mental health worker agree with another in their evaluation of problem behavior. Reliability plunges precipitously between adults who view the same child in different situations, such as parents and teachers, teachers and mental health workers, or even teachers who see the child in different settings. This last finding suggests that many problem behaviors are situation-specific. Thus reliability is affected both by the implicit definitions and biases of the observers, and the different information input they have in terms of the situations in which they have observed the child.

The question of reliability is not as crucial to behavioral clinicians as it is to researchers. Up to a point they can say that the objective existence of the problem behavior is not as important as the fact that parents or teachers perceive the behavior as the problem. But they cannot always say this. In certain instances they may judge that the behavior falls within normal limits or that the parent is too disturbed to give an accurate account of the child. In such cases focus shifts from child to parent. Once again, the relative objectivity of the behavioral assessment does not exempt the clinician from acquiring highly developed clinical skills. (For a comprehensive discussion of naturalistic observation, see Kent and Foster, 1977.)

CLINICAL ASSESSMENT: ART AND SCIENCE

While differences in assessment procedures can best be understood in terms of clinicians' different theoretical and therapeutic allegiances, there is another, related source of disagreement. As scientists, psychologists strive for objectivity and precision, which require, among other things, clearly delineated procedures that are available to the scientific community. It is no accident that psychologists in the past championed intelligence tests in particular and the mental measurement movement in general over impressionistic evaluations. Nor is it by chance that behavioral assessment, with its explicit procedures for observation, its relative disinterest in historical antecedents, and its dismissal of inferred personality characteristics and motivations, is exercising a similar appeal. Concomitantly, there is a mistrust of the hypothesis-testing clinician initially described in this discussion. While utilizing theoretical and experiential guides, the process by which this clinician generates, tests, accepts, and discards ideas is nearer to an art than a science. He or she may indeed come up with impressive insights but also may be seriously in error; more important—and this is what concerns the critical psychologist—there is no clearly established procedure for deciding in favor of one outcome over the other.

This tug-of-war between the art and science of assessment took the form of clinical versus actuarial prediction thirty years ago; today it may well take the form of clinical versus computerized prediction. Suppose, for example, that the PIC were perfected and information concerning all possible profiles fed into a computer. Could not the computer print out a personality evaluation as valid as that of the clinician utilizing any other assessment technique? Thirty years ago a strong case was made in favor of the actuarial-computer approach and documented by research findings, although the issue was never settled. (For a rebuttal and reevaluation of the issue, see Janis, 1969, pp. 778–801. See also Wiggins, 1981.)

Certain clinicians might answer that scores are only one kind of information to be gained from a test, as we have seen in discussing intelligence tests. To limit assessment to such scores would be to eliminate the added behavioral data so vital to understanding an individual child. If such data have yet to be standardized and are of unknown reliability, their clinical utility justifies their use for the present.

These clinicians rightly claim that there are a number of important areas for which no standardized, clinically useful instrument exists, family interaction being the most prominent example. Thus, they can do no more than put the pieces of assessment data together as best they can. Moreover, it is just such efforts to understand complex, heretofore unsystematized data that can ultimately serve as the basis for objective assessment techniques. Recall that the PIC relied heavily on the accumulated clinical experience of its authors for its categories and items. Instead of polarizing the clinician and actuarially inclined psychologist (or the computer) the two should complement one another, the clinician exploring the territory which one day will be formally structured into objective assessment techniques whose reliability and validity can be tested.

While techniques and goals may vary, all clinical assessment requires a high degree of professional competence. Clinicians must be skillful and sensitive in handling the many interpersonal problems inherent in dealing with troubled parents and children; they must be knowledgeable concerning the procedures they utilize and the problems they are called upon to evaluate; they must be well acquainted with and abide by the ethical principles of their profession; and they must have received adequate academic and professional preparation, which for a clinical child psychologist typically involves a PhD or PsyD from an accredited university and at least two years of supervised experience (American Psychological Association, 1979).

The dovetailing of assessment and psychotherapy which has been emphasized will become clearer after we learn more about the major schools of psychotherapies themselves. This topic is covered in our final discussion.

14 ▪ Remediation and Prevention

Our discussion will now turn to some of the ways in which psychopathological behavior can be changed and ways to prevent it from occurring in at-risk populations. In the realm of remediation, three of the major psychotherapies—psychoanalytic, client-centered, and behavioral—will be presented, with emphasis on the conceptualization of development that provides the basic rationale for the therapeutic techniques each employs. After a brief survey of group and family psychotherapy, the effectiveness of psychotherapy in general will be discussed. Prevention will take us into the realm of the community mental health movement. The origins and nature of this movement and some of the many efforts at prevention it has generated will be described and evaluated.

THE PSYCHOANALYTIC APPROACH

Classical psychoanalysis is a highly specialized technique appropriate for only a limited range of psychopathologies. Here, as in the remainder of this section, the presentation will be based on Anna Freud's writings (A. Freud, 1965; Scharfman, 1978. Another influential figure in this field is Melanie Kline, who disagreed with Anna Freud on many points concerning child psychoanalysis (see Segal, 1973).)

The Developmental Model

Since classical psychoanalysis grows directly out of the psychoanalytic theory of neurosis, we need to review briefly what we have learned about this theory. Recall that psychopathology originates in the psychosexual stages, when the possessiveness, rivalry, death wish, and castration anxiety of the Oedipus complex act as particularly fertile breeding grounds for neurosis. Not only is the preschooler overwhelmed, but also the forces for growth are not sufficiently strong to overcome the traumatic impact.

Unable to master the psychosexual anxieties, preschoolers are tempted to regress. Returning to more babyish behaviors, however, is unacceptable to the mature elements in their personality. Thus, they are trapped, being able neither to progress nor to regress. If they cannot master the anxiety, at least they can defend themselves against it, using repression and other defenses, such as displacement and projection. In certain instances the defenses work in the sense of providing developmental pathways that will be serviceable throughout life. But there is always the vulnerability attendant upon an unmastered phase of development, and subsequent experiences may exacerbate the underlying disturbance, the special combination of fixation point and defenses producing the specific neurotic symptoms of hysteria, phobias, obsessions, or compulsions.

The essence of psychoanalysis consists of reversing the defensive process, reconfronting the individual with the original trauma so that it can be mastered belatedly. Successful psychoanalysis is epitomized by Freud's aphorism, "Where id was, there shall ego be." The once-overwhelming hates, jealousies, and fears can now be revived and viewed from a more mature perspective. The ensuing insight into the root of the problem exorcises it. The result is a "widening of consciousness" in two senses: the individual both can face previously unacceptable aspects of his or her personality, and the energy used for defensive maneuvers can now be employed in growth-promoting activities.

The Therapeutic Process

Psychoanalysis depends on the establishment of a *therapeutic alliance* between therapist and patient—a bond sufficiently strong to sustain the patient through the many stormy sessions which lie ahead. The sessions themselves are held four to five times a week for a period of three years or more. Another general feature of psychoanalysis is the maximizing of free expression during the psychoanalytic hour. Adult patients are initially instructed to lie down on the couch, facing away from the analyst, and say everything that comes into their mind—a technique called *free association.* It is from the basic data of free association that the analyst tries to understand the patient's life as the patient perceives it. Suggestions, advice, directions as to how to handle problems, and medication are minimized and ideally avoided altogether.

There are two major techniques for undoing the work of defenses. The first is called analyzing the *resistance.* Since defenses protect the patient from anxiety, he or she will find numerous ways to retain them. This accounts for the paradox that in spite of great suffering the adult neurotic will resist attempts at cure. The maneuvers used to resist bringing painful ideas and feelings into consciousness are numerous. A patient may lie on the couch and say that nothing comes to mind, for example, or he may bring up a personal feeling and quickly change the subject or impersonalize it by talking about the current state of society, or he may steep himself in psychoanalytic theory so that he "knows the answer" to his problem before the analyst, or he may even engage in a "flight into health," claiming that all his problems have been solved and that he never felt better in his life! The analyst's task is constantly to call attention to such evasive maneuvers and help the patient to focus on the threatening material which prompted them, the therapeutic alliance giving the client courage to explore such material.

Next, classical psychoanalysis involves analysis of the *transference*. The intense, prolonged one-to-one relationship stimulates the revival of previous intense relationships to the parents. Thus, feelings once directed toward parents are transferred to the therapist. We had a foretaste of transference when we discussed the child's reaction to the examiner in psychological assessment: if a child is frightened by or enamoured with or defiant of the examiner far in excess of the reality of the situation, one begins to suspect that a transference may be involved. In psychoanalysis, such irrational feelings are much more pronounced. A child's seemingly innocent question, "Do you have children of your own?" may be the beginning of an irrational anger over imagined rivals, while a very disturbed 10-year-old's refusal to enter the therapy room because she literally feared the analyst would bite her head off shows how terrorizing such fantasies can be. Again it is the analyst's function to call attention to transferences, so that in exploring them, patients can begin to gain access to the distressing relationships which played a decisive role in their neurosis.

The patient's verbal productions form the leading edge of psychoanalysis. After a period of time, the analyst begins to make *interpretations* as to the meaning of these productions once the meaning seems reasonably clear. Such interpretations are often very simple: "You must have been angry at your older brother for always being so much better than you were." "Wasn't it frustrating to have such a 'perfect' mother?" "You seem always to run away from this idea that you are as sexy as any other girl." Correctly timed, such interpretations produce insights; prematurely timed they are rejected and fuel the patient's resistance. Nor does a therapeutic cure come in one blinding flash of insight. Instead, the same material has to be approached again and again from many different directions and through many different experiences in order for the insight to be firmly established—a process called *working through*. The defense of being a sweet little girl or a nonentity or a hellion, for example, is expressed in countless ways, so the patient must confront and reevaluate these variations on the theme of his or her core conflicts before insights can become stable and generally serviceable.

Child Psychoanalysis

Applying classical psychoanalysis to children has required certain major changes in procedures and techniques but not in the basic goal. For a number of reasons the therapeutic alliance is different with children than with adults. Children do not voluntarily seek therapy, nor do they necessarily suffer intensely from their neurotic problems. They live more in the present than do adults, so they cannot be expected to endure the pain of psychoanalysis for the sake of some future good. In attributing causes for their behavior, they tend to externalize and place the responsibility on others rather than examining their own actions. By the same token, they look to the therapist as someone who will change the environment, so that they will not have to go to school or obey their father, for example. Children often lack the capacity for self-observation or self-monitoring that enables adults to participate in an intense emotional experience while at the same time observing themselves reacting. One can readily understand how such an ability facilitates the gaining of insight. Finally, during times of developmental stress such as adolescence, children are reluctant to add to their emotional burdens by confronting their anxieties.

Children's personalities are also not as firmly structured as those of adults, who can maintain an intrapsychic conflict relatively independent of environmental events. A child is always more responsive to environmental influences even when neurotic; for example, the resolution of a phobia may come about by some growth-promoting forces within the environment and not represent a "flight into health." Thus the child analyst must keep track of reality to a much greater extent than is necessary with adults. Children's transferences, unlike those of adults, do not involve feelings toward parental ghosts dating back to the distant past. Because children are still living with and dependent upon parents, their transference tends to be more dilute and obscure; for example, the irrational anger a girl brings to a therapy session may be due to the fact that her parents have entered a stormy phase in their relationship or that a parent, envious of the therapist's influence, has begun catering to the child in order to win her over.

A radical change in technique is necessitated by the fact that children cannot free-associate, and *play* has to be substituted. However, play is not the equivalent of free association. Through associations, adults provide the key to the idiosyncratic meaning of events or dreams; since children provide no such key, the analyst must actively try to decode the meaning of their fantasies. In addition, adults are encouraged to say anything which comes into their mind, while children cannot be similarly encouraged to do anything they like; such a lure too often leads to aggressive acting out, such as damaging property, endangering their safety, attacking the analyst, all of which overwhelms their already weakened ability to reflect upon their own behavior.

The play material itself is the kind which taps fantasies rather than skills—a doll family, crayons, clay, etc. The analyst watches for signs that a theme is of special importance: repetition, excessive affect, an abrupt termination (which suggests anxiety), regression in the form of more infantile play or speech, loss of control, such as scattering the toys around, or a "they lived happily ever after" dismissal of a conflict situation (Peller, 1964). Interpretations are simple and closely attuned to the play: "I bet that family was really scared when the hurricane started coming toward their house." "I wonder why the little girl always wanted to look at the monkeys in the zoo." "Being locked in a closet for two years after being bad does seem a long time." After obtaining clues as to the meaning of the child's fantasy, both from play material and conversations, the analyst can begin building a bridge from the safe disguise of make-believe to the child's own feelings; for example, "That hurricane sounds like what you told me about your mother and father having all those fights." Through such interpretations the child, like the adult, is led back to the original traumatic situation and helped to recognize, reevaluate, and master it. And as with adults, the roadblocks of resistance must be overcome, while the transference is utilized for clues concerning feelings toward parents.

The analyst recognizes that age itself significantly affects the manner in which a psychoanalysis can be conducted; the play material which delights the preschooler becomes increasingly inappropriate toward the end of middle childhood and would be considered demeaning to the adolescent. In fact, adolescents are particularly difficult to help, since they eschew fantasy play, while their tenuous self-control makes them reluctant to explore their feelings via free association. Finally, psychoanalysis stresses the importance of analysts being aware of and learning to manage their own *countertransference*—the many difficult feelings, such as irritation, impatience, or sexual attraction, that children arouse in them during the long, intensive involvement.

Psychoanalytically Oriented Psychotherapies

Since the conditions necessary for a classical psychoanalysis are difficult to meet in childhood, numerous adaptations have been made in order to help a wider variety of disturbed children. At times these variations serve the basic goal of enabling the child to deal with and master traumatic, unconscious material; more often the goal itself is changed to a general one of helping the child adapt, even though the core problem may go unresolved.

A number of the modifications involve the use of techniques which, in classical psychoanalysis, play only a minor role or are regarded as obstacles to achieving the basic goal. One of the most important modifications is that of providing a *corrective emotional experience,* typically by encouraging inhibited children to express forbidden feelings so they can discover that they are neither rejected nor punished for doing so. A too proper girl, for example, may find that there are no disastrous consequences to getting angry first with the therapist and then with significant people in her environment. Closely related to the corrective emotional experience is *reassurance,* in which the omnipotence the child invests in the therapist is used to counteract disabling fears and bolster crippled self-confidence and self-esteem. The implicit message often is: "There is nothing to be afraid of; you can do it if you really try; you are worthy of love and respect."

The therapist can perform an *educational* function which has nothing to do with academic instruction despite its label, but which is more akin to good parenting. The child is still dependent upon adults for guidance in dealing with hostile and erotic feelings (the id), in effectively and realistically managing interpersonal problems of everyday living (the ego), and in deciding upon the morally proper course of action (the superego). If the parents are cooperative and mature, they can participate in the therapist's educative process, although there is always the danger that, in the absence of a congenial working relationship between therapist and parent, the child will begin playing one off against the other, just as one parent can be played off against the other.

The above techniques are differentially emphasized depending on the child's problems. Emotionally deprived children, say, from bleak institutions or bleak homes, need large supplies of love more than anything else; preschizophrenic children with a tenuous hold on reality need a therapist who will serve as an "auxiliary ego," helping them to define and cope with reality while distinguishing it from their own primitive fantasies; for certain delinquents, the therapist must first establish a positive transference and then build up a serviceable set of moral guides. Typically, however, disturbed children have a variety of problems rather than representing "pure" cases, so that the psychoanalytically oriented psychotherapists must utilize a variety of skills.

Techniques may be so different that one kind of psychoanalytically oriented psychotherapy may have little in common with another. Fritz Redl's Pioneer House, which was described in chapter 8, was designed to help acting-out boys develop internal controls by dealing with their impulsive behavior as it happened. A staff member's attempt to manage a violent fight between two Pioneer House boys seems to have little in common with a therapeutic playroom in which an inhibited little girl is acting out a family drama with a set of dolls. Or again, Ruttenberg's therapy for autistic children is predicated on the psychoanalytic principle that establishing a warm maternal relationship is the basis for all future development. The therapists, therefore, consist of nonprofessional child-care workers with an inexhaustible supply of love and patience. Only as the child begins to form an attachment to the worker are other remedial measures such as speech therapy and cognitive stimulation introduced (Wenar and Ruttenberg, 1969).

Thus, there seems to be no common denominator to psychoanalytically oriented psychotherapies other than the therapist's allegiance to the genetic theory of psychosexual development and to the structural theory of id-ego-superego. Yet, the psychoanalytic approach does champion certain concepts, even though such concepts may not all be included in a particular therapeutic variation. First is the importance of understanding the *developmental etiology* of psychopathology; hence the emphasis on history in assessment. Next there is an emphasis on the affect generated by intense interpersonal relationships. Freud's belief that the passions of love, hate, fear, and guilt hold the key to pathology clearly implies that such feelings and their interpersonal contexts should be central in correcting psychopathology. Hence, the emphasis not only on children's *relationship* to parents and sibs but also on their relationship to the therapist and the therapist's feelings toward them. There is the belief that broadly based *motivational systems* underlie specific behaviors and that, as much as possible, those systems should be changed. Castration anxiety, for example, has manifold expressions in terms of fear of authority and competition, as well as being expressed in maneuvers to circumvent such fears; as the anxiety is allayed, many behaviors will lose their reason for being. Finally, there is a belief in the therapeutic value of *insight,* of facing ideas and feelings that had been too threatening to admit into consciousness, thereby achieving a new understanding of the self and of significant interpersonal relations.

THE CLIENT-CENTERED APPROACH

15-YEAR-OLD GIRL: WHEN DAD STARTS that same old lecture (in a singsong voice) 'No nice girl *I* ever knew went around in dirty jeans, and no nice girl *I* ever knew let a boy touch her body on the first date,'' I could just explode on the inside.

THERAPIST: You feel all angry on the inside then.

GIRL: Yeah. But then (glumly) sometimes I look at him and he looks so worn out and there's this cancer thing he's got . . .

THERAPIST: It sounds like you feel sad about your father's condition—getting old and sick, I mean.

GIRL: Or just mixed up so I don't know where I'm going at times, except maybe crazy (with a little laugh).

THERAPIST: So it's as if the mad feeling and the sad feeling make you feel all mixed up?

The therapist is doing the two things which epitomize the client-centered approach—*reflecting* and *accepting* the client's feelings. The therapist's manner is sincere, interested, warm. This type of therapist will never interpret, unlike the analyst, or tell clients how to solve their problems, unlike the behavior therapist. Primarily the therapist will accept and reflect feelings.

On the face of it, the client-centered approach makes little sense, and its practice seems too simple to be regarded as a skill. In reality, the therapy is based on an explicit developmental model of psychopathology, is one of the most demanding of its practitioners, and has exerted a powerful influence on the professional community.

The Developmental Model

Our discussion will be based on the ideas of Carl Rogers (1959), founder of client-centered therapy. Rogers stresses the primacy of the individual's experience and of the individual's self. Maturity is the ability to *experience a feeling fully* so that there is congruence between experiencing the feeling, awareness of the feeling, and expressing the feeling. If the three elements are not present the individual is apt to be disturbed; a repressed individual cannot allow certain feelings into consciousness, an overintellectualized individual talks about feelings in an impersonal manner, while an inhibited individual is afraid to act upon feelings. The *self* is the concept of who one is and of one's relations with others. While it may not be totally conscious, it is available to consciousness.

Rogers is explicit about the conditions which facilitate or block the attainment of maturity. First he postulates an *actualizing tendency,* which is an inherent tendency in each organism to develop all of its capacities in ways which serve to maintain or enhance it. This is the growth principle—an innate push toward expansion, differentiation, and maximization. It includes the tendency to be creative, to learn new things painfully rather than to settle for the complacency of acquired learning, to develop toward autonomy rather than to be controlled by external forces. Moreover, each organism has an *organismic valuing process,* which leads it to value positively those experiences that maintain and enhance it, while valuing negatively those that have the opposite effect. Thus, each individual has a built-in guide to what is best for personal growth, innately seeking enhancing experiences and avoiding those that are detrimental.

The *self* begins to emerge as a portion of the toddler's experience becomes differentiated and symbolized in an awareness of being and an awareness of functioning. Thus, both "I" and what the "I" can do become part of conscious awareness. As awareness of the self emerges, the individual develops the *need for positive regard,* which is a universal need for warmth, respect, sympathy, and acceptance. With time, the need can become more potent than the organismic valuing process.

An essential requirement for healthy growth is that the need for positive regard continues to serve the organismic valuing process; in other words, it is essential that the people the child loves and values continue to foster the child's need to experience and decide for himself. In our terminology, affection must enhance initiative. This can be done only if the child receives *unconditional positive regard.* Here, no experience of the child is perceived by others as more or less worthy of positive regard. Children are intrinsically valued, and their experiences are not viewed judgmentally as being "good" or "bad" by adult standards.

But Rogers does not advocate total permissiveness. He recognizes that children cannot be allowed to do everything they like. However, discipline should take place in the context of an explicit and sympathetic recognition of the children's feelings: "I know you are mad at your baby brother, and I understand why, but I just can't let you hurt him because he has his feelings too." When this is done children never have to view themselves as "bad" and never have to disown their feelings. Consequently, their openness to experience and feelings is preserved.

Normal development goes awry because

of what Rogers calls *conditions of worth.* Instead of unconditional positive regard, significant adults, particularly parents, say, in essence, "I will love you on the condition that you behave as I want you to." If children do what parents consider to be good, they are loved; if they do what parents consider to be bad, they are not loved. Because of the strong need for positive regard, children eventually make parental values into self values. At this point children are no longer in touch with their organismic valuing process, no longer open to experience and capable of deciding for themselves whether an experience is growth-promoting. By incorporating alien values they become alienated from themselves. Because of alienation, children begin to distort experiences in order to fit the imposed model of a "good boy" or a "good girl": the aesthetic boy believes he has to be a competitive go-getter because this is his father's ideal, the bright girl is hounded by feelings of inadequacy because her mother disparages intellectual achievement. Self-alienation is also a state of vulnerability to anxiety as the organismic values continue to press for their rightful place in the self. Children do not recognize such values but can only try to defend themselves against them. When distress becomes too intense, anxiety runs rampant and therapy is required.

How different the Rogerian model is from the Freudian. Freud sees humanity as endowed with primitive drives that must be socialized or else society itself could no longer exist. Rogers follows Rousseau's idea that the child, like the primitive "noble savage," is innately good, and it is socialization that has the potential for destroying the natural tendencies to growth and self-actualization. Understandably, Rogers has had a strong appeal for those who turn their backs on convention in order to "find themselves" and search for a way of life which would express "the real me." He is also in harmony with the existential emphasis on the primacy of the individual's experience and the importance of individual choice. One hears echoes of Shakespeare's "To thine own self be true" along with the "me" generation's "If it feels right, it is right."

The Therapeutic Process

In light of what we have learned, we can understand how the client-centered therapist, by offering the child unconditional positive regard, will help undo the damage of conditional love. The focus is continually on feelings because these hold the key to maturity. And because of the growth principle, the therapist has complete confidence in the client's ability to solve his or her own problems with the minimum of direction—hence the general name, *nondirective therapy.*

A number of therapists have adapted Rogers's principles for children; Axeline's (1964, 1969) approach is presented here. The major change in procedure is the introduction of play material for children below the preadolescent age range. The material is simple and conducive to self-expression—dolls, animals, clay, sand, building materials. Construction toys and games of skill are avoided as being too structured to produce varied and individualized behavior. While the formal arrangement resembles that of psychoanalysis, the purpose is quite different. Rather than using play as the basis for interpretation, therapists limit their activity to reflecting the themes and affects the child introduces.

Some of the basic features of nondirective therapy deserve to be elaborated. Therapists are, quite literally, nondirective. After discussing the ground rules for the therapeutic hour and describing the procedure in general terms they leave the direction of the sessions up to the child. Even if the child asks such a simple question as, "What is this toy?" the therapist shifts the decision back to the child by a neutral comment such as, "What does it look like to you?" or, "It can be whatever you like." As we have seen, therapists do not interpret the meaning of the child's behavior, nor do they introduce any material from the child's past, from the reality of the child's present situation, or from previous sessions. If, for example, they learn that the child has started setting fires, they wait until the child is ready to make such behavior part of the therapeutic session. Thus, responsibility is always on the child's shoulders. What therapists communicate implicitly is a faith in the child's ability to decide what is best for his or her own growth.

We can now understand both why the past has little intrinsic value and why diagnosis plays only a minor role in nondirective therapy. Therapists have no need to "know the answer" ahead of time; in fact, such a need might well interfere with the therapeutic process. Not only do they want to learn about the child only through the child, but as much as possible they also want to experience life as the child experiences it. Their reflection of feeling is not a mechanical technique; with it goes a genuine effort to feel their way into the child's experience. Therapists are not onlookers; they are empathetic participants.

We can also understand why it is so demanding to be a nondirective therapist. First it means relinquishing the role of authoritative adult. Moreover, the therapist's acceptance of and respect for the child must be genuine. As we have already learned from Anna Freud, when children are given freedom to do what they like, many of them begin to gravitate toward destructive acting out. Not only that, but they also have a genius for finding ways of teasing, testing, and provoking adults. For the therapist to maintain an attitude of acceptance and understanding rather than self-defense and retaliation requires a forebearing disposition and self-discipline.

However, not everything children do is accepted; certain limits are essential. There is the limit of time, since the children must leave at the end of the session whether they want to or not. Children are not permitted to do things which deviate significantly from the world of reality; specifically, they are not allowed to attack the therapist or themselves physically or to destroy the playroom and its contents. However, the therapist, like the good parent, is understanding of the motive, even while preventing the behavior, thus avoiding judging the children as "bad."

One final word about the technique of reflecting feelings. Its *structuring* properties are obvious, since the therapist is implicitly sending the message, "While we are together, feelings are what we will be dealing with." But there is more than that. In the permissive atmosphere of the therapeutic session, the child begins to explore feelings which formerly had to be banished from conscious awareness. In fact, some of these feelings may never have been clearly recognized for what they were. Thus, reflection also serves a *defining* function rather than being a mere echo of what the child already knows. What is more, as feelings are explicitly defined, they come under conscious control. As the boy realizes his resentment for being pushed into the alien role of a go-getter, as the girl can face her fear of being rejected by a nonintellectual mother, such feelings become part of the self. The once-divided self is whole again.

THE BEHAVIOR THERAPIES

Behavior therapy is the most vigorous psychotherapy on the current scene. The past twenty years have witnessed an exuberant expansion of therapeutic techniques that has been somewhat disconcerting to those concerned with conceptual clarity—just as theoretical physicists are presently wondering what model can accommodate the quarks and gluons and other exotic particles that are being revealed by technological advances. And if behavior therapy represents the marriage of the clinic and the laboratory, there are signs that the honeymoon is drawing to a close; little irritations are surfacing, and the two partners are searching for a more sober and mature basis for their relationship.

First, a conceptual framework sufficiently broad to embrace all the behavior therapies will be presented. Then the therapies themselves willl be sampled in terms of their underlying rationales. Finally, we shall turn to some of the practical and theoretical problems that have accompanied the field's rapid growth.

Note that a special discussion of the *developmental model* will not be presented. Because of their origin in learning theory, behavior therapies have inherited an emphasis on universal laws of behavior acquisition and elimination. The ways in which such laws are translated into action depend on the particular culture into which the infant is born. Instead of a universal sequence of behaviors, as found in Freud's and Piaget's theories, progression is determined by the particular behaviors a given society values at different ages. While allowing for physiological maturation, behaviorists ever since Watson have favored an environmentalist position.

However, a developmental dimension is implicit in the laws of learning behavior therapists utilize. A reinforcer is neither an object (such as a candy) nor a behavior (such as praise) but anything that is likely to increase the probability that a behavior will occur. What a reinforcer will be, therefore, clearly is a function of the child's developmental level. In a like manner, implementation of cognitive behavior therapy obviously depends on the level of the child's cognitive development, even though behavior therapists eschew the notion of universal stages.

Conceptual Framework

Behavior therapies are characterized by attention to specific, currently *observable behaviors* of the client, by a concern with *objective measures* of the outcomes of their interventions, and by a reliance on the *research laboratory* to provide general principles of behavior change that can be used as the basis of therapeutic intervention and as a place to put clinical findings to rigorous experimental tests. Rather than being a special set of techniques, behavior therapies are "an *approach* to abnormal behavior . . . characterized by (an) empirical methodology" (A.L. Ross and Nelson, 1979, p. 303. Our presentation follows Ross and Nelson, pp. 303–335. For a more detailed presentation, see Ross, 1981.).

To elaborate: pragmatic considerations have dictated the emphasis on specific behaviors, since these are most amenable to change. Behavior therapists would not deny that such behaviors may be rooted in the past, but the past cannot be altered, the present and the future can. Among ongoing behaviors, the therapists deal with three response systems—overt-motor, physiological-emotional, and cognitive-verbal. All must be considered in a comprehensive treatment program, since they are not necessarily correlated; a boy who is constantly fighting in school may tell the therapist that "everything is OK" and he only fights "a little every now and then." Incidentally, this concentration on the present has resulted in a relative neglect of etiology; thus, the behaviorists' contributions to the field of developmental psychopathology do not match their contributions to remediation.

In the constant interplay between the clinic and the laboratory, principles of learning have been extensively utilized to generate therapeutic procedures, while both social and developmental psychology have provided conceptual underpinnings for therapeutic techniques, although to a lesser degree. Perhaps even more significant than the application of laboratory findings is the incorporation of experimental procedures into psychotherapeutic practice. Behavioral assessment (as described in chapter 13) sets the stage for the objective, reliable measurement of target behavior, as well as providing leads to the specific antecedents and consequents that elicit and maintain these behaviors. The behavior therapist then proceeds to reason very much like his or her experimental counterpart: If behavior X is due to antecedent Y and consequent Z, then as Y and Z are changed, so should X. The therapeutic intervention, like an experiment, consists of testing out the hypothesis, the crucial measure being a change in the base rate of the target behavior X in the desired direction.

The simplest design in evaluating therapeutic effectiveness is the A-B design, in which the dependent measure is evaluated both before intervention (baseline or A) and during intervention (B). Such a design is adequate for clinical work because it demonstrates whether or not change occurs. However, for a more stringent test of the hypothesis that change was caused by the intervention rather than by other variables, the reversal or A-B-A-B design is used in which the therapeutic procedure is repeatedly applied and withdrawn. If change in the target behavior occurs only in the presence of the intervention, then a causal relationship can be more readily assumed.

While the behavior therapist's procedure is akin to the experimentalist's, therapy cannot be equated with experimentation. Uncontrolled variables (such as a boy improving because his father obtained a better job), ethical considerations, and the inevitable complexity of dealing with ongoing problems of living prevent therapy from having the required purity. However, questions raised by therapeutic efficacy can be referred back to the laboratory to be examined under properly controlled conditions. If, for example, a child with a snake phobia begins to handle snakes after watching movies of other children doing so, is it because the anxiety has diminished or because the incentives and techniques for handling snakes are now enhanced, even though the anxiety level itself remains unchanged? The general question of whether it is better to diminish anxiety or enhance coping skills, along with a number of other questions raised in the context of behavior therapies, has provided grist for the experimental mill. In sum, the interaction between the clinic and the laboratory and the objective documentation of the efficacy of various intervention techniques are the hallmarks that clearly distinguish behavior therapies from other approaches to remediation.

Behavior Therapies Derived from Learning Theory

In the prototypical instances of behavior therapy, principles of learning—specifically, classical conditioning, operant learning, and imitation— have formed the bases of intervention procedures. Exemplars of the application of each principle will be examined. (For a more comprehensive account of the behavior therapies, see A. L. Ross, 1981.)

CLASSICAL CONDITIONING. *Systematic desensitization,* as developed by Wolpe (1973), is a procedure for eliminating anxiety-mediated problems. In such problems, initially neutral stimuli come to elicit powerful anxiety responses as a result of classical conditioning. The bond between the conditioned stimulus and the anxiety response can be broken, however, by *reciprocal inhibition,* in which the stronger of two incompatible responses tends to inhibit the weaker. The therapist's task, therefore, becomes one of pairing anxiety-eliciting stimuli with a more powerful, incompatible response. The response Wolpe utilizes is deep muscle relaxation, since obviously an individual cannot be simultaneously anxious and relaxed.

Two preliminary steps are needed in order to implement the therapy. First the child must be instructed in the technique of relaxing various muscle groups throughout the body. The child is also required to make up a graduated sequence of anxiety-eliciting stimuli, going from the least to the most intense. A girl with a school phobia, for example, may feel no anxiety when she awakens and dresses, mild anxiety at breakfast, increasingly strong anxiety while waiting for the bus and approaching school, while the most intense anxiety comes in the free period before classes start.

In the therapy proper, the children imagine each of the steps, pairing them with the relaxation response. If the anxiety is too strong at any particular step and they cannot relax, they return to the preceding step. Over a series of sessions the children gradually are able to relax in response to even the most intense anxiety-producing stimuli. For adults, around sixteen to twenty-three treatment sessions are required to reach this goal. It is interesting that the therapeutic gains which relate solely to imagined representations of reality transfer to reality itself. While Wolpe's rationale has been questioned and the specific variables responsible for improvement have not been satisfactorily isolated, the therapy itself has been successful in treating a host of problems, including school and hospital phobias, examination anxiety, fear of authority, maternal separation anxiety, and asthma.

OPERANT LEARNING. Behavior therapists have made extensive use of the operant principle that behavior is controlled by specific antecedent and consequent stimulus events. *Contingent management,* or the manipulation of rewards and punishments which follow or are contingent upon the response, has been particularly potent in decreasing the strength of undesirable behaviors or increasing the strength of adaptive ones. There are two kinds of positive consequences: reward or positive reinforcement, and removal of an aversive stimulus or negative reinforcement. There are also two kinds of negative consequences: positive punishment or administering an aversive stimulus, and negative punishment or the removal of a pleasant stimulus. Two procedures are used if the behavior one wishes to strengthen is not present in the child's repertoire or is infrequently emitted: *chaining* or *shaping,* in which components or successive approximations of the desired behavior are differentially reinforced, and *prompting,* in which instruction, modeling, or physical guidance is used to elicit the desired response. Behavior therapists frequently combine these various ingredients in order to increase the effectiveness of their therapeutic program.

Examples of the application of operant principles are legion, some involving a therapist, others involving parents who not only can be taught how to implement a therapeutic program with relative ease but who also are in a position to control a wider range of behaviors than can be elicited in a therapeutic setting. (The examples are from Ross and Nelson, 1979.) We shall begin with instances of simple reward or punishment and proceed to programs combining both. The language skills of 2- and 3-year-old children were enhanced when their mothers reinforced naming of objects with praise or bits of food, while the tantrums of a 21-month-old were extinguished when the mother ignored them, thereby withdrawing the attention that had been sustaining them. In programs combining extinction with reinforcement, aggressive dependent behavior was ignored while cooperative independent behavior received parental attention; the mother of an effeminate boy ignored his feminine behavior while praising his masculine behavior; self-stimulation and self-injurious behavior in severely disturbed children was punished by a brief electric shock or a slap, while adaptive behavior was rewarded.

Instead of direct reinforcement, a child can be a given a *token,* which subsequently can be redeemed for rewards such as prizes or privileges. In one therapeutic program children were given tokens for cooperative behavior and doing chores while losing them for undesirable social behavior. In *time out,* the child is isolated for a brief period, thereby being punished by the withdrawal of reinforcers. In one complex program an acting-out boy was isolated for two minutes when he was aggressive and disobedient, while less severe misbehavior was ignored and cooperative behavior was rewarded by special attention and treats. In another complex program, the tantrums of a $3\frac{1}{2}$-year-old autistic boy were treated by time out. A shaping technique was used to teach him to wear glasses, since he was in danger of losing his vision. First he was rewarded for holding the empty frames, then for bringing the frames to his eyes, and finally for wearing the prescriptive lenses. To treat his echolalic speech, he was first rewarded for saying the label for a picture the therapist held and then rewarded for saying the label without the therapist's prompting. His eating problems were decreased by temporarily removing his plate when he ate with his fingers and by temporarily removing him from the dining room when he threw food or took it from someone else's plate.

Training parents to be behavior therapists is not without its problems. The parent must be motivated to learn the techniques and sufficiently conscientious to utilize them over long periods of time. While parents typically want their children to change, they are not uniformally agreeable to the idea that they must also change. The problem of parental involvement may be compounded when the complaint originates in the school or in the court, as it often does. Thus, parents themselves may need special reinforcement from the therapist.

OBSERVATIONAL LEARNING. Observational learning or modeling has not been extensively employed as a primary (rather than an auxiliary) therapeutic technique. However, observing fearless children interacting with a phobic stimulus, such as a snake or a dog, has successfully eliminated phobias. The model may be presented either in real life or on film. Modeling is often combined with reinforcement of the desired behavior; for example, in teaching verbal behavior to autistic children, the child is immediately rewarded with food upon each successful imitation of the therapist's vocalization.

While modeling procedures are comparatively new, they are promising, especially for children.

Cognitive Behavior Therapies

Cognitive behavior therapies are the newest and most controversial additions to the family of behavioral techniques. Not that there is a strict dichotomy between traditional and cognitive behavior therapy. Traditional procedures employ cognitive elements as a means of achieving behavioral change: in desensitization, for example, children imagine various situations and instruct themselves to relax, both of which are cognitive activities. For their part, cognitive therapies are concerned with changing specific overt behaviors, are ahistoric, systematically monitor the relation between intervention and behavioral change, and retain allegiance to the clinic-laboratory symbiosis. However, cognition now becomes the primary object of the therapeutic thrust, since the basic goal is to change the way the child thinks. When this has been accomplished, behavior will also change. Of the varieties of cognitive therapies, only two will be discussed, those concerned with self-control and with cognitive restructuring. (For a comprehensive discussion of cognitive behavior therapy, see Mahoney, 1974.)

SELF-CONTROL. There is an Achilles heel to traditional behavioral techniques: the very design that proves their effectiveness—the A-B-A-B paradigm—leaves the child forever dependent upon external agents for maintenance of the new, more adaptive behavior. Such a situation presents practical problems, since therapists cannot see children indefinitely, while the enthusiasm of parents and teachers may wane. The situation is also ethically unacceptable to a society which values self-determination so highly. Therefore, behavior therapists have set about finding ways by which external control can become internalized. One technique, within the traditional model, is called *fading* and involves the gradual removal of contingencies. Delinquents, for example, were first given tokens for every acceptable specific behavior but, after reaching a level of consistently high performance, were placed on a merit system, where privileges were freely available as long as the delinquents continued to behave appropriately.

Other behavior therapists have attacked the problem of self-control directly (Kazdin, 1980). Rather than equating self-control with some vaguely defined trait, such as will power, these therapists conceptualize it as a deliberate undertaking by the individual to achieve a self-selected outcome. This involves, among other things, forgoing immediate rewards for future ones (for example, doing homework instead of looking at television), selecting cues congruent with eliciting the desired behavior (leaving the recreation room and finding a quiet place to study), monitoring one's behavior and rewarding or punishing one's self as the goal is or is not realized. Each component can be subjected to study in a laboratory setting and, individually or in combination, can serve as the basis for intervention techniques. For example, elementary children's writing improved when they administered tokens to themselves which could later be exchanged for rewards such as free time or games.

One of the most successful techniques involves increasing self-control in impulsive or hyperactive children by means of *self-instruction* (Meichenbaum and Goodman, 1971). The rationale is the familiar one that verbal symbols (words) serve both to delay and guide behavior. Impulsive children, who are presumably deficient in "self-talk," should perform better on specific tasks if they learn how to instruct themselves properly. The procedure relies on modeling, reinforcement, and a graduated performance task. For the purpose of illustration, the task of copying a rectangle has been chosen. First the adult performs the task, talking aloud in order to delineate each step in the procedure: defining the task ("Let's see, what do I have to do? I have to copy this picture"), focusing attention ("I'm going real slow and careful"), self-monitoring and self-reinforcement ("I did that corner really well"), and self-evaluation ("That's pretty good, except next time I could get that line straighter if I went slower"). Next the children perform the same task with the therapist giving explicit instructions. Then the children perform the task, first instructing themselves aloud, then whispering the instructions, and finally guiding their performance via private speech. In short, the children's haphazard, impulsive self-instructions are replaced by planful and critical ones.

Understandably, self-control procedures are not without shortcomings. While partly designed to alleviate the problem of maintaining gains in traditional behavior therapies, they themselves can begin to deteriorate over time in the absence of external reinforcement. Schoolchildren, for example, who have been taught to reward themselves for acceptable behavior in the classroom might gradually begin rewarding themselves for disruptive behavior. Once again we see how tenuous self-control is in middle childhood and the concomitant dependence on adult guidance.

COGNITIVE RESTRUCTURING. Long a therapy in its own right, Ellis's (1970) Rational Emotive Therapy (RET) has recently been included under the behavior-therapies umbrella. Ellis assumes that psychopathology results from misperceptions and mistaken cognitions. He lists twelve such irrational ideas, such as "Everyone must love me for everything I do," "I need someone stronger than myself to rely on," "It is easier to avoid than to face life's difficulties." The therapist, through a kind of Socratic dialogue and logical examination of the clients' ideas, helps them achieve emotional insight into erroneous beliefs while assigning specific tasks which enable them to put their newfound understanding into practice.

Like all behavior therapies, cognitive restructuring emphasizes specific behavioral change. With self-instruction, it shares an emphasis on the importance of private monologues and provides reinforcement for systematic observation and alteration of dysfunctional thought. While its technique of rational self-examination makes it poorly suited for young children, it has been presented in order to highlight some of the problems with cognitive behavior which will now be discussed.

Practical and Theoretical Problems

The principle *practical* problem with behavior therapies is not with producing but with maintaining change (Ross and Nelson, 1979). In learning-theory terms, the problem is one of generalization over situations and over time. Generalization over situations, or stimulus generalization, cannot be assumed; behaviors changed in the home, for example, may remain at their pretreatment level in the school situation. This is congruent with the behaviorist's view that behavior is situation-specific rather than the result of underlying traits. (Parenthetically the concern over stimulus generalization has its counterpart in the psychoanalytic concept of "working through," in which the patient must apply an insight to a host of situations that were previously handled in a neurotic manner.) Generalization over time is another problem. In our discussion of various psychopathologies we have seen many instances in which initial gains fail to be maintained, while even self-control techniques may deteriorate.

In order to increase the likelihood of generalization, a number of procedures are recommended. Among them are the transfer of behavior control from the artificial therapeutic setting to contingencies in the natural environment, training the behavior in multiple situations or training multiple behaviors for the same response class (the former being stimulus generalization, the latter response generalization), utilizing partial reinforcement or occasional noncontingent rewards, and deliberately training for generalization by using specific instructions to generalize behavior change, or by making the appropriate response class deliberately broad (Ross and Nelson, 1979).

The principle *theoretical* issue is whether cognitive behavior therapy should be regarded as behavior therapy at all. (See Ledwidge, 1978. For a lively exchange of ideas, see Mahoney and Kazdin, 1979, and Ledwidge, 1979.) In the discussion of neurosis we saw that some conservative behaviorists are reluctant to deal with "mental" events because the major thrust of behaviorism historically involved a rebellion against mentalism and a defining of psychology as the study of objective behavior. However, cognitive behaviorists maintain that inner events such as thoughts or feelings are perfectly admissable as long as they can be operationally defined in behavioral terms and their inclusion increases the predictability and control of behavior. Those who admit private events, moreover, disagree as to whether such events conform to the classical laws of learning or whether some new theory is required. While there is some preference for an information-processing model among the revisionists, there is no generally accepted cognitive theory. Mahoney (1974), for example, presented his own theory which he regards as more attuned to psychopathological behavior than information processing.

Furthermore, conservatives object that cognitive restructuring, in particular, lacks all the hallmarks of the behavioral approach: Ellis's twelve irrational ideas are nearer to the broad motivational systems of Freud and the self-systems of Rogers than they are to target behaviors; the theory is not buttressed by a body of research findings; and the interaction between the clinic and the laboratory is tenuous at best. The final irony is that cognitive therapies in general lack the record of proven effectiveness which more traditional behavior therapies have accumulated (Ledwidge, 1978). In short, cognitive behavior therapists have sold their behavioral birthright for a mess of cognitive porridge.

Champions of cognitive behavior therapy would be the first to admit the preliminary nature of their venture while strongly defending its worthwhileness. Certain techniques, such as self-instruction, are within the tradition of the laboratory-clinic interaction and, if a satisfactory cognitive theory is not yet available, serious efforts are being made to find one. More importantly, the chance to place cognition on a solid behavioral basis is too important to miss, while reports of initial therapeutic successes are too promising to neglect. Since the potential of cognitive behavior therapy has excited a talented group of scientist-practitioners, its fate will be decided as it should be—not by arguments and counterarguments but by data from the clinic and the laboratory.

THE BEHAVIORAL APPROACH AND PIAGET. Why should cognitive behaviorists be searching for a theory when Piaget's is so readily available, when it has the required ties to the laboratory, and when it is beginning to generate behavior-specific therapies? (Recall Selman's training program for reducing egocentrism in acting-out children which was discussed in chapter 8. Also see Urbain and Kendall. 1980.)

Piaget's theory is not congenial for a number of reasons. In postulating an invariable sequencing of stages, the theory is too much on the nativist side for behaviorists who traditionally uphold an environmental position. Piaget also postulates qualitative changes in cognition at each stage, while behaviorists are analytic and reductionistic, believing that complex phenomena can be reduced to the workings of basic laws governing behavioral change. In such a scientific program there is no room for qualitative changes which represent the emergence of new, irreducible organizations of cognition. Finally, behaviorists have traditionally been pragmatists and doers. In addition to asking whether a theory can be verified or not, they also ask of what use it is. Piaget's theory does not readily lend itself to practical applications in the realm of psychopathology. Some etiological and therapeutic bridges have been built, but they are few. While this is not surprising in light of the fact that Piaget had little interest in psychopathology, it does mean that his followers have not produced a corpus of therapeutic techniques which could serve as lures for the cognitive behavior therapists.

Research on Psychotherapy

After reading the literature on psychotherapy one comes to two conclusions: everything works, and nothing works.

The impression that everything works is partly due to the policy of professional journals of accepting only articles which show positive results. Thus, it is never clear how often a given therapy was tried and failed. There may also be a common element to psychotherapies, perhaps a compound of the therapist's understanding and confidence interacting with the client's desire to change, which guarantees a modicum of success to anyone attempting to help children, no matter how strange or exotic the technique might be. Finally, everything may seem to work because standards of research design and objectivity of evaluation have been lax in regard to evaluating therapeutic outcomes. Whatever the reasons, the literature on outcome of psychotherapy is almost an unbroken series of success stories.

On the other hand, Eysenck (1952) rocked the therapeutic community with a survey showing that a variety of psychotherapies with neurotic adults were no more effective than the improvement which could be expected from spontaneous recovery. After conducting a similar study with children, Levitt (1957) reached a similar conclusion. The ensuing debate has yet to die down. Eysenck claims, with some justification, that subsequent studies have confirmed his findings; yet other surveys clearly show the effectiveness of psychotherapy except with cases in which it would not be expected to succeed, such as with chronic schizophrenics and delinquents. There is even some evidence that the better a study is designed, the more it is apt to yield results favoring psychotherapy.

A critique of Eysenck's research will not be attempted; since the problems with his study are common to all research on therapeutic *outcome*, it would be more fruitful to present these. Then we shall review objections to outcome studies and discuss the shift to a *process* analysis of psychotherapy. Unfortunately, the lion's share of the literature is concerned with adult clients, and it is not clear what modifications might have to be made for child psychotherapy. (For a more complete coverage of the topic of outcome research in psychotherapy, see Bergin and Lambert, 1978.)

The first problem in studying therapeutic effectiveness is one of *matching* groups. Since psychopathologies differ in amenability to change, the groups should at least be equated in terms of the nature and severity of disturbance. But other variables might also affect outcome, not only demographic ones such as age, intelligence, and socioeconomic status but also therapy-specific ones such as motivation for treatment and expectation of being helped. The problem of matching is particularly difficult in the therapy, no-therapy study, since it is unethical to withhold treatment from a group of needy clients solely for research purposes. Other strategies must be adopted, none of which is totally satisfactory. Some studies have utilized matched clients on the waiting list, although there is no guarantee that such clients will not receive help from other sources during the waiting period. Another possibility is to use the client as his or her own control, as in the behavior therapists' A-B-A-B design.

The therapy or therapies being investigated must be competently conducted, and therapeutic *competence* is difficult to measure, although years of experience has served as a practical guide. *Criteria of outcome* differ radically among psychotherapies; the specific changes a behavior therapist might accept as defining successful completion might be rejected by a Freudian or Rogerian. *Follow-up* evaluations are important to insure that initial differences in effectiveness do not wash out in time or even reverse themselves. Finally, research on psychotherapy, like all psychological research, is hampered by lack of adequate *measuring instruments.* It is chancy to accept either the therapist's or the client's judgment concerning outcome, both of whom are subject to bias; for example, parents report their children have continued to improve after therapy when objective measures indicate that they have not or that their behavior has actually worsened. To avoid bias, individuals not involved in the therapy should evaluate the client by means of objective instruments before and after treatment. Standardized tests may be used, but they may not be sensitive to crucial therapeutic variables, while specialized assessment techniques run the risk of being inadequately standardized.

A number of investigators are now maintaining that outcome research that broadly questions the effectiveness of psychotherapy is futile, since it rests on the false assumptions that patients, treatment, and outcome are uniform and therefore can be lumped together. The more refined question, Which therapeutic approach is superior to all others? is equally simplistic. As we have discovered in previous discussions, the therapy of choice varies depending on the psychopathology. For autism and neuroses, therapy is superior to no therapy, but among therapies there is no evidence of any one being more effective if it is skillfully implemented. For enuresis, a mechanical device based on conditioning principles is the therapy of choice; for severely retarded children, behavioral techniques are most effective; and hyperactivity responds best to psychopharmacological agents. Even treatments of choice are not absolute in their effectiveness. Hence, a clinician should be sufficiently versatile to change a therapeutic approach when it is not proving helpful or sufficiently ethical to refer the child to someone who has a skill the clinician lacks. The day of the all-purpose therapy has yet to dawn.

Instead of studying outcome, researchers are now asking the process question: "What combinations of therapist, client, and technique produce what kinds of change?" In the résumé that follows, the findings are primarily derived from research with adults unless otherwise specified. (For a more complete summary, see Gomes-Schwartz, Hadley, and Strupp, 1978. For comprehensive coverage, see Garfield and Bergin, 1978.) We will first discuss nonbehavioral psychotherapies, which have been primarily interested in the effects of patient and therapist characteristics, of patient-therapist match, and of specific therapeutic techniques on improvement.

For adults and children alike, the general rule is that the more disturbed the client, the less likely is improvement, and that sociopaths and psychotics are less amenable to psychotherapy than are neurotics. Younger children improve more than older ones, while sex is not systematically related to improvement. The long-standing belief that individuals from the lower socioeconomic status do not respond to psychotherapy has been successfully challenged; evidence suggests that a good deal depends on how competent and comfortable the therapist is in dealing with racial and class differences between the client and himself or herself. The client's motivation to change is positively related to outcome; the role of expectations is more ambiguous, but the evidence suggests that if these are realistic and if the client is willing to work to fulfill them, they are facilitative. The client's willingness to collaborate actively in the therapy and to assume responsibility for change are also facilitative, while readiness to reveal intimate information and feelings is not clearly related to outcome.

In regard to the therapist, a good personal adjustment facilitates positive change, perhaps because the client identifies with the healthy aspects of the therapist's personality. On the other hand, the importance of warmth, empathy, and genuineness has been recently challenged, while there is no evidence that the therapist's value systems or biases per se have a direct impact on therapeutic outcome. In the realm of the therapeutic alliance, it is important that therapist and client like one another, that there is relaxed rapport and open communication, that the therapist conveys a capacity to understand, and the client feels understood. Anger, boredom, or detachment on the part of the therapist hamper therapy or lead to termination. Therapy can be enhanced if both parties either share similar values or have complementary ones, such as a submissive client matched with an authoritative therapist.

In regard to therapeutic approaches, the effectiveness of psychotherapies and behavior therapies is essentially comparable. However, the effectiveness of specific techniques—that is, of interpretation, anxiety-provoking confrontations, and catharsis or release of affect—has not been clearly established.

Client variables such as motivation to change carry the most weight in determining outcome, with therapists' personal characteristics coming next and techniques running a weak third (Bergin and Lambert, 1978). Thus, research findings contradict the widely held and strongly defended position that the choice of therapy is the most important determinant of outcome. The evidence suggests that in training therapists, the cultivation of interpersonal skills may be more advantageous to future clients than the teaching of a particular technique.

Research on behavior therapies has been both exciting and disappointing in that "the bulk of the behavioral literature [is] replete with methodological deficiencies" (Gomes-Schwartz et al., 1978, p. 447). However, as behavior therapists are no longer on the defensive in regard to proving the effectiveness of their techniques, they are increasingly turning their attention to understanding the variables responsible for their success. Interestingly, a number of these variables are the very ones which have concerned nonbehavioral psychotherapists—the client's expectations, the client–therapist relationship, and (as we have seen) cognitions. The research findings contain some surprises; for example, behavior therapists tend to be warmer, more natural, and more involved than psychoanalytically oriented psychotherapists, who place the relationship at the heart of the therapeutic process (Sloane, Staples, Cristol, Yorkston, and Whipple, 1975).

As behavioral and nonbehavioral therapists have begun dealing with the same variables, they have started talking to each other more than in the past. Instead of "my therapy" versus "your therapy," there is recognition of overlap, of sharing common techniques and problems. Such a development is all to the good in terms of advancing understanding of the therapeutic process and utilizing a variety of techniques in helping children.

FAMILY THERAPY

While various schools of psychotherapy, the psychoanalytic in particular, have adapted their techniques to treating families rather than individuals, it will be more fruitful to examine those conceptualizations that have broken new ground by regarding family interaction as an entity to be studied and understood in its own right. (Our presentation follows Whiteside, 1979.) Through the discussion of anorexia nervosa and schizophrenia, we are already familiar with the basic premise and some of the concepts generated by the family approach. Now we need to examine both in greater detail.

The basic premise is that the family is a superordinate unit, an entity over and above the interaction of its individual members. In searching for a congenial theoretical framework, family therapists have gravitated toward viewing the family as an *open system.* It is a system because it is the product of the dynamic interaction among a set of mutually interdependent components. It is open because it interacts with other systems. Expressed concretely, family members are in continual interaction with one another and each family interacts with other families as well as with other social institutions. As an open system, the family has certain characteristics:

WHOLENESS. Families, like individuals, have their own defining characteristics, which cannot be derived from the personalities of its members. At times, families are characterized by psychological terms, such as *hostile, inhibited,* or *inadequate;* at other times, therapists use colloquial expressions, such as *tough* or *slippery.* Thus, family therapists subscribe to the principle that the whole is greater than the sum of its parts.

INTERDEPENDENCE. The family is formed by highly complex interlocking relationships, so that a change in any one member will affect the remaining members. The nature of relatedness ranges from trivial to profound, from routine functions such as putting out the garbage to meeting the deepest needs for love or for respect.

FEEDBACK. Family therapists reject linear causality, in which *A* causes change in *B,* for a circular conceptualization in which *A* both affects and is affected by *B.* Since the family is a system, this feedback may well involve multiple reverberating influences among family members. At the dinner table, for example, a mother's remark concerning what a cute baby the adolescent son was may elicit a protest not only from the son but from his younger sibling as well, in response to which the mother quickly changes the subject by suggesting that the daughter clear the table, which she does, thereby reducing the general tension level. Thus, the pattern is one in which the son is in league against the mother, while the daughter is the peacemaking ally.

HOMEOSTASIS. A family limits the variations in behavior which each member is allowed, thereby bringing stability to the system. When the limits are exceeded, feedback functions to bring the system back in balance. Some states of equilibrium are maintained at the cost of curtailing individuality; for example, all the family members may be required to behave as if there were never any disharmony. Other states of equilibrium can allow for both individuality and adaptation to changing circumstances.

RULES. These are the persistent and observable regularities in family relationships. Rules may govern trivial behavior such as, "Brush your teeth before bedtime," or they may define broad areas of relationships such as, "Female family members are inferior to male members." While some rules are conscious and explicit, others are implemented without awareness.

COMMUNICATION. Communication, the warp and woof of the fabric of family interaction, is the means by which interactions are established and negotiated. Indeed, a family member cannot avoid communicating, since silence itself can send potent messages such as "I will not do what you want me to do" or "I do not consider myself part of this group." A communication has a given content, an expressive component, and an implied relationship. "Go upstairs to bed," spoken in an angry voice, conveys both the literal message, the anger of the speaker, and the fact that he or she is in command. The same content could be conveyed in such a manner as to indicate meekness and uncertainty as to authority.

CHANGE. In first-order change, variation occurs within the rules of the system. Therapists have noted, for example, that if the system requires a disturbed member in order to maintain homeostasis and if one member of the family improves, another may become disturbed. In second-order change, the system itself is altered; instead of using a disturbed child as an excuse for not facing its basic conflicts, the family is helped by a therapist to confront such problems. Naturally, both first- and second-order change can occur outside of therapy, and the latter can be in the direction of greater or less adaptability.

A well-functioning family system is characterized by explicit rules, clarity of communication, flexibility, openness to change, and respect for individuality. Such qualities enable it to successfully perform its functions of socializing the child while enhancing autonomy. A malfunctioning system is characterized by covertness, manipulation, and rigid, ambiguous, or amorphous rules; individuation is sacrificed to a false image of togetherness. The child feels bewildered or imprisoned or betrayed but, in the most insidious cases, is prevented by family maneuvers from realizing what is happening. We have seen many exemplars of such faulty systems. In Minuchin's concept of *enmeshment* and *overprotection*, family members are highly involved with one another in an intrusive, overconcerned manner that robs each member of a sense of individuality (Minuchin, 1975). Bateson's concept of the *double bind* turns communication into an insolvable dilemma of being condemned regardless of what one does, while being prevented from calling attention to the trap which has been laid. Wynne (1979) describes the *diffuse* and *fragmented* family structure, along with the inability of family members to maintain an appropriate *psychological distance*. Lidz (1973) delineates the *skewed* family with its dominating mother and passive father, and the *schismatic* family in which conflicted parents compete for the child's loyalties.

The systems approach redefines the nature of psychopathology. The disturbed child becomes merely the "identified patient," the symptom, as it were, that something has gone wrong. The pathology itself is in the system. The child may be a *scapegoat* protecting parents from facing their own unresolved problems; concern over antisocial acting out, for example, may divert parents from facing their own chronic conflicts in regard to who makes decisions in the family. In fact, confronting parents with the fact that the entire network of familial relationships must be examined and changed may be the jolt which initiates the process of change.

Therapy

At the beginning of therapy families are trapped in defensive maneuvers which block growth and distort reality. Therapists initially try to cut through defenses, to facilitate openness, and to uncover sources of pain. They are especially skilled in sensitizing families to mixed, contradictory, obscure, and vague communications, often pointing to the expressive as well as to the manifest content. They help family members face conflicting needs and the self-defeating results of their defensive protection. At times they support the system in order to convey a message of understanding and trustworthiness; at times they upset the system's equilibrium in order that the underlying issues may be brought to light. One such technique involves confronting parents with an alternate interpretation of the child's behavior, such as pointing out that an immature adolescent boy wants to spare the parents the pain of his growing up and becoming independent of them. While catharsis or release of pent-up emotions might well take place in the process of therapy, this is not the goal. The goal is restructuring the family system. Only then can experiences which have been avoided or denied be mastered.

While there are many kinds of family therapy, we have chosen to discuss Satir's, since she pays greater attention than most therapists to the role of the child. (See Satir, 1967. For a comprehensive presentation of family therapies, see Goldenberg and Goldenberg, 1980). Satir regards self-esteem as the basic human drive and defines the mature individual as one who is in touch with his or her own feelings, can communicate clearly, and can accept the individuality of others. Separating from the family and becoming a clearly delineated self represent the key to maturity or pathology.

There are a number of ways in which self-differentiation can be blocked. If either or both of the parents have a poor self-image they will tend to view the child as a means of achieving self-esteem. Consequently the child is not viewed as an individual and is saddled with the burden of fulfilling parental needs. Any difference in the child's outlook is translated as a lack of love for the parents. Since the parents themselves may well be in conflict, the child who turns to one for help risks losing the other. (One catches glimpses of Rogers in Satir's theorizing.)

Satir, like many other family therapists, emphasizes the role of communication in enhancing or blocking development. The parent who has low self-esteem does not communicate clearly. The messages are vague or uncertain or contradictory or there is a disjuncture between the content and the expressive component. Since the child's self is formed partially by interactions with the parent, such communications prevent the child from achieving a clearly defined self-image.

Finally, there is the matter of family rules. Ideally the rules should give children the freedom to disagree, to ask questions when they do not understand, and to acknowledge their own feelings. However, family rules may be rigid and unrealistic such as, "Only good feelings may be expressed," or "You must not feel angry or jealous of your sibling." Family rules can also be uncertain or contradictory, leaving children baffled as to where they stand and what they should do.

It follows that one goal of therapy is to help the family discover the rules regarding emotional interchange in order to ascertain which are still valid and which no longer apply. This emphasis on rules has the advantage of relieving the child of the role of "the sick one," while relieving parents of guilt over having done something "wrong." In the good sense of the word, the situation is depersonalized as all member of the family set out to understand the causes of the pain they are feeling. As the rules causing pain are exposed, the family has a chance to change them, which, in turn, enhances the family's feeling of being in control of its destiny. Families must also learn to communicate and to individuate so that each member can report completely and congruently what he or she feels and thinks, while uniqueness is valued and differentness is openly acknowledged and used for growth.

Being both an experienced professional and an outsider, the therapist is in a favored position to detect incongruent, covert, and confused messages and to articulate implicit rules. But even more important, the therapist must model open communication by being warm, empathetic, and involved while sending messages that are clear, congruent, and reality-based. Thus, while the family is examining the faults in its system that produce pain, they have constantly before them a model of what communication and a mature relationship should be like.

Research

Research indicates that family therapy is as effective as and possibly more effective than individual therapy for a variety of problems, both individual (such as asthma and diabetes) and interpersonal. Systems therapies may even be the treatment of choice for decreasing hospitalization rates for some chronic and acute inpatients, for anorexia, for juvenile delinquency, and for sexual dysfunctions. Behaviorally oriented family therapy has not proved its effectiveness at this point. Short-term therapy is as effective as long-term therapy in many instances, most of the positive results being achieved in less than five months. The father plays the major role in the efficacy of family therapy when a child or adolescent is the identified patient, an interesting finding in light of the fact that child guidance clinics deal primarily with the mother and child. (For further details concerning research, see Gurman and Kniskern, 1978.)

GROUP THERAPIES

Group therapies are difficult if not impossible to epitomize. They involve such diverse ages (from preschoolers to adolescents), psychopathologies (the entire gamut has been treated on a group basis), special-interest groups (father-absent boys, teenage pregnant girls), techniques (structured tasks, games, discussions ranging from dreams to current happenings, fantasy play, role playing, dance, body movement, and art), goals (release of inhibitions, relief of anxiety and guilt, increased controls and coping skills, modification of the self-concept, insight), conceptual models (psychoanalytic, nondirective, behavioral, gestalt, and transactional analysis), and they are performed in such a variety of settings (child guidance clinics, private practice, schools, hospitals, detention homes), with the therapist's role varying from passive observer to active director, that adequate coverage would take us far afield (see Kraft, 1979). Unlike family therapy, group therapies have a catch-as-catch-can quality resulting from the lack of an overall integrating framework. Therefore our discussion will be limited to a presentation of some of their general characteristics.

The rationale of group therapy derives from the inherently social nature of human beings that is clearly evident from infancy on. The general goal is to enable children, isolated from healthy peer contact by withdrawal or hostility, to establish growth-promoting social interactions. A number of curative factors are at work in a group setting (Yalom, 1975). One is *universality,* or the reassuring discovery that many others share the child's feelings and experiences. There are various sources of *interpersonal learning experiences,* some coming from direct interaction among the group members, others from imitation of peers and modeling of the therapist's behavior, and still others from group cohesiveness and the sense of "we-ness" which develops with time; for example, groups may form clubs which serve to check the impulsive behavior of its members, bolster self-esteem, deepen the sense of loyalty, and serve as a forum for reality-testing discussions. The therapist is also a source of information concerning ways in which children can get along together constructively. The group experience may involve *catharsis*, or the release of pent-up feelings in an accepting and sympathetic setting, as well as providing a chance to relive and correct *distortions originating in the family;* for example, the manipulatively helpless child finds no support from the group or the therapist, the disconfirmation of expectations serving as the opening wedge to change. There is the opportunity for children to see themselves as others see them, thus gaining *perspective* and ultimately a sense of responsibility for their actions; for example, if aggression starts getting out of hand, the therapist can call a halt, either challenging the group to examine the cause and suggest remedies or taking the lead in discussing the value of self-control. There are positive feelings which accompany *altruistic* behavior on the child's part, as well as the *hopefulness* which comes from the knowledge that previously insoluble problems can be resolved.

It has been suggested that groups progress through similar stages of development (Yalom, 1975). Initially, there is a period of orientation, hesitant participation, and a searching for significance, accompanied by dependence on the group therapist. The second stage is one of conflict, dominance, and rebellion, group members engaging in power struggles with one another and with the therapist. Finally, the group develops cohesiveness, marked by an increase in morale, mutual trust, and self-disclosure. In the final stage, the group develops independence from the therapist.

The above generalizations are helpful attempts to capture some of the characteristics of group therapy, but they probably will have to be modified in terms of the developmental status of the participants, since their applicability to younger children is uncertain. The developmental literature has been more concerned with the change in techniques with age, preschoolers and children in early middle childhood primarily engaging in play, while verbal exchanges increase with age, although even adolescents may engage in structured activities and games during their sessions.

Recommended group size ranges from three to eight, with a balance of sexes, although the latter is difficult to achieve, since disturbed boys typically outnumber girls 3 to 1. Suggested age groups are 4 to 8 years, 9 to 11, 12 to 13, and then early, middle, and late adolescence. Good candidates for group therapy include children who are withdrawn, immature, phobic, ones with conduct disorders, and effeminate boys. Excessively aggressive, sociopathic, actively psychotic children and ones with overt sexual deviance are usually not included, although they have been treated in groups specially designed to meet their needs. There is general agreement that there should be a mixture of problems in a given group so that, for example, inhibited and acting-out children may serve as models for one another. The therapist identifies group goals, instructs the group as to how it should function, keeps it task-oriented, facilitates cohesiveness, and serves as a model. In the process, the therapist may clarify reality for the group, analyze the interactions, empathetically acknowledge the feelings of the members, as well as describe his or her own feelings and educate when there is ignorance or misinformation. (For further details, see Slavson and Schiffer, 1975.)

In addition to its intrinsic merit, group therapy helps solve the practical problem of inadequate facilities to help disturbed children. Individual therapies, even if they were 100 percent effective, would still be grossly inadequate. In fact, the pressing need to help a wider population of children than was being seen in mental health clinics was one of the forces behind the community mental health movement and its concern with prevention. (This presentation of psychotherapies has been selective; for a comprehensive coverage, see Noshpitz, 1979a.)

PREVENTION

The Community Mental Health Movement

In the 1960s, community mental health was heralded as the third mental health revolution. If Pinel had unshackled the insane in 1792, thereby proclaiming their right to be treated as human beings, if Freud had shown that neurosis conformed to the same principles which accounted for normal behavior, then community mental health would prevent psychopathology through social interventions. (Our presentation follows Korchin, 1976.)

Mental health problems were viewed as intimately connected with social problems—poverty, primarily, along with racism, crime, inadequate housing and education, job discrimination, and unemployment. Concern shifted from the individual to the social institution, from therapy to prevention, from clinic to community. The mental health worker's place should be in the community rather than in an office, both to make services readily accessible to populations most in need of them and to mobilize human resources within the community itself. Social action and advocacy were added to the mental health worker's functions. As if that were not enough, the movement aimed at maximizing human potential as well as ameliorating psychological suffering.

A number of factors were responsible for such a radical departure from traditional clinical thought and practice. The connection between poverty and psychopathology had been convincingly demonstrated prior to the 1960s, but largely ignored. Ironically, the greater need of the poor was accompanied by an equally great inequity in the delivery of services to them. The largely middle-class clinician preferred to treat the middle-class client, while the poor tended to be shunted into custodial hospitals where they received grossly inadequate care. It was the *social ferment* of the 1960s—the riots, the protests, the demands of impoverished Blacks for equality—which opened the eyes and seared the conscience of mental health workers. That there was both ideological and financial support at the national level assured the translation of community mental health goals into actual programs.

The second factor contributing to the momentum of the community mental health movement was a *dissatisfaction with psychotherapy,* which was viewed as both ineffectual and inefficient. Eysenck's outcome study with adults and Levitt's similar study with children have already been discussed. While the claim of ineffectualness subsequently proved to be exaggerated, the verdict is still a qualifed one: psychotherapy may be superior to no psychotherapy for certain psychopathologies, but it is least effective for populations which are most troublesome to society—the sociopath and the psychotic. But even if it were completely effective, psychotherapy is costly in terms of time, effort, and money. Moreover, the task of providing sufficient numbers of therapists to conduct it is a hopeless one. To take only one example: it has been estimated that of the 12 million disturbed children and adolescents, 90 percent are not receiving appropriate services (Cummings, 1979). To offer services would therefore require a vast expansion of training and clinical facilities. And this does not even include adults and the aged, whose needs are equally great.

Finally, the deplorable condition of *mental hospitals* at the end of World War II was a factor underlying the shift from individual to institution. Not only were many of these hospitals grossly understaffed, but the requirement that patients be submissive and accept a role of being inadequate and incompetent also fostered regression rather than recovery. Nor was brutality and inhumane treatment unknown; children were beaten, deprived of clothing and toilet facilities, placed in solitary confinement, and sexually abused. Mental institutions were a major disgrace in the affluent American society, just as prisons continue to be to this day.

One of the visible results of the ferment just described was the establishment of *comprehensive mental health centers,* much of the funding for construction and staffing coming from the federal government. "Comprehensive" means that all services would be available to all people. Mandated services include inpatient and outpatient care, partial hospitalization such as night hospitals for patients able to work during the day, 24-hour emergency services, and consultation to community agencies and professional personnel.

The shift to *prevention* took its cue from the history of medicine, which shows that no major disease has been eliminated by therapeutic measures alone, but only through preventive ones. In addition, prevention captured the spirit of the mental health movement, in that it required professionals to reach out to the most needy populations and to show members of these populations how to assume responsibility for helping themselves. Along with its high-minded ideology, the outreach approach had the potentiality for solving the practical problem of understaffing.

The Concept of Prevention

Prevention is seen as a threefold system: primary prevention aims at averting the appearance of a psychopathology; secondary prevention refers to early diagnosis and prompt treatment in order to shorten the duration of a psychopathology; and tertiary prevention promotes maximal psychological functioning in individuals whose psychopathology is irreversible.

Classifying programs is not as important as the fact that many psychopathologies are multidetermined and require a variety of preventative measures. Poverty is an economic concept. Therefore the correlation between poverty and psychopathology says nothing about the variables responsible for the relationship. Some are undoubtedly psychological, others biological, medical, and sociological. It is an ongoing challenge to discover exactly what these crucial variables are. In all probability, no variable is unique to the poor, but among the poor there may well be a higher incidence of them, as well as a compounding of their noxious effects; as we have seen, the developmental fate of two equally damaged neonates depends on whether they are born to lower- or middle-class parents, the chances being greater that the former will continue to be deviant and the latter will function normally eventually.

For the purpose of discussion, it will be helpful to divide preventative measures into biological, psychological, and sociological, discussing each in turn. (For a brief description of psychological programs, see Clarizio and McCoy, 1976. For a detailed presentation of the entire field, see Noshpitz, 1979b.)

BIOLOGICAL APPROACHES. Since the physiologically damaged or defective neonate is at risk in regard to subsequent psychopathologies, among them mental retardation, hyperactivity, and schizophrenia, a number of programs have been instituted to prevent such damage from occurring. Sterilization, birth control, and therapeutic abortions are highly controversial issues in American society, while involuntary sterilization is generally unacceptable. *Family planning,* in which the adults concerned discuss voluntary sterilization, contraception, and abortion with a qualified professional, is more palatable. As the number of pediatric disorders found to have a genetic base is increasing, *genetic counseling* is becoming increasingly important as a preventive technique. The degree of genetic risk, the severity of the abnormal condition, and the effectiveness of existing therapies are presented, along with the psychological and social consequences of the abnormal condition. As with family planning, the purpose of counseling is to enable parents to arrive at an informed decision concerning the present fetus and future pregnancies.

PRENATAL CARE. A number of prenatal factors can increase the risk of neurological impairment with concomitant intellectual and behavioral deficits in the newborn—infectious diseases such as rubella, malnutrition, obesity, radiation, drugs, and possibly emotional stress. In order to reduce the chance of prematurity and congenital anomalies, the mother should receive adequate medical, dietary, and emotional care during pregnancy. There has been a special concern for the pregnant teenager of lower socioeconomic status, whose age alone places the fetus at risk and whose class membership increases the likelihood that her diet ("Coke and junk food") is deficient, that she has received inadequate medical care, and that emotional support from the father and family is lacking. Providing adequate prenatal care to the poor has involved both increasing the facilities and devising ways to make such facilities more accessible than they have been in the past.

The Maternal and Infant Care (MIC) outreach program decentralizes services into neighborhood settings and provides prenatal and postnatal care and family planning in areas where there are few private physicians. The multidisciplinary staff, aided by community members, carries out case findings in churches, stores, schools, laundromats, and other gathering places. In addition to medical attention, dental care and counseling for emotional and vocational problems is available. The clinic is open in the evening and on weekends, and staff members make home visits. The program has been effective in reducing infant mortality among the high-risk population it serves (Millar, 1979).

PSYCHOLOGICAL APPROACHES. *Parent education* is not new to the preventive scene, as witnessed by the enduring popularity of Benjamin Spock's book and other advice-to-parents publications. What the community health movement added was a concerted effort to reach lower-class mothers who need the information most but have least access to it.

Early intervention programs concentrate on the first year or two of life. They may have any of a number of goals:

1. To impart information about normal development to mothers, many of whom (particularly teenagers) literally do not know what behavior to expect.

2. To instruct mothers in ways to stimulate cognitive growth. Some mothers do not understand why they should talk to their infants, for example, since infants "don't answer back and don't know what I'm saying anyway," as one mother put it. They are also taught how to use simple household materials, such as string, plastic cups, cereal boxes, and aluminum foil, to make mobiles

and other objects that will pique the infant's curiosity.

3. To encourage mothers to express warmth and pride in their infants so as to foster the bond of affection.

4. To enhance the mother's own feelings of competence. This may involve not only increasing her caregiving skills but also helping her with realistic problems in regard to her future and her family.

Some programs are conducted on a group basis which allows the mothers to compare notes on their infants' development, share problems, and learn from one another as well as from the leader. It is often helpful to conduct the groups in the hospital where the mother delivered the infant, since she knows both setting and staff. However, many mothers cannot or are unwilling to manage the demands of scheduled meetings. Programs are therefore conducted in the home at their convenience.

The Florida Parent Education Program is a relatively extensive effort in parent education. In many ways it resembles Heber's preventive program discussed in chapter 11 (Gordon, 1975). Between infancy and 2 years of age, two trained disadvantaged women make weekly home visits to teach mother–infant activities largely centered around Piagetian tasks. Between 2 and 3 years of age a backyard center is added, preschoolers being transported to specially equipped home centers twice weekly for more individualized cognitive stimulation. At the same time the parent educators instruct the mothers both in the rationale and mechanics of the activities, encouraging them to continue the stimulation in the home. Finally, the parent educator works with the child in kindergarten through third grade, spending part of the day in classroom activities, part of the day discussing with the mother ways to continue the learning taking place in the school. Such contacts with the mothers help prevent the rift between home and school noted in Heber's project. The fact that the program is conducted by paraprofessionals, with disadvantaged mothers helping other disadvantaged mothers, is very much in keeping with the goals of the community mental health movement. (For a résumé of other programs, see Beller, 1979.)

PREVENTION IN THE SCHOOLS. Since a vast number of disturbed children are not brought to mental health clinics but are dealt with by community caregivers such as pediatricians, the clergy, lawyers, and the police, it seems logical that trained mental health professionals offer their services as *consultants* to such caregivers. Of all community settings, the school has the most direct and continuing impact on the child's development. Consultation in the schools may take a number of forms. It may be client-centered, the psychologist evaluating the child presenting problems and making recommendations in regard to management. Another kind of consultation involves increasing the remedial skills of the teachers themselves. Because of mainstreaming, for example, teachers are suddenly required to deal with learning disabled, hyperactive, and autistic-like children for whom they have had little or no professional preparation. Special workshops conducted by knowledgeable mental health workers can be helpful in such cases. (For a more comprehensive discussion of the consultant role, see Clarizio and McCoy, 1976.)

The school is also an ideal setting for early diagnosis and remediation, because of the large population of children it services. Unfortunately, psychologists lack the assessment instruments for implementing an effective early detection and intervention program. As we saw in the general discussion of predictability and the specific discussions of acting-out behavior and brain damage, prediction in the preschool period is subject to significant error. In the early part of middle childhood a certain proportion of the children who will continue to be disturbed can be identified, but there is still a large number who will outgrow their problems, and a large number of adequately functioning children who will "grow into" problems. While early detection is an impossible dream at present, the challenge has spurred the development of new assessment techniques, which, it is hoped, will be more effective than the ones extant.

SOCIAL APPROACHES. Recall that the community mental health movement aims at changing the social context in which psychopathology is apt to develop. This involves both the establishment of new community resources and changing existing ones.

New community resources include community mental health centers, crisis centers, hot lines for the potentially suicidal, 24-hour drop-in drug clinics, all of which make professional help more readily available than previously. Halfway houses help those adolescents who had previously been institutionalized for various psychopathologies and for mental retardation make the transition to independent community living. In the realm of education, Head Start is an accepted fixture on the social scene. Still in the experimental stage are classes in parenting and supervised experience in infant care for teenagers, the argument being that learning how to become a parent is at least as important as learning how to drive a car and deserves the same expert instruction. Day-care centers enabling mothers to work or to further their education without neglecting their children have mushroomed and also have become permanent fixtures. Not to be neglected is "Sesame Street," the pioneering effort to use the mass medium of television to stimulate cognitive and social development, whose success is responsible for a number of similar television shows for children.

Among *institutions*, the community mental health movement has had the greatest impact on mental hospitals. In part, the decline in population there has been due to the discovery of more effective psychopharmacological agents; but it also has been due to professional and public concern over the detrimental effect many large state hospitals were having on their patients. There has also been a vigorous movement protecting the rights of psychologically disturbed and mentally retarded children in regard to the decision to institutionalize them, as well as their right to humane treatment, appropriate therapy, and periodical evaluation once institutionalized. While programs to capitalize on the therapeutic potential of mental institutions have been inaugurated, they cannot be said to have had a major impact. The same is true of programs for improving the juvenile justice system.

Another important feature of the current scene is *legislation* that has countered society's tendency to insulate itself from the fate of the deviant. Notable are the Education for All Handicapped Children Act of 1975, Public Law 94-142, which prescribes free appropriate public education for children who are mentally retarded, deaf, orthopedically and visually impaired, seriously emotionally disturbed, and learning disabled; legislation in regard to the mentally retarded; and the Child Abuse and Treatment Act, Public Law 93-274, which serves as a legal deterrent to child abuse by encouraging the reporting of such abuse and requiring that the abused child receive appropriate treatment.

Problems and Reevaluation

Because the mental health needs of the poor had been ignored, community mental health programs were largely formulated on the basis of ignorance rather than experience. Predictably, the high idealism, optimism, and enthusiasm which marked its birth were subsequently tempered by innumerable problems which surfaced during its implementation. While some mental health workers have been disillusioned, most are now more cautious, sober, and realistic concerning the potential of the movement. Some of the difficulties it has encountered will be touched on briefly.

There are two *ideological* problems. When a parent figuratively knocks on a clinician's door and says, "My child needs help," the clinician is being requested to intervene in the lives of parent and child. But when a mental health worker figuratively knocks on a parent's door and says, "You and your child need help," the situation is quite different. On what basis does the worker have the right to make this statement; at what point does help become intrusiveness and a violation of privacy? The question is a particularly sensitive one in these days of heightened concern for the rights of minorities, and there have been court rulings that the community worker has no right to change a family's life-style in the name of mental health (Korchin, 1976).

The second ideological problem concerns the "different versus deficient" issue. The initial conceptualization of the poor was in terms of deficit—they were culturally deprived. Closer acquaintance revealed that this deficit model was not accurate, since the poor may have their own culture, which is different from that of mainstream America. But if the poor were merely different, would this not undermine the basis for trying to change them? Our democracy was founded on respect for diversity. Why then should not American society accommodate to the culture of lower-class Blacks, for example, rather than trying to homogenize them? The question has no easy answer. All concerned parents might agree on certain issues: a child should not suffer from sickness or malnutrition or brutality or neglect. But regardless of a certain fundamental agreement, the line between "disadvantage" and "stylistic difference" in child rearing is not clear. At what point does openness in expressing feeling become bewildering parental inconsistency? At what point does an extended family shade into inadequate love and care from adults?

The community health movement has encountered *resistances* at both the individual and the social levels. The assumption that the poor were thirsting to become middle class proved naive; there were many who saw no reason to exchange lower-class "soul" for middle-class "success." The well-intentioned mental health worker also has had to contend with the poor's suspicions born of many years of being treated with indifference, disrespect, and contempt. In the volatile 1960s it was not unknown for the community worker to become the target of the pent-up rage of the poor. Finally, the poor are often preoccupied with immediate problems of living—how to pay the rent, how to buy food and clothes—from which they rightfully want relief. And immediate relief of needs is at variance with prevention. It is difficult to convince a sorely beset mother that she should play games with her toddler because three years from now the child will do better in school.

Nor were institutions ripe for reform. While the ills of mental institutions might have originated in inadequate budgets and staff along with a depreciated social status, institutional organization and operation had been codified into rules and regulations which, for one reason or another, had been accepted as the way things were going to remain. Change was upsetting and intrusive. Other social institutions—the schools, the police, the hospitals, the courts—were also uncertain as to how much they wanted to go along with the new movement, and few wholeheartedly agreed to be the vehicle for realizing the mental health ideology.

Such resistances were complemented by ineptness owing to the inexperience of many mental health workers. Clinicians, accustomed to treating middle-class clients, had to make radical shifts in their approach and techniques as they went out into the community to work with parents. Initiating and sustaining change in institutions also required special skills different from those acquired in one-to-one psychotherapy. Thus community mental health professionals had to develop expertise commensurate with their ideology almost on a trial-and-error basis.

In response to the urgent need for social remedies in the 1960s, community health programs proliferated. As the crisis subsided, proven merit and *accountability* entered the picture. What was the evidence that the intended population was really being helped and, since federal money was often involved, that taxpayers were getting their money's worth? Most programs either lacked evaluation or were unsatisfactorily evaluated; still others failed to demonstrate significant improvement in the population served. (See Clarizio and McCoy, 1976, in regard to day care, parent education, and school programs.) Consequently, community mental health programs are in a situation comparable to that of psychotherapy after the Eysenck-Levitt studies. Evidence of significant and sustained effectiveness is being increasingly required, while program evaluation has become an important specialty in its own right (Perloff, Perloff, and Susna, 1976).

The community mental health movement has had to be content with innumerable *practical* problems. As we have seen, secondary prevention with children has been hampered by inadequate assessment instruments, the uncertainty of predicting the course of early development, and inadequate facilities to help the populations involved. Moreover, both ideological and financial support at the federal and local levels has waxed and waned. In times of crisis and relative prosperity, funds are forthcoming; when the crisis is past and economy in government prevails, funds are cut. While many features of the community health movement have become part of the national scene, the movement is far from playing its envisioned role, and a number of programs are barely able to survive, much less expand. Finally, the proliferation of programs has led to needless overlap on the one hand, fragmentation on the other, while "turf protection" significantly hampers cooperation among agencies (Lourie, 1979). The effective delivery of services has therefore become as important a professional concern as program evaluation. The overall picture is made even more gloomy by interprofessional rivalries, such as those between psychiatrists and psychologists, which represent chronic, unresolved power struggles and prevent the coordinated mobilization of all professional resources to serve the needs of the disturbed child.

Children's Rights, Advocacy, and Political Action

The concern for *children's rights* arose from the recognition of children's helplessness when adults failed to discharge their responsibilities—in the brutally abusing home, in the court, in mental institutions. In 1970 the Joint Commission on the Mental Health of Children listed a set of rights which apply to all children: the right to be wanted, to be born healthy and live in a healthy environment, to obtain satisfaction of basic needs, to receive continuous loving care, to acquire the intellectual skills necessary to cope effectively with society, to receive appropriate care and treatment, and to be as close as possible to their normal setting. What had formerly been regarded as "needs" were thereby transformed into "rights."

In the case of child abuse, adjudication, and in some states, institutionalization, children's rights are enforced by laws. Whether more rights should have legal backing is a matter of debate. The rights of children must be weighed against those of parents and siblings, and the legal profession has traditionally been reluctant to intrude in family life except under the special conditions of divorce and custody litigation. The developmental dimension further complicates the picture, 13- to 18-year-olds being able to make decisions, such as receiving therapy, which would be meaningless for a child under 6 years of age. It may be that children's rights are too complex and individualized to be codified and implemented by lawyers and judges whose own training includes little or nothing of child development. (For a more extended discussion, see Hayes, 1979.)

Another response to the "child as victim" has been *advocacy.* An advocate is a person who tries to insure that programs and services based on sound developmental knowledge are available to all children. Advocates perform diverse functions. Case advocacy is concerned that the individual child is appropriately treated by an agency: for example, an advocate might hear individual grievances, investigate, and render a judgment in a state training school for delinquents. There is class action litigation on behalf of a class of children where abuse raises the issue of deprivation of constitutional rights, such as the case of handicapped children being excluded from public school or students suspended without due process. Monitoring involves watching the conduct of those serving children in order to hold the systems accountable for what happens; for example, seeing that judicial decisions are complied with and that funded agencies are implementing legislation. Legislative advocacy attempts to insure that statutory provisions serve the needs of children as well as protecting their rights (Knitzer, 1976).

There have been instances in which advocacy has been effective; recall the success of parents of mentally retarded children in helping to pass legislation and obtain funds for treatment and research. In spite of such successes and of strong endorsement by national experts, advocacy continues to be "fragmented, disorganized and, for the most part, ineffective" (Shore, 1979, p. 1019). However, the role of advocates is a new one which those concerned with the welfare of children may well learn to perform more effectively with time.

It is clear that the community mental health movement has placed the clinical child psychologist and other mental health professionals in the *political arena.* One cannot strive to alter public policies and institutions, change laws, and accept federal, state, and local funds while avoiding politics. However, political activism has another root. Our actual record of achievements has for years belied our stance that we are a nation deeply concerned with the welfare of our children. The infant mortality rate, for example, is higher here than in thirteen other industrialized countries. The need for psychological care has been repeatedly documented and largely ignored. The 1978 President's Commission on Mental Health explicitly stated that the mental health care for children and adolescents was inadequate or nonexistent, and that an alarming number of children suffer from indifference, neglect, and abuse. Drug and alcohol abuse and suicide rates among adolescents have increased dramatically in the past two decades. Troubled children and adolescents, especially of racial minorities, are often shunted from one service to another, increasing their confusion and despair. While 90 percent of the 12 million disturbed children and adolescents do not receive appropriate services, federal funds were proposed (not appropriated) to serve only 15 percent, these being the psychotic, autistic, chronic, or "grossly maladaptive" children whose problems are most intractable. The children for whom intervention would probably be most fruitful were ignored. (For further details, see Cummings, 1979.) It is argued that one reason for national apathy is that children have no political constituencies; consequently, professionals along with concerned members of the community must spearhead the adoption of political measures on their behalf.

The nature and extent of political involvement remains a controversial issue. Clinicians who publicly opposed the Vietnam War as "bad for the mental health of children" or who advocate adopting a national guaranteed minimal income might be said to be dabbling in political and economic matters which lie beyond the realm of their expertise, while at the same time undermining their credibility in regard to psychological issues which fall within their province. At the other extreme conservative psychologists claim that we know far too little about developmental psychopathology even to attempt to shape national and local policy. Yet it can be argued that, whenever such policies are to be made, input from an experienced clinical child psychologist would probably be more valuable than from most lawmakers.

Traditionally, clinical child psychologists have not been political activists. In the political arena, as in other aspects of community involvement, they are learning a new role without a clear mandate from colleagues as to what this role should be and with little or no formal training for it. Since there is every evidence that political involvement will become increasingly important, the clinical child psychologist, of necessity, will become more seasoned and skillful, as well as better trained for political encounters.

Summing Up

If the community mental health movement represents a third revolution, it is a revolution which will take decades to accomplish its goals. While not changing the direction of mental health care, it has had a significant impact on the etiological theories of psychopathology, on attitudes toward and programs for the needy, as well as on prevention and remediation. It has added the essential and neglected ingredient of the societal context.

Child clinicians have much knowledge and skill to offer society and should be included as shapers of appropriate social policies; in turn, they have learned a great deal from their efforts to reach out and help the poor and racial minorities. There is every reason to believe that this mutual enhancement of the profession and of society will continue to characterize the community mental health movement.

15 ▪ A Summing Up and a Challenge

A literal summary of what we have learned about psychopathological development would be extensive and repetitious. However, it is worthwhile looking back to make some general points about the guiding hypothesis that psychopathology can be regarded as normal development gone awry. We began with two time-honored exemplars of the hypothesis—fixation and regression. However, we quickly discovered that they were inadequate and needed to be supplemented. Let us review the many different versions of psychopathology as deviant development that we have encountered and look at examples of each.

PSYCHOPATHOLOGIES OF TIMING

In psychopathologies of timing the child exhibits behavior which, while part of normal development, is not age or stage appropriate. In addition to *fixations* and *regressions*, this category includes deviant *rates* and *sequencing* of development. The deviations may be *within* a given psychological function or *between* and *among* functions. Let us examine each variation briefly.

In *fixation*, children continue to evidence behaviors appropriate to a given developmental level long after they should have acquired more advanced, age- or stage-appropriate behaviors, while in *regression* children, having progressed, revert to behaviors appropriate to a younger age or a former developmental stage. Fixations are exemplified by the enuretic who never achieved bladder control, by the preschooler who continues to be negativistic (chapter 6), by the mentally retarded school-age child who continues to use position as a solution to a discrimination learning task (chapter 11). Regression is exemplified by the return of separation anxiety in symbiotic psychosis, by enuresis in a previously toilet-trained preschooler (chapter 6), by the reappearance of magical, omnipotent thinking in the schizophrenic adolescent (chapter 10).

Developmental *lags* and *precocities* are the psychopathologies produced by a deviant rate of development. A developmental lag is an unusually slow rate of development. Some of the best documentation comes from studies of the mentally retarded, indicating that personal self-sufficiency develops extremely slowly in the severely retarded, while Down's syndrome preschoolers become mischievous after their intellectually normal counterparts have passed through this stage. An interesting variation in developmental lags is the case in which both the rate and pattern of growth are deviant; for example, the mental age scores of Down's syndrome children, instead of evidencing the smooth progression found in children of normal intelligence, proceed by a succession of spurts and plateaus (chapter 11). Incidentally, the dearth of developmental data makes it difficult to decide whether a given psychopathology represents a developmental lag or a fixation. The poor self-control which Redl studied, for example, may result either from a fixation or from a sluggish rate of growth (chapter 8). When behavior is sampled at only one point in time, the choice between fixation or lag may be impossible to make.

We have come across no well-documented instances in which precocity produced psychopathology, although the finding that obsessive-compulsive children have a high level of guilt is congruent with the clinical observation that such children have a precociously developed conscience (chapter 7). Our failure to find such instances may be owing to the selective coverage of psychopathologies; while we explored the psychological problems of the retardate and the learning disabled, we did not discuss the intellectually gifted.

Marked developmental *discrepancies among psychological functions* (some lagging, some progressing normally, some being precocious), combined with *deviations in the sequencing* of development within specific functions, are particularly devastating and characterize children with childhood schizophrenia (chapter 4). Here both the orderly unfolding of components of personality and the growth-enhancing interplay among them are disrupted, resulting in the bizarre behaviors which define the psychopathology.

PSYCHOPATHOLOGY OWING TO DIFFERENCE IN FUNCTIONING

In the psychopathologies discussed up until now, the behaviors were part of normal development; it was primarily the timing and sequencing of such behaviors that marked them as deviant. As the deviations from normal development became more pervasive and extreme, so did the psychopathology. However, we have also encountered behaviors which seem to have little or no counterpart in normal development; on the contrary, the difference here seems to be one of a kind. Recall the drivenness and the piercing cry noted in the hyperactive infant (chapter 12). Difference in kind does not mean that the behavior is totally absent from the normal repertoire, since all children share a common heritage; however, it does mean that behavior which is exceptionally rare, and that appears only under special conditions in normal development, is habitual and characteristic in disturbed children.

Autism supplied the clearest instances of behavior which seems to reflect a different way of responding to the social and physical environment, in that normally interesting and pleasurable stimuli become aversive (chapter 4). Research is beginning to tease out a more differentiated picture of this psychopathological condition by discovering which functions are intact (for example, there is no sensory impairment, and rote memory is normal) and which are grossly deficient (such as imitation and the ability to extract meaning). We can expect even more insights as progress is made in understanding both how autistic children function and how normal infants and toddlers function in comparable situations. Only then will we know what developmental models provide a comprehensive accounting of the baffling behavior.

Conceptualizing psychopathology as deviant development has proven to be a fruitful approach to understanding disturbed children. Obviously, there is much to learn both concerning the nature of the psychopathologies themselves and the varieties of developmental models necessary to link them to normal functioning. Advances on both fronts are needed. Ad hoc theorizing on the basis of meager data does little to increase understanding. Data collection without the organization properties of a developmental model results in clutter. Progress results when research and model building complement one another, as we have seen throughout our discussion.

THE CHALLENGE: DEVIANT DEVELOPMENT AS PSYCHOPATHOLOGY

There is an even greater challenge than trying to understand psychopathology as deviant development, however: that of *defining* deviant development as psychopathology. Recall that, from chapter 3 on, we have relied upon the GAP Report and DSM-III to define the realm of psychopathological behavior. Both classifications represent giant steps toward evolving a child-appropriate diagnostic system, rather than one which merely extrapolates down from adults to children. Neither of them has gone far enough in tailoring abnormal behavior to child development, however. The more daring step is to begin with our present knowledge of normal development and then state that significant deviations should be considered psychopathological.

This new approach would not replace the traditional classifications; indeed, all of the psychopathologies which we have discussed would still appear because they represent significant deviation from normal development. However, it would allow the inclusion of other variables which are slighted or omitted in current classifications. In our first discussion, for example, we learned that a brutal or an impoverished environment can significantly hamper normal development (chapter 4). Yet DSM-III has a classification covering only the failure to form an attachment in the first 9 months of life because of neglect (Reactive Attachment Disorder of Infancy), while child abuse is casually mentioned as only one of many parent–child problems. The reason for such shortcomings is apparent. It would be difficult to justify an environmental variable such as bleakness or brutality as a psychopathology or a mental disorder in the traditional sense. A thoroughgoing developmental approach would have no such problem.

Such an approach would also include variables which are now absent from diagnostic classifications. The most important of these is peer relations. As we learned from longitudinal studies, peer relations is one of the best predictors of adult psychopathology, yet neither the GAP Report nor DSM-III recognizes that the rejected, friendless child may be as disturbed as a phobic child, while being at a much greater risk for developing crippling problems as an adult. Ironically, this neglect of peers comes at a time when the study of peer relations is burgeoning in developmental psychology.

Regarding extreme deviation as synonymous with psychological disturbances requires that the clinician work hand in hand with individuals investigating normal development. It also requires that deviant development be defined sufficiently broadly to allow for the many normal variations within developmental patterns and within individual children. The suggested shift per se would not solve any of the substantive issues we encountered in our previous discussions. Yet it comes closer than any current classification system to defining psychopathology in ways which are exactly suited to the child's particular age or developmental stage. It would bring into being—at long last—a truly developmental psychopathology from infancy to adulthood. And that, after all, is what we have been seeking.

Glossary

Abilities tests. Tests designed to evaluate abilities directly related to academic achievement.

Abused child. An infant or child suffering from repeated physical injuries, such as bone fractures and neurological damage, along with psychological trauma inflicted by a parent or parent surrogate. Sexual molestation by such caretakers is also a form of child abuse.

Achievement tests. Tests designed to assess academic achievement.

Acting-out behavior. Children who act out their feelings or impulses toward others in a socially unacceptable fashion. Also called tension-discharge disorders or conduct disorders.

Actualizing tendency. In Carl Rogers's theory, the inherent tendency for an organism to develop all of its capacities in ways that serve to maintain and enhance it.

Advocacy. See *Child advocacy.*

Aggression. Behavior for which the goal is physical or psychological injury or destruction; anger or hatred may be the accompanying affect.

Anaclitic depression. The infant's reaction of despair following the loss of a loved and needed caretaker.

Anal stage. In Freud's psychosexual theory, the second stage of development, in which pleasure is derived from retaining and evacuating feces and the toddler confronts the issue of autonomy versus compliance.

Anorexia nervosa. A prolonged refusal to eat, often due to a fear of being obese and resulting in at least a 20 percent loss of body weight.

Anoxia. Deprivation of oxygen during or immediately following birth; may cause damage to or destroy brain cells.

Anxiety. As used here, anxiety refers to the anticipation of a painful experience.

Anxiety disorders. See *Psychoneurotic disorders.*

Anxiety hysteria. See *Phobia.*

Anxiety neurosis. A state characterized by intense, diffuse anxiety, which may be "free floating." Also called anxiety type and overanxious disorder.

Anxiety type. See *Anxiety neurosis.*

Attachment. The bond of love that develops between infant and caretaker.

Attentional deficit disorder with hyperactivity. See *Hyperactivity.*

Autism. See *Early infantile autism.*

Avoidance learning. A form of learning in which an organism, having experienced an aversive stimulus, behaves so as to prevent future encounters with that stimulus.

Baseline. In behavioral assessment, the frequency of the natural occurrence of behavior targeted for change by behavioral techniques.

Behavior therapies. A group of therapies characterized by attention to specific, current behaviors; objective measurement; and reliance on principles of behavior change derived from the laboratory.

Behavioral assessment. Procedures designed to locate specific behaviors—along with their antecedents and consequences—that subsequently can serve as targets for modification through behavioral techniques.

Behaviorism. A theory inaugurated by John B. Watson according to which the study of overt behavior is the sole basis for a scientific psychology.

Brain syndrome (or *organic brain syndrome*). A group of disorders caused by impairment of brain tissue, particularly the cerebral cortex. They may be characterized by impairment of cognitive functions, lability of affect, and personality disturbances.

Castration anxiety. In Freud's psychosexual theory, the universal fear among preschool boys in the oedipal stage that the rivalrous father will emasculate them for wanting to possess the mother.

Central nervous system (CNS). The part of the nervous system that includes the spinal cord and the brain.

Chaining. See *Shaping.*

Child advocacy. The attempt to insure that programs and services based on sound developmental knowledge are available to all children.

Childhood schizophrenia. A psychosis appearing in middle childhood; characterized by marked withdrawal, bizarre thinking and behavior, loss of reality contact, and inappropriate affect. Also called schizophreniform psychotic disorder.

Client-centered therapy. See *Nondirective therapy.*

Coalition. Salvador Minuchin's term for a family pattern in which a child sides with one parent against the other.

Community mental health movement. The effort to eliminate the social conditions responsible for the production and perpetuation of mental health problems.

Compulsion. An irrational act that an individual is compelled to do.

Conditions of worth. Carl Rogers's term for conditions set by parents under which they will grant their love and respect for the child.

Conduct disorders. Behaviors that indicate poor self-control but are not antisocial.

Conversion hysteria. See *Conversion type* (*of psychoneurotic disorder*).

Conversion type (*of psychoneurotic disorder*). Primarily, the loss or alteration of bodily function attributable to an internalized psychological conflict.

Corrective emotional experience. In psychoanalytic therapy, the discovery that expression of anxiety-laden feelings does not lead to punishment or rejection.

Critical period. The assumption that early experiences have disproportionately potent influence on later development.

Defense mechanisms. Strategems for reducing anxiety. (See also *Repression, Reaction formation, Projection,* and *Displacement.*)

Delusion. A firmly held, irrational belief that runs counter to reality and to the individual's culture or subculture.

Depression. In its psychopathological form, depression is marked by a depressed mood, loss of self-esteem, intense self-deprecation, and guilt. Eating and sleeping disturbances as well as agitation may also occur.

Deprivation. See *Privation.*

Detachment. The final phase of an infant's reaction to the loss of a loved caretaker when socially acceptable but superficial contact is established. Also called restitution.

Detouring. Salvador Minuchin's term for parents who avoid their own conflicts by regarding their child as their sole problem.

Developmental crises. Crises inherent in normal development.

Diathesis-stress hypothesis. The hypothesis that abnormal behavior results from a genetic predisposition combined with environmental stress.

Displacement. A mechanism of defense in which an impulse is directed toward a target that is safer than the original one.

Dissociative hysteria. A psychopathology characterized by disturbances in consciousness, such as trances, personality disorganization (including multiple personalities), and odd motor expressions (including sleepwalking).

Double bind. A communication pattern that traps the recipient between two negative and inescapable injunctions. There is also a prohibition against drawing attention to the bind itself.

Down's syndrome. A form of mental retardation caused by a chromosomal abnormality and accompanied by distinctive physical features. (Once called mongolism.)

Drug abuse. Significant impairment of functioning caused by a pattern of pathological use of a chemical substance.

DSM-III. The third edition of the *Diagnostic and Statistical Manual,* a diagnostic classification system adopted by the American Psychiatric Association.

Early infantile autism (or *infantile autism*). A psychosis of infancy marked by extreme aloneness, a pathological need for sameness, and mutism or noncommunicative speech.

Ego. In Freud's structural theory, the psychic component responsible for learning the nature of reality in order to gratify the id's demands for maximal pleasure, on the one hand, and avoid the painful censure of the superego, on the other hand.

Ego ideal. In Freudian theory, the individual's idealized self-image.

Egocentrism. In Jean Piaget's theory, the tendency to view the physical and social world exclusively from one's own point of view. In psychoanalytic theory, the tendency to judge others in terms of their ability to satisfy one's own needs.

Electra complex. The female counterpart of the Oedipus complex in the preschool girl; characterized by the desire to take possession of the father and eliminate the rivalrous mother.

Electroencephalogram (EEG). An instrument used to record electrical activity in the brain by means of electrodes attached to the scalp.

Encopresis. In children 3 years of age and older, withholding of feces and involuntary defecation not directly caused by physical disease.

Enmeshment. Salvador Minuchin's term for a family in which individual members are excessively involved with one another and there is no strong sense of individuality.

Enuresis. Involuntary urination during the day or night in children 5 years of age or older.

Extinction. The gradual disappearance of a learned behavior through the removal of reinforcements.

Fading. In behavior therapy, the gradual removal of reinforcements so that the desired behavior may become autonomous.

Family therapies. A group of specific techniques based on the assumption that it is necessary to treat the entire family in order to correct the faulty pattern responsible for producing a disturbance in single members.

Fixation. The persistence of normal behavior beyond the point where it is developmentally appropriate. This arrest of development may be psychopathological, depending on the degree or intensity.

Fragmentation. A thought disorder in which tangentially related or unrelated ideas disrupt the chain of thought.

Free association. The basic psychoanalytic technique for uncovering unconscious material by encouraging the patient to say whatever comes to mind.

Functional disorder. A designation given to disturbances that are primarily psychological rather than primarily organic in origin.

GAP report. A diagnostic classification system devised especially for children by the Group for the Advancement of Psychiatry.

Gender identity. Self-classification as male or female.

Group therapies. Therapeutic techniques in which individuals work together to solve their problems through social interaction guided by a trained leader.

Guilt. Judging oneself as bad and the painful affect accompanying this judgment.

Habit disorders. Psychological disturbances centering on the social regulation of bodily functions, particularly eating and elimination.

Hallucination. A sensory perception occurring in the absence of any appropriate external stimulus.

Homosexuality. A preferential erotic attraction to members of the same sex.

Hyperactivity (or *hyperkinetic syndrome*). Excessive gross-motor activity, restlessness, fidgeting. Also called attentional deficit disorder with hyperactivity.

Hysterical neurosis. A condition characterized by overly dramatic emotional expression, suggestibility, and a magical view of the world.

Id. In Freud's structural theory, the biologically based source of all psychic energy.

Identity. In Erik Erikson's theory, the search for inner continuity and interpersonal mutuality that begins in adolescence and is evidenced by a vocational choice.

Imitation (modeling). Learning by observing the behavior of others (models).

Impulse-ridden personality (or *undersocialized aggressive type*). See *Psychopathic* (or *sociopathic*) *delinquent.*

Initiative. Self-reliant expansiveness.

Intelligence quotient (IQ). A measurement of intelligence derived from the relation between the child's mental age and chronological age.

Intelligence tests. Standardized techniques for measuring intellectual functioning.

Interactional psychotic disorder. See *Symbiotic psychosis.*

Internalization. The process by which behavior that was once dependent on environmental factors for its maintenance comes to be maintained by intraindividual factors.

Internalization-externalization. A classification of psychopathologies based on whether the child suffers (internalization) or the environment suffers (externalization).

Interpretation. In psychoanalytic therapy, interpretations consist of the therapist pointing out the meaning of material which the patient is not aware of.

Intrasensory integration. The process of perceiving the equivalence of stimuli presented in different sense modalities.

La belle indifférence. A lack of concern for the physical symptoms resulting from a conversion hysteria.

Lateralization hypothesis. The hypothesis that the cerebrum undergoes progressive left-hemisphere specialization as language develops.

Learned helplessness. Nonresponsiveness to a noxious stimulus that has occurred independently of the organism's efforts to avoid it.

Learning disabilities. Learning problems due to a disorder in one or more of the basic psychological processes involved in understanding or in using spoken or written language and not due to mental retardation, emotional disturbance, environmental disadvantage, or specific perceptual or motor handicaps.

Lesbianism. Female homosexuality.

Libido. Freud's term for the biologically based drive to obtain erotic bodily sensations; also equated with sexual drive.

Mainstreaming. The term given to placing retardates in regular classes.

Marasmus. René Spitz's term for infants who waste away and sometimes die due to a lack of adequate mothering.

Masked depression. Children in middle childhood whose underlying depression is masked by a wide variety of deviant but nondepressive behaviors.

Medical model. A model of psychopathology emphasizing the role of organic dysfunction in the etiology of psychopathologies as well as classification and interpretation of psychopathological behaviors in terms of diagnostic entities.

Mental retardation. Significantly subaverage general intelligence and deficits in adaptive behavior; manifested during the developmental period.

Milieu therapy. A mode of treatment in which the daily environment is ordered so as to be therapeutic.

Minimal brain damage (or *minimal brain dysfunction*). Children of average or above-average intelligence in whom deviations of function of the central nervous system are manifested by hyperactivity; perceptual-motor impairment; emotional lability; coordination deficits; disorders of attention, memory, thinking, and speech; and specific learning disabilities.

Modeling. See *Imitation.*

Moral treatment. A humane, psychologically oriented treatment developed by Philippe Pinel; popular in the early nineteenth century.

Multiaxial classification. Diagnostic system whereby individuals are assessed in terms of a number of dimensions rather than in terms of a single classification.

Mutism. Refusal to speak in spite of an ability to do so.

Negativism. A heightened state of opposition to adults which flourishes in the toddler and early preschool period.

Negative reinforcement. Increasing the probability that behavior will occur by removing unpleasant or aversive consequences.

Neurotic delinquent (or *neurotic personality disorder*). Children whose antisocial acts are limited and repetitive, suggestive of a specific underlying conflict.

Nondirective therapy. Carl Rogers's therapeutic procedure, which utilizes warmth, acceptance, and reflection of the client's ideas and feelings to remove the obstacles to self-actualization. Also called client-centered therapy.

Object concept. In Jean Piaget's cognitive theory, the infant's separation of self from the physical world and the realization that objects have independent existence.

Object relation. In Freudian theory, the term used for an emotional attachment to another person.

Obsession. An irrational thought, the repeated occurrence of which is beyond the individual's conscious control.

Oedipus complex. In Freud's psychosexual theory, the universal desire of the preschool boy to take possession of the mother and eliminate the rivalrous father.

Omnipotent thinking. Belief that one can control events that, in reality, lie beyond one's power.

Operant conditioning (instrumental conditioning). A form of conditioning in which the persistence of a response depends on its effects on the environment.

Oppositional personality. Children who express their aggressiveness by oppositional patterns such as negativism, stubbornness, or dawdling.

Oral stage. In Freud's psychosexual theory, the first stage of development, in which pleasure is derived from sucking and biting and attachment to the caretaker is formed.

Organismic valuing process. In Carl Rogers's theory, the innate tendency for an organism to value experiences so as to optimize its development.

Overanxious disorder. See *Anxiety neurosis.*

Overinclusiveness. A thought disorder in which ideas flit from one tangential association to another.

Overprotection. Excessive and unrealistic concern over another's welfare.

Perseveration. A thought disorder in which the individual dwells on a single idea.

Personality disorders. Deeply ingrained, maladaptive behaviors that, while more pervasive than the psychoneuroses, still do not significantly diminish the individual's reality contact.

Personality inventories. Personality assessment technique in which a series of statements are judged as characteristic or not characteristic of the individual.

Phallic stage. In Freud's psychosexual theory, the third stage of development, in which the preschooler is expansive and assertive and derives pleasure from stimulating the genitals.

Phobia (or *phobic neurosis*). An intense, persistent, irrational fear of an animate or inanimate object or of a situation.

Pica. The ingestion of substances not ordinarily considered edible.

Play therapy. Using play to encourage the child to express important ideas, conflicts, and feelings symbolically rather than through direct verbal communication. The procedure depends on the kind of psychotherapy being used, such as psychoanalytic or nondirective.

Positive reinforcement. Use of rewards to increase the probability that behavior will occur.

Precausal thinking. In Jean Piaget's theory, the tendency to view the physical world in animistic terms, as having life and purpose, for example.

Preconscious. In Freudian theory, the region of the mind that contains material that is not conscious but can be brought into consciousness.

Prevention. The emphasis in the community mental health movement on forestalling the development of mental health problems rather than on treating them after they have appeared. *Primary prevention* averts the appearance of psychopathology; *secondary prevention* involves early diagnosis and prompt treatment to shorten its duration; and *tertiary prevention* maximizes the psychological functioning of those with irreversible psychopathologies.

Primary-process thinking. In Freudian theory, unrealistic thinking based on immediate need gratification rather than on reality.

Privation. A lack of growth-promoting stimulation from the social and physical environment. Privation refers to infants who never had such stimulation; *deprivation* implies that such stimulation was available but was withdrawn.

Process schizophrenia. Schizophrenia characterized by a long, gradual onset.

Projection. A mechanism of defense in which anxiety-provoking impulses are denied in oneself and attributed to others.

Projective techniques. Personality assessment methods using ambiguous or unstructured stimuli. The most popular are the Rorschach, consisting of a series of ink blots; the Thematic Apperception Test (TAT), consisting of a series of ambiguous pictures; and human figure drawing.

Prompting. In operant conditioning, the utilization of instructions, modeling, or guidance to elicit a desired response.

Pseudo-mutuality. L. C. Wynne's term for families which use a facade of harmony to cover pervasive feelings of futility.

Pseudoneurotic. According to Lauretta Bender, a basically schizophrenic school-aged child who presents a number of neurotic symptoms.

Pseudopsychopathic. According to Lauretta Bender, a basically schizophrenic school-aged child who presents a number of acting-out symptoms.

Psychoactive drugs. Drugs that affect the central nervous system so as to alter subjective states of feeling.

Psychoanalysis. A psychotherapeutic technique relying upon free association, dream interpretation, play, and the analysis of resistance and transference to provide insights into the unconscious roots of disturbed behavior.

Psychodynamic theory. The Freudian and neo-Freudian theories that aim to understand the basic motivations of human behavior. Both emotions and unconscious motivations play a major role.

Psychoneurotic disorders (*anxiety disorders*). A group of disturbances characterized by intense, chronic anxiety.

Psychopathic (or *sociopathic*) *delinquent.* Children whose difficulty controlling aggressive and sexual impulses leads to impulsive acting out, often regardless of consequences. Also called impulse-ridden personality.

Psychopathology. Abnormal behavior that may have psychological and/or biological causes. As used here, psychopathology is synonymous with abnormality, deviance, and psychological disturbance.

Psychophysiological disorders. Physical symptoms arising from the dysfunction of and structural damage to an organ caused primarily by prolonged psychological and social stress.

Psychosexual theory. Freud's developmental theory in which each stage—the oral, anal, and phallic—is marked by a change in the source of erotic bodily sensations and a distinct personality development.

Psychosis. A disorder so severe and pervasive as to interfere with the individual's capacity to meet the ordinary demands of life.

Punishment. Presentation of an aversive stimulus which decreases the probability that the response leading to it will occur.

Rational emotive therapy. Albert Ellis's cognitive restructuring therapy, in which the client is helped to identify and correct irrational ideas responsible for disturbed behavior.

Reaction formation. A mechanism of defense in which a child's thoughts and feelings are diametrically opposed to an anxiety-provoking impulse.

Reactive schizophrenia. Schizophrenia that appears suddenly, often in reaction to a specific traumatic event.

Reading disability. Failure to learn to read or to make appropriate progress in spite of normal intelligence and adequate instruction.

Reciprocal inhibition. The inhibition of the weaker of two incompatible responses by the stronger one. Utilized in systematic desensitization.

Regression. The return of behaviors that once were developmentally appropriate but no longer are. Whether or not the behaviors are psychopathological depends on the degree or intensity of regression.

Reinforcer. Any stimulus that increases the probability of a response.

Reliability. The consistency with which an assessment instrument performs.

Repression. The basic mechanism of defense in which anxiety-provoking impulses and ideas are banished from consciousness.

Resistance. In psychoanalytic therapy, devices used by patients to avoid bringing painful material to consciousness.

Restitution. See *Detachment.*

Rigidity. Excessive and unrealistic resistance to change.

Rorschach. See *Projective techniques.*

Schismatic family. Theodore Lidz's term for families of schizophrenic children; characterized by overt conflict between parents, mutual depreciation, and competition for the child's loyalty.

Schizophreniform psychotic disorder. See *Childhood schizophrenia.*

Self-actualization. See *Actualizing tendency.*

Self-control. The ability of the child to behave in a socially acceptable rather than a socially unacceptable manner when the two are in conflict.

Self-instruction. A behavioral therapy designed to increase self-control by teaching impulsive children how to guide their behavior by first talking out loud and then to themselves.

Separation anxiety. The anxiety engendered by the caretaker's departure after an attachment has been formed in infancy.

Separation-individuation. Margaret Mahler's term for the toddler's healthy assertion of autonomy in relation to the mother.

Sex role. Culturally approved behaviors and attitudes for males and females.

Shaping. An operant-conditioning technique in which responses that successively approximate the desired one are reinforced.

Situational crises. Crises that, while not inherent in normal development, are frequently encountered and are typically weathered.

Skewed family. Theodore Lidz's term for families of schizophrenic children in which the mother is dominating and overprotective and the father is weak and passive.

Sociosyntonic personality disorder. See *Subcultural delinquent.*

Soft neurological signs. A group of behavioral criteria from which, in the absence of demonstrable impairment, minimal CNS dysfunction is inferred.

Stage theories. Theories that assume that development proceeds by qualitatively distinct reorganizations of behavior and that the sequence of such reorganizations is invariant.

Stimulus generalization. The tendency of an organism, conditioned to a particular stimulus, subsequently to respond to similar stimuli.

Stimulus overselectivity. The tendency to respond to a limited number of cues in the environment, to the detriment of adaptation and learning.

Subcultural delinquent. Antisocial behavior resulting from conformity to familial or group standards that deviate from society's standard. Also called sociosyntonic personality disorder or socialized, aggressive type.

Substance abuse. See *Drug abuse.*

Superego. The moral component, or conscience, in Freud's structural theory. Initially, it is perfectionistic, requiring absolute obedience and punishing transgressions with guilt feelings.

Symbiosis. The interdependence and mutual enhancement of mother and infant.

Symbiotic psychosis. An early psychosis evidenced by intense separation anxiety, extreme ambivalence toward the mother, and fragmented speech. Also called interactional psychotic disorder.

Symptom. A psychological, behavioral, or biological manifestation of a disorder or illness.

Systematic desensitization. A behavior therapy for extinguishing anxiety by pairing a graded series of anxiety stimuli with the incompatible response of relaxation.

Tension-discharge disorders. See *Acting-out behavior.*

Thematic Apperception Test (TAT). See *Projective techniques.*

Therapeutic alliance. In psychoanalytic therapy, the positive bond between patient and therapist.

Time out. In behavior therapy, isolating the child for brief periods in order to extinguish undesirable behaviors.

Token economy. A behavioral therapy in which socially desirable behavior is rewarded by tokens that can subsequently be exchanged for rewards of the client's choosing.

Transference. In psychoanalytic therapy, the projection onto the therapist of intense feelings once directed toward significant figures, typically the parents.

Transsexualism. Gender identity with the opposite sex.

Transvestism. Obtaining sexual gratification by dressing in the clothes of the opposite sex.

Triangulation. Salvador Minuchin's term for a

family pattern in which the child is forced to side with one parent against the other.

Unconditional positive regard. In Carl Rogers's theory, the parents' intrinsic valuing and acceptance of the child.

Unconscious. In Freudian theory, the region of the mind that contains material that has been repressed or has never been conscious.

Undersocialized aggressive type. See *Impulse-ridden personality.*

Validity. The degree to which an instrument evaluates what it intends to evaluate.

Work. The ability to do what is required to be done; task orientation.

Working through. In psychoanalytic therapy, the process by which the patient gains insight into the many ways in which a single conflict is expressed.

Bibliography

Abramowitz, R. Parenthood in America. *Journal of Clinical Child Psychology,* 1976, **5,** 43–46.

Abramson, L. Y., and Sackeim, H. A. A paradox in depression: Uncontrollability and self-blame. *Psychological Bulletin,* 1977, **84,** 838–851.

Achenbach, T. M. The classification of children's psychiatric symptoms: A factor-analytic study. *Psychological Monographs,* 1966, **80** (7, Whole No. 609).

Achenbach, T. M. *Developmental psychopathology.* New York: Ronald Press, 1974.

Achenbach, T. M. Psychopathology of childhood: Research problems and issues. *Journal of Consulting and Clinical Psychology,* 1978, **46,** 759–776.

Achenbach, T. M. The child behavior profile: An empirically-based system for assessing children's behavior problems and competencies. *International Journal of Mental Health,* 1979, **7,** 24–42.

Achenbach, T. M. DSM-III in light of empirical research in the classification of child psychopathology. *Journal of the American Academy of Child Psychiatry,* 1980, **19,** 395–412.

Achenbach, T. M., and Edelbrock, C. S. The classification of child psychopathology: A review and analysis of empirical efforts. *Psychological Bulletin,* 1978, **85,** 1275–1301.

Achenbach, T. M., and Lewis, M. A proposed model for clinical research and its application to encopresis and enuresis. *Journal of the American Academy of Child Psychiatry,* 1971, **10,** 535–554.

Adam, K. S. Childhood parental loss, suicidal ideation, and suicidal behavior. In E. J. Anthony and C. Koupernik (Eds.), *The child and his family: The impact of disease and death* (Vol. 2). New York: Wiley, 1973.

Adams, P. K. Psychoneuroses. In J. D. Noshpitz (Ed.), *Basic handbook of child psychiatry. Disturbances in development* (Vol. 2). New York: Basic Books, 1979.

Ainsworth, M. D. S. Object relations, dependency and attachment: A theoretical review of the mother-infant relationship. *Child Development,* 1969, **40,** 969–1025.

Ainsworth, M. D. S. The development of the infant-mother attachment. In B. M. Caldwell and H. N. Ricciuti (Eds.), *Review of child development research* (Vol. 3). Chicago: University of Chicago Press, 1973.

Alexander, F. G., and Selesnick, S. T. *The history of psychiatry: An evaluation of psychiatric thought from prehistoric times to the present.* New York: Harper & Row, 1966.

Alexander, J. How psychologists can help stop child abuse. *Journal of Clinical Child Psychology,* 1976, **5,** 13–14.

American Psychiatric Association. *Diagnostic and statistical manual of mental disorders* (3d ed.). Washington, D.C.: Author, 1980.

American Psychological Association. *Revised ethical standards of psychologists.* Washington, D.C.: Author, 1979.

Ames, L. B., Métraux, R., Rodell, J. L., and Walker, R. N. *Child Rorschach responses: Developmental trends from two to ten years* (rev. ed.). New York: Brunner/Mazel, 1974.

Ames, L. B., Métraux, R. W., and Walker, R. N. *Adolescent Rorschach responses: Developmental trends from ten to sixteen years* (rev. ed.). New York: Brunner/Mazel, 1971.

Ansbacher, H. L., and Ansbacher, R. R. (Eds.), *The individual psychology of Alfred Adler. A systematic presentation in selections from his writings.* New York: Harper & Row, 1956.

Anthony, E. J. The syndrome of the psychologically invulnerable child. In E. J. Anthony and C. Koupernik (Eds.), *The child and his family. Children at psychiatric risk, III.* New York: Wiley, 1974.

Anthony, E. J. Preventive measures for children and adolescents at risk for psychoses. In G. W. Albee and J. M. Joffe (Eds.), *Primary prevention of pyschopathology (Vol. 1). The issues.* Hanover, N.H.: University Press of New England, 1977.

Anthony, E. J., and Gilpin, D. C. (Eds.), *Three clinical faces of childhood.* New York: Spectrum, 1976.

Anthony, S. *The discovery of death in childhood and after.* New York: Basic Books, 1972.

Appel, L. F., Cooper, R. G., McCarrell, N., Sims-Knight, J., Yussen, S. R., and Flavell, J. H. The development of the distinctions between perceiving and memorizing. *Child Development,* 1972, **43,** 1365–1381.

Appleton, T., Clifton, R., and Goldberg, S. The development of behavioral competence in infancy. In F. D. Horowitz (Ed.), *Review of child development research* (Vol. 4). Chicago: University of Chicago Press, 1975.

Arend, R., Gove, F. L., and Sroufe, L. A. Continuity of individual adaptation from infancy to kindergarten: A predictive study of ego-resiliency and curiosity in preschoolers. *Child Development,* 1979, **50,** 950–959.

Ariès, P. *Centuries of childhood.* R. Baldick, trans. New York: Vintage, 1962.

Asher, S., and Gottman, J. M. (Eds.), *The development of children's friendships.* New York: Cambridge University Press, 1981.

Axeline, V. *Dibbs in search of self.* New York: Ballantine, 1964.

Axeline, V. *Play therapy.* New York: Ballantine, 1969.

Bakwin, H., and Bakwin, R. M. *Behavior disorders in children* (4th ed.) Philadelphia: Saunders, 1972.

Bandura, A. A social learning interpretation of psychological dysfunctions. In P. London and D. Rosenhan (Eds.), *Foundation of Abnormal Psychology.* New York: Holt, Rinehart & Winston, 1968.

Bandura, A. *Principles of behavior modification.* New York: Holt, Rinehart & Winston, 1969.

Bandura, A. *Social learning theory.* Englewood Cliffs, N.J.: Prentice-Hall, 1977.

Bandura, A., and Walters, R. H. *Social learning and personality development.* New York: Holt, Rinehart & Winston, 1963.

Barkley, R. A. A review of stimulant drug research with hyperactive children. *Journal of Child Psychology and Psychiatry,* 1977, **18,** 137–165.

Bates, J. E. The concept of difficult temperament. *Merrill-Palmer Quarterly,* 1980, **26,** 299–319.

Battle, E. S., and Lacey, B. A context for hyperactivity in children over time. *Child Development,* 1972, **43,** 757–773.

Bayley, N. *Bayley Scales of Infant Development*

manual. New York: Psychological Corporation, 1969.

Beadle, K. R. Clinical interaction of verbal language, learning and behavior. *Journal of Clinical Child Psychology,* 1979, **8,** 201–205.

Beck, A. T., Sethi, B. B., and Tuthill, R. W. Childhood bereavement and adult depression. *Archives of General Psychiatry,* 1963, **9,** 295–302.

Becker, W. Consquences of different kinds of parental discipline. In M. L. Hoffman and L. W. Hoffman (Eds.), *Review of child development research* (Vol. 1). New York: Russell Sage Foundation, 1964.

Bell, A. P., and Weinberg, M. S. *Homosexualities. A study of diversity among men and women.* New York: Simon & Schuster, 1978.

Bellak, L. *The Thematic Apperception Test and the Children's Apperception Test in clinical use.* New York: Grune & Stratton, 1954.

Beller, E. K. Early intervention programs. In J. D. Osofsky (Ed.), *Handbook of infant development.* New York: Wiley, 1979.

Belmont, L. Epidemiology. In H. E. Rie and E. D. Rie (Eds.), *Handbook of minimal brain dysfunctions. A critical review.* New York: Wiley, 1980.

Belsky, J. A theoretical analysis of child abuse remediation strategies. *Journal of Clinical Child Psychology,* 1978, **7,** 117–121.

Belsky, J. Child maltreatment: An ecological integration. *American Psychologist,* 1980, **35,** 320–335.

Bemis, K. M. Current approaches to the treatment and etiology of anorexia nervosa. *Psychological Bulletin,* 1978, **85,** 593–617.

Bender, L. Childhood schizophrenia: Clinical studies of 100 schizophrenic children. *American Journal of Orthopsychiatry,* 1947, **17,** 40–56.

Bender, L. Specific reading disability as a maturational lag. *Bulletin of the Orton Society,* 1957, **7,** 9–18.

Bender, L. *The Bender Visual Motor Gestalt Test for Children.* Los Angeles: Western Psychological Services, 1962.

Bender, L., and Faretra, G. The relationship between childhood schizophrenia and adult schizophrenia. In A. Kaplan (Ed.), *Genetic factors in schizophrenia.* Springfield, Ill.: Charles C Thomas, 1972.

Bendiksen, R., and Fulton, R. Death and the child: An anterospective test of the childhood bereavement and later behavior disorder hypothesis. *Omega,* 1975, **6,** 45–59.

Bergin, A. E., and Lambert, M. J. The evaluation of therapeutic outcomes. In S. L. Garfield and A. E. Bergin (Eds.), *Handbook of psychotherapy and behavioral change: An empirical analysis.* (2d ed.) New York: Wiley, 1978.

Berkowitz, L. Control of aggression. In B. M. Caldwell and H. N. R. Ricciuti (Eds.), *Review of child development research* (Vol. 3). Chicago: University of Chicago Press, 1973.

Berry, K., and Cook, V. J. Personality and behavior. In H. E. Rie and E. D. Rie (Eds.), *Handbook of minimal brain dysfunctions. A critical view.* New York: Wiley, 1980.

Bibring, E. The mechanism of depression. In P. Greenacre (Ed.), *Affective disorders.* New York: Hallmark-Hubner, 1953, pp. 13–48.

Biller, H. B., and Davids, A. Parent–child relations, personality development and psychopathology. In A. Davids (Ed.), *Issues in abnormal child psychology.* Monterey, Calif.: Brooks/Cole, 1973.

Binet, A., and Simon, T. *The development of intelligence in children.* Baltimore: Williams & Wilkins, 1916.

Birch, H. G. The problem of "brain damage" in children. In H. G. Birch (Ed.), *Brain damage in children, the biological and social aspects.* Baltimore: Williams & Wilkins, 1964.

Blank, M., Weider, S., and Bridger, W. H. Verbal deficiencies in abstract thinking in early reading retardation. *American Journal of Orthopsychiatry,* 1968, **38,** 823–834.

Blatt, B., and Kaplan, F. Christmas in purgatory: *A photographer's essay on mental retardation.* Boston: Allyn & Bacon, 1966.

Bleuler, M. The offsprings of schizophrenics. *Schizophrenia Bulletin,* 1974, **8,** 93–107.

Block, J., and Haan, N. *Lives through time.* Berkeley, Calif.: Bancroft, 1971.

Bootzin, R. R. *Abnormal psychology. Current perspectives* (3d ed.). New York: Random House, 1980.

Bowlby, J. Grief and mourning in infancy and early childhood. *The psychoanalytic study of the child* (Vol. 15). New York: International Universities Press, 1960.

Bowlby, J. *Attachment and loss series. Separation: Anxiety and Anger* (Vol. 2). New York: Basic Books, 1973.

Brackbill, Y. Extinction of the smiling response in infants as a function of reinforcement schedule. *Child Development*, 1958, **29,** 115–124.

Brazelton, T. B. *Neonatal Behavioral Assessment Scale.* Philadelphia: Lippincott, 1963.

Bronfenbrenner, U. Toward an experimental ecology of human development. *American Psychologist*, 1977, **32,** 513–531.

Bruch, H. *Eating disorders: Obesity, anorexia nervosa, and the person within.* New York: Basic Books, 1973.

Bryan, T., and Pearl, R. Self-concepts and locus of control in children with learning disabilities. *Journal of Clinical Child Psychology*, 1979, **8,** 223–226.

Buros, O. K. (Ed.), *The eighth mental measurements yearbook* (Vol. 1 and 2). Highland Park, N.J.: Gryphon, 1978.

Burton, R. *The anatomy of melancholy.* New York: Dutton, 1968.

Calhoun, J. F. *Abnormal psychology: Current perspectives.* New York: Random House, 1972.

Calhoun, J. F., Acocella, J. R., and Goodstein, L. D. *Abnormal psychology: Current perspectives* (2d ed.). New York: Random House, 1977.

Callner, D. A. Behavioral treatment approaches to drug abuse. A critical review of the research. *Psychological Bulletin*, 1975, **82,** 143–164.

Campbell, S. B., Douglas, V. I., and Morgenstern, G. Cognitive style in hyperactive children and the effect of methylphenidate. *Journal of Child Psychology and Psychiatry*, 1971, **12,** 55–67.

Cantwell, D. P. The diagnostic process and diagnostic classification in child psychiatry. DSM-III. *Journal of the American Academy of Child Psychiatry*, 1980, **19,** 345–355.

Caplan, M. G., and Douglas, V. I. Incidence of parental loss in children with depressed mood. *Journal of Child Psychology and Psychiatry*, 1969, **10,** 225–232.

Carlson, G. A., and Cantwell, D. P. A survey of depressive symptoms, syndrome, and disorder in a child psychiatric population. *Journal of Child Psychology and Psychiatry*, 1980, **21,** 19–25.

Carr, J. *Young children with Down's syndrome. Their development, upbringing and effect on their families.* London: Butterworth, 1975.

Cass, L. K., and Thomas, C. B. *Childhood pathology and later adjustment. The question of prediction.* New York: Wiley, 1979.

Chandler, M. J. Egocentrism and antisocial behavior: The assessment and training of social perspective-taking skills. *Developmental Psychology*, 1973, **9,** 326–332.

Chess, S. Autism in children with congenital rubella. *Journal of Autism and Childhood Schizophrenia*, 1971, **1,** 33–47.

Children and the law. *Journal of Clinical Child Psychology*, 1978, **7.**

Chilman, C. S. Programs for disadvantaged parents. Some major trends and related research. In B. M. Caldwell and H. R. Ricciuti (Eds.), *Review of child development research* (Vol. 3). Chicago: University of Chicago Press, 1973.

Ciminero, A. R. Behavioral assessment: An overview. In A. R. Ciminero, K. S. Calhoun, and H. E. Adams (Eds.), *The handbook of behavioral assessment.* New York: Wiley, 1977.

Clarizio, H. F., and McCoy, C. F. *Behavior disorders in children* (2d ed.). New York: Thomas Y. Crowell, 1976.

Clarke, A. M., and Clarke, A. D. B. *Early experience: Myth and evidence.* New York: Free Press, 1977.

Coleman, J. C. Friendship and the peer group in adolescence. In J. Adelson (Ed.), *Handbook of adolescent psychology.* New York: Wiley, 1980.

Coles, R. *Migrants, sharecroppers, mountaineers.* Boston: Little, Brown, 1971.

Coles, R. *The South goes north.* Boston: Little, Brown, 1971.

Conners, C. K., and Werry, J. S. Pharmacotherapy. In H. C. Quay and J. S. Werry (Eds.), *Psychopathological disorders of childhood* (2d ed.). New York: Wiley, 1979.

Corah, N. L., Anthony, E. J., Painter, P., Stern, J. A., and Thurston, D. Effects of perinatal anoxia after seven years. *Psychological Monographs,* 1965, **79,** (3, Whole No. 596).

Costello, C. G. Childhood depression: Three basic but questionable assumptions in the Lefkowitz and Burton critique. *Psychological Bulletin,* 1980, **87,** 185–190.

Coulter, W. A., and Morrow, H. W. (Eds.), *Adaptive behavior. Concepts and measurements.* New York: Grune & Stratton, 1978.

Croake, J. W., and Knox, F. H. The changing nature of children's fears. *Child Study Journal,* 1973, **3,** 91–105.

Crook, T., and Eliot, J. Parental death during childhood and adult depression. A critical review of the literature. *Psychological Bulletin,* 1980, **87,** 252–259.

Cummings, N. A. Funding for children's services. *American Psychologist,* 1979, **34,** 1037–1039.

Davis, C. M. Self selection of diet by newly weaned infants. *American Journal of Diseases of Children,* 1929, **36,** 651–679.

Davis, C. M. Choice of formulas made by three infants throughout the nursing period. *American Journal of Diseases of Children,* 1935, **50,** 385–394.

Davis, E. J. Personality development. In T. J. Ryan (Ed.), *Poverty and the child: A Canadian study.* Toronto: McGraw-Hill Ryerson, 1972.

de Hirsch, K., Jansky, J., and Langford, W. *Predicting reading failure: A preliminary study of reading, writing, and spelling disabilities in preschool children.* New York: Harper & Row, 1966.

de Mause, L. (Ed.), *The history of childhood.* New York: Psychohistory Press, 1974.

DeMeyer, M. The nature of the neuropsychological disability in autistic children. In E. Schopler and R. J. Reichler (Eds.), *Psychopathology and child development.* New York: Plenum Press, 1976.

Doane, J. A. Family interaction and communication deviance in disturbed and normal families: A review of research. *Family Process,* 1978, **17,** 357–376.

Doehring, D. G., and Hoshko, I. M. Classification of reading problems by the Q-technique of factor analysis. *Cortex,* 1977, **13**(3), 281–294.

Doleys, D. M. Behavioral treatments for nocturnal enuresis in children: A review of the recent literature. *Psychological Bulletin,* 1977, **84,** 30–54.

Douglas, V. I. Treatment and training approaches to hyperactivity: Establishing internal or external control? In C. K. Whalen and B. Henker (Eds.), *Hyperactive children: The social ecology of identification and treatment.* New York: Academic Press, 1980.

Douglas, V. I., and Peters, K. G. Toward a clearer definition of the attentional deficit of hyperactive children. In G. A. Hale and M. Lewis (Eds.), *Attention and the development of cognitive skills.* New York: Plenum Press, 1980.

Dunn, L. M. Expanded manual for the *Peabody Picture Vocabulary Test.* Minneapolis: American Guidance Service, 1965.

Dupont, R. I., Goldstein, A., and O'Donnell, J. (Eds.), *Handbook on drug abuse.* Washington, D.C.: National Institute on Drug Abuse, 1979.

Edelbrock, C., and Achenbach, T. M. A typology of child behavior profile patterns: Distribution and correlates for disturbed children aged 6–16. *Journal of Abnormal Child Psychology,* 1980, **8,** 441–470.

Elkind, D. Cognitive development and psychopathology: Observations on egocentrism and ego defense. In E. Schopler and R. J. Reichler (Eds.), *Psychopathology and child development. Research and treatment.* New York: Plenum Press, 1976.

Ellis, A. *The essence of rational psychotherapy: A comprehensive approach to treatment.* New York: Institute for Rational Living, 1970.

Elmer, E., Evans, S., and Reinhart, J. B. *Fragile*

families, troubled children. Pittsburgh: University of Pittsburgh Press, 1977.

Emde, R. N., Katz, E. L., and Thorpe, J. K. Emotional expression in infancy. Early deviation in Down's syndrome. In M. Lewis and L. A. Rosenblum (Eds.), *The development of affect.* New York: Plenum Press, 1978.

Erikson, E. *Childhood and society.* New York: Norton, 1950.

Erikson, E. *Identity. Youth and crisis.* New York: Norton, 1968.

Escalona, S. Some considerations regarding psychotherapy for psychotic children. *Bulletin of the Menninger Clinic,* 1948, **2,** 126–134.

Essen, J., and Peckham, C. Nocturnal enuresis in childhood. *Developmental Medicine and Child Neurology,* 1976, **18,** 577–589.

Etaugh, C. Effects of nonmaternal care on children. Research evidence and popular views. *American Psychologist,* 1980, **35,** 309–319.

Evans, I. M., and Nelson, R. O. Assessment of child behavior problems. In A. R. Ciminero, K. S. Calhoun, and H. E. Adams (Eds.), *Handbook of behavioral assessment.* New York: Wiley, 1977.

Evans, R. B. Childhood parental relationships of homosexual men. *Journal of Consulting and Clinical Psychology,* 1969, **33,** 129–135.

Everly, K. New directions in divorce research. *Journal of Clinical Psychology,* 1977, **6,** 7–10.

Exner, J. E. *The Rorschach, a comprehensive system* (Vol. 2). *Current research.* New York: Wiley, 1978.

Eysenck, H. J. The effects of psychotherapy: An evaluation. *Journal of Consulting Psychology,* 1952, **16,** 319–324.

Eysenck, H. J. *Handbook of abnormal psychology.* London: Pittman, 1960.

Felner, R. D., Stolberg, A., and Cowen, L. Crisis events and school mental health referral patterns of young children. *Journal of Consulting and Clinical Psychology,* 1975, **43,** 305–310.

Ferster, C. B., and DeMyer, M. K. A method for the experimental analysis of the behavior of autistic children. *American Journal of Orthopsychiatry,* 1962, **32,** 89–98.

Fish, B. Contributions of developmental research to a theory of schizophrenia. In J. Hellmuth (Ed.), *Exceptional infant: Studies in abnormalities.* New York: Brunner/Mazel, 1971.

Fish, B. Biological disorders in infants at risk for schizophrenia. In E. R. Ritvo, B. Freeman, E. M. Ornitz, and P. E. Tanquay (Eds.), *Autism: Diagnosis, current research, and management.* New York: Spectrum, 1976.

Fisher, S., and Greenberg, R. P. *The scientific credibility of Freud's theories and therapy.* New York: Basic Books, 1977.

Flavell, J. H. *Cognitive development.* Englewood Cliffs, N.J.: Prentice-Hall, 1977.

Fraiberg, S. *Insights from the blind. Comparative studies of blind and sighted infants.* New York: Basic Books, 1977.

Freeman, T. *Childhood psychopathology and adult psychoses.* New York: International Universities Press, 1976.

Freud, A. *The ego and the mechanisms of defense.* New York: International Universities Press, 1946.

Freud, A. *Normality and pathology in childhood. Assessment of development.* New York: International Universities Press, 1965.

Freud, S. Three essays on the theory of sexuality (1905). In *The standard edition of the complete psychological works of Sigmund Freud* (Vol. 7). London: Hogarth Press, 1953.

Friedlander, D. Personality development of 25 children who later became psychotic. *Journal of Abnormal and Social Psychology,* 1945, **40,** 330–335.

Friedrich, W. N., and Boriskin, J. A. The role of the child in abuse: A review of the literature. *American Journal of Orthopsychiatry,* 1976, **46,** 580–590.

Frostig, M. Visual perception, integrative functions and academic learning. *Journal of Learning Disabilities,* 1972, **5,** 1–15.

Furman, E. *A child's parent dies: Studies in childhood bereavement.* New Haven, Conn.: Yale University Press, 1974.

Furman, R. A. A child's capacity for mourning.

In E. J. Anthony and C. Koupernik, *The child in his family: The impact of disease and death* (Vol. 2). New York: Wiley, 1973.

Garfield, S. L., and Bergin, A. (Eds.). *Handbook of psychotherapy and behavior change: An empirical analysis* (2d ed.). New York: Wiley, 1978.

Garmezy, N. Current status of a sample of other high-risk research programs. In L. C. Wynne, R. L. Cromwell, and S. Matthysse (Eds.), *The nature of schizophrenia. New approaches to research and treatment.* New York: Wiley, 1978.

Garmezy, N. Children at risk: The search for antecedents of schizophrenia. Part II. Ongoing research programs, issues and intervention. *Schizophrenia Bulletin,* 1974, **9,** 55–125.

Garmezy, N., and Streitman, S. Children at risk: The search for antecedents of schizophrenia. Part I. Conceptual models and research methods. *Schizophrenia Bulletin,* 1974, **8,** 14–90.

Gendreau, P., and Ross, R. Effective correctional treatment: Bibliotherapy for cynics. *Crime and Delinquency,* 1979, **25,** 463–489.

George, C., and Main, M. Abused children: Their rejection of peers and caregivers. In T. M. Field (Ed.), *High-risk infants and children. Adult and peer interactions.* New York: Academic Press, 1980.

Gesell, A., and Ilg, F. L. *Child development: An introduction to the study of human growth.* New York: Harper, 1949.

Gesell, A., Ilg, F. L., Ames, L. B., and Bullis, G. E. *The child from five to ten.* New York: Harper, 1946.

Gibson, D. *Down's syndrome. The psychology of mongolism.* Cambridge: Cambridge University Press, 1978.

Gibson, E. J. *Principles of perceptual learning and development.* New York: Appleton-Century-Crofts, 1969.

Gibson, E. J., and Levin, H. *The psychology of reading.* Cambridge, Mass.: MIT Press, 1975.

Gilpin, D. C., and Worland, J. Symptomatic oppositionality as seen in the clinic. In E. J. Anthony and D. C. Gilpin (Eds.), *Three clinical faces of childhood.* New York: Spectrum, 1976.

Gittelman-Klein, R. Definition and methodological issues concerning depressive illness in children. In J. G. Schulterbrandt and A. Raskin (Eds.), *Depression in childhood: Diagnosis, treatment and conceptual models.* New York: Raven Press, 1977.

Gold, M., and Petronio, R. J. Delinquent behavior in adolescence. In J. Adelson (Ed.), *Handbook of adolescent psychology.* New York: Wiley, 1980.

Goldenberg, I., and Goldenberg, H. *Family therapy: An overview.* Monterey, Calif.: Brooks/Cole, 1980.

Goldfarb, W. Psychological privation in infancy and subsequent adjustment. *American Journal of Orthopsychiatry,* 1945, **15,** 247–255.

Goldfarb, W. Childhood psychoses. In P. M. Mussen (Ed.), *Carmichael's manual of child psychology* (Vol. 2). New York: Wiley, 1970.

Gomes-Schwartz, B., Hadley, S. W., and Strupp, H. H. Individual psychotherapy and behavior therapy. In M. R. Rosenzweig and L. W. Porter (Eds.), *Annual review of psychology* (Vol. 29). Palo Alto, Calif.: Annual Reviews, 1978, pp. 435–471.

Gordon, I. *Human development: a transactional perspective.* New York: Harper & Row, 1975.

Gottesman, I. I. Schizophrenia and genetics: Where are we? Are you sure? In L. C. Wynne, R. L. Cromwell, and S. Matthysse (Eds.), *The nature of schizophrenia. New approaches to research and treatment.* New York: Wiley, 1978.

Graham, F. K., Ernhart, C. B., Thurston, D., and Craft, M. Development three years after perinatal anoxia and other potentially damaging newborn experiences. *Psychological Monographs,* 1962, **76,** (3, Whole No. 522).

Graham, F. K., and Kendall, B. S. Memory for Designs Test: Revised general manual. *Perceptual and Motor Skills,* 1960, **11,** 147–188.

Gray, W. S. *Gray Oral Reading Tests.* Indianapolis, Ind.: Bobbs-Merrill, 1963.

Graziano, A. M. Behavior theory. In B. J. Wolman (Ed.), *Handbook of treatment of mental disorders in childhood and adolescence.* Englewood Cliffs, N.J.: Prentice-Hall, 1978.

Graziano, A. M., DeGiovanni, I. S., and Garcia,

K. A. Behavioral treatment of childhood fears: A review. *Psychological Bulletin*, 1979, **86**, 804–830.

Green, R. *Sexual identity conflict in children and adults.* New York: Basic Books, 1974.

Green, R. Masculinity and femininity during boyhood: 100 families. In A. Davids (Ed.), *Child personality and psychopathology: Current topics* (Vol. 3). New York: Wiley, 1976.

Gregory, I. Retrospective data concerning childhood loss of a parent. *Archives of General Psychiatry*, 1966, **15**, 362–367.

Group for the Advancement of Psychiatry. *Psychopathological disorders in childhood: Theoretical considerations and a proposed classification* (Vol. 6, No. 62), 1966.

Gurman, A. S., and Kniskern, D. P. Research on marital and family therapy: Progress, perspective and prospect. In S. L. Garfield and A. E. Bergin (Eds.), *Handbook of psychotherapy and behavior change: An empirical analysis* (2d ed.). New York: Wiley, 1978.

Haggstrom, W. C. The power of the poor. In L. E. Sneden II (Ed.), *Poverty: A psychosocial analysis.* Berkeley, Calif.: McCutchan, 1970.

Hare, E. H. Masturbatory insanity: The history of an idea. *Journal of Mental Science*, 1962, **108**, 1–25.

Harms, E. *Origin of modern psychiatry.* Springfield, Ill.: Charles C Thomas, 1967.

Hartman, H. *Essays on ego psychology.* New York: International Universities Press, 1964.

Hartup, W. W. Peer interaction and the behavioral assessment of the individual child. In E. Schopler and R. J. Reichler (Eds.), *Child development, deviations and treatment.* New York: Plenum Press, 1976.

Hayes, M. Rights of the child. In J. D. Noshpitz (Ed.), *Basic handbook of child psychiatry* (Vol. 4). *Prevention and current issues.* New York: Basic Books, 1979.

Healy, W., and Bronner, A. F. The child guidance clinic. Birth and growth of an idea. In L. G. Lowrey (Ed.), *Orthopsychiatry, 1923–1949: Retrospect and prospect.* New York: American Orthopsychiatric Association, 1948.

Heber, F. R. Sociocultural mental retardation: A longitudinal study. In D. G. Forgays (Ed.), *Primary prevention of psychopathology* (Vol. 2). *Environmental influences.* Hanover, N.H.: University Press of New England, 1978.

Heinstein, M. I. Behavioral correlates of breast–bottle regimes under varying parent–infant relationships. *Monographs of the Society for Research in Child Development*, 1963, **28** (4, Serial No. 88).

Helper, M. M. Follow-up of children with minimal brain dysfunction: Outcomes and predictors. In H. E. Rie and E. D. Rie (Eds.), *Handbook of minimal brain dysfunctions. A critical view.* New York: Wiley, 1980.

Herbert, M. *Emotional problems of development in children.* New York: Academic Press, 1974.

Hermelin, B. Coding and sense modalities. In L. Wing (Ed.), *Early childhood autism. Clinical, educational and social aspects.* New York: Pergamon Press, 1976.

Hersov, L. Fecal soiling. In M. Rutter and L. Hersov (Eds.), *Child psychiatry: Modern approaches.* Oxford: Blackwell Scientific Publications, 1977.

Hersov, L. A. Persistent non-attendance at school. *Journal of Child Psychology and Psychiatry*, 1960, **1**, 130–136.

Herzog, E., and Sudia, C. E. Children in fatherless families. In B. E. Caldwell and H. N. Ricciuti (Eds.), *Review of child development research* (Vol. 3). Chicago: University of Chicago Press, 1973.

Hetherington, E. M. Effects of father absence on personality development in adolescent daughters. *Developmental Psychology*, 1972, **7**, 313–326.

Hetherington, E. M., Cox, M., and Cox, R. The aftermath of divorce. In J. H. Stevens, Jr., and M. Matthew (Eds.), *Mother/child, father/child relationships.* Washington, D.C.: National Association for the Education of Young Children, 1978.

Hetherington, E. M., and Martin, B. Family interaction. In H. C. Quay and J. S. Werry (Eds.), *Psychopathological disorders of childhood* (2d ed.). New York: Wiley, 1979.

Hetherington, E. M., and Parke, R. D. *Child psychology. A contemporary viewpoint* (2d ed.). New York: McGraw-Hill, 1979.

Hilgard, J. R., Newman, M. F., and Fisk, F. Strength of adult ego following childhood bereavement. *American Journal of Orthopsychiatry,* 1960, **30,** 788–798.

Horowitz, F. D., and Paden, L. Y. The effectiveness of environmental intervention programs. In B. M. Caldwell and H. R. Ricciuti (Eds.), *Review of child development research* (Vol. 3). Chicago: University of Chicago Press, 1973.

Huelsman, C. B. The WISC subtest syndrome for disabled readers. *Perceptual and Motor Skills,* 1970, **30,** 535–550.

Hunter, R., and Macalpine, I. *Three hundred years of psychiatry.* New York: Oxford University Press, 1963.

Hurlock, E. B. *Child development* (4th ed.). New York: McGraw-Hill, 1964.

Jacob, T., and Grounds, L. Confusions and conclusions: A response to Doane. *Family Process,* 1978, **17,** 377–387.

Jacobs, J. *Adolescent suicide,* New York: Wiley-Interscience, 1971.

Jacobson, E. *The self and the object world.* New York: International Universities Press, 1964.

Janis, I. L. (Ed.). *Personality. Dynamics, development, and assessment.* New York: Harcourt Brace & World, 1969.

Jastak, J. F., and Jastak, S. R. *The Wide-Range Achievement Test* (rev. ed.). Wilmington, Del.: Guidance Associates, 1965.

Jenkins, R. L. *Behavior disorders of childhood and adolescence.* Springfield, Ill.: Charles C Thomas, 1973.

Jessor, R. Marijuana: A review of recent psychosocial research. In R. I. Dupont, A. Goldstein, and J. O'Donnell (Eds.), *Handbook on drug abuse.* Washington, D.C.: National Institute on Drug Abuse, 1979.

Jessor, R., and Jessor, S. L. *Problem behavior and psychosocial development. A longitudinal study of youth.* New York: Academic Press, 1977.

Johnston, L. D., Bachman, J. G., and O'Malley, P. M. *Highlights from: Drug use among American high school students, 1975–1977.* Rockville, Md.: National Institute on Drug Abuse, 1977.

Jurkovic, G. J. The juvenile deliquent as a moral philosopher: A structural-developmental perspective. *Psychological Bulletin,* 1980, **88,** 709–727.

Jurkovic, G. J., and Prentice, N. M. Relation of moral and cognitive development to dimensions of juvenile delinquency. *Journal of Abnormal Psychology,* 1977, **86,** 414–420.

Kaffman, M., and Elizur, E. *Infants who become enuretics: A longitudinal study of 161 Kibbutz children.* Monographs of the Society for Research in Child Development, vol. 42, no. 2, 1977.

Kail, R. *The development of memory in children.* San Francisco: Freeman, 1979.

Kandel, D. B. Convergence in prospective longitudinal surveys of drug use in normal populations. In D. B. Kandel (Ed.), *Longitudinal research in drug use. Empirical findings and methodological issues.* Washington, D.C.: Hemisphere, 1978.

Kandel, D. B., Kessler, R. C., and Margulies, R. Z. Antecedents of adolescent initiation into stages of drug use: A developmental analysis. In D. B. Kandel (Ed.), *Longitudinal research in drug use. Empirical findings and methodological issues.* Washington: Hemisphere, 1978.

Kane, B. Children's concepts of death. *Journal of Genetic Psychology,* 1979, **134,** 141–153.

Kanner, L. Irrelevant and metaphorical language in early infantile autism. *American Journal of Psychiatry,* 1946–1947, **103,** 242–246.

Kanner, L. *Child psychiatry* (4th ed.). Springfield, Ill.: Charles C Thomas, 1977.

Kanner, L., Rodriguez, A., and Ashenden, B. How far can autistic children go in matters of social adaptation? *Journal of Autism and Childhood Schizophrenia,* 1972, **2,** 9–33.

Kantor, R. E., Wallner, J. M., and Winder, C. L. Process and reactive schizophrenia. *Journal of Consulting Psychology,* 1953, **17,** 157–162.

Kastenbaum, R. Childhood: The kingdom where

creatures die. *Journal of Clinical Child Psychology,* 1974, **3,** 11–14.

Katz, P., and Zigler, E. Self-image disparity: A developmental approach. *Journal of Personality and Social Psychology,* 1967, **5,** 186–195.

Kaufman, A. S. *Intelligence Testing with WISC-R.* New York: Wiley, 1979.

Kazdin, A. E. *Behavior modification in applied settings.* Homewood, Ill.: Dorsey Press, 1980.

Kelley, T. L., Madden, R., Gardner, E. F., and Rudman, H. C. *The Stanford Achievement Test.* New York: Harcourt Brace Jovanovich, 1964.

Kelly, E. W., Jr. School phobia: A review of theory and treatment. *Psychology in the schools,* 1973, **10,** 33–42.

Kelly, J. B., and Wallerstein, J. S. The effects of parental divorce: Experiences of the child in early latency. *American Journal of Orthopsychiatry,* 1976, **46,** 20–32.

Kenny, T. J. Hyperactivity. In H. E. Rie and E. D. Rie (Eds.), *Handbook of minimal brain dysfunctions. A critical view.* New York: Wiley, 1980.

Kenny, T. J., and Burka, A. Coordinating multiple interventions. In H. E. Rie and E. D. Rie (Eds.), *Handbook of minimal brain dysfunctions. A critical view.* New York: Wiley, 1980.

Kent, R. N., and Foster, S. L. Direct observational procedures: Methodological issues in naturalistic settings. In A. R. Ciminero, K. S. Calhoun, and H. E. Adams (Eds.), *Handbook of behavioral assessment.* New York: Wiley, 1977.

Kephart, N. *Learning disability: An educational adventure.* West Lafayette, Ind.: Kappa Delta Pi Press, 1968.

Kernberg, P. F. Childhood schizophrenia and autism: A selective review. In L. Bellak (Ed.), *Disorders of the schizophrenic syndrome.* New York: Basic Books, 1979.

Kessler, J. W. *Psychopathology of childhood.* Englewood Cliffs, N.J.: Prentice-Hall, 1966.

Kessler, J. W. Nosology in child psychopathology. In H. E. Rie (Ed.), *Perspectives in child psychopathology.* Chicago: Aldine-Atherton, 1971.

Kessler, J. W. History of minimal brain dysfunctions. In H. E. Rie and E. D. Rie (Eds.), *Handbook of minimal brain dysfunctions. A critical view.* New York: Wiley, 1980.

Kinsbourne, M., and Caplan, P. J. *Children's learning and attention problems.* Boston: Little, Brown, 1979.

Kinsbourne, M., and Hiscock, M. Cerebral lateralization and cognitive development. In J. S. Chall and A. F. Mirsky (Eds.), *Education and the brain. The seventy-seventh yearbook of the National Society for the Study of Education* (Part 2). Chicago: University of Chicago Press, 1978.

Kinsey, A. C., Pomeroy, W. B., and Martin, C. E. *Sexual behavior in the human male.* Philadelphia: Saunders, 1948.

Kirk, S., McCarthy, J., and Kirk, W. *Illinois Test of Psycholinguistic Ability* (rev. ed.). Urbana, Ill.: University of Illinois Press, 1968.

Klausmeier, H., and Allen, P. S. *Cognitive development of children and youth: A longitudinal study.* New York: Academic Press, 1978.

Klopfer, W. G., and Taulbee, E. S. Projective tests. In M. R. Rosenzweig and L. W. Porter (Eds.), *Annual review of psychology* (Vol. 27). Palo Alto, Calif.: Annual Reviews, 1976.

Knitzer, J. E. Child advocacy: A perspective. *American Journal of Orthopsychiatry,* 1976, **46,** 200–216.

Knopf, I. J. *Childhood psychopathology. A developmental approach.* Englewood Cliffs, N.J.: Prentice-Hall, 1979.

Kohlberg, L. Moral stages and moralization: The cognitive-developmental approach. In T. Lickona (Ed.), *Moral development and behavior. Theory, research and social issues.* New York: Holt, Rinehart & Winston, 1976.

Kohlberg, L., LaCrossee, J., and Ricks, D. The predictability of adult mental health from childhood behavior. In B. J. Wolman (Ed.), *Manual of child psychopathology.* New York: McGraw-Hill, 1972.

Kohn, M. *Social competence, symptoms and underachievement in childhood: A longitudinal perspective.* Silver Spring, Md.: V. H. Winston, 1977.

Kolvin, I., Ounsted, C., Humphrey, M., McNay, A. Studies in childhood psychoses. Part 2.

The phenomenology of childhood psychoses. *British Journal of Psychiatry*, 1971, **118**, 385–395.

Kolvin, I., Ounsted, C., Richardson, L. M., and Garside, R. Studies in childhood psychoses. Part 3. The family and social background in childhood psychosis. *British Journal of Psychiatry*, 1971, **118**, 396–402.

Koppitz, E. M. *The Bender Gestalt Test for Young Children*. New York: Grune & Stratton, 1964.

Koppitz, E. M. *Children with learning disabilities: A five year follow-up study*. New York: Grune & Stratton, 1971.

Korchin, S. J. *Modern clinical psychology. Principles of intervention in the clinic and community*. New York: Basic Books, 1976.

Kovacs, M., and Beck, A. T. An empirical-clinical approach toward a definition of childhood depression. In J. G. Schulterbrandt, and A. Raskin (Eds.), *Depression in childhood: Diagnosis, treatment and conceptual models*. New York: Raven Press, 1977.

Kraft, I. A. Group therapy. In J. D. Noshpitz (Ed.), *Basic handbook of child psychiatry* (Vol. 3). *Therapeutic interventions*. New York: Basic Books, 1979.

Kubicek, L. F. Organization in two mother–infant interactions involving a normal infant and his fraternal twin brother, who was later diagnosed as autistic. In T. M. Field (Ed.), *High-risk infants and children. Adult and peer interaction*. New York: Academic Press, 1980.

LaVietes, R. Mental retardation: Psychological treatment. In B. J. Wolman (Ed.), *Handbook of treatment of mental disorders in childhood and adolescence*. Englewood Cliffs, N.J.: Prentice-Hall, 1978.

Ledwidge, B. Cognitive behavior modification: A step in the wrong direction? *Psychological Bulletin*, 1978, **85**, 353–375.

Ledwidge, B. Cognitive behavior modification or new ways to change minds: Reply to Mahoney and Kazdin. *Psychological Bulletin*, 1979, **86**, 1050–1053.

Lefkowitz, M. M. Childhood depression: A reply to Costello. *Psychological Bulletin*, 1980, **87**, 191–194.

Lefkowitz, M. M., and Burton, N. Childhood depression: A critique of the concept. *Psychological Bulletin*, 1978, **85**, 716–726.

Lefkowitz, M. M., Eron, L. D., Walder, L. O., and Huesmann, L. R. *Growing up to be violent. A longitudinal study of the development of aggression*. New York: Pergamon Press, 1977.

Lefrançois, G. R. *Psychology*. Belmont, Calif.: Wadsworth, 1980.

Leif, A. (Ed.), *The commonsense psychiatry of Dr. Adolph Meyer*. New York: McGraw-Hill, 1948.

Leland, H. Theoretical considerations of adaptive behavior. In W. A. Coulter and H. W. Morrow (Eds.), *Adaptive behavior. Concepts and measurements*. New York: Grune & Stratton, 1978.

Lettieri, D. J., Sayers, M., and Pearson, H. W. (Eds.), Theories on drug abuse. Selected contemporary perspectives. *NIDA Research Monograph 30*. Washington, D.C.: National Institute on Drug Abuse, 1980.

Levitt, E. E. The results of psychotherapy with children: An evaluation. *Journal of Consulting Psychology*, 1957, **21**, 189–196.

Levy, D. M. Oppositional syndrome and oppositional behavior. In P. H. Hoch and J. Zubin (Eds.), *Psychopathology of childhood*. New York: Grune & Stratton, 1955, pp. 204–226.

Lidz, T. *The origin and treatment of schizophrenic disorders*. New York: Basic Books, 1973.

Lindquist, E. F., and Hieronymus, A. M. *Iowa Tests of Basic Skills manuals*. Boston: Houghton-Mifflin, 1955–1956.

Livson, N., and Peskin, H. Perspectives on adolescence from longitudinal research. In J. Adelson (Ed.), *Handbook of adolescent psychology*. New York: Wiley, 1980.

Lotter, V. Follow-up studies. In M. Rutter and E. Schopler (Eds.), *Autism: A reappraisal of concepts and treatment*. New York: Plenum Press, 1978.

Lourie, N. V. Child advocacy. In J. D. Noshpitz (Ed.), *Basic handbook of child psychiatry* (Vol. 4). *Prevention and current issues*. New York: Basic Books, 1979.

Lovaas, O. I. *The autistic child. Language development through behavior modification.* New York: Irvington, 1977.

Lovaas, O. I., Koegel, R. L., and Schreibman, L. Stimulus overselectivity in autism: A review of research. *Psychological Bulletin,* 1979, **86,** 1236–1254.

Lovibond, S. H., and Coote, M. A. Enuresis. In C. G. Costello, *Symptoms of psychopathology: A handbook.* New York: Wiley, 1979.

Lucas, A. R. Muscular control and coordination in minimal brain dysfunctions. In H. E. Rie and E. D. Rie (Eds.), *Handbook of minimal brain dysfunctions: A critical view.* New York: Wiley, 1980.

McConaghy, M. J. Gender permanence and the genital basis of gender: Stages in the development of constancy of gender identity. *Child Development,* 1979, **50,** 1223–1226.

McCord, J. A thirty-year follow-up of treatment effects. *American Psychologist,* 1978, **33,** 284–289.

McCord, W., McCord, J., and Verden, P. Family relationships and sexual deviance in lower-class adolescents. *International Journal of Social Psychiatry,* 1962, **8,** 165–179.

McDermott, J. F., Jr. Parental divorce in early childhood. *American Journal of Psychiatry,* 1968, **124,** 1424–1432.

Macfarlane, J. W. Perspectives on personal consistency and change: The guidance study. *Vita Humana,* 1964, **7,** 115–126.

Macfarlane, J. W., Allen, L., and Honzik, M. P. *A developmental study of the behavior problems of normal children between 21 months and 14 years of age.* Berkeley and Los Angeles: University of California Press, 1954.

McGlothlin, W. H. Drugs and crime. In R. I. Dupont, A. Goldstein, and J. O'Donnell (Eds.), *Handbook on drug abuse.* Washington, D.C.: National Institute on Drug Abuse, 1979.

Machover, K. *Personality projection in the drawing of the human figure.* Springfield, Ill.: Charles C Thomas, 1949.

Mahler, M. S. On childhood psychosis and schizophrenia: Autistic and symbiotic infantile psychosis. In R. S. Eissler, A. Freud, H. Hartmann, and E. Kris (Eds.), *The psychoanalytic study of the child* (Vol. 7). New York: International Universities Press, 1952, pp. 286–305.

Mahler, M. S. On early infantile psychosis: The symbiotic and autistic syndromes. *Journal of the American Academy of Child Psychiatry,* 1965, **4,** 442–468.

Mahler, M. S., and Furer, M. *On human symbiosis and the vicissitudes of individuation. Vol. 1: Infantile psychosis.* New York: International Universities Press, 1968.

Mahler, M. S., and Furer, M. Child psychosis: A theoretical statement and its implications. *Journal of Autism and Childhood Schizophrenia,* 1972, **2,** 213–218.

Mahoney, M. J. *Cognition and behavior modification.* Cambridge, Mass.: Ballinger, 1974.

Mahoney, M. J. Reflections on the cognitive-learning trend in psychotherapy. *American Psychologist,* 1977, **32,** 5–13.

Mahoney, M. J., and Kazdin, A. E. Cognitive behavior modification: Misconceptions and premature evacuation. *Psychological Bulletin,* 1979, **86,** 1044–1049.

Mahoney, M. J., Kazdin, A. E., Lesswing, N.J. Behavior modification: Delusion or deliverance? In C. M. Franks and G. T. Wilson (Eds.), *Annual review of behavior therapy, theory and practice* (Vol. 2). New York: Brunner/Mazel, 1974.

Malmquist, C. P. Depressive phenomena in children. In B. B. Wolman (Ed.), *Manual of child psychopathology.* New York: McGraw-Hill, 1972.

Marcia, J. E. Identity in adolescence. In J. Adelson (Ed.), *Handbook of adolescent psychology.* New York: Wiley, 1980.

Markusen, E., and Fulton, R. Childhood bereavement and behavior disorders: A critical review. *Omega,* 1971, **2,** 107–117.

Martin, B. Parent–child relations. In F. D. Horowitz (Ed.), *Review of child development research* (Vol. 4). Chicago: University of Chicago Press, 1975.

Martin, H. P., and Breezley, P. Behavioral observations of abused children. *Developmental Medicine and Child Neurology,* 1977, **19,** 373–387.

Martin, H. P., Breezley, P., Conway, E. F., and Kempe, C. H. The development of abused children, Part 1: A review of the literature. In I. Schulman (Ed.), *Advances in pediatrics* (Vol. 21). Chicago: Yearbook Medical Publishers, 1974.

Martin, H. P., and Kempe, C. H. *The abused child: A multidisciplinary approach to developmental issues and treatment.* Cambridge, Mass.: Ballinger, 1976.

Massie, H. N. Pathological interactions in infancy. In T. M. Field (Ed.), *High-risk infants and children. Adult and peer interaction.* New York: Academic Press, 1980.

Mednick, B. R. Breakdown in high-risk subjects: Familial and early environmental factors. *Journal of Abnormal Psychology,* 1973, **82,** 469–475.

Mednick, S. A., Schulsinger, H., and Schulsinger, F. Schizophrenia in children of schizophrenic mothers. In A. Davids (Ed.), *Child personality and psychopathology: Current topics* (Vol. 2). New York: Wiley, 1975.

Mednick, S. A., and Witkin-Lanoil, G. H. Intervention in children at high risk for schizophrenia. In G. W. Albee and J. M. Joffe (Eds.), *Primary prevention of psychopathology* (Vol. 1). *The issues.* Hanover, N.H.: University Press of New England, 1977.

Meehl, P. E. Theoretical risks and tabular asterisks: Sir Karl, Sir Ronald, and the slow progress of soft psychology. *Journal of Consulting and Clinical Psychology,* 1978, **46,** 806–834.

Meichenbaum, D. H., and Goodman, J. Training impulsive children to talk to themselves. A means of developing self-control. *Journal of Abnormal Psychology,* 1971, **77,** 115–126.

Meier, J. H. Dyslexia and other learning disabilities. In P. R. Magrab (Ed.), *Psychological management of pediatric problems. II: Sensorineural conditions and social concerns.* Baltimore: University Park Press, 1978.

Meissner, W. W., Mack, J. E., and Semrad, E. V. Classical psychoanalysis. In A. M. Freedman, H. I. Kaplan, and R. J. Sadock, *Comprehensive textbook of psychiatry* (Vol. 2). Baltimore: Williams & Wilkins, 1975.

Menyuk, P. Language: What's wrong and why. In M. Rutter and E. Schopler (Eds.), *Autism: A reappraisal of concepts and treatment.* New York: Plenum Press, 1978.

Mercer, J. R. *System of multicultural pluralistic assessment: Technical manual.* New York: Psychological Corporation, 1977.

Millar, H. E. C. Health care for high-risk mothers. In J. D. Noshpitz (Ed.), *Basic handbook for child psychiatry* (Vol. 4). *Prevention and current issues.* New York: Basic Books, 1979.

Miller, L. C., Barrett, C. L., and Hampe, E. Phobias of childhood in a prescientific era. In A. Davids (Ed.), *Child personality and psychopathology: Current topics* (Vol. 1). New York: Wiley, 1974.

Miller, L. C., Barrett, C. L., Hampe, E., and Noble, H. Comparison of reciprocal inhibition, psychotherapy and waiting list control for phobic children. *Journal of Abnormal Psychology,* 1972, **79,** 269–279.

Miller, N. E., and Dollard, J. *Social learning and imitation.* New Haven, Conn.: Yale University Press, 1941.

Miller, R. T. Childhood schizophrenia: A review of selected literature. *International Journal of Mental Health,* 1974, **3,** 3–46.

Minuchin, S., Baker, L., Rosman, B. L., Liebman, R., Milman, L., and Todd, T. C. A conceptual model of psychosomatic illness in children. *Archives of General Psychiatry,* 1975, **32,** 1031–1038.

Minuchin, S., Montalvo, B., Guerney. B. G., Jr., Rosman, B. L., and Schumer, F. *Families of the slums.* New York: Basic Books, 1967.

Mischel, W. Processes in delay of gratification. In L. Berkowitz (Ed.), *Advances in experimental social psychology* (Vol. 7). New York: Academic Press, 1974.

Mischel, W. How children postpone pleasure. *Human Nature,* 1978, **1,** 50–55.

Mishler, E. G., and Waxler, N. E. Family interaction and schizophrenia: A review of current theories. *Merrill-Palmer Quarterly,* 1965, **11,** 269–316.

Money, J. Sexual dimorphism and homosexual gender identity. *Psychological Bulletin,* 1970, **74,** 425–440.

Money, J., and Ehrhardt, A. A. *Man and woman, boy and girl. The differentiation and dimorphism of gender identity from conception to maturity.* Baltimore: Johns Hopkins University Press, 1972.

Money, J., and Higham, E. Juvenile gender identity: Differentiation and transpositions. In A. Davids (Ed.),*Child personality and psychopathology: Current topics* (Vol. 3). New York: Wiley, 1976.

Mosher, L. R., and Keith. S. J. Research on the psychosocial treatment of schizophrenia: A summary report. *American Journal of Psychiatry,* 1977, **136,** 623–631.

Munro, A. Parental deprivation in depressive patients. *British Journal of Psychiatry,* 1966, **112,** 443–457.

Nagera, H. Early childhood disturbances, the infantile neurosis, and the adult disturbances. Problems of a developmental psychoanalytic psychology. *The psychoanalytic study of the child.* Monograph No. 2. New York: International Universities Press, 1966.

Naylor, H. Reading disability and lateral asymmetry: An information-processing analysis. *Psychological Bulletin,* 1980, **87,** 531–545.

Nihira, K. Dimensions of adaptive behavior in institutionalized mentally retarded children and adults: Developmental perspectives. *American Journal of Mental Deficiency,* 1976, **81,** 215–226.

Nihira, K. Factorial descriptions of the AAMD Adaptive Behavior Scale. In W. A. Coulter and H. W. Morrow (Eds.), *Adaptive behavior. Concepts and measurements.* New York: Grune & Stratton, 1978.

Nihira, K., Foster R., Shellhaas, M., and Leland, H. *AAMD Adaptive Behavior Scale, 1974 revision.* Washington, D.C.: American Association on Mental Deficiency, 1974.

Nodine, C. F., and Steuerle, N. L. Development of perceptual and cognitive strategies of differentiating graphemes. *Journal of Experimental Psychology,* 1973, **97,** 158–166.

Noshpitz, J. D. (Ed.), *Basic handbook of child psychiatry* (Vol. 3). *Therapeutic interventions.* New York: Basic Books, 1979a.

Noshpitz, J. D. (Ed.), *Basic handbook of child psychiatry* (Vol. 4). *Prevention and current issues.* New York: Basic Books, 1979b.

Offord, D. R., and Cross, L. A. Behavioral antecedents of adult schizophrenia. A review. *Archives of General Psychiatry,* 1969, **21,** 267–283.

Olweus, D. *Aggression in the schools. Bullies and whipping boys.* New York: Halsted Press, 1978.

Olweus, D. Stability of aggressive reaction patterns in males: A review. *Psychological Bulletin,* 1979, **86,** 852–875.

Orlando, F. A., and Black, J. P. The juvenile court. In N. Hobbs (Ed.), *Issues in the classification of children* (Vol. 1). San Francisco: Jossey-Bass, 1975.

Ornitz, E. M. The modulation of sensory input and motor output in autistic children. In E. Schopler and R. J. Reichler (Eds.), *Psychopathology and child development.* New York: Plenum Press, 1976.

Ornitz, E. M., and Ritvo, E. R. The syndrome of autism: A critical review. *American Journal of Psychiatry,* 1976, **133**(6), 609–621.

Ortony, A., Reynolds, R. E., and Arter, J. A. Metaphor: Theoretical and empirical research. *Psychological Bulletin,* 1978, **85,** 919–943.

Osofsky, J. D., and Connors, K. Mother–infant interaction: An integrative view of a complex system. In J. D. Osofsky (Ed.), *Handbook of infant development.* New York: Wiley, 1979.

Palmer, J. O. *The psychological assessment of children.* New York: Wiley, 1970.

Parke, R. D. Perspectives on father–infant interaction. In J. D. Osofsky (Ed.), *Handbook of infant development.* New York: Wiley, 1979.

Parke, R. D., and Collmer, C. W. Child abuse: An interdisciplinary analysis. In E. M. Hetherington (Ed.), *Review of child development research* (Vol. 5). Chicago: University of Chicago Press, 1975.

Patterson, G. R., Littman, R. A., and Bricker, W. Assertive behavior in children: A step toward a theory of aggression. *Monographs of the Society for Research in Child Development,* 1967, **32** (5, Serial No. 113).

Paul, G. L., and Lentz, R. J. *Psychosocial treatment of chronic mental patients.* Cambridge, Mass.: Harvard University Press, 1977.

Paulson, M. J., and Stone, D. Suicidal behavior of latency-age children. *Journal of Clinical Child Psychology,* 1974, **3,** 50–53.

Peller, L. E. Libidinal development as reflected in play. In M. R. Haworth (Ed.), *Child psychotherapy.* New York: Basic Books,1964.

Perloff, R., Perloff, E., and Sussna, E. Program evaluation. In M. R. Rosenzweig and L. W. Porter (Eds.), *Annual review of psychology* (Vol. 27). Palo Alto, Calif.: Annual Reviews, 1976, 569–594.

Peterson, D. W., and Becker, W. C. Family interaction and delinquency. In H. C. Quay (Ed.), *Juvenile delinquency, research and theory.* New York: Van Nostrand, 1965.

Peterson, R. C. (Ed.), Marijuana research findings. *NIDA Research Monograph 31.* Washington, D.C.: National Institute of Drug Abuse, 1980.

Pfeffer, C. R., Conte, H. R., Plutchik, R., and Jerrett, M. A. Suicidal behavior in latency-age children. An outpatient population. *Journal of the American Academy of Child Psychiatry,* 1980, **19,** 703–710.

Phares, E. J. *Locus of control in personality.* Morristown, N. J.: General Learning Press, 1976.

Piaget, J. *The child's conception of physical causality.* London: Kegan Paul, 1930.

Piaget, J. *The moral judgment of the child.* London: Kegan Paul, 1932.

Piaget, J. *The construction of reality in the child.* New York: Basic Books, 1954.

Piaget, J. *Six psychological studies.* New York: Random House, 1967.

Pines, M. Superkids. *Psychology Today,* 1979, **12,** 53–63.

Poznanski, E., Krahenbuhl, V., and Zrull, J. Childhood depression: A longitudinal perspective. *Journal of the American Academy of Child Psychiatry,* 1976, **15**(3), 491–501.

Premorbid adjustment and schizophrenic heterogeneity. *Schizophrenia Bulletin,* 1977, **3**(2), 180–182.

Prior, M. R. Cognitive abilities and disabilities in infantile autism: A review. *Journal of Abnormal Child Psychology,* 1979, **7,** 357–380.

Prior, M. R., and Chen, C. S. Short-term and serial memory in autistic, retarded, and normal children. *Journal of Autism and Childhood Schizophrenia,* 1976, **6,** 121–131.

Proctor, J. T. Hysteria in childhood. *American Journal of Orthopsychiatry,* 1958, **28,** 394–407.

Provence, S., and Lipton, R. C. *Infants in institutions.* New York: International Universities Press, 1962.

Quay, H. C. Classification. In H. C. Quay and J. S. Werry (Eds.), *Psychopathological disorders of childhood* (2d ed.). New York: Wiley, 1979.

Rapoport, J., Mikkelsen, E. J., and Werry, J. S. Antimanic, antianxiety, hallucinogenic, and miscellaneous drugs. In J. S. Werry (Ed.), *Pediatric psychopharmacology.* New York: Brunner/Mazel, 1978.

Redd, W. H., Porterfield, A. L., and Andersen, B. L. Behavior modification. *Behavioral approaches to human problems.* New York: Random House, 1979.

Redl, F. Oppositional behavior in everyday life. In E. J. Anthony and D. C. Gilpin (Eds.), *Three clinical faces of childhood.* New York: Spectrum, 1976.

Redl, F., and Wineman, D. *Children who hate. The disorganization and breakdown of behavior controls.* New York: Free Press, 1951.

Reese, H. W., and Lipsitt, L. P. *Experimental child psychology.* New York: Academic Press, 1970.

Reitan, R. *Manual for administering the scoring of the Reitan Indiana Neuropsychological Battery for Young Children.* Indianapolis: University of Indiana Medical Center, 1964.

Rholes, W. S., Blackwell, J., Jordan, C., and Walters, C. A developmental study of learned helplessness. *Developmental Psychology,* 1980, **16,** 616–24.

Richardson, S. A., Goodman, N., Hastorf, A. H., and Dornbusch, S. M. Cultural uniformity in reaction to physical disabilities, *American Sociological Review,* 1961, **26,** 241–247.

Rie, E. D. Effects of MBD on learning, intellectual functions and achievement. In H. E. Rie and E. D. Rie (Eds.), *Handbook of minimal brain dysfunctions. A critical view.* New York: Wiley, 1980.

Rie, E. D., Rie, H. E., Stewart, S., and Rettemnier, S. R. An analysis of soft signs in children with learning problems. *Brain and Language,* 1978, **6,** 32–46.

Rie, H. E. Depression in childhood: A survey of some pertinent contributions. *Journal of the American Academy of Child Psychiatry,* 1966, **5,** 653–685.

Rie, H. E. Historical perspective of concepts of child psychopathology. In H. E. Rie (Ed.), *Perspectives in child psychopathology.* Chicago: Aldine-Atherton, 1971.

Rie, H. E. Definitional problems. In H. E. Rie and E. D. Rie (Eds.), *Handbook of minimal brain dysfunctions. A critical view.* New York: Wiley, 1980.

Rie, H. E., and Rie, E. D. (Eds.), *Handbook of minimal brain dysfunctions. A critical view.* New York: Wiley, 1980.

Rimland, B. The differentiation of childhood psychoses: An analysis of check lists for 2,218 psychotic children. *Journal of Autism and Childhood Schizophrenia,* 1971, **1,** 161–174.

Rincover, A., and Koegel, R. L. Research on the education of autistic children: Current status and future directions. In B. B. Lahey and A. E. Kazdin (Eds.), *Advances in child clinical psychology* (Vol. 1). New York: Plenum Press, 1977, 329–361.

Roberts, M. Persistent school refusal among children and adolescents. In R. D. Wirt, G. Winokur, and M. Roff (Eds.), *Life history research in psychopathology* (Vol. 4). Minneapolis: University of Minnesota Press, 1975.

Robins, L. N. *Deviant children grown up: A sociological and psychiatric study of sociopathic personality.* Baltimore: Williams & Wilkins, 1966.

Robins, L. N. Follow-up studies of behavior disorders in children. In H. C. Quay and J. S. Werry (Eds.), *Psychopathological disorders of childhood.* New York: Wiley, 1972.

Robins, L. N. Addict careers. In R. I. Dupont, A. Goldstein, and J. O'Donnell (Eds.), *Handbook on drug abuse.* Washington, D.C.: National Institute on Drug Abuse, 1979.

Robins, L. N. The natural history of drug abuse. In D. J. Lettieri, M. Sayers, and H. W. Pearson (Eds.), *Theories on drug abuse. Selected contemporary perspectives. NIDA Research Monograph* 30. Washington, D.C.: National Institute on Drug Abuse, 1980.

Robins, L. N., Davis, D. H., and Nurco, D. N. How permanent was Vietnam drug addiction? *American Journal of Public Health,* 1974, **64,** (Suppl.), 38–43.

Robinson, N. M., and Robinson, H. B. *The mentally retarded child. A psychological approach* (2d ed.). New York: McGraw-Hill, 1976.

Roff, J. D. Adolescent schizophrenia: Variables related to differences in long-term adult outcome. *Journal of Consulting and Clinical Psychology,* 1974, **42,** 180–183.

Roff, M. *Some childhood and adolescent characteristics of adult homosexuals.* Report No. 66. University of Minnesota Institute of Child Development, 1966.

Rogers, C. R. A theory of therapy, personality, and interpersonal relationships as developed in the client-centered framework. In S. Koch (Ed.), *Psychology: Study of a science* (Vol. 3). *Formulations of the person and the social context.* New York: McGraw-Hill, 1959.

Rohrlich, J. A., Ranier, R., Berg-Cross, L., and Berg-Cross, G. The effects of divorce: A research review with a developmental perspective. *Journal of Clinical Child Psychology,* 1977, **6,** 15–20.

Rosen, M., Clark, G. R., and Kivitz, M. S. *Habilitation of the handicapped: New dimensions in programs for the developmentally disabled.* Baltimore: University Park Press, 1977.

Rosenthal, D., Wender, P. H., Kety, S. S., Schulsinger, F., Welner, J., and Rieder, R. O. Parent–child relationships and psychopathological disorder in the child. *Archives of General Psychiatry,* 1975, **32,** 466–476.

Ross, A. O. *Psychological disorders of children. A behavioral approach to theory, research, and therapy* (2d ed.). New York: McGraw-Hill, 1980.

Ross, A. O. *Child behavior therapy. Principles, procedures, and empirical basis.* New York: Wiley, 1981.

Ross, A. O., and Nelson, R. O. Behavior therapy. In H. C. Quay and J. S. Werry (Eds.)., *Psychopathological disorders of childhood* (2d ed.). New York: Wiley, 1979.

Ross, D. C. *A classification of child psychiatry.* 4951 McKean Ave., Philadelphia, Author, 1964.

Ross, D. M., and Ross, S. A. *Hyperactivity: Research, theory, and action.* New York: Wiley, 1976.

Routh, D. K. Activity, attention and aggression in learning-disabled children. *Journal of Clinical Child Psychology,* 1979, **8,** 183–187.

Routh, D. K., and Mesibov, G. B. Psychological and environmental intervention: Toward social competence. In H. E. Rie and E. D. Rie (Eds.), *Handbook of minimal brain dysfunctions. A critical view.* New York: Wiley, 1980.

Rubin, H. T. The juvenile court's search for identity and responsibility. *Crime and Delinquency,* 1977, **23,** 1–13.

Rubinstein, E. Childhood mental diseases in America: A review of the literature before 1900. *American Journal of Orthopsychiatry,* 1948, **18,** 314–321.

Ruttenberg, B. A., Kalish, B., Wenar, C., and Wolf, E. G. *Behavior rating instrument for autistic and other atypical children* (BRIACC). Chicago: Stolting, 1978.

Rutter, M. Psychiatry. In J. Wortis (Ed.), *Mental retardation. An annual review* (Vol. 3). New York: Grune & Stratton, 1971.

Rutter, M. *Maternal deprivation reassessed.* New York: Penguin, 1972.

Rutter, M. Brain damage syndromes in childhood: Concepts and findings. *Journal of Child Psychology and Psychiatry,* 1977, **18,** 1–21.

Rutter, M. Diagnoses and definition. In M. Rutter and E. Schopler (Eds.), *Autism: A reappraisal of concepts and treatment.* New York: Plenum Press, 1978.

Rutter, M. *Changing youth in a changing society. Patterns of adolescent development and disorder.* London: Nuffield Provincial Hospitals Trust, 1979a.

Rutter, M. Maternal deprivation, 1972–1978: New findings, new concepts, new approaches. *Child Development,* 1979b, **50,** 283–305.

Rutter, M., and Shaffer, D. DSM-III—A step forward or back in terms of the classification of child psychiatric disorders? *Journal of the American Academy of Child Psychiatry,* 1980, **19,** 371–394.

Safier, G. A study in relationships between the life and death concepts in children. *Journal of Genetic Psychology,* 1964, **105,** 283–294.

Saghir, M. T., and Robins, E. *Male and female homosexuality. A comprehensive investigation.* Baltimore: Williams & Wilkins, 1973.

Sameroff, A. J., and Chandler, M. J. Reproductive risk and the continuum of caretaking casualty. In F. D. Horowitz (Ed.), *Review of child development research* (Vol. 4). Chicago: University of Chicago Press, 1975.

Sameroff, A. J., and Zax, M. In search of schizophrenia: Young offspring of schizophrenic women. In L. C. Wynne, R. L. Cromwell, and S. Matthysse (Eds.), *The nature of schizophrenia. New approaches to research and treatment.* New York: Wiley, 1978.

Sander, L. W. Adaptive relationships in early mother–child interaction. *Journal of the American Academy of Child Psychiatry,* 1964, **3,** 231–264.

Satir, V. *Conjoint family therapy: A guide to theory and technique* (2d ed.). Palo Alto, Calif.: Science and Behavior Books, 1967.

Sattler, J. M. *Assessment of children's intelligence and special abilities.* Philadelphia: Saunders, 1982.

Schacht, T., and Nathan, P. E. But is it good for the psychologists? Appraisal and status of DSM-III. *American Psychologist,* 1977, **32,** 1017–1025.

Scharfman, M. A. Psychoanalytic treatment. In B. B. Wolman, J. Egan, and A. O. Ross (Eds.), *Handbook of treatment of mental disorders in childhood and adolescence.* Englewood Cliffs, N.J.: Prentice-Hall, 1978.

Schneider, G. E. Is it really better to have your brain lesion early? A revision of the "Kennard principle." *Neuropsychologica,* 1979, **17,** 557–583.

Schulterbrandt, J. G., and Raskin, A. (Eds.). *Depression in childhood: Diagnosis, treatment and conceptual models.* New York: Raven Press, 1977.

Schwartz, S., and Johnson, J. H. *Psychopathology of childhood. A clinical-experimental approach.* New York: Pergamon Press, 1981.

Sears, R. R. Your ancients revisited: A history of child development. In E. M. Hetherington (Ed.), *Review of child development research* (Vol. 5), Chicago: University of Chicago Press, 1975.

Segal, H. *Introduction to the work of Melanie Klein.* New York: Basic Books, 1973.

Self, P. A., and Horowitz, F. D. The behavioral assessment of the neonate: An overview. In T. D. Osofsky (Ed.), *Handbook of infant development.* New York: Wiley, 1979.

Seligman, M. E. P. *Helplessness: On depression, development and death.* San Francisco: Freeman, 1975.

Selman, R. L., and Byrne, D. F. A structural-developmental analysis of levels of role taking in middle childhood. *Child Development,* 1974, **45,** 803–806.

Senf, G. M., and Comrey, A. L. State initiative in learning disabilities. Illinois project SCREEN Report 1: The SCREEN early identification project. *Journal of Learning Disabilities,* 1975, **8,** 451–457.

Serafica, F. C., and Cicchetti, D. Down's syndrome children in a strange situation: Attachment and exploration behaviors. *Merrill-Palmer Quarterly,* 1976, **22,** 137–150.

Serafica, F. C., and Harway, N. I. Social relations and self-esteem of children with learning disabilities. *Journal of Clinical Child Psychology,* 1979, **8,** 227–233.

Shaffer, D. Enuresis. In M. Rutter and L. Hersov (Eds.), *Child Psychiatry: Modern approaches.* Oxford: Blackwell Scientific Publications, 1977.

Shaffer, D., Chadwick, O., and Rutter, M. Psychiatric outcome of localized head injuries in children. Outcome of severe damage to the central nervous system. Ciba Foundation Symposium, 1975, **34,** 191–209. (new series)

Shakow, D. Experimental psychology. In R. R. Grinker (Ed.), *Midcentury psychiatry.* Springfield, Ill.: Charles C Thomas, 1953.

Shantz, C. U. The development of social cognition. In E. M. Hetherington (Ed.), *Review of child development research,* (Vol. 5). Chicago: University of Chicago Press, 1975.

Shapiro, S. Disturbances in development and childhood neurosis. In S. L. Copel (Ed.), *Behavior pathology of childhood and adolescence.* New York: Basic Books, 1973.

Shore, M. F. Legislation, advocacy, and the rights of children and youth, *American Psychologist,* 1979, **34,** 1017–1019.

Singer, M. T., Wynne, L. C., and Toohey, B. A. Communication disorders and the families of schizophrenics. In L. C. Wynne, R. L. Cromwell, and S. Matthysse (Eds.), *The nature of schizophrenia. New approaches to research and treatment.* New York: Wiley, 1979.

Skeels, H. M. Adult status of children with contrasting early life experiences. *Monographs of the Society for Research in Child Development,* 1966, **31,** (3, Serial No. 105).

Skinner, B. F. *Walden Two.* New York: Macmillan, 1948.

Skinner, B. F. *Science and human behavior.* New York: Macmillan, 1953.

Slavson, S. R, and Schiffer, M. *Group psychotherapies for children: A textbook.* New York: International Universities Press, 1975.

Sloan, R. B., Staples, F. R., Cristol, A. H., Yorkston, N. J., and Whipple, K. *Psychotherapy versus behavior therapy.* Cambridge, Mass.: Harvard University Press, 1975.

Smith, F. *Psycholinguistics and Reading.* New York: Holt, Rinehart & Winston, 1973.

Sorensen, R. C. *Adolescent sexuality in contemporary America. Personal values and sexual behavior, ages 13–19.* New York: World, 1973.

Sours, J. A. Anorexia nervosa: Nosology, diagnosis, developmental patterns, and power-control dynamics. In G. Caplan and S. Lebovici

(Eds.), *Adolescence: Psychosocial perspectives.* New York: Basic Books, 1969.

Spitz, H. H., and Nadler, B. T. Logic problem solving by educable retarded adolescents and normal children. *Developmental Psychology,* 1974, **10,** 404–412.

Spitz, R. A. Hospitalism: An inquiry into the genesis of psychiatric conditions in early childhood. *Psychoanalytic study of the child* (Vol. 1). New York: International Universities Press, 1945.

Spitz, R. A. Anaclitic depression. *Psychoanalytic study of the child* (Vol. 2). New York: International Universities Press, 1946.

Spitzer, R. L., and Cantwell, D. P. The DSM-III classification of the psychiatric disorders of infancy, childhood and adolescence. *Journal of the American Academy of Child Psychiatry,* 1980, **19,** 356–370.

Spivack, G., Platt, J. J., and Shure, M. *The problem-solving approach to adjustment.* San Francisco: Jossey-Bass, 1976.

Spock, B. The striving for autonomy and regressive object relations. *Psychoanalytic study and the child* (Vol. 18). New York: International Universities Press, 1963.

Sroufe, A. L. Socioemotional development. In J. D. Osofsky (Ed.), *Handbook of infant development.* New York, Wiley, 1979.

Strauss, J. S., Kokes, R. F., Carpenter, W. T., Jr., and Ritzler, B. A. The course of schizophrenia as a developmental process. In L. C. Wynne, R. L. Cromwell, and S. Matthysse (Eds.), *The nature of schizophrenia. New approaches to research and treatment.* New York: Wiley, 1978.

Strauss, J. S., Kokes, R. F., Klorman, R., and Sacksteder, J. S. Premorbid adjustment and schizophrenic heterogeneity. Part I: The concept of premorbid adjustment. *Schizophrenic Bulletin,* 1977, **3,** 182–185.

Sullivan, H. S. *The interpersonal theory of psychiatry.* New York: Norton, 1953.

Suran, B. G., and Rizzo, J. V. *Special children: An integrative approach.* Glenview, Ill.: Scott, Foresman, 1979.

Sykes, D. H., Douglas, V. I., and Morgenstern, G. Sustained attention in hyperactive children. *Journal of Child Psychology and Psychiatry,* 1973, **14,** 213–220.

Terman, L. M., and Merrill, M. A. *Manual for 3rd revision, Form L-M, Stanford-Binet Intelligence Scale.* Boston: Houghton-Mifflin, 1973.

Teuber, H. L. Recovery of function after brain injury in man. Outcome of severe damage to the central nervous system. *Ciba Foundation Symposium,* 1975, **34,** 159–190. (new series)

Thomas, A., and Chess, S. *Temperament and development.* New York: Brunner/Mazel, 1977.

Thomas, A., Chess, S., and Birch, H. *Temperament and behavior disorders in children.* New York: New York University Press, 1968.

Thompson, N. L., and McCandless, B. R. The homosexual orientation and its antecedents. In A. Davids (Ed.), *Child personality and psychopathology: Current topics* (Vol. 3). New York: Wiley, 1976.

Torgensen, J. Problems and prospects in the study of learning disabilities. In E. M. Hetherington (Ed.), *Review of child development research* (Vol. 5). Chicago: University of Chicago Press, 1975.

Townes, B. D., Trupin, E. W., Martin, D. C., and Goldstein, D. Neuropsychological correlates of academic success among elementary school children. *Journal of Consulting and Clinical Psychology,* 1980, **48,** 675–684.

Urbain, E. S., and Kendall, P. C. Review of social-cognitive problem-solving intervention with children. *Psychological Bulletin,* 1980, **88,** 109–143.

Voss, H. L. The predictive efficiency of the Glueck Social Prediction Tables. *Journal of Criminal Law, Criminology, and Police Science,* 1963, **54,** 421–430.

Waelder, B. *Basic theory of psychoanalysis.* New York: International Universities Press, 1960.

Waldron, S., Jr., Shrier, D. K., Stone, B., and Tobin, F. School phobia and other childhood neuroses. A systematic study of children and their families. *American Journal of Psychiatry,* 1975, **132,** 802–808.

Wallerstein, J. S., and Kelly, J. B. The effects of

parental divorce: The adolescent experience. In E. J. Anthony and G. Koupernik (Eds)., *The child in his family: Children at psychiatric risk* (Vol. 3). New York: Wiley, 1974.

Wallerstein, J. S., and Kelly, J. B. The effects of parental divorce: Experiences in the child in later latency. *American Journal of Orthopsychiatry,* 1976, **46,** 256–269.

Watson, J. B. Psychology as the behaviorist views it. *Psychological Review,* 1913, **20,** 158–177.

Watson, J. B. *Psychology from the standpoint of the behaviorist.* Philadelphia: Lippincott, 1919.

Watson, J. S., and Ramey, C. T. Reactions to responsive-contingent stimulation in early infancy. *Merrill-Palmer Quarterly,* 1972, **18,** 219–227.

Watt, N. F., and Lubensky, A. W. Childhood roots of schizophrenia. *Journal of Consulting and Clinical Psychology,* 1976, **44,** 363–375.

Wechsler, D. *Manual for the Wechsler Intelligence Scale for Children-Revised.* New York: Psychological Corporation, 1974.

Weiner, I. B. *Psychological disturbances in adolescence.* New York: Wiley, 1970.

Weiner, I. B. Psychopathology in adolescence. In J. Adelson (Ed.), *Handbook of adolescent psychology.* New York: Wiley, 1980.

Weiner, P. S. Developmental language disorder. In H. E. Rie and E. D. Rie (Eds.), *Handbook of minimal brain dysfunctions. A critical view.* New York: Wiley, 1980.

Weiss, G. MBD: Critical diagnostic issues. In H. E. Rie and E. D. Rie (Eds.), *Handbook of minimal brain dysfunctions. A critical view.* New York: Wiley, 1980.

Weisz, J., and Zigler, E. Cognitive development in retarded and nonretarded persons. Piagetian tests of the similar sequence hypothesis. *Psychological Bulletin,* 1979, **86,** 831–851.

Wenar, C. *Personality development from infancy to adulthood.* Boston: Houghton-Mifflin, 1971.

Wenar, C. Executive competence in toddlers: A prospective, observational study. *Genetic Psychology Monographs,* 1976, **93,** 189–285.

Wenar, C. On negativism. *Human Development,* 1982, **25,** 1–23.

Wenar, C., and Ruttenberg, B. A. Therapies for autistic children. In J. H. Masserman (Ed.), *Current psychiatric therapies* (Vol. 9). New York: Grune & Stratton, 1969.

Wenar, C., and Ruttenberg, B. A. The use of BRIACC for evaluating therapeutic effectiveness. *Journal of Autism and Childhood Schizophrenia,* 1976, **6,** 175–191.

Werner, E. E. Environmental interaction in minimal brain dysfunction. In H. E. Rie and E. D. Rie (Eds.), *Handbook of minimal brain dysfunctions. A critical view.* New York: Wiley, 1980.

Werry, J. S. Organic factors. In H. C. Quay and J. S. Werry (Eds.), *Psychopathological disorders of childhood* (2d ed.). New York: Wiley, 1979.

West, D. J. *Homosexuality.* Chicago: Aldine, 1967.

West, D. J. *Homosexuality re-examined.* Minneapolis: University of Minnesota Press, 1977.

White, E., Elsom, B., and Prawat, R. Children's concept of death. *Child Development,* 1978, **49,** 307–310.

White, R. W. Motivation reconsidered: The concept of competence. *Psychological Review,* 1959, **66,** 297–333.

Whiteside, M. F. Family therapy. In J. D. Noshpitz (Ed.), *Therapeutic interventions. Basic handbook of child psychiatry* (Vol. 3). New York: Basic Books, 1979.

Wiggins, J. S. Clinical and statistical prediction: Where are we and where do we go from here? *Clinical Psychology Review,* 1981, **1,** 3–18.

Winsberg, B. G., and Yepes, L. E. Antipsychotics (major tranquilizers, neuroleptics). In J. S. Werry (Ed.), *Pediatric psychopharmacology.* New York: Brunner/Mazel, 1978.

Wirt, R. D., Lachar, D., Klinedinst, J. K., and Seat, P. D. *Personality Inventory for Children.* Los Angeles: Western Psychological Services, 1977.

Wohl, T. H. Other assessment techniques. In H. E. Rie and E. D. Rie (Eds.), *Handbook of minimal brain dysfunctions.* New York: Wiley, 1980.

Wolfenstein, M. How is mourning possible? *Psy-*

choanalytic study of the child (Vol. 21). New York: International Universities Press, 1966.

Wolff, S. Nondelinquent disturbances of conduct. In M. Rutter and L. Hersov (Eds.), *Child psychiatry: Modern approaches.* Oxford: Blackwell Scientific Publications, 1977.

Wolpe, J. *The practice of behavior therapy* (2d ed.). New York: Pergamon Press, 1973.

Wright, J. C., and Vliestra, A. G. The development of selective attention: From perceptual exploration to logical search. In H. W. Reese (Ed.), *Advances in child development and behavior* (Vol. 10). New York: Academic Press, 1975.

Wynn, L. C., Toohey, M. L., and Doane, J. Family studies. In L. Bellak (Ed.)., *Disorders of the schizophrenic syndrome.* New York: Basic Books, 1979.

Yalom, I. D. *The theory and practice of group psychotherapy* (2d ed.). New York: Basic Books, 1975.

Yarrow, L. J. Separation from parents during early childhood. In M. L. Hoffman and L. W. Hoffman, *Review of child development research* (Vol. 1). New York: Russell Sage Foundation, 1964.

Yarrow, M. R., Campbell, J. D., and Burton, R. V. Recollections of childhood: A study of the retrospective method. *Monographs of the Society for Research in Child Development.* 1970, **35,** (5, Serial No. 138).

Yussen, S. R., and Santrock, J. W. *Child development: An introduction.* Dubuque, Iowa: William C. Brown, 1978.

Yuwiler, A., Geller, E., and Ritvo, E. R. Neurobiochemical research. In E. R. Ritvo, B. Freeman, E. M. Ornitz, and P. E. Tanguay (Eds.), *Autism: Diagnosis, current research, and management.* New York: Spectrum, 1976.

Zigler, E., and Balla, D. *Mental retardation. The development-difference controversy.* Hillsdale, N.J.: Lawrence Erlbaum Associates, in press.

Zubin, J. Concluding comments. In L. C. Wynne, R. L. Cromwell, and S. Matthysse (Eds.), *The nature of schizophrenia. New approaches to research and treatment.* New York: Wiley, 1978.

Name Index

Subject Index

About the Author

Charles Wenar is professor of psychology at The Ohio State University. He heads both the developmental area and the clinical child program in the department of psychology there. A graduate of Swarthmore College and Iowa State University, Dr. Wenar was both a clinician and a researcher at Michael Reese Hospital, the Illinois Neuropsychiatric Institute, and the University of Pennsylvania. His two previous books and numerous articles, as well as his current research on autism and on negativism in healthy toddlers, attest to his longstanding interest in both normal and disturbed children.